Musformation Presents:

GET MORE FANS: The DIY Guide To The New Music Business

Everything You Need To Know About:

Twitter • Bandcamp • Facebook • Spotify • Apple Music • SoundCloud • Getting Fans Excited • Kickstarter • Using Free Music To Make You Money • Tumblr • Getting On Blogs • YouTube • Going Viral • Licensing Your Music • Getting More Fans At Shows • TopSpin • Next Big Sound • Getting Publicity • Hype Machine • Snapchat • Booking Shows • Selling More Merch • Pandora • Direct-To-Fan • Instagram • Using Torrent Sites To Your Advantage • Limited Run • Managing Your Band • Amazon • Pinterest • Targeting Potential Fans • ReverbNation • TuneCore • ArtistGrowth • Last.FM • CD Baby • Maintaining A Mailing List • FanBridge • WordPress • Music Industry Rules • • Apple Music • Making A Great Website • ASCAP, BMI or SESAC • SoundExchange • Marketing Ideas • Reddit • Choosing A Record Producer • TikTok • Going Viral • THOUSANDS OF CREATIVE IDEAS ON HOW TO PROMOTE YOUR MUSIC

Thousands Of Tips For Musicians Of Every Size, Whether You Have Zero Or 1,000,000 Fans

A Detailed Look At How To Get More People To Hear Your Music & Build Your Fanbase

By Jesse Cannon And Todd Thomas
Musformation.com
GetMoreFansBook.com
Copyright @ 2013, 2014, 2015, 2016, 2017, 2018, 2019, 2020, 2021 by
Jesse Cannon and Todd Thomas
This work is licensed under a Creative Commons Attribution-
Noncommercial-ShareAlike 3.0 Unported License.

Published by Musformation, 62 Ten Eyck St. #1
Brooklyn, NY 11206 United States
For more information visit musformation.com

Library of Congress Cataloging-in-Publication Data

Cannon, Jesse
Get more fans: the diy guide to the new music business / by Jesse Cannon
& Todd Thomas
p.cm
ISBN-13: 978-0-9885613-0-4
ISBN-10: 0988561301
1. Music Business 2. Music Resources

Manufactured in the USA

Credits:
Authors: Jesse Cannon and Todd Thomas
Editor: Thomas Nassiff (bit.ly/thomasnassiff)
Cover Design: David Ahuja (amoebalabs.com)
Additional Editing and Insight: Jeremy Winter (jettbrando.bandcamp.com),
Jackie Brennan (jackiebrennan.com), Mike Oettinger
(cannonfoundsoundation.com), Michael Davidson and Erica Sackin
Book Website: Matt Hucke (mhucke.com)

Table of Contents

Introduction - The Flat Playing Field Of Today's Music Business

"How do we get more people to hear our music?"

"How do we get more fans?"

"How on Earth does a band get thousands of plays on Spotify?"

"How do we get signed to a label?"

"How do I make a living from my music so I can stop working at Chipotle?"

I hear these questions from musicians every day, whether I'm out at a show, party, bar or in my recording studio. These questions are common, because their answers aren't obvious. It takes a lot of time and dedication to get the kind of fanbase where the answers to these questions become clear. The fact is, this information has never been readily available and there isn't a "one-size-fits-all" answer. Instead it takes a vast understanding of what is happening in the music business to make good decisions for your music.

Today's music business has allowed musicians to take matters into their own hands. Gone are the days of musicians waiting for a gatekeeper (someone who holds power and prevents you from being let in) at a label, late-night talk show or radio station to say they are worthy of the spotlight. In today's music business, you don't need to ask for permission to build a fanbase and you no longer need to pay thousands of dollars to a company to do it. Every day, musicians are getting their music out to thousands of listeners without any help from industry bigwigs. They simply deliver it to the fans directly, without asking for permission or outside help to receive exposure or connect with thousands of listeners.

The Music Landscape Today

While the Internet has opened new doors for musicians, many still think these opportunities are exceptions to the rule. They're not. Unlike in 2008, musicians who do it themselves have nearly identical opportunities to major label musicians who receive tens of thousands of dollars in promotional budgets. Musicians can now sell their albums in the same stores as their idols, play concerts in the same venues and get their music on where listeners are finding new music each day; it just requires a smart,

9

diligent work ethic. As long as fans enjoy the music you make, you can build a fanbase just as easily as any musician with a huge budget behind them.

Every day there is more news of doom and gloom in the music business being shared by your friends on social media. What these click bait articles don't always note is that the gloom is reserved for those who have traditionally held power in the industry, not those who are presently rising up in the business. In the old music business, gatekeepers (major labels, record stores, booking agents, radio, MTV, A&R, etc.) with questionable values and even more questionable methods held back musicians who didn't fit into a certain mold. The musicians at the mercy of these gatekeepers had no way to access essential tools to build a fanbase. That old music business crumbles a little more every day, simultaneously leveling the playing field between all types of musicians. Just a few years ago, there were many outlets and opportunities that a DIY musician could never gain access to. Today, there are very few opportunities that aren't open to those who do it themselves.

A decade ago, it seemed a musician's only option was to put a song on Myspace, add friends, play shows and hope for the best. If they were any good, they might start to gain some fans and experience a small amount of success. But as Myspace disappeared and as major studios and record labels collapsed, we were suddenly left with a variety of blogs to dictate the cultural zeitgeist and now the majority of how music is discovered is fans sharing the acts they love and building them up by word of mouth or algorithm (more on that later). The music business had changed and the way musicians approached building a fanbase had to change with it. Acts like Metric, Brockhampton, Nine Inch Nails, A Day To Remember, Mac Miller, OK Go, Circa Survive, Coheed & Cambria, Run The Jewels, Amanda Palmer and Radiohead have now successfully selling records without a label to support them. In 2013 Macklemore & Ryan Lewis even had a Platinum selling #1 single and album (one million copies shipped) as a DIY act on their own label. In 2016 Chance The Rapper scored a #8 on a self-released album, after never having released a record on an indie or major label. There are also countless artists who self-released their music before going on to a huge career like FKA Twigs, A$AP Rocky, Ed Sheeran & countless more. New musicians are starting to wonder how they can emulate these larger acts, no longer just in sound, but in business practice.

While major labels are getting weaker, DIY musicians are growing stronger. Every day, the record stores that used to give major labels preferential treatment--in exchange for behind-closed-doors cash--are closing up shop and the power of the major labels that bought exposure for their acts dies a little more. Instead of discovering music through this unethical product placement, fans hear about music through more organic means. The result of hearing about new music in a word-of-mouth fashion, whether it be from close friends, playlists or bloggers you've never met, is a more pure, egalitarian method of selection in terms of which musicians get discovered by new listeners. Each day, music fans are exposed to musicians who earn their fanbase by listeners responding to their music, instead of benefitting from promotions paid for by major label bucks.

Staffing at major labels has gone down 60 percent in the last decade and a half, as a result, labels outsource many of the tasks they used to do in-house--and they hire the same services and firms that indie or DIY musicians have access to themselves. A major label musician's manager now controls much of the band's revenue, making decisions about hiring publicists, producers and other members of the team. This is the same approach a DIY musician takes. With each passing season, the tools used in the world of major labels and the tools used by DIY musicians become more and more similar. For example, MailChimp is used by both relatively unknown musicians and by worldwide phenomenon. TuneCore aggregates records for everyone from the smallest indie bands to award-winning acts like Nine Inch Nails.

Musicians no longer have to waste their time and energy trying to convince some jaded gatekeeper at a record company, radio station or booking agency that they're doing something great. Instead, they can work hard on a smart strategy and implement it themselves, eventually getting noticed on their own merit. As more and more people begin to enjoy the music created by these DIY musicians, the rest of the world begins to hear it via the power of social networks and live performances. We've finally reached an era where good music is shared not only by record labels, but music fans themselves in increasing numbers. Instead of the gatekeepers getting musicians in front of listeners, it's blogs; fans and tastemakers who spread the word of what's good, before the gatekeepers even get the chance. Major label signings used to dictate who got a following, but now the majors sign bands that have already earned a following on their own terms. Today, if you're making music that the world wants to hear, it's only a lack of hard work; knowledge and imagination that can hold you back.

Think of the main ways we all regularly discover new music. Friends tell each other what they're listening to on social networks like Facebook, Twitter and Instagram--or even in person. Online radio services like Pandora or Spotify suggest new artists for listeners to fall in love with, using an algorithm based on their existing personal tastes. Hype Machine is able to make a chart of what's being listened to across the blogosphere, enabling tastemakers and music fans to collaborate on what gets pushed to the musical forefront. Last.fm allows music listeners to bond with others that share similar tastes, connecting people who have never met through their love for music. Thanks to all these tools, it's a like-minded kinship in music taste that helps fans discover new artists--not some out-of-touch, jaded loudmouth telling you what you should like.

The field is wide open and there's never been a more exciting time to make music. While many bemoan the fact that anybody can easily create and release music with the advent of home studios, this creates a culture of excitement when you find someone who does it well. When everyone is able to create music and get it out there, it becomes easier to find music that suits your particular taste and to experience that amazing sensation when you find a record that makes you feel alive.

There are great things on the horizon. Revenues for independent musicians are up, while those of the dinosaur major labels are down. If you listen to the chatter of the lame-stream music media, you may get scared that going into the music business means being broke for the rest of your life. We wrote this book to tell you the contrary. If you make smart moves, work hard and write great songs, you have the benefit of living in an age in which--now more than ever--your music can get discovered and you can earn a living from it. I hope that after you read this book, you'll be as excited as we are.

About Us

Jesse Cannon
In order to understand this book, it may be helpful to know where I am coming from and how I learned what I know. Over the years I've worked in nearly every aspect of the music business. It started when I was 15 years old and entered a recording studio with the punk band that I played drums

in. When our record didn't sound exactly the way I wanted, I decided to buy recording equipment and take matters into my own hands. At 17, I started recording bands in my town in exchange for food and beer. By 18, bands from nearby New York City were hiring me for a modest fee to produce 7"s and CDs that would then be sold nationally.

Soon after, I was doing live sound at local shows and at my high school, where I attracted the notice of America's largest and most esteemed freeform radio station, WFMU (wfmu.org). A DJ at the station was impressed by my mixing skills and I began to record live on-air performances at the station. I stayed there for nine years working with groups like The Magnetic Fields, The Sea and the Cake, Spoon and countless other indie bands. This gave me daily experience of speaking with many great minds in up-and-coming groups that would eventually go on to influence millions of musicians.

While still a teenager, I began promoting concerts at Anthony Trance Presents, which put on shows at now-legendary venues like The Pipeline, Connections and NYC's Coney Island High. For three years, we booked national acts like AFI, Jimmy Eat World and My Chemical Romance before they would gain the huge fanbase they have today. Years before today's festival craze, I promoted a 24-band, two-day festival that drew thousands of people to see groups like Saves The Day, Converge, Dillinger Escape Plan and Cave In.

Through all these years, I was taking my writing to the masses, self-publishing half a dozen zines under various monikers. I learned to oversee every aspect of these zines and learned what went into selling ads, getting albums reviewed, publishing a zine and distributing it into stores. I also made freelance contributions to widely read zines like Tape Op, Punk Planet, SoundViews and Maximum RockNRoll.

I played in bands called The Dyslexics, Yakub and Jett Brando. During that time, I did what a manager does for all of these bands: I chose producers, booked shows and maintained the group's presence. All the while, my friends and I would self-release our own bands' records and learn the ropes of every aspect of promoting a record. Everyone I hung out with had their own DIY label and would release their own 7"s, CDs, compilations and demo tapes. I credit the DIY punk scene (*scene - a sub-genre of music that has a community*) with teaching me how to promote music

13

independently and get it spread across the country with no budget or corporate backing--all in a pre-Internet music world.

At 20, I took on the role of retail marketing and publicity at Go Kart Records and became the buyer for Soapbox Records, the record store in front of Go Kart's office on St. Mark's Place in Manhattan's East Village. That job meant I was doing publicity, tour promotion, radio promotion and helping decide what bands we signed, working with groups like Weston, The Lunachicks and The Buzzcocks. It was here that I learned what makes people buy records as well as why they ignore them.

The next year I took a job at Alan Douches' West West Side Music, the top-mastering studio for indie labels in America for the past three decades. While there, I interacted with some the country's largest indie labels like Epitaph, Fueled By Ramen, Astralwerks and Roadrunner--all the while, learning recording, mastering and the ropes of dealing with big-name acts like Fatboy Slim, Brand New, RUN DMC and Fall Out Boy. Every day I got to talk with people who were responsible for running the careers of the biggest indie musicians out there. I got to see their creative process while picking their brains about the music business.

At 25, my skills producing records became so in-demand I had to leave West West Side in order to grow. The first album I recorded on Pro Tools got picked up by Atlantic/Lava and gave the group, Little T and One Track Mike, a hit with their single "Shaniqua." The song received tons of attention on MTV until the September 11th attacks gave a quick death to the group's airplay. With the money I made from this record, I was able to buy an expensive Pro Tools system and build Cannon Found Soundation Recording Studios (cannonfoundsoundation.com). This studio is a three-room facility where I produce, mix and master records on a daily basis. Over this time, I have had in a hand in the production, recording, mixing and mastering of over 1,000 records.

Over the years, I got to produce and engineer groups like Animal Collective, The Misfits, The Menzingers, Northstar and Lifetime. I go to work under producer Steve Evetts and make records with Say Anything, Senses Fail and Dillinger Escape Plan. I travelled the world with producer Ross Robinson to work on records with The Cure, Limp Bizkit and Chase Pagan.

In 2003, I decided to take on a manager role for a group I had produced and loved called The Escape Engine. The group was the first release on a small indie label, Fidelity Records. Despite the lack of distribution, our team worked hard and the band toured year-round. Through our hard work mobilizing fans in the pre-Myspace era, we managed to get their video heavy playtime on MTV's *Extreme Music* show. The group ultimately recorded another album with me and was told by an A&R man at one of the biggest indie labels that their record was amazing, but they were too old (their late-20s) to be marketed in the emo genre. This sickened me and inspired much of my ire toward the way the music business was being run. Consequently, the group disbanded and I swore off management.

I stuck by that pledge until 2008, when I met a group called Man Overboard. Shortly after I produced their first EP, I started Musformation-- the blog from which this book was sprung. I decided that since I was writing about the music business and DIY marketing for musicians, I should try my hand at putting all of this information into practice. So, I took on the most promising band I knew.

It worked! With our hard work, the group went from a band with no Facebook page to one with 50,000 Likes by the time I stopped managing them. During this time, I managed every detail of their strategy to build a fanbase and in two short years, I helped turn them into a group that made tens of thousands of dollars a month, sold hundreds of merch items each week, packed venues all over the world and had releases available in every record store in America. Along the way, I also took on managing a group named Transit. Under my guidance, Transit, along with Man Overboard, signed with one of the world's largest independent labels, Rise Records. I also managed smaller groups named Repeater, Unifier and Washington Square Park. I've once again retired from management to focus on new goals and spreading what I have learned to every musician I can.

I also have the pleasure of teaching classes for a great company called CreativeLive (creativelive.com/audio). They do amazing, free, live streaming courses on everything from business to Photoshop and design onto maker crafts. I teach classes on recording and the music business. These courses are a high quality, immersion into each subject and are so good; I even watch the other courses when they air since I learn so much watching them.

In 2014, I decided to go into the world of podcasting and launched Off The Record (offtherecord.fm) and discuss the music business each week with people doing cool things within it. Each week we discuss the changing music business and the consumption of music and the tech around it. I also launched an interview series for Noise Creators (noisecreators.com) where I discuss creativity and get to know the best producers in music today.

In 2016, along with my co-founder Johnny Minardi (Self Titled Management, Equal Vision records and formerly Fueled By Ramen) we launched a service called Noise Creators (noisecreators.com). We allow musicians to get to know producers through interviews, discographies, podcasts, Spotify playlists and more. We allow musicians to find a better fit for producing their record or have us help them with that fit and get them a better deal to work with a producer who can help bring their music to its full potential.

In 2017, I released the book *Processing Creativity: The Tools, Practices And Habits Used To Make Music You're Happy With,* which details the countless pitfalls of the creative process. It is currently the best-selling book on songwriting and recording of 2017 and has received high praise from Alternative Press, Tape Op and countless other outlets as well as many of the top producers and musicians in music today. If you want to explore how to make songs you are happy with and avoid the many common ways musicians fail to make their songs as good as possible, go to https://processingcreativitybook.com for more information.

In 2018, I began developing podcasts at Atlantic Records that show how the biggest artists in the world develop their amazing records. The first of these shows, Inside The Album documents the creative process of artists like Dashboard Confessional, Vance Joy, Jason Mraz, Brent Cobb, Wallows, nothing.nowhere and a ton more. In 2019 I released more podcasts through Atlantic including Landed which has extensive interview with music business veterans. Atlantic granted me unprecedented access to their creative process with these interviews and I am incredibly proud of them.

In late 2019 I launched a YouTube channel titled Musformation to accompany my work as a music marketing consultant and my two books. It is quickly becoming acclaimed as the "realest" YouTube channel on music. I hope you will look it up and follow it.

Todd Thomas

The other half of Musformation is Todd Thomas. Todd contributed to this book immensely and while it is written in my (Jesse's) voice, this is only to maintain clarity for the reader. Todd's contributions to this book make it his as much as it is mine.

Todd went to school at the University of North Carolina in Wilmington and graduated with a degree in creative writing. After a stint writing music reviews at the university newspaper, he took a job writing for the Star News (a New York Times company) as a music and entertainment journalist.

Todd's music industry perspective comes from real world experience. In 2005, he was the singer and guitarist in a buzzed-about band from North Carolina called The Fashion Brigade. After touring and putting out their own EP, he took his band halfway across the country to record their 'big record,' spending loads of money to work with a big-name producer (who will remain nameless) in a swanky recording studio in Dallas. The results were less than staggering. Todd was shocked at the lack of interest this high-price-tag producer had for his music and the band was completely unimpressed with the producer's attitude and effort through their sessions. After taking out big loans to pay this producer, it was extremely frustrating for Todd to see him come into the studio and merely 'phone in' his job, even while his band worked their hardest to write and record songs that meant the world to them. Following this musical misstep, Todd took it upon himself to take a different path--one that involved DIY ethics and empowerment, the basis of Musformation and this book.

As part of this ethos, Todd and his band moved to New York to pursue their music on a bigger scale. Todd now plays in and self-manages a burgeoning Brooklyn band called Sensual Harassment. If you frequently read dance music blogs, there is no avoiding their name. The god of all that is indie, Pitchfork Media, featured Sensual Harassment in their Forkcast section and the band has since been featured on Big Stereo, Vice, MTVu, Dazed and Confused, Brooklyn Vegan, Oh My Rockness, Purple Magazine and Hype Machine. They record and mix their own records, book their own shows and tours, do their own press and are all the happier (and arguably successful) because of it.

Todd also works as freelance marketing specialist. His latest venture includes an extended stay at Aegis Media, one of the world's largest media marketing agencies. He has worked on projects for major brands like Gatorade, General Motors, Macy's, Bailey's and Procter & Gamble.

Jackie Brennan
Jackie is Musformation's web developer and handles the online tasks that are too technical for Todd and I. I've known Jackie since the mid-90's when we were both hanging out in the New York City punk scene and met at a Misfits show.

Jackie moved to St. Louis in 2004 to get a degree in interactive digital media from Webster University. She has been working as a freelance web developer ever since and in addition to her work for Musformation, has done work for musicians, record labels, small businesses and major corporations.

She recently moved back to NYC in the summer of 2012 and the Musformation team is now together again. Jackie has been working for an advertising agency on projects for Gatorade and T-Mobile and is now the senior front-end web developer for the Smithsonian Channel in NYC. She also runs a freelance web business, Adapted Reality (adaptedreality.com), with her partner, Matt Hucke.

When the musicians and labels Musformation works with need help making cool websites or are in need of new marketing tools, Jackie is the one who makes it happen.

Musformation
In the summer of 2007, Todd and I met by chance after his band posted on a local message board looking for a recording studio. I offered my services and within a week, they came by to cut some drums. We quickly realized that in addition to sharing the same taste in fashion, late night drinking and dancing with girls, we also shared a similar perspective toward the music business. After many impassioned discussions at wee hours of the morning, we decided to stop complaining about the lack of relevant information on the current state of the music business and do something about it.

We agreed there were exciting developments in the music business despite the state of disrepair and challenges it was facing. Musicians were becoming independent and successful without the help of a major record label. Technology was offering musicians more power than ever to write, record and produce their own demos, singles and albums. The influx of information on the Internet helped more informed musicians make better choices and, in the end, have a better chance of actually making money doing what they loved to do. The only thing missing in this equation was a community that offered resources, up-to-date information and daily insights into new developments in the industry. That's where our website and this book come in.

Unlike a lot of people who write books or blogs about "the music business," we actually *live* it (for better or for worse). We weren't in a band that was sort of successful 20 years ago, we aren't corporate funded, we don't go on and on about abstract ideas in the music business just because we have an audience that will listen to us. We put what we practice into writing and use our everyday lives as inspiration. Most topics you read on our blog and in this book are taken from an everyday discussion we had with someone.

Musformation was started not as a reaction to what was already out there in the music business, but as a reaction to what was missing. We felt there was no comprehensive website that provided a complete resource for musicians and others in the music business, who wanted a reliable and ranging wealth of information about the new music business.

We write pitches to bloggers. We book tours. We read music sites. We record bands. We mix our own records. We build websites. We listen to Hype Machine, Beats1 and other Internet radio services all day while we work. We use social networks. We deal with entertainment lawyers. We promote. We play shows. We read contracts. We go to bars and chat about the struggles of being a musician today. We get to work with some musicians who have huge budgets and some who have no budget at all. What we write about is how we make it work--no matter what. You name it, we do it.

We write about what we see, hear and learn. We don't concern ourselves with corporate stock quotes or who is in or out as CEO of some music startup. We are only interested in writing about the newest and best tools available and the ideas that can help push music forward. While Musformation's blog is no longer active, we still write and share our feelings on the new music business on websites like Alternative Press, Hypebot, Party Smasher Inc., Property of Zack, Medium and many more. Today most of Musformation's work comes in consulting for artists, making release plans and developing content ideas to surround their releases.

Writing This Book

When we decided to do this book, the standard advice was to go after a publisher or get some sort of corporate backing. After a short time dealing with the pains and frustrations of another often-clueless industry, we decided there was only one way to do this--ourselves--just like we advise musicians to do in this book. We tirelessly wrote, edited and laid out this book for more than three years and have updated it every single year with the most relevant information, even if that means re-writing hundreds of pages each year. It's our own work, with the help of some friends who have given us perspective and another close friend who designed the cover. For duplication and fulfillment, we employed Lightning Source (lightningsource.com) and direct publishing for the digital version. We ran small pressings at a duplication house, the same way many musicians do for a short run of CDs. All of the promotional methods we used to promote this book are straight out of what we preach in these very pages. We uploaded the digital formats the same way a musician would upload an album. We fulfilled the online mail order for this book using the same methods we describe in its merch chapter.

Every time you see this book somewhere, it means the theories and techniques we wrote about have been applied to its own promotion and distribution. Music isn't the only industry that is going through big changes. The best places to look for inspiration in how to promote your music are in other industries. What our experience in making this book showed us is that the whole world is changing, not just the music business.

Making The Most Of This Book

Filling In The Blanks
This book isn't for those with no knowledge of the music business. There's an insane number of books and blogs out there that would prefer to treat you as if you just bought your first copy of *Mel Bay's Guitar Chords Book*, but we recognize that you're here for a reason: You're serious about your music and want to build a fanbase for it. The tired echo chamber of music business books is filled with basics, background noise and outdated

material. Our goal is to offer a book filled strictly with pertinent knowledge--the most current and relevant kind you won't find anywhere else. If you ever have trouble keeping up with the terms in this book, we promise they can be easily looked up via Google. If you're looking for legal advice and want to read tirelessly about what is and isn't legal or every nuance of how to sue someone for stealing your music, there are 60 other books that talk about that. While there is some legal knowledge that's crucial to understand--in order to make sure your hard work isn't diminished by a lawsuit--that isn't the focus of this book. We're here to teach you how to grow a fanbase.

This book is inherently scattered, but the concepts are linked together like a spider's web. If you're not interested in reading about how you can use YouTube to promote your music, you'll miss out on how you can use it to draw more potential fans at your next show. If you don't read the chapter on preparing for the recording studio and skip right to the chapters about social networks, you'll be missing out on crucial knowledge about how to prevent your online promotions from going to waste. While we understand if you want to skip around the book, be warned that if you don't read it as a whole, you might be missing out on a lot of the information that makes this all work together. There are big chunks of important topics, but the glue that holds everything together is important as well. Small leaks in your knowledge can expand into larger holes--potentially sinking your ship.

Throughout this book, you'll see countless websites mentioned and thousands of little details. While some may not be directly relevant to you, we see success in the music business as building a haystack--it takes a lot of seemingly insignificant parts to build up the final product. Figuring out how to combine everything is what makes your personal strategy your own sculpture. And when I say "sculpture," I mean it. Figuring out the best way to promote your music is a delicate art of its own.

You may read parts of this book and feel like we're idiots. Part of the fun is voicing your opinion and discussing it, so we can all figure out the right answers. Our website and forum (*ahem, Facebook group*) are filled with some very smart users discussing cutting-edge music business information every day. We want to get to the bottom of every mystery in the business and present everyone with the information they need to make great decisions about what to do with their promising future in music. If you think we got something wrong or have a different take on a topic, meet us online and add to the conversation. What we're trying to do with this book is start a discussion. By publishing new versions of this book as often as we can, we would like to keep the discussion evolving and the flow of information steady.

By no means is this book a complete guide, just as no single book or blog could possibly claim to be. What's astounding to me on a day-to-day basis is how many new services and tools are constantly popping up. It's crazy how many people are doing interesting projects in the business. This book is a companion to our website and if you want to stay up to date, visit Musformation.com on a regular basis.

Also, note that websites change every day. One music service gets bought by another and sites always give up or go out of business. Within a week of pressing this book, some service will completely change or go under. Don't hate us if something in this book is already out of date by the time you read it. That is bound to happen. This world moves fast these days and we will update this book and our website as often as we can.

Innovate, Don't Emulate
While this book might tell you what you could be doing or what other successful musicians are doing, the point here is to give you ideas. Not every idea and tool are for every musician, nor are they necessary to emulate. All of the musicians who make a lasting impact must innovate and lead. If you want to be another sheep in the herd, then you can do what everyone else is doing. But the key to being remembered is innovation. Take these ideas and tools and do something new with them.

This book exists because the music business is filled with far too much emulation. There are too many musicians who sound exactly the same and too many industry zombies who parrot old ideas instead of changing with the times. Unfortunately, many young musicians don't know any better than to follow the outdated "wisdom" of industry veterans whose views and ideals have been spoiled by a fast-changing business climate. We're here to give you the tools you need to make something new and interesting. You need to take this book and use it as a springboard to come up with your own ideas and apply them to your music.

Legal Disclaimer:
Even though we often wear cheap suits, we are not lawyers. Nothing in this book should be taken as legal, health or business advice. Please consult

with a lawyer to make sure anything you may be thinking of doing that was inspired by this book is in fact within the bounds of the law.

The authors have exhaustively researched their sources to the best of their abilities to ensure accuracy and comprehensiveness. We assume no responsibility for errors, inaccuracies, omissions or inconsistency herein. Any slight against any of the subjects contained is unintentional. Readers should consult an attorney or accountant for any specific matter since many ideas in this book are spoken in generality and do not always refer to the exhaustive permission, laws and regulations you may need to abide by.

Thank You:
Todd and I would like to thank the following people, without whom writing this book would have been impossible: Jackie Brennan, David Ahuja, Mike Oettinger, Thomas Nassiff, Jeremy Winter, Erica Sackin, Dom Tucci, John Zaremba, Krikor Daglian, Matt Hucke, Martin Franscogna and all of our readers who bring new ideas to the table every day.

Jesse:
I would like to send a special thank you to my parents, Joanne and David Cannon, who provided constant inspiration and support to do everything I have done in my life. Alan Douches, who has always been one of the most inspiring visionaries in the music business, believed in me and inspired much of this book. Dean Rispler, Steve Evetts, Ross Robinson, Greg Ross and the fine folks at WFMU all believed in me enough to give me the opportunities to learn all of this information. Mike Gallucci, Sam Goldman, Spencer Ackerman, Ben Manners, Ivan Berko, Pat King and Elliot Aronow, all of whom I played and learned about music with. Lastly, I would like to thank Alap Momin, Benjamin Weinman, John Cafiero, Will Brooks, Ken Stewart, Zack Zarrillo, Justin Collier, Tim Landers, Finn McKenty, Dan Sassone and Jonathan Snyder, all of whom I regularly bounced ideas off of that contributed to this book.

Todd:
I would like to thank my bandmates, Mike Sherburn and John Barclay, for putting up with me during this time and for being an ongoing experimental guinea pig for many of the ideas and theories in this book. I'd also like to thank my parents, Ron and Freida Thomas, who have always kept me going with their continued support.

Chapter 1: How Do I Get More People To Hear My Music & Make Fans?

Obscurity

The biggest problem most musicians have is obscurity--not enough people know who you are. No one knows that they should listen to your music or give your song a chance to become their favorite track. Even if your music is readily available, people aren't aware that it's out there. When I'm in my studio working with musicians, I am asked two questions every single day: "How do we get more people to hear us?" and "How do we get more fans?" What musicians don't realize is that these are two different steps in the process of building a fanbase that leads to a career.

These are questions you'll be asking yourself for the rest of your life, even if you're U2, Kanye West, Metallica, Tiesto or some other huge act. You'll always want more people to be aware of what you do and to pay to be a part of it. Even when you're the biggest act within your genre, there are still potential fans that've never heard of you and these are people who might like your music if they did hear it. Part of keeping your fanbase growing is finding these untapped listeners, getting your music in their ears and converting them into fans.

When you're a lesser-known musician, this problem is much more daunting. No one is interested in writing about you and you can't just book gigs to get more exposure. You're fighting for every scrap of interest you can possibly get, even employing one-on-one interactions via social networks to persuade one potential fan to listen to your music.

In order to get more people to hear your music, you need to raise awareness about what you're doing. This could apply to your new music, tour dates, activism, unique merch or whatever it is that makes you special. While it's easier said than done, your ultimate goal is to raise awareness about your music and everything you have to offer with it. You might want to highlight the great interviews you do, the merch you make, the cool songs you have, the chats you hold with fans on Twitter or your insane live shows. If you focus on increasing public awareness about these things, most of your other problems will become much easier to deal with as fans discuss your band and spread the word about your music. If you do something remarkable, fans and writers will want to tell the world about you. If you aren't doing anything special, why would anyone want to talk about you?

Much of our focus with this book is to come up with ideas for raising awareness about your music. The more eventful promotions you create that get your fans excited, the easier it'll be for you to get more people to listen to your music. Every song you release, update you post, contest, item of merch you sell, gig you play and service your music gets posted to all have the potential to raise awareness and get another listener to hear your music. The question then becomes, "What does this look like in practice?"

Make Music Fans Love
Nearly every piece of writing about promoting your music emphasizes how important this is, so we'll spare you by not repeating it time and time again. The better job you do crafting your songs, the easier it is to transform listeners into diehard fans who want to spread the word about you and your band. The more remarkable your music is, the easier it is to promote. Now that we've got that out of the way, we won't mention this every few pages like every other book about promoting your music.

Always Be Available - You want to have your music in as many places as possible. The more places you have your music, the more chances there are for someone to discover it. If you make merch, you want to have it abundantly available and worn by as many fans as possible--not only so you can fund your music, but also so you can turn your fans into a walking advertisement. If your fans want updates from you on a social network they frequent, give it to them on the network they prefer. The more people see you, the more chances you have for them to listen to your music and become a fan. Be available everywhere you possibly can.

Be Eventful - Musicians who are good at marketing themselves online are well versed in doing cool promotions that get their fans excited. This is not a coincidence. This comes from putting hard work and thought into figuring out what will excite fans and how to turn every promotion into a major event that gets buzz. Being eventful means, you are doing something worth talking about. Unique, personalized events will be the topic of even more talk by being spread by your fans and writers alike.

Draw Attention - In order to get anyone to listen to you, you need to draw attention to yourself. This requires getting others to talk about you and actively taking part in eventful promotions. If you're not doing promotions worth talking about, there is no reason for fans to discuss you and point to your music.

Feed Your Fans - A constant stream of content (*music, videos, blog posts, video updates or anything else that a fan can ingest and enjoy*) will continue to make you an eventful act that tastemakers comment on and fans tell other potential fans about. Keep up a constant stream of eventful activity that your fans can discuss, so they always have something new to spread the word about. This helps put your name in front of more people, increasing the chance of making a new fan. If you're not creating new content on a regular basis, you lose your chance to raise awareness and you lose your chance to get discovered. The more content you create, the more opportunities you have to be discovered.

Friction - You need to make it as easy as possible for fans to do what you want them to do. This means they shouldn't pay for music before they even know whether they like it. The easier you make it for potential fans to discover your music, become addicted to it and then promote it to their friends--the easier it'll be for you to organically grow a fanbase. Anything that makes it harder for that to happen is *friction*. An example of this is making a potential fan click through pop up banners on your website in order to hear a song before they even know if they like you or not.

User Experience - Too many musicians spend time *wishing* their fans would think and act the way they want them to. This is a fool's game. Musicians who think about their fans' experience when interacting with them are musicians who gain fans. If you clutter your social networks with self-indulgent nonsense, inside jokes and irrelevant tweets, you aren't giving your fans an experience they will enjoy, since they will feel left out. Thinking about what your fans want to see--updates, promotions, contests and live experiences--will help keep them excited and supportive. Think about what your favorite musicians do and what you enjoy seeing them do. Think about how you can bring that enjoyable experience to your fans-- doing so will help you grow a fanbase that appreciates what you do.

All of these practices, along with the other concepts littered throughout this book, will help you get your music heard by more listeners and turn them into lifelong fans. If they like what you hear, you'll grow a fanbase.

How Do I Get More Fans?

There is a big difference between getting more fans and getting people to listen to you. A fan is someone who enjoys your music, listens to it and is curious about what you're doing next. Not everyone who hears your music will become a fan, but obviously, attracting more listeners increases the chance to gain more new fans. Once someone hears you and then decides they like you, it's important to give them the opportunity and resources to become a dedicated fan.

If someone hears your new single and likes it, that's great. But without more music, ways to keep in touch with you and additional content for this listener to bite into, they won't necessarily become a fan. You need other songs that this potential fan hasn't heard, merch, social network presence, videos or any other special fan-oriented content to develop this relationship. You want your content to be attractive, turning a first-time listener into a longtime fan who will support your music for years or even decades, to come. This is all a part of what goes into creating a fan. If you want fans you need to nurture these relationships by giving them content they want. In return, they will ideally pay for that content--if not now, then perhaps eventually.

While the evolution from listener to fan has remained the same for decades, the post-Napster-era has changed certain things. Gone is the idea that you'll make your fans pay to find out if they even like what you have to offer. There is so much free music in the world today that you need to offer free samples to get your foot in the door. Asking a fan to pay for your music before they even know whether they like it puts you at a disadvantage when compared to the millions of other musicians who are giving out free samples. These musicians aren't keeping their music behind a wall--they are putting it out there in the marketplace, letting people listen to it, enjoy it and then buy it. <u>Before going any further, you need to accept that part of turning an interested listener into a fan is giving them a free sample first, then building a relationship from there.</u>

The Goal Of Every Musician - <u>The goal of every musician is to get more fans</u>. Fans cheer you on when you play live shows, support you financially, give you praise that makes you feel good and spread your music to more people so the world can hear it. No matter what, the bottom-line goal of every musician should be to get more fans.

Turning Listeners Into Fans

If you have no fans, you can't make any money because you have no one to sell anything to. You need to first raise awareness of your music, give people a chance to hear it, then let them take their time to enjoy and become entrenched in your music. They will decide how much they like you and hopefully consume it and want to hear more from you.

When you see your idols in established acts like Taylor Swift withholding their music from streaming music services and only selling music to fans without giving away free samples, it's because they have already earned their fan base's' trust. Fans trust these acts to make a record they'll enjoy, so they will pay early in the process for the chance to hear it. When you have very few fans, you haven't earned that trust. You can help yourself build that trust by giving away as much free music as you can and getting in front of more listeners.

Just A Taste - If you have ever been to a mall food court, you've probably experienced the *chicken taste tactic*. You walk into the food court and you may know that you want to eat at a specific place like Chipotle or you may still be undecided. Along the way, there is an employee of the local Chinese food stand, giving out free samples of their kung-pow chicken on a toothpick. They call out, inviting you to have a free taste. Inevitably, you walk over, take the free sample and then decide whether you like it. Accordingly, you decide whether to eat at the Chinese food stand or make your way to an established favorite, like Chipotle.

If you do decide to check out the Chinese stand, they're hoping for you to see all the other awesome products they have to offer: Other types of chicken, more expensive entrees, soda, cheap appetizers, even a funny cashier. You have now become aware of everything this stand has to offer, all because of your free sample. You might buy the most expensive thing on the menu or even become a regular customer. Even though the free sample cost the Chinese stand five cents, you might start spending $30 a week at their business. That works out pretty well for them, huh?

This process is used in every supermarket and food court--and even in magazine advertisements that include a free perfume sample. All types of business give away small samples for free, hoping consumers will keep coming back for more and more. If your product--in this case, your music-- is good enough, you'll be able to use a free sample to create a new loyal customer--in this case, a new diehard fan.

In Music Terms - To draw a parallel to that chicken sample, as a musician you need to offer your fans a way to ingest your music for free, enabling them to decide if they're interested in seeing what else you have available. This is the most effective way to turn a listener into a fan. If a new listener enjoys your free song, you lead them to your website--where you have more streaming music waiting for them, along with videos, free downloads or other types of content. If they like what they see and hear, you have to make sure you introduce them to other content--this time, content they have to pay for.

New listeners should be presented with a multitude of options across a few different price points. These options can include EPs (the equivalent to an appetizer), LPs (small entree), a "deluxe package" that includes maybe a T-shirt paired with music (expensive entree) and finally some stickers, coffee mugs, etc. (soda and sides). Having options helps ease the transition from new listener to financially supportive fan. This is the goal of every interaction with a new listener--and since you can't communicate directly with every single person, you need to make sure your online presence is built to do this for you.

Once this listener becomes a paying customer and a new fan, they will hopefully help expose you to more potential fans. Maybe they will bring a friend to your concert or share your music with someone--like you might bring a co-worker to the Chinese stand with you. That co-worker becomes a regular customer of the stand and then tells another friend about it, just like what can happen when someone shares your music on Facebook or Twitter. All of this exposure is possible when you make free samples of your music available. You begin a process that opens the gates for your music to be spread around and you have the opportunity to attract listeners and turn them into fans with very little friction.

In a streaming music world where most of your potential fans are finding new music, they love through Spotify playlists, it means you have to do whatever you can to get yourselves on those playlists since this is where your fans are looking for samples.

The Price Of A Relationship - By eating the small cost of a free food sample, the Chinese stand created a regular customer. That customer now helps the stand make money on a regular basis by eating there and exposing the stand to other people. This is what you're trying to do with

29

each and every listener. If your song is only available for 99 cents on iTunes, you may get some interested parties who bite the bullet and pay for it without getting to listen to it beforehand. But after Apple takes its cut and after taxes, you only see about 40 cents of that dollar anyway. The potentially random income of 40 cents from an iTunes sale isn't worth the number of potential fans it deters from listening to your music. By having that song streaming for free, you're maximizing the relationships you build--opening up the door to many more real fans than you would ever gain if you keep your music behind a pay wall. This also helps you grow a genuinely interested fanbase in an organic way--these are the people that may support you with hundreds of dollars every year by purchasing music, show tickets, merch, etc.

Turning a listener into a fan and then a paying customer is how you pursue your dreams and further your career. This is why it's essential to first worry about making fans, then worry about making money from them. If you're having trouble building a following, there's probably too much friction in the road from listener to fan. Tear down those borders and you'll watch your fanbase rise faster than ever before.

If you're not convinced yet, we'll delve much deeper into the nuances of this topic later in the book.

Building Relationships
Look at it this way: You're not in the music sales business--as so many musicians think they are--you're in the *relationship business*. Think about how all of your relationships have grown throughout your life. You meet someone and develop an interest in them. Eventually, you might put a title on the relationship, like *friend, boyfriend, girlfriend* or in this case, *fan*. Now imagine if you proposed to a person that they should take on this new title when all they knew was your name. That would be a little uncomfortable, right?

This is what musicians are doing when they try to sell music to potential fans before they even hear it. This is a marriage proposal before the friendship has begun. It's much smarter to give your fans an introduction, showing them your awesome personality and talents. If they're impressed, you take the relationship to the next level. Take the time to impress this potential partner and fall in love before you get hitched and trade your financial information, just like you would a marriage.

Once upon a time, chunks of music sales occurred after a fan discovered a song on MTV or the radio. Now these outlets are becoming outdated and instead fans usually discover music through a streaming service like YouTube or SoundCloud--the two most popular ways to discover new music, according to MusicMetric. Usually, this exposure is the result of sharing via social networking. This opportunity is hindered when musicians hide their music in previews or don't post it online for fans to digest. It's very hard to build a relationship if you aren't active on the sites and services where people most often discover new music. This is why posting every song you make on every platform is so crucial in a streaming world.

Nurturing - When musicians take advantage of the ways a listener discovers music, they're nurturing a fan relationship. Instead of trying to get discovered by writing letters and emails to A&R people at record labels, DJs at radio stations or video reps at cable networks, musicians are turning to fans that give them strong endorsements until the right people notice them.

By focusing on your relationships with your fans instead of waiting for others to give you a chance, you can build an army of fans who not only promote your music, but also financially support you. Taking the time to connect with fans--feeding them the content they want--starts a mutually beneficial relationship. The fans enjoy the content you create and you get the financial support you need to create it all. Luckily, you can now connect directly with these fans, communicate with them, find out what they want and deliver it straight to them.

Perhaps the best part about the way we communicate today is the two-way relationship between fan and artist. In the past, musicians would mostly talk to their fans, with very little response back. Maybe a fan joined their mailing list or street team but staying in touch took a hugely concentrated effort. Sending out promos to a physical mailing list took hours of work and tons of materials and postage. That process cost record labels a significant amount of money--today, all it takes is 20 minutes and an Internet connection.

Just like what happens within a friendship, you can now exchange contact information with your fans via social media. You're able to get in touch with each other whenever you have something to say. If you want to tell your fans what you're up to, whether it's news about a new tour or just a funny story, you can deliver that message to them immediately and directly.

31

When your fans want to tell you it's been too long since you released music, that you should be playing this venue instead of that venue or that they just heard your song on the radio, they can do so in a heartbeat via Twitter, email or a handful of other outlets.

Best of all, this communication can start a meaningful relationship with fans that will allow you to connect and create superfans like never before. Surveys show that fans are more likely to spend money on musicians they feel they have a personal connection with. Even if your biggest concern is about getting rich, as opposed to the art of music, you still need to focus on building relationships with your fans. This means talking to concert attendees, distributing content on your social networks, demonstrating your personality and most of all, giving fans what they want. If your fans want hooded sweatshirts, print them and sell them. If they want live video broadcasts, you can do it in seconds on YouTube. If they want a new record and you don't have the money for it, you can start a crowdfunding campaign and create a new record your fans fund themselves.

If you're not willing to go out of your way to make one new fan at a time, you're at a disadvantage to the thousands of musicians who are. Most fanbases are built a few fans at a time. It's very rare that you're going to see huge jumps in fans in the early stages of accumulating your following. Instead, you're going to have to concentrate on going out of your way to do more than just spam potential fans on social networks. You're going to have to put effort into one-on-one connections until you have enough fans that you can empower them to make other fans for you on a regular basis. Even then, going out of your way for your fans will ensure they continue to become bigger fans and tell more of their friends about you.

You can build these relationships your own way. Some musicians do it through constant touring. Musicians like Justin Bieber and Lady Gaga built their followings through small interactions with fans on Twitter and connecting fans together on social networks based around their music--like Lady GaGa's Little Monsters network. The group Chester French takes more time to write their fans personal letters than they do pursuing press interviews. Alex Day makes countless YouTube videos and interacts with fans in the comments sections of the videos. By interacting with your fans, you strengthen your relationship and the support they give you. Studies show time and time again, <u>fans support musicians they feel they have the closest connections with.</u>

Decade-Long Relationships

Young musicians always seem to think of relationships as fleeting, short-term flings. When I mention decade-long relationships it doesn't seem plausible, especially to musicians trying to build their first fanbase. But to me, it's very real. From before I was born, my father has had a 45-year relationship with Bruce Springsteen. In January of 1973, my father went with my mother and his friend Doug Joswick, a music industry veteran, to Parsippany, NJ. At a club called A Joint In The Woods they plunked down $4 to see Bruce. There they saw him play a few times and were stunned by his diverse performances. Every time they saw him at a show, he would perform different arrangements of songs, playing acoustic guitar one night then maybe piano the next.

These performances turned my father into an instant fan, purchasing his copy of *Greetings From Asbury Park* the week it became available. By 1974, Springsteen was playing to a couple hundred fans at The Capitol Theater and my father was still there. Over the years, he has bought over 20 records (some on multiple formats) from The Boss within the first weeks they were released. He has followed him to shows with 75,000 other fans at Giants Stadium. My father has seen Springsteen about 15 times and he has friends who have seen him more than 100 times.

But it goes even further. Bruce's guitarist Little Steven throws garage rock festivals that my dad attends. Steven has a show on Sirius XM and it's the main reason my father has a subscription to the service. He even gave Little Steven's horrible series on Netflix a chance. This relationship has a vast reach and can help you and the careers of many musicians around you, for years to come.

I've been regularly buying records, T-shirts and going to shows by Blur, Tortoise, Daft Punk, Public Enemy and Lifetime for over 15 years. This type of relationship loyalty doesn't just apply to bands. Since I was a teenager, I've been following and buying everything I could from J. Robbins, John McEntire, Dennis Lyxzen and Richard D. James. As long as these musicians keep making music, I will keep following them. Even further, I got my Clash records from my father, who saw them play in the late 70's. This fan relationship was passed down to me and I've seen Joe Strummer and Mick Jones whenever I've had the chance and bought every record they've released, as well as numerous Clash T-shirts, posters and DVDs.

This is the relationship you can build. Not every fan is going to follow you for their whole life, but if you bond with your fans and maintain a relationship, they can last as long as you're making music. This relationship can make you a significant amount of money for years down the road. A small initial investment like talking to a fan on Facebook can end up in a huge payoff as long as the relationship is maintained.

Building Quality Fans
While you should try to get your music in front of as many listeners as possible, you also want to make sure you nurture and capitalize on your existing relationships. A relationship is a two-way street and you need to give in order to receive. Part of this giving from the musician's side is what gets fans to buy your music and promote you. What fans really want from musicians is a connection. They get those connections from personal contact, special experiences and most importantly, good music that affects them emotionally.

Fans also want to actively be a part of music. They want to listen to music that defines them. You can learn a lot about a person by looking through their iPod, because your taste in music is a huge part of your identity. As a Brooklyn resident, I identify myself as part of the community's music scene when I wear a Misfits, Morning Glory or Pup shirt. I choose to show my community parts of my personality through these shirts and the musicians allow me to be a part of what they do by selling me these shirts. When people choose to become a fan of your music, giving them the option to identify themselves as such will help you build a loyal and proud fanbase. By enabling fans to tell others about you, you encourage them to be a part of what you stand for. This depth gives them a reason to promote you.

If you continue to give fans what they want, they will give you the support you need, whether it's financial or otherwise. There are countless ways to upgrade your relationship with the fans you have and turn them into superfans that support you for years to come. This is the ultimate goal.

Seeing Is Believing - Musicians have trouble believing this can happen to them. But this process is simple to see. Today you can actually watch someone grow from a listener into a full-blown fan. Let's say you post a new song on YouTube. A listener then checks it out because their friend shares a link--they hear your song and love it. If you have a link to a free download of that song in the description under your YouTube video, you can get their email address in exchange for that free download. A week later, you can look at your email list and see that the same fan came back and downloaded some more songs you made available for free. Two weeks from now, you can see that their email address is now in your customers list, since they bought your latest record and a T-shirt.

I've watched this happen to the groups I work with and you can too, using the methods discussed throughout this book. There is plenty of technology out there to help you keep track of the patterns of your fans and help you realize how you have made new fans. If you utilize these tools, along with other smart practices, you may see those email addresses pop up in your customers list for decades to come.

What Turns A Listener Into A Fan

There's a concept often called "the listening barrier" which is how you get a potential fan to go from that potential status to actually hearing your music and becoming a fan. We've established that you need to first to make listeners aware of your music and then turn them into your fans. But what are the most effective methods of making that happen?

Hearing Is Believing - The most important and convincing way to gain fans is to actually have them hear your music. Nothing inspires a faster reaction in a listener than hearing a great song. This is why touring, radio, music videos, streaming playlists, recommendation radio and DJs are the most powerful ways to gain fans. Concentrating on some of these outlets can be expensive, but with the right ideas and efforts most of them can be tackled in a cheap and efficient way.

Getting placements, playing shows and having your music promoted by tastemakers is the way to make this happen. While this is easier said than done, many musicians put a high degree of concentration on this practice and work creative angles, reaping great payoffs when their music gets heard.

Friendly Recommendations - We've all discovered some of our favorite music from our friends' recommendations. We trust friends with similar taste--therefore, we are much more likely to explore something they recommend compared to recommendations that come from others. This is why Twitter, Facebook and Instagram are such powerful ways to discover new music. Since friends often have the same emotional lexicon as us, it makes sense that we would respond similarly to the emotional communication. Enabling this modern form of sharing is an important way to promote your music and the reason why so much emphasis is placed on making your music social and easily shared. While these shares are only spread to a small group of people at a time, these friendly recommendations are taken very seriously.

Make it easy for your fans to share your music with the countless tools available to do so. Encourage them to do so and offer them rewards like free downloads, retweets and other encouragements and you will see your music spread quickly.

Algorithmic Recommendations – The fastest growing way we find new music is algorithms giving us recommendations and while this is becoming more and more powerful it is still not equal to friendly recommendations. Listeners are overwhelming turning solely to the recommendation playlists served to them by the streaming services they use since they have data that can effectively predict what they will like more accurately than any of the other methods I just outlined. This is overwhelmingly the way passionate music fans now find new music and harnessing this method is crucial to building any fanbase today.

The most common way to work this promotion is submitting your music to influencers and following streaming services best practices. We will get into all of that in our chapter on digital distribution.

Influencer Recommendations - When a potential fan sees one of their favorite musicians, YouTubers, authors or actors recommending you, it can lead to that potential fan giving your music a chance. If a fan trusts or respects the source of a recommendation, it can go a long way in getting them to stop what they're doing and listen to your music. We all want to be closer with those we respect and learn what inspires them to be so great. Fans will investigate these recommendations so they can gain a deeper connection with those they respect. While less effective than a friend's recommendation, this is still a good source of getting listeners to investigate your music. While not as high a percentage of followers will listen to this influencer's recommendation as a friend's recommendation, influencers have so many followers that their recommendation is still very helpful. Even if not everyone listens, the sheer number of their fans that they influence can make this a huge step in gaining a fanbase.

Getting your musician friends to recommend you on their social network feeds is a perfect example of these recommendations' power in action. If you know a semi-famous author, having them plug your record in an interview can lead to tons of new listeners--even though they aren't a musician. Many musicians will send their music to celebrities with hopes of getting mentioned by them. Other musicians will identify their most influential friends, social network followers and fans, then concentrate on nurturing those relationships in hopes of getting promoted by those with a large audience.

Respected Recommendations - Record reviews, interviews, blogs, papers and news sites can all help get you discovered by potential fans. If a listener knows a paper, blog or site to have good taste, seeing your name there gives you a powerful endorsement. If you're able to get a good review, it will help persuade readers who trust the reviewer to give you a listen. While this form of recommendation is dramatically less effective than the two discussed above with power that seems to diminish every year, it's much easier to make happen--all you need is a little hard work. Many marketers are starting to see that even write-ups from huge outlets like The New York Times have less impact than an Instagram from an influential personality or streaming playlist.

The most common way to work this promotion is submitting your music to blogs and writers. Keeping your name in the news and getting reviews, interviews and song streams is the most effective way to take advantage of this promotion.

Community Recommendations - Having your music talked about all over the Web will eventually cause listeners to check you out. Seeing stickers, T-shirts, Facebook updates, flyers, online content and ads can create a tipping point where you seem to be so ever-present that a listener will check you out to see what the fuss is about. This potential fan may not always be someone who is likely to be into your music, coming to you from the critical mass of having seen and heard about you from all your combined promotions. While this takes a lot of work, if you can manage to become unavoidable, you'll get countless listeners to check you out.

The best way to enable this form of discovery is to diversify your promotions. Not only do you need to mount a local sticker campaign, you also need a strong social network presence. It's important to do a little bit of everything. Many fanbases have been built by concentrating on one area at a time, thinking about different ways to reach every possible potential fan in every different way. From physical promotions in your hometown to online marketing campaigns that engage fans across the country, getting people to interact with you will draw more new listeners.

Accumulating Subtleties - Discussed throughout this book are countless ways to promote your music. While many of the suggestions seem small, paying attention to the details will help form one giant structure to help gain a fanbase. Endless small promotions will eventually create a tidal wave that makes people take notice of you. Make time for every small detail and eventually all of them will add up to something bigger.

Advertising - Nothing is less likely to attract new listeners than an advertisement. Advertisements are helpful for keeping up promotion, helping with your familiarity and branding and reminding existing fans to give you a listen. The likelihood of gaining new fans from an ad is lower than all other forms of promotion. Advertising should only be employed in your promotions if you are using a diverse array of strategies in order to create the critical mass we described when discussing community recommendations.

One affordable way to help advertising work is using targeted advertising. In the Internet era, you can use Facebook, Google and a handful of other tools to target people who might be more likely to enjoy your music. Sadly, most people ignore ads and don't treat them the same as they would a recommendation. If you can find a way to target fans and tell them how you fit in with what they already like (for example, if you sound like Miley Cyrus, target Miley Cyrus fans and tell them you sound like her), you can see effective results for your dollar. But most advertising is essentially money down the drain, unless you pull out all the stops and employ some clever strategy.

Consistent, Sustained Repetition of Promotion - The key ingredient in getting a potential fan to discover you is consistent, sustained repetition of Promotion. All of the above methods of discovery need to be employed in order to gain a large fanbase, but they also need to be employed consistently and over a long period of time, with very few lapses in promotion. Many musicians suffer from absent periods where they drop off the radar of their fans. This inconsistency depletes your momentum.

When I am asked for the "secrets" of building a fanbase, I always point to consistent, sustained repetition of promotions. Building your fanbase is like pushing a snowball down a mountain: The more you roll it, the more it grabs other pieces of snow and grows. If you stop rolling it for a short time, the ball will begin to melt in the sun. The key is to not rest and keep pushing. As the ball gets bigger and bigger, others see it and want to come look at this humongous snowball, adding some snow to it themselves.

Continuing to feed your fans content in a consistent, sustained way keeps that snowball rolling and growing in size. When you stop, fans forget about you. They stop following you on a social network; they grow up and move on to another type of music. It's important to constantly make new fans so you can compensate for the ones that inevitably move on. Without this sustained and consistent promotion, you'll lose fans while you're absent and never gain the momentum you need to really take advantage of the fans you make and broaden your fanbase.

Two Methods Of Promotion Strategy
Once you're ready to start promoting your music, you can focus on one of two paths. Which of these directions you choose will decide whether you put your music's future in your own hands or someone else's. There are two viable ways to think about your promotions.

Trickle-Down Promotions - The first method of promoting yourself is referred to as trickle-down promotions. This is the attempt (*the key word being attempt*) to get big opportunities that trickle down and expose you to new fans. These are opportunities like getting to play Jimmy Fallon's late-night show, scoring a licensing deal to be in an Apple commercial or getting an opening slot on a huge tour. While these opportunities are important to go for, they're long shots. If this is all you spend your time on, the likelihood you will build a fanbase isn't great. Though these opportunities can give you a boost in your fanbase equivalent to months of consistent work, they're so unlikely to pan out that you might spend months begging for them and wind up with nothing.

Grassroots Promotions - The opposite of trickle-down promotions are grassroots promotions. These build your fanbase one fan and one small move at a time. Over time you're nurturing a fanbase that grows into a movement so big it can't be ignored. It's these promotions that make gatekeepers notice you--whether they're A&R people at a record label, music coordinators for Jimmy Fallon or booking agents for huge tours.

They approach you because they want exposure to *your* fanbase that you have built *for yourself*. Grassroots promotions are built on fan relationships and making sure that the size of your fanbase is obvious. Even if writers or late-night talk show bookers aren't feeling your music, they'll be inclined to work with you if you show them that you have a sizable audience because they will want to expose themselves to your fanbase.

Remember, musicians don't usually get huge opportunities because someone believes in them. They get an opportunity because someone else believes they can benefit from giving them that opportunity. If you try to get booked on Jimmy Fallon and have 50 Facebook fans, they would be doing you a favor where they get nothing in return. If you have 50,000 fans, all of who may watch you play when the show airs, you are now showing talk-show bookers that you are a worthy recipient of the time and opportunity they hold. If you build a fanbase yourself, you will become someone who others want to give opportunities to.

This Is How You Do It
This book is devoted to pursuing grassroots promotions. While you would be a fool to not find trickle-down promotions to take advantage of, usually that involves making industry contacts, begging them to listen to you and hoping for the best. That doesn't take a book to explain.

If you put your eggs in the basket of only pursuing trickle-down promotions, you are most likely going to be miserable at your day job for years to come. While you wait for gatekeepers to give you a present you haven't earned, other musicians will be steadily climbing their way over the gate by building a fanbase that these gatekeepers will want to have access to. Remember, the reason any gatekeeper lets you through--giving you the opportunity they hold the key to--is because they think it will be beneficial for them. Whether it's exposure with your audience or the "cool factor" you present, you're rarely going to get anyone in the music business to help you unless they think they can benefit from you. Once in a while, a powerful gatekeeper may love your music and want to work with you, even if you're just starting out. Sadly, you may be waiting a long time before you find that person. Instead of waiting, build a grassroots fanbase that demands attention and makes gatekeepers come to you.

Taking the time to write emails and mail press kits to A&R people, big time managers and booking agents who have never heard of you is a waste of time. You could be devoting that time to building a fanbase that makes you attractive to all the powerful players you want to work with. Don't sit around hoping an industry professional will discover you at your next show and solve your problems. Instead, you can solve them yourself. Build a team that mobilizes fans and attracts attention from those professionals.

Many musicians think paying a publicist, video promotion company or a label will get them a fanbase. However, using these resources to promote yourself is only useful once you already have fans. You have to build a grassroots following if you want any of these promotions to be helpful. Otherwise, you will waste money on promotions that do you very little good when your momentum dies.

This Isn't New - If you think I'm crazy for suggesting these things, understand that this has been happening for decades. Joan Jett went solo after leaving The Runaways and was turned down by 23 different major record labels (*back when there were 23 major labels, not 3*). She released her debut record on her own, in spite of having little-to-no budget. But she built a team that got her tons of attention for a fraction of what it would cost most groups and went on to sell 10 million copies of her record worldwide. She even made a music video about the process for her hit single "Bad Reputation." A little over a decade later Lisa Loeb would land a #1 single with her song "Stay" on her own label.

The punk scene of the 1980s turned out bands that put out records on their own indie labels, like Fugazi. Although they never pursued press opportunities themselves, their rabid fanbase demanded mainstream coverage. In the '90s, groups like The Offspring and Rancid sold millions of records--all without playing the mainstream music game--by building a smart infrastructure within their indie label, Epitaph Records.

Many musicians think managing themselves or releasing their own music diminishes the chance of getting exposure because it looks unprofessional. This has never been the case. Do you think MTV thought twice about playing Bad Religion or Black Flag music videos because the guitarist of each band ran their record label? I still saw them late at night on MTV and bought their records after seeing their videos. When Jay-Z was selling his own music out of the trunk of his car, no one did anything but drop their jaws at his talent. They definitely didn't check to see what major label executives thought of him. Metric gets stocked on shelves at major retail outlets and receives airplay on nearly every alternative rock station in North

41

America. No one thinks twice about the fact that they're the only act on their own record label.

The playing field is more level than ever before. As I write this, I'm being forced to add more names every month to the roster of successful musicians who are abandoning major *and* indie labels altogether and doing it on their own. A Day To Remember, Circa Survive, Macklemore, Coheed & Cambria and Metric all successfully self-released records during the writing of this book. Groups like Metallica are getting ready to do the same. They make smart business decisions, have control of their own music and most importantly, they don't have to worry about a record label making poor decisions, destroying their profits or ruining their relationship with their fans.

What You're Trying To Build
This book is about *building*. From a fanbase to income to followers on a social network to a great record to fans all over the country, you're trying to build an infrastructure that lasts. While the last thing I want to do is be some old geezer lecturing you about having a career decades from now, you should realize that I am also talking about getting you fans that throw underwear at you during every show and provide you the income to buy all 200 of the guitars you want. No matter what your ultimate goal is, the technique to achieve it is exactly the same. The theory behind building a fanbase is constant among all genres of music. While your specific promotions may differ from other musicians, the core theory is present in every musician who builds a fanbase in the new music business.

You're trying to build a multi-armed machine that can handle your entire music career on its own without waiting for support from a label, manager or anyone else. Get dropped from a label after you make the record of your life, like countless other musicians? Great! You'll still have all your fans' email addresses and they will still know where to go to get new music from you. Booking agent quits the business? Well that is sad, but you have all the contacts for venues and the means to promote every show from here to eternity, all on your own. Go through managers like Spinal Tap goes through drummers? You have built an infrastructure that is self-sufficient and rooted in the connections you have made with your fans--not in the strings your manager pulled for you.

Getting Signed

42

There was a time when getting signed to a label meant that a badass team of professionals would congregate to solve your problems as a musician. While that can still happen on occasion, it's much more common for a musician to assemble a team one member at a time, often over the course of several years. Slowly, they build a solid team devoted to working together and helping them build a substantial fanbase.

Many musicians think that once they sign to a big indie or major label, the label will create all sorts of opportunities for them. It's assumed that awesome tours, huge TV spots, lucrative publishing contracts, endorsements and all other types of cool stuff descends from the sky the second the contract is signed. But this isn't true and becomes less common every day. Your team--meaning your manager, booking agent, publicist, lawyer and maybe even a label--all make these opportunities happen by working together. Yes, getting signed to a popular label can open some doors, but tons of musicians on great record labels still fail because they haven't built an equally great team surrounding them.

<u>"Getting signed" should not be your ultimate goal, since it is both obsolete and shortsighted.</u> Instead, you need to be thinking about how to attract a team that can work together to build you a fanbase. There is no secret "getting signed method." The secret method is finding good people who will help build you up. Throughout this book, we'll discuss the things you can do to attract this team.

DIY Means Decide It Yourself, Not Do It Yourself
Derek Sivers, founder of CDBaby (his book, *Anything You Want*, is a highly recommended read), has a great saying that DIY doesn't mean do-it-yourself--it means decide-it-yourself. When you're a DIY musician, you can make the decision to write a record that sounds nothing like your older material without having to run it by anyone else. If you want to manage yourself, but hire an outside booking agent or publicist, that's your choice. If you want to sign to a label and have them take control of certain aspects of your business, that's your call--but you can also decide to call the shots yourself instead of taking the risk inherent in a record label that may make decisions based on an outdated, formulaic way of thinking. If you know your audience and you know the way you want to promote yourself better than a label would know, you can put yourself in charge.

DIY doesn't have to mean do it *all* yourself. If all goes as planned, you won't have the time to do it all on your own. Instead, your team will be there to help you make decisions and accomplish goals. Until you get that reliable team in your corner, you may have to shoulder more of the burden on your own. But the advantage is that by learning each job and how they combine to work toward a common endpoint, you'll know whether future team members are holding up their end of the deal. Remember, doing it yourself means you're not left thinking someone else is going to do a job that needed to get done.

Building Your Own Team
Regardless of whether you sign to a label, you'll need to amass a team that makes smart decisions, creates opportunities and efficiently follows through on those opportunities. Signing a record deal doesn't mean anything is going to automatically happen--your team still has to be vigilant. Just ask the thousands of musicians who signed to a major label and never even sold 1,000 records. Some musicians get signed to a huge label and never even release a record because their team fails to get things off the ground--despite the added resources provided by the label. Getting a great record label, booking agent, manager, publicist, etc., is just part of the puzzle of building a fanbase. Though getting on an established label or management team will open doors and give you some financial backing, it means little without a team in the background that keeps pushing you and helping you create a smart overall strategy. Getting signed is not the end-all, be-all answer to building a fanbase; the answer is assembling a reliable team, which you are an active a part of.

You don't have to answer to a major label A&R moron who asks why you changed your sound or whines about your singer's new haircut. Your team can be made entirely of individuals you trust yourself. You can book huge tours on your own and even avoid Ticketmaster and LiveNation by selling the tickets on your own website. Just like Radiohead, Circa Survive, Nine Inch Nails and Chance, you can sell tons of records on your own record label. You can fund the budget of your new record solely from fans' contributions through sites like Kickstarter and not have to worry about pouring your own money into a huge risk.

For the past few decades, smart musicians have built a business around their music. Groups like Metric have a manager who has built a record label of over a dozen employees--all of whom are devoted to working on their music. Because they don't need to split profits with an outside label, they're able to make this happen. While they have their own label, they can still outsource booking and other services. <u>They decided this themselves and you can too.</u>

When I managed Man Overboard, we started our own label dedicated to putting out smaller releases independent of what the band did with the much larger indie label they were signed to. We didn't want to lose the opportunity that came with putting out smaller releases that wouldn't have made sense for a larger label but were still worthwhile connections to our diehard fanbase. Releasing a limited run of cassettes or vinyl from friends' bands kept us in touch with our fanbase and made it possible to do the cool things we enjoyed doing. We decided it was important and made sure the deal we signed with their larger indie label included the freedom to continue doing these releases.

With Man Overboard, we also had our own merch mailing company where we would fulfill hundreds of online orders a month from all across the world. While this wasn't conventional, we decided that this was the way we wanted to build their career. It was important to make small connections with fans by doing our own mail order and communicating directly with customers. We would personalize orders, nickname packages and include funny messages our fans would enjoy while fulfilling their orders. This helped maintain a high level of control in communicating and bonding with fans and it kept profits high to boot.

Outsourcing - While it's great to have your own business and employees, what if that isn't your cup of tea? The great news is that if you don't want this to be all under one roof, it doesn't have to be. You can hire out any publicist, booking agent or manager if you so desire. Unlike the music business of decades ago, there isn't one way to do it. You can make up your own formula and decide for yourself how you want to build your team. The world is your oyster and the knowledge of how to make your own decisions is in the rest of this book.

If you want to achieve your musical dreams, you'll need to build an organization that allows you to sufficiently handle the potential of your music and grow it. There is no right way to do it--and down the road, you can adjust the organization you build as your needs and preferences change. Want to have your own record label and put out releases by musicians you like while making your own music? Tons of musicians are doing that every single day. Want to hire a competent team to handle the business side of things, leaving you to think about only music and video games? You can do that too.

Be So Great You Can't Be Ignored
The goal of every musician should be to make your music and presence so good that you can't be ignored. With some smart strategy, hard work and music skills, you can make your music hard to avoid. But why not just be who you are--be good and hope for the best? Because no one is interested in an artist that puts an average amount of effort into their songs and presence. You, along with every other music fan, want to hear something exceptional. When we all hear or see something exceptional, we stop what we're doing and take notice. Striving to be that exception and pursuing that quest every day will do more for building your fanbase than anything else.

Many musicians have an image of the industry as people writing emails to professionals they have never met, asking them for favors like getting on tours or passing their music along to labels. Instead, you should concentrate on being the best you can be and calling as much attention to yourself as possible. Make it so that potential team members reach out to work with you, rather than randomly asking people to please pay attention to you. You want to be exceptional to the point that fans, bloggers, labels and everyone else in between have to take notice of you. If a manager approaches you, you'll have much more leverage in getting them to work hard on your music as opposed to someone you had to beg to give you a shot. Instead of concentrating on how good of an email you can write to a manager you've never met, you can concentrate on getting your fans to talk about you so much that every manager hears about you on his own. It's easier, more fun...and realistic!

Whoever Cares The Least, Wins!
I know that phrase sounds crazy, but it's true. One of the reasons you're going to build your fanbase--without begging people you've never met to get involved--is so that you're not desperate to get help from anyone who comes along. You need to be exceptional and self-sufficient, so you don't sign with "professionals" who might destroy your future. There have been countless musicians who signed with the first team member that came around. Even though these team members weren't good enough to handle their talent, they signed on with them and then had their potential sunk when opportunities were squandered away.

Sadly, that happens every day. Talk to any musician that had a good buzz and went nowhere. They will usually tell you the reason they failed was they trusted their career to someone who didn't carry their weight. They trusted a manager or label to do something for them and, eventually, momentum died and they were no longer a rising star--they were falling fast. It's sad when you see an act you think are amazing that never takes off. Often, the hidden story behind that failure is that they trusted team members who ended up dropping the ball.

You need to gain momentum and make progress promoting your music on your own. This way, when a record label comes along--that you aren't totally convinced is the right fit--you can say, "I don't care if we sign with them, we're doing fine without their help." Even if you don't sign with the label, you still win. You're self-sufficient, raising awareness every day and continually expanding your fanbase. So even if you don't sign with the label, you are still operating full steam ahead. Eventually, a worthwhile manager or label will come knocking and you'll be able to work with them, strengthening your team even more.

Additionally, if you've been doing the groundwork that comes along with building a fanbase, you've become familiar with almost every job that is part of the process. This makes it easier to determine whether a potential team member is competent and a worthy addition.

This is the philosophy I have brought to any group I've worked with. I want the group to work as hard as it can on its own--and if someone worthwhile takes notice and can help us grow, we add them to our team. If not, we keep trucking along, knocking down doors and making sure the world notices how great we're doing on our own. This always makes potential team members take notice. Instead of begging people to listen to your music, you can demand attention by making them interested in the interesting things you do.

If someone asks to be a part of your team, they have to prove they're capable of pulling their weight and being on board. On the other hand, if you're writing people emails and begging them to work with you, they won't feel the need to work as hard because of how desperate you were to have them on in the first place. After all, you should be grateful they even gave you the time of day. Never be desperate for help. Instead, take charge of promoting your music so that you never waste time begging people for their assistance.

A lot of musician's trust team members who don't pull their weight and are too short-sighted to recognize the problem before it slows down their momentum and kills their dreams. You want to be able to create momentum on your own so you're never in the position of having to take on a lackluster team member.

Even if your ultimate goal is to get signed to a label and have a manager take care of everything for you, you have to work hard to build a team to make this possible. You can't become a rock star who dates celebrities and plays video games all day without promoting yourself and getting noticed early on, making it so you can't be ignored. Waiting around and hoping to be discovered from an email or half-filled live show is a fool's game.

Uphill Battle - Hearing about all this work may deflate your dream of having thousands of adoring fans. As someone who has witnessed this process, I can assure you that the hardest part comes at the beginning. Selling the first 5,000 copies of your record is much harder than the next 5,000. Getting the first 10,000 listeners on your Spotify page is harder than the next 10,000. Once you get the ball rolling, the people who you once begged for help--like promoters, producers, managers and label reps--will start asking you to work together. The more fans you get, the more they will spread the word about your music (with some encouragement).

This is not to say life becomes easy once you hit 10,000 Spotify listeners. Eventually you stop trying to scrape up every available opportunity and instead have the job of fielding many offers and choosing the right ones. You'll need to make smart moves that get you ahead instead of foolish ones that sink your career. Keeping your fanbase active and ever expanding is hard work--but as you grow that fanbase, your job becomes more enjoyable because you're growing as a musician and living your dreams.

Building a Great Team

Talking about a team can instantly bring to mind boring corporate talk, a la the movie *Office Space*. Rest assured, when I talk about teams, I'm just talking about a set of people who work together--much like a sports team. I promise there's no company retreat or exercises where you fall backwards and let your drummer catch you. We all know how that would pan out.

Whether you want to make everyone your own personal employee or have everyone working from their own agency, you need a great team. There are many jobs that go into what popular musicians do every day. Everyone has to be on the same page and doing a good job for you to be successful, so you want to find team members who are as excited and talented as you are. Remember, you and the musicians you work with can fill these roles yourselves, even when you're famous. Regardless of whether your band members all take on a piece of the work or if you decide to outsource each individual job, you're going to need to fill every role outlined below.

You want to find passionate, self-motivated, driven and competent people to fill each role. Maybe your bassist does graphic design as a hobby and can provide fantastic work for your band. Your drummer may aspire to be a manager one day and want to take on this role until someone better comes along or you need someone more experienced. There is no "right" way to get fill these roles, but in the end, you need smart, competent people focused on your band's future. The weakest links in your team always weigh you down. A strong team pushes everyone involved to do their best and raises the quality of everything you do. Recruiting passionate and talented people for all of these positions is one of the most important practices you can do to reach your potential and make something remarkable that fans want to talk about.

Members Of The Team
Below is a list of roles you'll need to fill to make a team. There is no rule that says each of these roles needs to be a separate person. In fact, when you first start off, you may need to fill all of these roles yourself. As you grow, the demands of each job will become too much work and you'll need to bring in more help. As you build a fanbase, you should assemble team members who do an exceptional job filling these roles and bring them on as these jobs become too much to handle. Throughout this book, I will further explain how to find the right person for each of these jobs.

Musicians - Until you build a fanbase and can afford to pay people to do most of these jobs, you're going to have to do them yourself. The musicians you work with are a crucial part of the team and will be responsible for many of these roles until you can afford to bring in other people. This is how you'll get things done when you're starting out and

49

keep your costs down. It's also important to note that if any of the musicians you work with aren't too wild about doing this work, the rest of the team may start to lose excitement as well. It's extremely important for the musicians involved to keep their heads up, take on their roles and keep the ship moving forward with enthusiasm so that all other members of the team feel motivated to do their jobs. Otherwise, they will find a more motivated set of musicians to work for and gain greater returns from.

Manager - Whenever you get an opportunity, no matter where it comes from, it's your manager's job to maximize its potential. Your manager is the hub that connects your team together. They're the go-to person to make sure everyone is on the same page and keep your strategy coordinated.

Your manager is also responsible for making sure your accounting gets done correctly, that everyone shows up at the right place and that your whole infrastructure is working well. It's your manager's job to make sure something gets done even if another team member is slacking off. In the next chapter, the many roles and duties of a manager are discussed more extensively. Your manager is by far the most important member of your team, outside of those you make music with.

Booking Agent - One of the hardest team members to find is a good, competent booking agent. Because of this, many musicians are forced to act as their own booking agents. Your booking agent will book your tours, take care of guarantees and submit you to get on tours with other acts. While this member of the team is usually hard to come by, taking this job seriously is do-or-die for a musician whose fanbase is built through live shows.

Lawyer - Once you're making money and getting new opportunities, you'll need a lawyer to take care of any contracts that come your way. In general, you're going to want to deal with a single lawyer for all of your matters. Oftentimes, a band will sign a contract with a lawyer where the lawyer receives a fee on all earnings that the band makes through the lawyer's help. A lawyer will also shop your music for record deals and licensing.

Record Label - If you choose to sign with a record label, they will handle various aspects of your career. In this day and age, this is not the Swiss army knife of duties like it used to be. Most labels will usually provide you with a publicist, distribution, some marketing money and--if you're lucky-- radio and video promotion. Most deals will bankroll your recording and help open some new doors for you. Some labels go far beyond these capacities, while others are much less prominent in your career. Every label does things differently and there are few universal standards in recording contracts, making it all the more difficult to assess whether you're getting a good deal.

While the record deal is thought of as a huge problem solver, these days it's more of a piece of the puzzle than anything else. If used properly, it can help you advance your career greatly. But if you don't properly take advantage of your spot on a label's roster, it won't do much for you and you'll be another one of the many musicians who got signed and went nowhere.

Distribution - If you don't sign to a label, you need to get a distributor for your music. Distributors get your music for sale in physical and digital outlets. Many distributors will work to get good placements for musicians who show promise and constantly promote their music. Developing this relationship can do a lot for you.

Publicity - Doing publicity is a time-consuming job that takes lots of marketing know-how and relationship building. Writing countless emails and searching out places that will talk about you is a never-ending job. Having someone good at it, with relationships that open doors, is an amazingly valuable asset.

Radio Promotion - Promoting to radio is still a huge piece of getting your music to break into the mainstream. Doing this on your own can be difficult unless you just want to focus on smaller radio outlets and online radio. But independent artists can still do it effectively, especially as online radio starts to dwarf terrestrial radio.

Creative Director – More and more artists have a creative director who is seeking out the artists, directors, clothing designers and others who will create the image around your look and maintain a brand identity for your music.

Video Promotion - Getting your videos promoted can be a huge step in gaining more exposure. While promoting to traditional TV outlets is nearly impossible to do yourself, you can get around this by utilizing online video promotion--by far the strongest method for promoting videos today.

Playlist Promotion – More and more musicians are outsourcing those with contacts to get them on popular playlists on the big streaming services.

Graphic Design - While musicians will use the talents of many different designers for various duties throughout their careers, it's smart to employ one person who can deal with the many graphic needs you'll have. Websites, advertisements, stickers, merch and album art all need graphic work. This can get expensive fast, so developing a relationship with a talented artist or learning to do it yourself is necessary.

Web Development - Sometimes your graphic designer can also be your web developer. No matter what, you're going to need someone to handle the more complex web coding duties that arise. These duties can also mean developing marketing tools for contests or making you a great website.

Publishing/Licensing - Your publisher can do a lot for you in terms of getting placements, licensing deals and making you money through these avenues.

Merch Fulfillment - You're going to need someone to make your merch and send it to people who order it online.

Recording Engineer/Producer - While musicians will change this up from record to record, having a constant person who can help you record alternate versions of songs, blog content and provide quick edits for placements is a plus. Learning to do many of these duties for your own music is extremely helpful.

Videographer - If you're going to do YouTube updates, acoustic videos, music videos or any other type of video content, someone is going to have to film and edit them.

Tour Crew - If you are touring with a live band you will need a crew that handles many roles like tour manager, merchandise, guitar and drum tech, soundguy, lighting technologies and countless other roles depending on the size of the tour.

Chapter 2: Managing Your Music

As the music business changes, old roles and definitions change with it. Even a few years ago, the role of a manager was completely different than what it is now. Today a great manager is much more of an online marketing expert, strategist and an independent spirit who can view your music as a long-term investment instead of a short stock. They're the taskmaster who holds the whole ship together, delegating responsibility and keeping your fanbase growing. They're the whip when someone isn't pulling their weight. The person who plugs the hole before it sinks as well as the person who builds a new sail to make your ship move faster.

Your manager can be a business-minded band member or an outside person who is knowledgeable about the business and loves your music. It could be your drummer (not likely) or your keyboardist. No matter what, when most musicians imagine a manager, the picture they get in their heads is far from the reality. The manager is the most important member of the team you're going to assemble over time. Choosing your manager is a huge decision; understanding the enormous responsibility behind your manager's job will help you choose a good one.

What A Modern Manager Does
It's hard for many musicians to tell whether their manager is doing a good job and what exactly their manager should be doing. While anyone can order merch, update social networks and book local shows, a manager who is going to be proactive in growing your fanbase also does a whole lot more. Below is a list of a few of the responsibilities that managers should take on, but this is just the tip of the iceberg.

- **Strategist** - A manager plans the strategy and coordinates the work between everyone on your team. They also figure out what technology and facilities are needed to accomplish your goals in marketing.
- **Coordinator** - A manager is the go-to person for everyone involved in the artist's music, like the publicist, record label and booking agent. They also help pick up the slack when needed for the booking agent, record label or publicist.
- **Salesman** - A manager is a salesman for your music. They need to make people excited about your music. When your fanbase

53

begins to grow, your manager will be focused on selling others on the idea that you're worthy of new opportunities.

- **Motivator** - Your manager has to keep everyone on their toes and make sure the wheels are turning. When momentum slows, they pick things back up and tell you what to do to keep growing your fanbase.
- **Opportunity Seeker** - A good manager creates new opportunities for you to expose your music to new listeners.
- **Problem Solver** - When problems inevitably arise, it's the manager's job to smooth things out and try to turn negatives into positives. If you become successful, you'll have many great opportunities to choose from--the manager determines which of these opportunities to pursue. When you're smaller, the hardest part of the job is figuring out how to maximize every opportunity and making sure none of your limited opportunities are missed.
- **Financial Supervisor** - Regardless of whether you employ an accountant, the manager oversees the finances and make sure everything is running optimally.
- **Hiring Manager** - It's important for your manager to constantly keep an eye out for new team members and determine who you will hire for certain tasks.
- **Endorsement Seeker** - Unfortunately, too many managers sole focus is this. But getting endorsements is an important part of keeping costs low and gaining further awareness through promotions.

Your Day-To-Day Manager vs. Your Main Manager
You'll hear the term "day-to-day manager" thrown around by established musicians. This refers to a structure where there's a day-to-day manager and a main manager. The main manager is in charge of strategy, big moves and decisions. The day-to-day manager is in charge of more common annoyances like email, tour managing, guest lists, updating show itineraries, merch orders and other mundane activities. This helps your main manager keep time free to make big moves, do important tasks and not be bogged down with small scheduling, social networks, tiny receipts and payment disputes with merch companies, etc.

The day-to-day manager is often a group member, tour manager or an aspiring manager. You might have a friend who wants to help out--someone with a good work ethic, who isn't experienced enough in the music business to do you any good as your main manager. This person is an ideal candidate to be your day-to-day manager. Finding someone to take on many of the day-to-day duties is helpful to keep progress moving, allowing your manager to focus on the big picture.

Self-Manage *Then* Get Someone Else To Manage You
Many musicians have a moral standpoint on whether they want to manage themselves or have a manager take control of certain aspects of their career. This inner argument happens to every musician and is a part of furthering your career. Neither choice is right 100 percent of the time. Instead, I like to think of this decision as more of a philosophy. You should manage yourself until the day it's holding you back--holding back the growth of your fanbase, your income, your music-making, etc. When your fanbase is growing and the world is taking notice of you, the opportunities eventually become overwhelming and it's not clear what to do next. This is the time to enlist a manager.

Many naive musicians think a manager does nothing but schmooze to gain opportunities. Many musicians waste many of their best years hoping to "get discovered" by a label or a manager who will magically erase all of their problems and "make them famous." In reality, this scenario is unlikely. Even if your ultimate goal is to get a manager and a big recording contract, you need to make progress happen on your own.

The other key to this philosophy is what happens when you get a manager or a label. Managers and labels both work hardest on the groups that work hard. They see the groups they have to do everything for as the bad bet on where to place their energy. When you help build the momentum for your music by working hard, they are excited that their work will go twice as hard. While this may not be discussed on musician's forums every day, ask any vet of the music business and they will tell you the same.

Manage Yourself Before You Get Someone Else To Manage You
Not only does self-managing build character, but it also helps lay some groundwork, making it easier to one day find a real manager to take some problems off your hands. Hoping you get lucky and find some mystical angel of a manager, who puts you on their wings and flies you to overnight success isn't only unrealistic, it's downright delusional. The most common rise to prominence is a hardworking act that takes on many managerial duties themselves and eventually gets noticed by a manager who can help build upon their hard work.

The Myth Of The Genius Manager
I've worked with hundreds of acts both big and small. The ones who do get popular and have a lasting career are the ones who take part in many of the decisions about their music. The musicians make the decisions *with* their manager. While there are a few genius managers who have ordered around some dummy musicians, that is the exception--not the rule. Usually, the musicians are just as involved with the decisions in their career as the manager is. The more you know about the business, the better you're able to help make good decisions that help your fanbase grow and allow you to make a living out of your music. Knowing what you're talking about in these discussions and being educated in the business will help your career last.

Begging Takes More Time Than Doing - All the time you spend stuffing envelopes, sending emails and begging someone to manage you could be much better spent by building yourself a following and attracting a strong management team. No manager is ever impressed by a group that begs and always annoys him to manage them. They're impressed when you make progress happen without their help.

Avoid The Lame - Many managers who are willing to take on musicians in their early days are not worth signing away your dreams with. These are the "professionals" who throw a lot of crap (musicians they only half-heartedly believe in) at the wall and see if anything sticks and catches on. Even worse, it could be a manager who does little to no work. This is detrimental to your progress since you assume someone is taking care of business for you when they're not. If you think of your music like a stock, the more passionate fans you have, the higher your stock's value is. When something has value, more people want to be a part of it. If your stock soars, you'll have many great managers and other team members trying to work with you. This allows you to make a great choice instead of going for the only lame candidate willing to take you on at the get-go.

Day-To-Day Duties - Even when you get a great manager with a powerful staff, it helps to be able to handle the day-to-day duties on your own. There's less money to split when you don't need to hire someone to do dumb tasks like update your Twitter feed or post your tour dates. If you're able to handle many of the small duties your manager has on their plate, your manager will have more time to concentrate on bigger moves to help build your fanbase. Instead of micromanaging your drummer, showing up at practice and lecturing your bassist on getting lessons, they can spend that time talking to someone about a great tour for you.

Scam-Proof - A lot of musicians worry about getting ripped off and scammed in this business. If you know the business and are an active part of the decisions for your music, there's less of a chance for you to get taken advantage of. If you're able to manage your own tours, you'll understand the finances behind everything. As these tours get bigger, you'll more clearly see where the waste and fraud happens. In today's music business, you need to always optimize finances in order to maintain a livable profit. In the end, no one will ever care about your share of the profits and your dreams coming true as much as you do. Learn the basics and you'll be able to help make sure both of these goals are more obtainable.

Making Better Decisions - Smart musicians have lasting careers. Though a lot of your favorite bands may appear to be vacuous party animals buried in groupies, there's often a quiet genius musician involved, concentrating on what's best to grow a fanbase. If you're able to take part in the decisions made for your music and have an educated opinion on them, you'll be confident you're making good decisions in your life, instead of hoping someone else is making them for you.

Paying Your Dues - While this is one of the worst clichés of the music business (*and boy are there many*), other musicians respect their peers who do it themselves--and the more musicians respect you, the easier it is to get ahead. Musicians don't like when others "have everything handed to them" and won't want to help them. If you're seen as one of those musicians, it may set you back a bit.

When Should You Get A Manager?
You want to wait as long as you can before you get a manager, within reason. As your music's value soars, you're only going to keep receiving more and more opportunities to work with talented people. With that said, below are some clear signs that you need a manager:

- **What Next?** - If you're starting to feel overwhelmed by all of the opportunities presented to you, it may be a good time to get a manager. While many musicians look for a manager to make opportunities happen for them (and a good manager will do this), what's most important is making the right decisions. If you're at a point where so many opportunities are offered to you that it's hard to decide what's best--the help of a manager can be vital.

- **Demand** - If there are many offers to manage you (not just one or two of your friends), it may be time to get a manager. Hold out if you don't feel you absolutely need it--or the candidates aren't good enough--but if a lot of managers are knocking on your door it means you're probably ready for the next step.

Choosing A Manager

A Good First Test For A Potential Manager

I am constantly asked by friends to help determine which of several candidates should manage them. Lots of sayings are thrown around that are used as credentials for these managers: "They have been in the business for a decade," "they used to be in this band" or "they worked for _____ management company for a year." While this is all great, there are plenty of people who have accomplished these things. There are more important ways you can choose a manager.

Think back to your days in high school. There were students who really paid attention in class, those who synthesized all of the information given to them and really understood it. There were other students who just showed up waiting for lunchtime. This still applies to what goes on when someone "works in the music business." Just because someone came along for the ride, doesn't mean they know how to drive you back down that winding road. I attended science class when they taught me what photosynthesis is, but I don't have a clue how it works today.

Having connections can get you somewhere but having ideas and a solid work ethic is what really counts. Connections can be formed by anyone who works at it. They're easy to get when people see you as a promising, upcoming act. And while work ethic can only be tested in the field, ideas are easily tested before you tie yourself to someone.

A Plan - When you're evaluating potential managers, you should have them write you a timeline for the next year of your career. It should be a realistic plan, not just "get you on tour with The Killers." How are they going to help develop you and make you stand out from the countless other musicians looking for the attention of the same people you want attention

58

from? If they come back with obvious ideas you could easily have thought of on your own, then why do you need to give this person a chance at managing you?

A large part of a manager's role is to think of fresh, new ideas and the means to accomplish them. They should have a clear and insightful vision how to build your fanbase, besides the usual "record, shoot promo pics, have a record release party, tour..." and repeat. Every great manager I know has a strategy and ideas for how to make the musicians they work with stand out from the pack. If a candidate can't demonstrate these ideas to you, they've flunked the test and won't be of much use to you. Look for someone who tells you something you don't know. If they can't, then why bother?

Why You Need To Choose A Great Manager The First Time
You may be wondering why I keep pressing the point that choosing a manager is important and why you should wait till you find a great one. It's because hopping from manager to manager on a regular basis is a huge mistake. While many successful musicians will do this, what happens behind the scenes is hurting their potential. It's common in most manager's contracts to keep earning royalties from the musicians they manage 6-12 months after the contract is terminated--this is called a sunset clause. This exists because most of a manager's work doesn't usually earn profits until many months later. If your old manager and the one you just hired are both taking 15 percent, you're now giving away 30 percent of your earnings to management. That's way less money for you each month and less of a budget to promote your music.

Piece Of The Pie - Every time someone gets involved with you as a manager, lawyer, label or booking agent, they're usually going to take a percentage of your earnings. Managers are usually going to take 10-15 percent. Booking agents are going to take the same off your touring funds. Your lawyer is going to want a percentage of either all of your transactions or everything they have to deal with, unless you pay them by the hour. You also may have a record label taking 50 to 90 percent of your album sales. This can mean a lot of your money is already gone. Having someone take another 15 percent when they're no longer working for you is hard on both your wallet and the funding for your progress.

Opportunity Cost - To make matters worse, others will contact your old management with opportunities that don't get passed on to the new management. Instead, they will try to make it work for the groups your old manager still works with. Avoid all this and make a wise, informed decision before you start working with anyone.

Making Your Management Work Run Smooth

The Downside Of DIY: The Good Cop/Bad Cop Need For A Manager
Doing it all yourself does have some downsides. One of these downsides is that when it's time to be an asshole (aka the "bad cop"), you don't have someone else to place that burden on. Many musicians think a manager makes all their business deals for them, but another key responsibility is to play the role of the fall guy when it's time to disappoint or argue with someone. This is an important role that managers play, making sure the musicians they represent don't come off like assholes.

If you start to get any sort of fanbase, there are bound to be conflicts: Show cancellations, missed interviews, royalty arguments, etc. When you manage yourself, you're in the position of being the one who lets your fans down and deals with the people you do business with. The promoter who gave you a chance early on in your career may still try to give you cut from a show for 100 people, instead of the 1,000 who just came out to see you. It's much better to let your manager be the bad guy in situations like that, so you can still have a positive and productive relationship with business partners.

With a good manager, you'll be able to keep your relationships on good terms by simply having someone else to blame in certain situations. It makes you seem like you were just listening to your manager, and that matters were out of your hands--helping keep relationships with business partners and fans on good terms. This is essential for your band's image when you start to gain more fans.

A Joke And The Lesson To Learn From It
Greg Ross of Go Kart Records told me a joke 15 years ago that I still think about on a regular basis. It helps explain why so many relationships in the music business go wrong:

Scene: *A man is taking a walk through a field when he looks up and sees a man in a balloon yelling at him.*

Man In Balloon: Hey, can you help me? I am in this balloon and I can't get down!
Man On Ground: Sure, you could find a mountain and try to jump out or wait for the balloon to deflate or maybe call someone who does this for a living for help?
Man In Balloon: You must work at a record label!
Man On Ground: How did you know?
Man In Balloon: Because you're trying to be helpful, but every bit of advice you have is obvious and doesn't involve you doing anything!
Man On Ground: Oh, well you must be a musician!
Man In Balloon: How did you know?
Man On Ground: Because you blame me for the stupid mess you got yourself into while trying to have some fun and now that you're in trouble you expect me to solve all of your problems!

It's tough working with others in the music business. Musicians often blame everyone else for the problems they incur instead of taking responsibility. You want to find team members you can have an open dialogue with when discussing flaws and what you do better. Most importantly, don't always point the finger outwards. Oftentimes it's not only one person's fault, anyway--and it's more important to find a way to solve problems instead of finding someone to blame. Accept that from time to time, things will go wrong and try to learn from those experiences and work better together, instead of pointing fingers.

Management Checks And Balances
When a musician is young and naive, they assume signing to a label will magically solve all of their problems. If it's a successful label, they think they'll be working with a smart team that knows the secrets of how to break a new act. Unfortunately, much of the time this isn't the reality. One of the most neglected aspects of the musician-label dynamic is the checks-and-balances system. This system is necessary not only for the management to make sure that the label is doing their job, but also to come up with a progressive strategy. Labels are tied to thinking in terms of what sells records (the way they make money), not what grows your fanbase (the way musicians and their managers make money). This also works in reverse--if management caters to the whims of musicians, appeasing their every "need," the labels can provide a much-needed reality check to let everyone know the musicians are slacking off.

Inevitably, once you have a few members on a team, it's easy for them to see what each member can be doing better. This doesn't mean a member of your team is bad at their job. It has always been basic human nature to see each other's flaws and try to help everyone improve. Finding team members who can work well together and give each other constructive criticism is a crucial part of having a well-oiled machine.

Don't Bother Your Manager With The Little Things - Be A Part Of Your Team
Many musicians believe that once they get a manager, their days of updating social networks, show lists and handling other boring tasks are over. What they fail to realize is that while it may seem relieving to hand this boring work to their manager, they should really want the manager to make bigger moves and concentrate on tasks they can't do themselves. Everyone has a finite number of hours they can put into a project in a given day. By placing the burden of small tasks on your manager's back, you're taking away from the time they have to make bigger moves for you. If your manager has the time to look at the big picture while you tackle the day-to-day tasks, you can get twice as much done.

Opportunity Cost
A lot of this book is about being organized and efficient, which seems a bit intense to some people. Once your fanbase starts to grow, the opportunities start to move fast--very fast. If you're doing tasks in an inefficient manner, things will begin to pile up and daily duties will start to overwhelm you. If you're inefficient, you might end up wasting away time that you could use to be creative, pursue new opportunities and build your fanbase.

This also goes for prioritizing what work is most important to get done. Some musicians will call their local top 40 radio station and request their song all day, thinking it will eventually get played. Instead, what they could use that time to target fans who are likely to like them, who will then eventually call radio stations for them once they're mobilized. Choosing how you spend your time is as important as making time to build your fanbase.

Do What's Important, Not What's Easy
As gatekeepers disappear, cracking into in the music business becomes more about how much you can do yourself in order to grow your fanbase. Critical to this point is the idea of getting important work done, not just the

task that's easy and fun. It's easy to sit at home and Facebook chat or tweet at potential fans. It's also easy to go to practice and rehearse your older songs, instead of writing new ones. If you really want to grow your fanbase, you must distinguish between what work is important to get done and what's easy and fun. It's important to know the difference and to prioritize your work accordingly.

In order to prioritize your work effectively, it is helpful to begin by organizing it. This is how I organize my to-do list every day:

Huge Steps - The first category in your to-do list is called *huge steps*. This is a list of tasks that could change your life. They're usually the tasks that are the hardest to do. Make sure these tasks are one step away, not leaps away like "get signed." Identify direct steps that work toward ultimate goals, like "give demo to DJ Big Butt next Friday at Don Pedro's." Little details help in this department. Keep track of tasks that you know will really help you--tasks that you probably won't enjoy doing, but really need to get done. After you get done with one, add the next step to the list and keep making progress on these big goals.

Preventive - *Preventive* tasks are just as important as *huge steps*, but for different reasons. These are tasks like paying parking tickets you got on tour or dealing with taxes and insurance. These items are just as important as what you have listed in the *huge steps* category, if not more, since they can slow down your progress. These are priorities to get done each day.

Stay On Top - The *stay on top* section includes items that aren't as important as those in *huge steps,* but still need that checkmark firmly drawn in next to them. You still need to get them done, but they aren't of utmost importance: Getting T-shirts made, calling a promoter back about a gig, etc. Keeping all of these tasks prioritized is very important. These are the tasks you do once the *huge steps* and *preventive* lists are out of the way.

Soon - There is a theory that it's unwise to put tasks on your to-do list that you will want to do six months or a year down the road. It weighs down your thoughts, preventing you from feeling like you are making progress. Put them on a list called *soon* so you can store those ideas in a way that doesn't clutter your main to-do list. If you're always looking at tasks you can't do right now, your thoughts will constantly be occupied and you'll be stressed out. Instead, concentrate on what's next. Making a *soon* list can keep you from forgetting these tasks while helping you focus on more pressing matters.

Do It Now - If it takes less than a few minutes to do a task, it's best to do it right then and there instead of putting it on a list. In my life, I keep a general rule that if I can take care of a task in less than 2-3 minutes, I will do it right away.

It should be noted that many of these ideas are my own versions of what I've learned from others and from reading Dave Allen's amazing book, *Getting Things Done*. If you want to be more efficient, you should read it.

Use SWOT Analysis To Help Figure Out What You Need To Do

One of the ways I keep organized and figure out what work I need to do is to figure out each act I work with SWOT (Strengths, Weaknesses, Opportunities, Threats). At the top of my To-do list I make sure to list these attributes and below I have listed how I use them.

- **Strengths** – I keep these listed so I can remember what to always tell anyone I am pitching as well as to remember to keep nurturing these strengths. This can be anything from great songs, to cute singer onto a T-shirt that is selling well.
- **Weaknesses** – I want to remember what the act needs to be improving and make sure I get work done on this everyday until I can erase the attribute from this chart. This can be a weak drummer, thin discography or too few YouTube videos. I will want to keep these on a list so I can think of how to correct them.
- **Opportunities** – I want to make sure any opportunity we have recently been given is followed up on. If someone said they want to hear our next songs or I heard a promoter looks the act's music I will keep this here.
- **Threats** – If the van is late on payments or someone is threatening a lawsuit, I will put those here. While these are listed last, these are the most important to get done since they can ruin your progress.

DWYSYD - Do What You Said You Would Do (When You Said You Would Do It)

There is a philosophy I abide by that keeps my relationships solid, the musicians I work with happy and myself productive. I take it very seriously that I always do what I said I would do, when I said I would do it. Being reliable is a quality everyone wants to see in those they deal with. Being reliable can also help you get many opportunities. A flaky musician who takes an inordinate amount of time to communicate is going to struggle to get the same opportunities as more responsible, responsive musicians. Because I take this quality seriously, I get many opportunities since others know I can be relied upon.

This applies directly to musicians--if you're reliable, you'll see yourself get more gigs, attract potential team members and earn great endorsements from those who have worked with you.

There Should Be No Lulls In Your Momentum

I always hear discussions about what to do during the lulls of momentum in building a fanbase. Many musicians' views lulls as if they are inevitable, as if there are built-in periods where you do nothing and stop building your fanbase. This is dumbfounding--every group I've worked with that successful built up a fanbase avoided lulls in momentum. Whether it's staying up later, waking up earlier or doing work on the weekends, you should never let anything get in the way of you promoting your music.

This is the mindset that separates musicians who stay stagnant and musicians who constantly progress and build a following. Make your music-related work a higher priority than hanging out, playing video games and whatever other hobbies you may have, and there will be no lulls in your momentum.

Use Parkinson's Law To Your Advantage

"Work expands to fill the time available for its completion." - Parkinson's Law

Let's say you want to schedule some recording time at a studio. You decide it's going to take three months to prepare the songs for this recording. Parkinson's Law dictates that if you decide you're going to take three months to do this, it will be very difficult to finish any sooner. You'll procrastinate for the first month, and then slowly start to get in gear and accomplish things until going all-out near the end of the timeframe, when most of the work gets done. In reality, you probably could have prepared those songs in one month, but you incorporated a bunch of extra time to procrastinate.

65

The lesson to be learned from Parkinson's Law is that you can do projects faster than you think. When planning a project, you usually give yourself a bunch of extra time just in case you need it. This time ends up being wasted. As the deadline looms, you end up cramming to get a majority of the work done. If you take a realistic view of how long tasks take and don't buffer in the "just in case" time, you can avoid wasting days or weeks. This doesn't mean you should rush yourself to an unreasonable extent, it just means not affording yourself the luxury of having time to slouch around.

The late Apple founder, Steve Jobs, became famous for using a *reality distortion field*. He would schedule projects in such a tight amount of time that many people didn't think it would be possible to meet the deadline. This would motivate his team to get tasks done and keep them progressing, eventually helping Apple become the amazing company it is today. As you do tasks like record, plan tours and make videos, take note of the time it takes and what you can do to make it more efficient.

Why Your Band Loses So Many Members - Pay Attention To Momentum
Has the number of drummers you've gone through put Spinal Tap to shame? If so, it's usually because your group consistently loses momentum. Human nature is to want to be a part of an endeavor where everyone involved can be proud. With all the dubious looks family members and significant others give you when you're a musician, it's very hard to keep up your pride if you aren't accomplishing anything. When a group is losing momentum it's like a sinking ship. And when a ship is sinking, everyone jumps.

Often when you talk to musicians that have left bands, they say happened because the band was "doing nothing." If you want to stop losing members, start staring at that calendar and make sure something is happening *every day*. When progress starts to slow down, make sure you remedy it with something new that keeps the ball rolling. Continued progress helps members feel like they're going somewhere with their dream and that tends to make them stick around. Members who feel like they're putting their time, money and effort into a dream that's going nowhere will eventually disappear.

Don't Pigeonhole Your Success With Too Much Planning

Having goals and a vision for your music is great, but too much micro planning isn't helpful. Building a fanbase is never a direct path, meaning no one knows exactly what opportunities you may be presented with and what may be the best route for you. You might be a rock band that has one very dance-y track you're unsure about, only to discover that it's far and away your best-received song. You might be a hipster dance producer that happens to find success at frat parties. You never know how you and your material are going to be received.

Take cues from where your success is coming from and follow the path that's working for you--not a pre-defined map you've created in your head of how your rise to fame is going to come about. Just because your favorite band moved from the burbs to the big city, doesn't mean that is your path to success. At the same time if you can't seem to find a fanbase in the burbs it may be time to pack things up and get moving. If something isn't working, don't be afraid to shift gears and try something new. There is no shame in admitting that you tried something you thought would work, only to discover it didn't go over well. Being resilient and adaptable keeps you moving forward and able to find a place for your music in this world. If you focus too much on a specific roadmap to success, you might miss out on the best avenues for your group.

Motivating Others To Stay On Deadlines
One of the greatest struggles with managing your music is you're often working with people who are underpaid, doing for you in their spare time. It often takes years of experience to learn how to keep people motivated to stay on deadline. These are a few techniques that can help keep your collaborators on track.

- **Hard Deadline From Day One** – Tell your collaborator you have a hard deadline that is reasonable and get them to agree on it. Ideally this should be a week before the real deadline in case there are problems.
- **Check-In** – Write a reminder in your calendar to check-in on the project every few days or weekly depending on the duration of the project. Creatives feel the pressure if they hear from you regularly, but long absences let the pressure down. The squeaky wheel will most often get the oil.
- **Get It In Writing** – Make sure all discussions of the deadline are in writing, so it can easily be referred to later.

- **Pay Structure** – Paying half up front and the rest when a usable product is delivered ensures your collaborator has motivation to get paid.

Habits! Habits! Habits!
As I update this book every year, I pay a lot of attention to what people criticize about it and one of the discussions I commonly have is that it doesn't talk enough about how to get all of this work done. While I tweak many parts of this book from this feedback, this criticism is much more about the person trying to implement in their life than it is about any knowledge I can give you. The fact is that 99 out of 100 times when I have coached anyone who is failing at their music connecting to a fanbase it comes down to either people don't like their music or they can never promote it consistently and they lose momentum and suffer from keeping the attention of their scene since they disappear intermittently constantly. If this is ringing true to what you have experienced, I do have a few suggestions:

- **To Do List Push Notifications** – Apple's Reminders app can be set to annoy you about the same things on a regular basis, every day even if you want it to. I regularly use this app to remind me how mad at myself I am going to be if I don't chip away at a project. Let it help you make time each day to get the work you need to and develop a habit of working. There are also tons of ToDo list apps I outline later that can get even more intense.
- **Learn About Habits** – Books like _The Power of Habit_ and my latest book, _Processing Creativity_ will teach you how to get in better habits so you continually make progress. There's a lot of science and some techniques that can really help get past the obstacles of life, so you achieve consistent progress.
- **Schedule** – If promoting your music really is a top priority in your life, use a calendar and schedule time you can't cancel every day. Most often musicians try to squeeze in the promotion in spare time instead of actually scheduling time to do it every single day.

Management Philosophies

For Every Five Promises/Opportunities You Receive, Usually Only One Will Come True

"Don't Put All Your Eggs In One Basket"

Everyone knows the music business is cutthroat. It's loaded with ego bruises and disappointment around every turn. When you're a musician, you'll be promised opportunities that will get your hopes up time and time again. Over the years, I've watched many close friends get their hearts broken when a powerful member of the music business guaranteed them an opportunity that didn't end up happening. I can tell you one concept that will ring true whether you're Madonna or a local band, whether you have 20 fans or 20 million: For every five opportunities you are offered, usually only one will come to fruition.

The Scenario - It happens all the time: Someone tells you an A&R man is going to listen to your song or you're going to get put on this tour. Maybe some musician is going to do a song with you. The music world abounds with promises that never come true. It's not because everyone is a liar, fake or whatever cynical cliché you want to throw around. It's usually good-natured and motivated by doing the same thing you're trying to do--make smart decisions that help build a fanbase.

The usual scenario is that someone who likes your music kind of knows an A&R guy whose label you'd love to be on. This person wants to help you out of the kindness of their heart and odds are they want to be cool... just like you! They want to make progress happen for the music they love, just like you do. For some reason, it doesn't work out and you're left disappointed. The person trying to help you has great intentions, but like many opportunities in this business, it didn't shape out the way you imagined. There is no reason to be mad at the person who was going to try to help you or at that A&R guy. You should be mad at yourself for putting all of your eggs in just one basket.

Reality - What you need to make it in this business is a deck of cards full of options. If you're waiting on one person to give you a big break, you're going to be waiting a long time. One person isn't going to be enough to build you a fanbase that kick-starts your career. There are far too many variables at play to guarantee that any single opportunity will pan out. Even if you have a song that would blow away a talent scout at a huge label, there's simply no way to know if they will ever even open your email. You

69

need to spread yourself out or else you're in for a life of disappointment. There is too much that can go wrong waiting for one or two opportunities to come through.

Getting Ahead - What about when someone calls you up and says they can get your band on a cool tour, and then they end up bailing on you for another act? Just like you, this person is acting in their own interests. You can't be angry if someone decides they may have more success without your band involved at that specific moment. Eventually, your group will probably disappoint someone else when you make a choice about which bands to bring on tour. It's not about how good you are it's about this person trying to do right by the act they represent. In fact, this happens to popular musicians so many times it no longer even phases them. By the time you're the biggest musician in the world, you'll have been passed over for so many tours, commercials, festivals, etc., that it will be second nature to doubt every offer you get.

Expand your options; never wait on anyone to give you a break and you'll be five steps ahead of the rest.

"Never Let A Good Crisis Go To Waste"
This is a famous saying attributed to Rahm Emanuel, the mayor of Chicago. Even though he was talking about politics, it applies to music as well. Later in this book, you'll read about how former MusforMGMT act Man Overboard handled the leaking of their record. What should have been a terrible situation became one where we gained tons of respect and new fans. This also goes for cancelled shows: Some of the best shows I've ever been to are punk shows that have been shut down by the cops. When a band suddenly decides to do a show in a friend's garage instead of the shutdown venue, it can become one of the most memorable shows you'll ever see. Bad things are going to happen throughout your music career and figuring out how to make the best of them is what separates the professionals from the amateurs. When a crisis happens, figure out how to turn it into opportunity.

The Power Of The Objective Perspective
The *objective perspective* is the idea of getting an unbiased perspective from someone who isn't as close to your situation as you are. The objective perspective has many uses in music. We've all had problems with our significant others--if you go talk to a friend about it, you might gain a newfound sense of clarity on the situation. Even if they just reaffirm what

you already think, sometimes you just need to hear it from someone else. The same goes with your music: You may have gotten so deep into a project and worked so hard on it that you've become insensitive to the finer details.

Songwriting - Record producers do a lot of rehearsing with musicians. The simplest viewpoint a producer can bring to the situation is as a new ear that wasn't around for the entire songwriting process. They can offer a genuine first impression of songs that they haven't heard in a zillion different arrangements during the writing process. If a part is being played too many times or if the bass player's busy line takes away from the vocals, the producer will be able to hear it on first listen. Your group may have gotten used to the way a song sounds over time, but the producer's objectivity allows him or her to immediately see things in a different way. Being objective doesn't always make your opinion right, but it's a valuable opinion to consider.

Mixing/Mastering - The quotable mastering engineer Alan Douches of West West Side Music (westwestsidemusic.com) often says that one of the most important parts of his job is offering an objective perspective toward the recording process. While you were mixing your record, hearing the songs hundreds of times, you may have gotten lost in some details. It's his job to try to compensate for any ways that you may have lost perspective during hours of working. He comes to the table with a new set of ears and can help get your head back on track with suggestions. Getting lost while recording a song is why many musicians will employ a separate mixer who has never heard the song during the recording process. Getting an opinion from someone who hasn't been involved in the tireless creation of what you do can be a crucial part in crafting a great final product.

Whose Opinion Do You Listen To? - Having many people give you opinions is a great way to make an informed decision, but it can also get confusing. You may have to consider possible hidden agendas from those giving you advice. If that isn't enough, some people talk a lot despite not having educated opinions. Who you take advice from is a lot of what makes you who you are. These decisions shape your career, how you're seen in the public spotlight and how your music is received. So, who do you listen to?

Your Songs - Friends will often give you their opinions on your songs. Since everyone loves music, most opinions have some validity. However, there are times when the average listener's opinion isn't always the one to cater to. For example, if your producer is telling you a part sounds sloppy or cluttered, but your significant other tells you it sounds just fine--you may want to pay more attention to the opinion of your producer. Many music listeners are not trained in hearing the potential a song can reach like great musicians or producers are. They may say your song sounds fine, but their ears simply aren't as tuned into every detail as someone who has devoted their life to listening to music and can identify your true potential. These producers can hear the flaws that a novice can't put their finger on.

Easy Way Out - Many times, humans want to take the easy way out and listen to whoever gives us a convenient opinion. But holding ourselves to the standards of those who are good at nitpicking is what can ultimately lead to achieving great things.

On the reverse side, if your friends and family who aren't trained musicians tell you something is wrong with a song, this can be a scary thing. When flaws jump out at an untrained ear, that's usually bad news. Musicians will often come to a producer after recording a great song and say, "That's the first time my mom has actually liked one of our songs." If you can please your Perry Como-listening mother with your latest prog-rock track, you're probably onto something (or she is excited at the idea of you moving out of her basement). However, if you play a song for some friends who actively listen to your genre of music and they say your songs are all too long; you probably need to shorten them up.

Agendas - It's shocking that musicians will listen to the advice of people without thinking about the agenda that person may have. Unfortunately, many people will give you advice that benefits their own interests more so than yours. Not everyone will do this, but it's all too common and a concept you should be aware of. Maybe your band is listening to a newly recorded song and you come to a vocal part where the singer belts out a lyric. The bassist says he hates it, but not because yelling the line is a bad thing, but because he hates any vocals that are belted in any songs. You need to take into account the biases, hang-ups and agendas of the opinionated party before you listen to their opinions.

If agendas aren't enough, some people are incapable of having their own opinions. Some friends and fans will tell you they love everything you do just because they're so enamored with you or insecure in their opinions. While this is good for your ego, it's not always what you need to hear if you're trying to get an objective perspective. It's more valuable to have honest friends that can offer constructive criticism.

Questions To Ask - When getting advice on a situation I always try to ask myself a few questions about each piece of advice.

- **Agenda** - What was this person's agenda, if any?
- **Educated** - Is this person educated on the topic? Are they up to date on their information? Are they stuck in the rules of the past?
- **Take The Hard Road** - What is the hard road? We all have a tendency to look at the hard answer and find a way around it. Keep reminding yourself about the harder road, and make sure that when you make a final decision about anything, that you aren't simply looking for the easy way out.
- **Occam's Razor** - What does a layman think of this situation? Those with no experience can see the forest instead of each individual tree, providing you with a valuable perspective.

How Do You Deal With Too Much Trust?

Recently, I came across a comment on Musformation's blog that asked, "What do you do when the rest of your band trusts you too much and thinks everything you say or do is gold?" While this is a rare instance, it's definitely an issue. One of the best things about music is that everyone is able to have an opinion. If everyone involved in a project is humble and reasonable, everyone's opinions are easily discussed and an easy consensus can be reached. But if everyone trusts a single person, the best ideas might stay buried.

When I'm producing records, every once in a while, I can sense that the band I'm working with is putting me into a situation where they trust me a little too much. Once my trust alarm goes off, I launch into a speech that goes like this...

"I've been doing this for a long time and you may like a lot of records I've done, but that doesn't mean I am perfect and that every idea I have is gold or better than yours. What makes a great record is everyone trusting his or her guts. When you feel something, say something and then we'll discuss it. We need everyone in this project bringing ideas to the table, and then we need to try them out to see what works best. Every time you feel something is wrong or has the potential for improvement, please speak up

73

so we can think about it more and make sure we're making everything the best it can possibly be."

This also goes for managing your music and songwriting. No one is perfect and no one is such a genius that they won't benefit from an environment where others are challenging them. In the end, the good ideas will shine if you're mature about discussing them. Most great things are built in a great environment with a team discussing each other's ideas in a constructive manner. Make sure you create that environment in your musical dealings.

How To Obtain The Quality Control Advantages That A Record Label Has
Much has been said about the zombie-like quality control at record labels when they reject a musician's "creative endeavor" and tell them to head back to the studio and start over. This happens when something doesn't fit a certain mold or isn't up to the standard of the record label. As easy as it is to find disdain for the way major labels are run, in this case they have a thankless job. If a label sends a musician back to the drawing board to re-record their latest "masterpiece" and the record comes out better than the original, no one ever points at the label and gives them an award for being a genius. However, the same label will be the subject of scrutiny if the world hears an album and finds it unlistenable.

This thankless job is often the difference between making classic records or forgettable one-offs. The balance of offering creative restriction and quality control is one of the toughest tasks labels are charged with. There are indeed times a musician needs to be told that they can do better. When the label model works well, the label has a vision and can hear when a record isn't being executed properly. Whether the mixing wasn't well done, the production is off, the vocalist wasn't concentrating, or the songs just aren't fully formed, it's up to the label and other team members to offer comments and directions that might be a make or break factor in creating a great record.

If you're self-managed, these decisions are often troubling since you have one less objective perspective. Most likely, if you play a lot of shows, you're going to meet some managers, labels, producers, booking agents, etc., who have expressed interest in you. If they understand your music, it's not a bad idea to keep in touch with them. Even if it's a record producer you can't afford yet or someone you want to work with, but your schedules don't align, stay in contact by updating them with your progress and sending them new music. You never know--perhaps they will end up helping you in an unexpected way or you'll work together in the future.

You Don't Need To Use Every Tool
Throughout this book, you'll be presented with hundreds of tools; services and apps that can help you promote your music. It should go without saying that just because a tool is mentioned in this book doesn't mean you have to use it.

For those who live under a rock, "Bruce Lee" wasn't only a great song from the electronic music outfit Underworld in the late 90's, but also the name of a famous actor and martial artist in the '60s and '70s. In addition to kicking ass in some sweet movies, Bruce Lee was famous for having a karate style that was sort of an aggregate. In other words, he took elements of multiple martial arts disciplines and crafted his own style. Apply the same idea to the tools you use to manage your music. There are lots of suggestions in this book. Clearly, they aren't all for everyone. Promoting music is not a "one-size-fits-all" task. Like Bruce Lee and his very personalized karate technique, learn all the options out there and then find what combination works best for you.

That being said, if you don't have a website or even a demo but are focused on building a huge Instagram following, your priorities are probably out of order. Don't be arrogant or get too far ahead of yourself--it only hurts you in the long run. If you don't have 100 Facebook likes, it doesn't make sense to drop $3,000 on merch and set up a complicated online store. Some of these tools and ideas will be new to you. Some of them will be familiar. Some will be very relevant and useful. Others are completely useless. Take an honest look at the wide variety of services and ask yourself what can help you advance your career. Be open-minded and evaluate each tool and strategy on its own. We're flattered to think you might take this book's advice seriously, but it's important to decide for yourself what to use.

Organizing Your Team

Make A Wiki To Keep Everyone On The Same Page
One of the biggest time wasters in managing your music is having to send emails to everyone on your team asking for passwords, addresses, press

clips, bios, etc. Making a *wiki* in Google Docs (drive.google.com) is a great way to solve this. A wiki is the perfect place to store individual band members' addresses, save press quotes, drop links for downloads of your music and art, and confidently store passwords for your various accounts. You can also share this document with anyone working on a given project (management, musicians, publicists, booking agents), so you don't need to repeatedly send people the same information.

An organized wiki can save countless hours of useless fetching and email writing. It helps keep information that can easily be forgotten in one easy place. Simply share it with the members of your team and start storing information.

Here is some common information kept in a band's wiki:

- **To-Do List** - Keeping a to-do list in the wiki can help tasks to get done and lets people know when something has been taken care of. When someone has free time or is motivated, they can look here and find out what still needs to be attended to.
- **Member Names & Contact Info** - When new team members come on board, having this information handy to refer to can keep work running smoothly.
- **Track Listings & Discography** - Often needed for press, publishing, licensing and other inquiries.
- **Current Bio -** Having an up-to-date bio in one spot helps make sure that everyone constantly has access to the most recent version.
- **Press Highlights & Quotes -** Various members of your team will need these from time to time. Having the greatest hits on hand makes life easy.
- **Credentials -** Having the login and password information stored for all of your different accounts is essential for team members to get tasks done without stalling.
- **Shipping Addresses -** There's nothing more annoying than typing out your whole address four times a week whenever someone needs it!
- **Publishing Information -** Having the songwriter and publishing information for each song written down can help when a licensing deal comes down the pipeline.
- **Emergency Contact Info -** Accidents happen. Knowing who to call if something goes wrong is important.

Idea Pad - As your fanbase grows, you'll have tons of ideas about marketing and releases, and you may also hear about services and sites you should check out. Having a group document serving as an idea launching pad allows everyone to share their new thoughts. There's nothing worse than a lost idea--and even the most fleeting thought can lead to a creative new way to make fans.

Building and Keeping Contacts

Perhaps one of the most important parts of promoting your music is finding those who will help you, retaining their information and making sure you can contact them later down the road. Whether it's a DJ who will play your music, a blogger who writes about you, or a coffee house that will hang your poster, organizing these contacts will make your promotions easier and more effective. If you keep a clean database of this information, you'll have a way to constantly build on each opportunity and keep in touch with those who will help you for years to come.

Who's On the List? - Whenever a blog features you, a record store carries your album, or a venue lets you play a show, you need to add contact information to a spreadsheet that will allow you to reference that information later. If you log everything, you'll be able to maintain and strengthen relationships with people who help your band grow. Keeping a list like this and having the ability to see who has helped you in the past is one of the ways that record labels continually help musicians grow. Here are some suggestions of who to keep on your list:

- **Writers** - Keeping a press database is one of the most important parts of promoting your music. Keeping track of the email address, Twitter handle and city of writers will help you hit them up for coverage when you play near them. Having this information handy means you don't need to look it up every time you have something to announce.
- **DJs** - If someone plays your music, be sure to write down their contact information so you can give them more music in the future. Also keep track of where they're from so you can meet up when you're in town and build that relationship.
- **Record Stores** - If stores carry your music, hang posters or are open to having you in for events, you'll want to come back again.
- **Promoters** - Make your touring life easier by keeping the contact information for promoters organized.

- **Convergence Spots** - These are places to hang out in each city, where you can put up posters and meet potential fans. These range from coffee shops to mom and pop stores to bars--anywhere your fans congregate that may let you brand yourself.
- **Street Team Members** - Having their information sorted by city can help with geo-marketing.

Sort - Having all of this information easily sortable is extremely helpful. Being able to look up contacts by publication, location, etc., can help you figure out who to contact at what point in time. I like to have a contact list with the following information:

- **Who** - What's the publication, venue, record store, etc.?
- **Name** - Who is the human you talk to at this organization?
- **What** - Is this a blogger, venue owner, promoter, DJ, street team member or record store?
- **Phone Number**
- **Email**
- **Twitter**
- **Mailing Address** - Good for record reviews, thank-you merch and mailing street team materials.
- **Social Network** - Music business types can be weird sometimes, but some of them might like to talk via Facebook or Twitter. Put that info here.
- **Location** - City and state.

Managing Files

Part of being a manager is also being a librarian of sorts. It's the manager's job to collect all the files the team will need, to know where they exist and to have them backed up, so they don't get erased. Having all of these on hand is important in keeping organized and being ready to take advantage of opportunities.

Below is a list of common files you'll encounter when managing your music:

- **Audio Multi-Tracks** - These are the files with the individual tracks of your record. You'll need these in the future. If you need to remix your song or if you want an alternate version down the road, you'll need these files.

- **Mixes** - You're going to want mixes of all your songs in a high definition format like a .wav and in a lower definition format like an MP3. The high-def versions will serve as your masters, whereas the low definition files are great for sharing and selling.
- **Stems** - If you do a lot of remixing and live DJ performances, stems are crucial.
- **Instrumentals and A Capellas** - If your song gets picked up for licensing you may need these mixes on very short notice. Knowing where they are and keeping them organized is helpful.
- **Art** - You'll accumulate tons of pieces of art for albums, logos, flyers, stickers, etc. Keep it all on hand in case it's ever needed. You never know when something random like a show flyer might be needed years down the road, even for stuff like bootleg releases or collages.
- **Art Source Files** - Album art, logos and any other complex pieces of art are usually made in a program like Photoshop, which will have a source file. Keep these files in case you ever need to tweak or edit anything.
- **Contracts**- You'll have digital copies of all your contracts in addition to physical ones. Keep these safe.
- **Much More** - If you think there is even the slightest chance you'll need a file, just keep it.

How - You should keep at least two copies of all physical files in separate locations. All digital files should have two or three copies. Here's my strategy:

- **Computer** - I keep a copy of everything in common use on my computer.
- **External Hard Drive** - I have an external hard drive where I back everything up.
- **Cloud** - I use services like Dropbox, Google Drive and Amazon Glacier to store files in the cloud. That way they will not be lost if a hard drive crashes or a disaster happens at my office.

Learn And Love Spreadsheets
Whether you use Microsoft Office, Apple's iCloud or Google Docs, it's undeniable that getting to know how to use a spreadsheet can help you stay organized and optimize your business. James Murphy of LCD Soundsystem fame talks about how knowing how to run a spreadsheet and see where money is being lost can often be the big difference between

79

profits and losses. As well, if your music career doesn't work out, knowing spreadsheets is crucial for most jobs in this world. It's a great skill to have that will help you throughout your life in whatever you do.

A Note About Security

When you start using the Internet to promote and manage your music, any service you use will make you more vulnerable to identity theft, as well as your passwords being exposed if a hack occurs. If any of your information is compromised and you haven't taken sufficient precautions, there can be serious consequences. Make sure you utilize a safe online strategy.

- Google, Dropbox and many other services have a two-step verification that ensures maximum security.
- Have one password you use for web services that have nothing to do with finances (Twitter, Facebook, Tumblr, etc.).
- Have a separate password for your email account.
- For every financial institution you use, make sure you have a password you only use at that financial institution and nowhere else. This means if a service or your email gets hacked, it will not make your finances vulnerable. If you have a bank, a PayPal and Square account, make sure you use a different password for each of these so that if one gets exposed, the damage is minimal.
- Try to avoid writing down actual passwords. If your password is your dog's name and its year of birth, write that down instead of the direct password. If someone finds it, they won't be able to do anything unless they are privy to that specific information.
- Change your passwords every year. Many web services get hacked or expose information as they go out of business. If you regularly change your passwords, this will make you less vulnerable to this exposure.
- Services like LastPass (lastpass.com) can make all of this much easier, but they do charge a fee.

Chapter 3: Tools For Managing & Promoting Your Music

Now that you understand how much work goes into managing your music, you can see why you'll need many different tools to help build a fanbase. There are vast arrays of options that can help you get tasks done efficiently. In this chapter, I will go over the most helpful tools that make your life as painless as possible, helping you get work done faster so you can concentrate on having fun and playing music.

You Need A Google Account

I hate to be a so forceful, but with the amount of features Google offers for free, it's hard to not give it a wholehearted endorsement. Their tools help you manage your music easily and efficiently. No one makes a better basic toolkit for keeping up with the day-to-day management of your group. Let's take a tour through their tools and some tips on how to use them fully.

Gmail

One of the best email services in the business, Gmail's (gmail.com) ease of use is second to none for establishing an organized workflow, complete with a great contact manager that can sync to most phones and a to-do list built right into the main window.

Here are some great Gmail features that can help you out:

- **Junk** - You're inevitably going to get countless pieces of junk mail in your inbox. Gmail has an amazing junk filter to sort it all out and let you concentrate on what matters.
- **Space** - Gmail is constantly increasing how much space you can use. You can send MP3 demos back forth to team members all day long and have plenty of space to keep them archived. They are also easily searched for using the email client's astounding search function.
- **Canned Responses** - If your music catches on, you'll get the same emails *constantly*. Thankfully, Gmail allows you to save the most common responses and quickly reply with them, instead of typing out the same old tired response, over and over again.

- **Labels** - Labeling emails can make your life easier in the future. Gmail's labeling system makes it easy to quickly find receipts, contracts and lists of tasks.
- **Multiple Inboxes** - Gmail allows you to have multiple inboxes. For example, you can make an email address for just your merch, another for your fans to contact, and a third for business. You can make it so each of these all go to a separate inbox in a single Gmail window.
- **Tasks** - Gmail offers a great way of organizing to-do lists right in the main email window. You can keep numerous lists there right in your face as you're answering emails all day long.
- **Chat** - The Google Talk feature allows you to chat with your contacts. This can be great for quick conversations and for getting to know people better.
- **Calls and SMS** - You're able to make free domestic calls and texts with your Gmail account. This means you can save on cell phone bills and get a lot done without leaving your email window.
- **Managing Your Contacts** - You can sync your Gmail contacts with any smartphone that has standard features. Google automatically adds your frequently emailed contacts.
- **Scheduled Send & Snoozing** – You can use Gmail to schedule emails so that you can write them when you have free time but send them at a time where someone is more likely to respond, like mid-week instead of during the weekend when the Monday morning email pile-up is more likely.

Google Calendar (GCal)

Having a calendar that your whole team can reference is crucial to making your ship run smoothly. This service allows everyone involved to edit and reference a master calendar that shows what you have going on, so nobody is ever lost and nobody ever has to ask questions about the schedule. This is especially great for touring when you can reference set times and load-in times. Here are some tips for getting the most out of Google Calendars (google.com/calendar):

- **Holidays** - Google has a list of US, Christian and many other religious holidays so that you don't accidentally book a big show on Christmas day and then have everyone be mad at you. Simply click on Google's suggested calendars.
- **Alerts** - You can get email alerts a certain amount of time before you're supposed to do something. This is great for the drummer

who forgets that she's supposed to be at practice instead of the bar on a Monday.

- **Repeated Events** – Putting in reminders to submit for festivals, get tax information or other events that happen every year can help you remember them. Simply select a repetition schedule for an event and be reminded of it each week, month or year.
- **Sync** - These calendars can sync to your phone--you can update them from your phone, too.
- **Obligations** - When members of your team can't move a personal event (wedding, funeral, graduation, etc.) you can add it to the calendar so that nothing gets booked then. The collaborative nature of GCal allows everyone to make sure their schedule is respected and keep everyone informed of each other's obligations.

Google Docs

Google Docs (drive.google.com) is essentially Microsoft Office in the cloud. It allows multiple users to collaborate on various documents, so that everyone involved in a project can edit, update and view them. These are some of Google Docs features and how you can use them to manage your music:

- **Documents** - These are standard word processing documents. These are great for storing press clippings, bios, lyrics, etc., and can also work as living wikis for idea management. These files should be shared so various members of your team can tweak them. This makes for a fast and easy way to get opinions and ideas on projects. (Side note: This book was written exclusively in Google Docs.)
- **Presentations** - This service is similar to Microsoft's PowerPoint software. You can make multimedia slideshows, which you can use for on-stage projections or proposals in meetings to impress investors or brands you want to get involved with.
- **Spreadsheets** - Spreadsheets are the lifeblood of your organization. These can help you do your accounting, organize tours, update mailing lists, and so much more. Anyone familiar with Microsoft Excel is familiar with the functionality of these spreadsheets.
- **Forms** - You can use forms for many cool tasks. You can put them on your website to poll fans, survey everyone on your team about a subject while allowing them to remain anonymous, or keep track of expenses.

- **Drawings** - If you need to wireframe a website or make a simple sign, this feature can be your best friend.
- **Any File** - You can upload any file type (within size limits) to Google Docs and then share it with whomever you want. This makes sharing promo photos, demos, input lists, etc., easy and accessible from a window you normally use.

Google Drive

Another helpful way to stay organized is Google Drive (drive.google.com). This Drive is a cloud-based storage locker that will let you store any files you want. If you want to keep a .zip file of your latest record and promo photos, you can store it here and easily send it out to press people or allow other members of your team to access it. If you hire a publicist, you can give them access to all your music, press photos and other materials with the click of one button. Just remember Google Drive handles audio very poorly and some people consider it an insult to be sent audio files on it. Some common files to keep in Drive include:

- **Bio**
- **Press Quotes**
- **Press Photos**
- **Album Art**
- **Your Music**
- **Riders**
- **Input Lists and Stage Plots**

Google Voice

Google Voice (google.com/voice) is one of the coolest tools Google has in its arsenal. You get a Google Voice phone number, which you can use to make phone calls, send texts and receive transcribed voicemails. You can do this all on your computer or your phone. Here are some applicable uses for Google Voice:

- **Business Phone** - You can put your Google Voice phone number in your email signature and have it forward to your cell phone only during the hours when you want to do business. This means no annoying business calls when you don't want them.
- **Bounce** - Send annoying people or unknown calls straight to voicemail, so you can learn what they want before getting caught in an annoying conversation from someone who shouldn't have your number.

- **Secretary** - You can use Google Voice as your own personal secretary. Callers are asked to announce their names and then you can choose whether to take their call or not.
- **Record** - Easily record phone calls for interviews or to remember business discussions.
- **Text** - Receive texts and voicemails in your email inbox so that you can easily respond to them on a full-sized keyboard.
- **Free** - Make free domestic calls and inexpensive foreign calls.
- **Phones** - There are iOS/Android for the service that can help you manage how you use Google Voice.
- **Compatible** - You can port your present number to Google Voice so that you can use Google's services without having to give everyone a new number.

Google Alerts
Google is most famous for being the world's best search engine. Whenever you are mentioned on the web, Google will email you a link to what was said. (google.com/alerts)

Google Analytics
Google Analytics (google.com/analytics) is your website's best friend. You can use this program to measure traffic to your site and record whether fans on your site also click through to your webstore.

Much More
Google has a tool for everything. Throughout this book, we'll reference other Google services like AdSense, YouTube, Checkout, Picasa and more. Google Chrome is the fastest web browser and is tailor-made to work best with Google's many features. No matter what your needs, how big or small your fanbase is, at some point you'll need a Google account.

More Tools To Make Life Easier

SongKick
One of the most annoying parts of being a musician is adding your concert dates to a bunch of different websites and social networks. Well, SongKick (songkick.com) is a service that updates all of them for you at the same time, meaning you only need to add the dates once to distribute them everywhere. It publishes your tour dates on sites like YouTube,

85

HypeMachine and even their own site, which is built around alerting fans when their favorite musicians are coming near them. They have Spotify integration that tells fans when the musicians they listen to are coming to their area. Many local concert listings use SongKick to harvest dates too; so having your dates here helps out with press. There are many advantages to an up to date SongKick.

In order to update SongKick, you simply use their Tourbox function (tourbox.songkick.com) and enter in your band's information. Once it's accepted, you can start entering tour dates and have them publish anywhere you'd like. SongKick might become the only site you need to use to announce tour dates, saving you a bunch of time. You can also add ticket-purchasing links to the service to make it efficient for fans.

Your dates are published to the following sites once you update your SongKick Tourbox:

- **SongKick**
- **Songkick's Facebook App**
- **SoundCloud**
- **YouTube**
- **Spotify (when fans land on your page they will show there)**
- **Bandcamp**
- **Tumblr**
- **WordPress**
- **HypeMachine**
- **FourSquare**
- **Flavors.ME**

BandsInTown
Like SongKick, BandsInTown (bandsintown.com) is a service that allows you to aggregate tour dates to a handful of services, making them visible to concertgoers. The service's Facebook App alerts fans' newsfeed, Twitter, Tumblr and WordPress when you add dates in their area. The Tour Manager app allows you to make Facebook events for your dates and aggregate them easily. This can help to make fans alerted to your tour dates by simply adding your dates to the service. If that weren't enough, the App creates playlists for their users of the acts playing local to them that are similar to other acts they listen to--enabling your music to get discovered by those looking for new live acts to see.

They also have great bells and whistles like:
- **In-App Ticket Purchases**
- **RSVIP** – A way for musicians to give away meet and greats and other experiences to random fans who RSVP to your show.
- **VIP Club** – Allow your biggest fans to buy tickets in advance.
- **Push Notifications** – The ability to send push notifications to the fans that have RSVPed to the show.
- **Unified Events Promotion Page** – The ability to make a page that shows all your events that you can push out via your streaming links hub, social media or website.
- **Geo-Targeted Messaging** – The ability to message fans in a geographical area about an upcoming performance.
- **YouTube Cards** – BandsInTown is eligible to be linked via YouTube cards.
- **Analytics** – The service is able to present you with a map of where fans that are tracking you live, so you can make sure to go to their town.
- **Play My City** – Many of their products have the option for a play my city button so you can know where to tour.

Dropbox

Dropbox (dropbox.com) is one of the best organizational tools you'll find for your music. It also offers an easy way to share files with your contacts. By downloading the Dropbox application to your computer, you can take files from your hard drive and put them in the cloud, making them publicly available with a Dropbox URL that you can send to anyone, or keeping them private for only your team members to access. Dropbox has multiple pricing plans depending on how much storage space you need, so costs remain low or even free if you need only a few gigabytes of storage.

It's a huge time killer when you need to send new files to everyone on your team. With a private shared folder on Dropbox, a group of people can add and remove content from that folder and everyone can reference the materials when needed. So all of your songs, press photos, input lists, merch designs and whatever else you may need multiple to have access to can be kept organized. This is crucial when working with a half-dozen team members on a project, so no one is waiting to receive important materials.

If you have been working in the music business for any time at all, you have received file transfers from sites like WeTransfer, HighTail, Mediafire,

87

etc. These sites are slow and blast you with ads and pop-up windows. They don't offer the best first impression when you want to send someone your music. Instead, you can use Dropbox to share files with a simple URL that gives a fast, clean download of the file you wish to share--all for free.

As an added bonus, Dropbox has a mobile app that works on Android and iOS. With this app, you can run into a potential contact and send them your music right away, instead of waiting until later in the week and seeming like a slacker. You can also access your files at any time, so workflow never slows down.

Slack

Which App who J (unt.

Slack has been a life-changing app for me. It allows you to invite members of your band and team to a chat room to hold meetings, discussions, or just chat. You can use it in your web browser, a stand-alone desktop app, iOS, Android or whatever. You may be asking why you should use Slack instead of a text message group? Slack is infinitely searchable, so when your drummer can't remember what was agreed upon in a meeting, he can look it up later. This does wonders for not having to fight about what was discussed as well as remembering good ideas you may soon forget. I have gotten so into Slack I don't like to have meetings on the phone or Skype anymore, since Slack is an easily accessible record that can always be revisited. Every project I work on is done solely in Slack, eliminating dumb, unread emails, texts and phone calls.

The ability to drop files into chats and have team members who missed a meeting easily be able to revisit what was said in a few minutes. There's also direct messaging and the ability to make private chats if certain members shouldn't be included in a discussion. Slack is free for most band's needs, otherwise it's $6 per person, per month. (slack.com)

Front

Front is a cool app that allows you to manage a busy email inbox. If you find it confusing who in your team is answering emails and spending far too long forwarding emails, Front is for you. Front allows you to assign responsibility for emails and to see if someone else has already answered an email. It also allows canned responses for common responses. This app works great when your email gets too hectic. (frontapp.com)

OmniFocus

There's a million ToDo list apps, but to me OmniFocus is the best one for getting things done and keep a mess organized. While the App is dramatically more expensive than others, the tool and system allows you to get whatever you need done. (omnigroup.com/omnifocus)

ToDoist
If you need a ToDo list where you whole band or team can collaborate and make sure what needs to be done is getting that way, Wunderlist is the best in the business. The app allows you to invite other users to a list and see the tasks at hand and begin to get them done. (todoist.com)

Trello
While ToDoist and other ToDo apps are great, the flexibility and features of Trello allows your team to manage tasks and track progress on group projects. Trello is my favorite app for organizing a band/team and making sure everyone is making progress. (trello.com)

iCloud
Apple developed the iCloud (icloud.com) site (initially under the name .mac or MobileMe) to be their Gmail rival. While the site has never come close to being as useful as Gmail, it's still a great tool that can help you stay organized. It's now free for up to 25 gigabytes of storage. It has the following feature set which can be helpful for musicians:

- **iCloud** - The iCloud (formerly iDisk) is very similar to Dropbox in that you can share files and folders with other users. You can also use a mobile app to send files on the spot and share files with nice, clean downloads.
- **Email** - With the me.com moniker, this popular email service can be accessed like any other. With easy drag-and-drop facilities, it's great for sharing files.
- **iCal** - Like the Google Calendar, iCal has the ability sync with numerous users and send you reminders.

Skype
Skype (skype.com) revolutionized communications with a desktop application that enables you to conduct audio, video or text chats for free across continents as long as you're connected to Wi-Fi. It's a very valuable tool for hosting meetings with team members spread across the country in a way that doesn't sacrifice audio and video quality. It's especially useful

for those that like to carry on their business from the desktop of their computer.

Zoom
Skye competitor that offers similar services and often superior clarity in meetings. (zoom.us)

SoundOut
Are you looking for some honest feedback on your song before it hits the world? SoundOut (soundout.com) plays your music for a panel of music listeners who listen and critique it. You get a PDF report of how people reacted to your music, and you can learn from this. Like we talked about before, objective perspective is important if you're not sure about the decisions surrounding your latest tracks. While not all of the feedback from SoundOut is helpful, my experience with the service is that the majority is both accurate and honest.

SoundOut also offers licensing and radio placements to those who use their service. The service costs $30 to $150 depending on how fast and extensive a review you want. If you want to submit more than one song, they offer discounted packages--this could be useful to help determine a single.

AudioKite
Similarly to SoundOut, AudioKite arms you with user feedback and analytics. (audiokite.com)

SkyClerk
Keeping track of your accounting is a tough task. Google Spreadsheets and other basic services include accounting facilities, but eventually you'll have too much money coming in and out and you'll need a more advanced tool. Skyclerk (skyclerk.com) is a great web-based accounting tool with a clean, user-friendly interface.

FreshBooks
If you want the ability to invoice and keep track of your accounting Freshbooks has some of the best and most affordable tools to do so. (freshbooks.com)

PDFPen

Need to alter contracts or paste your signature into them without going through the trouble of printing them out? PDFPen (pdfpen.com) is a great way to mark up PDFs in your computer. The $60 software lets you edit any PDF easily, and helps you save a bit on printing costs to offset the price. While this software can be helpful for thorough contract markups, the free Preview app in a Mac allows many of these features as well as the mark up features in the iPhones pictures app.

DocuSign

If you are doing lots of work with contracts it can be extremely annoying and expensive to send print contracts back and forth. Docusign allows you to send digital legally binding documents across the web and have them easily signed by novices. (docusign.com)

Band Management Services

While Gmail solves many problems within one holistic umbrella, there are a few services specifically designed to organize musicians and have tailored themselves to provide exactly what musicians need to make themselves more functional. These sites all have specific features that could help you get work done faster and in a more organized fashion.

Artist Growth

It's often unclear what you should be doing on a day-to-day basis to get more fans. Artist Growth (artistgrowth.com) aims to change that with their band management system. Simply input concert dates, recording dates or select actions like getting press or making a business plan, and their app will tell you what you should be doing on a day-to-day basis. With an extensive reminder system and what they call "action packs," Artist Growth gives you tutorials on everything.

If you have an upcoming gig, the system will remind you to take certain actions on a daily basis. It will also allow you to access a list of local press, radio, venues and other contacts to make promotions easier. It can do the same for your recording slots and album release campaigns with an extensive list of what you can be doing to ensure growth in each step. They have a free trial and subscriptions are $10 a month. The app also boasts the following features:

- **Mobile** - iOS and Android apps so you can do tasks on the go.
- **Social** - Update Facebook and Twitter.
- **Concert Aggregation** – You can synch with BandsInTown to automatically upload your concert dates.
- **PRO Submission** – You can submit your set lists to get royalties from your PRO.
- **Information Storage** - Manage set lists and publishing info.
- **Tutorials** - Watch countless tutorials on nearly any subject in the music business.
- **Financials** - Manage your finances and merch inventory.

Use AtVenu To Manage Merch And Sell More Of It
One of the biggest pains of selling merch can be inventory, especially when you need to do count-ins and count-outs for venue percentages. Thankfully, AtVenu (atvenu.com) has made this pain along with many others, far less painful. It allows you to evaluate merch sales data analytics to determine what merch to stock along with reporting venue scans for SoundScan so your sales of music at shows count towards the Billboard charts. You can also sell merch to fans via Square integration. Depending on your needs the tool is priced at $10, $50 or $90 and is available on iOS and on desktops.

MasterTour Organizes Your Touring In One App
MasterTour (eventric.com) is an app that allows you to manage tour itinerary, travel, accounting, production, guest list, setlists and everything else a tour manager could need. The software allows management and tour/day to day management interact and keep the small moving parts of touring moving seamlessly. There's both a desktop and mobile version, which cost $49.99 a month.

Analytics Services

Analytics are one of the most important technologies changing the music business today. As the playing field is leveled, the effectiveness of your promotions becomes more and more important as you try to get a lot of bang for very few bucks. How do you know how to market your music, unless you know what works? The statistics you gain from analytic software are important to make decisions in promoting your music. The following services are aimed at helping musicians gain these stats.

The ChartMetric

While many analytic services offer tools for bigger artists ChartMetric (chartmetric.com) offers insights any musician can use. Their most helpful feature is the ability to look at other artists insights in order to get a grasp on your strategy including their Spotify playlist placements. Pricing ranges from free to $140 per month.

The Appreciation Engine

If you're looking for a graphical representation and analysis of your top fans, The Appreciation Engine (theappreciationengine.com) has a lot of answers. It harvests information from Facebook, Twitter, YouTube, Instagram, SoundCloud, FourSquare, Last.fm, Spotify and Deezer. It sets up an actionable list of what fans you should communicate with and has many visual representations of their geographic location and the metrics of their engagement.

The premise of the site is that it identifies and tracks your top fans, then gives you information you can use to strengthen relationships with them. Their pricing depends on the scale of your communication with fans, starting at free and going up to $75 a month if you have thousands of fans.

ForTunes

If you are tired of having to search across numerous platforms for your analytics ForTunes (fortunes.io) aggregates SoundCloud, Apple Music, Spotify YouTube, Instagram, Facebook and Twitter all in one place. This free app does this along with a host of other targeting features making it a very worthwhile tool.

Next Big Sound

NextBigSound (nextbigsound.com) has an awesome view where you can get verified and then add your various social networks to the site. You can then compare plays and new fan gains against up to four other acts, so you can see how you're doing compared to other related groups. The service has an extensive feature set that includes the following:

- The ability to track stats across sites like Facebook, Twitter, YouTube, Last.fm, Pandora, Bandcamp, PureVolume, ReverbNation, Soundcloud, Wikipedia, VeVo, OurStage and Vimeo.
- By adding you stats to NextBigSound you allow yourself to be tracked by Next Big Sound's Social 50 chart which is printed

weekly in Billboard magazine and watched by many potential team members who are looking for hot new talent.

- The ability to track events and press mentions with increased plays, for deeper analyzing. The software will pull in press mentions and other notifications for you.
- A global view that can be examined to show where your fans live so you can plan tours more effectively.
- Demographic breakdowns by age, sex and location of your fans.
- The ability to import other stats like Facebook interactions and iTunes sales data for deep processing. Simply connect the available analytics to your profile and see a thorough breakdown to learn about your fans.

SoundCharts Analyses The World Of Music
If you are looking to measure streaming services, playlists and other social metrics SoundCharts (soundcharts.com) can put this all in one dashboard, organizing the data so you can accurately analyze data and see where growth is coming from.

Chapter 4: Selling Direct To Your Fans & The Tools To Do It

The phrase "direct-to-fan" may seem like cheesy marketing talk from some nerds trying to sell you their advice, but in fact, it's the foundation of how you build and maintain a following for your music. The easiest way to explain the concept is to look at iTunes. When you sell a song on iTunes, Apple gets the email address of a customer who was a big enough fan of yours to buy your music. Then *Apple* is able to annoy that customer every time a Yanni or Bhad Bhabie album comes out that they're hyping, instead of you being able to contact them with news about your new release. Pretty lame right?

Instead, if you sell your music through a direct-to-fan method, you're able to gain the email addresses of your fans and build a relationship with them for years to come. You can contact them directly with news about you--the act they were interested in from the get-go. You gain the ability to send your fans details of what you are doing whenever you want. This is the best way to never lose contact with a person who already likes your music and has already supported you. You can build lasting relationships instead of just getting a single sale, allowing you to maximize the relationship with every fan that's interested in your music.

Middle Man
By going direct, you cut out a middleman (or two sometimes), so you're able to sell your music for less and still make more money. For example, if your direct-to-fan method takes a 15 percent cut and iTunes takes 33 percent cut, you're making 18 percent more selling direct to your fans and gaining an email relationship with them. This adds up when you're selling albums for about $10 each. And not only are you making more money immediately, you also have the future possibility of making a sale to that fan again because you have their contact information to remind them about new releases.

Building Fan Relationships
Direct-to-fan isn't just about sales, either: There are countless tools that trade email addresses or tweets for free music. If a potential fan is interested enough to check you out, you can gain their email address in

exchange for a free MP3 download, then introduce them to what else you have to offer that they can then pay for.

This is how you build a fanbase that stays informed and is constantly paying attention to you. These reminders not only help remind fans to spread the word to their friends, but they enable a fanbase that keeps growing for years to come. Routing both listeners and fans to your direct-to-fan method is how you turn fans who occasionally check in to see what you're doing into die-hard fans that stick by your side for years to come. Figuring out marketing techniques and how to get your fans to use this method as much as possible is the difference between taking big steps towards building a fanbase or squandering an opportunity.

Doing Direct-To-Fan The Right Way

There are a number of tactics you can employ in order to make your direct-to-fan method as effective as possible.

Selling Digital Music
While it's best to make sure your music is for sale in every possible digital outlet, you need to sell direct to your fans as much as possible. The more you sell direct, the better chance you have of keeping that fan for a longer period of time. While it's good to have your music on iTunes and Spotify, you'll always prefer for your fans to buy from your direct-to-fan method--so be sure to link them there instead.

Give Reason To Buy
Adding bonus tracks or other content to your direct-to-fan method gives fans an incentive to buy from you instead from the larger digital outlets. If you have exclusive peripheral content from your direct-to-fan method, fans will be encouraged to buy from there. You can do this through your website and even tell your fans it's a special thank-you to those who come to the website.

Discount
When you sell direct, you cut out a middleman who would otherwise take a cut of your sales. You can pass this savings on to your fans. By selling your music and merch for less through your direct-to-fan method, you can drive sales there.

Bundling

One cool way to get fans to buy from you is to give a free sampler with every purchase. You can bundle free music with every online sale as an extra incentive. Webstore services like TopSpin, Limited Run, Bandcamp and BigCartel all allow you to bundle merch and digital merchandise together.

Call Attention

Find as many ways to drive your fans to your direct-to-fan method as possible. When you get covered by blogs, ask them to embed an email-for-download widget (more on that later) in the post. This gives you the chance to gain the email address of a potential new fan around every corner.

Personal

One of the best things about direct-to-fan is you can make a fan feel special. If you see a new name that has bought your music in your email list, write them a personal letter thanking them. When you first start out this can turn fans into diehards who spread the word about your music. Little personal touches like this can accelerate your fanbase growth.

Profit

Linking to your direct-to-fan method is way more profitable than selling on iTunes or Amazon. There is very little benefit to giving someone else a sale when you could make those sales yourself.

Direct-To-Fan Management Tools

Managing your interactions with your fans, as well as selling to them directly, isn't something every musician does well today. However, it's the future of the music business. Having a strong set of tools to manage your interactions with fans and maximize them is valuable.

Limited Run

Limited Run (limitedrun.com) is a merch platform that allows you to pay a flat monthly fee based on how many items you offer for sale. The price for their service is a flat 5% of sales with a cap of $250 a month. You can bundle digital items and also sell physical items; you can also include a blog, SoundCloud player and many individual pages. They also offer the following features:

- **Custom Domains**
- **Discount Codes**
- **Digital Format Choices** - The ability for fans to choose which digital format they get their download in.
- **Free Digital Files** – If you give away free music, Limited Run doesn't charge you for it.
- **Ticket Sales** - The ability to sell tickets to your own events, including will call abilities.
- **SoundScan** – The ability to report sales to SoundScan and get your music on the Billboard charts.
- **Preorders and cart limiting** – When there's a high demand for your merch and music they have features that helps you sell the most copies including the ability to notify people who missed out on an item when it comes back in stock.
- **Mailing List** – Limited Run has a great mailing list feature that comes with their standard fees for the service.
- **Numerous Shipping Options**
- **Bundles** – You can bundle music with digital and physical releases and create VIP packages for fans.
- **Deep Analytics**
- **Email Collection** – Collect fans emails including those of fans who try to order unavailable merch.

ReverbNation

ReverbNation (reverbnation.com) is one of the most essential tools for musicians looking to build a fanbase. This is why over two million musicians have signed up for it. Their vast array of tools (most of which are free of charge) is astounding. As if that isn't enough, they're a huge social network of musicians and fans. When you sign up for RN, you get a page on their network that resembles what Myspace should have been, providing yet another great way for fans to discover your music. Below are some of their many features:

- **Distribution** - RN has a two-tiered aggregation service for musicians to get their music in various online stores. You can get your music on iTunes, Amazon, Spotify, etc. This service is discussed more thoroughly in the chapter about distribution.

- **Widgets** - ReverbNation offers good-looking widgets you can embed all around the web to spread the word about your music.
- **Facebook Page** - ReverbNation makes one of the most popular Facebook music pages in the business. It holds a music player, wall, concert listings, mailing list signup and much more. This is covered in depth in the chapter on Facebook.
- **Promote It** - RN can help you develop efficient Facebook ad campaigns, including in-depth analytics.
- **Electronic Press Kits (EPKs)** - The ability to design great-looking press kits, easily, from the media you have already uploaded to RN.
- **AudioKite** – ReverbNation provides a service they integrated from AudioKite that allows fans to give you feedback on your songs.
- **Banner Ad Generator** - RN has an easy-to-use banner ad generator for your website.
- **Mobile App Builder** - If you want an iPhone app, RN has a customizable app builder that you can upgrade to.
- **Website Builder** - The website builder on RN is a partnership with Bandzoogle. You can make a fantastic site with thousands of templates and access to Bandzoogle's facilities.
- **SocialSync** - The ability to update your ReverbNation profile, Facebook, Twitter and YouTube all at once.
- **GigFinder** - ReverbNation probably has the greatest venue database on the net. With a vast listing of venues and promoters across the country, you can use your EPKs to submit for gigs within their system.
- **Opportunities** - They also have many other opportunities you can apply for with their service, including festivals and licensing deals.
- **Fair Share** - If you're getting heavy plays every month on your profile, you can apply to be a part of the ad revenue and earn money.
- **iPhone App** - You can perform many actions from the ReverbNation website on your iPhone with their app.
- **ReverbStore** - ReverbNation teamed up with Alliance Entertainment to make the ReverbStore. This allows fans to buy merch on demand. This means that merch is printed as it is ordered, rather than paying fees up front to print tons of merch you may never sell.

FanReach - ReverbNation's FanReach service has some of the best mailing list management tools you can buy (for a great price, too). With a free trial period and a $10 per month entry point (the price goes up as you acquire more email addresses), this is one of the least expensive email tools that includes a wide variety of features:

- The ability to install widgets on your web page that trade email addresses for tracks.
- The ability to have simple forms that allow fans to sign up for the mailing list.
- The ability to geo-target your fans so you can increase show turnouts and send emails only to fans who may want to hear about a certain appearance.
- A wide variety of templates.
- Analytics that show how many people opened your email, how many people clicked a link, etc.

TopSpin Media

TopSpin (topspinmedia.com) is one of the most heavily mentioned services in this book. A direct-to-fan suite of tools that comes from a company owned by the merch giants Cinder Block/Band Merch, they offer tools that help out with sales, promotion, email management, merch fulfillment, analytics and more. They're some of the loudest proponents of direct-to-fan on the web, constantly developing new tools that help musicians grow their fanbases.

TopSpin currently takes 15 percent of your sales as a fee and offers a plan where you pay $10, $50 or $100 per month depending on the features you need. There is also a $999 yearlong plan for users who need a more complicated tool set. While these prices seem high, TopSpin actually offers a lot more bang for your buck than its peers. If you bought each individual tool separately, you would pay considerably more.

Widgets - TopSpin probably has the best embeddable widgets in the business. Their widgets handle a wide variety of chores that musicians need to market their music. They offer a wide set of HTML5 widgets that can perform a wide variety of tasks.

- **Email For Media** - The ability to trade emails for downloads. You can also make this a simple email capture tool. It's customizable to match color or messaging needs.

- **Streaming Player** - The ability to put audio and video in a customizable player that allows fans or blogs to embed, tweet or Facebook share it.
- **Single Track Player** - Perfect for blog embeds, this enables you to stream songs for exclusive blog placements.
- **Download Link** - Allow fans or business contacts to download your song or record in a clean, logical format.
- **Sales** - Everything you sell through TopSpin is available in an embeddable widget that you can place on your website or blog.

More - While TopSpin's widgets are littered around the web, they still offer so much more.

- **Analytics** - You have the ability to see data about where your fans are and how they behave. This can range from trends in sales or how traffic on your website relates to social media.
- **Stores** - TopSpin allows you to sell merch and music through their SpinStore feature. The SpinStore offers a great interface to do everything from create new product pages to fulfill the actual orders.
- **Merch Management** - They have an amazing merchandise management system, so when you are making sales, you're able to retain all of your customers' information and ship orders in a fast and easy manner.
- **Music Management** - In addition to being able to sell merch, you can also sell digital music and bundle digital products with physical goods.
- **Mailing List** - Their mailing list platform makes it so that once you have your email list, you can keep contacting them using TopSpin's ahead-of-the-curve email software. They offer many different ways to target the customers who are most likely to purchase from you again.
- **Ticketing** - A ticketing system where you're able to sell tickets directly to fans and then scan them with TopSpin's iPhone app.
- **Fulfillment** - TopSpin has a partnership with BandMerch/Cinderblock to fulfill your merch orders. You can also plug many other merch partners into their system. There's much more about this in the merch chapter.

Bandcamp

Bandcamp (bandcamp.com) is one of the most popular ways musicians sell and give away music directly to their fans. The ability to capture contact information, sell or give away your music, sell tickets and also sell physical merch make Bandcamp an amazing service. Bandcamp is discussed in great depth in the chapter about digital distribution.

MusicGlue
MusicGlue (musicglue.com) offers a wide variety of services, most notably a widget to collect fans' emails in exchange for content. The site offers both a free basic model and a paid model that offers more features. Their website lists their features as:

- Control wholesale and retail prices.
- Create 'product offerings' that include multiple tracks, encouraging consumers to purchase whole albums or EPs.
- Gain invaluable information on fans, including email addresses, listening habits and location (city & country).
- Bring fans closer to the musician, with personalized messages and branding on all web pages. Furthermore, send out automated emails reminding fans of release dates.
- Load unlimited tracks.
- Design your own flash music player that can be added to your website.
- Switch off certain countries, depending on your licensing situation.
- View real-time reports of sales with total financial transparency.
- Accept PayPal and credit card sales worldwide.
- Quarterly accounting.

BandZoogle
While BandZoogle (bandzoogle.com) is mostly known as a website-building service, they're also a direct-to-fan sales platform, using a store that allows you to sell digital or physical merchandise through a PayPal checkout system. Once you set up your monthly account with BandZoogle, you're able to sell your goods without giving them a percentage. They will also allow you to sell any digital file you wish through their system, so if you want to sell a documentary or any other cool file, you can easily do it through them.

More Ways To Sell Direct-To-Fan
If you're just starting out and only have a couple of items to sell, these are some solutions that can help you easily sell directly to your fans.

- **GunRoad** - GumRoad (gumroad.com) allows you to sell to your fans online by creating a simple webpage (and even run pre-orders). Afterwards, you can keep in touch with your fans when you have new items to sell.
- **BigCartel** - Big Cartel (bigcartel.com) is a merch store that is easy to set up and takes no fees. More details about them in the merch chapter.

Chapter 5: Targeting & Researching Other Musicians For Effective Promotion

Whether it's getting press, booking shows, writing your bio or figuring out your social network presence, you need to reference other musicians to get an idea of what you should be doing to promote your music. Having a list of musicians you follow allows you to easily find fans and outlets that'll be likely to be interested in you. This is the easiest way to grow your fanbase and is part of an essential chore in promoting your music each day. *I am often asked what readers of this book overlook the most and my answer is this very chapter. Read this and incorporate it into your daily life.*

Target
What I mean by "targeting" other groups is that we want to identify similar acts that have the attention of fans, writers, promoters and other key players. By identifying these acts, we can find people who have the potential to be interested in you. This helps immensely in making sure your promotions are as effective possible, since your targets will be those who have a high likelihood of being interested in your music.

Potential Fans
You have already read the words "potential fans" about a thousand times in this book. What this means is that there are some people who are never going to be your fan, no matter how hard you try. I like a lot of music--my music library is equal parts punk, classic rock, dance music, pop and hip-hop. But if you sing about your pickup truck and going to church, my subway-riding-Atheist-self cannot relate in any way. One of the reasons it is important that we target all of your promotions is we want to try to find fans who are likely to enjoy your music, instead of wasting time and money trying to market to listeners who will most likely ignore you.

Finding The Targets
You want to create a list of 10 to 20 acts (this list can grow later, if need be) that you're going to keep track of in order to make your own promotions more effective. When making this list, you'll be researching which musicians may be best to target. The following are some qualities you want to evaluate:

- **Similar In Sound** - All of the musicians you target should have a somewhat similar sound to your group. If you make diverse music, it's fine to target a few different acts that each share a part of your sound. The more similar each of the musicians you target are to you, the easier it is to make these targets effective.
- **Local** - While every musician you target doesn't need to be located near you, it helps to have some who are. The more nearby musicians you keep track of, the better--especially if you're just starting out. If you need to build a bigger regional following, you can follow local bands that might not sound the same as you. In fact, it can help to target a few local musicians who aren't even near your genre, but work hard on their music, in order to find some local opportunities that you may not discover otherwise.
- **Smaller** - This may be irrelevant if you're just starting out, but it helps to target musicians who are less popular than you. If they're getting covered by a blog, have some fans or are playing shows somewhere, it'll be easy for you to get all of the opportunities this smaller musician has.
- **Similar In Size** - The majority of the musicians you target should have a similar amount of fans to you. This means they have a similar amount of followers on their social networks and have been around for about as long. Within reason, you should find as many of these musicians as possible, since the majority of what they have going for them, you can also get.
- **Bigger** - Targeting musicians who are extremely popular in your genre may seem like a waste of time, but it can really help. They have more fans and press coverage than you and can help you form an idea of where you want to go.
- **Spreading Out** - If you have exhausted the targets in your local scene, begin to target musicians in another city you want to build fans in.

Better Targeting Through Science
What if you don't even know where to start with finding acts who are similar to you? Relax, there are many ways to find these musicians. Even if you think you know who may be best to target, all of these methods can show you some musicians you may have missed.

- **Bandcamp** - Bandcamp (bandcamp.com) has a fantastic searchable tagging system. You can search tags of the genre of music you play, or you can search by state or city. Try any search criteria that you think may find musicians similar to you. If they seem similar enough that you might share fans, then you have a target.

- **Last.fm** - If you have some plays on Last.fm, their algorithm will already have suggestions for musicians who are similar to you. This is a fine way to find similar artists that you can reference.
- **Jango** - If you go into your Spotify profile, as long as you have more than a few plays you can get a list of ten acts you are similar to.
- **Facebook** - When you've begun to target a band, you can see who they play shows with and who they talk about--those are other potential bands to target.

What To Do With Your Targets?
Now that you have this list of targets, what do you do with it?

Alerts – There are a few different alert systems that will alert you whenever a name is mentioned on the web. Each of these services will allow you to find opportunities once they begin to follow your targets.

- **Google Alerts** – While free, Google Alerts (google.com/alerts) will email you every day with links to where your targets are mentioned. While they are somewhat flawed and can miss a lot of mentions of your targets on the web, their price cannot be beat.
- **Google Image Search** – By typing your targets into Google Image Search you can easily see what blogs write about them and submit your music to them. This can often be faster than a blog search.
- **Talkwalker** - Talkwalker(talkwalker.com) is a free service that will track your targets both on the web and over social networks. Their extensive alerts can be customized to learn to not bring up false triggers and you can disable social network mentions if they get to be too annoying.
- **Awario** – A modestly priced service that will allow you 10 targets at a time for $20 a month with extensive monitoring. (awario.com)

Once you have chosen your alert system, type each target's name into it, to become notified when news is posted about each target. Each day when you begin to work on promoting your music, open your alert system and there will be a list of the blogs, promoters and fans that've been talking about your targets. This will continue for as long as you keep the target's alert active, giving you a constant dose of new places to try to market yourself. Here are some ideas of what to do with the results:

- **Press** - Add all of the places that write about these targets to your press list. Look around for their contact information and add them to your database. In a few weeks, you'll start to have a great list of blogs, news sites and newspapers that will hopefully write about you.
- **Venues** - This will give you show announcements so you can find out where you should play.
- **Fans** - Fans who blog about your targets will come up. These are fans that share and promote the music they love and will do the same for you if they like your music. Make it a priority to interact with them and get them your music.
- **Community** - Message boards and other communities will come up on these lists. Participating in these communities is a fast way to find potential fans.
- **Potential Team Members** - Record labels that put out compilations, writers, managers and others who work with your targets will show up. You can add them to your contacts database and try to get in touch with them in the future.

Twitter Search - Using Twitter search (search.twitter.com) will let you see who is tweeting about your targets. You can then follow all of these people, interact with them and subtly try to introduce them to your music. On this search, you'll find active fans of your targets that promote the music they love, that you can follow and develop a relationship with (more on that in the Twitter chapter). This will also alert you to more blogs, news sites and venues that cover these targets.

TweetDeck - Using TweetDeck (web.tweetdeck.com) you can create a column of a search for your name or targets that you can scan each day in order to find more targets. I find TweetDeck to be the easiest way to get through my promotional Twitter duties each day. The service is free which makes it even better!

What You Should Do With The Targeted Musicians, Contacts, Promoters And Press You Find
- **Follow** - Like and follow all of the targeted acts on all of their social networks. Watch and take note of the smart things they do and the ways they interact with their fans. Look for more press outlets and

107

venues you can play. Note their superfans and try to develop relationships with them. Bookmark their website and take note of the smart strategies they utilize on it. Follow everyone interacting with them.

- **Community** - This is who you should build rapport with. Play shows with the musicians you find, attend their shows, meet their fans and pass them flyers. Team up with them for promotions and build friendships. Trade shows with them if they're from out of town and venture out on tour together when you're both ready.

- **Find Sneezers** - In his book *Unleashing the Ideavirus*, Seth Godin uses the word "Sneezers" to define people who are influential, have a lot of social media followers and like to spread the word about what they love. A Sneezer is someone who enjoys spreading their opinions. By finding the fans of your targets that talk about what they love all the time, you can target these fans and make sure you develop a relationship with them.

- **Connections** - When you identify these targeted musicians, be sure to look at the contacts section of the social networks and website. The managers, lawyers, record labels and booking agents you'll find here are who you should target for your team. Find them on social networks and participate in their word.

- **Refine**- Most alert systems allow you to tell it when they alert you to terms that aren't quite looking for. Whether it is using minus keys for words you don't want them to include or flagging bad results, most of them will allow you to target more effectively if you take a few seconds to tweak them.

Finding Community

One of the most crucial parts of building a fanbase is finding where the fans and the tastemakers in your genre hang out on the Internet. One of the reasons targeting is so important is it can expose you to where you should be hanging out to find like-minded people who you will target to become fans, play shows with, exchange music with, collaborate or become teammates with. The Facebook Groups, Twitch streams, subreddits and other message boards that you will come across are where you should be spending a good deal of your time since finding these people is one of the most crucial parts of building a fanbase.

Chapter 6: Getting Potential Team Members Excited About Your Music

While this book is very much about doing it yourself, at some point you're going to have to get others in the music business excited about your music. There is now more you can do yourself than ever before--but you're still going to need to get other people to believe in you and excited about working with you at some point.

Getting potential team members excited about our music will make them want to help you, even when they may get very little return on their investment at first. One of the greatest things about music is that many people are willing to help just because they love what you do. However, if you turn off potential team members, you'll find yourself working the same dead-end job you already have as you grow older, still getting yelled at by your mom to clean your room. If this picture horrifies you, hopefully you'll take this chapter very seriously.

Being Social

Throughout this book, I tell you that writing to strangers about your music is a waste of time. That is exactly why you need to be social and work on introducing your music to as many people as possible. If people get a recommendation from a trusted source, they are more likely to get excited about your music. An email you send them when they have no clue who you are is much less effective. Concentrating on getting as many fans as possible to spread your music will get you heard by important industry players. Not emails you write to them out of the blue.

What About Your Friends?
We've all seen opportunities go to the friends of powerful industry leaders instead of hard-working musicians with great songs--and we've all gotten rightfully pissed off about it. You or a friend gets passed up for a record deal and a terrible band gets signed instead. You go on an enraged rant every time you hear the name of the band that got signed. What do they have that you don't? They probably had friends in high places. While I am

109

not writing anything Earth-shattering here, one of the not-so-secrets to getting ahead in this business is to be likable and not act like a rock-star asshole. Making friends and being personable can put you ahead.

Organic Referrals - As we talked about before, the best way to get someone to check out something new is by recommendation from a trusted source. You have probably checked out countless musicians you now love after being referred to them by someone you hold in high regard. In marketing dork speak, that is called an *organic referral*. The way to put this into use for your music is to have others recommend you to potential team members that you're trying to get in good graces with.

Live And Learn - Being friendly and talking to other musicians is a great way to get good recommendations. Throughout this book, you'll hear about participating in the community you want to be a part of. This could mean following people who you want to know about your music on Twitter, going to the shows of other musicians in your scene or participating on an online message board. All of these things help you get recommended, gain contacts and moved up in the music business. Being a hardworking act that makes great music and keeps in contact with other musicians is the easiest way to get potential team members to hear you.

Labels, managers, booking agents and other potential team members depend on the musicians they work with to tell them which young musicians they should keep an eye on. Musicians are perfect scouts since they're out on the road seeing up-and-coming talent all the time. Countless musicians have received amazing opportunities on the basis of this type of recommendation. If you play a killer live set and make friends with other musicians, these other musicians are likely to recommend you to their team members. Socialize and find common ground between you and the other acts. Offer help with any issues they're having, if you can. Everyone has loopholes in their knowledge--even if a musician is much more popular than you, you may still be able to offer them a hand. Once you help them, they'll be happy to help you.

Being Nice - Today's small-time house show promoter is tomorrow's label owner, manager or booking agent. That kid who runs a blog with 400 followers will be an editor of your favorite website in two years. Being nice to everyone not only feels good, it makes a world of difference for you. It helps you gain contacts that will lend you an ear throughout all of your endeavors. Never underestimate the power of helping other people. It takes years of being in this industry to recognize that the dorky 17-year-old kid at your show will one day become someone in a position of power. Taking the time to nurture a relationship with that kid can help you down the line.

Friend Of A Friend - Everyone has a friend who likes their music, who in turn has another friend who is some big shot in the music industry. Keeping track of these relationships and getting your songs passed on to potential team members is one of the most efficient ways to get recognized. If you're a good friend and they're a true fan of your music, they should have no trouble recommending you to their important friend.

Send An Email - Keeping in touch with potential team members and the musicians you meet is a smart move. Whenever you have new songs, simply notify your contacts and ask for advice on who you should send those songs to. Be specific. Write them a personalized email asking them if they know anyone who would be into your new tracks and if they can introduce you. Though it's preferable for them to pass it along themselves, keeping in touch and extending the same courtesy to everyone you meet can help your music spread.

The Difference Between Networking and Being A Total Douchebag
I grew up in the punk rock scene of the '90s. The last thing you would do in the scene I grew up in was "network." To this day, if someone talks to me about networking, I throw up in my mouth. When people "network," we hear what they're really saying: "What can you do for me?" When someone is blatantly trying to get my help--using empty compliments and ego inflation--I instantly tune them out. They are, for lack of a better term, "being a douchebag." Networking feels slimy and too business-like. The "I'll scratch your back if you scratch mine" transaction disgusts me and contrary to popular belief, many in the music business feel the same way.

In punk rock, we knew we needed to be social and work together in order to make our scene stronger. We were genuine in helping each other because of the common bond we all shared. We worked to help each other without sliminess or a sense of expectation. This friendly, egalitarian approach works well and can get you much of what you want in building a fanbase without the lies and ass kissing of "networking."

Social Skills For The Unsocial

I was not born an outgoing person but working in a club and a studio during my teen years did a world of good for my social skills. I was forced to converse with new people every single day while doing these jobs. Time and time again, I've seen friends come out of their shells and really enjoy being social once they learn how to do it. If you have decided that you're sick of your day job and are committed to doing whatever it takes to build your fanbase, it's time to accept that a lot of it revolves around being social.

We've all seen countless musicians become successful because of who they know--even though you think they suck. You can either hate them for it or you can learn to be social. Odds are you'll actually enjoy it once you get past the initial fear of conversing with your fellow humans. Social skills are not the only key to building a fanbase, but they do help good musicians get noticed by the world. You can be the best band in your region, but it doesn't make a difference if potential fans don't hear about you.

The good news is that you have an advantage if you're not a natural-born socialite. It keeps you a little more honest. For those of us not born with the gene to ask for favors and schmooze, it can keep your compliments humble and honest. If you speak with inherent kindness about real things rather than talking out of your ass, those on the receiving end will like you more.

Be Yourself - While "be yourself" may be a time-honored saying, there is a part of that saying that gets taken the wrong way. "Be yourself" means if you're not a kiss-ass, don't be one. Don't pretend to like things you don't like and don't change your opinions just to fit in. "Be yourself" doesn't mean you should remain complacent with the flaw of not being able to make new contacts. It doesn't mean you should give up on self-improvement. And it definitely doesn't mean that you should never change yourself when you see that you can do something that will help you achieve your dreams.

Musicians will hide behind this saying and retort, "I'm just being myself and I'm not very social." We all have room for improvement in our lives. I will ask you a simple question: Do you like your day job enough that you're OK with being antisocial and never accomplishing your dreams? If not, get out there and try being social with other musicians and potential team members. I promise it won't be that bad once you try it a few times.

Being Social
Let me put your mind at ease:

- You don't have to tell anyone you love their music.
- You don't have to ask for favors (nothing makes me sick to my stomach like asking someone to do me a favor).
- You don't have to sleep with anyone to get ahead or even buy anyone drinks (*but it is nice to buy drinks for the authors of this book if you see them out on the town*).

Being social is simple: Just talk to others about what you may have in common--if there isn't much, then move on. Those who you have a bond with, who you can keep talking to, are the ones to focus on. If you don't like someone and they rub you the wrong way, then move on. No one is saying you have to get on your knees and commit to partying with Satan after signing a pact with him. Find like-minded friends and work with them on promoting your music and theirs. Even if someone is more successful than you, it doesn't mean that you can't help them and they can't help you. If their band draws 250 fans and you bring 10 of your fans to their next show--trust me, they're going to be appreciative. When you get to that point, you'll appreciate it too. Being social means getting out of your house, finding others you get along with and starting a movement to help one another--not telling someone that you think their awful music is great.

Your Movement - In the punk rock movement, we worked hard to help each other because we wanted the world to know about our ideals to make the world a better place. If you aren't into the whole political movement thing, and simply think that you're better than some of the other music out there, think about that as the movement you're trying to spread. Show people that your music and your friends' music is worth their time. Band together. Promote yourselves and what you have in common.

Kurt Cobain started a massive movement in the '90s by simply telling everyone about all of his favorite bands. He wasn't trading favors since a lot of the bands he promoted were way smaller than his or already broken up. He was simply promoting what he liked while trying to bury what he didn't. You can make your movement be whatever you want it to be, but you need to make it substantive while being generous in promoting those who are in it with you.

Networking
Even typing that word makes me shudder. The second I feel like someone is talking business with me in that fashion, I want to run out of the room.

Unfortunately, dealing with these types is necessary in business, since so many musicians adopt this sleazy tactic as they become successful. Even worse, as you become successful, you'll see more and more of these people.

Many people want to scratch each other's backs and use favors as currency in the music business. I don't think they're bad people--this is just how they were taught to do business.

It doesn't have to be this way, though. The corporate networking practice is one of the stupidest things we all have to deal with in music. Talk like humans: There's no need to brag or "exchange contacts." The funny thing is that when you try to do business with someone who rubs you the wrong way, you both end up unhappy. I've passed up many opportunities in my life after getting a bad feeling about someone. While they may have gone on to be successful, I know my life is always much happier when I deal with people I like on a daily basis. If someone rubs you wrong, walk the other way--and please, don't "exchange contacts."

People Being Douchebags
There is no cure for you if you a douchebag, so I will advise you on how to avoid becoming one. I don't want you to be influenced by the ways of the douche. So you'll know what to look out for, here are the actions of a douchebag:

- **"I Love Your Music"** - If you don't love someone's music, you don't need to say it. Most musicians can tell when someone is a real fan. Anyone can tell when someone is kissing their ass to get a favor. If you're asking for a favor like an opening slot, you don't need to lie about your fondness of the person you're asking. Everyone can tell when you're lying. Tell them the truth about why it would be good to have you as an opener, don't bribe them with lies and false compliments. Relate to them--and if you two gel, you can usually get much more than the favor you're asking for.
- **Buying Drinks And Expecting A Favor In Return** - It's obvious when someone is being nice because they want a favor. Be real. Find a bond with the other person as a human. Are you both into politics, guitar pedals, picking up girls, Harry Potter, UFC, whatever? It doesn't matter how classy or shallow it is--if you're the same type of people, that creates a real bond. People want to help

114

others they have a real bond with, not the douchebag who bought them drinks hoping they would get a favor in return.

- **Insisting That Someone Has To Help You** - When I used to book shows, musicians would tell me they should be on a show because they "deserved" it. Unfortunately, life doesn't work like that and if you try to be intimidating and overly persuasive, you're losing your chance at getting what you want, as well as closing doors for yourself in the future. If you believe you should be on a show, sell the promoter on it with something tangible don't insist or try to play mind games. If you're playing these games, you've already lost.

Getting Out Of The House
As comfortable as it is to stay inside watching *Here Comes Honey Boo-Boo* with your boo, if you say your goal in life is to grow a fanbase, you're going to have to go outside. I say this as someone who is often a shut-in (the book you hold in your hands was written indoors, after all). We all have heard enough stories of artists who met one person with connections who changed their life, so there is no doubt that while the Internet can introduce you to those people, these in person interactions can often foster a relationship that can be life-changing. It helps to have at least one band member go out and be an ambassador for your music.

Your Scene - When musicians are in my studio, they always ask what they can do to make progress while not on tour. The simplest action is to go to local shows when there are musicians who may be similar to you in sound. When I say this, I mean that if a musician comes through town and you think that their fans may like you at all--get out there, meet people and tell them about your band. Sometimes musicians won't go to these shows because they don't like the band playing. But it's not about whether they're good--it's a matter of you going out to a show where you'll meet people who could be interested in your music and interacting with them. Is there a bar where they play your style of music? A place where musicians are playing that share a similar audience? A party with a band similar to yours? Actually going to all of these real-world events can do a lot more for promoting your music than sitting at home Facebook messaging your Internet girlfriend.

Be Helpful - Did you make friends with someone from another band that you would like to work with? There is plenty you can do for them. Are you at an awesome party? Text them and let them know! Got a good show hookup? Share it. Read an awesome book you think they should be reading (hint, hint)? Musicians think that other, more popular musicians know much more than they do. This isn't the case: Everyone has gaps in their knowledge and you might be able to teach those with more experience than you. Sometimes I work with musicians who have been alive for less time than I've been playing music--yet I learn new things from them all the time. If someone sees that you're trying to be helpful, odds are they will want to help you. Just don't do it expecting a favor: Do it because you believe in the other musician and have a genuine bond with them.

I Hate This Part - I know so many great musicians who hate leaving their comfortable circle of friends. Unfortunately, it's necessary if you want to stop working your crappy day job. I would rather hang out with my friends at a bar or a nice restaurant instead of going to a show, since I am often burnt out at the end of a week of producing records. But if my goal in life was to build a huge fanbase, I would go out at least a one night a week to any show or bar where other musicians are hanging out. By making friends, music fans want to come see you play, promote you and pass your music on to friends in higher places. Even small towns have a scene like this, so don't feel like this only applies in New York, Austin or Los Angeles.

Friends Like To Help Friends - If you make lots of friends and are a genuine, nice person, others will want to help you. You know what's crazy? Even if they think your music is average, being a good person makes others more likely to get on board with what you're doing. If you're a good person making good music, you won't even need to ask others to show your music to an A&R person--they will want to do this on their own accord. So, forget the stories you hear of that rockstar asshole being a terrible person to everyone in their path. The real trick is to be someone who others want to see succeed.

Make Relationships, Not One Night Stands
I'm often shocked at how fast musicians think relationships develop. In all my years of working with musicians, I've rarely seen a veteran A&R person or manager come out on the first night they see a musician and say they want to sign them. Despite what you may have seen in the movies, this isn't how it usually goes. There is no contract waiting to be signed inside a briefcase. But many musicians act like it's the end of the world if they don't get a contract the night, they meet a potential team member. They don't understand that this is the beginning of a relationship. Just as someone isn't a fan after they hear your song one time, it also takes time to develop and explore a working relationship with potential team members. Slowly

showing someone how enjoyable it would be to work together is the way to build a team...not asking for a contract on night one.

I've never said yes to any musician who asked me to manage them the first time they asked. While I respect their ambition of asking, I've usually waited until we got to know each other better, did an album together, had some beers and saw enough of their personality that I was convinced it would be a good idea. In the same way you (usually) don't want to jump in someone's pants the first night, you want to focus on building a long and meaningful relationship with the people you're going to work with. If all doesn't happen on the first night, that's fine. Hit them up a few days later and say hello! Tell them a few more reasons why they should want to be a part of your team. Maybe they will want to see you again. And maybe, if all goes well, you can sign a contract that allows you to go through absolute hell if you break up. Just like dating and marriage!

Music Industry Red Flags

There are many different behaviors that can turn off potential team members, making them decide not to work with you. These are what I like to call "red flags."

You Must Have Velocity
Here is a great example of a giant red flag that goes up in relation to how fast your band moves: Let's say you recorded music in September, then for whatever reason you master that record in March. Maybe you were waiting on artwork, a new website or whatever? You then get it to the ears of a manager who you want to work with and mention that you just had it mastered last week--but he or she realizes you recorded it back in September. The manager is going to wonder what you did for the last six months. I hope you have progress to show for those months, or you're going to look like a slacker.

Motivated team members (the type you want to be working with) want to see that you're also motivated. They have enough problems and don't want another one--like motivating you to stop playing *Guitar Hero* and actually start playing your guitar. They want to see that you're working hard and want to get your music out to the world so badly that you can't wait to do it. When you can wait six months (or even two) for your master that shows

117

you aren't hungry. They want to see you get tasks done fast without suffering lapses in motivation. If you don't know how to manage your time to get tasks done, your talent can easily go to waste. The amount of hard work that goes into building a fanbase is insane and no matter how much someone likes your demo, team members will find more motivated bands if they think you're a slacker.

So how do to show you have velocity? Take six months off to find a new drummer? Ehhhh, find a fill in! Book mastering ASAP after recording is done. And after you get a master, start getting it into the right people's hands the very next day. Don't wait on artwork for three months. If someone is taking too long, it's time to move on. There are plenty of artists out there. Even better--get artwork started once you begin recording. Play shows! If there is one thing that shows you're making progress with your music, it's a full calendar of concert dates on your website. Just keep your momentum going. If you stay busy and show that you know how to work hard, this will often forgive other flaws that a potential team member may notice.

The Stupidest Things You Could Say To A Potential Team Member

"We were waiting until we got a label behind us to promote our record." –
Some Idiot Musician

An experienced team member is looking musicians with good songs and a hunger to succeed. No hard-working potential team member wants to work with musicians who are happy sitting at home and enjoying their lives. A friend who used to work for a successful indie label always said that he looked for musicians who hated their lives at home so that they'd always want to be on tour. This is not news to most people, yet so many musicians think it's smart to say that they were waiting for someone else to solve their problems. Prove you can solve your own problems and build your own fanbase, and those who can help you build a better fanbase will want to work with you.

"We were going to wait until we got a label behind us to go on tour." –
Some Idiot Musician

We understand it's not feasible for a lot of musicians to tour. You may have commitments, bills and even a family. But saying the above statement to a potential team member paints you as someone who waits for things to happen to them rather than someone who makes things happen for them. Instead, talk about what you have been doing or say something like, "We've been concentrating on building a local following first." At least that sounds like you've been making progress, instead of waiting for the record label fairy to drop a contract under your pillow while you were passed out on the couch.

"We wanted to shop it around before we released the songs." – Some Idiot Musician

It's the digital age and there is this thing called the Internet where everyone can listen to music--instantly! No potential team member is going to consider it a deal-breaker that you put some songs online to get some hype for your music. If anything, they will gauge the reaction to your songs as a measuring stick before they invest a ton of time and money into you. Get the songs out there once you have a master. Show that you're hungry. A musician that is too eager is much more welcome in this business than one who is lazy and waiting for someone to make things happen for them.

"We wanted to get the perfect lineup before we started to promote these songs." – Some Idiot Musician

My head hurt just typing that one. Getting the perfect lineup can take a lifetime. If you were actually hungry--and by hungry, I mean you can't wait another day for listeners to hear your music--you would never say this. Get your music out there and start showing it to the world. If you play shows and gain a following, you'll have many more options for great members and the perfect lineup. In fact, you may meet the drummer for your perfect lineup in a band you play a show with. In the meantime, work with the one you have and upgrade along the way.

"We Are No Good At The Business Side Of Things"
Years of reading rock journalism and watching rock-doc movies teaches musicians very stupid myths about how the music business works. One of those myths is that if you're good enough musicians, you'll get taken under the wing of some amazing manager or A&R guy. Unfortunately, this is rarely the case.

Many musicians don't realize that most successful managers and A&R people aren't rocket scientists or even hard workers. There've been countless successful careers in this industry built on finding musicians who have the whole package--they are good songwriters and smart businessmen--and the suits ride their coattails to the top. Even when the music business figure has a great work ethic, they don't want to be carrying all of the weight, especially in this age of smaller budgets. All of this adds up to why being "no good at the business side of things" is a one-way ticket to your parents' basement for the rest of your life.

You may have seen movies where musicians party all night and sip margaritas poolside while some guy in a suit yells into a phone for them. I hope you realize this is fiction. Musicians constantly need to be helping themselves out. With decreasing budgets, it becomes all the more important that you can conduct business on your own. The days of being able to sit back and hang out while your management takes care of your career are over.

You Are Not An Unsigned Band, Even If You Don't Have A Record Contract
One of the worst terms musicians use to describe themselves is "unsigned band." There is no other self-professed title that does more harm to a musician's image. This title tells potential fans that you aren't someone who should be paid attention to yet. It says that you are an amateur who hasn't been deemed ready for the world's attention. It says no gatekeeper has endorsed you and no one thinks you are good enough to "be signed." You describe yourself as being unsuccessful in your goal, since you don't think of yourself as successful until someone else says you are.

Instead, tell the world you are an "independent musician" or even just "a band." There is no need to classify yourself with a term associated with being an amateur. If you decide one day to sign to a record label, that's great because you decided to do so (remember, DIY means decide it yourself, not do it yourself). Until then, you can be signed to your own label, showing everyone your ambition at the same time. You are making things happen for yourself and if someone else wants to come on board and help--well, that can be discussed. In the meantime you are making things happen on your own terms, which is an attractive quality in the eyes of potential team members and music fans.

Get Used To Meeting With Potential Team Members

120

In the same way that it helps to play a few smaller shows before playing a big one--so you can get over the awkwardness and work the kinks out--it helps to meet with smaller-level potential team members before meeting the members you really want to work with. Even if you don't have any interest in working with a particular person, you can sit through a meeting to get a feel for how working together would go, leaving you more confident when better options come along.

When you meet with potential team members, it's often an audition to make sure your social skills are up to par and that you won't make drop the ball when you meet this team members contacts. No one wants to work with an act that is shy and awkward to talk to. They want to see that you know how to be charming and fun. Charming and fun musicians make friends easily and are able to help themselves. This is the type of person everyone wants to work with. Most people who work in music are here because it's fun (or at least they thought it was when they got started). If you're no fun, you aren't going to fit into most people's vision of who they would like to work with.

If you're excited at the prospect of working with someone you're meeting with, don't be shy or nervous. Realize that no matter how cool you think they are, they're just like you. Trust me, if you end up working with them, you'll eventually get to know all their flaws and think of them as a peer. Realize that being cool, fun and talkative is the key to getting where you want--not trying to be safe by not saying anything dumb.

Saying The Same Old Tired Things
Every week I get sent an electronic press kits (EPKs) from musicians and brace myself for the inevitable pain of what I'm about to watch. In nine out of ten of these EPKs, I witness musicians recite the same clichés we've all heard thousands of times. While the tendency among young musicians is to watch and imitate, most smart potential team members are looking to work with someone who can lead. Musicians who are in demand make a good impression by avoiding saying stupid clichés when dealing with potential team members.

A musician who knows how to give answers that aren't your typical interview fodder will get a lot more press than those who always talk about how grateful they are to have fans, how much they love being on the road or any of the other things we've all heard a million times. There's a reason why every writer wants to interview Amanda Palmer, Thom Yorke, Tyler

121

The Creator, Kanye West and Offset: The press knows that every time you put a recorder in front of them, they're going to say something quotable and interesting. Part of building a fanbase is the ability to get the press to ask for interviews, rather than having to beg for every single interview you do. Finding your voice is essential.

Don't be shy! When you're doing an interview, meeting someone important or doing your EPK, it's time to say the opinions that give you a personality. Don't stick to safe answers. Instead, say how you really feel. If you think you have a unique perspective on a subject, find a way to work it into the interview. Asking if you can talk about a specific subject is welcomed by most interviewers who are desperate to have good content in the interviews they print. I am not telling you to go into Marilyn Manson-esque hyperbole each time you see a red light on a recorder--in fact, please don't. But if you have something to share that isn't being discussed, this is the time to get it out there.

Having Bad Photos Speaks Toward Your Work Ethic, Not Just Your Look
Many musicians don't care about their image and hate that they even have to think about it. I can't blame them--it is disheartening to see "cute" musicians get ahead of talented ones. Spending tons of time and money on clothes and your hair can be mind-numbing beyond belief. What most musicians don't realize is that if you have bad promo photos, it shows that you have no concern for the quality of the product you represent.

There are tons of different ways to make an act with no concern for their image look great. Think of it this way: During the hair-metal era, photographers still managed to make both Nirvana and Hootie and The Blowfish look fresh despite the fact that they looked nothing like what the world was used to. Every local scene has great photographers who do great work. Simply scroll through Facebook photo galleries of local acts and look for photo credits on good-looking photos. It will speak to your work ethic, your ability to be self-sufficient and your ability make a positive first impression when you have a great-looking press photo--no matter what kind of fashion sense you have. Promo photos are one of the first indicators of whether you're up for the job. Don't skimp.

Keep The Trash Talk In The Back Alleys
A few years ago, I was working with a young band that was getting a lot of attention. They were signed to a new label with a clueless, drug-addicted

moron for a label boss--who also happened to be very social and have great connections. Thankfully, other labels and management were starting to express interest in this young band and they hadn't finished signing with this sad excuse for a label guy. After a great day in the studio, we hit the local bar and began to talk trash. The band was very vocal about what a clown their label boss was and disparaged him loudly for a while. No big deal--it happens at numerous bars all across New York City every single night.

Except it was a big deal. The label guy's lawyer was right next to us, not only chuckling away, but videotaping everything on his iPhone. The next day, they both came by the studio and we recognized his lawyer immediately. He played back the recording and the session ground to a halt. The label was no longer paying for the recording and he no longer wanted to work with this band. Shortly after, all the managers and labels showing interest in the group heard this legendary story and passed on working with them.

You never know who's listening and where the word will spread when you start talking trash in public. There is no blacklist in the music business--if there was, plenty of famous musicians would already be on it. But no one wants to work with an ungrateful bunch of musicians who were stupid enough to run their mouths where everyone could hear. Everything the group said was true, but it didn't matter. They were now the punchline of a joke and shortly thereafter, they broke up.

Impressing The Music Business

Recognizing The Cluelessness Of The Music Industry To Help Yourself

I am constantly saddened by the mistakes I see young musicians make. Many musicians don't realize that most of the music business is guessing at what they do. When they aren't guessing, they're making very uneducated decisions. Unfortunately, success (often through the luck of riding someone else's coattails) and admiration can cloud musicians' views. A musician can be left thinking that everyone in the industry who has seen moderate success is a genius and is making decisions based on concrete theories and ideas.

One of the prime examples of this point are the choices A&R people make when signing musicians. This part of the business is riddled with guessing. Many musicians think that in order to get signed, some wizard is going to find them after they work hard for a while and scoop them up because they fit into a formula some A&R person has sitting on their desk.

So if many people in the music business are clueless, what do you do about it?

Trust, But Verify - Walking around doubting everything that comes out of someone's mouth is no fun. Most of us have the instinct to tell when advice seems shady. Do research and make sure the advice you're getting is accurate.

Use Others' Ignorance To Your Advantage - If you're trying to get someone in the music business to notice you, spell it out for them--leaving very little to the imagination. I know so many musicians with a lot going for them, but they don't let anyone know about it. Since much of this industry makes uneducated decisions, if you educate them about why you're so great, they have less work to do themselves. Memorize your best attributes. If you have 20 fans that followed you up and down the east coast on tour, make sure there's a video of it. Don't assume that any potential team member can see your merits. Like you, the people who you want to be on your team are waiting for good opportunities--be sure to make yourself an obvious opportunity.

Pick A Bragging Right - Find something you have going for yourself and figure out a great way to brag about it. If you get 100 YouTube comments a day, that is worth telling someone about. If every larger act you open for ends up DJing your latest single, make it known. If a famous guitarist says your guitarist is inspirational, that's pretty notable. Figure out some way to tell others you're remarkable. Trent Reznor famously marched into TVT with a full presentation on why Nine Inch Nails would succeed with marketing data and more, leading to the label signing them.

Make Your Music Speak For Itself - Having demos, rough mixes or unmastered tracks gives these clueless guessers room to think and you don't want them using their limited imagination. Many musicians get excited and want their dreams to come true tomorrow. They then play their music for potential team members when it isn't finished. This leaves the listener room to imagine. Many listeners can't hear how much better the

124

final product will sound, walking away unimpressed instead of blown away. The team member you're trying to impress feels like the song sounds "off." Instead of immediately grabbing them the way a finished song does, they think "this isn't right" and they turn you down.

Don't play demos, rough mixes or unmastered tracks for people you want to impress, since they rarely can hear how much better they will be when you finish them.

Demonstrate That You Don't Have To Beg
A funny fact about the music business is that most industry folks don't listen to the type of music they work with. I will confess to being a part of this lot. Most of the bands I work with have rabid fans that are primarily 15-year-old girls. I am a guy in my 30s and while I love the music of the groups I work with, it's a bit of a guess whether the audience they appeal to will actually enjoy it. Because of that, I have to look at fan reaction to gauge whether their music is connecting.

What many potential team members are looking for is a genuine reaction from the public that demonstrates you don't have to beg for fans. They want to see that listeners get excited when they hear your music. They want to see that when someone discovers your music organically, they like it immediately. This makes their job and everyone else's job involved in pushing your music much easier.

We all sadly remember the days when musicians begged for comments or pictures of fans wearing their merch on Myspace. We've all been spammed by bands to vote for them in online contests. While everyone in the music business wants to work with musicians who work hard, if all they ever see you doing is begging your fans for favors, they won't be impressed.

There are some fan responses you simply can't fake. Fans getting your logos or lyrics tattooed on them demonstrates a true passion for your music that can't be faked or bought. Having established musicians willingly promote your music is another demonstration that speaks volumes about your talent and potential. Anyone who's been in this business for a minute knows that an endorsement from another musician can lead to great sales.

Every day I meet musicians who have qualities they don't realize they should be putting in plain sight for all to see. Posting this content on your Facebook, Instagram and YouTube can give the hint to potential team

125

members that you're worth their time. Whenever you have fans demonstrating their passion for you, find a way to make it visible. It'll encourage similar action from other fans and show potential team members that you're a force to be reckoned with.

Being Too Proud To Beg

"Do not wait to strike 'till the iron is hot; but make it hot by striking." -
William B. Sprague

Musicians are often disappointed when I don't have some sort of magic secret to make their goals come true. While this wisdom doesn't exist, there is one philosophy I abide by that works time and time again in getting the attention of the music business. If you spend all of your energy asking potential team members to listen to your music, you won't be as effective as those who force the world to listen to them.

As I stated earlier, I have a philosophy that has held true for every band I work with: Work so hard that everyone has to hear you. Put your energy into that work rather than contacting strangers with your SoundCloud page. Instead, make them take notice by being everywhere you can possibly be. Word travels fast when you start making fans and getting press and when a potential team member discovers you organically, you come across as much more appealing.

When I make a strategy to promote a group, I think about how to make the group self-sufficient. I think of ways to make them a mainstay in the press, even during "down time." This is essential because you want to get discovered by industry leaders naturally, not by begging them to listen to you--you'll always make a better impression that way.

Potential team members always check out the acts that fans are getting excited about. Nothing speaks louder than having thousands of fans and dozens of blogs buzzing about you. Building this buzz up will draw everyone's attention. Hungry, hard-working potential team members always have their ears to the ground looking for musicians on the rise. Becoming one of those musicians should be your goal.

This is all easier said than done, but if you start devoting your time to getting heard rather than finding addresses to mail demos, you'll be on a constructive path rather than one that is less likely to pan out. Devote your time to building fans through one-on-one connections, promoting your music and not hoping your "connections" will magically help you garner attention.

Don't Astroturf
"Astroturfing" is the term for fake grassroots. If you think of grassroots as having true, passionate followers, AstroTurf is having fake grass that isn't quite right and has all of the character and personality missing from it. There are tons of services where you can buy Facebook likes, Twitter followers, and YouTube plays. They're not worth the money and because of that, this book avoids giving them any lip service.

You may be able to fool some clueless manager who doesn't notice that you paid for fake fans. But at some point, they're going to figure out that you were faking it and their enthusiasm towards you will end. Just like heavy metal rockers who used to stuff their pants with a sock, eventually they would get the groupie backstage and they would discover the sad truth. It's easy to spot musicians who AstroTurf their fanbase and getting exposed for doing so can be very embarrassing. It also makes your real fans look dumb. It's not worth your time or money to pay for fake fans.

Engagement - Any potential team member worth working with, knows that having 10,000-plus Facebook likes isn't the only metric that matters. Your fans need to be excited and if you aren't getting tons of likes and comments on your posts, it shows your fans aren't very passionate and are probably fake. This is all the more reason that astroturfing is a fool's game. The astroturf-ed fans don't engage your page, so devote your time instead to real fans that are excited about your music.

Obituary Of A Theory: Waiting Till Everything Is Perfect To Release A Song
It's hard to argue with being a perfectionist--well, maybe against *Chinese Democracy*-level perfectionism. While perfectionism can lead to great things, there are points when it becomes silly.

I've known musicians with amazing songs already recorded who do nothing but sit around and write more songs for nine months. While they might have great songs in their pocket, they have been waiting until they can put out something "perfect." Unfortunately, this theory is flawed.

I'm not arguing against perfecting your sound. Instead, I'm trying to get you to think about stagnancy and not waiting to let listeners get a taste of your music. I see so many musicians wait too long to get everything ready before their release, not realizing you also need to be building a fanbase so you have ground to stand on and fans to help spread the word when it's time to unleash your new music.

No One Likes To Start At Zero - If you have been sitting in the rehearsal studio for six-plus months and not building a fanbase, you're reverting yourself to square one. Let's say there's a potential team member who hears you and loves your music. Much of the time, they don't want to start from scratch--they want you to already have a foundation. It's one thing if you're Radiohead and take six months off. It's another thing when you have a minimal following and can't clear 1,000 CDs from your car's trunk. Even if you have a few followers on Spotify it will dramatically help you get discovered each time you release a single since their algorithm introduces you to one new fan each time you release a single for each follower you have.

You Need To Demonstrate That Listeners Like Your Music - Many music business types just want to make a buck. They want to like your music, but more importantly they want to see it's an easy sell. If you've never put out music and gauged fan reaction, you have no way to demonstrate this. So when you sat in the studio for all those months while you should have been growing your fanbase, you put all your eggs in one basket and now don't have a strong case to argue that you're worth working with.

Your Dreams Take Time To Build - Forget about building a team for a moment. It's rare for anyone to be an overnight success. Start building a fanbase. Record the best song you have, even if you're going to re-record it later. Let listeners begin to hear what you're about. This way, when you release your future masterpiece, you already have some fans that want to help spread the word. Without those fans, it's very hard to get noticed and the material you slaved over may go remain under the radar.

Shopping Your Music To Potential Team Members
After you record something new, it's customary to send it to music industry professionals who you would like to be a part of your team. For some reason, this practice is known as shopping. Make sure you constantly

update your contact book so when you need to shop some new material, you know who to send it to.

This shopping consists of sending an email to the potential team member with a link to your new unreleased recording. This is usually done with the hope that they will get on board and help you promote this new release. The downside is that this is usually an annoying process for most members of the music business and unsolicited links are often ignored.

To Shop Or Not To Shop?
Shopping your music to potential labels, managers, etc., is a smart step whenever you have a new recording. Many musicians waste months of momentum trying to shop their record without doing much of anything else. Shop it to anyone you have already met who seems interested, but make sure this gets done fast. Waiting more than 30 days to gauge whether you have interest from your shopping is a huge waste of time. Instead, if you have lukewarm or small reaction you should put your music out into the world. If it gets a good reaction, the people who are letting your new album stream sit in their email inbox will be forced to check it out.

Many potential members of your team will get much more excited if you're working hard, gaining a fanbase and doing some of the promotion work for them. They can always re-release your record or jump on board for the next release. Don't stall your promotions waiting for potential team members to climb aboard. Instead, make progress on building your fanbase all the time and entice others to join you. That is much more impressive than getting another email asking if they listened to your record.

As a record producer, I finish records with bands all the time and I have seen one thing over and over: The groups who get signed, get signed fast in the shopping process. The one's who don't sit around waiting months and months for nothing. Usually if someone is interested you hear back in a week or two at most. If you haven't heard back in two weeks, odds are you are being strung along. Get moving and force the world to get excited about you. In fact, many A&R people I know will wait to see how the world reacts to a song even if they enjoy it. Trust me, music sounds better to potential team members when everyone else is talking about it.

Joining An Adventure Rather Than Saving A Lost Ship
While stories exist of musicians being discovered from unsolicited messages, these stories are the exception and not rule. I've never known

or been part of an act that has gotten discovered from an unsolicited message. Instead, these relationships usually start from a recommendation or a chance meeting that develops into a relationship. This is also the case for all of my friends who work at labels or as managers. Sending unsolicited messages shows you aren't a part of a social circle. If you were, you could find an inside way to contact the people you want to work with.

In my time as a manager, label employee and producer, I've always noticed that I pay much more attention to musicians who are making progress than those who want me to get on board and make progress for them. Most of the musicians I've ended up working with go out and make progress for themselves and ask me to come on board their already moving ship. It's a turn-off when you ask for help rather than inviting someone to join an actively changing adventure.

Connect - The best way to shop your music is to send it to people who you have an insider connection with or people you've already started a relationship with. I find it's best to update your contacts with a personal letter after each release, asking them to check it out and seeing if they have any feedback. If they react positively, stay in touch. Develop the relationship by showing what it would be like to work with you. Update them with your happenings and if you get a big opportunity, you can ask them for some advice--a great way to show you would like to be working together. If all goes smooth, ask if they'd like to be on your team.

Community - The best way to get potential team members interested is by being a part of their community. If a label has a message board, join it, participate in it and have your signature link to your music. Don't be overly self-promotional. Instead, be subtle and a valuable member of the community. Follow potential team members on social networks and be a friendly member of their social circle. Find where they congregate and be a part of that community as well--this can even be clubs, bars, Facebook Groups or parties. You can also build relationships with the musicians they work with.

Introduction - If you don't know someone in the music business but a friend does, the best thing you can get is an introduction via email. Ask for an introduction, where both you and the person you're being recommended to are included on an email, so it's a rock-solid start to a relationship. That will usually get a much better response than you sending an email saying your friend said to contact them. This can start a dialogue and shows that your mutual friend likes you enough to give you an endorsement. Always ask for introduction emails when friends offer to recommend you.

How To Show The Music Business That You Mean Business

One of the first questions I'm always asked is what you should send or show to someone in the music business to impress them. With the advent of Myspace, glossy laminated press kits became a bit of a joke. With the death of Myspace, it just became confusing--what you should show potential team members to get them interested in you? There are a few simple options you can present to anyone you aim to impress and if you're worthwhile, these should help you make a great impression.

Demonstrate Your Progress With Next Big Sound

As stated before, many potential team members might not be fans of the genre of music they work in, so they like to see that your music will be easy to sell. Next Big Sound's (nextbigsound.com) comparison charts can help you demonstrate whether your music fits the bill. These charts can clearly spell out that fans are listening to your music. You can show how much they're listening to you compared to other musicians within your genre. Never before have you been able to so clearly show someone that your music has potential.

Lately, when lesser-known musicians ask for my help, I've been saying that if they can make the graph maintain at least a 45-degree angle for the next three months, I'm happy to give some advice on what they should do next. This is also a great way to motivate and set goals for your music to make some serious progress.

Understand What Makes You Special

Odds are there are tons of other musicians out there who are just like you. But there has to be a quality that sets you apart. I don't mean something as crazy as being a polka band that dresses in costumes that look like Slipknot. You have to know what makes you special and be able to tell others in a way that gets them excited. Do you make bangers that make Cardi B sound like Muzak? You need to be able to describe that in a compelling way. This doesn't mean being an arrogant and bragging as much as it means being able to sell yourself. Without knowing what sets you apart, it'll be hard to get doors opened for you.

What Do You Show To Someone You're Trying To Impress?

This question is a nuanced one and will differ from musician to musician. Throughout your time in this business you'll see different musicians get team members on board in all sorts of different ways. Many will never have to show a label or a manager a stupid press kit. Team members are interested in working with them strictly based on their accomplishments and hype. If you're reaching out to potential team members who don't know how amazing you are, it's a good idea to have tangible and presentable evidence to show them.

- **Music -** Duh! That's why we're here. Give anyone an easy way to download and stream your record. If you're going for physical promo packages, at least include a burned CD. Be sure to recommend a few tracks that give a first impression as opposed to your twelve-minute prog-rock closing track.
- **Photos -** Live photos and press shots are both good. If you're too cool for school and don't want to do press shots, you may want to skip the whole thing.
- **Bio -** Who are you? Why does anyone care? A few short sentences that tell someone what makes you special and why they should care goes a long way. Your bio should be between two and five paragraphs that concentrate on your strong points and history.
- **Metrics -** If you're experiencing a lot of growth on your social networks, getting tons of plays or having a huge uptick in engagement every time you release a song, this is great to show potential team members. <u>Find one statistic or number from your social networks, concert attendance or sales that sounds impressive, dress it up and make it sound as awesome as possible.</u>
- **Video -** Live YouTube streams and video updates are a big deal these days and they do a great job of getting your personality across.
- **Press Clippings -** Got good press? Let them know! If you have tons of it, show it off.
- **Contact Info -** It will never cease to amaze me how many musicians forget this part.

Physical Press Kit?

If you were unfortunate enough to work in the music business before 2003, you were most likely flooded by heavy packages, demos and press kits.

These kits would consist of a custom-made folder, 8" by 10" glossy photos, a CD (or five) and loads of press clippings and bios. Thankfully, Myspace killed all of this expensive, tree-killing, wallet-draining, time-consuming nonsense. Despite the fact that these kits are now irrelevant, you still need to get this *content* to people you want to work with.

If you're going to present something physical to a potential team member, you no longer need to give much more than a CD and a one-sheet with bio and press highlights. Link to your social networks and if the person is interested, they'll be able to find out more about you online.

EPK (Electronic Press Kit) Are A Thing Of The Past
For years many struggling artists would put together press kits to pitch A&R but that is no longer the case. Please under no circumstances make a press kit, instead focus on making your socials look good to fans and anyone in the business checking you out. Let's be glad you can spend your time on content that fans will enjoy instead of something that was usually never even opened by most music businesspeople it was sent to.

Getting Your Music To Potential Team Members

How Do You Send Music?
Many times, you'll be asked to send music you haven't yet released. In these times it's important you deliver it in a smart manner. HighTail, WeTransfer, MediaFire and other similar websites are all terrible. They're public and can cause a leak when exposed by services like FilesTube. These sites will often discourage people from downloading your songs since they bring up annoying pop-up ads, offer slow download speeds and have confusing interfaces. Instead, here are some smarter options:

- **YouTube Private Links** – If you are concerned about unreleased material being linked, YouTube has privacy features that allow videos to remain unlisted so that only those you are trying to impress will see. This is generally preferred by all.
- **SoundCloud** - SoundCloud (soundcloud.com) gives you the option to make tracks private and password-protect them so that only those who you invite can listen. You can even check if someone has listened to your track after you send it to them.

- **Dropbox** - Dropbox (dropbox.com) provides a clean way to send a .zip file to anyone and it will download both quickly and free of any ugly banner ads.
- **Google Drive** – Many people dislike receiving Google Drive links so avoid this.
- **FTP** - If you're good with your web skills, you can setup an FTP transfer and password-protect it. Make sure your server gives a decent file transfer rate. It's very easy for someone to get discouraged by long download times and give up.

Stream AND Download - Keep in mind many potential team members can be finicky. I know a few music writers who hate having tons of music on their hard drive, so they will no longer automatically download music just to give it a listen. They stream it first and if they're interested, download it then. It's a good idea to give the option to both stream and download your music--in case they want to take it for a listen on a jog or drive later. Using Soundcloud or a TopSpin streaming player and download link are easy solutions to these problems.

How Most A&R Scout New Artists Today
The fact is in the years since I first wrote this book, the ways A&R discover new artists has changed a lot. Nearly every label now employs scouting software that show them when artists are trending and they mostly use that software along with connections to hip them to who is making good music. With that said there are a few alternative ways they hear about music, but all of the methods listed in the next few sections are dwarfed by software and connections doing 99% of the work.

Hit The A&R Blogs
We've told you repeatedly, there is a better way to get noticed by potential team members than by writing them cold letters. One of the overlooked ways to get the attention of labels big and small is to get featured on one of the Internet's many A&R blogs. These are sites that aggregate which musicians are worth checking out for the labels of the world. They are a respected source of information declaring who is and isn't worth checking out. If you play music that is massively accessible, it's a huge mistake to not try to get your music to the writers who run these sites. The following are some of the most respected A&R blogs in the business:

- **Singles Jukebox** – The Singles Jukebox is a collection of journalists and bloggers who discuss the latest tracks that many A&R keep their eye on. (thesinglesjukebox.com)
- **Kings of A&R** - These guys been on the Internet since dinosaurs ran it using a mouse in a wheel. They have always been a current and relevant source of which acts are up-and-coming in the industry. KOAR keeps it mostly to buzz and industry news, with the occasional rant thrown in for good measure. They take submissions via email. (kingsofar.com)
- **Pop Justice** - One of the best pop music blogs out there. They cover strictly pop music and the main writers' intense worship of Lady GaGa. They also put up fantastic musings and interviews about pop music. They have contact info on their site to submit them tracks. (popjustice.com)

A&R Submission Services
There are also services where you can submit your music to A&R people who are looking for new acts to work with. The following all facilitate this, some with fees and some without:

- **OurStage** - OurStage (ourstage.com) runs a battle of the bands and spotlight service where, if you win, you qualify for showcases that help you gain the attention of a wide variety of music industry professionals.
- **Music XRay** - In addition to being able to submit your music for tons of licensing opportunities, you can also submit yourself to A&R. (musicxray.com)
- **SonicBids** - With a price you can submit yourself to A&R opportunities. (sonicbids.com)
- **Broadjam** - Have your music reviewed by prominent A&R people. (broadjam.com)
- **SpinnUp** – Universal Records has an aggregator to get your music on Spotify, iTunes and other services and get discovered by their A&R pool. (spinnup.com)
- **MusicRegistry** - Their service sells an A&R Directory where you can contact and submit to many of the top A&R people. While I don't recommend this practice, the option is there. (musicregistry.com)

Fluence Allows You Access To Influencers For A Price

Fluence (fluence.io) allows you access to some of the biggest writers and influencers in music. They allow these influencers to put a price on how much it costs to send your music or video to them and they will listen and evaluate it. While this can be costly and goes against many of the principles of this book, the option is available to buy your way into having access with the people you want to hear your music.

Submithub Allows You To Pay To Get Blogs To Listen
Many musicians bemoan submitting to blogs since they never even listen to their tracks. Submithub (submithub.com) changes that by allowing you to pay $1 per blog for them to listen. If a blog doesn't listen you receive credit for future submissions. The service allows you to at least know your music is being considered by blogs that will have influence on both avid music fans as well as other blogs but I will warn you they have a laundry list of customers all over social media that don't feel the service is worth it and few who endorse it.

Utilizing Blog Coverage When You Don't Make Mainstream Music
Many musicians don't fit in to the "major label mold" that the above blogs cover, but that doesn't mean blogs can't help you. Many indie and dance labels use music blogs as their A&R scouts. There are countless indie music blogs that labels are always looking for new musicians. More and more musicians talk of getting signed by being "blog hits." If you're in dance music, a post on the latest hip dance blog (*sadly this changes so fast, I have had to change the name of the "hip dance blog" every edition of the book, so I am leaving examples out of the book from now on*), can mean a flood of opportunities in your inbox the next day. If you are trying to get noticed in this business, placing an emphasis on blog coverage is key. The CEO of McDonough booking has said that one post on Pitchfork Best New Music can ignite the bidding war between numerous labels and agents for an act and the way you get there is by being covered by small blogs that Pitchfork keeps track of (*but more on that later*).

Get A Lawyer

One of the oddest practices in the music business is that entertainment lawyers often do a lot of the legwork in shopping musicians around to various labels. This isn't to say a manager, publicist, booking agent, friend or musician can't also pass along music, but lawyers are often overlooked as an ambassador for your music. Many of these lawyers have made strong bonds with A&R through daily dealings. Unfortunately, over the years, musicians have had it branded into their heads that some sleazy manager will shop them to all of their connections. In reality, a lawyer--who is super busy, always late on every project you need and a little too socially active, is who calls a label and mails over a press kit.

How It Goes Down
Since nearly every deal made in this industry needs a contract, lawyers have a lot of contact with labels. Over the years, this began a tradition of them handing labels new music. Subsequently, some acts got signed and this became common practice. While not every entertainment lawyer shops musicians, this is one possible way to get your music heard by A&R people at the label you want to be on.

Anyone who hasn't dealt with a lawyer and is unfamiliar with this process is probably thinking this is going to cost them a lot of money. In reality, most of these deals come down to signing this lawyer on to handle all of your legal transactions. They will take a 10-15% cut of your profits (sometimes only the profits they do a deal for you on) so basically--if you're making money, they're making money. This is no sweat since, while you may be able to self-manage, there are many transactions you simply can't do without a lawyer's touch. In this case, you kill two birds with one stone by finding a lawyer who will shop your music and take care of your legal problems, like negotiating a record contract.

How To Find One
Put down the Yellow Pages! A majority of entertainment lawyers specialize in certain genres and don't handle every walk of music. We're in the digital age, so you don't need the lawyer to be close to you. Try to find out who some similar bands use as a lawyer. Talk to friends in the business and see if they know anyone who they can introduce you to.

Five Reasons You Need To Hire A Lawyer
While a lawyer can be difficult to hire, especially if you're looking locally, there are times you definitely need one. Here are some clear signs you need to hire one:

- **Record Deal** - If your record deal has any financial or time commitment past a few thousand dollars, you need to hire a lawyer to read it over.

- **Band Agreement** - If you plan on taking your music seriously and think you'll be splitting up a lot of money, it's smart to have a lawyer look at your band agreement.
- **Publishing Deal** - Most publishing deals need lawyer involvement.
- **Management Deal** - If you're signing with a manager, it would be smart to have your lawyer look at the deal to make sure the person who is going to be looking out for your best interest isn't already trying to do wrong by you.
- **Licensing Deal** - Any exclusive licensing deals should have a lawyer's eye.
- **Booking Agent** - Especially if you're signing a revenue-sharing agreement.

Signing To A Label - Is It Even Worth It?

This book is littered with tips on how to do the job of a traditional record label without being on one. But what if you're offered a record contract? It's hard to turn down a team member willing to sink time, money and effort into your career. While this help is enticing, it can either be an opportunity or a stone that weighs down your progress. Below are some considerations before you decide whether to sign to a label.

Too Soon?
When you're a young musician with a small following, it's especially enticing to sign with a label and have them help grow your fanbase. The downside is that without sufficient promotion, this growth may never happen. Many labels are reluctant to include free music in their marketing plans, especially after they shell out thousands of dollars for you to record it. This can put you at a huge disadvantage against all the other musicians who are giving away free music. Make sure any deal you sign accounts for how to handle the recruitment of new listeners and doesn't hold back your ability to get new fans by enticing them with free music.

Promotion Dollars
Many labels these days offer little more than connections and distribution. While this isn't the case for every label, there are a shocking number of labels that offer you very little. Without a promotional budget, you're at a disadvantage to every other act who is selling their own records and able to reinvest a sizable chunk of their money into future promotions. Instead,

you're paying this label 50 to 90 percent of your royalties in exchange for services you could have done on your own, but now have less funds to invest in yourself with. Many labels have access to great press options, but it helps to talk to others who have used their promotional facilities before to make sure it's worth the tradeoff of not having the control and means to invest in your own promotions.

Research and ask about the benefits any label is offering you. Don't assume they exist. Ask for concrete examples of what they have done for the other musicians on their label.

Distribution
If the main benefit a label is offering is a recording budget and distribution, it may not be worth it to go with them. With the demise of physical distribution, you can have much of what most labels offer all on your own. Talk to them about their digital and physical distribution. Most DIY musicians can get the same distribution as many small indie labels, all in a half-day's work and by reading the rest of this book. Unless you have a big release that is highly promoted, most record stores are never going to take it on. In the digital world, anyone can get themselves into every major digital outlet for about $50. Make sure your label has more to offer you than you can do on your own.

Exclusivity In A Small Indie Label Recording Contract
I am constantly shocked by how many recording contracts still look like they were drafted in 2002, when majors and large indies were still buying musicians out of their small indie contracts like there was no tomorrow. In the past, small indies hoped to sign musicians and then be bought out of their contracts for insane prices. While this prospect gets increasingly rare, many labels haven't adjusted their contracts to the current climate. They ask to keep a musician bound to their label for 12 to 48 months, which not only holds potential sales back, but can hold back the growth of both the label and the musician.

Keeping a musician in a contract for 18-plus months after their release can be like a prison term. I don't mean to demean any label by saying this, but the music business is moving faster than ever before, and a term this long is now ancient. If a musician moves on to a bigger and better label, it's obvious that there is potential to increase sales previous releases. This benefits everyone, so contracts should be adjusted to reflect the new pace of the industry.

Contracts should allow musicians to sign to other labels while the current label holds exclusive rights to the recording of a predetermined amount of songs from the releases they put out from the musician. Depending on how much the label invested in the musician, the terms of how long the label owns the recording and exclusive rights to a release should be determined as a tradeoff with this investment. There are also many smaller labels offering only pressing, physical distribution and minor marketing budgets-- obviously the compensation should be smaller if this is all that is offered. The length of exclusivity and how many songs the label retains is negotiated on a case-by-case basis, since no two deals are the same.

Contracts With Incentives Are Always The Best Way To Go
The music business is full of big promises. Unfortunately, most of them are not kept. Using incentives can make sure your team stays motivated on your project. Management and record contracts can easily have milestones built into them so you're not stuck in a situation you wish you'd never gotten into. When negotiating a contract with someone, make sure to get each party's responsibilities put into the contract, so that if relationship isn't going the way you planned, it's easy to make an exit.

A great example of this is using sales marks for each release in a record contract. If a certain amount of records are not SoundScanned, then the label or musician will have the option to leave the contract or renegotiate. This makes sure that if both parties are unhappy, they're free to move on with no real hassle. In management contracts, you can set milestones of income and if they're not reached, you can opt out of a manager's sunset clause.

Establishing goals and making sure both sides are meeting their responsibilities not only makes it easy to leave a bad situation, but it also establishes what to work towards. If both parties know that earning $10,000 a month and selling 3,000 copies of your latest release is the goal, both parties are able to make sure that happens. It also that means you have a clear way to judge whether or not your relationship is working or not.

Chapter 7: Writing A Great Biography (Bio)

The dread of every musician. Writing a bio can be an agonizing and annoying process--but it doesn't have to be. Biographies can seem ridiculous and unnecessary, despite that sentiment they are an essential part of getting press. No musician is above having a bio, so take the time to create one that is both useful and original.

What's In a Bio?

Write Three Biographies

Those three words may turn your stomach. No one hates writing a bio more than me. In fact, the only thing I hate more than writing a bio is reading one. However, they're a necessary evil that gives potential fans an idea of who you are and whether they should be interested in what you do. Unfortunately, I've written over a hundred of them in my life and read even more, so I've taken note of what works and what doesn't.

Why do you have to write three biographies? At different times you're going to have space restraints and need to tell the world who you're at different lengths. Below are the three bios you'll need and where they're used.

- **Two Sentence** - The shortest summation of who you are and why anyone should care. Some call this an "elevator pitch." It's your job to make someone interested in learning more within two sentences of describing yourself. Your social media profiles, especially your Twitter profile (limited to 160 characters), will use this bio. It's also handy to know a short, quick bio for when you meet people in person.
- **One Paragraph** - In five sentences or less, inform fans why they should care about you. This bio is published on venue websites, the "About" section of your Facebook page, your Spotify profile and tons of other places.
- **Five Paragraphs** - This bio will mostly be for writers and music business people. You'll use this for your EPK, press pitches, website biography and tons of other places where you need to give people more background about yourself.

Thankfully, once you have written your five-paragraph biography, you can usually cut it down to make the other two. Because of this, start off by writing that one.

Objectives
In your five-paragraph biography there is an easy structure to follow in order to get readers interested. Outlined below is what to do in each of the five paragraphs. This is intentionally vague since you don't want your biography to be a cookie cutter of what everyone has read countless times. You want to make a bio unique while following a formula that will keep readers interested.

- **Lure** - In the first paragraph you want to give the reader a reason to care. You want to create a question that will make them want more by telling them a reason they should care about what you do. Find some way to convey that you're exceptional. Most people who read biographies have read a lot of them. Give them interesting content to lure them in so they want more.
- **Compel** - Tell the reader why they should be excited about you in further detail. Remember, your bio is trying to get someone to either listen to your music or to work with you. Now is the time to present why the world should care about you. Ask yourself "what would make me read about an artist and then want to hear them?" and reverse engineer that into your own bio. Until you have answered that question you should not publish your bio.
- **Inform** - Now that you've gotten the reader excited, you need to present them with some relevant information. Give them some less exciting details that they would want to know if they were writing an article about you. Maybe you talk about ex-members, notable team members or an interesting story about your band or how you formed.
- **Current/Future** - Tell them what you're doing now and your future plans. Describe your current release and how it stacks up to the rest of your music.
- **Hit It Home** - Your last paragraph is a place to sell yourself one last time. If the reader has made it this far, you can usually get a bit hyperbolic and make a bold exclamation about how you're going to change the world in some way. And if they buy it, it will give them reason to be excited.

Essential Tips

In order to write a great bio, there are certain solid practices that you want to use and other clichés you want to avoid. While this is what I've found to work, you should be willing to go outside the box. Anything you can do to spice up this boring part of music-making is certainly welcome.

Sneak A Peek
Find a musician you admire, perhaps in your own scene, who has achieved some level of success. Take a look at their bio. See what they're doing that works (or doesn't) and ask them about how they formulated their biography. If you're having trouble getting started, seeing the angle that others took will help you get perspective on what you might try out. This can also help you determine tone; bios can be funny, snarky or dead serious. Try to figure out a tone that will blend well with your music.

Your Own, Personal, Bio
If you have a logo or letterhead--use it. If you have specific colors and fonts you use for your image, use them. The more original and distinctive you can make it, the better. Personalizing also means that if humor is a part of your songs or attitude then use that in your bio, too. Don't worry if it doesn't appeal to everyone--your music isn't going to appeal to everyone either. Just remain focused on your target audience and don't be afraid to step out a bit and be yourself.

If you played a show in Savannah last year and everyone started dancing on the bar, throwing wooden chairs around the room, prompting the bartender to offer free shots of whiskey, that might be a story worth relaying. And of course, make sure that you start the bio with a hook (something interesting that makes the reader want to know more) so readers will want to keep reading. This hook invites mystery and a reason to keep following. You want to create curiosity.

Not everyone has an interesting story, but even somewhat boring stories can be made to sound intriguing. A great example is my former bandmate, Jett Brando. In his late-thirties, Jett doesn't have the coolest story anymore. A high school English teacher by day doesn't exactly have the same allure as Kathleen Hanna being a stripper pre-Bikini Kill. He still finds a way to tell his story in an intriguing way. Check it out below:

"If you've ever wondered what an Indiana Jones movie would be like if the titular character was a high school English teacher by day and a struggling indie rocker by night, then you may be en route to imagining a day in the life of Jeremy Winter, the man behind the myth that very few people have heard of – the myth of Jett Brando."

Practice Brevity

Be brief, especially since most people reading your bio don't know anything about you and have already read a million of these. Keep it to the meat and skip all the fluff. Of the bios I've read, almost all of them are too long. It's not that people hate you or your music, they just don't have time to care about you...yet. The sight of a bio that is too long is enough to make most people stop reading. Especially in these times of Twitter-speak and abbreviated everything, don't overwhelm the reader. If the bio is printed, it shouldn't be longer than one page in a 12-point font, with a logo/letterhead, a list of the musicians and what instruments the play, and your social network links at the bottom. If it's online, try to keep those five paragraphs as brief as you can.

No One Cares... No, Really, NO ONE CARES

No one cares about what your names are or what instruments you play. Instead, you should add this at the end of the bio or in a sidebar. The only time you should be putting your names and instruments in your bio is if you've previously played in recognizable bands. Otherwise, don't take up space with a rundown of what instrument everyone plays. Add a list of personnel at the end, in case a writer needs it.

Classify/Compare Yourself

Of course you think you're the most original sounding group on the planet, but guess what? You're not. And even if you are, readers need some sort of comparison to drive their interest. Mentioning musicians you actually sound like helps--not who you wish you would sound like.

This is a case where it might be good to ask some trusted people who you remind them of. Not your mom, your girlfriend or your roadie, but someone who will give you their honest opinion. Musicians are often too close to their own music to be honest with themselves about the influences on their sound, so feel free to call in an unbiased listener for help on this one.

Mentioning a genre can help readers know you're part of a movement they also feel a part of. But if you only describe the genre, it doesn't invite much curiosity. Write an intriguing mix of musicians that you could compare yourself to; this is your "comparative pitch." A description that says, "If the Sex Pistols had read Noam Chomsky," or "We take the robot out of Daft Punk by adding the MC5," will make readers curious about that you sound like. Writing, "A unique blend of Fall Out Boy and Blink-182" will hardly excite huge fans of both of those groups seeing as this isn't very unique. Instead, it leaves them thinking you sound like two very similar groups. The music business doesn't want to be a part of a dying movement that already exists; they want to be a part of a new, exciting, up-and-coming movement. Write a description that makes the reader curious--not just, "For fans of Pink!" since that basically says you're a generic, boring version of Pink.

It is important not to try to appeal to everyone. In fact, standing against something can be more helpful. If you pride yourself on not abiding by a fashion of a certain genre, feel free to tell everyone. Writing that you put "maximum in minimal techno," can invite some curiosity. Try and avoid saying you're a little Grateful Dead, Red Hot Chili Peppers and Skrillex, with a hint of Creed, which just muddies the waters with too many comparisons and would most likely make someone cringe. When you try to appeal to too many people, it scares away the majority of listeners who are looking for something new.

Also, try to avoid going overboard with the superfluous adjectives - everyone thinks they're the "craziest, sexiest, coolest guys in Brooklyn," but it doesn't make for a good bio. Keep the adjectives brief.

Think Of It As A Resume
When you're sending out resumes for a job, my guess is that you send out different versions to different job openings. The same goes for your bio. Different readers are going to be looking for different pieces of information, so don't forget to keep the recipient in mind when you're penning this masterpiece.

Just like with a resume, know your audience. If you're sending to smart, snarky writers, know that most of your claims may get mocked. If you're a country-rap hybrid, you may want to make two bios to sell yourself to each audience. You wouldn't apply for a job at an ad agency and talk more about your hamburger flipping experience than your writing skills. Know who you're writing to and try to create a narrative that will make them interested.

You also need to tell readers what you did in the past, what you're currently doing and what you're going to do. Just like with a job, no one wants to hire someone with no experience who isn't doing anything currently and has no future plans. Make sure you explain your past accomplishments, what you're currently promoting and your future plans. This section of your bio will need to be updated frequently.

Brag (Briefly)
Parts of your bio involve talking about yourself - who you've shared the stage with, where you've toured, what you've accomplished, etc. Keep this sounding humble but do take a little time to tell others about what you have done. Don't make stuff up and don't stretch the truth because these half-truths have a strange way of being found out. At the same time, make the truth as pretty and persuasive as you can get away with.

If you fill up two sentences worth of space of every act you've opened for, this may impress promoters, but record reviewers don't care. Meanwhile, talking about your record for two paragraphs when trying to get live shows makes no difference. Change your bio depending on who you're pitching, focusing on your album for record reviewers and who you've opened for when you submit to promoters.

If you're writing a bio for the world to read, please do not tell us everyone you have ever opened for and toured with. It's boring and tedious.

Speak Your Audience's Language
Ol' Morrissey was quite the literary bloke--always jawing on about quotes, highbrow literature and the like. So, make like the magnanimous Mancunian wordsmith and use quotes to your advantage. If your audience is going to be impressed by highbrow language, then use it. However, if you appeal to a bunch of illiterate stoners, it may be best to keep it d-u-m-b and spell everything out for them.

I Can't Help Quoting You
If someone has actually called you "the greatest jug band since Sexy Vampire Tooth," then by all means, use that quote in your bio. In fact, use quotes early and often. Any other credibility that you can add to your clout will help. Don't turn your bio into a bad movie poster littered with irrelevant

reviews but do name-drop where it's tasteful and appropriate. Quotes from esteemed writers, musicians or other influencers will make an impression.

Write What You Want Them To Say
If you've had any experience sending out bios, you might notice that many writers often copy a bio verbatim into their articles. Many writers are looking for shortcuts, so if you bother to write a decent description/bio, writers will happily cut and paste it. So, why not use this to your advantage?

Keeping this in mind, you need to pay careful attention to every word in your bio and updates, since odds are this is exactly what's going to end up in front of tons of readers' eyes. Conveniently, whatever would capture a reader's eye will make a writer want to write about you. Make sure you describe what you do thoroughly and describe what's unique about you in a clear and coherent way. If you do this right, you're bound to end up with much better press.

If you're able to pull off daring proclamations of your greatness, especially with other writers' words, this can make for a great bio. If your record got named "album of the year" by a website, be sure to put that in there. This might set a precedent for writers. If this writer is feeling good about your release, they'll be more encouraged to heap on the praise. In fact, telling people it's OK to think your release is amazing often makes them like it more. You can always go a small step past reality in your bio and it'll get passed on by lazy writers as true. Just don't go too far.

Let Five Pairs Of Educated Eyes See It Before The World Does
We have all seen writing nightmares, from typos to sentences that make no sense (hell, you might have seen a few on our website) when receiving email blasts, web updates, bios, etc. This stems from not having enough people check your writing. A great rule from the advertising world is to have five sets of educated eyes read your writing before it goes out to the world. This will help ensure that you have no communication breakdowns or typos.

There are many times when those involved in a project may understand what you're trying to convey, but the outside world isn't picking up what you're putting down on paper. Let some outside eyes see what you're trying to say before your next message goes out into the world and no one has a clue what in the hell you are talking about.

Try Again
Remember, if you wrote your bio and the message doesn't seem to be generating a response, it may be time to think of a new pitch and story. Much of what gets readers to give you a chance is the pitch and story you bring with a bio. If it isn't getting you through doors, it may be time to think of another angle.

Points To Make Sure You Didn't Miss In Your Bio
Be sure to not miss these key pieces of information in your bio:

- **Location** - Make sure you tell readers where you're from. Even if you claim to be from outer space, this is important for every writer and potential team member.
- **Sound** - Make sure you give some idea of what you sound like.
- **Current** - Let readers know what you're currently promoting: A tour, a new album, etc. Update your bio as you move on to new things.
- **Special** - What sets you apart and makes you special compared to all the other musicians vying for this person's attention.
- **Contact** - Make sure there is contact information at the end of your bio, even if it's elsewhere on the page. Don't make readers search for it.
- **Social** - Be sure to list your website and your social networks at the end.
- **Personal** - After the body of your bio, list the members and what they play.

Your One-Paragraph Bio
After you have this five-paragraph monstrosity finished, it's time to take your hard work and whittle it down to one paragraph. Think of this as the greatest hits of your bio. You want to give relevant information about why someone should care and nurture curiosity so that the reader wants to learn more. Here are some points to make sure you capture in your one paragraph bio:

- **Location** - Where you are now and where you are from if it's relevant.
- **Sound** - Use the comparative pitch you came up with to get potential fans curious to learn more.

- **Current** - Tell fans what you're currently up to. Are you about to release a new record or go out on tour? Please inform and tell them about something to check out that you're currently in the process of doing.

Your Two-Sentence Bio

This is the shortest description of your music and career. It's the bio you use for some social networks and what you tell someone when they ask you about your music in person. It's important that this is smart and snappy since every time you meet someone with the potential to help your music, they will ask you, "What do you sound like?" Having a witty answer that invites curiosity is great. My suggestion is to say what you came up with for your sound in the comparative pitch as well as your location. If you can find a witty way to say this, it will help new fans become interested in hearing you. It should hit these points:

- **Who** - Who are you? Think about what draws you in when you hear about a new band and use that as a guide.
- **Sound** - What do you sound like?
- **Location** - Where you're from, in as few words as possible.
- **Unique** - Talk about what makes you unique.

Getting Your Bio Done

Like many musicians, your strength may not be writing. This happens a lot. If that is the case, hope is not lost. Here are a few ways to get a bio done with some help from others.

- **Writer** - Ask a writer who likes you or has written about you kindly in the past for help with this.
- **Crowdsource** - Take to your social networks and see if any fans can help.
- **Friends** - Nearly everyone has a friend who can write decently. Get some help from this friend.

Chapter 8: Dealing With Money And Funding Your Music

One of the best problems you can have is having money and needing to manage it. In the past even a small indie group would need to have a C.P.A. to deal with accounting. But now, it's easier than ever to manage the money that comes in from your music.

Dealing With Money

You won't be making any money early on in your musical endeavor. Despite this fact, many musicians feel the need to "look professional" and form an LLC, get a bank account, etc. This is not always the wisest use of time and money, since you can exist for years without ever needing to get this formal. There are some simple tricks that can keep you from having to spend unnecessary time and money when you first start out.

Let's also note that this is how I've done it. I'm sure some accountants or even the IRS will have issues with some of these techniques. I am in no way telling you what to do; I am telling you how I've done it. Proceed at your own risk.

First, you need some way to collect the money you make:

Cash Drawer
If you get paid in cash, you'll need someplace to put it. You want to get a cash drawer with a lock and then never let it leave your sight. Whenever you do take your eyes off of it, have it in a very safe place. You'll use this at shows to collect money from merch or put in money you make on the road. This also means that if it gets stolen, you're going to lose all the cash you have. A cash drawer is also unavoidable since you'll always be paying out cash as you go through your life as a musician, for various expenses. You'll also be constantly collecting it, which means all of your hard work can go down the drain unless you develop a smart system to keep this money safe.

PayPal

PayPal (paypal.com) is one of a musician's best friends. In order to get payments from many online music and merch sales outlets you'll need to have a PayPal account. While some fear this institution, it can be a great ally in your music career. Their fees are still very reasonable and they offer many awesome features:

- **Debit Card** - They offer a debit card free that comes free of charge, which means you can use it for the purchases.
- **App** - You can also use their smartphone app to take pictures of checks you receive and deposit them directly into your PayPal account. This means you can use your PayPal account for all finances connected to your music and do easy accounting within it.
- **Credit Card Reader** - You can accept credit cards and checks with your phone at shows. PayPal has the added bonus of giving you the money the moment you scan someone's card.
- **Micro Payments** - One of the best tools PayPal offers is micro-payments. If you're going to be selling lots of music through services like BigCartel or Bandcamp, this can dramatically increase your profits.
- **Merchant Accounts** - PayPal also offers vendor accounts where they take less of a fee than standard accounts as long as you're making a certain amount of sales through their service every month.

It also helps to have an account since many merch companies, vendors and promoters will want to PayPal you for easy accounting. You should have a PayPal account the second you start selling your music or merch.

Square

Square (squareup.com) is that neat little white dongle that reads credit cards. If you go to live shows, you see these at merch tables all the time. It works with any iOS or Android device. You simply download the app, sign up at their website and go through the process of linking your bank account to Square. The charges you make get deposited into your bank account every evening (unlike PayPal who adds the money immediately). This is crucial if you're selling merch on tour since you'll have the money the next day to get you to your next stop. You can get a free credit card reader either by signing up at their website or simply typing in everyone's credit card numbers. You can also use this to take credit card payments from promoters or over the phone for merch or anything you can think of.

Band Agreement

One of the most important tasks to do right now--before you start making any money--is to write up a band agreement. Before you have any money and your egos all get too big, it's smart to make sure you can all agree on how money is split within the group. While this seems like a big commitment, the faster you do this, the easier it is to come to an agreement on. Once the financial security of everyone involved is dependent on the income of the group, these negotiations become less and less rational.

Splitting it Up - There are a handful of issues to be discussed in the band agreement. Most importantly is the overall profit split. Some bands decide the core members should get one percentage and all the hired musicians or "expendable musicians" (aka the musicians who don't play on the record or contribute to the songwriting) should get another. While some bands have one member who writes all of the songs, it's often agreed that all the profits for the publishing will be split evenly amongst everyone, since other members may contribute to duties like tour management that don't receive significant compensation. This can help minimize fights and make it so that when money is tight, everyone in the band can afford to stay on the road. If one member is making dramatically more money than the others it can become hard to keep the group together.

When you form an LLC, these percentages become legally binding. You'll also choose how the publishing is split when you register with your publishing company. Once these forms are filed, they're also legally binding.

Democracy - When making decisions, does everyone have an equal say? Do some members have more say than others? Does the manager vote as a member of the group or outside with a veto power? These are important concepts to figure out before the tough decisions come (and they will). If you want to keep the band intact and not have members feel like they're in a prison with no say, it helps to make it as even a democracy as possible.

Investments - When you're an up-and-coming group and putting your own money into your music, not everyone invests equal amounts. One way to make this a little more even is by agreeing to keep track of who invests the most money. Then if the group becomes profitable, the members who invested more than the others are repaid as profits come in. Other groups will say that on the day they start being profitable, all previous investments are zeroed out.

What Happens When a Member Leaves - Very few bands keep their original lineup forever. It's important to establish beforehand what happens if a member leaves. Are they paid back for any investments they made with their money if the band becomes profitable? Many bands allow the members who played on each recording to keep their publishing and sales royalties, but they will no longer be paid for merch sales or live performances.

The Band's Name & Logo - Names and logos become big money when you're a huge band. Whoever controls these rights is making a lot of the money even after the band is broken up. It's important to establish who makes money from this name. Often, it's divided amongst the founding members, but this is a highly personal subject that each band deals with differently.

Your Investment: The Reality

To make a living from your music, it's going to most likely take a pretty substantial investment from you or an outside investor. Especially when you're just starting out, you are constantly putting more money into paying for promotional tools and other expenses. It's a long ride, but it's also really fun and will bring you the best times of your life. But most of all, don't quit your day job to focus on your music on day one. You're going to need it so you have a good amount of money to put into your career.

Invest - Once you do start getting paid, whether it's royalty checks, fees from live performances or publishing--keep putting it back into your music until you have a good amount of money in your savings account. Just like any business, you need to keep reinvesting your early earnings back into your career so it can become a sustainable way to make a living and gain a following.

So When Do I Start Making Money?

The question on many musicians' minds is: *When do we stop putting money in and start making a living*? If you have gotten anywhere near this point, it's probably a very pressing issue, since your life is fully consumed with working on your music, leaving little time for your "real job." If you have hit this point, congratulations! It doesn't happen to everyone. Time to figure out when to start cutting the payroll checks...or rather, doling out the scraps.

$10,000 - You shouldn't be paying out more than per diems (daily living expenses for the band while out on the road) until you have $10,000 saved. Why that number? Time and time again, that is the magic number. You shouldn't be paying out profits until there is $10,000 in your savings account (this means you also have money set aside for monthly expenses), in case anything happens. If your van's engine seizes, that's what it costs for a new van on the spot. This savings will make it so you have a nice cushion if things go wrong. Things always go wrong and if you keep growing your fanbase you'll want even more than this amount in savings. But $10,000 is where you start.

This also means you need to account for monthly operating costs. If you need to order $4,000 of merch every month and have $1,000 in van fees, you need to factor that all in to the cash you have on hand before you do payouts. This $10K cushion will help when you inevitably do the math wrong or have a bad month.

When You Have $10,000 - Once you have reached this magic number, the way many musicians deal out the profits is by calculating how much they have in upcoming expenses like. If you have $14,000 on hand at the end of the month and $2,000 of monthly bills and expenses, you then have $2,000 to split amongst the band. Once those costs are covered, they then split the profits up amongst the members of the group. As long as you're staying on the road and selling merch, it should be easy to keep making money and paying out profits to everyone.

You'll need to raise this $10,000 threshold as you incur larger merch purchases, production costs, bus rentals, etc. Thankfully, if you are spending money on these expenses, your profits should be increasing. Modify the plan as you go along but be sure to have a cushion of savings in case things go wrong.

Forming An LLC (Limited Liability Corporation)
An LLC is the right step to take once you're playing out a lot and becoming profitable. By becoming an LLC, you become a legitimate business in the government's eyes. What that also means is you'll need to pay a couple hundred dollars of filing fees and will start to pay a minimum of $800 to the government in taxes. This also means you can start to deduct van

payments, insurance and drumsticks on your taxes. If you begin to become involved with a label or booking agency, they will also need your tax identification information to be able to write off what they pay you. It also will ensure that the percentage of profits you split is legally binding. This is useful for bands that don't trust each other to break up money in an appropriate fashion.

If you wish to form an LLC, each state has different fees and guidelines. One of the easiest ways is to have your entertainment lawyer guide you through it. You can also use sites like LegalZoom (legalzoom.com), which will take care of the filing for you (for a fee). Most filings come in under $600 and more than $200.

Band Bank Account - The main reason to form an LLC--aside from Uncle Sam unleashing his fury on you--is to get yourself a bank account for your band. Once you have the business identification number--which you get with your LLC papers--you can now open a business account at a bank. It definitely helps to open this account at a bank that has branches throughout the country so you can make easy deposits while on the road.

When you setup this account you can choose who has access to it. This means if your bassist is a junkie, he doesn't need to be listed on this form. However, it does help to get a few cards for anyone who handles any financial duties since they will need a debit card with their name on it to pay for gas or order merch.

Most of all be sure to keep good track of this account since everything you put into it needs to be explained to the IRS once a year.

Alternate Methods To Fund Your Music

There are many other ways to fund your music aside from taking money from your day job and reinvesting your royalties.

How To Pursue A Business Sponsorship To Get Funding For Your Music
We all flipped our lids when we saw OK GO's "This Too Shall Pass" video spread around the Internet--yet again, they had made one of the best viral videos the world had ever seen. The small detail that made this video a bit

more interesting was that it was sponsored by State Farm Insurance and contained a little message from them at the end. We've long been told that the future of music is in corporate sponsorships and partnerships, but the question is how do you go about getting one of these?

Identifying - First, you need to identify a business that would benefit from visibility with your fanbase. Every musician with a fanbase will have fans that fall into some company's target demographic. Depending on the size of your fanbase, you should decide whether you want to pursue a local or national company to get in bed with. If you have a small following, odds are national companies aren't going to be as interested, though you may be able to dream up an interesting opportunity for them.

If you have a great marketing idea, you may be able to convince just about anybody to get involved, pending they have a forward-thinking marketing team. It's a good idea to find a few different companies who might potentially work with you. Once you develop the idea of what you can do for them, it will probably apply to a few different companies, so you can slightly tailor your proposals to each of them until you find a partner.

What To Do - Once you have found a few companies who could benefit from being seen by your fanbase, you need to write up a proposal. Make a simple PDF file that you can email to various marketing people. In this PDF you should identify the following:

- **Elevator Pitch** - What you want to do with this company and why they would benefit from aligning themselves with you in two paragraphs or less.
- **Who Are You?** - Give a brief bio and remember that this isn't for rock writers. Make the bio show why you're a good potential partner.
- **Why Are You Relevant To Them?** - The first thing anyone who you may partner with will want to know is why they should choose you instead of someone else. Make a good case for why you're an ideal partner and outline some key points on how you can help them.
- **What Do They Get?** - Are you going to put their logo on your merch booth, the back of shirts or in your new YouTube video? Everyone wants to know what's in it for them, so let them know!

- **Why It Will Work** - Give a thorough explanation of why this is a foolproof partnership. If you can't come up with a solid argument for this, odds are you're wasting your time.
- **Conclusion** - Make some solid points on your way out, wrapping all of this up.
- **Passion** - The last ingredient in this is that you need to show them you're either passionate about their product or passionate about making this work for them. It's rare for businessmen to give money to a bunch of irresponsible musicians. They want to see passion for this relationship and what it can do for you both.

Once this is done, contact that marketing head at your ideal partner's office and see if you can work some magic. Good luck!

Business Of All Sizes - It doesn't need to be a humongous corporation that you pursue sponsorship with. Local businesses can also benefit from your coolness--especially if there is an aspiring brand looking to get some cool recognition. If the next Snapple is starting nearby, they may need help in getting their message out to cool kids like your fans. The local all-night pizzeria may want to give you money to mention they are open all night and you hang out there after your shows.

Endorsements: Promotion And Free Stuff!
Endorsements are one of the coolest parts of being a badass musician. Your favorite gear companies give you discounts. And if you get good enough and show an influence over other musicians, they will give you free stuff. And for them? They get business from other musicians who want to use what you use. While there are many tasks that are a bigger priority than chasing endorsements, they can help promote your music as long as you can find the right brand to form a mutually beneficial deal.

Getting An Endorsement - Equipment companies are encouraged to give endorsements because they think it will lead to business from musicians you influence. That is the only incentive these gear companies have to give you free or discounted gear and to give you free promotion by putting you in ads and videos. It's not because they think your music is good or that you can twirl a drumstick.

Because prospective sales from your imitators are their only incentive, if you want an endorsement, you're going to have to convince them you're someone who others want to imitate. Every gear company that does endorsements usually has a contact form for those looking to get one. They will then send you an application. When you get this application there are a few things you can do to make your endorsement have a good chance of being approved:

- **Sell** - Remember, they want to see that you'll convince others to use their product. You need to find ways to show them that you'll put their gear in front of eyes and that you're someone others want to imitate.
- **Authentic** - If you already use their gear, show them places where you have been seen using it in front of a lot of people.
- **Talent** - A lot of gear companies want to see you play. Invite them to your show and put them on the guest list if you're in their town. Send them whatever materials they want. Make videos of yourself playing solo if your latest pop single doesn't show off what a badass you are.
- **Don't Lie** - They've been around the block. They smell a lie from a million Facebook likes away. Be honest while selling yourself.

A Discount Is The Start Of A Relationship - A lot of musicians are disappointed when a gear company only offers them a discount instead of free gear. They don't realize that this is the start of a relationship with a company. What a discount says is that they believe in you, but you haven't demonstrated you're at a high enough level that you'll give them enough business to justify free gear.

If this is a company you believe in and want to be involved with, take the discount and build a relationship. Keep in regular contact with your rep, talk to them about doing videos, contests, ads, appearances or whatever you can do together. If you work for them, they will want to work for you and promote you. These companies can spend tons of money on advertising, promoting you on their website and exposing you to new potential fans who will check you out after seeing your name and that you're badass enough to earn their endorsement.

Bartering
Another way to get funding is to barter a skill you have. Whenever you need to purchase recording time, a van, merch, or really anything else, you can approach the seller with the idea of bartering. As a recording studio owner, I've bartered construction work, dental work (any licensed Dentist or whoever wants to barter this again, please get in touch), photography and

graphic design in exchange for my services. Offer any skills you have and see if it can get you a discount.

Your Credit Card As A Record Label & What You Should Know Before You Go There
As much as credit card debt is an evil thing to get involved with, it can be a useful tool to fund your music. Many musicians have used it to make their dreams come true in place of investors, record companies and fan support. Using this easily acquired capital, you can make an investment in yourself. As the model of DIY instead of a record label becomes more popular, the idea of funding your music with credit cards can be a light bulb that goes off in a musician's head. But should it be one that you explore?

The Realities Of Paying Off $X A Month - The first thought to consider when going into credit card debt is whether you'll really be able to pay it off. Credit cards have a monthly minimum payment you're going to need to meet every month. While many musicians can get anywhere from $300 to $30,000 of credit--depending on their credit score--it isn't going to be a great idea if you can't pay it off. When musicians get the bright idea that every member of the band should go into debt, it becomes a dangerous road. If you acquire $10,000 of debt, you'll need to pay off around $300 a month. This means for every $10,000 of debt, you're going to need to make $300 that month aside from all the other expenses you already have. This may seem very feasible to you or it may not. If that seems obvious, here are some other things you may not have considered:

- **Time Off** - What about the months you take off? A month to record your new album? What happens in January when there aren't many good gigs to make money with?
- **Interest** - Paying $300 on $10,000 of debt takes a little more than three years if you have a reasonable interest rate. Do you really want to be paying off all of that debt years later if things don't work out?
- **Life Happens** - If you get booted from the band, if you break up or whatever else may happen, you're still responsible for that debt and will need to find a way to pay it off.
- **Savings** - If you usually save up for tour in "off months," you now have the added burden of this debt to pay that month, making saving tough.
- **The Hidden Fees** - The credit industry is ruthless these days and if your payment is three days late because you were trapped in a

snowstorm in Wyoming, you can go from a 4 percent interest rate to a 22 percent rate or higher. This can make paying off a debt painful. One slip up these days and credit card companies have the right to make your life a living hell.

The Reality - You can take a credit card and conceivably use it in place of a label. If everyone in your group were to have amazing credit, you could have $30,000 each in credit. So a five-piece band would have $150,000 to spend. This isn't a very likely scenario, but let's entertain this for a second: $150,000 is more than enough to fund a great recording, hire the best publicist, extensively promote a tour and push your videos to major networks. The problem is that you now have at least $4,500 to pay in minimum fees every month. That is a hard profit margin to manage for the next few years. You can always go bankrupt if it doesn't work out.

Let's take this down to a more reasonable number like $30,000. You're still paying off $900 a month in fees. While you no longer need to give a label their cut and you'll keep as much as 97 percent of your record sales and many other income streams, this still doesn't add up if you aren't selling records. Depending on how much you sell, you may as well consider your credit card company a label with them taking such a huge cut. If you aren't gigging, you need to sell almost 100 full-priced LPs a month to break even with your debt (being generous with $9 profit per LP). If you're on tour for the whole month, you're going to need to turn a profit of $30 every day to pay off this debt. Think about all the other expenses you have to pay for like gas, a van, food, etc., and you'll see that this extra $30 per day is often tough to come by. In order to gauge whether you can pull this off, it's best to have a thoroughly thought-out budget.

The Cushion - Many people find credit cards useful in an emergency. What if your equipment is robbed or the van dies? These are the pitfalls that credit cards come in handy for. If you have spent all of your credit on funding, you may be out of luck in the event of an emergency.

Playing It Safe - I've seen the credit card as a record label work well in only one scenario: Keeping a low amount of debt such as $2,000 or $3,000. Let's say you record some songs funded by a little bit of credit debt to get gigs. You take it slow and use the gig money to pay back the debt. After you have played out a little and you're profitable locally, you go into another $1,000 of debt for merchandise and another $2,000 for a van (please don't pay $2,000 for a van unless you have a great mechanic in your group). Then you tour a little bit and pay that off. This is actually a feasible model and does work for many people.

While you still are paying a heavy fee to a lender, it can also enable you to get somewhere for the price of your interest rate. When weighing credit card debt, you have to consider whether the interest fee and the burden of a monthly payment is worth it to get what you want. As much as it turns my stomach to say it--credit cards have in some ways made my dreams come true. I got ahead by using them to pay off things I couldn't afford when I was younger. Even though I still have debt from purchases made nearly a decade ago, it was worth all the bills, pain and fees since it got me where I wanted to be in life. Despite all of those benefits, this takes slick calculations and realistic number crunching. Beware of the pitfalls and be realistic before you use your credit card to finance your career--it's a dangerous field that can turn into a bad situation with one misstep. If you do not plan realistically, you're headed for a life of pain that can last long into the future.

Distributors Fronting You Capital
A recent advent of many artists becoming their own record label is that digital and physical distributors are often willing to front you an advance on your royalties to fund your next release. If you have millions of streams many digital distributors are willing to do this and STEM even has a capital program that will use an algorithm to determine your streams and how much money they will front you.

Team Up With A Charity
Once you're starting to make some money with your music, find a charity that is important to you and build a relationship with them. Not only can you get a tax deduction for work on a cause you believe in, but a good charity relationship will also get you new fans and promotion from the charity. As you grow this relationship, many charities will sponsor concerts and help your promotions, perhaps even helping to bankroll a tour. Cozy up to a charity. Do some good with the popularity you have so you can both sleep at night and promote your music.

Chapter 9: Crowdfunding To Fund Your Music

Crowdfunding has become a popular method for musicians to release music on their own. The traditional model of putting out your record through a label, then having record sales support your career, has become less and less necessary for success. Crowdfunding has become a more viable means to fund your musical endeavors and continue to build a fanbase. It's also a great way to build your relationship with fans and give them something special in exchange for their support of your career.

While crowdfunding is an amazing opportunity to fund your music and get press for your project, there are lots of bumps in the road that can send you off course. Under 50 percent of the projects that attempt to get crowdfunding actually reach their goals. This means that taking the time to understand what goes into crowdfunding can help you make it a success and get your music a financial backing you may never be able to accomplish on your own.

Crowdfunding Services

Kickstarter

Kickstarter (kickstarter.com) is a name that is synonymous with crowdfunding. Fans "pledge" money to fund your project and only pay if your goal is reached. This also means you don't get any funding unless your goal is reached. For example, if you want to get fans to fund your upcoming album and your goal is to raise $5,000, you have to gain that much money in pledges to get any donations at all. If only $4,999.99 is pledged, no money will be collected from your fans and you will receive none at all. If your fans pledge more than your total (or your project explodes and you get way more money than anticipated, like what happened to Amanda Palmer, Murder By Death and countless others) you get that money, too.

Currently, Kickstarter takes 5 percent of the money earned if you meet or exceed your funding goal. They handle payments through Amazon, which takes an additional 3 to 5 percent cut off your credit card payments. There is no fee to launch a Kickstarter, but they do need to approve it (usually you get approved as long as you follow their guidelines). Kickstarter allows you to keep a blog page where you can provide updates to fans and those interested in your project. You're able to give incentives to pledge more and make it so that those fans that pledge the most get better rewards for their larger investments.

Kickstarter is the most popular site for musicians to fund their musical projects. Over the site's existence, we've seen members of Animal Collective fund an African tour, Murder By Death fund a vinyl release, Amanda Palmer fund a record and tour and the group Drug Rug fund a new van. You can really fund just about anything, within reason.

Kickstarter also offers the following features:

- Kickstarter encourages you to make a video to show off your campaign. You can easily embed this video on your blog, website and on other blogs.
- Show off your incentives.
- Sorting for local and popular projects so that new fans are able to easily discover your project.
- A space to upload bio and social network information.

IndieGoGo
IndieGoGo (indiegogo.com) is a crowdfunding service that has a slightly different format than Kickstarter. There is no fee or application process, which means there's a very wide variety of projects on the service. They take 4 percent off the top of your project and a 3 percent credit card processing fee, which is noticeably cheaper than Kickstarter. They offer two payment models:

- **Flexible Funding** - A funding model where you do not need to reach a goal and are strictly using the platform to raise as much as you can. They take 9 percent if you do not reach your goal on top of the 4 percent they already take, so it is still important to set a reasonable goal.
- **Fixed Funding** - You set a goal and you need to reach it in order to receive your funding. They don't take a fee if you don't reach your goal.

The service has a wide variety of tools to help you get your funding:

- Sharing and email campaign tools to help raise awareness among your fans.
- The ability to take payments from around the world.
- Deep analytics to help analyze your campaign.
- Customizable templates so you can change the look and feel of your campaign page.

Patreon

Whenever you read discussions of music on the Internet, it's only a matter of time before someone throws down the trump card of "I buy records to support the musicians I love." Then someone writes back that they're glad they don't have to buy records to find out if they like a record or not and that's why leaks and illegal downloads are great. Then we get into discussions about how Spotify is about to kill iTunes and the like and musicians get paid very poorly by Spotify at the present time. We also see musicians pleading with their fans via Kickstarter campaigns that they need money to do things like tour, make videos or records etc. To put it lightly there's a big problem where musicians aren't compensated for their work and often need help getting it together to do the things you enjoy from them.

There's another problem many fans don't often see in the music world. Musicians (even the big ones) get very irregular paychecks. As someone who has handled accounting for musicians, you'd be shocked at how much of a castrophe a week late check can be in a musician's life. One month you may get a huge check because you did a huge tour and put out a record, but around the winter when you're not touring it may be a pretty pitiful check since you're not doing much and still need to pay rent, for the van, health insurance etc. This is pretty soul sucking to your creativity when it comes time to pay rent and your significant other or parent has to bail you out (again) or worse yet you need to sell a guitar in order to make the rent. Trust me, I've lived and worked with musicians for a decade and a half, I've literally seen it on the 31st of every month hundreds of times.

Musicians want to live a stable life and while they have a cool job, it really is disheartening to always wonder if you're going to have enough money to survive from month to month. This is where Patreon (patreon.com) steps in. As a music fan, you tell Patreon which acts you enjoy (as long as they are signed up with the service) and how much money you are willing to give to the musicians you love each month to fund what they do. You set a maximum amount of money to be billed each month and if a musician you love does something (like put out a new song) they will get paid by you. If you start to hate what they do, outgrow them, join a cult, go broke or whatever—you can always stop funding them. Because of your generosity the musicians will give you benefits like presales, hangouts, lessons or whatever they choose.

In return, musicians have money to fund their lives that comes in steadily as long as they are creating and they can budget for this creation. They have the time to work on making you things you'll enjoy in a steady monthly paycheck so they know they can make their rent. Let's be honest here, a lot of us don't need another CD or piece of vinyl, but we sure want our favorite groups to keep touring and making music. This is a great way to lend that support that can really help musicians do what you love in a more comfortable way. Instead of having to beg you to support the latest Kickstarter, you can choose to say, I support this band on a regular basis because they make my life better. This also encourages the musicians you love to regularly churn out music for you, since they know they will be paid a certain amount of money each month.

They have launched a toolset that gives patrons exclusive content in exchange for their support that includes the following:
- The ability share content such as text, images and audio to patrons for a limited time.
- A live streaming tool from Crowdcast which can host gated, patron-only livestreams.
- A mobile app called Lens that makes sharing stories, photos, and videos easier.
- The Patron Relationship Manager allows analytics to enhance your benefits for patrons.
- The ability to release exclusive videos, songs, podcasts and other content to those who support you.

You can join Patreon by signing up for their service and then telling your fans about it on your social networks.

IgnitionDeck
IgnitionDeck (ignitiondeck.com) is a WordPress plug-in that you can install on your blog to help you crowdfund. They offer a no-fees, no application process and a highly customizable format to raise funds on your own

terms. It can also automatically add the email addresses of your fans to MailChimp and Aweber.

GoFundMe
A fundraising platform that allows you to set up a fundraising campaign where you don't need a goal and can simply fundraise to build money for whatever you wish. They take a 5% cut of all funds raised and a 3% credit card fee is applied. (gofundme.com)

Making Crowdfunding Work

The Ingredients To A Successful Crowdfunded Project
It may seem very simple to pull off a successful crowdfunding project, but a lot goes into it. If you understand what makes them work, you have a better chance of getting the funding you need.

This Isn't A Bake Sale – Many people see this crowdfunding as being just like a bake sale where you are raising funds for a good cause. But really, most fans are just purchasing what you are selling as incentives. While fans may believe in your cause, most of them just want the cool things you have come up for as incentives. In a bake sale, your funders will purchase stale cookies in order to make sure a good cause happens. In crowdfunding this is really just a way to sell your fans something they would want to buy with some added incentives and urgency. If you sell them stale cookies, you will probably fail. If you sell them Cronuts and some unique artisanal cake with a personal touch, they will most likely fund you.

Confidence - Crowdfunding only works when you have established trust with your fanbase. <u>Your fans need to have the confidence that you'll follow through and do something great with their money</u>. Since fans are giving you money before they hear the product or see you play live, they have to be passionate about what you do and trust that you will do good again. This means you shouldn't waste your time crowdfunding for your first release, but rather after you have earned the trust of fans that you'll make something great. Without this earned trust, crowdfunding will not work for you.

Relationships - Every single successful crowdfunding musician says the same thing: "This didn't happen overnight." They have been building relationships with fans for years and tending to the growing of these grassroots for a long time. Fans are more likely to give money to a musician they feel a personal bond with. If you build that bond with a lot of fans, you'll have a much easier time crowdfunding.

A Story - Are you trying to fund your record? Surely you have gone through a lot in the process. A compelling story of why you can't do this on your own helps a lot. Got shafted by your last label? Fans love those stories and the idea that they can help you when you are down. Do you have a kid at home? Other parents can understand what that's like. Make your project appeal to fans. If you want to tour but need money, you can talk about how much fans enjoy seeing you. Develop a story that is more than just "Ugh, we're broke and I smoke a lot of weed, so like, can you help us out, so I don't have to get a day job and stuff?"

Know The Terrain - Look at what others are doing on the crowdfunding various crowdfunding. Take notes. What prices are they charging? Do they have good incentives? The more you look around at what others are doing and take notes, the more likely you'll have a successful funding campaign. I know homework sucks, but this can't be the worst assignment you've ever received.

A Video - Nothing spreads faster online than an intriguing, honest video. Honestly, it's a lot more engaging than an essay about the same topic. This video and your incentives are going to be the most important parts of your project. That means you need to make a video that tells your story and gives fans a reason to fund you. You want to upload this video to your crowdfunding site, YouTube and Vimeo. You also want to get all the blogs on your press list to post and ask fans for help sharing it. This is the easiest way to spread your message. If you make the video fun, interesting and worth watching, it will spread even more. Remember: if you make a boring video, it'll say a lot about the effort you're going to put into your project. Make as many videos as you want!

Sell Incentives Don't Just Ask For Money - When telling your story, make sure to focus on what the fans get. It's pretty boring to just tell everyone you're broke. Show fans all the cool benefits they get if they fund your project; it makes it much more enticing for them to lend support. Having cool incentives you can show in your video helps a lot.

Updates - Crowdfunding sites have blogs where you can keep your funders updated. You want to keep them in the loop about anything new going on with the project so they know you aren't slacking. This also helps remind fans to tell their friends about you campaign. Make sure to do written as well as video updates.

Budget - You need a certain amount of money, but all of these incentives also cost money, as do the fees your crowdfunding site takes. Make sure you thoroughly think through your budget before making it official.

Tiered Incentives - Incentives are what make fans what to fund you. Your story is important, but at the end of the day fans want special prizes from you. The prizes need to be great rewards that they get in return for giving you their money before you have even done anything for them. You need to be creative and offer a wide variety of rewards that fans may want.

Not everyone has $2,000 to pay for the grand reward of hanging out with your grandmother who makes killer pancakes. You need to make numerous price points so that fans with different sized wallets (and enthusiasm towards your music) can choose how much they would like to pay. Starting at $1 and going all the way up to your full funding amount is the best practice. In between those, you want to make many different price points. How to do this depends on the incentives and how much it will cost to fulfill them.

Limited Edition - What helps die-hard fans feel special is limiting the quantity of these opportunities. If everyone is able to access to a reward, it's not special. Be sure to limit some of the opportunities at the top of the price range so fans will feel this is a truly special experience.

Fans - If you're lucky, 3 percent of your social network followers will contribute to your project. Doing that math against how many fans you're asking to contribute to you can be a very sobering experience. You need to have a strong and enthusiastic fanbase that is supportive and already giving you money. If you're having trouble getting 1,000 YouTube views or 100 hundred fans at your shows, you're going to have a lot more trouble getting any serious funding.

Space - You can't crowdfund everything. Fans need some space between campaigns. Even if you have a successful crowdfunding campaign, this doesn't mean you can have another one three months later. Use your head and make sure you keep some distance between campaigns, so you can keep getting funded.

Have The Time To Work It - Most musicians need to put a lot of work into getting funded. This means that if you have a month-long campaign, you're going to be having to devote a lot of time to creating incentives, making updates, videos, getting press and shaking down friends with money, etc. If you're going to be on vacation or busy at work, you should wait until a different month to launch your campaign. Most crowdfunding sites allow you to choose a timeline. While longer crowdfunding campaigns can lose momentum, shorter campaigns require more intensity. Make sure you know what you're capable of.

Charity - Having a charitable element helps projects get funded. Not only can you use it as a tax write-off (*if done correctly*), it's also a good thing to do. It can help get press for your project since supporters of the charity and the charity itself will often help you raise money for it.

Adapt - If your campaign isn't working out and it looks like you may not reach your goal, you need to adapt. Adding more incentives and tiers to your campaign can often get those who were on the fence about donating to you to become contributors.

Raising Awareness - You have to get people talking about your crowdfunding project. You need to hit your press list (if you don't have one, get started building one or else you need to hire a publicist) and get them informing fans that you need help. Obviously, the best way to get people talking is to do something worth talking about. Interesting projects and weird incentives will get bloggers blogging and fans tweeting.

Keep the press updated and find new outlets to write about what you're doing. Find ways to get fans talking and this all becomes a lot easier. You should be collecting press who may write about it well in advance of your campaign. You'll only have a limited amount of time to raise the money for your project and you want blogs writing about it from day one. In fact, you want fans talking about it before it has even started. It would be a good idea to give fair warning to fans about what you'll want them devoting their money to in the next week, so you can get some funding on day one. Also, don't forget to get your friends and fellow musicians to help raise awareness too.

What Incentives You Can Give Fans

- **Your Release** - Whether you're funding a new record or a new van--fans love music. If you want to get the word out and raise lots of small donations, put up the digital version of your record for $1 to $5. While the price may seem cheap, these fans are paying for something they have yet to experience in advance. Because they're putting their faith in you, a lower rate should be expected. The low price point will also bring in many backers who wouldn't normally contribute, which will up your overall haul. Amanda Palmer charged $1 for her latest digital release on Kickstarter and this brought in 4,743 pledges. This also will bring in a lot of fans that stole your last album but liked it enough to give you some spare change for your next one.
- **Your Discography** - You can deliver your entire discography to bigger donors. You may even include rare demos, covers or live recordings that no one else has.
- **Music Lessons** - Every musician can give a fan a lesson. This can fetch you a pretty penny and take very little time. It will also help build your relationship with every fan you give this great experience to.
- **Handwritten Items** - Lyric sheets, song meanings and--if you're a real rock star--autographed items all carry a special value to your die-hard fans.
- **Hangout** - Offer your fans some of your personal time. Take them to dinner, for a bar crawl or whatever you do for fun. You can even invite them to practice or dinner at your house. You can put a high price tag on this, as long as you think there are fans that will pay to spend time with you.
- **Contact** - Offer to mail fans postcards from the road or sing them a song if they're nearby. Some sort of personal contact goes a long way.
- **Personal Concerts** - A lot of musicians offer to play a private concert when they're in town.
- **Art** - Are you good at art or do you work with a great artist? Unique art that accompanies your music in a high-quality format can help get you funded.
- **Guest List For Life** - A big donor can receive free entry into any show you do forever.

- **Access** - You can give these fans backstage or in-studio access to entice them. I've even seen musicians sell the chance to come on tour for a couple of days.
- **Credit** - If you're funding an album, you can sell thank-you credits or even an "executive producer" credit.
- **Fan Club Access** - Give fans discounts, exclusive content, access to web streams, Q&A's, etc.
- **Build A Setlist** - Allow a fan to choose a setlist for a show they attend.
- **Perform With The Band** - Some fans would kill to play one song with you at a show. While this has the potential to be a disaster, it can also gain you serious funds.
- **Personal Talents** - Is your drummer a hairdresser? Of course, he is! Well, he can cut someone's hair in every town in exchange for donations. Do you knit a mean Christmas sweater? Get ready to knit 10 of them for your top donors. Use your personal talents to offer fans something special.
- **Fun With Low-Priced Incentives** - You can use humor to reel in fans with low funds. Campaigns offer everything from writing a fan's name on a bathroom wall to the ability to watch the band listen to a song or watch a bad YouTube video on Skype. This can gain you a few dollars and some fan bonding.

Achieving Your Goal Successfully

The Money
What this is all about is getting some money to fund a project. Granted, it's nice that it can help you promote your music and bond with fans, but really--you need money. There are a lot of considerations you need to make for all the time and effort you'll put into getting this funding.

Goal
Remember not to make the goal as high as possible, but a reasonable amount of money you can actually achieve. It's possible to get over-funded, but keep in mind that fans are less likely to fund you if you fulfill your goal since it doesn't seem like you need the money anymore. The exception is if you have good incentives--more fans may want to take advantage of them and keep funding you even after your goal is reached.

171

Let's say you need $1,000 (most projects never ask for more than $10,000, but some do) as the bare minimum to make your project happen. You'll need to ask for about 10 percent more than you actually need to make up for the fees associated with crowdfunding. So, that already means you need to ask for about $1,150 to meet your goal.

What about the cost of the incentives you're selling? Let's say you're offering a T-shirt that costs $5 to make to everyone who pledges $15. Let's say 20 fans funded you on that level. You're now out $100 and that's before postage costs. Remember you also offered to take your biggest fan out for a bar crawl when they pledged $200. Sadly they drank $60 of beer that night. Make sure the overhead of fulfilling incentives is factored into your final goal.

Budgeting
Keeping in mind that you need to budget for a whole bunch of purchasing scenarios. You also need to make sure you're making a profit that is worth the trouble you're going through. Just because you find this to be a pain in the ass doesn't mean you can charge $30 for T-shirts. Fans aren't giving you a gift, they're buying things they want with the added bonus of helping you. And they don't want to help someone who is ripping them off.

Look around at the prices other musicians charge on crowdfunding sites and figure that into your own expectations. A lot of the benefits you're pricing are intangible. It's important that fans don't feel ripped off, but that you also don't get ripped off. Try to find a happy medium and you'll have a great match for your crowdfunding.

Targeting
It's important to have all sorts of price points. Even having a few options within the $20 to $35 range is especially important since the most common pledge on all platforms is $25. You also want to have many options well above that to enable enthusiastic fans help you.

Pricing
One of the most important considerations is to not overcharge your fans. It's very important to do a lot of research on how much other musicians charge for similar rewards. It can be hard to put a price on how much to charge a fan to go to IHOP with you but looking at what other musicians charge for a similar experience and pricing accordingly can ensure your fans don't see you as unreasonable.

Hack It

The trick many musicians employ is that if it doesn't look like they're going to make their funding goal, they bail themselves out by funding the rest themselves. This obviously requires some savings, but you can always pledge your saving at the very end to reach your goal. You lose the money from the fees the services take, but at least you have all the other money that was pledged.

More Thoughts On Crowdfunding

While crowdfunding is great, there's a lot of skepticism about this emerging avenue. There's a lot to think about before you throw yourself blindly down this path.

I Look Desperate

You don't look desperate unless you make yourself look that way. Some musicians are very concerned with looking like they're rich. How are you supposed to look like a rock star when you're begging like a homeless person on the street? Don't beg. Tell your fans the truth: The music business is a broken, horrible system and now you're doing business the right way. Tell your fans that they're now the record company. Isn't that cool?

Fans Hate Crowdfunding

Yes, there are some fans that resent crowdfunding for taking the music business back to the days where we all paid for records before we even got to hear if we liked them. But some people just hate everything. More and more fans get used to this new model every day. It's also your responsibility to sell them on this being a great cause. We're still in the stage where music fans are getting accustomed to this as a normal concept. Lead them to it and they will follow. I've seen many music communities like AbsolutePunk and Punknews poll their readers and the majority of them embrace this new form of funding.

Constantly Asking For Favors

Fans can get tired of you if all you ever do is ask instead of give. They like you for what you create, not for being a beggar. If all you're ever doing is asking them to come to shows, vote for you or check out your content, your relationship is very one-sided. This also goes for fan-funding everything you need to do. The day may come where fan-funding everything you need to do is commonplace, but we're not there yet.

Chapter 10: Planning Your Recording

There was a time when you could have just recorded the best album of all time, but unless you got it in the hands of the right record label, it would remain unknown (watch the documentary *Big Star: Nothing Can Hurt Me*, if you don't believe me). Now that music industry gatekeepers hold less power, the quality of your recording determines your music's potential more than ever. If you don't put your all into writing the best song possible, tweaking it and then getting an amazing recording for it, any work you do afterwards may prove to be useless. Now more than ever, your actual product will dictate your success.

As the playing field levels with the Internet's dominance over music sales and buzz, physical distribution is no longer a major force. Independent musicians can get in every online store that a major label musician can get in. This means your music can spread like never before if fans take a liking to it. Your music is your strongest marketing tool. No amount of touring, promotion or marketing tricks are going to get you as far as a musician who records a great, well-executed song and puts in some serious hard work.

I've worked as an album producer, recording musicians 300 days a year for well twenty years. Oftentimes, a musician will make some mistakes before they come to me (or wherever else they're recording) and sometimes these mistakes can hinder their ability to promote their music. In this chapter, I've assembled as much advice as I can to try to make sure you don't make these mistakes.

What You're Up Against

The Tyranny Of Dead Ideas
Labels and management companies have tried it a million times. They spend countless hours and dollars promoting a record that isn't that great and no one cares about it. A musician will get promoted to death with tons of money poured into them, but it never seems to go anywhere because they don't have the music to back it up. They may get a little flash-in-the-pan fame, but in the end they're forgotten. We can all think of musicians whose posters we saw everywhere, with commercials for their music all

over TV, but somehow, they ended up going nowhere. Usually, they were promoting a project where the songs and recording didn't resonate, despite pouring tons of money into it.

Musicians love to think that if there is enough promotion and muscle behind them, anything they put out will become popular, no matter how mediocre it may be. This myth is derived from hearing a song so bad you can't believe anyone likes it. While hard work can earn musicians some popularity, they're never going to get lasting fans and a career in music unless the world loves their songs. Every time the major labels spend countless dollars on posters and radio promotion for a musician that flops, the idea that money leads to a career in the music business is disproved. The second you realize that anything can become popular, you'll understand that you need to take the craft of recording your music very seriously and make sure it comes out the best that it can be.

Perspiration Doesn't Always Equal Domination
Some musicians tour for years, keep their social networks up to date and put out countless records. You hear their albums and their songs are underdeveloped with weak production, and the musicians never realize their full potential. You can be an amazing live musician and have the best-looking promo shots in the biz, but if no one can listen to your recording and feel good when they hear it, then all of this promotional hoopla isn't going to take you very far.

If you write a great song, fans will talk, tweet and spread the word without you having to pay a dime for them to do it. This is an essential part of promoting anything, since word of mouth promotion is more trusted and important than any advertising. If you promote your music to death but your song isn't up to par when it comes tumbling down a Tumblr stream, the blogs of the world are going to promote another musician that they actually enjoy listening to. Your song needs to be good enough that your fans want to spread it on their own free will.

You Can Fool Some People Sometimes, But You Can't Fool Everyone All The Time
There will always be friends and fans with low enough standards that they'll enjoy anything you put out, even if it's you singing in the shower. There are certain listeners that are enthusiastic toward anything that's shoved down their throats enough. You can aspire be loved by these people only, or you can put the time and preparation into making a great record that will

impress even the most discerning of listeners. It's possible to win over many easily impressed people to make a small fanbase, but this is a fool's game. It's much more fulfilling--and often easier--to put time into your songwriting and recording and try to appeal to the average listener who actually evaluates what they listen to. This expands your potential to reach more people.

If you want to be successful and loved by the world of music listeners, you're going to need to work long and hard on your songwriting and recording. Working long doesn't always mean three months in the studio as much as it means working smart. You need to be researching, planning and tweaking until your music has found the right direction. Making wise decisions about your music is important. It makes all of your efforts in promoting your music and building a fanbase a much easier battle.

If You're Releasing A Demo, You're Already Dead In The Water
By definition, a demo is a demonstration of what you could do if you had a budget and some more help. If you plan for your next recording to be a demo, I have some sad news: No one is going to care. This isn't to say you shouldn't record demos of your music for your own evaluation or maybe to get fans hyped up, but a demo shouldn't be something you promote for an extended period of time. As access to great recording equipment has become abundant during the home studio revolution, music fans are now used to hearing finished songs that need no caveats or apologies.

One of the many mistakes musicians make is releasing a demo to the public to attract label attention. Perhaps back in 2001 this was still a way you could get somewhere in the music world, but that's no longer the case. Music fans have now grown accustomed to hearing a well-executed recording by even the newest groups. The world of music has changed and if you don't adapt to this reality, you're going to be living in your mother's basement forever.

No Vision - When you consider putting out a demo instead of a well-executed, fully produced version of your song, remember listeners have no vision to see the potential you have. Even A&R people who are supposed to see the potential in young musicians don't always have the ears to hear the potential in a demo. Some do have this gift, but 90 percent of the A&R people I've encountered do not. If you're recording a demo, you have to hope you find the 10 percent who do. Most gatekeepers aren't trained or tested for their abilities to hear a hit in its rawest form. In fact, the opposite is often true--they have limited vision and look for musicians who already have a great recording and then run with it.

The majority of the A&R world is not picking a musician out of demo obscurity and envisioning how much better it could be with a bigger budget. They are picking up acts that already have recordings that sound and feel great to listen to. They're finding musicians who have already made music that is getting them a buzz and then giving them the tools they need to take it to the next level.

The Story Doesn't Matter--The Song And The Execution Does
"We recorded our album ourselves 100 percent DIY!"

"We only had $1,000 and we still managed to make a full length!"

"Our friend gave us a great rate on recording, but he didn't know what he was doing."

"We recorded in this studio that looked so amazing! It was so nice, the console was the size of a jet airplane."

How many times have you heard these statements before someone plays you their music? If you need to explain your music for people to appreciate it, what happens when you aren't there to explain it? Each day musicians are making music that needs no explanation that's so good that everyone wants to hear it again, without any provided context. Those songs are what we all will listen to and what will take up space in our iPhones. No one wants to hear a song where they have to think about how much better it could be; they just want to hear something that feels good. If you have the right plan, you can release a song to the world good enough to speak for itself.

Planning For The Studio

Write A Great Song First, Get A Great Recording Second
You've spent countless hours and thousands of dollars in the studio. You're equipped with the best microphones in the world. You've gotten the most amazing vintage gear and have learned how to master all your effects pedals, as well as every plug-in known to man. You even managed to

scrape the money together to get the best producer that your collective bank accounts can buy. What could possibly stop you now? Well, your songs can still stink.

As a record producer I care about recording techniques and other intricate details, but the point I want to stress is that great songs surpass any problems that might come with bad gear or a poor recording. The time you spend crafting a song is far more important than the time you spend recording it. Before musicians' step into the studio, I tell them every hour they spend before they arrive is vital compared to the hours they spend while here. No one buys a bad song that sounds pretty. These days, good recordings are a dime a dozen. People listen to music for the content, not for the microphone used to record it.

Great production is a key ingredient in realizing a song's potential, but it can't turn a bad song good. The song itself is what determines whether a first-time listener will come back to it. Concentrate as hard as you can on demoing and making sure a song is great before you ever set foot in the studio. And if you work hard at capturing that song and producing it properly, you'll have a winning combination that spreads very easily.

Quality Versus Quantity
Part of making a great record is striking a balance between quality and quantity. One of the defining factors of every musician's discography is how much material they release as well as the quality they let the world see. Some musicians write 24 songs over four years and every one is solid, whereas others release that many songs in one year, but only a handful are appreciated by the majority of their fanbase. Making a decision about the quality you'll show your fans is very important.

Many musicians will leave countless songs on the cutting room floor, never recorded nor released to their fans. Others will record many songs but save the gems for their LPs and EPs, releasing lesser-quality B-sides and bonus tracks along the way. The way you unleash this output is a large part of how your fans see you. Saving the best 10 tracks you have for your LP and shelving the rest can be a great idea, but it doesn't allow you to feed your fans music on regular basis. However, if you let every song you write go out to the public, you risk overwhelming fans or putting out songs that could be better. Finding the right balance--so that you turn out a consistent quantity of quality releases--can be the key to keeping fans happy and making sure your fanbase keeps growing.

Write More Songs Than You're Going To Record

Many musicians improve their recorded output by writing more songs than they're actually going to record. While it's heartbreaking that some of your work may be left unheard, it can help you immensely in improving your creative output. It's rare that every song a musician writes is a masterpiece or even a good song to make public. Having too many songs means you can choose from the best material you have.

You can always hold onto extra songs and revise them to use later. No matter what, if you have a wide variety of material to choose from, the chance that it's exceptional enough to get you exposure will increase dramatically.

How Many Songs Should I Record?

A decision that every musician faces before recording is how many songs they should include in their next release. This is a complex question and is best answered by focusing on the following things:

Goals - When I'm working with a band, I always question how many songs they want to record.

Here are two frequent answers:

1. "It's how many we wrote."
2. "This band did it on their last record and their record was awesome."

Both of these answers aren't good enough to justify employing either as a strategy. Instead, the first thing you need to think about is what you're trying to accomplish with your next recording.

Value vs. Viral - Are you trying to get signed, get some fans or do you need a release to sell at shows? If the answer is all of the above or you need a release to sell at shows, you need to make at least an EP or LP. If you're just trying to create some buzz among fans or attract potential team members, you just need to record your absolute best material.

Going Viral - If you're trying to ride a single to glory, you only really need to focus on that one song. This philosophy has worked for many musicians over the years. While a lot of musicians get scared that potential team members will want to hear more from them, it's a better strategy and more cost effective to only record the songs that are solid gold. If someone is interested, they will ask to hear more and by that time, you'll have had a chance to write more strong material.

Recording mediocre material is not going to help impress listeners or team members. It's just going to show that you're capable of writing duds. But if you focus on only a few of your best tracks then give yourself time to write a few more that are also that good, you become a smarter musician because you're using time wisely.

Why Not Record A Few To Choose From? - Plain and simple: The more songs you record, the more money and time it takes to record them. If money and time aren't an issue, then by all means just record every song you can imagine. Otherwise, you're going to need to stretch your dollars as far as they can go. Stay focused and remember that the better each track comes out, the more it will be shared to get you new fans.

EPs and LPs - You have decided you're going to make either an EP or an LP. But how many songs should you record?

Why Are You Recording An EP Or LP?
First, let's make sure you're recording an EP/LP for the right reasons. Before you decide you want to go down this route, there are two points you should consider:

1. The music business isn't what it was even a few short years ago. While many of your favorite musicians still turn out LPs, it may not be the best strategy for you. Many musicians are choosing to put out a series of EPs or singles that they later assemble into a full-length. Smaller releases can help you to get attention more frequently and get fans excited about your music more often.
2. How good your release is, will determine your maximum potential until you have the chance to record again. This means you need to be certain you have the right songs in order to make a great record. If you make a filler-loaded album or you don't have enough time in the studio to bring the songs to their full potential, you're going to waste a lot of time promoting a record that fans aren't excited to share. The better you make this record, the easier it is for the release to promote itself.

3. Because of Spotify & YouTube's algorithms you are now rewarded by releasing singles instead of an EP or LP. So if you are self-recording or releasing a larger release consider how releasing a string of releases plays into your recording planning and if it is better to concentrate on one or a few at a time.

Budget vs. Aspirations - You need to establish a budget and whether or not it realistically lines up with your aspirations. You're going to have a finite amount of time to record, depending on your budget. The more songs you record, the less time you're going to have to make each one perfect. The fewer songs you record, the more time you have to tweak each song and make sure they turn out great.

It's In Your Head! FILLER! - Music fans--especially record reviewers--love calling songs on records "filler." Making a 54-minute album before you have a huge budget and you're sure you have written 54 minutes of great material isn't the best idea. Everyone would rather hear a few perfectly executed songs than 54 minutes of music that isn't properly developed. Recording every song you wrote can bring down the quality of your record immensely, whereas concentrating on making a few songs exceptional will make you and your listeners happier. In simple terms, record the least amount of songs you can execute perfectly.

Records You Have Enjoyed - Everyone has different ideas of what a great record is and what it contains. It's common practice to get together with the musicians you'll work with and assemble a couple of records that are considered favorites. Whittle that list down to a handful of records you all consider classics and think about the following things:

- How many songs do these records have on them?
- How many minutes long are these records?
- What do these records consist of?
- Are there interludes? Skits?
- Were there three singles in the album's marketing? Five singles?

These are important considerations. There is no exact formula, since different ideas work depending on what genre you're in. Rancid consistently makes great punk records with nearly 20 songs on them while many dance musicians make only eight songs that combined exceed 60 minutes of music. You need to find what works for your record and your genre. Some musicians do their best by bucking these trends and that's what makes them interesting. Knowing these standards can help you make wise decisions and help you to figure out how you should assemble your own record. You may decide that you're the group that is going to show prog-rock that two-minute songs can work, like they do in punk. If so, I applaud your courage.

It's important to see how your record matches up with the records you consider classics. If you often enjoy 36-minute records with 12 songs, but all of your songs are four minutes long, you need to consider what to take away from that. Do you shorten your songs? Do you record 12 songs and have a 48-minute record? Or do you record nine songs and get a 36-minute record?

You can use your own experiences with records that give you a great listening experience. Do you feel ripped off when you buy a 28-minute LP, even if it has great songs on it? On the other hand, are you happy to pay $10 for 28 minutes of consistently good songs versus a 54-minute record that is half filler? This is an important consideration.

Time vs. Boredom - No matter how classic some records are, there are some albums you never make it all the way through. I love every millisecond of Mew's *And the Glass Handed Kites*. In fact, it may be one of my favorite records of the past decade. However, it clocks in at 54 minutes--so no matter how much I love it, I rarely get through the whole record in one sitting. Despite enjoying every song on the album, it's hard to digest the record all at once. This is certainly a thought to consider when piecing together your album. Your results may vary, but this is an important consideration since there is no reason to waste your time and recording budget on the excess fat of a record.

The Benefits Of An EP
- **Focus** - An EP can give you good focus. You don't need to make a big statement, instead assemble a few songs that work well together.
- **Time** - It takes less time to write and record.
- **Enjoyment** - While singles can sometimes leave music fans wanting more, an EP is enough for a fan to bite into, enjoy and have the confidence to declare you a great group they want to keep up with.

183

- **Budget** - You can have a dramatically smaller budget to record an EP compared to an LP. You still come out with a great record that does your music justice.
- **Changing Times** - The EP is becoming more and more powerful. Skrillex was arguably one of the biggest musicians of 2012 and had only put out two EPs and zero LPs at the time. As the music world becomes more and more about songs than records, EPs open up the possibility of taking your fanbase to greater heights than ever before.

The Benefits Of An LP

- **Statement** - An LP can be a big statement. It takes a lot of work and when you make a great one it says a lot about your status as a musician.
- **Newsworthy** - An LP is eventful. It is newsworthy and others take notice and get excited.
- **Love** - While fans fall in love with songs, the love we all have for a full-length record that really affects us is unrivaled.
- **Press** - It's much harder to get your single or EP reviewed than it is an LP. An LP is a bigger deal.
- **Profitable** - Selling an LP can net a much higher profit than an EP or single.

Make Sure You Record All The Tracks You Will Need

Musicians often think of making a record as recording only the songs that the public ends up hearing. However, in reality this isn't usually the case. Many musicians (if they can afford it) will record extra tracks to throw by the wayside. Other times, musicians will plan to record too many songs and use them for marketing purposes, such as B-sides or incentives for fans.

There is a huge demand for extra tracks, whether they're bonus songs for foreign regions (often required to get licensing deals), B-sides, or exclusive tracks to help sell more copies on iTunes, etc. It's smart to plan on recording more tracks for the main release than you need. Before you schedule recording time, make sure you think about what extra tracks you may need to market your record effectively.

Use Bonus Tracks To Make Your Releases More Appealing To Buy

Having bonus material on your releases can increase sales, as well as get fans to buy a release in a particular format. For example, if you really want your fans to buy your album on vinyl, you can throw in a few bonus songs as an incentive for them to purchase that format. It's now a common and smart strategy to include bonus material on your direct-to-fan sales method so that you can earn your fan's email address and make a larger profit.

There are many types of bonus materials you can include on your release. Some of them include:

- **Acoustic/Stripped Down Versions** - An easy way to show the basic core of your song.
- **Remixes** - For many genres, remixes offer a great way to give your song cross-appeal, not to mention lure in fans of whoever does the remix.
- **Instrumentals** - Releasing an instrumental version of your song can allow listeners to focus on an instrument the vocals may be distracting them from. It also allows for easy sampling, if this is something you would like to encourage.
- **Live Performances** - A live version of your songs can show why fans should come see your live shows. It can also be a great way to show the different feeling you give to a track when it's played live.
- **Alternate Mixes** - Sometimes a song works with two very different mixes. Listeners are greatly amused by a subtly different version on a record.
- **Extra Tracks** - Sometimes the best bonus tracks are more original songs from a musician. While this takes the most effort, it usually offers the most reward.
- **Covers** - A cover is a great bonus track that saves you the trouble of writing another song.
- **Demos** - Do your demos shed light on what a genius you are? Are they dramatically different than your main versions, in a cool way? Your superfans could be interested.

Pre-Production

Pre-production is the work you do before you enter the studio. Much of the time this involves recording rough demos to reference and gain a new perspective on your material. If you're working with a producer, they will often come to a rehearsal, listen to demos and work with you on your songs. Other times, musicians will work with an outside songwriter who will help tune up their songs before they get to the studio. Pre-production is different for every project but putting some time into this process before you hit the studio can make a huge difference in your next recording.

Demo Your Music To Make A Better Record
Most musicians understand that they should record themselves. The perspective you obtain when you hear a song played back loud and clear through speakers is much different than what you hear when you're rehearsing. Even if you're going to an outside producer later, every producer loves a good quality demo to work with, to help provide a clearer vision of what to do with your song.

As a producer, it's astounding to me how much better off musicians are when they record themselves before coming into the studio. Musicians who create detailed recordings by doing numerous overdubs and putting down every possible idea--as opposed to a one-take demo of the song played live--always walk out of the studio with better results than the musicians who don't do this. When you have well thought-out demos, everyone involved in the project is able to feed off ideas and be more creative with a greater vision of where the song should go.

While programs like GarageBand are great tools and capable of demoing, it's amazing how much it helps a musician's creativity when they learn how to use more advanced DAWs like Logic, Ableton, Pro Tools or Reaper.

Why? - Musicians who record themselves are able to be more creative in the studio. They know what they want and how best to achieve it--one of the most important skills in trying to realize your creative vision. Musicians who understand the recording process and have done a lot of it have the comfort and vision to get a recording they're happy with. It takes a lot of practice to understand why something doesn't sound right and how to get it to sound the way you want it to. Whether you want to write better songs or be happier with your recordings, this is an essential practice in order to be happy with what you record.

Going Beyond GarageBand
What GarageBand doesn't show you is the real options a good DAW (Digital Audio Workstation aka recording software) gives you. GarageBand is a great tool, but if you want to advance your songs and recordings, there comes a time where you need to start tracking every

single idea you have and learning how to manipulate and play with sound in a more advanced DAW.

Cheap - Most musicians have a laptop that can handle recording but are afraid to dip their feet too deep in the water. It's amazing how cheap it is to actually make a reference demo that's clear enough to work off of and helps make your song better. As long as you have a fairly new computer, all you need to do to get started is simply purchase a cheap audio interface. There are many to be had in the $150 range that have two audio inputs and outputs. As long as you have two ins and outs and two microphones, you can record any instrument and get quality that is good enough for these demos. Since most musicians already have a few mics lying around, this process shouldn't cost much at all. If you have a Mac laptop you can even use the built-in mic to record drums with a very usable result.

For entry level DAW's, Ardour (ardour.org) and Reaper (reaper.fm) are both great and insanely cheap. Logic is great and affordable software that gives you amazing features for $199. Pro Tools has a few different affordable options that all include Audio Interfaces. Pro Tools LE will give you a light Pro Tools version that can be had for around $25 a month.

Make A Reference Mix
When trying to communicate the way you want your record to sound--or even just a guitar sound--it's often tough to put it into words. Words like "warm," "pretty," or "slick" all mean different things to different people. No one hears each of these terms the same way, so communicating through words is difficult. Instead, show your examples of the sounds you like. I often ask musicians to give me references to a couple of records they like the sound of. I then talk to them about what they like about each record. They can make me a Spotify or Apple Music playlist, then we can sit down for a few minutes and they can tell me what they like about each recording. As the producer, this helps me give the musicians a release they're happy with and also helps us find a medium where we can better understand each other.

Come to the studio with some notes on sounds you like and a playlist on your iPod. It is a small and easy task that can make you dramatically happier with the end result of your recording.

Choosing a Producer & Recording Studio For Your Next Record

Choosing a producer and recording studio for your recording is one of the most important decisions you'll make for your music. The right combination can make your song come alive, whereas choosing the wrong producer can mean your songs never reach their full potential. Making the wrong choice is a decision you may regret for the rest of your life. Understanding the common mistakes that go into finding a producer or recording studio can help make your music truly shine.

Working With A Producer/Engineer
Many musicians think that you go to a recording studio and get a good recording, just like you go to a Jiffy Lube to get your oil changed. This is not the case. The producer and engineer you work with imparts their personality, taste and skill on your music in a big way; finding one who fits with your music is crucial to making your recording come out the way you want. A great producer/engineer can make the equipment in any studio sound good. In fact, the studio you go to is far less important than working with a person who knows what they're doing.

When discussing hiring someone to do your record, seek out a producer instead of a recording studio. The person with the vision behind the board is what matters, so go to them directly.

Hiring An Engineer Instead Of A Producer
A producer is someone who is in charge of getting good performances, working with the musicians on song ideas and overseeing the quality and vision of the recording. An engineer is the person who handles all the technology in the studio. Some musicians don't want to work with a producer because they don't want an outside opinion on their songs. In this case, you should pursue and engineer instead of a producer. These jobs are often one in the same, but there are plenty of engineers who will keep their mouths shut, do as you say and just make sure you get a good recording.

Recording Studio - While many studios have employees, most are owned by the main producer and engineer there. When deciding who to work with, it's important you don't just go to a studio that has made great records, but that you get to work with a person who has recorded albums you like.

Walking into a great studio but working with the wrong producer can lead to a very bad outcome.

Self-Recording - This next section bears very little use for those who enjoy self-recording their music. While I am a producer, I think that musicians recording themselves is a great thing if they're making songs that make them happy. There are countless musicians who do a great job recording themselves. Todd and I met when I recorded drums and would mix tracks for his group, Sensual Harassment. They do a great job recording themselves and I have worked with countless other groups who do a great job doing the same. No one says you need to go to a producer to make legitimate recordings. You can decide that for yourself.

Three Things You Need To Do Before You Choose Someone To Record With
Regretting your most recent recording experience makes it very hard to be enthusiastic about promoting your music. If you're embarrassed about the music you're supposed to promote, that doesn't give you much motivation to try to get the world to hear it. There are a few things you can do before entering the studio to avoid this from happening:

- **Take It Home** - You need to hear multiple records a producer or studio has made on a stereo you usually listen to music on. Listening to songs in the studio is fine, but make sure you take it home. Studios have great sounding speakers--but if you don't listen to this music on a system you're familiar with, you won't know whether the mixes translate well or if hearing music in a sound-treated studio is just blowing you away.
- **Recommendation** - Talk to a few musicians who have recorded with the person you're recording with. Many studios can talk a great game and show you their best work. While there are many great studios, some are able to consistently scam musicians over and over again. No matter how awesome the records are that come out of some studios, if they're abusive and don't listen to the musicians they work with, they may not be right for you.
- **Meeting** - Meet your producer or talk to them. There are some people who you can tell you're never going to get along with from the moment you start talking to them. When choosing a studio you need to trust your gut and if someone rubs you wrong...run! You may be having aggravating fights and disagreements with this person for the next few months of your life and waste your time,

189

money and dreams working with someone you didn't like from day one.

You Don't Need To Go To Just One Producer For Your Next Record
Many musicians are locked into recording their music with a single producer, under a single roof. However, musicians often like one trait about one producer's work and something else about another producer. In this day and age, audio files are so easily interchanged from one studio to another, there's no reason not to have multiple producers work on one song or a whole album. If you like the drums that one producer does but don't care for their vocal production, why are you going to that producer for vocals? One of the areas where albums often fall flat is when rock musicians enlist rock producers to do electronic elements to their productions. If you want to incorporate synths and programming into your music, why not enlist someone else who does just that?

You'll be paying a majority of producers on day-to-day terms; there is no reason you can't manipulate your budget to make it so you can track each element with someone you feel is an expert in each field. As the playing field levels and gatekeepers continue to disappear, it's easier for your music to be heard if it's executed perfectly. In order to get it executed properly, you may need to enlist experts in different fields.

This also applies to musicians who record themselves, too. If you feel you never get the sounds you're looking for on drums, you can always go to a studio to just record drums. Perhaps you're looking to have some help with vocal arrangements? There are plenty of producers who can help with this. When self-recording, it is wise to figure out what you aren't doing well and admit it. Find someone who can help you overcome your shortcomings and make an even better record.

DIY - This also means you can take tracks home and work on them yourself. In this day of home recording and soft synths, if you want to work on parts on your own, this is often an option when working inside DAWs. Save time and money by trying out ideas on your own or even getting down solid MIDI parts and recording on your own. Then take it back to your producer and put it together.

Recognizing Past Failures In Choosing A Producer
Making a great record is what every musician wants to do. Unfortunately, one of the most common causes of a bad record is a poor choice in who

should record it. Many smart music business folks still use flawed logic when making this crucial decision. Over the years, we've all heard records with great songs, but flawed production. It happens all the time and many times it holds back your enjoyment of the record. Let's discuss the flawed ideas that have ruined many records and then discuss how to understand and fix them.

Budget - The first problem you can run into when making a record is not having the proper budget. In this day and age, you don't need $100,000 or even $20,000 to make an album that changes the world. You do, however, need to be realistic about whether you're budgeting enough money to accomplish your goals. Most musicians can't create a good record for $1,000. More often than not, a lack of budget is what kills an album before it's even recorded.

Personality - While it's important that you get a good feeling from your producer/engineer, that isn't everything. There are plenty of producers who are aces at meetings but are not the right person to get the sound you're looking for. Just because someone was the coolest person at a meeting doesn't mean you should work with them. On the flip side, if you have a bad vibe from someone from the get-go, in all likelihood it will only get worse once the pressure of the studio is upon you.

Dog & Pony Show - A fancy studio with a huge console, glass windows and a high ceiling doesn't make great records. A talented person with great ideas for your music does. These days, great-sounding records are often made in bedrooms. High studio prices, fancy equipment and comfortable lounges don't make music sound any better. Listen to 90 percent of the records that come out of big studios and you'll realize this instantly. The right person can make a fantastic record using limited equipment.

Filling In The Blanks - Just because someone has made a successful record in the past doesn't mean they're the right producer for you. Every musician has flaws that they need help with. What makes a great record is a musician teaming up with a producer who fills in their blanks. For example, if you're a musician with perfect vocals but a drummer who is inept and you get a producer who offers no drumming input, your record will most likely be dead from the moment the rhythm tracks are laid down. Just because a producer made a great record with a few musicians you love doesn't mean they're a genius and can deliver the same results for your music.

Planning - One of the most overlooked parts of making a great record is good planning. If a musician doesn't have the songs or their performances down, the record may take longer than average to make. That said, if the producer is on a tight schedule and the project has to be done on time, this can kill a record instantly. Improper planning has killed more records that I can count. Make sure the producer you want to work with doesn't put you on a schedule that will hinder your creativity and ability to make a good record.

Budgeting
Now that we've established the usual mistakes, let's start to plan on how to fix them. If you have a great record in you, the first way that it may end up not living up to its potential is by making a stupid decision on how to budget it. I've seen more records die of this particular death than from any other cause.

A smart way to figure out your budget is to call all of your potential producers and ask a simple question: "Can you listen to our music and tell us how much you would need to make a recording of _____ quality?" Most producers will take a listen to your music and help determine this. When asking this question, don't fill in that blank with something dumb like "to get signed." Ask about specific recordings they have made and their professional opinion of how long it will take to achieve a recording of similar quality. Next, you should talk to other musicians and ask the same question so that you don't get conned by a studio looking to fill as much studio time as possible. If you get a few opinions on this subject, you will begin to have an educated idea on how to achieve a great recording that will take you to the next level.

Reality - While some musicians may have made an amazing record in five days, you may not be tight enough to do this. An important part of this process is to make sure you are realistic about whether you've rehearsed enough and how fast or slow your creative process moves. Depending on the answers you come up with, you may need to book more or less time. If you have a singer whose voice blows out after 25 minutes of singing, you may be in for one hell of a studio bill to make a fantastic record. But if you are the type of musician that is insanely tight live, you may be able to knock out tracks faster than most.

Don't Stop Short - A common mistake is thinking that you have to be done once the budget is up. Often, this leads to a lackluster recording that an act spends the next year or two promoting with no success. If you know that one or two more days in the studio could make your recording better, make sure you find a way to make it happen. I have witnessed so many records where, had the act put in 10 percent more of their recording budget to punch in some vocals or tweak a mix, their record could have been exceptional instead of just good. Don't sell yourself short by trying to stick to a budget limit when you are so close to something great.

Five Things That Don't Matter When Choosing A Producer or Recording Studio
After having a terrible recording experience, musicians love to tell the world about it. While sometimes it's the recording studio or producer's fault that the recording went bad, ultimately, it's usually the musicians' fault for making a poor decision on who to work with. These are a few mistakes that musicians commonly make when choosing a recording studio.

A Huge Console Means Nothing - Anyone experienced in recording knows that it's the person operating the console that makes the console sound good. While you may think it takes some experience to operate such a monstrosity of technology, that's not the case. Over the years, any experienced musician will hear terrible sounding records come out of expensive studios with big consoles. To make this matter even more complicated, many studios now have huge controller consoles *that don't even run audio through them*. That's right, they simply move the faders inside the computer. Every day, records are made in bedrooms that sound just as great as records made in nice studios.

Looks And Slanted Glass Windows Mean Nothing - To reiterate, it's all about the operator. Just because you see slanted glass windows (which many engineers believe make the room sound worse, though they do look cool) doesn't mean a room is going to sound good. When recording nerds get together, we love to discuss the countless studios we've entered that spent tens of thousands of dollars on looking good, but ultimately didn't sound any better than some rundown hellhole where we once recorded (watch Dave Grohl's movie *Sound City* if you want further proof). If you ever took a look at Cello Studios where many great rock records from the past 50 years were made (the Beach Boys' *Pet Sounds* among others), it wasn't the bright wooden studio you see in the fancy pictures of today. It was a dark, ugly room. But the second you heard a drum set being played in that room, it felt like magic. Just because a room looks nice doesn't mean it sounds nice or that the person you're working with can make it sound good.

A List Of Records Someone Made Doesn't Mean They Can Make Yours Sound Good - Credit lists are often very deceiving. Just because someone worked on a record doesn't mean they had a part in shaping the sound. There are many times the producer of a record didn't do much and let the musicians do most of the work. What makes a great producer is not one good record but producing great results for every musician they work with. Secondly, just because a producer made a good record with a musician you like doesn't mean they're right for your record. A good musician/producer combination comes from complementing each other's strengths and weaknesses.

Tape Machines Do Not Make Great Records - Just because someone records on tape doesn't mean Merlin the Magic Tape God is going to cast a spell on your record and give it a perfect feel. Musicians turn to tape as a way to recapture the old awesome vibes of yesteryear. If you have great outboard gear, a great engineer who understands how things work and solid songs to perform, tape can help you build the character of your music. But if you're short in any of these departments, tape isn't going to make a difference or give you any added edge.

A Huge Drum Room Doesn't Always Make Huge Drum Sounds - A big drum room doesn't translate to big drum sounds, and most records don't even call for such a room. In fact, drum rooms can sometimes be too big! The engineer at the board has to understand how to use the room and shape it properly. Don't judge a book by its cover or it may smack you upside your head.

Testing It - One idea is to test out producers by doing a single together; this helps test your relationship. Some musicians will even go as far as recording the same song with a few different producers. Again, this is one of the most important decisions you can make, so make sure you put some thought into it. I've worked with acts that recorded their first few songs with a different producer each time until they found the one that fit to do their next LP. Many musicians test out producers by recording B-sides, soundtrack songs and other bonus material and then chose the producer they prefer.

Determining Your Blanks To Help Choose A Producer

After the first edition of this book was released, one of the most common questions I received was how to determine what blanks you need filled. Here are a few ideas:

- **Weakness** – Is there a weak member of your group? Are you bad at drum programming but great at synths? Whatever you know you aren't the best with, you need to find a producer who is strong at this skill.
- **Feedback** – Taking record reviews to heart can be a tough concept to navigate. But, if you see common complaints about your music, it may be good to find a producer who can help you with them—especially if they are complaints you would like to improve upon.
- **Insight** – If you don't have a clue how to write harmonies or program drums on a drum machine, but want these attributes on your record, make sure your producer is proficient in them.

The Musician's Bill Of Rights Upon Entering A Recording Studio

At Musformation, we think the home recording studio movement is a blessing, not a curse. We work hard every day, trying to give everyone the knowledge they need to make their music the best it can be. We want to hear the amazing music you will make with this knowledge. With that said, there has been an obvious deterioration and lack of professionalism that recording engineers uphold.

Every day, I hear horror stories of what a studio owner or a producer did to some random musician. It angers me because there are so many great engineers out there who would never indulge in any of these shenanigans. Musicians should be working with professionals instead of these con men who destroy hopes and dreams when they are being paid to do quality work. Unfortunately, some musicians don't know the questions to ask when stepping into a studio and don't know what to expect upon entering the recording environment.

There are some producers who work very effectively using the craziest methods imaginable, but understand that this is the exception, not the rule. Most of the rules we are about to outline are fine to disobey as long as long as they are discussed with the musicians in advance. I am outlining what most dedicated producer/engineers do. If a producer has a family and can't work 10 hours a day, that's totally cool--just make sure it is discussed beforehand. I am not saying great records can't be made unless you follow these rules; I am trying to tell musicians the bare minimum they should expect when walking into a studio.

The Right To A Coherent Producer/Engineer - Listen, this is the music business...everyone likes to party! However, if you're paying for studio time you should at least have someone who is sober enough to communicate. The boundaries for excess should be set in advance. Some professionals claim they don't know a mix is right until they smoke a little weed before hearing it. However, some musicians want everyone at their most attentive state of mind, so make sure lines are drawn in advance to ensure there are no disagreements after the fact.

The Right To Have Your Producer/Engineer At Work When They Are At Work - The biggest complaint about the modern "engineer" is the lack of attentiveness to their work. You have the right to your producer's undivided attention--he doesn't need to be texting talking to people on the phone during a session. A producer doing this while a musician has an instrument in hand is completely unprofessional. The session should come first over petty distractions like Skype chatting. With that said, everyone has emergencies sometimes. All of this obviously doesn't apply when there is a serious incident. If a studio is holding you to how many hours you paid for, you can hold the producer accountable for excessive phone calls that interrupt the session and the time should be compensated in some form.

The Right To Have The Producer/Engineer At The Session - I've heard countless stories of engineers bailing to go take a jog, watch an episode of Friends, etc. They teach the musicians to punch themselves in and leave them to record themselves. Just like with a "real job," a producer/engineer is supposed to actually show up to work. We all know life hands us some serious drama sometimes and we all have responsibilities, but musicians have a right to know if the producer/engineer has prior commitments. This includes charging musicians a huge rate and then sticking them with the assistant engineer the whole time.

The Right To Hear It Your Way - The title "producer" doesn't give anyone veto power, unless you set that standard beforehand. Musicians have the right to hear their ideas. It's one thing to be told you will go over budget if you try out an idea, but it's another to deny you the right to hear your music the way you'd like. Most of the time this comes down to making simple alternate mixes, which can take five minutes. All too often, producers won't like an idea for a track and refuse to explore it since it doesn't fit with their concept what they think the song is supposed to be. Typically, the time it takes to argue over these things is usually how long it would take to hear the idea.

The Right To Have Competency - Every producer/engineer is learning on the job to some extent. But it needs to be established in advance if they're going to be watching tutorials or looking in a manual every hour to learn how to do the tasks that come with recording musicians of the genre you're working in. If you're a modern pop band and the engineer doesn't know how to use auto-tune, they shouldn't be charging you for the time it takes to figure out their recording program. Producers/engineers are supposed to be charging their clients for the time it takes to execute their ideas. If there is extensive learning on the clock, the musicians should either receive credit or it should be discussed first.

The Right To Understand What You're Paying For - The days of studios charging $20 for a nine-volt battery are over--the free market of home studios has obsoleted them. Every musician has the right to an honest estimate and hourly rate with no hidden fees. You have the right to see every fee that you may run into with your budget in advance so there are no surprises. With that said, Murphy's Law is often a reality. So, if a snare head breaks and you're expected to pay for it, don't blame the producer/engineer.

The Right To Not Be Insulted - With no exception, no producer/engineer has the right to call you a derogatory term. Joking around is all well and good and the occasional jab is all in good fun. However, any producer/engineer should have enough class to know when it's appropriate to throw a hurtful insult around. Racist, sexist, xenophobic and homophobic terms meant to hurt someone else are never justified under the studio's roof.

The Right To Not Pay For Data Loss - If a track, a take or a whole record is erased because of an engineer's error, you have the right to not pay for it. Data loss is not a fact of life; it's a plague of being unprofessional. And you don't need to put up with it or pay for it.

The Right To Receive Your Music In A Timely Fashion - Musicians that pay for their studio time should get their music returned to them by the studio within a predetermined timeframe. Musicians have schedules to uphold (like tours and mastering dates, etc.) and should never have their lives put on hold because a producer/engineer is slacking. Not having your music on time can mean lost revenue and missed opportunities. Studios must be honest about when mixes will be finished. Musicians who fail to get their music back in a timely fashion should be entitled to a partial refund.

The Right To Have Changes After The Mix Is Done - No one likes a musician who changes their mind too many times, but a certain number of small changes to a mix aren't unreasonable. Sometimes only time and a little distance from the project can tell you what adjustments need to be made. While too many changes are annoying and exhausting for an engineer, the first few changes are no big deal and often take little time. At the end of a session, it should be made clear that changes are expected and should be done expeditiously. This should always be the standard practice.

The Right To A Clean & Comfortable Studio Environment - We're all artists in a sense and artists aren't usually known for their cleanliness, but at some point, we must draw the line. You're not at a country club, but a studio shouldn't smell like a locker room, be overflowing with trash bags or be rat-infested. In addition, musicians shouldn't have to worry about how they're going to play well because it's freezing inside the live room and the owner won't turn on the heat. Furthermore, musicians shouldn't need to be concerned about their gear being ruined because a roof is leaking or their allergies going crazy because there's mold all over the place. While there is nothing wrong with having a relaxed "home studio" vibe, it should be a comfortable environment where musicians can concentrate on more important things--you know, like the music.

The Right To A Functional Studio - Most of us have been through a DIY stage in our musical careers where we opt for cheap fixes and workarounds, but there are some things that are unacceptable. For example, a singer can't give his or her best vocal performance if they can't hear themselves because the headphones keep shorting out. If the studio states they will have certain equipment (drums, amps, etc.), they should have those available for you and in some sort of working order, especially if they're necessary for the project's sound.

In Closing - Musicians entering a recording environment--especially one they have never worked in--should ask their engineer if they agree with their terms. The bright side is that it gets a lot of communication out of the way in advance. By discussing all of these concepts before working together, there'll be less fighting and bitterness in the studio. Both musicians and producers can understand where each side is coming from before a project even starts. This will lead to both parties being happier in the end.

How To Handle When Your Recording Goes Wrong

When You Need To Retrack, Remix or Remaster Your Record
Sadly, like everything else in life, everything doesn't always goes as planned when making a record. Throughout my years as a record producer, mixer and mastering engineer I have been the person who is called to save the day when things go wrong with a recording. Unfortunately, many times when I get this call, the solution the management and act has determined is the cause of the problem isn't always the one that will save this record from being an unlistenable mess.

In order to know what to do when a record goes wrong often takes years of experience and an acute understanding of the process of making records. Thankfully, there are a few common mishaps that can easily point you in the direction to go, to make sure you properly rescue your record.

When You Need To Retrack Your Record
The worst-case scenario you can have when making a record is it being recorded poorly and you need to start all over again or re-track some elements of the record in order to get the result you would want. These are some calling cards for needing to re-track your record.

- **Sloppy** – If you feel your record as a whole is sloppy and off time, it was probably tracked with little scrutiny. If it wasn't recorded to a click track and you feel the rhythm tracks and the feel is off, you will need to start from scratch. If the record was recorded to a click, it's possible that a good editor can reign in the performances and get the recording to work again.
- **Something Is Off** – Maybe the vocals or bass is out of tune or a couple instruments lack the proper voicings in power. If this is the case, for relatively little money you should be able to find a competent producer to help you get back on track, by only re-

recording an instrument or two in a song and leaving the majority of what was recorded intact. If you feel there's a few elements off, it can often be great to just get your songs to another producer and get a new set of ears on it.

- **The Feel Is Off** – Sometimes, you cannot deny that the emotion of a song wasn't captured properly. The demo may have had a better feel or the songs just sound a million times better in the practice space. This is usually in the performances, but many uneducated ears will blame the mix. While the mix can occasionally be the culprit; often times the feel, tempo or emotion was sucked out in the recording. There is no way to mix this back in. It's often best to take it to a competent producer/mixer and see what they recommend to revive the tracks.

When You Need To Remix A Record

A great mix on a great song can really take it to a new level. Often times, the mix is blamed when the recording is off and performances need to be retracked. Before I outlined when to blame the retracking, but the mix can be a problem. Here is how to know when it is.

- **Rough Was Better** – When you feel like the rough mix was better, it often means the mixer sucked the life out of the track. Have the mixer give it another approach and perhaps give them some songs you feel they could aim for. If this doesn't work try having some other mixers do "test mixes." This is an affordable way to try out a new mixer or 3 and find out whether the potential of your song is being reached. By hearing what a few other people can do with your song can be an affordable way (often only $200-$400 per test mix or even less, if the mixer really wants the job and there are many more songs to be mixed on the project) to get a perspective on whether you have the best mix possible for your record.
- **Something Just Isn't Gelling** – Sometimes the mixer just can't find the sound you want. It's very easy to lose perspective on a mix after hearing it in so many rough forms beforehand. This doesn't mean who you worked with is incompetent, many top producers hire outside mixers to bring a fresh perspective to a song. If you feel like there's something wrong and the mix isn't 90% of the way there it may be time to get a fresh perspective.

When It's Time To Get A New Master

Many people will hope a master can save a bad mix, but sadly if you feel your mix is a C on the letter scale, it will usually only make it a C+ or at best a B. If you have bad feeling about your mix, remember great mastering only slightly improves it. With that said, things can go wrong in the mastering process.

- **The Life Is Gone** – There are far too many mastering engineers with big credits out there who have bad taste. While their taste may have worked for someone else's record, it may not be on par with what you want. Trust your ears, if you don't feel the mastering job you got back sounds better than your mixes, have the mastering engineer re-think it or get a test master from someone else. Far too many mastering engineers push the volume too far or just clip in an unmusical way. Give it to someone else or provide your engineer with examples of what you would like but trust yourself if you don't like what you get.
- **It Sounds Worse** – Sadly, many times I get back masters from mastering engineers I don't trust, my mix sounds worse. While they may have expensive toys, what they came up with isn't the band's vision or my own. Don't be afraid to say it sounds worse. Figure out what you don't like and do not let this crucial last part of the recording ruin what you wanted by trusting that cause their title says "master" that they know what they are doing.

How To Evaluate Your Mixes And Masters Properly
One of the most common reasons people are unconfident in their opinions on how to judge a mix or master if they don't know how to listen properly. They trust the people they work with cause they don't trust their own ears or get confused by what to listen for. If you follow these simple steps you can easily reference and know how to listen properly to your music and make good judgments.

- **Familiar** – When you listen to your mixes or masters, don't go to your friend's Dad's system that he paid $10,000 for. You want to listen on the systems you listen to music on every day. It doesn't matter if this is your laptop, car, earbuds, studio monitors or all of the above. You want to listen on the systems you listen to music on every single day. This is why it's important to not trust your mixer or mastering engineers speakers as much as your own. You know when a song sounds good or bad on your speakers and you need to trust that intuition and relationship you have built with these speakers. As well, odds are most people will listen on these speakers than the expensive studio monitors your mixer uses.

- **References** – Put on a playlist of 3-5 songs you have listened to a lot and that are similar to the type of music you make into iTunes (if you use iTunes make sure you turn off "SoundCheck" in the preferences) or your phone's media player. Next, load your mixes into the same media player, otherwise this comparison won't work. As long as you have heard them a bunch on this system and they are close to what you do, they will work well. Don't go crazy trying to find songs exactly like your own, just relax and listen to them. Put them on at a volume you like to listen to music at.

- **Volume Match** – Most of the time, your mix won't be as loud as the songs you compare it to. Because of this we want you to get a VU Meter from the App Store on your smart phone. Once you have it, set the reading to "average" and take note of what volume you are listening to your reference mixes at. 82db is a great place to aim for, but you can also set the volume to an average listening level, that feels good to you.

- **Compare** – After you have listened to 3-5 of your references, relaxed and taken note of how they sound, it's now time to put on your mix. Use the VU meter and turn up your mix to the volume of the other songs you are listening to properly evaluate it. As you feel different opinions about the songs, jot them down and feel free to go back and forth between your references and mixes. This will get you a confident result. Now trust yourself enough to tell your engineer what you heard.

- **Evaluating A Master's Loudness** – If you want to make sure your master is as loud as another release, you should not turn up the volume when your master comes on. Make sure it plays at the same volume as your reference. If it isn't loud enough or too loud, have a conversation with your mastering engineer. It isn't always to make your master as loud as what you reference, make sure you work with your mastering engineer on finding an appropriate volume that brings out the best of your song.

Chapter 11: Getting Your Music Mastered & Audio Quality

Why You Have To Master Your Music

Mastering is one of those processes that can be easy to skip out on. If you haven't ever had great mastering done, it can be hard to hear the difference between a mastered and unmastered record. Unfortunately, many people you want to impress with your music do know the difference.

As we previously discussed, one of the worst things you can do is leave something to the listeners' imagination. Music listeners are used to a finished product that feels great without apologies. Mastering is one of those differences that's hard for laments to pinpoint: while many listeners can't place exactly what's wrong with a track, they can tell whether something just isn't right.

A good mastering job will make your record work better than it did before. Whether you make lo-fi art rock or polished pop, the mastering will add the finishing touches. You don't want to miss out on crafting a perfect album by skimping out on some decent mastering.

What Good Mastering Does

Many people will discuss what goes into mastering in technical terms (compression, equalization, loudness maximization, song sequencing), but this can all be nonsense when you don't understand what these technical terms mean. To clarify, I've assembled a list of what mastering generally does:

- **Louder** - While some records have their dynamics already perfected, most records need the help of a little loudness maximization. This helps make it so that when your song comes on next to another, it's equal in volume and has an improved resolution. Great mastering houses have expensive loudness maximizers that make your record louder without sounding tinny and boxy.
- **Clearer** - Good mastering will bring out more resolution and clarity in your recording. It will not only be clearer, but the recording as a whole will be a more coherent work.

203

- **Sequencing -** A good mastering job will nail down the proper spacing between tracks and help make the album flow properly.

Get What You Need From Your Mixer
When your record is being mixed, you need to know what mixes you'll need from that engineer to bring to the mastering house. It's important you know this in advance, since recalling your mixes can take a long time for your mixer to get around to, costing you tons of extra money--compared to doing it during the mix. Here are some mixes you may need:

- **Main Mixes** - You'll need a stereo mix of the track. Often alternate mixes are made with the main vocal up or down a bit in case you need that to make the record more consistent in the master.
- **Radio Edits** - If your song has curses or is too long, you may need to make radio edits. Singles over four minutes or songs with curse words will need edits if you want to push them to mainstream radio.
- **Instrumentals** - These can be very important for karaoke and licensing. Sometimes having the instrumental on hand right in the moment can be the difference between getting a five-digit licensing deal or losing the opportunity. Be sure to have it when you need it.
- **A Capellas** - Just the vocal tracks; you'll need these for remixes.
- **Backing Tracks** - If you used certain instruments in the studio but won't have them when you play live, you may need backing tracks. This is crucial in pop music.
- **Stems** - Stems are extremely helpful if you plan to do remixes or want to submit to Rock Band-type video games.
- **B-Sides & Bonus Tracks** - If you recorded more songs than you're going to put on the record, it's best to master them with the rest of the record. It's always good to have a mastered version on hand to be able to release on a compilation, soundtrack or if you think of a great marketing idea. You never know when you'll need them.

When Do You Book A Mastering Session?
As I told you before, you need to maintain momentum in order to attract potential team members. I constantly see musicians getting their records mastered nearly a year after their record is finished. Not only does this slow down your momentum, but it makes you look bad to potential team members. The smartest practice is to book your mastering time at the

same time you book your recording dates. Schedule it for two weeks after your recording session is supposed to be done (to leave room in case your recording time goes over budget) and you'll be on the fast track for a timely release. Many mastering houses are booked far in advance, so setting this up early is essential. Also, if your recording session ends up taking longer than you expected, most mastering houses are happy to accommodate you and switch your session with someone else as long as you keep a clear line of communication with them.

Choosing A Mastering Engineer
Choosing a producer and a mastering engineer is based on more than locality or availability. Choosing a mastering engineer based on a quick turnaround or "having a hookup" can be the weak link in your recording. You have worked too hard on this record to then have it be ruined in this crucial final step.

Trust Your Producer On Their Mastering Engineer Choice - Most good producers develop a relationship with a mastering engineer that is crucial to their sound. The two of them learn from each other about how to achieve an optimal sound. Just as important as a mastering engineer's talent is their ability to understand your producer's vision. This relationship takes time to build and it's often why you should trust your producer. Your producer is always thinking about how to help your sound become the best it can be. The business guys are busy thinking about budgets and schedules. If you're trying to make an exceptional record, it's obvious who you trust.

The Search - What if you're self-recorded or haven't found a mastering engineer whose work you like? My first suggestion would be to look at who was used on your favorite records. Odds are you'll see the same names over and over. Sometimes these names are out of your budget range. You can write some producers you admire and ask them who they trust. They're usually shockingly forthcoming about this. The one thing not to do is master with an engineer because they're local to you. The world is flat when it comes to sending files over the Internet, so no need to master with the guy in your town. With a little research, you can find someone who can best handle this fragile job with a precise hand.

When "Young And Hungry" Is Not What You Want - One of the pieces of advice I offer to musicians early in this book is to find someone young and hungry to work with and help them in various aspects of the business.

As much as I love this philosophy, it does have exceptions. Sometimes musicians will say, "Our label wants us to go with a mastering guy who is young and hungry."

It pains me to the bone to think that musicians could end up with a sub-par record after following the advice of a label that thinks someone new can just walk into a highly precise field like mastering and get a great result.

Who Would You Choose? - As someone whose primary job is being a record producer, I believe you need an objective perspective in your mastering and I would never master my own records unless forced to. I go to Alan Douches (as well as Jamal Ruhe) at West West Side Music (westwestsidemusic.com), who is truly one of the most amazing and talented human beings I've ever met. If you check out his discography, you'll see that he has worked with everyone in the business. When you need the best quality you can get, there are none better at any price than Alan and Jamal at West West Side. No matter what style of music you do, if you can afford them, they are by far your best choice for any budget in my humble opinion.

Now would also be the time to mention that I master tons of records a year and if you can't afford West West Side, I do a less expensive mastering job for those on a budget. You can find me at Cannon Found Soundation (cannonfoundsoundation.com). I master lots of indie rock, punk, dance, emo, metal, hardcore, hip-hop and prog records. I also am honest enough to say when I am not up for the job. I know some genres well, but if you do smooth jazz or solo clarinet, I will send you elsewhere to someone who can give you a great master.

Don't Use LANDR – While you may be berated by endless adds, algorithmic mastering services don't compare to using a human. There are plenty of mastering services that are affordable that do great work.

Ten Tips To Prepare Your Music For Mastering
You made the final decision about your music and you've decided to go the full nine yards and have your record mastered by an actual professional. But now you've come all the way down to the wire and your record is getting mastered tomorrow--so what do you do? Relax and follow these tips and your session will be go smooth:

1. **Make Sure The Mix Is Great** - Mastering is not the time to make huge mix changes. Instead, it should accentuate what you've already done. While some mastering engineers can perform miracles, don't always expect you can "fix it in the mastering." If you've gotten a great mix, you've made the mastering engineer's job much easier. In addition, make sure everyone is happy with the mix before you send it to master. Your mastering session is the last place you want to be arguing about the level of the kick drum at a super high hourly rate.

2. **You Don't Need To Normalize Or Get It As Loud As Possible** - Keep in mind most mastering engineers like some headroom to work with (6-12db for you nerds out there). Do what they ask and everything will be fine.

3. **Make Sure The Bounce Is Done Properly** - When bouncing your files, it's common to use the WAV format. Pay attention and make sure that you're bouncing at the same sample rate you recorded at (if you recorded at 96k then make sure to do the bounce at 96k)-- and keep bitrates the same as well. As stated above, normalizing is not necessary. If you're using a compressor you like that helps get the tone you want, feel free to bounce it with the compressor. However, also remember that your engineer will most likely have higher quality gear than the plug-ins you may be using.

4. **Come With An Open Mind** - Keep in mind that a mastering engineer is an objective perspective. They're giving you fresh ears. If you have been listening to your mixes for a month before your mastering date, you may be used to the huge size of the bottom end--but the mastering engineer may find this hugeness to be sloppy and point out that it's getting in the way of your vocal. Keep in mind that in 30 days when you have fresh ears, you may actually agree with him. Give the mastering engineer the benefit of the doubt. However, if you have a clear vision of what you want and they missed it, be sure to tell them.

5. **Know Your Sequence Before You Arrive** - You're going to be choosing song order and spacing for the songs. Some musicians make this up as they go along, but you pay a high price to do this, since mastering time isn't cheap. Anyone with iTunes can use a playlist to test it out beforehand.

6. **Email Your Engineer The Files Before You Meet With Them** - If there is a problem with your mix bounce, you don't want to find out when it's too late. Most engineers will take a quick listen to your mix earlier to make sure there are no inexplicable errors. If there

are, having your mixes checked first could save you a lot of headaches. Use a service like Dropbox, Google Drive or MobileMe to send your files to the engineer and everyone will feel more at ease when the actual day comes around.

7. **Have A Copy Online And With You** - It's much better to be overly cautious with backups. Even if you email the files to an engineer ahead of time, something can still happen to them. Make sure you take a copy with you and for extra protection, keep a copy somewhere online where you can access it. You probably won't need it, but with something this important, you'll want to be sure.

8. **Bring Reference Tracks** - Sometimes you'll be dealing with an engineer who understands your music and perhaps even appreciates it, but this is not always the case. For volume and style comparisons, you'll want to bring in high-quality MP3s or WAVs of other music you like or want to imitate. This will help the individual mastering your record immensely and can show you how your recording compares with your heroes.

9. **Skip The Sauce & Get Some Sleep** - Just because you finished your record doesn't mean it's time to pop bottles yet. The night before your mastering session is not the time to get crunked up on booze (or whatever else). Save that for another date. Make sure you get plenty of rest so that you'll be as fresh as possible. Listening to your music at loud volumes repeatedly and helping the engineer make the important decisions is the last thing you want to do while hung over, with every crash cymbal pounding in your head. You've come too far at this point to screw it up, so hold out until after the mastering is done to hit the bar.

10. **Be Prepared With Money** - Mastering sessions are almost always estimated beforehand, which means it's possible you may go over the time limit and over budget. Be prepared for this to happen and be prepared to pay for services at the time they're rendered. Especially when dealing with a professional, you don't want to look like an amateur when it comes down to business. Remember that many engineers are connected in the business and you don't need anyone spreading word that you're an irresponsible musician. Besides, it's likely you won't walk out of the session with a disc in hand until you put down some cash. It's time to end the cliché of musicians being cheap bums who are always broke. If you're serious enough about your music to have it mastered, you should certainly have the money--and then some.

Why Attending Your Mastering Session Can Hurt Your Record
Control is a hard thing to give up, especially when you're handing your brand-new record to someone for crucial final tweaks. If botched, it can ruin the experience of your record. If done properly, mastering can accentuate your record, giving it a breath of fresh air. Mastering is the last creative step for a potentially great record to reach full fruition. Unfortunately, trying to keep control at this stage can bring down your product.

The relationship between an engineer's speakers and his or her ears has a value that can never be calculated. That said, many times musicians and producers will walk into a mastering engineer's room and try to make critical decisions on the sound of a record when they don't know the room or speakers very well and can't make proper judgments. You should just stay at home and have the engineer send you files to listen to on your own speakers in your own room, that you are familiar with. This will let you make educated decisions about how you want the record to sound. By being in your own comfortable environment, it's much easier to know you're making the right decisions about how your record should sound.

How To Tell How Loud Your Record Should Be
Loud records get a bad name these days and how loud you'll want to make your own particular record is a huge creative decision. Unfortunately, many musicians don't know how to properly make this crucial judgment call.

Standards - Every musician is going to have a different sound they're going for. Get together a few records that you like the sound of and would like to draw comparisons to. It's also smart to find records your producer has done so you can use them for reference. Once you have assembled these records, you have to do a proper comparison of them against your recordings.

MP3 Woes - If you're going to be comparing MP3s to your master, make sure you have good rips of your reference material. Low bitrate MP3s or webrips do not provide accurate references. You can click to get info in iTunes to see the bit rates for these MP3s and see if they're up to par.

Evaluating - All of these records need to come from the same source. If you're going to listen to your master from iTunes, you then need to listen to your references through iTunes as well. If you're going to listen to your master from a CD, then you need to listen to your references from CDs as well. You then need to put your music on at a reasonable volume. If you have a smartphone, download a decibel meter (iOS and Android both have them) and turn up the volume of your stereo until you hit an average of 82db (for scientific reasons this is an ideal listening volume, for further reading look up "The Fletcher-Munson Curve"). If you don't have one, turn your stereo up to a volume that you could talk loudly over the top of. Once this volume is set, don't touch the volume knob again until the whole process is over.

Once the volume is set, put on your reference material and then put on your song (in that order). Keep doing this and take notes on what you hear. Listen back and forth for a while and make honest judgments about whether your record is as loud as the records in your reference material. In the end you should have a clear perspective on where your record stands in this process.

Sequencing Your Record - Pitfalls
Sequencing your record is an important part of crafting a great final product, yet many musicians use flawed logic.

Concepts Over Content - Sequencing your record can be an unexpected trouble in the process of finishing your album. One of the biggest mistakes young musicians make is coming in with a list of what the song order should be without ever having listened to that order. In this day and age of DAWs and iTunes playlists, there is no reason to ever do this. Before coming into the studio, experiment at home with iTunes, GarageBand or your own DAW and you may discover a much different perspective than the order you thought the songs should go in. This usually brings good results. The way the moods of different songs blend together is hard for many musicians to conceptualize. Instead, use your ears and your emotions. Listen back to how they blend together and you'll make much better decisions.

From Best To Worst - If you're an unknown musician, it's usually smart to make the first song on your record one that blows everyone away. But this isn't always the right path. Countless musicians decide that they should sequence their record from the best song to their least favorite. While there are exceptions, this idea will fail more often than it will work. What most listeners are looking for in a record is an emotion and when you scatter the emotional movements of a record in a random way, it can be very disruptive to the flow of the album. Having your record's ballads come on tracks 2 and 9 can give the listener an emotional roller coaster. While every record requires a new approach to its emotional sequencing, be sure that you don't have a party rocking song segue right into the ballad just because they go in sequence of your favorite to least favorite. Think about the emotional experience a listener will have and you'll have a record that listeners enjoy much more.

Sequence On Beat - Determining the space between your songs on your record is one of those subtle details that can make a big difference in the flow of your record. One of the subtle tricks that can make a record work a little better is to sequence your record so that each song comes in on beat. Making a song come in based on the tempo of the previous song can provide a natural flow. This can be especially important on recordings with rigid tempos, like many dance records.

Go High Definition! - One of the ways many musicians are still making money is by selling high definition files to fans. Most recordings are captured at a much higher quality than MP3s. The good news is that a lot of fans want to hear how great it sounded in the studio and are willing to pay for it. Sites like TopSpin and Bandcamp make it easy to deliver high definition files to fans. iTunes has even gotten hip to it with their "Mastered for iTunes" category that allows you to sell these files over their platform. If you made a great recording, be sure to also ask your mastering engineer for high definition files so that these files can be delivered to your fans.

Chapter 12: Choosing Which Songs To Promote

The Difference Between A Single & An Album Track

Odds are there are a good amount of your songs that while you may love them, are not the best introduction to your music for a new listener. In the context of songs on an LP, there are two types of tracks:

- **Album Tracks** - Songs you love but are not the best introduction to your music for a new listener. They can even be great songs but are not the ones that are going to get the world hooked on your music. Once someone is a fan of your music, they may think the album tracks are your best stuff, but if they had heard this song first, they may never have become hooked on your sound.
- **Singles** - In the same way that sometimes you need to dress up a little, put on some snazzy clothes and make a good impression, you sometimes need to put the poppy, accessible songs out to the masses first. While this song may not be the one that best shows everything you have to offer, it will invite listeners to get to know you better.

The way you look when you dress up is your single--an accessible, fancy version of you. The person you really are, when you're reading a book in your Snuggie laying around the house is your album track. Both are fantastic, but it's definitely crucial to recognize the role of each.

You're The Worst Person At Choosing A "Single" - THAT MEANS YOU!

It happens right at the end of nearly every record I make. A musician says, "Which of the songs we just recorded should we release as a single?" I tell the musicians the honest truth: Everyone in this room is the worst person to make this decision. The people at your record label and your manager are also the wrong people to make this crucial choice.

We have all bought records and wondered why a certain song was chosen as a single when there are much better tracks on the record. By choosing the wrong song to promote, you hold back your potential and make your goals harder to accomplish. This decision can make a difference in how easy it is to build your fanbase.

There are some songs that aren't a good introduction to your music, even though your fans may love them once they get to know you. An objective perspective can help get you a clear opinion. Often the only way to get that is to ask the opinion of someone who doesn't have an investment in your music and can clearly see the forest from the trees. If you're able to gain some objectivity, you can avoid the fatal flaw of promoting the wrong song on your record. If you think you have too good of an ear or are too smart to fall into the trap of picking the wrong single, I will challenge both your intellect and your ear.

Why The Band Can't Choose Their Own Single - In my opinion, no one is worse at choosing which song to promote than the musicians that wrote the album. Every day, I see the tragic mistakes of musicians who could become a little more popular if they didn't pretend to be brilliant marketers and instead let someone else give them a fresh perspective. Let me count the ways why the musician's perspective on which song to promote is unbelievably flawed:

- **"My Favorite"** - Musicians constantly choose the single based on which song has their favorite part in it. Do you know how many times I've seen the drummer want to promote the song with his favorite drum fill? Musicians often think about what makes them look good or are biased because of what the song means to them, personally. This has very little bearing on what songs fans will enjoy the most.
- **Sick Of It** - Musicians get sick of their best song. Most musicians even acknowledge that they do this. You wrote a great song, but now it's six months old and you aren't as excited about it. However, to a first-time listener, the older song is way better than your newer tracks. Unfortunately, this doesn't stop musicians from wanting their newest songs to be the singles.
- **Taste** - Your musical tastes may not be in the right headspace for picking a single. There is nothing worse than when a musician first discovers the Mars Volta, Aphex Twin, Radiohead, Battles, Dillinger Escape Plan or other similar groups and starts to become "progressive." They then want to show all their "mature" material and suddenly hate their catchy songs. They think the song with the beat in 7/8 is their best one and will show the world what awesome musicians they are. Do I even need to mention how silly this is? You know what all of the musicians I listed above have in common? Even though they're known for being weird, progressive

213

and playing "musician's music," they still put their most accessible songs out to the public first. This is what gets a musician who makes adventurous music heard.

Why The Producer, Engineer Or Mixer Can't Choose It - Despite being a record producer for half of my life, I am the first to admit my flawed perspective in this situation. Producers mess up this decision but love to throw their opinion around like it's made of gold.

- **Jaded** - Producers are some of the most jaded music listeners in the business. We have heard it all, done it all, seen it, flipped it, stomped on it and reinvented it a million times. Since most music fans and passionate music listeners are young and haven't clocked half as many hours analyzing music as a producer, we tend to over-think everything.
- **"My Favorite"** - Just like musicians, we often think about which song we like our production or mix best on and want to show it off. We all get selfish and biased, just like the musicians we frown upon.
- **Sick Of It** - Like the musicians, we hear the songs a million times and lose the feeling a listener gets when they first hear a song they love. We don't know what it's like to hear the finished product for the first time since we have heard the song grow from a demo into a monster.
- **Over It** - Most producers who succeed in a given genre don't even listen to that genre too much. Usually, what makes you able to be an amazing producer is being so totally over a genre that you're an expert. Producers bring the tools of the other genres they listen to into the one you play.

Why Your Team Can't Choose It - Music business types love to claim to be the expert at this game. While there are some people with great ears in this business, many have received credit for making very obvious choices. We've all heard records with one amazing single while the rest of the record is unlistenable. To make matters worse, even if they make a poor choice, the single may succeed from the amount of promotion put into it. Then, even though the song wasn't the best choice, the record may succeed because that song was still great. Though the record might have never reached its full potential since the best song never got promoted, no one ever truly knows the difference.

Odds are your team is just as bad as the musicians and the producers: They have heard demos, rough mixes and many other incarnations of the album, so they have lost the experience of a first-time listener. Record labels suffer from the same blind spots as producers in that they have heard way too many musicians and are really jaded. To make matters worse, most team members are not in your target demographic. If you make music for young people, odds are that a lot of your team is not in your target demographic. When letting the label take charge of this decision, be sure to analyze any flaws their opinions may hold.

So, Who Should Choose It? - The fans that are actually going to buy it. The easiest way to get a great perspective on which songs you should promote is to play it for fans of your music (this doesn't mean your significant other or best friend) and some people who may potentially like your music. These listeners will have a fresh, unbiased perspective.

But, how do you find these people? Your fans are easy to find. Someone you see at your shows that you don't know too well is a perfect example. Tell them you want them to help select your new single. They'll be excited to participate and it will undoubtedly help build your fan relationship. Do this with two or three fans and they'll be ecstatic that they had the chance to be a part of music they love. Next, reach out to some fans of the musicians you previously targeted and see if they will help you decide. Do this with another three listeners and you'll have a great perspective of what potential fans think is your best material. As an added bonus, I bet you just made a few new fans.

Use The Pizza Parlor Jury To Decide Your Next Single - I remember listening to the radio when I was a teenager and always hearing the myth that whenever Bon Jovi would finish a record, they would invite fans to a pizza place to hear his new songs. They weren't doing this just to be cool to their fans, even though it really is a great promotion--they wanted their opinion on which songs should be singles on their recently recorded album. Having a listening party or a pizza parlor jury decide which songs jump out at them is a great way to pick a single and give fans an experience they will never forget.

Give Your Single To A Tastemaker - Every city has a radio station or local DJ who plays music at clubs. This person is usually one of the biggest tastemakers around. Whether it's the local club DJ, a college radio DJ or someone with an Internet radio station, it's not hard to find someone that might be into your music since so many of them exist these days.

Approach this tastemaker and ask them for input on picking your single. DJs are some of the biggest music fans around and are usually into the idea of doing this (as long you pick one that is into your genre). This will help you make a connection and a lot of the time, a new supporter. This can help get you get more radio play and hear wise advice from someone in the forefront of your music scene.

A Vision - The manager of legendary acts the Misfits and the Ramones, John Cafiero, had some further thoughts on this subject. In addition to handling these classic bands, John also makes his own music under the moniker Osaka Popstar (osakapopstar.com). He produces these songs and manages himself (along with producing, directing and editing other people's works), so he understands what it's like to be on every side of this situation. If you have ever seen the quality he maintains during a project as I have, you will know this advice to be true:

"While I agree in many cases, some managers or producers might not always be the best person to pick a single, and while the pizza parlor method might work in some circles, as a whole, in my experience a fair share of fans all have a difference of opinion, and too many cooks can leave you with a serious corrosion potion.

I firmly believe there are anomaly cases of those so invested in the acts they work with, that they do have the right sensibilities to pick the single for their artists, and do know what is in the best interest of the band, and in tune with the fan's sensibilities above most. Granted it's the anomaly, but it does exist.."

I do have to agree, and if you have seen the projects John gets involved with, you know he is this guy. There are some cases where someone involved with a project is so perfectly in tune with the direction that they are able to single-handedly make an informed, self-aware decision. But if no one has an opinion that is this well-honed, it can help to get an objective perspective.

Chapter 13: Releasing & Spreading Your Recorded Music Effectively

Once you have recorded some music, you obviously want to release it in a way that makes a big splash. Because we're in a new era of music where the way to make that happen is always evolving (and is full of competition), it's important to get educated on all your options to ensure that your music release goes as far as possible.

Solving The Problem Of Obscurity

Starting in 2018 digital download stores like iTunes & Bandcamp now sell less than streaming music. Your biggest problem and the reason you're reading this book is that you want more people to hear your music. The easiest way to solve this problem is by allowing them to hear your music, listen to it wherever they like to listen to music and begin to get addicted to it. Streaming music allows you to put no friction, border or money between you starting up a relationship with a potential fan. If you want fans, this will give you a way to turn them from casually interested listeners into light fans and possibly even grow them into super fans who buy from you on a regular basis. Remember: If a listener checks you out by downloading your music and adding it to their library (be it CD, Spotify or iTunes) -- even if they haven't decided they like you -- they are reminded of you every time they scan past your music on their music player. So your goal is to get exposed to as many listeners as possible and have them add you to their library in whatever form they prefer.

Streaming Music Can Build You A Fanbase Of Paying Customers

We should start this discussion by remember that streaming music is the gateway to a huge fanbase for every artist today. We've all seen YouTube turn a nobody into a high selling somebody with just one video. Platinum-selling musician Ed Sheeran, who was cited by MusicMetric's (musicmetric.com) torrent study as the most torrented musician of 2012, is now one of the biggest artists in the world. He sees torrents (giving away free music) as "part of promoting a record." Metric, one of DIY music's biggest successes, said, "The songs that we give away the most are the songs we sell the most of." Suzanne Vega gave away a song for free and later found that 61 percent of the fans who received that free download later made a purchase from her directly. Fitz and the Tantrums initially gave away free MP3s of their music to spread the word and went on to sell 120,000 copies of their record.

Streaming music is about exposure, which also goes for the streams on streaming subscription services. A 2014 study by the NPD Group showed that those who listen to music on the streaming service Spotify are twice as likely to buy music compared to those who don't. Music fans will buy the music and merchandise from the artists they love, but they need to be exposed to it first.

Why People Purchase Music Today
You have to remember that listeners are not buying music just to hear it and they aren't buying merchandise randomly like many other capitalistic fashion ventures. They can find tons of music to sample through countless different avenues and most merchandise isn't appealing to anyone but fans. Fans buy from musicians they feel a bond with and a sale rarely occurs for any reason other than that.

Music Is A Want Not A Need - Music fans still buy music for a few reasons. Overwhelmingly they're buying it because they want it in a convenient format they enjoy. This could be the fidelity of vinyl, a CD so they can play it on their car stereo or iTunes so it can easily get on their phone. Fans are not buying music because they are forced to; they're buying music because they want to. You can always find a way to not buy a record. But if you want it a certain way, at a certain time, you have to buy it.

Your Music Doesn't Always Have To Be Free – While many people get scared of devaluing their music if they give away free CDs or downloads on their website it's not the case. In fact, I have good news. If you give away your music for free at first, it doesn't always have to be free forever. One of MusforMGMT's former acts, Man Overboard, released their debut EP for free and gave away over 10,000 copies, both digitally and on burnt CDs. Over time--as they grew a fanbase from giving away this free music--they were able to start selling this EP to fans who heard about how great it was and 5 years later it still sells and has millions of listens on Spotify. They eventually recorded five bonus tracks and repackaged them as a collection release with the EP they had given away for free. They've since sold thousands of copies of this collection release and it sells years later.

218

The Secret of Why Many Musicians Embrace Illegal Downloads

One of the questions I often hear from musicians is, "How do you have the time to take down all the links posting your record illegally?" They're shocked when my answer is, "Who cares?" Yes, I don't care whatsoever if others download the music of the groups I work with, because I've made a decision: I would rather have as many potential fans hear the music of the groups I work with than to try to curb them from stealing it and limit our fanbase (*note: I am presenting this argument as one aimed at those who haven't grown a huge fanbase they're happy with; groups with established fanbases set up a whole new set of problems when it comes to managing illegal downloads*).

I would rather spend my time getting more people interested in the musicians I work with than spend time trying to force potential fans to discover them in the ways I wish they would (a futile endeavor, if ever there was one). I am grateful for the interest from these potential fans and the interest of fans we've already made because I know it leads to a bigger fan relationship.

If you want fans that go to shows, buy merch or purchase your music, you need to first have them become a fan. It takes tons of backbreaking work in order to get listeners to become your fans. Most musicians pay lip service to wanting as many people to hear their music as possible, yet some get mad at the idea of the same people stealing it in order to hear it and become a fan. They're angered by fans disobeying their approved methods of music consumption. I find this is counter-intuitive, since they could be making good money from other outlets while gaining more fans.

More Profitable - The profits from most records released on an indie label for upcoming musicians comes in somewhere between $1.25 and $5 per physical LP (we don't even want to get into the silliness that goes on at many of the major labels, where $1.25 is nowhere near the royalty rate). But selling concert tickets and merch can be profitable from $2 up to $15 in some cases. If you expose your music to more potential fans--letting piracy run wild--you stand the chance of seeing the fans you've converted buying concert tickets and merch that give you a higher profit margin than you would make off of an album sale.

Letting your music be a gateway to buying allows you to make fans that will keep coming back year after year, giving you money every time you do something eventful like play show or put out a new release. Taking down a link to your record is disabling the person who wants to share this link from telling their friends they should be fans of your music. It closes a gateway to continued, long-term support that is much more profitable than the one record you're trying to sell them. Friends and blogs telling their friends and followers about you is a powerful recommendation for your music that can lead to many new fans. Deleting links and taking down these files shuts down the ability for these tastemakers to do their job and tell others they should be listening to you.

Many will argue that you need the money from the sale of recording in order to have the budget to properly promote a release. Devoting time to keeping fans away from music instead of putting your time into having more of them hear it rarely yields a result that will grow your fanbase. Embrace streaming sites like Apple Music, Spotify and Tidal, which allow you to profit (minimally) from fans consuming your music. Don't spend your time thinking about how you can make less people listen to your music by taking down links and fighting torrents. Spend your time thinking about how you can get more potential fans to hear your music that will have the money to pour into other avenues that can fund your music.

A Piece Of The Puzzle - For most musicians music sales are only 5-10% of their earnings. If you are going to spend your time trying to maximize that percentage, instead of opening the doors to get more merch sales, concert attendees, licensing deals and the many other ways to make music, you are shutting down the ability to make money through many of the other avenues setting your music free enables.

Your Free Music Page
While most music is consumed on streaming site, it is still smart to have some rarities for fans on a page on your website so you can begin a relationship with them. The best tool you have for turning listeners into fans and growing the relationship from there is a free music page. You can promote this page on postcards, wristbands, stickers, your social networks and anywhere else you can possibly plaster the URL. The idea of this page is to give the listener content to grow their interest in you. Even in a streaming music world with Spotify and Apple Music converting fans to the idea they won't own music and only rent it, these pages can allow fans to "own" your music and begin a relationship with them. For listeners who have never heard you, this is a way to sample your music and become interested in being a fan. For fans that aren't yet diehard fans, this is the

content that helps them get more addicted to you and become an even bigger fan. For the already diehard fans, this is how you give back to them.

This page should contain as much free music as you can in order to give fans content to listen to and get addicted to. It should include streams of songs as well as downloads. In exchange for downloads, you can collect email addresses or trade tweets and Twitter followers. The combination of these two elements can help you build fan relationships and keep traffic coming back to your page as fans tweet out the address and tell their friends to come check it out.

Advertising this page in as many places as you can lets the world know that when they want free music they can get it from you. If you regularly update this page you can keep fans checking back to see what you're up to and your relationship with them will continue to grow. Putting the address of this page in album liner notes, social network links, bios, stickers, postcards, wristbands and anywhere else you can think of gives fans an easy way to get to you.

The Elements Of A Successful Free Music Page - There are many attributes that go into a great free music page:

- **Solid Material** - Give away free singles that will make a great first impression on a fan. These should be at the top of your page or even bundled together in a sampler.
- **Bonus Material** - Give away material that makes your existing fans happy. B-sides, alternate versions, covers, etc.
- **Stream & Download** - Make sure you have both streams and downloads, in case fans aren't on a device that can download music or just want to test out your material without committing to downloading it.
- **Trade** - Make sure you get an email address from fans that want this content, so you can continue to keep in touch and grow your relationship.
- **Spread** - Don't just use email capture widgets; you can also trade emails for Tweets so that your fans tell their friends about you in exchange for the content they receive. You can also use tools that trade Facebook "likes" for tracks as well. Many major label musicians who implore this method do it to attract viral attention to tour dates, a new release or merchandise.

Building Your Fan Relationships With Every Song Released

Every time you put out a new song, you have the potential to capture new fan contacts, stay in touch with them, develop a relationship and then have them spread the word about your music. This opportunity is another chance for someone to fall in love with your music and form a lasting relationship. In order to maximize the opportunity to take them from listener to fan, you need to employ some smart strategies.

The Follow, Subscribe, Playlist Adds & Library Adds Are The Start Of A Relationship

Today, most fan relationships begin with streaming a song on one of the many streaming platforms. Your goal is to always encourage the fans to then add you to playlists, their library or Subscribe/Follow you on their preferred streaming site. This way the fan will get updates from you and hopefully continue to build a relationship with you.

Building Fan Relationships With Email-For-A-Download Tools

Trading an email address for a track is the most powerful way to start a relationship with a fan. It allows you to keep them updated whenever you have something new to share. If you give away your music without asking for an email address, you lose the chance to stay in touch with fans and grow your relationship with them.

Stream First, Download After - It's always best to let a fan to stream a track and then allow them to download the song if they're interested. This allows them to audition your song and become a fan before they're forced to trade information with you.

Always Be Available – You have to remember fans are finicky and usually only listen to music through 1-2 methods (most likely YouTube and a streaming music service). So your music needs to be everywhere they may want it. It's crucial with each release you allow your potential to grow by putting your music on every platform possible so you can allow your relationships to grow and for fans to become addicted to your music and tell others.

Tools For Retaining Fans

The following are tools you can use to retain fans' email addresses in exchange for your content:

- **Show.co** – This service offers ways to gate YouTube, Soundcloud or Spotify content for an email address or Gate content for a Soundcloud follow. They have a free tier for a single compaign.
- **ToneDen** – ToneDen has similar features to Show.co with a free tier on up to $200 tiers for more accounts(toneden.com)
- **Distrokid Hyperfollow** – If you release your music through Distrokid they have a free service that allows you to presave Spotify albums that is worth its weight in gold.
- **TopSpin Email For Media Widget** - All a fan needs to do is enter their email and it will send them a link to whatever you're giving away--whether it be a single track or your whole record. (topspinmedia.com)
- **Bandcamp** - You can direct fans to your Bandcamp page if you have a free download there. Make sure you make them enter their email address to get the track. (bandcamp.com)
- **NoiseTrade** - NoiseTrade will allow your fans to either get a free download or name their own price. (noisetrade.com)
- **Fanbridge Video Gating** - Fanbridge has a video gating tools that allow you to collect email addresses from fans in order to watch your video. (fanbridge.com)
- **Tweet For A Download** - If you have a bunch of content and you've already traded emails for downloads, you can also trade Tweets for downloads. This will allow your fans to get your song in exchange for tweeting about it with a link to your free music page, introducing their friends to your music. Employing this, along with an email for download tool, can help keep traffic coming to your free music page. Most of these tools will also have the fan follow you on Twitter in exchange for this download, keeping them connected to you and updated about your happenings.
- **MailChimp** – While a bit complicated you can trade a song for an email through MailChimp automation, but it is free until you have 2,000 email addresses.

Some Common Ways To Build Fan Relationships Through Song Downloads
One of the greatest feelings is to post a new song, capture a fan's email address and then look at all the email addresses of the fans you have sold music to and see the same names. This shows the relationship of your fanbase is growing and you can watch it grow through your analytics. Below are a few scenarios of how you can start this relationship and begin to watch this happen.

Blog Posts - Getting a blog to link back to your free music page or embed a stream that has an email-for-a-download widget can allow you to capture interested potential fans. If you're pitching a blog to post a stream or video of your music, be sure to try to get them to embed your widget.

YouTube - Putting the address of where a fan can download a track for an email in your YouTube description is a great way to grow this relationship. I can't tell you how many times I've put up a song on YouTube that has a link to an email-for-a-download widget and then seen the addresses collected from the widget turn into paying customers.

SoundCloud - You can use the same technique described for YouTube on SoundCloud.

Website / Free Music Page - Just have a simple email signup page that offers fans a song or sampler in exchange for their email address.

Upselling - Remember, if you want to do more than expose your fans to your music and profit from this, you need to present them with items they can then buy from you. If they like your music and become addicted to it, they will most likely buy music and merch from you--if you show them where they can get it.

Using Streaming Music Effectively To Build A Fanbase

Understanding How Streaming Music Builds A Fanbase By Giving It What It Wants To See

So while we just talked a lot about downloading music, it is mostly to give you an education on how listener's consume music so you can make good strategic decisions in your marketing. Today, streaming is the most consequential way a fanbase is built. The algorithms and the way streaming sites reward artists is crucial to building a fanbase as it will deliver your music to more fans that are likely to enjoy your music than any method you can get by spending no money or for that matter even tens of thousands of dollars. So, what do we do to take advantage of streaming music?

Release More Singles – Singles are the name of the game today and even if you are the type of artist who's fans need an album for you to be considered an artist of merit, you still need to release more singles BEFORE your album is released if you want to take advantage of the algorithms. Many acts now release 5 singles before their album comes out and sometimes the whole album comes out as singles and gets wrapped up in a package at the end. Since YouTube's subscription feed will put you in front of more eyes, along with Spotify's Release Radar and social media announcements your existing fans are reminded of you more often and therefore your chances of getting attention go up. But that it isn't even the biggest part of it. For every follower you have on Spotify, they present you to one new fan in Discover Weekly. YouTube rewards you since they look for artists who are putting up consistent content their viewers watch to the end. Since Spotify and YouTube are the number one- and two-ways fans take in new music this is crucial.

Focus Tracks- Have you ever noticed the artists you love don't always release their best tracks as the first track? This is called a focus track and since Spotify and YouTube reward consistent content what many marketers do is release a song that reminds fans to follow an artist but really they are gearing up for the fact that fans are going to see the artists name more often and by the time the second and third single are released potential fans are curious what all the fuss is about and now they hear the superior material and can go back and hear other songs and get addicted to the artist. The artist is intentionally not putting their best foot forward in hopes that the best impression is yet to come.

Consistent, Sustained Singles – What I advise every new artist to do is release a new single every 6 weeks for 12-18 months which when figuring in holidays that accounts for 8 songs a year or 12 over 18 months. In order to take advantage of algorithms and your potential audiences interest I encourage the release of first a stream of the song and a single frame video on YouTube. 2 weeks later a lyric video should be released and two weeks after that release a music video. This allows YouTube to recognize you are releasing music regularly and for fans to see you are eventful and an artist that is continually feeding them and they should keep up with you.

Chapter 14: Planning Your Press Strategy

Once you have some music recorded, you need to effectively release it to the public in order to gain more fans. It takes some smart strategy and planning to make your promotions go as far as possible.

The Album Cycle

Releasing new music is the biggest chance you have to grow your fanbase and get attention from new fans. Despite the fact that most musicians don't put much thought into the album cycle, understanding it is essential if you want to successfully promote your music and grow your fanbase.

When you put out new music, you need to have a plan for how you will continually promote so that it keeps increasing in popularity over at least nine months, as opposed to the death most albums suffer after only 30 days. Your album--as well as your song releases--are your biggest chance to make huge leaps in popularity. Let me put this even more intensely – **Your biggest chance to gain fans comes down to the strategy and execution around each release.** You need to make sure you plan how to sustain your promotions as best you can.

Dead Conventional Wisdom: Caring More About First Week Sales Than Nine Months Later
Many labels still base the emphasis of everything they do for a record on first week sales. They tend to give up on acts that don't perform to their standards in a one-week competition against other releases in the same week. While this may matter for Top 40 acts, it's totally irrelevant for anything outside of that world. Even if you put out the record of the year and make the *Dark Side Of The Moon* of our generation, you want to have a sustained campaign of sales for months on end. *Dark Side* is actually the perfect example of what you want your record to be: An album that breaks all records and stays on the charts seemingly forever--not a record judged by having an amazing first week.

The record with the second-longest chart run (after *Dark Side*) is Guns N' Roses *Appetite For Destruction*. Twenty-five years after its release, *Appetite* still has never had a week where it sold fewer than 5,000 copies! The funny thing about this record is it took some time to catch on. The band was basically unheard of when this debut album was released and its first single, "Welcome To The Jungle," stalled. Now no one remembers this, since the single found a new life after the record caught on and was pushed to radio a second time nearly a year later. It took almost nine months into their album cycle before they released "Sweet Child O' Mine" and the record started to see a serious increase in sales. Millions of album sales later, the world forgets that if their label had given up on them and stopped the relentless promotion--after lackluster early sales--they would be missing out on one of the biggest sellers and most important records in rock history.

More recently, Macklemore only started to achieve big chart success after "Thrift Shop" was released, being the fifth single off *The Heist*. This means it took 5 separate pushes, after almost two years before the album had a #1 song. When climbing the mountain of promotion – especially while doing it yourself – remember, this is a long game and you need to put sustained effort for the pay offs you want to receive.

Don't Post Teasers!@!#$!!!
If there is one thing that has come to crashing death in the attention economy, it is the practice of posting teasers when you are an artist that has a small fanbase. The fact is with so much going on each day every time you can get your audience's attention it should be taken advantage of to its fullest extent. When you post a teaser the chances of anyone making a reminder to check back is under 0.01% and you have lost a chance of having someone's attention to get them to become addicted to your music. Save all of your promo for after you have a release out and if you have more than a single release out, be sure to always link them to a playlist which will keep them listening to you so they can develop a bond and addiction to your music.

Consistent Sustained Promotion
Big labels often go guns blazing trying to ensure a record has a strong first week, but then have spent most of their budget by the time the album actually starts gaining traction. Most musicians who build a fanbase and go on to be legends in their genre accomplish it through a sustained push, not necessarily an amazing first week showing. Was the most important week

for Taking Back Sunday's *Tell All Your Friends*, Tame Impala *Currents,* DeadMau5 *Random Album Title or* Phoenix's *Wolfgang Amadeus* (their fourth record, I might add) the first week? No. It took months to ramp up the buzz and establish their following. For some acts it even took a few records to make them the huge sellers they are today. This sustained promotion is what sets them up to do a strong debut on their next release--a concept that's often forgotten when promotions budgets are blown on making a strong first week.

A perfect example of how this sustained promotion works well is the recent success of Gotye, whose record came out in the US in August of 2011 and peaked at No. 1 in the US in April of 2012. He went from being a nobody to a somebody after a sustained push of a single for months on end. Brockhampton, believed in their single "Sugar" enough to release 3 different videos for it, one remix and continue the push on it for over 6 months to push it to have millions of streams. Usually, a musician's first release is not the one that brings them success, but with sustained promotion, you will have a release down the road that puts you out in front of everyone.

It's the Internet age and if you are promoting a song no one can hear yet when you're not yet an artist people are waiting on every move of, you are wasting attention that is very hard to come by today. In fact, attention has never been harder to get since so many people know how to demand it, so if you actually get it from someone it should be as optimized as possible. Let's get over the idea of promoting a record to death to get that strong first week--it's a dead idea in the age of the Internet. Invest in promoting your record over time and don't think about competing with every record that's coming out the same day. The shelf life is as long as you can sustain a buzz, not the length of time a CD gets dusty on a shelf before it gets returned to a distributor. Make sure you budget your promotions so the first week isn't most important thing in the world. If you have a record fans are enjoying, make sure there's money to keep gaining fans over the entire cycle of your album.

Planning Your Next Release & How To Stay In The News Cycle For Longer
There's a bell curve when it comes to the interest fans have in your record. There is a certain amount of time leading up to the release and during the album cycle that where this album is the most important way for you to make new fans. But after a while, it becomes a back-catalog release,

losing importance to prospective fans. One of the keys to a successful record is making the top of this curve sustain itself for as long as possible.

When I say planning a release, I mean going above and beyond the obvious promotions every musician does. Most musicians simply decide that they're going to release their record, possibly tour and play some shows, maybe make a video and put out some songs as "singles" and post them a few months apart on their social networks. This is about as exciting to your fans as watching paint dry. If you want to make a huge mark with your next release, think about this curve and everything you can do to sustain the peaks of it keeping fans' interest. Put some thought into keeping this peak going and keeping fans talking about your music. Think about how you make a sustained promotion that stays strong for months instead of hitting its high point during the week of release.

Smaller Releases, More Frequently
We previously discussed the idea that your promotions can only go as far as the quality of your last recording. With that in mind, why not increase your chances of going far by putting out new songs more often? If you want to buck the idea of the album cycle and the music business that lives and dies by it, you can do this easily by putting out smaller releases more frequently.

In this age of disappearing gatekeepers, the Internet makes it easier for every musician to be heard by the world. The lifespan of an album is now smaller than ever since there are more musicians competing for fans' attention. While there are some exceptions with records that can still push singles two years down the road, most small or mid-sized musicians are lucky if they can get anyone to pay attention to their records three to six months later.

One way to solve this is to put out releases more often. Getting regular press coverage helps you stay in the news cycle and gives your fans fresh material more often. We've all seen musicians lose their fans' interest by taking too long to release new material. This goes tenfold for musicians targeting teenagers, since 18 months later they will have moved on to the next trend.

The Hype Machine - The best examples of this technique in action are modern dance acts that release one-off singles to blogs, helping them stay in the news cycle on a regular basis. Look at most of the top musicians on

Hype Machine (hypem.com). Most of them never go more than two months without posting a new track or remix. What you often see with dance acts on that site is that every month they either put out a remix, a DJ mix or an original track--keeping them relevant in this fast-paced blog news cycle. The big musicians getting all the buzz at the moment are the musicians who put out one or more tracks every month, keeping themselves on everyone's radar and generating more press with each track.

Taking two years between releases might as well be called 700 blog years--meaning you have been out of the news cycle for an eternity. There's so much music pushed on fans these days that, when you consider how painstaking it is to make a record, it makes sense to make smaller releases. The benefits work in your favor when it comes to profit, press and giving your fans a steady diet of music that they appreciate. Get with the times, because the times have already changed.

This is also smart financially. Let's say you're selling your LPs for $10 and your EPs for $6. You make a little extra money if you can sell a fan two EPs instead of one LP, and you retain their attention over a longer period of time. In these tough financial times, fans are more likely to buy cheap content, even if it doesn't have as much value. Releasing new material throughout the year will help all of your releases get press and get you to the ears of more fans. The lower entry fee will also help, since it's cheaper and less of a discouraging price for new fans. If you offer a quality product by employing this method, you can expect to see your fanbase grow.

Living Proof - When I was working with Man Overboard, there was a point when we released 51 songs in about 18 months. That sounds pretty insane, right? This high output is what kept the group in the news cycle all the time and gave their fans a body of work to digest and share--keeping fans excited on a regular basis. Did it help that the Nik the bassist/singer had his own studio, or that since I was their manager we could also record new stuff in my studio? Absolutely. They also had a prolific songwriter in Zac, which was the main reason we were able to make this happen. But this extends to other groups like Brockhampton (who admittedly have tons of members) released 78 songs in less than 4 years.

No matter what the circumstances, there's no doubt in my mind this was one of the reasons the group was able to get a large fanbase so fast. We were being written up and talked about a lot for a young band and had an oddly huge discography for fans to get excited about. Don't underestimate how much regular doses of material can get the world buzzing and keep your fans happy and enthused.

Exceptions - There is an exception to small releases being the key to success. There are some bands that live and die with full-length releases. Wilco, Radiohead, The Shins, Green Day, etc., are all bands that are expected to make genius albums. While smaller releases can really help smaller bands get noticed, it doesn't work if you're the type of band who needs to impress their audience with a large statement like an LP. Some bands are never recognized for their greatness until they can assemble a coherent LP, no matter how great their singles are. While singles can help establish a fanbase early on, some bands will never be truly recognized until they can assemble an amazing full-length.

Take this technique and apply it however you will. Release new singles in between albums. Make a follow-up EP of B-sides between each album. Release a new single bi-weekly or whatever. No matter what, implementing some small releases into your plan is a smart move.

Compile Singles To Make A Record
Many musicians worry about not having an LP to promote or profit from financially, even though releasing singles one at a time can undoubtedly get you more attention. One solution is to have patience and when you have enough material, compile all the singles you released into an LP. You can always record a handful of new songs for the release, which will give existing fans a reason to purchase it. You can also look at this compilation as a way to get reviews, make some news and introduce your music to new listeners who didn't check out the singles. It also gives fans a chance to get songs they may have missed.

More Chances To Be Discovered
The most popular way passionate music fans discover music today is through algorithms. So it makes sense to structure your release strategy around catering to them. Algorithmic playlists are giving an advantage to artists who release singles regularly. With Spotify's New Music Radar, Discover Weekly Playlists and both Spotify and Apple Music's email blasts about new releases or YouTube recommendations, these are some of the most popular ways avid music fans discover music, these playlists look at your tastes and suggest what you may like based on what you have listened to in the past and similar listeners. These playlists add on songs from new releases, so each time you release a song you have another

chance to get on it. Whereas when you release an album you lose this chance for your songs to be a marketing tool.

Spotify says it presents your music to 4 times the amount of followers you have on the service, so if you are releasing singles regularly and accumulate followers you have a far better chance of gaining new fans through their algorithm, especially if you are releasing songs often.

Staying In The News Cycle: Consistent, Sustained Promotion

Promoting your music successfully is a long haul. It's not just about promoting for a month before and after your latest release. Every successful musician promotes every day for years on end until the world has heard so much from them that they're tired of it. Then they can finally take a few months off. If you're planning to build a fanbase, you need to be thinking of promotional ideas many months ahead of time, not for just a few weeks around a big event. It never stops. Coming up with ideas that keep raising awareness of your music is one of the most crucial elements that go into building a fanbase.

Why Would Your Fans Tell Their Friends About This Promotion?
Whenever you are thinking of a new promotion to do for your music, make sure to ask yourself, "Why would my fans tell their friends about this promotion?" Give them something worth talking about that is eventful and interesting enough to want to tell their friends who don't know about your music and you will see tons of listeners checking you out.

Do Something Weekly And Something Eventful Every Month
Apple Music's Ian Rogers is a big evangelist for a theory that many publicists have been suggesting for years. If you want potential fans to discover your music, bring it up again and again. This will get your name seen constantly by potential fans, inviting curiosity and eventually getting them to listen to your music. If you release an EP with six songs and one single this year, you'll see a good amount of coverage once during the whole year. But if you're putting out a song every couple of months, you have the potential for writers to be writing about you every time you put out a single. This also means fans won't only hear about your progress as a

musician once a year, but that you can keep winning over fans as you get better and better.

When you hear about a marketing plan, this is a lot of it. You should have ideas for eventful promotions you can announce every week for months to come. The smaller events can be YouTube updates, a big show, a cover song you recorded, some cool new merch, a DJ mix or whatever clever idea you can think of that will excite your fans. The big events are a new single, album, video, tour or special event. Figuring out how to place these events in your calendar can keep your momentum going and keep your fanbase growing. If you're looking for ideas on what to do, the rest of this book is riddled with them. Coming up with eventful promotions you feel will work for your music is the most important part of building your event calendar.

Make It A Calendar
When I work with a band, we have a Google Calendar titled "Press." Every entry on it lasts a week and it says what we're doing each week to promote the band's music. For that week we focus on promoting one event, that we hope will excite fans and continue to get the word spread. Once a month (sometimes every three to five weeks), we do a big promotion: Release a record, video, tour or announce huge news like a new record label signing, etc. We may promote that event for more than a month at time, but in between you'll be doing other promotions every week that help keep your name in the news cycle. These events should help raise awareness by making them the type of events both fans and press write about. An example of a calendar is below:

- **Week 1 Big Announcement:** We started recording our new album. We send out this announcement to press and tell fans.
- **Week 2:** In-studio video update--posted to social networks.
- **Week 3:** Announce a contest to come to the studio.
- **Week 4:** Announce winner of contest and post video of them there.
- **Week 5 Big Announcement:** New album is done. We're going out on tour to promote this record. Here are the dates--sent out to everyone.
- **Week 6:** Post another video from the studio.
- **Week 7:** Hold a chat with fans about new record.
- **Week 8:** Announce pre-order, track listing and album art.
- **Week 9: Big Announcement:** Pre-Order is up, release first song from new record.

- **Week 10:** Release lyric video of first single.
- **Week 11:** Post to YouTube a behind the scenes video for the record.
- **Week 12:** Release acoustic video of a song from the record to a blog where you trade a download for a download.
- **Week 13: Big Announcement:** Record is now out. Post single frame videos of every song from the record on YouTube.
- **Week 14:** Play record release show, start tour.
- **Week 15:** Post all the awesome interviews and reviews you have done.
- **Week 16:** Tour update video.
- **Week 17 Big Announcement:** Music video for first single is out.
- **Week 18:** Announce contest to come to your lead singer's family reunion as his date.
- **Week 19:** Release remix of first single.
- **Week 20:** Tour ends, release another video update from it including sneak preview of a new song you played one night.
- **Week 21 Big Announcement:** Post full concert video from last tour. Announce your new tour and post video from your last tour, showing fans why they don't want to miss this one.
- **Week 22:** Post lyric video of all of the songs from your new album on YouTube.
- **Week 23:** Post video of you doing a new, alternate version of a song from the record.
- **Week 24:** Announce DJ set you'll be broadcasting to the web and then have the recording of it posted to a blog for download.
- **Week 25 Big Announcement:** Announce giveaway of new single in conjunction with the release of the music video for it.

Creating all of this press takes a lot of time and effort and in all likelihood you'll have to re-arrange the order of events. Every musician will do this a little differently. The first week of your campaign may even start two months before you start a crowdfunding campaign. Many of these announcements may not work for you, but with some time and imagination you can make a similar calendar of your own that's effective in keeping you in the news, gaining new fans and raising awareness.

Attention Explosions – Some acts like to come out with a very big bang and seemingly be everywhere with content for a few days. Announcing an online game, then a video, then a weird ad campaign all in the matter of a week or two. This can be great to get a groundswell of attention, but it does often grab a lot of attention that you then have to sustain for another 9 months or more and makes that much harder to sustain.

The Newest Way Bands Are Using This Calendar
A common trend I have seen with many acts who are going from playing small clubs to 1,500 seat venues by the time their first album is released is to use the power of getting regular attention on social media and gearing their releases towards discovery algorithms. They do this by making every song a three legged six week event that they often do for a year to a year and a half where they finally collect the best songs along with a few unreleased tracks onto an LP once the buzz has swelled demand for the artist to make a big statement like an album.

The method I see in this release strategy is they first release a stream of the song, then two weeks later a lyric video, then two weeks after that a music video. Sometimes they will even put up remixes for the song every two weeks after that if they really want to push the song. This creates a groundswell since they are continually staying in the news cycle and demanding attention, while getting put on discover playlists regularly.

To spell this out more clearly:
- **Event One: The Single Screen/Streaming Release** – Release your single on all streaming platforms along with a single screen video.
- **Event Two: Lyric Video** – 1-2 weeks after you premier your single follow it up with another reason for fans to listen again with a lyric video.
- **Event Three: The Music Video** – Depending on your press calendar, release the music video for your song to spread the song further and give another eventful reminder to fans to listen to your single again.

Many of these acts delay the release of a debut EP or LP with a string of singles for over a year as they find their sound and use the Internet news cycle to continually keep them top of mind. This harnesses every element of how attention works presently and there's a reason I see tons of groups utilizing it. This year alone I have seen massive artists like Billie Eilish, Pale Waves and countless "SoundCloud Rappers" use it to rise to prominence. I personally suggest this to every single group I work with now.

236

Episodic Releases – Many artists are starting to string their videos or other content into a narrative so it is released in episode forms so you are encouraged to discuss it, anticipate it and follow along longer. Particularly with videos and putting together pieces in picture content.

But I Have No Fans, Press Contacts Or Means Of Touring? - You should still follow this pattern. Instead, make a big deal out of your local shows. Make live videos from your sets, record cover videos--create as much content as you can for potential fans to dig into. Release a new song once a month, so that you have the chance for new fans to hear about you as often as possible and begin accumulating material for potential fans to dig into when they find you. It's hard for you to become someone's favorite musician if you only have two songs. You'll then have reason to keep trying your hand at getting written about on the blogs you target. Getting material out early--in a steady schedule--can help keep you in the news cycle.

Ideas For Staying In The News Cycle With Releases

Release a Hype EP

The speed of the Internet news cycle has brought on a need for up and coming musicians to release music more often in short bursts, so they stay on the minds of their fans and the music media. If you're a touring act, the prospect of releasing three-song EPs can be nauseating since LP sales account for a good amount of a touring act's revenue. While you want to stay in the news cycle, if you aren't making enough money to cover recording and touring costs, your plans will become irrelevant. If you're married to the idea of putting out an LP or even an EP of six or more songs, the "hype EP" is a great way to get a little more mileage out of your next release and still be able to reap the rewards of an LP.

So what is a hype EP? It's a release of three to five songs that will appear on your next full-length. This will get the buzz going about a current release and offer you the chance to get excitement brewing for your upcoming LP. You'll still have the forthcoming larger release to sell on tour, but you'll also have a means to get more press and fan excitement before it comes out. This EP is usually only released digitally to save money on pressing physical copies.

Some will tell you that your fans will get pissed that they're buying the same songs a second time when they buy your hype EP and then your LP. There are easy ways to fix this problem. Since they are already your fans, you can offer them the songs not on the EP but as a pack from your direct-to-fan sites for a reduced price. You can make this special release priced lower than iTunes, since your profit margin is higher if you sell your music directly.

Another way to make the EP more worthwhile to fans is to add extra content like bonus tracks, live tracks, acoustic versions, remixes, etc. You can offer this bonus content on either the hype EP or the LP, depending on which one you want to aim the incentive towards.

The hype EP not only works to get hype for your release but can also work to raise some extra funds to promote your upcoming release. You can take the money from the sales of this EP and put it into further promotion of your LP.

When Your Record's Value Expires, Use It As A Promotional Tool
It's always a sad day when you check out your record sales and see numbers that were once steady have now stalled. Obviously, the first thing to do is get ready to start recording a new album (if you haven't already), but the next consideration you should make is how to get some extra mileage out of your last release. If fans are no longer buying your old record, consider that it may have lost its original value. Logically, the best thing to do is to set it free. Instead of letting all those copies sit around in your closet (or your endless digital closet), make the record available for free, allowing it to gain interest in your next recording. Accepting that your record has lost value can be a tough thought to swallow but realizing that it can still have value in helping to spread the word about your music can be an empowering prospect. It can also help your next record gain even more value.

Make one of your recent releases free for a few months on a site like Bandcamp while the press rush ramps up for your next release. While you're getting tons of attention for your new release, fans will have more to bite into and an easy way to get some more music from you. This allows fans to get a taste of your music and, like an addict, get hooked and excited for your next release. Acknowledge when your release has lost the value it once had and give it a new price tag in order to move more copies and better set up your next release.

Deluxe Edition – You can also cure your record's diminished value by releasing a deluxe edition, which can call attention to you. If you have B-sides laying around you never put out or a few songs that don't fit your next album's sound you can always gain a bit of attention at the end of an album cycle with a deluxe edition.

Other Releases You Can Put Out
Putting out releases is one of the most eventful ways to stay in the news cycle. Below are some ideas that your fans will love to spread the word about:

- **Singles** - Obviously, the easiest way to get press is to put up a one-off single.
- **Compilation** - Compile B-Sides, singles, demos or spare tracks.
- **Covers** - Make a covers record. This always seems to be a fan favorite if you can make great versions of some past tunes.
- **Remix Record** - Fans are always eager to hear a re-imagining of a familiar song.
- **Live Record** - This may interest casual fans and listeners who are "on the fence" about whether or not they like your music. It may even help bring more fans to your shows since it can show that you're not merely a product of "studio magic."
- **Acoustic/Stripped Down Record** - Fans still continue to respond well to the courage some musicians show by letting their songs speak for themselves and "letting it all hang out."
- **Collaboration -** Work with a musician who brings a new element to your songs.

Give Fans Content To Chew On With Podcasts
While podcasts are usually reserved for nerds talking about news and other nerdy things, musicians can use them too. After all, a podcast is an audio or video file that is 30 to 120 minutes long, available through a free subscription--making it a very open format. They're regularly delivered to your fans via an RSS feed or the podcast provider of their choice (usually iTunes). You'll want to make a theme for your podcast and give your fans a format they've come to expect. Here are some ideas for podcasts that you can do:

- **DJ Set** - Dance music stars like Sebastian Ingrosso, Avicii, Tiesto and Eric Prydz all do podcasts that give a preview to what they're DJing in upcoming sets. This can help fans get excited to go hear this amazing mix loud in the club.
- **Influences** - Diplo's Mad Decent podcast is always a surprise: He chooses a theme and introduces his fans to a whole new style of underground music. I listen to his punk rock mix all the time. Showing fans where you come from and a look at what you're interested in can do wonders for your relationship with your fans.
- **Mixtapes** - With Man Overboard we would issue "Defend Pop Punk Mixtapes." The band would play music from other bands they were friends with and who were a part of their movement. They would tell stories of fun times with these bands and give them an endorsement. The fans of the bands on the mixtape and our fans would all download it, spreading the word around and growing everyone's fanbase.
- **Talk Show** - Host a talk show. Interview your friends. Make it like a variety show. Get comedians on, do skits, whatever. The possibilities are endless.
- **Exclusive** – You can make a podcast and only give the feed to fans that are in a fan club or subscribe to your Patreon.

After you create a podcast you need to get it so others can listen. SimpleCast (simplecast.com) is the best tool for professional podcasters but Anchor.FM's free tool can be great for those who don't want to commit to much. Put your Podcasts up on Soundcloud or even Bandcamp (you'll have to break it up into parts for Bandcamp) to make sure all your fans see them. You can trade emails or tweets for downloads of the Podcast or give it away. No matter what this free content is appreciated.

Album Commentary Tracks
Fans always love the stories behind songs, especially if they're good stories told in the musician's own voice. Lately, album commentary tracks on streaming sites like Apple Music and Spotify are another approach. These can easily be recorded by speaking into a microphone in GarageBand and then sent to a blog to get a feature, embedded on your album stream on streaming services or traded for email addresses/tweets. No matter what, album commentary is content many musicians use as added content to give fans a deeper look into their releases. As long as you can tell a compelling story about each of your songs, these tracks are easy to make and enjoyable for fans.

Hip-Hop Mixtapes

In the world of hip-hop, one of the most powerful tools to spread your music is the mixtape. Sometimes called "street albums," these mixtapes are released without the help of a label to get out of contractual obligations and to avoid dealing with copyright laws on sampled material. No matter what the intent, they have long been the way underground talent gets discovered in hip-hop and are an essential part of promoting your music in this world. Make sure you give a track listing for any music you use so that fans can discover new music from it.

Mixtape Hosts - Below are some sites that will host your mixtape and help get spread the word:

- **Datpiff** - Well-respected source to download mixtapes. (datpiff.com)
- **LiveMixtapes** - Another host for your mixtape. (livemixtapes.com)

Not Just Hip-Hop - Personally, I would like to see more musicians outside the world of hip-hop embrace releases like this. It's easy to have musicians drop different interpretations on one another's material. You can add new elements to pre-existing songs, do remixes, etc.

iBook's

Apple's iBook Author (free in the Mac App Store) gives you the ability to author an insanely in-depth experience for fans. While these are in a book format, you can do many cool things with them like include intensive graphic design, art, photo galleries and videos. You can also link to content you have littered across the Internet. This can be great if you want to make footnotes for what your lyrics mean or write references for fans to gain a greater understanding of your message. The bad news is they only work on iOS devices or a Mac, so it will exclude a portion of your fanbase that doesn't own these devices.

Personalized Songs For Fans

A cool way to build bonds with your fans is to write personalized songs. Allow fans to choose the topic, then you'll write and deliver a song to them. Max Bemis of Say Anything has done this to great effect with The Max Bemis Song Shop (maxbemissongshop.com). Not only will this be something your fans cherish for a long time, it can build an intense bond that fans will share with everyone they know. As an added bonus, it can help you turn a profit.

Tour Diaries
If you go to a huge arena tour, you may get what's called a concert book: An expensive colorful book with writing and pictures all about the tour. The good news is that you don't need to be an arena rocker to make this happen. Simply compile some pictures from your tour and some writing and you can print it or sell it in e-book format to all your fans that saw you while you were out. Services like 48HrBooks (48hourbooks.com) can make you awesome, inexpensive books that look great.

DJ Sets
Many blogs are happy to post a DJ set from you. Simply record it and post the audio file to a site like SoundCloud and you'll have another way to stay in the news cycle. You can also host a DJ set live on a streaming video service and then release it for others to listen later. If you add unreleased material to the set, it will gain all the more attention. Fans of all genres will appreciate this.

Mashups
Everyone loves mashups. Every time someone combines two songs that shouldn't seemingly belong together into a coherent piece of music, the world is stunned. There are no rules when it comes to mashups except to make something that sounds cool. Sadly, they're usually illegal since you're not authorized to use the track. This doesn't mean you can't post a mash-up on a rogue blog or SoundCloud...at least until you get in trouble. If you think the world will love the mash-up of your latest single and Jenna Rose's "My Jeans," then have at it: Maybe it will get you some attention.

Using Remixes To Promote Your Music

The power of a remix is infinite. They can take a song the world is lukewarm on and create a new and vibrant buzz around it. The remix of a song is often the version that the world knows. Whether you're the person remixing a track or the person getting your song remixed, this re-contextualization can do a world of good for getting your name and music spread further than it could have in its original form.

Crossover

Getting a single to appeal to more than one genre has always been one of the keys to successfully marketing a track. At some point in the 80s, the music industry realized that there was crossover appeal from genre to genre among most singles. The label could market the original version of a song toward one market and the remix version of the song toward another. This trend has always continued and today you may have a several remixes of the same song on a remix release.

Name Recognition

One of the benefits of a remix is introducing your music to another crowd. If your music is remixed by someone else, you're introduced to their following and their fans see your name and learn about your music. You also introduce the remixer to your crowd by promoting this version. Not only is it a great way to give your songs a new life, it allows you to introduce other musicians to your crowd and vice-versa.

I'm Not Sold

You may be thinking, "What good does having a dance remix do for my indie rock band?" A lot. If the remix of your song gets lots of plays, there are tons of potential fans that will investigate the original. And if they have diverse tastes, they may become fans of your music. It also makes your name familiar to more people. While the whole world was discovering Gotye in 2012, I had known to give him a chance since I'd heard an incredible remix Ocelot had done for him years before he broke through. Fans will often hear a singer's voice and want more of it, only to find a whole catalog waiting for them to discover. Remixes can open plenty of doors for you.

It Is For Everyone - A lot of musicians think their music shouldn't be remixed or won't work in this context. When I hear Gotye and Adele being pumped on dance floors, I start to question the limits on which songs can be remixed. You may be morally against remixes and that's fine--but never underestimate the limits of how far your music can travel when it's reimagined by a talented remixer.

You Can Remix Too

Remixing songs is an easy way to get paid, get your name out there and easily finish a song (it sure is easy to write a song when the hook is already established). In an age where it's important to constantly feed your fans new music, remixes are an easy way to get that done. All you need to do is put your interpretation on what you think another song should sound like.

How To Encourage Remixes
If you want your music to be remixed, the best way to get it done is to make the files be available for download by anybody and everybody. Tell everyone you can about them, alert the press, do your social media thing and label it clearly on your website. Below is a list of what you should give potential remixers to work with. It's smart to ask your mix engineer for these files while you're mixing your song if you know you want to go down the remixing road.

- **The Session** - Groups like Nine Inch Nails and Phoenix have allowed their fans to download full multi-track files from their sessions. This can enable your music to be used in all sorts of new contexts, creating endless incarnations of your music that are easily spread.
- **Stems** - The most common way to feed potential remixers is to give them four to eight sub mixes of instruments to work with in a remix.
- **Instrumental & A Capella** - Most common in hip-hop, you can give instrumental and a capella tracks for remixers to use.
- **BPM & Key** - If you want to be helpful, include the BPM and the key you recorded the song in, to make your remixer's life easier.

Open Sourcing - By releasing the stems or multi-tracks to your record, you'll allow your music to take on new life while getting a burst of press. You open up an endless amount of possibilities for your music to be used by others and allow the world become more aware of you. The possibilities literally become endless once you set your music free.

Hosting - Once you have all of these files together, you need a way to get them to potential remixers. Here are some ideas of how to do that:

- **FTP** - Post them on your website and enable download via FTP.
- **TopSpin** - TopSpin allows you to make download links or even trade the stems for an email address. You can zip them or give away individual files.
- **SoundCloud** - You can post each stem (best to not do a full multi-track) as a downloadable SoundCloud stream on your feed.

- **STEMS** – Native Instruments has introduced a new format for delivering remix parts. (nativeinstruments.com)

Commissioning

Open Sourcing is an open call for remixers, but what if you don't want to be so open and only give your files to the few remixers you have in mind? That is totally fine. While I think you should get as many remixes as you can to get your name out there, it can also be good to contact only those you know will do a great job. Simply contact the musicians you'd like to do the remixes. But remember, this is a world where people are used to getting paid for their work. Remixes can often cost thousands of dollars, so be prepared to shell out some serious cash if you reach out to bigger names.

If you're going for remixers who you're not friendly with and they're asking for a lot of money, you can try to sweeten the deal for them. Explain the promotion going into the remix and offer shares in the profits and/or publishing. You have some bargaining chips: Use what you can if you really want the remix.

Indaba Music - Indaba Music (indabamusic.com) is a forum that allows musicians to host and participate in remixing, composing and mixing contests with musicians both big and small. These contests offer cool prizes and can give you a chance to get press for your remix skills. They also allow you to encourage artists to remix your music so you can gather press that way.

Collecting - Once you have some remixes, you can let the creators put them up on their own pages or you can do some extra promoting. It's not uncommon to release a single with multiple versions of a song or even a whole record with the best remixes for each song on the record. You can release this as a record or compile them as a SoundCloud playlist and post it around the web. Give the good remixes you get as much promotion as you can between you and your newfound collaborator.

Doing A Successful Pre-Order For Your Record

If you've achieved some success with a few thousand fans on your social networks, it may be a good idea to do a pre-order for your next record. This can be a nice press bump for your new record and raise funds to promote your album after its release day, which can be a nice asset after having plunked down tons of cash for recording and setting up your release. Starting a pre-order four to six weeks before your album release, complete with different tiers of packages for all different types of fans, can raise funds and give you a chance to sell your superfans some cool packages.

Doing these pre-orders through your direct-to-fan method can help acquire fan emails and get fans to your website so they're trained to go there for information about you throughout this upcoming album cycle. It can also help improve profits, since you're cutting out the fees of stores and vendors.

Tiered Packages
When doing a pre-order, it's important that you allow fans to purchase packages of varying cost. This means having different packages priced in different ranges, with more and more incentives as they go up the price ladder. Start pre-order packages in the $5 to $10 range and have one or two packages in the $20 to $25 range. You'll also want to have a high-priced option for those fans willing to go all-out for you. Having your highest tier be priced in the $75 to $100 market can ensure you can gain profits from super fans. Below is a list of common packages that musicians will do.

- **Point 1** - The entry-level package is usually just a digital download. You can include a bonus track to encourage fans to buy direct from you.
- **Point 2** - Digital with CD for a slightly higher price.
- **Point 3** - If you have vinyl for this release, include it here with a digital download.
- **Point 4** - Your digital download, a T-shirt and the fan's choice of physical format.
- **Point 5** - A special piece of merch and everything else in Point 4.
- **Point 6** - Another special piece of merch, usually with a limited quantity and high price tag. Everything in the previous packages will usually be included.

Incentive Ideas
Below are some ideas on items you can include in your pre-order.

- **Bonus Tracks** - The most common incentive to get fans to order an album in advance.
- **Extra Art** - Extra art or offering a poster for the album art is a great incentive for fans to buy.
- **T-Shirts** - An exclusive merch design that only comes with your pre-order package is a common part of a bundle.
- **Other Merch** - Any merch you sell can help boost pre-orders.
- **Personal Drawings** - You can make drawings for every fan that orders this package. This works especially if you have a band member who loves to draw all day in the van. Personalize every drawing, then put the fan's name on it. Fans will love it.
- **Books** - You can make a neat book that offer song meanings, lyrics, stories or whatever you have to say for your fans. 48HrBooks make affordable books that look great and are perfect for this purpose.
- **DVD** - If you have exclusive footage and some video editing skills, DVDs are still loved even in this Netflix and YouTube world. While they can be sold to your fans as their own release, a DVD packaged with a pre-order always offers a big incentive for an item that could be hard to sell otherwise. Furnace Manufacturing has great and affordable options for pressing DVD's.
- **Sheet Music/Tablature** - If you play music that's beloved by musician nerds, sheet music and tablature is a huge calling for your fans to drop some extra dollars.
- **Mixtapes** - A personalized mix for the fan; just remember this is technically piracy and your fellow musicians may not appreciate this.
- **Enhanced CDs** - While they have fallen out of favor, Enhanced CDs still exist. At one time you would put video features and other goodies on a CD to encourage a purchase--this has become less popular in the Internet and YouTube world. However, if you want to give fans that buy your CD some special fun, these can still be authored and made. I recommend West West Side Music's authoring (westwestsidemusic.com) and development services if you decide to do an Enhanced CD.

Tips For A Successful Pre-Order
Getting the word out about your pre-order gives you a chance to alert the press to your release. Below are some ideas to make sure it goes well:

- **Price Accordingly** - While pre-orders are a great chance to get some money back into your wallet while you promote your music, you need to make sure the packages are priced in a way that fans don't feel ripped off. Look at other musicians' pre-orders and make sure you observe common pricing practices.
- **Don't Limit** - Don't put limiting merch in your pre-order. While it can be cool to put a skateboard up as part of you pre-order, not everyone wants a skateboard. Include merch that is desired by the majority of your fans.
- **Promote** - Make a video and great pictures for your pre-order. Make a big deal out of it so fans want to spread it around.
- **Release** - Many musicians release the first single of their record on the day of their pre-order and will stream it right on the page that has their pre-order packages to help raise awareness of what they have for sale.

Services That Will Help You With Your Pre-Order
- **Limited Run** – Limited Run offers facilities to sell merch, packages with physical and digital merchandise and enable pre-orders.
- **TopSpin** - One of the services TopSpin is best known for is enabling pre-orders. They make facilitating them easy and have many options for how you would like to run them.
- **Bandcamp** - Bandcamp enables pre-orders and time-released digital assets to fans who pre-order. Their service enables a clean way to show the different packages you offer and sell them to fans.

More Ideas To Stay In The News Cycle

Bad Idea: Unknown Musicians Heavily Promoting Their Record Before Fans Can Download It
If you're an established musician, building anticipation with constant promotion for weeks and months on end before a new release is common practice. After all, the pressure is on to make sure you debut high on the charts.

But for little-known acts, topping the charts is never going to happen. If you're an unknown musician, the world doesn't care about your in-studio updates or crazy teaser videos showing you in a dark corner hiding your new CD. In fact, this wastes everyone's time and you lose a chance to sell a record and gain a fan. <u>Musicians have the tendency to imitate their idols, but promoting your record in the same way U2, DeadMau5 or Metallica does is not going to turn you into them.</u>

While it's a great idea to keep the few fans you have updated, many unknown musicians gear up for their release like many of the biggest musicians in the world do. Instead, unknown musicians should focus their promotion energy and budget on after their release is out for listeners to consume. Most of those great ideas you have will get much better results if your song is available and fans can hear your masterpiece and spread the word about it, since they have no reason to stick around and wait for it.

How Far In Advance Should You Release A Single Before Your Record Comes Out?

This is a question I am asked time and time again and the fact is, there's no one-size-fits-all answer. If you haven't released a song in some time, it is helpful to show fans you're alive and release a song months in advance to get your fans excited. The group Cut/Copy did this very effectively before their breakthrough record *In Ghost Colors*. After a long absence, the first single came out nearly nine months before the record, helping build hype and get fans excited for the record that followed the single. For most musicians, releasing the first single when it's available to buy or download for free is the best strategy. This way you don't lose any chances for fans to get more from you and keep devouring your music.

The rules for this are changing fast as we see more groups go to a releasing infinite singles model to package them on an album. I encourage you to see this as a lawless country where you can do what works best for you.

Skip The Friday Release

Many musicians try to seem legitimate by releasing their new music on a Friday like everyone else. This is often a bad idea. Trying to compete with a fan's favorite act releasing a new record on that day--when they're bound to have it on repeat and not have room for much else--isn't the best idea. It's one thing if you're putting your album up on iTunes, etc., on Friday, but it's another thing to premiere your new song and expect to get a lot of attention on Friday. Fans only have so much time for new music and new acts aren't always top priority. Put out your new song on another day when fans will have room for it in their listening diet.

Friction Is Important
At the beginning of this book, I briefly discussed friction. While it isn't the most fun subject, understanding it can make a huge difference in how well your promotions work. Let's make this simple--friction is how difficult it is to do something. This is important to your music marketing in one easy way: The more effort you ask your fans to put toward something, the less likely they are to do it. For example, if you're trying to get your fans to tweet for a track and it takes them four clicks to do this, they're much less likely to do it than if you can find a way for them to do it in two clicks. You can lose 20 to 80 percent of your potential fans for every click you ask them to make. This means that paying attention to making things easy for fans is very important.

This is why it is crucial to maximize your promotions by having music players showing up in a listener's Facebook timeline as well as having an easy checkout system for your merch. Don't lose the potential of your fans helping you by making it difficult for them to do so. Friction can also be how hard it is for a fan to find the info they want to know about you. If they have to go tearing through numerous pages of a website to find tour dates or can't see them clearly on your Facebook page, they may give up and never find out that you're playing in town next week.

Friction isn't only about clicks and making fans work, it's also about how much you charge. Free is always the least amount of friction and overpricing something is the most friction. If you're having trouble making your marketing work and getting your music to spread, think about how easy you're making it for listeners to discover your music. Always think about the experience of your fans. When you make it easy for those who are interested in you to become active in your music, your promotions will go far.

Chapter 15: Getting Press And Covered By Blogs

The Need For Press

No musician is able to build a huge fanbase without getting writers to write about them. Even if you aren't a critic's darling, you still need someone writing about you. Despite assumptions that the press is only looking for cool musicians, this isn't actually the case. While some writers are passionate fans that only write about what they love, many are constantly looking for new acts that are easy to write about to make their jobs easier to get through. This is why you must "feed" the press as much as you can. If you learn the tools and techniques that publicists use, you can easily make headway on getting your music out to the world and get written about in both print and online outlets.

Raising Awareness

Your goal is to raise awareness, not just get written about. Raising awareness means not thinking about press as just getting placements or building relationships with bloggers. You want to be doing promotions that get talked about and spread through social media. While a fan may find out about your latest news from a news item, blog post or website write-up, your main goal in doing promotions is to make people talk about you, increasing the likelihood that more people become aware of what you're all about. Do they know that you have three other albums or do the best cover of Crash Test Dummies anyone has ever heard? Or that you're also a novelist? You need to always be thinking of how to raise awareness about everything that's interesting about you and how to keep the press and fans constantly mentioning these assets.

It's important to remember that most of the writers who will write about you are fans of your music or writers who feel like you deserve coverage. Thinking about what gets fans excited and creating content accordingly is also what will get the press to write about you.

Don't Pass Go

Before you think about doing any press you want to make sure you have the following together:

- **Music** - Duh! If you don't have any yet, there is no reason anyone will ever write about you--unless you're friends with a writer already or were in a really cool band before the one you're in now.
- **Bio** - Writers need a story to write about and it's hard for them to know what to say if they only have music.
- **Photos** - These don't need to be press shots, but their needs to be a visual element that looks good to accompany anything written about you.
- **Presence** - The more together your website and social networks are, the easier it is to pour gasoline on the spark you get from press. If there is content for new fans, writers and potential team members to check out, it increases the likelihood they'll get more excited about you. The more you have going before you get some press, the more potential you have for it to be a big step instead of a little one. It may even be helpful to read the rest of this book before you pursue any press, to make sure you get everything ready in advance.

Tools For Getting Press

Google Alerts
Google Alerts is one of the most important tools for getting press. Google Alerts (google.com/alerts) makes it so that every time someone writes about you on the Internet it will show up in an email in your Gmail account. This will alert you when you get an awesome review, someone talks about how much of a loser your drummer is or puts your music up on a blog. The uses for this feature are infinite and a key part of getting press that builds a fanbase.

When setting up alerts, make sure you set it up to give you "comprehensive alerts." If you're putting a name with one or more words, use quotations. For example, the searches I use for myself would be "Jesse Cannon", "Get More Fans", or "Musformation." Get started on this ASAP.

Twitter Search

When you get written about, it will usually get tweeted. Using Twitter's search engine (search.twitter.com) will let you see who's tweeting about you. You can then follow all of these people, interact with them and thank them. If you use Twitter's TweetDeck tool (tweetdeck.com) you can set up a constant feed in your deck of everyone mentioning you in a Twitter search.

Pictures
Blogs like ours and nearly every other blog across the Internet love good pictures and videos. At Musformation, we don't write articles unless we have an awesome image and preferably a video of the subject to put with the article. If you have some nasty, blurry picture that your half-drunk significant other took, it may be enough to make some writers give up on your article. I am constantly shocked at what graphic snobs some writers can be. But I can also understand, since I put a lot of time into making my blog look good and I don't want to litter it with crappy images. Very quickly you'll find the sprawling paragraph blurb you were about to get on your favorite blog whittled down to one sentence if you don't have an eye-catching graphic.

You should have great, quality press shots uploaded to your Facebook, website and social media so that writers can easily find these pictures. Make sure you administer a Creative Commons license on the pictures and that they don't have watermarks from your photographer on them.

YouTube
If it weren't enough that you needed press photos, some taste-making blogs only use YouTube videos for their posts. If you don't have one, you're out of luck with their blog. In order to get good press, make sure there are links to a few different great videos on your YouTube channel.

SoundCloud
Many blogs want to host streams through SoundCloud (soundcloud.com). If your music isn't there, a blogger may pass because they can't get a stream of your music in their post. Be sure to have your music easily found (read: linked on your website and social networks) on SoundCloud.

Spotify
Spotify has this neat button called "The Play Button" that allows any blog to post your song if it's on Spotify. Many blogs are starting to use this button.

Making sure your tracks are on Spotify was already a smart move, but this makes it even more crucial for getting press.

SongLink
The big problem with linking streaming services is that is someone who isn't a member or doesn't want to sign up for the service can't listen to the track. SongLink (song.link) changes that by scouring all the streaming services including Apple Music, Spotify, YouTube, Google Music, Deezer and more and making a page where you can link to where a listener can hear your song on every service.

SmartURL
Similar to Linkfire but you can program it to be aware of the country and integrate into Google Analytics. There's a free tier as well as premium for extended features. (smarturl.it)

Getting Written About On Blogs

Once you have all of your tools set up, it's time to find some blogs who will write about you. One of the most unpleasant parts of pitching blogs is how hard it is to get placements. Getting 5 to 15 percent of the blogs you pitch to write about you is a great success. I know that sounds crazy, but most bloggers will turn their head the other way until they hear enough hype about you to take notice. In fact, if you do eventually get some success, you'll find many of the bloggers who once ignored you, are now your biggest fans. This isn't because they're awful people, but because they never even gave you a proper chance.

Much of your time will be spent locating the blogs that are most likely to cover you. This will also mean devoting time to becoming a part of their community so they will give you the time of day. Be prepared for a frustrating experience, but one that is extremely rewarding once you get it to work. Once you get a few blogs writing about you, it only gets easier.

Blogs Are For Everyone
A lot of musicians live under the assumption that their music is too uncool to get written about on blogs. Not the case! The greatest thing about the blogosphere is that anyone can start one. And trust me, there are blogs out there for every type of music and fan. There are fans waiting for every new

blog post to come down the pipe so they can hear about the latest Martha Wainwright cover song. No matter how boring, obscure or uncool your music is, someone is ready to blog about it. Sure, there may not be half as many bluegrass blogs as there are electro-house music blogs, but that doesn't mean these blogs can't help you reach rabid and influential fans. They even trickle over to other facets of the music, like being what ends up being put on Spotify's popular Fresh Finds playlist.

The good news is that while it's very hard to get written up by blogs at first, it eventually becomes easy. In fact, blogs will start to find you without you even pitching them, all because you were written about on another site. Once you get through the doors of a couple of blogs it's almost like pushing a button. You do something eventful and they write about that event.

Targeting

The first thing you need to do is identify some musicians whose fans would like your music. It's best to find a couple of them, some bigger than you, some at about your level and some smaller than you. It would help even more if they were local to you. If they're not, it's helpful to also add a local act to this list. Variety helps, so do as many as you can handle. The next thing you need to do is to add all of these similar acts into your Google Alerts and have these alerts sent to your email.

After a day or so, you'll start to see some results coming back into your email. What you'll begin to see is:

- Blogs, websites and magazines that've written about these acts and would potentially write about you.
- Shows that they're playing, where you can track down the promoter and talk to them about booking you.
- Fans who are writing about listening to the musicians you targeted. You can then add them to your social networks and start building a relationship with these influential fans.

Every day you'll only have a couple of alerts (at most) in each feed, which makes this easy to stay on top of. Simply dedicate yourself to looking at these alerts every day and take a few minutes to add each of the bloggers and promoters to your contact database and follow the fans of these musicians. To begin to do the job of promoting your music to blogs you will want to assemble the blog that write about your targets and start pitching them your latest track.

Stay Organized
As you find these blogs that will potentially write about you, be sure to keep track of them. Adding the relevant information for each blog to your contact database can help when you have to do this all over again the next time you release a song. Keeping the blog name, URL, contact info, preferred music submission format and notes on what they cover can help make your relationships with these writers grow. Keeping this list organized means you don't need to start from scratch every time you have a new release to promote.

Why Both Little Blogs And Big Blogs Matter
When musicians are looking to get press, they often ask whether they should target big blogs or small blogs. The answer is both.

Musicians sometimes get it in their head that the small blogs don't matter because no one actually reads them or the big blogs aren't worth trying for because they will never make it. While both of these points may be true, there is another side to each of those stories. Both of them have the potential to be a big break for you, so don't limit yourself to pursuing a single narrative of how your success is going to happen.

Small Blogs - It's true--not too many people actually read the smaller blogs. Often, the few who do read them are the die-hard music bloggers at bigger sites, who look to the smaller blogs to see what's going on. I've seen this happen countless times. Todd's band Sensual Harassment ascended up the blogosphere as they went from a small, unknown blog. This small blog was read by a bigger blog and that blog was read by Pitchfork, who then wrote them up. The small blogs can help get you started up the ladder to the bigger ones. Remember, no one reads more blogs than other bloggers. Do you want to see the nearly 1,000 blogs I have in my Feedly RSS Reader as proof?

Big Blogs - It can also work from the top down. Sending your music to big blogs can sometimes work out. You never know when the editor at one of the big blogs is going to be thinking, "I really wish there was a band that sounds like The Spin Doctors meets The Baha Men." When they get your bio and see that you describe your music as the melding of the two, you're now being championed as the band that saved music. Once this big-time blogger writes about you, tons of other smaller blogs who watch this blog will then applaud you as well.

There Is No Single Path To Success - Keep in mind is that there is no system in the blogosphere. There is no one way to getting discovered; it happens a different way every time. Keep your mind open.

Blog Graveyard - Sadly blogs come and go quickly. The average lifespan for a blog is three months (*I read that on the Internet, so it must be true*). This means that the Internet is ripe with dead blogs. When you find a blog that looks like it may cover you, make sure it's still posting updates. Sometimes even if it isn't and it seems like a perfect fit for you, it can be worth sending your music anyway. Yesterday's blogger is tomorrow's A&R person, promoter or tastemaker.

Use Blog Aggregators Like Hype Machine To Find Writers Who Will Write About You

If you're like me, you find Hype Machine (hypem.com) to be the greatest thing that ever happened for easily finding music by the acts you like. Aside from being able to easily find tracks by your favorite under-the-radar musicians, it also acts as a great way to find blogs that would potentially write about your music (provided that you're in the genres covered on their site). Getting blogged about is one of the best ways to get into the good graces of the Internet elite and this is the chart that shows which groups are getting blogged about.

Head over to Hype Machine and the first thing you'll see on the right-hand side is a field to "search blogs." In this field, you're going to type a musician that has fans that would like your music. For example, let's say you sound similar to Madeon (one of my favorite dance producers). Once you type in his name, you'll be taken to a list of all the times Madeon has been blogged about.

In each example of the search results, there are two links. The small text in blue writing has the name of the blog that blogged about the song and at the end it says, "Posted ___ ago". Both of these are links to a blog post that mentioned the musician you did a search for. The next thing to do is follow the links and then find the blogger's contact information and approach them about writing about you. This may be tricky since, despite bloggers' love of the Internet, they sometimes fail at web page design and make it difficult to find their contact information. Some blogs may have a

SoundCloud Dropbox, whereas others may have an email listed. Always submit to them in the way they prefer and take note of this when you add them to your contacts database.

Other Blog Aggregators - Although HypeMachine is the most popular blog aggregator and covers most everything you'll need, there are other good aggregators out there like Elbo.ws. These sites have similar facilities for finding blogs who will write about you. While they all cover similar music, some of them aggregate blogs that the others don't. If you find yourself having more time to pitch blogs, these services are a great way to find more.

Google Blog Searches - A little-known fact is that Google has a special blog search function. Google Blog Search is another place to find the artist and album of a similar artist and start going deep into the search results. This does take a while: You sometimes need to go back a few pages in the Google search to find usable results.

StoryAmp Connects Musicians To Writers - StoryAmp (storyamp.com) is an easy idea: It connects musicians with a story to writers who need a story. You can submit your press and what you're currently pushing to writers who have signed up for the service. The pricing goes from free for simple concert listings to $50 per city for placements.

Keeping In Contact With Writers
Don't over-communicate with writers. Sending them a weekly update would be annoying. Instead write to them whenever you do something eventful. If you're going to send a bulk email to them, be sure to have a unsubscribe function and respect them if they don't want email updates anymore. Otherwise, you could be on the bad side of an influential writer or get marked as spam and then you'll have trouble communicating with everyone you email. You can use your mailing list for this function if you keep the writers tagged in a separate tag and blast out to only that tag with updates. It's a good idea from time to time to check contact info. On bigger sites, writers often come and go. You may need to update your contacts if you aren't getting a reaction from some bloggers over time.

Pitching Bloggers

Now that you know who to approach with your music, how do you approach them? First off, you absolutely want to avoid sending carbon copy (CC) or blind carbon copy (BCC) mass emails. This is another place where you're trying to build relationships. These relationships are extra important since these writers have the power to expose you to hundreds or even thousands of potential fans. Giving a personal appeal and attention to detail will help you build a relationship with those who can help you for years to come.

There Are Less Music Journalists, More Music Fans
In this day and age there are fewer music "journalists," and more music fans blogging about their interests. You're rarely going to get covered on a blog unless this person is a fan of your music. Sure, sometimes writers will cover musicians they don't care for--who have tons of fans--to get more pageviews and increase their popularity. But when you're first trying to get covered by blogs, this will not be an asset you have on your side. You want to connect with writers the same way you would talk to a fan, since more often than not, they're your fans. Writers become successful because they're passionate about what they write about and their readers find that passion interesting. They have good taste in up-and-coming musicians and become a trusted source because they're fans of good music. Make sure you treat them like you would a fan--a fan that has a lot of power to help your music.

Understanding Bloggers To Get Closer To Them
If you're going to spend all this time trying to get closer to someone, you might as well understand what makes them tick. Here are some general truths about bloggers:

- **Consume** - They consume more music than anyone else. They're rabid music fans. In fact, they're so rabid they're willing to sift through all the awful music of the world just to find that one song that makes their day. That is serious devotion.
- **Addicts** - They read tons of other blogs and they're looking to feed their addiction to great music. They'll do almost anything to get more great music, including dealing with slacker musicians who are terrible at keeping promises and staying in touch with them.
- **Sneezers** - These are the same people who love to DJ, make mixtapes and tell others at a party about a great song they've never heard of. They pride themselves on discovering secrets on

their own and being the one who gets to tell the world this secret. If you make them feel special, they will give you special treatment.

- **Attention** - They're looking for attention and that attention comes from being credited as the person who finds great, new music.
- **Good Intentions** - Despite a lot of these qualities sounding awful, they're generally good people. They enjoy spreading the joy they get from music and making new friends.

Best Practices For Pitching Bloggers

> *"It's not that people are cruel or mean, they're just busy"*
> - Steven Pressfield

Don't forget, these bloggers don't know you. And of those who don't know you, even fewer care about your music the way people who know of you do. This means you need to take the time to research each blogger and make a personal appeal to them. A casual conversation that doesn't sound like a corporate press release is going to be really helpful here. There are many little things you can do to make your chance of getting written about on blogs more successful. While many of these tips seem trivial, they can make the difference in whether or not you get blog coverage that gives a huge boost to your fanbase.

Do Your Research - It will help to find out some information about the blog. Make sure you're pitching to the right blog for you. Blogs tend to be pretty narrow in scope and if you don't fit in this scope, you're wasting your time pitching them. You'll want to make sure you're sending an email to the correct person at the site. With a little research you can find out which writers are more apt to like your music and post something favorable about you. Doing your research also means finding out what their submission requirements are. Some blogs like full bios, some prefer links to your streaming music and some just want you to use SoundCloud or Spotify.

If you're gearing up to do press for your next release, it can help to search out these blogs well in advance so you have time to get to know them and find a way to be a part of the blog's community. Subscribe to their RSS feed, Twitter or Facebook and get to know them. You'll probably find some good music and learn a lot along the way. When you find a blog that would potentially write about you through Google searches, Hype Machine, Twitter or wherever, always hit subscribe and get to know them. Take notes on your favorite blogs (or put them in a folder in your RSS Reader) and keep track of what you like about each one and use this information when you pitch them. Post your name in the comments regularly so your name seems familiar and you're more likely to get your emails opened.

Mention Similar Musicians - It helps if you mention someone that the blog has written about before. If you're finding blogs on Hype Machine that will likely write about your music, you might want to mention the musician that you searched for to find their blog. Remember that writers receive tons of emails all the time and they don't know you. Even worse, they get added to tons of email lists that send them music they would never write about. This then numbs them to the submissions of musicians, including those they may want to write about. Make sure you demonstrate early in the pitch why they should be interested in you.

Be Complimentary - No one like an ass-kisser but having a nice comment to say about their blog or music taste can really help. Blogging is an underappreciated service that helps tons of music fans find happiness, with very little thanks. You're writing them because you share a common interest in this style of music. You should have a lot to talk about.

Exercise Brevity - A great piece of advice in most writing is to say whatever you have to say in as few words as possible. It isn't necessary to write a dissertation about your music and all the great things you've done. Keep everything you say to a paragraph or less if you can. No successful introduction to a blogger has ever lasted more than 2 paragraphs (unless they ask for a bio or press kit, make sure those are below your introduction as we will show you below). These writers often see hundreds of emails a day and just the sight of your long-winded jabber will cause them to throw your email in the trash bin.

Talk About Yourself Last - Keep in mind these blogs don't know you and almost certainly don't care about you yet. Although you're really excited to announce that you just released an awesome new 7" that looks like a sweet pepperoni pizza, the blogger couldn't care less. First, show them you're interested in them (with insights into their work and site) and then you can tell them why they might be interested in you. Leave your links and announcements for last.

Here is an example of what Todd's band Sensual Harassment sends out and the pitch that gets them blogged about on sites like Pitchfork, Vice, Magnet, XLR8R and countless others. Notice that Todd keeps his

261

message brief and then includes a lot of information in his signature, including other reviews they've received and bio information. This keeps writers from being intimidated by a multi-paragraph message and allows them to read more if they're indeed interested. Check out this masterpiece of blog pitching:

> Hey Joey,
>
> I recently discovered your site Peacock Rock through Hype Machine and really enjoyed it. Saw you're into Sexy Vampire Tooth's new single "The Magic Is Happening" so I thought I'd send you some of my band's new singles, since a lot of our fans like them too. We're a relatively new act out of Brooklyn, called Sensual Harassment, but we've had some pretty good responses to our stuff so far. Below is a link to two of our new singles. Recorded with Jesse Cannon (The Misfits, Animal Collective) and mastered by Alan Douches (Chemical Brothers, Mastodon). We're pretty happy with how things came out. Our info is below if you're interested in checking us out.
>
> sensualharassment.com
>
> cheers.
>
> Todd
>
> ~v^-()^-(http://www.sensualharassment.com)-^-- - --
> ==
>
> *"The dance floor has just found a new hero..."* - XLR8R
>
> *"It'll make you feel like you're in Tron, but in a Don Johnson suit..."* - Junk Magazine
>
> *"They water board their idols with layers upon layers of nostalgic noise that one can only imagine would amount to a deluge of monolithic tones heard live."* - Impose
>
> Sensual Harassment is a Reptilian Humanoid alliance utilizing sonic mind control through beat-driven psych-pop. In their debut

broadcast, the scaly Brooklyn trio seamlessly shape-shifts from reverb-drenched post-Apocalyptic new wave to epileptic space disco.

Recorded at their clandestine headquarters in South-side Williamsburg, the band wisely recruited Jesse Cannon (Animal Collective and The Misfits) to help engineer the cerebral revolution.

Bold yet subdued, **"Soldier"** is an electrified symphony soaked in icy analog synths concluding in a melodic crescendo that is reminiscent of Flaming Lips and Pet Shop Boys.

Cut with razor sharp synths, **"Daddy Long Legs"** is a cosmic dance party that combines grimy Moroder arpeggiators with the throbbing funk and aggression of Afrika Bambaataa.

Listen, Download & Post: 'Soldier' and 'Daddy Long Legs' from sensualharassment.com

*Please note that this is **not** something you'll want to copy and paste, but a good place to start. Add your own flair and ideas to this and make it your own. And most importantly, make it honest and personable.*

What Do You Send?
What you send to a blogger is different every single time. Do some reading on the blog you're pitching and see if the blogger tells you what they prefer. Sometimes a blog will have a SoundCloud drop box or something similar where you can upload files. Other times they tell you that they want MP3s attached to an email with a bio. In the above example, there is a link to songs on the Sensual Harassment website that then provides downloads and streams in plain sight. When a blogger's preference isn't known, it helps to offer them choices. Ideally, you'll want to send them to a place where there are both streams and downloads. Because of the nature of email filters, most email has size limitations. If you attach your song it can go to junk or never get to the blogger at all. Unless they ask you to attach an MP3, never attach it.

There are many great streaming players out there, but we've all become very fond of SoundCloud. Not only is SoundCloud (mostly) free, but it plays nicely with Hype Machine, ensuring your track is much more likely to be used by bloggers. It has become an industry standard with its beautiful customizable player and ease of use, so it puts you far ahead of any competition still using the generic players out there. You want to give bloggers content that is in their language and most of them understand SoundCloud. You can also make the file downloadable, letting the blogger have the choice to stream or download. You can even keep the file private for only those who have the URL, so it won't be easy to leak.

With that said, Dropbox links, SoundCloud and Spotify links all work great, too. You don't need to include every one of them as an option but having a stream and download option at the very least is essential.

What Not To Send
There are some things that no blogger ever wants to see in a pitch in this day and age:

- Your ReverbNation profile.
- A full LP of music, without noting the standout tracks (aka singles).
- A 100 MB+ file of your video or record. Link to streams of videos and if you send a record it doesn't need to be of audiophile quality. High-quality MP3s are great.
- A Spotify, Apple Music, Napster, Tidal or other subscription service link. While these can be fine as an additional link, making this the only thing you send means every blogger who doesn't belong to this service can't hear what you sent.
- Any email attachment, unless the blogger specifically asks for it.

Keep It Current
Even if you are pitching an old song, bloggers are the type of people who want to be up on what is fresh and new. Put a release date in your press release that is a few weeks in the future or 6-8 weeks ahead for a print publication.

When?
My best advice is to never send an email between Friday and Monday. Let me explain what a writer is thinking when they get an email on the days you shouldn't send it to them:

- **Friday** - At work, cramming to finish all the work I didn't finish during the week. All the new releases are out today. Or maybe I already left for a 3-day weekend.
- **Saturday** - Partying, relaxing, not at work. Duh!

- **Sunday** - Are you kidding me, you bother me on my one day off? I don't even read emails on Sunday.
- **Monday** - So many people emailed me the past three days, I don't have time to hear about your stupid music.

But what if those are the only times you have to send emails? That's OK! Most email providers have a scheduled send function so your email can be sent whenever you want, even if you want to write it on a different day than you should send it. If you're using Gmail it will allow you to schedule your email to send whenever you like.

Do I Really Need To Personalize My Blog Pitches?
Todd and I have been a part of a lot of blog pitches and time and time again we see some general rules:

- If you mass mail with no personal touch, if you even get a response from 1 out of 100 writers you're going to be lucky.
- If you personalize them a little if you get 5 out of 100 to write about you you'll be lucky.
- If you become a big follower of a blog, comment, interact on social networks and really make yourself a part of a community you can get written on 1 out of every 4 blogs.

The effort you put in goes a long way. There are countless other acts trying to get the same attention you want and even if your music is great, it will probably be ignored by people who would love it. What I do like doing is personalizing a bit and then using the app TextExpander (textexpander.com) to fill in the rest of the pitch I have written.

Carpet-bombing And Personalizing Effectively
One dirty secret of the blog world is that some of the bigger artists have more than one PR person. If you have a large press list and few relationships, you can always try carpet-bombing from one account and sending out impersonal emails to a large number of bloggers from a more personal account to your coveted bloggers.

Try And Try Again
Odds are your first pitches to most blogs won't go well. As Malcolm Gladwell advises in his excellent book *The Tipping Point*, you should change something small each time you do a new promotion. Keep tweaking and making things better and better and observing what made other promotions successful. If a pitch didn't work for a certain blog, try

changing it up a little next time and putting some time into improving your message.

Time Is Of The Essence

There is a joke in the blogosphere that information now moves so fast that one day is actually a "blog year." For Twitter addicts, posting two-day old news can get you laughed out of the blogosphere and awarded an Internet dunce cap. This is one of the keys to making sure any opportunities you may have to be written up in blog world will actually come into fruition. I've seen some friends lose great opportunities because they were too slow to keep up in the world of blogs. Hours can be a big deal when looking to fill content. Checking your email daily and always having easy access to any files needed for your project is often the difference between an opportunity turning into big leaps for your music or another failure. If a blog requests something and it takes you a day to get back that is sometimes 23 hours too late. Get with the times and realize you need to move fast if you want to be covered in a fast-moving world.

Send A Crazy Package

A tried and true method in music for the past 40 years has been to send blog, record labels, journalists or anyone else you want to impress a really crazy package so they remember you or display the item in their office. Many outlets have their address listed upon request for physical packages and you can often get a listen or make a big impression if you can come up with the right thing to send and think outside the box.

Non-Music Blogs

There are huge opportunities in submitting your music to non-music blogs. While blogs are everywhere and have become incredibly powerful, they do have their downsides. Because there are so many blogs, some of them have very few readers. In addition, many blogs have a very short lifespan. There is also an incredible amount of competition out there because of the amount of submissions. Take into consideration that blogs receive tons of music submissions, so what you're sending them is probably not very special.

Pursuing Non-Music Blogs

Let's say that you're in a band that plays retro '60s mod-style music. You dress the part, you speak the lingo and you live the mod life. Perhaps you could send your music to a mod culture blog or a blog about '60s style. If you send that same MP3 to a blog who doesn't usually receive that sort of thing, they may be much more excited to post about it. Submitting to non-music sites/magazines/blogs can open you up to a whole new audience.

Get creative. If your whole record is about your divorce, you should pitch divorce blogs. Are you a sexy librarian by day and Goth singer by night? There's bound to be a blog about cool librarians that will profile you. Are you a Libertarian and decided to write a song about how much you love the free market? There are tons of political blogs who feel the same way and will embrace you for being much cooler than they are. Somewhere in your life there is a blog that isn't music-centered but is interested in your life as a beekeeper, stamp collector or whatever other weirdo hobby you have.

Don't Forget Your Local Press
As much as blogs and websites are a great place to focus on, they're not the only place that can give you big bumps in fans and sales. Even though it may not be as cool or as highly esteemed as the blogs, having your local area or state paper write you up can give you giant spikes in awareness. If you have a song about living in a town--especially if it mentions a part of the town--this is always a way to get coverage in local press. I'm constantly shocked at the huge traffic bumps I see whenever musicians I work with get these placements.

Getting Aggressive
On some websites/blogs, the writers don't make their contacts readily available. This doesn't always mean they don't want to be contacted as much as their web design may simply be flawed. If you want to get your music to one of the print magazines that still exist, you may have even more trouble finding a writer's contact. Surprisingly, it's actually pretty simple to find them.

Type their name into Google and odds are you'll find another site the writer does writing for. If not, try to type the words "blog" or "Twitter" after their name. Before you do this, make sure you do some investigative work--read their reviews (this helps you understand the music world anyway and is helpful in getting your head around the blogosphere), find something you like about a review and start off by contacting them by commenting on that.

After you have done your sucking up, it's time to be a total creep and ask if you can send your music. Trust me, everyone does this and there isn't a writer who isn't used to it. Writers are huge music fans and are always looking for new music, just make sure you're giving it to someone who is likely to enjoy your music. As long as you aren't carpet-bombing everyone who ever wrote a review on the Internet, you should get good results if you send them something they would seemingly like.

What To Do When Your Pitches Keep Failing
Sadly, even with all this knowledge your blog pitches may be falling on deaf ears. Here are some ideas of what you can do to get through if your pitches haven't been working.

- **Zoom** – When comparing yourself to other acts, you may be comparing them to acts that are too mainstream or maybe too obscure. Try switching up your theory on who you should be comparing yourself to.
- **Language** – Try talking in a different way. Maybe talk much more the way you normally do or be more professional cause you may be coming off as the burnout you are.
- **Humor** – Adding humor can often make a big difference in being likable and getting in good graces with a blogger.
- **Interact** – Remember, being a part of the blogger's community goes further than any great pitch, find relevant (not annoying!) ways to be a part of the bloggers community. Retweet, Reblog the stuff from them you like and comment on it. BE a real part of the community and your pitches will go better.
- **Quality, Not Quantity** – <u>Many people make the mistake of thinking that having tons of blogger emails is more important than a few solid relationships. What is much more important is your relationships with them and being a part of the community, they are in.</u>

After You Get Written Up

Substance
We all know blogs; news aggregate sites and reviews help listeners discover music every day. Let's say a writer has just heard your music and wants to write about it. Usually you're not yet their favorite musician of all time, but they like what they heard and want to tell the world about you. Do they have anything to tell the world about? You need to have some information about your music--<u>a story</u>--whether it's a bio or even a recent blog that is easily accessible. Do you find this stuff cheesy? Well, guess what? After your music has gotten some attention you can make a website

with a cloud of mystery, but until the world knows something about your music, you have to give them a story.

When I say a story, I don't mean how your band got together or all of the members' names and what they play. Tell a story we all haven't heard before--a story that makes you unique--and there is a much better chance a writer will write about you. In fact, many writers are lazy and will literally copy whatever you gave them.

Steady Diet Of Nothing
Let's say you get a writer's attention: They love you and want to make it their mission to tell the world about you. How do they keep hearing about you? Sure, they can look up your Facebook, but Facebook's search engine often goes haywire. Maybe your Twitter name isn't exactly your band's name. This is yet another reason you need a website. A website gives these writers the option to stay in touch with you in any way and as many ways as they would like. Here is what you should have available to make sure writers can stay up to date with you and keep giving you free and effortless press:

- **Easily Accessible Email List -** If you have a website, on every page of your website there should be an email signup form. Put it in the sidebar and make sure it's on every page.
- **RSS Feed -** RSS is how press and news is spread in this day and age. Every site that isn't run by a bunch of morons has one. How do you get one of these? Every blog and website platform offers an RSS feed.
- **Link All Of Your Social Networks -** Some writers don't want more email or to subscribe to your YouTube and follow you on Facebook. Let them have it their way. Make it easy for them to find all of this information.
- **Twitter –** At the very least you should be updating the world to your news on Twitter. Most music writers use Twitter to get their news today, so be sure your news goes here.

A lot of musicians wonder why it's so hard to get press. Difficult-to-find information is often one of the reasons. The press isn't going to jump through hoops to find a way to stay in touch. Make it easy while they're excited about you.

Collect Interested Ears

Once you see anyone writing about you, add them to your contacts database, follow them on Twitter and like their blog on Facebook. This will make it so you can get to know each other better and grow your relationship. If you get written up on a blog, show your accessibility and write a comment thanking them. All of these techniques will ensure good press in the future.

Thank Bloggers With Traffic
Make sure to link any nice writing on your social networks. Bloggers greatly appreciate you giving them traffic and new readers, just like you appreciate them giving you new fans. Writers are much more likely to write about you in the future if they see that they get traffic from your fanbase whenever they write you up. This is how you give them thanks. Plus your fans always like seeing which blogs cover the groups they love, so they can then follow them and look for new music.

Collect It All
Part of the job of being your own publicist is the ability to collect and sort contacts. One of the main duties of a publicist is collecting, saving and neatly labeling your press clippings so they can be referenced later. If you're looking to add members to your team, like management, booking, etc., having all of your good press handy is an easy way to impress them. If you're going to go at it alone, having every press clipping, interview and review readily available can open doors to better shows, better distribution and other opportunities when you're asked by a gatekeeper to show what you've got. There are tools you should be using anytime you get press no matter how big or small.

- **Screen Capture** - If you get a good or even mediocre review online, take a screen capture of it. Once you've captured the screen, you can either add it to a program like EverNote (evernote.com) or keep it on your Google Drive or Dropbox in a folder.
- **Public** - If you want to make all the good press you get easily discoverable consider making a Pinterest (pinterest.com) board for it all.
- **Digital Camera** - If you get some press in a print publication, simply use your phone or digital camera to shoot it and put it in your press folder. If the print is hard to read, take numerous pictures of the same clipping.

- **Video Capture** - Know how to get videos off TV or YouTube appearances. There are countless methods used to do this and each situation requires a different set of skills.

Alerting Writers About What You're Doing

Feed The Press

Writers need content to chew on to be able to write about you. You need to give them substance. Once a blogger has written about you and you've given them a way to stay in touch with you, they'll be looking for news to write about from you. Delivering this news to them in a casual manner will help spread it to both fans and writers alike.

Do Not Write Press Releases

Press releases are obsolete. Even major companies don't even use them anymore. What you're trying to do is raise awareness and talk to fans in a way they will want to read about it and then tell others. Remember, since there are few music journalists left, most writers who write about you will also be fans that will spread this word. Talking to fans in a comfortable language that is fun for them to spread helps them to spread that word. Since your ultimate goal is to have writers and fans share what you're trying to tell them and raise awareness through articles and social network shares, it makes sense to talk to them in a fun way they appreciate. You know what your fans will never share? Some boring corporate-ish press release. What they will share is content written in the language they speak. In fact, writers and fans will often repeat exactly what you write if you write it in a fun and natural way.

You need to blog, email and update your fans in a casual, informative conversation. Look at even the most popular startup blogs. It's always written in a fun, casual manner. Despite the fact that they're a startup living in a corporate world and making tons of cash, they never put out a corporate-speak press release. Instead, they take a fun conversational tone that updates readers on what they are doing. This also gets the press writing about them.

Casual - This is the same way you should think about your blog entries and social network updates. You never want to write press releases. Instead write a casual conversation with your fans and tell them what's going on. Got a new song? All you need is one paragraph about it. If it got some great reviews--or your last song did--that can go in paragraph two.

What builds relationships is making sure your fans feel like they're hearing from you, not your publicist or some corporate dork at a record label that wrote a press release. Writers also feel this way--they want to see your personality, which is much more interesting than a boring press release.

Have some new merch and think it's "dope?" Say so! Would you describe your new track as "bangin" or "heavier than the balls of a giant alien?" Say it! <u>Writers and fans all fall in love with an artist's personality along with their music.</u>

Some Traditions To Adhere To
While you don't ever want to send a boring, formulaic press release to anyone, you also don't want to send an update that is complete chaos. Here are some formatting ideas that will make sure your updates are appreciated by your fans and writers.

- **Headline** - In half a sentence, tell everyone what the big deal is. For example: "Maxwells Show With BeBe & The Boo Boos 8/23" or "New Song Up Now On Our Website."
- **Two-Sentence Summary** - You gave away the secret in the headline, but now you have two sentences to say all of your info. This can go right under the subject or at the top of the body of your email. If you have more than one promotion to announce, tell the reader it's below. This way, if they're waiting for your new T-shirt, but your announcement is about your new single, they will know that information is coming later.
- **Get Excited** - You now have one paragraph to get everyone excited about what you're talking about. This is when you really let your personality loose and talk to your fans about why they should care about your news.
- **Sell It Some More** - Got other exciting news going on? Did something cool happen since your last update? Tell them.
- **Other News** - If you have relatively boring news or want to remind your fans about a promotion you're pushing, you can now do it here. If your fans got this far, they actually care.
- **Thanks** - Always thank your fans for their support and caring enough to read this far. Do it in your own words and please don't

write exactly what I just wrote. Write a sincere "thank-you" in your own words and it will have a much greater impact.
* **Links** - What social networks are you currently trying to get fans to follow you on? Take the time to link two of them here.

Where Do I Do These Updates?
So now that you know how to talk to your fans, where should you provide them with these updates? And what news needs what type of updates?

Level 1
Action - Playing a small show, got a new T-shirt, restocked some merch, reminding fans of your song, video release, did a mediocre interview, etc.

Response - Update Facebook, Twitter, Tumblr, your blog.

Level 2
Action - Playing a cool show, just finished recording your new EP/LP, have a track listing or album cover art, reminder about crowdfunding project, put up a cool YouTube video you want to push, did a great interview or got a cool piece of press.

Response - Update Facebook, Twitter, Tumblr and your blog. Send an email to your press list.

Level 3
Action - Releasing a new song, EP, LP, new video, tour dates, crowdfunding project.

Response - Post in your news feed on your website and then link to it from your Facebook and Twitter. Post the update to your Tumblr and your blog. Send an email to your press list. Send an email to all of your fans. Make a picture on Instagram and write about the news there.

Your Blog And Your News Feed Are Not The Same Thing
If you want your news to spread, you have to separate the blog where you cry about your ex-girlfriend, talk about your lunch and write your thoughts about how Rand Paul is secretly a robot sent from outer space from the place where you talk about huge news, like your new video and tour. This separation ensures that writers and casual fans don't stop paying attention to your updates.

News Feed - You need a place on your website where you only update big news. This is your news feed. Don't update your news feed every time someone reviews you or with the 40th reminder about your new song or the fifth reminder about your upcoming show. This is a place you post big news. Update this space twice a month, at most. It can even be a digest of everything you have to say every two weeks. The news feed is separate than your blog content, so writers don't get frustrated trying to find your news in the sea of pictures of your cat. It can also be a place fans go to check in who don't want to hear about the great meal you had in Austin last night.

Blog - Your blog is a place where you can show your fans personality; share the news from your news feed and talk about anything you want. Your blog should be a different feed than your news--each should have its own RSS feed that only posts the appropriate content. Your blog is where you tell the world crazy stories, your feelings and interests, whereas your news feed is where you post news and only news.

Remember, you can still have a personal blog and link to that on your social networks and website. Tons of musicians do this and it can really help build relationships. It also keeps your social networks and news clean and free of annoyance for fans that love your music but don't care about your life. Remember you can retweet, reblog and share between accounts to bring attention to your separate accounts, so that fans that follow one become aware of the other.

The Secrets Of Getting Press

Exclusive Content Gets You Press

Often, the blog you want to get on is not sure about whether they want to write you up or not. The easiest way to get them over the fence is to offer them exclusive content. This means you'll let them be the only website that has this content from you. Most commonly, this is a song stream or a download. Maybe for the first week your video is out, you'll have it exclusively stream on their site. There is lots of different exclusive content you can do and you can get creative with what you make to both entertain your fans and get the press to cover you. The more traffic this exclusive content will draw, the more likely the blog is to give you the spot to do it.

Pitching - If you're going to try to use exclusive content to get press, it's smart to try to give it to the blog that will raise the most awareness for you. Obviously, if you're someone no one has heard of and you approach Rolling Stone or Pitchfork, this probably won't work out too well. Find a blog that is as big as possible and pitch them what you have to offer first. If this doesn't work out, go down to your second, third choice, etc.

Remember when you give them this exclusive, you should post to your social networks that you're doing this exclusive with them and giving them traffic. Blogs love this and you'll be able to get news and your other happenings posted much more easily in the future. If you draw them a lot of traffic, this is a chance to start a great relationship with a place that regularly raises your awareness.

Content - What you give them is important. An exclusive interview that you're recording with your no-name producer isn't going to cut it. Below is a list of exclusive content that works well and will entice many bloggers.

- **Song Stream/Download** - The most common types of exclusive content. Offering to let them to host this song exclusively for a few days is often enough to entice.
- **Video Premiere** - Another great way to get placements. You hold off on posting your video on YouTube for a few days and tell all your fans they can see it on a blog first.
- **Behind The Scenes Video** - Video of you recording, touring, etc.
- **Cover Song** - Made a quick cover. This can work, but it helps if your originals are already getting coverage on this blog.
- **Acoustic Version, Remix, Alternate Version** - Blogs love this content.
- **DJ Sets, Playlists, Mixtapes, and Freestyles** - These help if you're established with the site and can be big news when you do them.
- **Blogs** - Have a tough experience in life? Maybe you did a tour or recording diary. Blogs love this stuff. If you can form a coherent sentence, writing this is great content for a lot of blogs.

Getting Covered - Look at what gets other musicians written about and do the same things. Does a blog write about Grimes' new haircut? Well, that is because she has a large fanbase and they cover her every move. Instead of looking at her, observe what the up-and-coming acts are doing. Observe the promotions that other musicians of your size do to stay in the news cycle. Does a blog write about musicians doing cover videos? Do a cover video! Keep tabs on the blogs you want to be on and do the promotions they write about on a regular basis--you'll be written about more often.

Using Spotify Playlists For Exclusive Placements
While the world buzzes about Spotify, Tidal and Apple Music, one of the coolest things about these services is that they open up a whole new world of promotional opportunities for musicians. By sharing playlists that show what you've been listening to or influenced by, you can bring a listenable element for blog features that give fans an enjoyable way to build a deeper bond with your music by understanding what inspires you.

Album Commentary
A new trend in press placements is for musicians to do a song-by-song commentary of their record. Blogs will present this commentary before each song is played in a playlist. It can be a great way to give fans insight into your new record, get a great press placement and grow bonds with fans. These commentaries can easily be recorded and assembled to give to blogs.

Keeping It Exclusive
If the content is going to be exclusive, you have to make sure other blogs don't use it. Many blogs have song and video players they can use to make sure the song won't be stolen by other blogs. If they don't, there are a few tricks to make this happen. Vimeo's "pro" package has a feature where only the author can embed the video. Meaning only you have the embed code, so you can keep the video exclusive. YouTube, Bandcamp and Soundcloud all have streaming players can disable sharing to keep it exclusive as well.

Have An Interesting Image To Go With Your Song
Bloggers love strong images. Some of Todd's successes getting press for his band, has come from always having a strong, interesting image to go with every song they push. Making exclusive art for each of your singles and giving it to blogs can greatly increase your chances of getting a placement.

Animated GIFs Will Help You Get Placements
The Internet and especially blogs love animated .gif images. If you have a cool animated .gif for your press photo, you can receive blog posts just so

the blogger can have that cool image on their blog. Get creative and take advantage of the excitement bloggers have for these images.

Musicians Who Give Good Interviews Get More Interviews

If you have something interesting to say, an interview is a great time to say it. Interviews drive traffic for blogs. Interesting interviews with memorable quotes drive even more traffic and buzz around the web. If you make news and say interesting things, other writers will want to interview you. If you have boring answers and say the same thing every time, putting no effort into making your interviews memorable, you aren't going to get as many interview opportunities. Just remember, trashing other musicians isn't interesting, it's immature. And sadly, it will also get you tons of press.

Bad Interviews Are Your Fault, Not The Interviewer's

Musicians are constantly complaining about how dumb interview questions are. Unfortunately, this is part of your job as a musician and inevitably you're going to have to deal with some brain-dead, uninformed questions in most interviews. Sadly for you, it's your job to learn how to compensate for the interviewer's stupidity.

If an interviewer asks you a stupid question, make like a politician and answer it a different way or change the subject after one sentence with a "by the way." Sometimes you can avoid answering the question entirely and say something much more interesting. Musicians who blame the interviewer for the questions and "gotcha questioning" are morons and should be treated as such. Smart musicians like James Murphy, Jack White and Marilyn Manson find a way to always spit out what's on their mind, rather than what the interviewer is asking. This technique will take you much further than answering questions about your latest cover song or what your influences are.

Bullet Point Your Interview Answers

A hidden secret of good interviews is that the interviewee is often armed with a list of things to make sure to mention. Top publicists develop a list of what they are trying to promote, good stories and interesting points a musician should be sure to say in an interview. If you're doing phone interviews this is particularly easy, otherwise make this list and read it over before each interview.

More Thoughts On Giving A Great Interview

- **Express Yourself** - Never answer interviews with one-word answers. You can do better.
- **Last Thoughts** - Most interviewers ask for last thoughts. This is the time to talk about everything you wanted to say they didn't ask.
- **Talking Points** - Many publicists hand musicians the points they shouldn't forget to mention during interviews. Having a list to refresh your memory can be extremely helpful. Mentioning cool stories and all the attributes that make you special can make big difference in how much an interview helps grow your fanbase. If you released 50 songs for free this year and forget to mention that, it's a huge opportunity lost to let every person who learns of you from this interview know that they can have tons of cool new music.

Be A Part Of The Community

Writers are way more likely to write about someone who is approved of by their community. If you're commenting on their forums, conversing with them on Twitter or in SoundCloud comments and talking with others they know, they're much more likely to take you seriously. If a blogger writes about your friend's band and sees you two tweeting about each other, they're likely to see you as someone they should cover, instead of as some nobody. Seeing a familiar name in the inbox goes a long way for getting an email opened.

How To Join The Club - When I want to be covered by a blog, I add them to my personal Twitter feed, add the blog to my RSS reader and like them on Facebook. Interact and say what you think about subjects. Try not to be overly self-promotional and this technique can get bloggers to see you as a part of their community that they should be covering. Following these writers tells you a lot: They will often show you the other blogs, DJs and musicians you should know.

Ridiculous Contests Can Help Raise Awareness

In the battle to get press, a nuclear weapon on your side is having a good story to tell the world. One of the ways to get your foot in the door with blogs and newspapers is to run a ridiculous contest so that there is an interesting story to be written up. Case in point: The amazing band Manchester Orchestra once ran a contest for their tour where they asked fans to submit pictures of their bitch (aka their dog) and whoever had the most awesome bitch won free admission to a show (all while satirizing hip hop culture). This contest got them written up on tons of websites that didn't usually cover them--getting them free press for their upcoming tour.

Unless You Know The Person, Never Follow Up
One of the advantages of having a professional publicist work for you is they often have strong relationships with writers. They can annoy a writer to death asking if they got a chance to check out a track, consider an interview, etc. If the blogger gives the publicist lip, they may lose the chance to interview the big act on the publicist's roster that the blogger is in love with. You, unfortunately, don't have that advantage when doing your own press. If the blogger doesn't reply and you don't know them, don't write a follow up email. Assume they weren't interested and put your energy into finding someone else who is more interested in your music. Just email them the next time you have a promotion to announce. If you do have a relationship with them, following up 14 days later is common practice for reviews and two days later for more time-sensitive news.

How To Handle Bad Reviews
One of the worst things you can do is to lash out at fans or bloggers who don't like your latest release. Aside from the fact that it makes you look immature, fragile and unconfident—it's just bad business. Many musicians start out with bad reviews, and their next release gets a great one from the same reviewer. If you lash out at that reviewer, the odds of that happening drop pretty fast. Let it go and realize it's just one person's opinion. When you see a fan or former fan tweet something bad about your latest release, instead of lashing out, write them something polite like, "I'm sorry you aren't enjoying it, hopefully you'll like what we do next." This makes you seem cool and will allow the fan to give you another chance, instead of closing a door on a relationship you once had.

Getting In The Mainstream Press

Obviously, it would be amazing to get featured in the mainstream press. Most musicians are smart enough to realize that the uneventful news of putting out a new record rarely gets an unknown musician into the mainstream press. Instead, you need to develop or find a story that is part of a narrative that bloggers will write about. Most writers in the mainstream press need to find a bigger story than the basic occurrence of a musician releasing music. Writers need to figure out how you fit into the larger audience they appeal to and what your place in there would be.

Submitting To Magazines And Local Papers
A lot of local mainstream press will take your music submissions, but you need to class up your operation in order to get covered by them. These submissions need to be in a much more old-school form to fit their old-school paper. You're going to want to submit print publications with real CDs, vinyl and printed-out press materials. If you can find where the writer of your local paper blogs online, it's much better to approach them like you would a blogger and send them material digitally. But sometimes this isn't possible. If this isn't the case, every paper has an address. Simply address it to the writer you think would write about you and write a follow up email if you can find their address (this is one instance in which writing follow-up emails can help).

Getting Reviews
Sadly, most of the mainstream press is reserved for hyped releases that readers are waiting for and those who advertise in a publication. Many advertisers will ask for preferential treatment to make sure they get interviews and reviews for their releases in the pages, in exchange for them keeping the paper in business with their ad dollars. With that said, you can still try to get into these pages with some smart tactics.

- **Writers** - Mail your record to the attention of writers who reviewed similar musicians to you. Send it to the main review address but mark it to their attention. If you want to submit to more than one writer, send multiple packages.
- **Material** - Mail them your physical album (singles are tough to get reviewed when you're a unknown). If you have vinyl, mail both CD and LP versions.
- **Press Sheet** - Send a sheet with a short bio and some reviews you've gotten. These reviews can convince a reviewer to check you out, especially if they know or respect the other writers.
- **Something Fun** - If you have a unique piece of merch or something fun to send the reviewer, do it. Usually it will end up in their office and it will keep you on the magazine's radar.

Keeping Friendly Press Relations

Say Thank You

If you're fortunate enough to have writer's say nice things about you to their audience, you should certainly make an effort to thank them. You'll be surprised at how happy some writers are to hear from you. One of the reasons writer's blog is to make connections with the musicians they love. Most writers love to hear from the musicians that they write about.

If the writer seems to like your music, it's not out of line to offer them some merch like stickers or a free shirt. <u>Remember: Don't bribe them, just thank them for their kindness.</u> Although the music business has changed in many ways, what hasn't changed is most progress is built on personal relationships. Offer to get them into shows for free whenever you're in their town and make sure to hang out with them at the show.

The biggest difference between you and a label or a publicist is that they're using the company credit card to buy drinks, dinners and schmooze press people. In this instance (and with a limited budget), it helps to use whatever resources you can. Remember that just because someone writes about your music doesn't mean they'll do it again--there are a lot of musicians dying for attention and you have to separate yourself somehow. The more you can build genuine friendships with writers, the easier it is to get written about by others. Writers like musicians who they think are great people, more than they do ones who have never been nice to them. Kindness goes a long way. It also helps that writers are usually interesting and have great advice for you. Nurture these relationships and reap the benefits.

Give A Phone Number When Putting Writers On The Guest List

We all know that it's a good idea to put local press on the guest list for a show, but there is a quick way to make this writer your enemy instead of your friend. Some venues are strict about the guest list and if there is the slightest transcription flaw in someone's name on the list, they will not allow them into a show. If you have a standard email you send out to everyone you put on the guest list, make sure you also put the cell phone number of the tour manager and/or responsible band member. If something goes wrong, you shouldn't have the writer left out of the show after making the effort to come see you.

Some More Thoughts On Doing Press Well

- **Keep Up The Conversation** - If you get blogged about, make sure to follow the blogger on every social network you can. Commenting and socializing can really go an extra mile.
- **Tip Them Off** - Want a big press outlet to help you out? Tip them off about some big news you have in a private email and let them post it before you do. This can endear them to you and help nurture your relationship. They will appreciate the help and the traffic it brings them.
- **Hide Tour Date Announcements In A Guest List Invite** - Have some tour dates to announce? One of the best ways to stay in your blogger buddies' good graces and get them written up is to lace it in a nice gesture. Whenever MusforMGMT's acts had dates, I would email our press list and start it with "Let me know if you want guest list or photo passes for any of these dates?" This would keep my email blasts in the good graces of blogs, get a post on their site for the tour and often land the groups we work with a show review or positive tweets about the show from influential bloggers. Win-win-win.
- **Keeping Up With The Guest List** - Once your fanbase is established, the guest list for press can get out of hand. If you're charged with doing the press for yourself, you need to make a spreadsheet and an itinerary for your tour. Make sure the guest list is updated and you give it to the promoter every night. Sometimes there are too many requests for how many spots you have. These are people who can greatly grow your awareness, so it makes sense to pay the promoter to expand the guest list.
- **BCC** - Always use BCC on any mass email. You don't want every writer to see everyone you sent your mass email to.
- **Staff Lists** - Many bigger websites list their whole staff, sometimes along with all of their social networks. Follow these people and socialize with them.
- **Tips** - If you see some news or are privy to news you think a blogger would like to know, send them tips. This can help you get more favorable coverage.

Music Submission Services
Nearly every day I'm asked whether you can buy a list of thousands of music writers to pitch your music to and see who will bite. The answer is yes, but with a caveat. While there are services that do this, in my experience they are never worth the money. Instead, you do in fact have

you music sent to thousands of writers who do not trust these services and send the emails directly to their junk box.

Hiring A Publicist

While it helps to start getting press for yourself, there comes a time when getting to the next level in the press requires a professional who can devote a lot of time to helping you get into bigger outlets. While this isn't cheap, it's a step nearly every musician takes after a certain level of success.

One of the biggest mistakes that Todd and I--as well as many other friends--have made is hiring a publicist when we didn't have enough momentum in building a fanbase yet. If you expect to get a huge buzz and lots of placements when you haven't even gotten write-ups on small blogs, nine times out of ten you're going to end up disappointed. Most publicists can get you some easy placements, but they're best at taking you to the next level. If you're only on level one, it's not going to be worth it to spend thousands of dollars to get you to level two when you could devote a few afternoons to doing it yourself. If you have 600 Facebook likes and expect to get the coverage that the big indie bands get, by throwing a few thousand dollars at the problem, you are most likely going to be wishing you had that money back to spend it in a more helpful way. Hiring out a publicist is a great way to build on top of some good press you've already gotten. But if you're still struggling to get any medium-sized blogs to post about you on a regular basis, I suggest working hard on your own press for a bit longer. Before you spend lots of money that you barely have, I suggest giving your publicist some existing press and content to work off of.

When you feel you've gotten through to all the bloggers who will talk to you, it's time to hire someone else. Below are some people Musformation has had great experiences working with.

- **Girlie Action** - Pam at Girlie Action (girlieaction.com) has been doing this forever with the biggest names in music, in nearly every genre. She is one of the top people in PR.
- **Earshot Media** - Mike did a fantastic job doing press for Man Overboard and Transit while MusforMGMT were with them. (earshotmedia.com)

Chapter 16: Going Viral & Exploits

Going "viral" is the goal of many musicians these days, but it's an extremely weird goal to me. After all, when it comes to music, if someone goes viral it's usually because they're being laughed at--Tay Zonday, Rebecca Black and Antoine Dodson all come to mind. Even when you aren't being laughed at or treated as a sad one-hit wonder freak of nature, going viral usually means you're going to have to be a novelty act who is known for a silly video instead of your great musical impact on the world. It's an odd goal to have, but for some people, it's what they want.

How To Go Viral

The best-case scenario for going viral is making content fans really want to share. After all, when we talk about going viral, we're talking about the type of content that people feel compelled to spread. Of course, that's the goal of everyone's promotions. While that's the goal, most people usually don't succeed. What makes people want to share content is because it's remarkable. Seth Godin calls this a "Purple Cow" in his book by the same name. He asserts that no one is going to write about a cow because they see that all the time, but a Purple Cow is an eventful piece of news people will tweet, Facebook share and post about on Instagram for years to come.

When we talk about going viral, the main ingredient is to do something really special. *Something that blows people's minds.* Many musicians think they're going to go viral with a funny song or a quick joke in a video. It takes much more than that. In fact, the threshold gets higher every day. You need to do something that is truly remarkable so that people tell everyone they know about it.

When I hear musicians talk about going viral, I ask them what they think people are going to say about their "viral content." Funny isn't enough to go viral. Funny will get shares but it isn't going to spread your content to every single person. Think about other viral videos you have enjoyed--they are never just funny or crazy. What makes them special can usually be summed up in quick sentence describing what the viewer has never seen before. For example:

285

- **Rebecca Black's "Friday"** - "The stupidest lyrics I've ever heard in a pop song, with one of the weirdest videos ever."
- **Duck Sauce's "Big Bad Wolf"** - "Oh my god, everyone has animals coming out of their crotches"
- **Tay Zonday's "Chocolate Rain"** - "Did you hear the voice coming out of that man-boy, WTF?"
- **Psy's "Gangnam Style"** - "Well, there's a million pieces of ridiculous in this one, but mostly the crazy dance and scenarios. It's a surreal assault of ridiculous dancing scenarios around every corner."

What are people going to say about your viral content? What about it is exceptional and remarkable and will make people want to tell their friends? Figure that out and you're halfway there.

Going Viral In Practice
Whenever going viral is discussed, there are some pieces of advice that come up time and time again.

- **25 Ideas** - Develop your viral idea as much as possible. Come up with twenty-five different ideas on how to approach your viral content and figure out how to meld them into something special that is worth sharing.
- **Titling** - You need to write a title that grabs your potential audience's attention. You can also apply the 25 ideas rule to your title. Think of as many titles as possible and then test them on your friends and see what they would click on.
- **Spreading** - Research where viral content is spread. Submit your content to podcasts, Redditt and any of the countless forums and blogs who cover viral content.
- **Devote Time** - If you plan on your content going viral, it's probably going to be a full-time job for a few days. You are going to have to work hard for a few days on getting it everywhere you possibly can. Prepare by finding outlets, communities, blogs and whoever else will post your content and begin participating in their community in advance, so that you are a familiar face and your content is easily accepted.

So You Went Viral! Now What?

Let's say you do go viral or even suddenly get a huge amount of attention from going viral. Going viral doesn't mean you're going to have any further success. In fact, tons of musicians go viral and it ends up netting them little-to-no lasting fanbase after a few days when the attention dies down. Most of the time, this is because they weren't prepared to go viral. The difference between being a blip on the radar or launching the start of your career is being prepared before you get all of this viral attention and then making sure you take advantage of this attention by building upon it.

Being Prepared
If you do happen to go viral, you need to prepare properly for it. When something goes viral, there is often a huge rush of traffic--sometimes within only a few hours. If you aren't properly prepared to capture fans and make the most of this opportunity, you can lose the chance to convert thousands of listeners into fans. While you may get lucky and notice a huge traffic spike, it may be too late to take advantage of all these new listeners and make the most of this opportunity.

Capture
If you go viral, take all of the people who discover you and turn them into fans. This means if they're watching your YouTube video, you should inform them about your other social networks. You should have a way to trade an email for a download of your song. Point them to a free music page where they can dig deeper and become a fan of more than just the one song and get addicted fast. Find some way that you can stay in touch, even if it's asking them to subscribe to your YouTube channel.

If you get tons of attention and everyone is now looking at you, you want to make sure you give these new fans content they can chew on. Release a new song, give new content away and most of all keep momentum going.

Be Available
Your music should be everywhere so that if these listeners want to start listening to you, they can do so easily. Let's say your YouTube video heats up but your music isn't on Spotify, the place where this listener does all of their music listening. You have squandered the chance for them to get addicted to the rest of your songs. Last of all, you should have the ability to sell content to these new fans who are now interested in you. These new fans are much more likely to spend money on you right after you blow their

minds rather than a month from now when you finally get your merchandise act together.

Build
The next thing you need to do is pour gasoline on this spark. Once many blogs, news outlets and other gatekeepers see that your content is going viral, they will want to jump on board and gain traffic from it. Make sure you research as many places that you can to send your content to. Even if someone turned you down before, they may now reconsider when they see you have a much bigger audience that they can exploit.

Lastly, you need to interact with your new fans. Since you had all of your social networks linked and got fans' emails, you can now contact them and offer prizes and contests if they help spread your content even more. Make sure to socialize with them and get them excited and talking about you. All of this can help get your new fans to keep spreading the word and give your viral content more legs.

Using Exploits To Your Advantage

In hacking culture an exploit is a whole in a system where you can get in and get a massive payoff without anyone realizing how you did it. This is why your apps always have to do security updates since some nerd has figure out how to exploit their system and get your grandmothers credit card number. So what does that have to with your music? In music marketing there are always exploits that allow similar for building a fanbase, just it doesn't usually involve robbing anyone blind. These exploits can either expose you to a ton of fans via a platform or by getting you a lot of press.

If you aren't catching my meaning let's discuss some past exploits.

- **Vulfpeck** – The group Vulfpeck put out a silent record they encouraged their fans to play in order to fund a tour. It got them tons of publicity and grew the group's funds and fanbases immensely. They also have their own font which got them press and allows fans to express themselves through the identity of it.
- **Bots** – For years before bots were known to the world hackers were driving up plays on videos making their groups seem bigger than they are.

288

- **YouTube Features** – YouTube regularly rolls out new features that help artists do bigger numbers or sales. When you stay on top of them you can often get promotions.
- **Emerging Technology** – Platforms that are emerging often allow artists who experiment with the format to reap huge benefits. See all the artists who got big from Vine before the major label artists knew to rush in. Right now Twitch and TikTok have tons of exploits to take advantage of.

Exploits are essentially hacks you can spot that will get you a huge result from very little effort. So the problem becomes that while these offer a huge ROI how do you make them happen?

How Do I Exploit Exploits?

The fact is most exploits are hidden in plain view all the time, you just need to take advantage of them. Here are some ideas on how to spot exploits.

- **Watch Marketing Boards** – There are tons of marketing message boards that are always showing examples of these exploits. Subscribe to their YouTube channels and message boards and get inspired. Even if they are message boards for other things aside from music you can often bring some of the marketing ideas to what you do in music and reap huge rewards.
- **Follow The Blogs Of Social Networks** – YouTube, Spotify and other services have blogs where they literally tell you how to take advantage of their exploits. In 2018 Spotify made a whole video series called The Game Plan that told you best practices to follow so they will promote your music since if you follow them it makes their service a better place.
- **Keep Your Ear To The Ground** – Most exploits come from seeing a crack in the system.
- **New Technology Is A Publicity Opportunity** – There have been SO MANY careers bolstered by taking advantage of a new technology. Think about how many articles you've seen about someone who "recorded their whole record in the Apple Store" or was "The First Record To Only Accept Bit Coin For Payment". Look at new technologies and figure out how you can use them to create a story around your music

Chapter 17: Spreading Your Music With Your Live Show

It seems like we hear someone declare that live music is dying every other year. And then in the subsequent year, we hear that it's booming again. Despite the prevalence of iTunes DJs, online streaming, free MP3 downloads and more music available than ever, the live music experience still remains unique and impossible to replicate. There is so much good music available (mostly for free) that it's hard to argue that recorded music hasn't become, in a way, disposable. What isn't disposable is the memory created by a great live show.

As humans, we value safety and structure, but we also experience boredom when life is too predictable. Live music has always appealed to that need. You never know what emotion you will feel when you go see a great act play. Watching the visceral intensity of musicians recreating their songs live in front of you still has the power to amaze the masses and perhaps more importantly, to grow your fanbase. Playing amazing shows is the best kind of advertising you can do for yourself. But the competition is fierce, as there are a lot of live acts out there trying to make a dollar. In order to survive and thrive, you have to separate yourself from the pack and bring a special experience to the stage every single time.

Improving Your Live Show To Spread The Word

A great live show is one of the great marketing tools for growing a fanbase. When you're great live, fans talk about it. I still talk about great live sets I saw 15 years ago. There is no better promotion than blowing the faces off a room full of people. When fans experience a memorable live show they tell everyone they meet about it for a long time to come. With that said, there are some not-so-obvious pieces of advice for getting your live show above the fray, enabling your live set to become a tool for getting more fans.

There Are No Excuses In Live Shows!

As we all know, the competition is stiff in the world of live music. No one cares how hard you have to work; all the audience wants is to see a good final product. In the movie *The Runaways*, there is an amazing scene where producer Kim Fowley hires some teenage boys from the neighborhood to throw bottles and dog crap at the girls in the band while they play. He says it teaches them that they still need to be able to play a great show, even when the crowd hates them. While you will hopefully never deal with that level of abuse, you'll probably have to deal with crappy monitors and equipment failures on a regular basis.

Part of being an amazing live act is ensuring that no matter what the circumstances, you still deliver a great live set. If you use a lot of MIDI in your set, part of your practice is taking this complex gear apart and putting it back together. Playing a lot of VFW halls and house shows on tour? Practice without being able to hear the vocals and your amp turned down lower than the level you're comfortable with. If you get good at playing amazing shows--even in the worst scenarios--you'll blow everyone away when you're in the best-case scenario.

How To Turn A Show In Front Of Eight People Into One Of Your Most Important Shows
If there is anything that can be traced to musicians' antidepressant prescriptions, it's the immense disappointment of playing to small crowds night after night. It even happens to arena-level acts. We've all seen great musicians play at decent-sized venues that are almost completely empty (whether due to a competing show, poor promotion or even a declining fanbase). Despite the lackluster turnout, smart musicians take the stage and play a great show regardless of the circumstances. This makes every concertgoer an even bigger fan. Here are a few scenarios where you can make a heartbreaking show into one that will grow your fanbase for years to come.

Socialize
While not always the case, many musicians get opportunities because they're friends with another musician. The single best thing you can do at an empty show is to get together with other musicians and discuss real things. Are they on SoundCloud? How is it working for them? Which of the tools are they using? The guitarist has that new Dr. Z amp? How does it sound? You just read a fantastic book that they should read <cough> <cough>? Tell them what you think! Talk about what you have in common.

When you make friends with other musicians, they want to help you, play more shows with you and maybe even tour together. Whether this leads to them getting you on shows or playing your songs to their team member who you'd love to work with--it pays to be friendly in these situations. You never know which acts are going to get huge. And even when you think a musician sucks, they could get a whole lot better in two years and take you with them. If you haven't figured this out by now, being an asshole doesn't make you seem like a rock star--it just makes you seem like an asshole.

Audience - It's not just musicians that you can socialize with. You can talk to the audience too. Something weird happens when you walk into a bar and it's filled to the brim with people. It makes it a little harder to approach people, because the situation isn't very exclusive or special. On the other hand, if you walk into the same size bar and it's kind of empty, suddenly everyone starts talking to one another. This same thing happens at shows. It's totally acceptable to hang out and make good friends with people and in an empty venue it's more welcome than ever. No matter how big or small a show you play, meeting the attendees can turn them into fans and turn the fans you already have into super-fans.

Impress - Once, a long time ago, I was in a band. We rolled into a desolate town and played a show to a dozen people. There were more musicians in the bands that played than audience members in attendance. Despite this fact, we went on stage and did what we always did: We gave it 110%. After the set, 10 of the dozen people in attendance came up to us and said they had never seen a band go so crazy, despite no one being around. Everyone rewarded us--and I mean everyone in the audience--buying tons of our merch to make up for their town being so lame that no one had come to see what ended up an amazing show.

It turned out that in attendance that night was a girl whose brother was A&R at one of the largest indie labels in the country--a label we dreamed of being on. After listening to our demo, the girl called her brother and said she'd just seen the second coming of Christ (aka our band) and that even though no one was there to see us, we destroyed the stage and had the most amazing demo ever. The next thing you know we're on the phone with an A&R man being courted. You understand the point--you never know who's watching, so always play shows as if the rooms are completely packed. While it is highly unlikely that there will be some connection to a powerful music business player at the show, you have zero chance of impressing anyone if you're not trying your best.

Word Gets Around - When you give it your all-in front of a small audience, it isn't just about the sibling of a famous A&R person who might be in attendance. When I see musicians give amazing performances to small crowds, I tell everyone. The fewer people at a concert, the more powerful an amazing performance feels. Fans, especially tastemakers, bloggers and huge music fans, love to tell friends about an experience that was amazing--this is even more true if very few people experienced. If you play a great show, the eight people in attendance will tell 16 friends how great you are and the word will keep spreading. Trust me, I have heard my father talk about seeing Bruce Springsteen in front of a dozen people over a hundred times--and I've told almost everyone I know about seeing Refused in front of less than a hundred people. When this word of mouth happens, the next time you roll into town it's likely the show won't be so empty.

Keep It Clean - I'm not going to be unrealistic and tell you to play every show sober. Some great musicians play their best sets intoxicated out of their minds. What I will say is this: Don't use the show when no one is there as the time to test if you can actually drink a whole bottle of absinthe and still get through the set. As stated above, this is an opportunity to blow potential fans away, not become Internet famous after the picture of your vomit all over the drum set gets turned into a .gif by Stuff You Will Hate (on second thought, this may help you). This is the night to get eight people telling every one of their friends, "I saw ____ and even though no one was there, they blew me away with how amazing they were." Save the drinking contest for practice or the next time you play a party.

Take Requests! - If you're playing a show and the eight people there are actually fans of your music, make it fun and engaging for them. Bribe your fans by offering them what they want. I once saw one of my favorite major label bands play to a quarter-packed room and they made it one of the best shows I have ever seen. They had a tambourine and said that if we rocked out hard on the next song, whoever danced the hardest got to play it in the chorus. The crowd went crazy!

After taking requests they even attempted to play a song they'd never played live. The crowd was so psyched and we told everyone we knew about how great it was. Because of me going on and on about them, some of my friends got into their music and they made new fans. Don't look at an empty room as a letdown, look at it as an opportunity to get your fanbase talking.

Video Tape Your Performance

Your mom loves your show. Your boyfriend gets SO HOT when he sees you sing. Your bandmates are convinced that The 1975 has never sounded as good as you did last night. Your manager swears a "big deal" is right around the corner. What do all them have in common? They don't know what the hell they're talking about. Perspective (especially the objective kind) from others is good, but no one knows your music like you do. You can't be there in the crowd to hear how you sounded and see how you looked, but luckily you can videotape yourself and watch it later.

For You - If you ever took a public speaking class, you learned the same lesson. As painful as it can be, facing up to the truth of what you look and sound like is vitally important to improving your live set. Vocalists can attest to the tricks of perception: Many times you may have walked out of a vocal booth convinced you just eclipsed Rufus Wainwright with your sonorous sounds, only to head into the control room to discover you sounded like a tuneless frog with whooping cough.

While some cameras have better sound than others, videotaping yourself *really* comes in handy when trying to improve your live performance. Are you active and animated (*read: enjoying your own music*) or rigid and amateurish? Does your drummer get tired and lose steam after the first half of the set or can he keep up? Are the long pauses between your songs losing the crowd? Is your "witty banter" with the crowd necessary? Were those light bulb costumes you wore on stage actually worth the money? Get a camera and find out.

For The Rest Of The World - If you want people to come see you in this modern world, you need to record your live set and put it on YouTube. Live videos attract potential fans to shows. Videotape your shows seriously and you'll get more heads to your show and help you become a better live act.

Get Feedback - Everyone wants someone to congratulate them and tell them they're a musical prodigy, but the only way to improve is to get honest feedback. This means asking people who you trust, not groupies and those who won't be completely candid for an honest opinion. The most valuable question to ask someone is, "How can we improve our next show?" Even great musicians have room for improvement, so let your ego take a backseat and instead be honest with yourself so you can take you to the next level.

Watch Shows Of The Other Acts In Your Scene

No band is an island (that is, unless you're in the band Islands or Future Islands). As unappealing as it may sound, you need to get out and see the other acts in your town and especially in your scene. Not only will you see what your competition is up to and how good they are, but you might actually learn from their music and stage show. One of the easiest ways to do this is to watch the sets of the other musicians you play with. Not only is it polite and a great way to make friends, but you can learn a lot by watching them.

Make It Interesting With A Visual Element

Most of us spend our teenage years dreaming of playing arenas and getting to do cool things like blow up a tyrannosaurus rex on stage, shoot lasers through our legs during a guitar solo or project images of frogs being blown up like a Jodorowsky film. Okay, maybe those were my teenage dreams after watching too much Beavis & Butthead, but you still want to do something that looks totally awesome on stage. The good news is you don't have to wait until you get to the arenas to do something cool. By going the extra mile, you'll give fans something to talk about. This word of mouth promotion is a powerful way to build a fanbase.

Light Show - You know your stoner friend who hangs around your practices flicking his lighter while you rock out? Well, he would probably be the perfect guy to run the light show at your next gig. This can mean everything from playing with the lights that the club already has to bringing your own lighting rig, which you can piece together easily and do tons of creative visuals with.

TVs - These days everyone is throwing out a TV that isn't flat or the size of most small Manhattan apartments. These TVs are great to scatter around the stage and play your film-student girlfriend's college videos on while you look at your shoes and hide in your bangs pretending to be deep. Even better--with some cheap wiring and knowledge, all of these TVs can be fed by one DVD player or computer that is chained together. Get creative.

PowerPoint Presentation - While you may think of these as what your mom does when trying to show quarterly earnings to Bob from accounting, they are a cheap way to project images while you play. They can easily be synced up to Apple, events or even the click of a pedal. You can learn to do many cool tricks if you spend time with the program. You can make these presentations for free by using Google Docs. Either hook into the club's projector or get one yourself and bring along a laptop to play the presentation and start entertaining your audience with cool visuals.

Projection - Many a drugged-out college band has played behind a white sheet while projecting an Andy Warhol film in front of it. Then later, when sober, they've looked back at these shows and sworn it wasn't them acting out this cliché. Despite this obvious faux pas, it doesn't mean you can't get a projector and show some really cool images while you play. Many clubs have projectors and screens that you can use to pull this off. Bring your laptop, some cables and you're set.

Doing It On The Cheap - These ideas are cool and all, but this all costs tons of money, right? Lights, TVs and projectors can all be had for little to no money by scouring friends' basements, Craigslist and eBay. With a little effort, creativity and hacking, you can do some amazing things on the cheap.

Give The Soundguy A Shirt
Perhaps you've heard this joke?

What's the difference between a sound guy and a toilet?
A toilet gets crapped on by one asshole at a time.

That's why you want to be nice to him! Not only is today's sound guy usually tomorrow's top record producer, tour manager, A&R person or show promoter, but he also has it hard and everyone at every show blames them for every problem there is. One of the best promotional moves I've witnessed is to give the sound guy a T-shirt at every show. Usually, he is broke and if he likes you, he'll wear it all the time. This is great promotion for you since he is one of the most visible guys in the club every night, giving you a free ad and a friend every time you come back to his venue. He is usually the key to local fun and sometimes might offer a place to stay, so be nice and reap the rewards.

Give Other Musicians Your Shirts
One of the single best ways to get free advertising is for other musicians to wear your T-shirts on stage in front of all of their fans. One of the cheapest ways to get a lot of promotion is by always giving the musicians you play with free T-shirts. If this seems like an expensive promotion, you can ask to trade merch with them, so you get something in return. In my eyes, this

promotion costs a few dollars and you can spend your money on much dumber promotions. It's effective and offers a high reward. Plus, you'll make up whatever it cost you when that musician's fans check out your music.

Tell Them How To Get More And Have Some Fun With It
It can be like groundhog day when going to see live acts night after night-- in between songs all you hear about is, "There are T-shirts in the back" and how they "gotta get to the next town" and their website URL is repeated non-stop. Despite how tired a cliché this all is, you have to make sure that you remind fans they can get more. If you have a free music page, this is one of the best ways to develop a fan relationship, so obviously you want to inform all of these potential fans about your free material.

Spelling out a full Bandcamp URL can be pretty lame, so if you have stickers, make sure the URL to your Bandcamp is stamped on the back. Maybe make postcards, wristbands or flyers that say how to get free music. You can throw these out into the crowd or leave them for free on your merch table. Remind the audience that they can find out how to get free music and make it easy to remember. Also, remember the ability for fans to get freebies lures them to your merch table, where they can see all of your merch while they're still high on your live performance.

A fun way to do this is to tell fans to go talk to you or your merch guy about some dumb subject. Is your merch guy obsessed with Pokemon? Tell your fans to be sure to go talk about that with him after the set and get some free music. Another way to make it fun is to buy a URL that has a free download of your music on it with a really funny URL. It could be <yourbandname>lovespokemon.com or whatever other weirdo obsession you have. Think of something fun and catchy and it will help with the response.

Booking Shows

Until the day you are headlining arenas, every musician will always wonder how to book better shows. While a lot of these answers are frustrating to hear, you need to accept the reality of the situation. <u>You're trying to get paid to do something a lot of people want to get paid to do.</u> After you've accepted this, you can now realize you're going to have to make some smart moves and do hard work to get the privilege of getting paid for something this awesome.

Where To Start?

At some point you have to play your first show. Trying to get your first show is often one of the more frustrating moments of a musician's life. You have to start somewhere and that somewhere usually sucks. The way you should always view your early shows is that they're a way for you to work out the kinks so you don't embarrass yourself when you get bigger opportunities. In this time, you should figure out your strong points, weed out the kinks and most of all, get experience you can use to get to the next level.

When you haven't yet built a fanbase, you're going to have to play anywhere that will have you. Obviously, scouring the local paper and looking at flyers in the town center, record stores and coffee houses are all great places to find the names of local venues. Then hit the Internet and see who will have you. If a venue seems like they book your style of music, this will make your life a lot easier. Sadly, sometimes the cool venue isn't going to let your unknown band play quite yet and you'll have to resort to open mics, battle of the bands and the crappy venues who will have anyone or, worst of all, pay-to-play venues.

When playing your early shows there are a few habits to get into in order to make sure you can skip ahead through this process as fast as possible:

- **Visual Recording** - Videotape and photograph every great moment and get them on your YouTube channel in some way. This can mean uploading the best song performance of every show. Even if the quality isn't amazing, it's at least some online presence. If someone is debating seeing you or booking you, they have a basis to make their decision if this visual evidence exists.
- **Draw** - Keep track of how many people you brought to the show so you can give future promoters an honest estimate of how many people attended a show. Even if the number seems pathetic at first, getting that number to 20 people as opposed to only your significant others is the difference between getting to the next step or still playing horrible shows.
- **Build Fans** - Make sure anyone who enjoyed your music signs the email list. One of the biggest mistakes musicians make is not

collecting the emails of those who would potentially come to
another show from day one. Start now!
* **No One Leaves Empty Handed** - Everyone who watched you
  should get something from you, be it a burned CD, sticker,
  download card or something else. *Much more about this later.*

Your Live Show Strategy Is Insane

The definition of insanity is to keep doing the same thing over and over
again, expecting different results. Coincidentally, you'll constantly see
musicians drive from town to town where they have no fans on a Tuesday
night and expect a miracle. They think they will roll into town and play a
sold-out show, because by some miracle they have 250 fans hiding under
a rock in this town. Another fantasy is arriving at a show and somehow one
of the acts you're playing with is secretly a huge act with a humongous
draw. All of their fans will show up early enough to catch your set, love your
music and show you this in merch sales.

This is insanity and unfortunately we all watch friends do this on a daily
basis. Many musicians have their momentum, wallets and time drained by
driving for days to cities that don't care about seeing them in order to fulfill
some myth about paying their dues. If this is what you're doing, please
stop.

If you play a show somewhere and it has a bad turn out, don't play there
again unless you're going to do something that will improve that outcome
next time. If you played in a town and no one came, don't go back until
you're sure the situation will improve, by doing some further promotion and
proactive work. Those six hours you were going to drive to a far-off show
are often better spent talking to other musicians who could help you draw a
crowd one day or taking care of one of the hundreds of other tasks you
could do to build a fanbase.

The Next Step

Look at you! You've played some shows and, believe it or not, fans that
you've never met have come to a show to hear your music. Now you want
to take the next step up to a venue that hasn't let you in its door yet.
Perhaps it's the cool club in town where touring acts come through and you
want to be the local opener for a cool headliner. How do you convince that
promoter to give you a chance?

Draw - You need to write them and tell them how much you can draw. This needs to be a real number of people based on a concert attendance you've had before and can replicate again in the future--not a lie or a guess. Believe me when I tell you that any good promoter will know you're lying. Either from asking the venue you played or by their own natural wits. Sure, you can probably inflate your draw by 10 percent and get away with it, but anything more risks a promoter not believing you in the future, when your draw really will increase. When I was booking a couple hundred shows a year, I prided myself on calling musicians out on lies about their draw. I was often at the shows watching the band that time they claimed they drew 50 people. So I knew firsthand it wasn't 50 people, it was 10 (me being one of them). Don't embarrass yourself and burn this bridge by being a liar.

Usually, if you get the gig, the venue will say that you need to sell X amount of tickets and that if you don't, you won't be booked again. Worse, you may be asked to put up a deposit for the money for those tickets, so if you don't sell all the tickets the promoter will still get paid and you'll be out of the money. Granted, this can also be a great chance to get a fantastic opening slot if you're willing to shell out the cash.

Music - Obviously, you need to link your music. Sometimes the venue's website will tell you how they want links to be sent. Some promoters only want to listen to your Facebook page, others want you to attach your best song as an MP3 to the email. Others may only want to see YouTube videos of you playing live (more and more common).

Who Are You? - Give them a one-paragraph bio. Got any members who were in bands that drew a local crowd before? Opened for big acts? Worked with a big producer? These can all be great assets to describe instead of listing your band's personnel and what instruments you play. Keep it short and simple, tell them about your sound, but don't get long-winded and poetic.

Social Networks - One of the ways promoters gauge your draw is by looking at your social networks. If you claim you draw 50 people and only have 100 Facebook likes, they're not going to believe you. Link your Facebook page and one other social network that has impressive content on it. Do you have a fantastic video on your YouTube channel? Point the promoter there. Does your Soundcloud have a bunch of comments or followers? Just as good! No need to link them to every social network on earth, just the impressive ones.

Photo - Unless they ask for it, please take a pass on this. They will see your photos on your social networks.

Be A Part Of The Scene - One of the easiest ways to get booked at a venue is to go there often. If the promoter sees that you know other regulars and are a part of what's going on, they're more likely to see you as being on the level of who should play their venue. Usually being out and friendly at shows in your scene will also increase your draw, since many people go to these shows to be a part of a scene. They're at the show to be a part of what is going on and the act playing that night is inconsequential. You and the promoter may end up becoming great friends and developing an awesome working relationship.

Many promoters are lazy and will often tell an act that already has a draw to pick someone to open for them. The headlining act also understands they need to pick someone that will help them draw or else it's their neck on the line. Musicians usually choose their friends, so meeting other musicians when going out to shows helps your chances of making this happen. Going to other musicians' shows and showing them support can also help get you these gigs.

Next Big Sound - When I talk to promoters, many of them tell me they're looking at Next Big Sound to see if an act is worth booking. They want to see enthusiasm and metrics rising and whether there's already a good fanbase in place. Just one more reason for you to make sure your metrics on NBS are going up.

Offer Promotion - A great way to convince a promoter to give you a gig is to offer special promotion. Perhaps you have a friend at the local radio station and they'll play your song. Will you put up 1,000 flyers for the show? Will you take an ad out in the college paper that your sister edits? Will the city's coolest blog write up the show and say that everyone needs to go? Use your imagination and resources and be sure to mention any of the assets you can offer. Just make sure whatever you're offering will happen or else you risk burning this bridge.

Persistence - If they reject you, feel free to try back in three months. It sometimes takes a little more growth before you're qualified to move up to the next level. Did you play a great opening show for a national act? Do

302

you have a new recording that is WAY better than your last? Update the promoter, but don't overdo it. Every three months is a nice interval.

Get Nerdy - Facebook, Instagram or Google Analytics and let you look at how many fans you have in each city. Look in their analytic sections and if these numbers are impressive, be sure to list them. You can also do the same with your mailing list by using geo-targeting features. Type in the zip code of the venue and tell them you have X amount of fans in their area on your email list. This nerdery can be impressive: Just make sure it's true.

Want Better Gigs? Get A Picture Of Yourself Playing To A Big Crowd - When looking for better gigs, have a picture of yourself playing to more than just your relatives, friends and significant others. Even if it registers with a promoter subliminally, having a few pictures that show concertgoers don't run out of the room the second you strap on your instruments can help you get better gigs. Showing someone has believed in you enough to put you in front of a large crowd is a vote of confidence for an insecure promoter and a small step toward getting a better show. Anytime you play to a larger-than-usual crowd make sure you capture it and show it's possible for you to hold an audience's attention.

Keep Track Of Attendance - Asking the promoter how many people were at each show should become a habit whenever you settle at the end of the night. In addition, if you sold tickets to a show, that information needs to be kept track of. Having this information in an organized format helps you show that you mean business. It can also help you learn what to expect as you start to tour around the country and explore other areas.

Look For Magnet Clubs
Musicians are always wondering how to get on bigger shows. A lot of musicians' questions don't have a simple answer, but this one does. Most cities have an ecosystem: Larger clubs look at certain smaller venues to find talent to open for the bigger shows in town. In New York City, the concert promotion company Bowery Presents has a magnet system where small acts play their smaller venue, The Mercury Lounge, and as they move up, they get picked up to open shows at their much larger venues like Bowery Ballroom, Music Hall of Williamsburg and Terminal 5 (as well as the venues they own in other cities). Pulling impressive numbers at the smaller venues gets you bigger shows opening for huge national acts and the chance to play in front of 3,500 people at their largest venue.

Many other cities have a similar network. It's important to research which clubs you should play at in order to give yourself the best chance to grow. In every city, there are some insular venues that don't help elevate musicians and others that will. Finding and researching these avenues is one of the hidden tricks to making big moves and building your fanbase.

Contact Other Musicians, Not Promoters
Another hidden tip to making booking easier is that you don't always need to contact promoters, at least at first. Social networks allow you to research gigs in towns you've never even been to. By using the information in the targeting chapter of this book, you can find other musicians who play your type of music in every city.

Once you do find these like-minded musicians, it's good to contact them and see where they recommend trying to play. If you have solid connections with booking agents in cities they want to play, you can exchange shows. This is helpful for getting a good show in another town. If you're able to play for a strong local act in their home city and you can do the same for them, both of you benefit enormously. If you aren't able to play together, at the very least you can get a good contact for a promoter.

If the acts you find are unresponsive, you can at least look at their upcoming tour dates and get a good idea of where you should be playing. Finding acts that are similar in size in other cities can show you many different things and the time spent doing this research is priceless. These connections can last and benefit the both of you for years to come.

Book A Residency
A residency can be a great step before you start touring and playing out of town more than in town. The idea behind a residency is to make your presence at a venue a regularly scheduled event. For example, you may play every Tuesday at your favorite bar in town. Each week you'll be charged with booking musicians to play with you, so that fans that come out each week see a new and refreshing experience. Perhaps you'll collaborate with the other acts you invite. Maybe you incorporate different DJ sets into the night or make a theme of each night. No matter what, if you can bring a new and interesting flavor to each night of your residency, you can thrive in your local scene and give fans a place to have fun and enjoy music every week. This can gain you a great reputation and if you're able to bring depth to this residency, gain you a buzz and respect as fans spread the word about your talent.

304

Check The Local Calendar Before Booking A Show
Imagine booking a show at your apartment for the middle of the summer with a few of your friends' bands and a touring band. Your large loft apartment can hold 300 or so people, so you promote it pretty heavily. You flyered, posted to every Internet listing, texted everyone you knew and--by your count--had at least 150-200 people confirmed to come. Unfortunately, the day you had scheduled was also the day of a huge annual music festival with multiple acts. At that huge show, everyone in attendance gets sunburned to a crisp and totally exhausted. Though your show started after the festival was over, it didn't seem to matter. Around 8 PM you receive tons of texts saying everyone was too tired and beat from the earlier festivities (aka soaking in 98 degree heat all day) and your attendance is down to about 50 people.

Had you picked up the local concert listing paper in advance, this disaster could have been avoided. The excitement of finally getting an awesome gig can be overwhelming and lead you to be delusional about your chances of getting attendance if it's up against another huge event. Try getting a good crowd out the night before Thanksgiving in NYC when everyone has gone back to the suburbs for the weekend. In some cases, no amount of promotion is going to get you a good crowd. Stay aware of what else is going on if you're going to pour hundreds of dollars into promotion for a gig or invite important people out to show off your huge following. Otherwise, you could be left looking like a chump.

Canceling Shows
Bands are a dime a dozen. Despite what most musicians believe, they're not unique. And even if you are unique, it's unlikely most people have realized it. With that in mind, remember that canceling a show is one of the worst things you can do to your fans and reputation. Sure, there are times that sickness or unexpected circumstances prevent you from playing, but it should always be your goal to play every single show that you commit to. When you're unreliable and cancel shows, word travels fast. Even if it's a tiny show on a weeknight in a small town, there might be fans that were anxiously waiting to see you. These fans are a valuable resource you can't afford to disappoint. If you don't think it's a good show, don't commit to it. Otherwise, you should follow through with every show you schedule, for no other reason than to maintain the reputation of an act that lives up to their word and respects everyone they're involved with.

Change It Up

No matter what style of music you play, if you want to keep fans coming to shows again and again, you need to give them a different show from time to time. Many musicians are able to start selling out shows in one town or another, but keeping fans coming back every time you play is a real challenge. Finding ways to keep your fans curious about what you'll do next is crucial in getting the same fans to keep coming to shows for years to come. Whether it's having interesting stories or banter between songs, improvising arrangements, crazy dance moves or just having fresh material to play, you need to find a way to show your fans you'll give them a new experience every time they see you. One way to advertise this is to make sure multiple sets of yours are on YouTube, so fans can see how different each experience can be.

Selling Your Own Tickets Can Help Build A Fanbase

For years, disgusting and greedy companies like Ticketmaster have found every way to gouge concertgoers for every dollar possible. Whether it's setting up their own scalper services or tacking on insane fees--music fans have despised these cretins for a long, long time. Unfortunately, they held a lot of power in the music industry and it was near impossible to work without them. Thankfully, that's changing.

Many new services allow you to sell tickets directly to your fans and scan them at the door of the venue. This means you can take out extra fees, be good to your fans (aka leave them with dollars to spend on merch) and most of all, capture their email so you can tell them the next time you're playing. The possibilities are endless, but you need to work out a deal with each promoter to make it happen.

Here are some ideas of how you can sell tickets for shows yourself.

- **DIY** - The easiest way to do your own ticketing is by putting on a show yourself. You can reap huge financial rewards since you don't need to pay the promoter's fees. Many venues will let you rent them out for a private event, then you can sell tickets through your website. Make sure you can sell enough tickets to turn a profit or else it's your own money lost. Hopefully, the extra money you get from taking the promoter out of the loop will help you make this a profitable experience.
- **In Conjunction** - You can work out a deal with a promoter to sell tickets from your website as well as theirs. This way you can

arrange to get a higher percentage on the tickets you sell yourself. As long as you're bringing in people, many promoters are open to ideas.

Tools To Sell Tickets

- **Limited Run** - Limited Run (limitedrun.com) have an awesome multi-platform ticket-bundling program that even sends amazing reminders to concertgoers the day before the show.
- **Bandcamp** – Has a great facility for selling tickets to fans.
- **TicketFly** - Sell tickets through TicketFly's (ticketfly.com) website and then scan them at the venue afterwards.
- **Eventbrite** - Popular ticketing platform that allows you to sell tickets on their website and scan them at your venue. (eventbrite.com)

Taking It Out Of Town

You're now the opening act or maybe even headlining at some local venues. You don't even know the people showing up at your shows for a change. What's even cooler is that you're doing so well the venue even lets you choose one or two of the opening acts for your shows. It looks like it's time to take it out of your local area and begin to build a fanbase in another town. But how do you do it? Is the next city is so far away that none of your fans will come? You're starting over from scratch. Don't have a nervous breakdown--it's time to leverage the awesomeness you've acquired in your hometown.

Connect - The first thing to do is look around and find the big local acts in your genre. Check to see that they have a similar level of concert draw or social network followers. Maybe offer to have them open up for you at your next gig if they do the same for you. Not only will you be making friends with another act, but you'll get introduced to an established fanbase of potential fans who will most likely love your music when they see you. You can find these acts by using the techniques in the targeting chapter. This will also serve the purpose of helping you build up a scene and create a network of like-minded musicians that will come in handy throughout your career. The musicians who you play shows with are often the people who will help you for years to come. You'll become so close with them you may play in bands with them or even have them at your wedding. These are your future friends and this is how you make them.

If you're having trouble with this you can also talk to the promoter in your hometown and see if they have a hookup in another city. You could ask fans on your social networks where and with whom you should be playing.

It's Alright, You're OK - There's something venues find cool about hosting musicians from out of town. Suddenly it's a bigger deal: There's this mysterious traveling act coming through town and it creates an event. Use this to your advantage. Talk it up and demonstrate how huge your buzz is in your city. Brag a bit when you talk to the promoter in this other city.

Guarantee - One of the other great benefits of your cool status is that you can now say, "Hey, if I am going to leave the cool place where I am popular and come to your little town with my big show, I need X amount of money." If you say the same amount of money you just made at your hometown headlining gig, you're going to get laughed out of town before you even get there. But if you give a modest price that covers your expenses in getting there, you'll probably be in. Sometimes the first time you come from out of town you'll not get a guarantee and just be paid off the door. While not ideal, this is a first step to growing your fanbase in this new town.

Door Deal - If you can't get a guarantee, it is customary to agree on a percentage you will get of the money collected at the door. You can ask that if the show reaches a certain amount of capacity that you will get an increased percentage. This is a standard nearly every promoter will agree to.

The Myth Of Needing To Tour--Take Weekend Trips Instead
Somewhere in the stories musicians tell each other, there became this myth that the first thing you do to prove yourself--even when you can barely draw a crowd in your hometown--is drive to the opposite side of the country and play to people who have never heard of you. This makes no sense at all.

Don't Tour As Fast As You Can - There is an ever-growing herd of musicians who think that if they get out there and start touring, they'll get attention from booking agents, labels and fans. While I wish the world was this fair, it's not. Many musicians walk into this methodology thinking that they should abide by the mantra "look professional and you'll be perceived as professional." Here's the problem: While a long tour looks professional on a website, it doesn't look professional to all the musicians, promoters, loved ones, etc. that played to eight people each night instead of spending that time building a fanbase the smart way.

Spreading Your Franchise

The smart way to build this fanbase is to slowly grow from one city to the next. Let's pretend you're a hamburger shop. You open up shop in your hometown. Imagine you're having a lot of trouble getting customers to come to your hamburger shop. Is the answer to now all of a sudden drive to every town on the opposite side of the country and sell your hamburgers for a single night and hope people talk about it? Of course not. There may be some logic to the idea that if customers aren't liking your hamburgers, going one city over and where fewer vegans live could help you get customers for your burger shop. While the people in the next town over might start liking your burgers more than those in your hometown, it makes no sense to drive all the way around the country selling hamburgers out of the back of your van.

So what does make sense? For one, if your hamburger doesn't seem to be selling in the town you live in or the next one over, perhaps you need to work on your recipe, get a little better and maybe come up with a new formula (think of this like getting a better recording or improving your live show). And when a hamburger shop finally has customers lining up for hamburgers, what does a hamburger shop usually do? It spreads to the towns surrounding it. This is why you see In And Out Burger littered across the west coast but not the east coast and Shake Shack being a mostly NYC-based operation.

Practical - Let me put it to you another way. Being a musician is expensive. I know you want to quit your job and move out of your parents' basement. But let's be smart about this. Clock in at that crummy Monday-Friday job or keep going to college. This way, you're going to make money to support your music. Then on the weekend, play in three different cities Friday, Saturday and Sunday. You won't go broke and you won't be thousands of miles from home playing to only a handful of people.

Smarter - When you're on tour, odds are Monday or Tuesday you aren't even going to be playing. This means you're going to be playing 5-6 shows a week. The other downfall is that even if you do play Monday, Tuesday and Wednesday, you'll have small crowds. Worst of all, there are a lot of times you're playing cities where barely anyone likes your style of music. Trust me, it's not easy getting people out for a dance-punk show in

Alabama compared to New Jersey. Usually on tour, one of these nights is spent playing in a city you booked just to get to the next town.

However, in two weekend trips you can play just as many shows as you would play on one week of tour. You'll also be able to make money to afford better studio recordings, more promotions and all sorts of other things since you didn't quit your job to go on tour. In most of the country, cities are grouped close together enough you can do this on a pretty regular basis without playing the same cities twice in a month.

Think Of It As Going Viral - A much more fun way to think of this concept is making your live show go viral. Though we usually only think of videos going viral online, this is how you should think about your live show strategy. If you've ever watched a horror movie about how some crazy zombie disease spreads, you know it starts in one city and then slowly starts to spread out in a circular pattern to the next cities. These zombie diseases are usually a "virus" which is where the term "viral" comes from. You want to emulate this movement and make your live show strategy viral. Once your virus has infected much of your local area, it's time to spread out in this circular motion. As you conquer this circle, you can make the circle spread wider and wider, infecting more and more people.

Momentum - Another upside to constantly playing weekend shows is that it's an easy amount of work to schedule during your week. It can keep your momentum going with a steady climb of fans without having to save a bunch of money to tour all the time. You can make new relationships every single weekend and see consistent growth all while being able to get promotional work done during the week and accomplish the other parts of promoting your music from the comfort of your own home--keeping your family, friends and significant other a little happier.

Logistics - In general, you're going to want to book a show on Friday that's close to home, go further on Saturday, then play a show on the way home Sunday. You can make Sunday's show the farthest away but you may be driving home through the night and going to work feeling pretty lousy the next day. You can route a variety of different weekend tour routes to keep things fresh each weekend.

Myth: Booking Agents Won't Book You Unless You Have Toured The Whole Country

Many of the musicians who walk through my studio embark on these ridiculous cross-country tours thinking this will land them a booking agent and a record deal. This is insane. I know a lot of booking agents and none of them care if a musician does this. What they do care about is working with a great act that fans like to go see. They want a professional act that is starting to pick up a draw in multiple cities. Yes, obviously they want to know that you'll tour, but if they see your calendar filled up with upcoming out of town shows and that fans are coming out to these shows, the last thing they're going to care about is whether these dates are on the opposite side of the country.

If you're drawing big in a bunch of cities that aren't your own, have a good buzz and keep getting increasing returns every time you play out of town, booking agents will care about you. Traveling 3,500 miles from home doesn't prove you are worth anything to booking agent.

THIS SUCKS! I Want A Booking Agent - Yes, I know you do. Every musician that doesn't have a booking agent wants one. One of the reasons there are few booking agents in the world is because the job sucks and it sucks even more when you aren't a booking agent with a huge roster. So, how do you get one? There is no single answer, but there are some usual cases. Usually, you show that you're able to convince 100-300 people to come see you in a few different towns every time you come there. If you can do this, you'll usually begin to get attention from potential team members and some booking agents will hear of you.

You can try writing a booking agent a cold email, but in all my years of doing this, I have never seen that work. Gaining a crowd, keeping a busy calendar on your social networks and meeting the right people will get you one. The sooner you accept that your cold email will not work, you can start working on techniques that will actually get you a booking agent.

Be Willing To Play For Free
A lot of folks will tell you that you should value your art and that when you give something away for free, people value it less. That's a nice armchair philosophy, but the reality is that music is everywhere and most people don't have to pay very much to get it. People like to think of "market value" as some evil political term that shouldn't be thrown around with something sacred like art, but even art has to face economic realities. By opening yourself up to playing for free, you can reach a huge group of potential fans that would never have otherwise heard your music.

311

It's important to think of playing free as an investment, not as a waste of time. Free shows can produce money from merchandise and can add addresses to your email list. Most importantly, it starts word-of-mouth promotion and gives potential fans a "risk-free" trial of your music. The whole "support the arts" movement is fine and dandy, but if you want to build a fanbase, some shows are worth investing in to get a bigger outcome of new fans that will later support you. That's an investment I would make any day.

Let's imagine you're a quirky electronic producer and Flying Lotus is coming to town, but they have no openers touring with them. You have a decent following, but so do 20 other musicians like you. Naturally, the competition for opening act slots is going to be fierce, but if you're willing to play the gig for free, the promoter can relax a bit and worry about meeting the headliner's guarantee. I've seen this technique effectively used at some of the biggest venues in New York City. After you've built up some more clout and proven yourself at a large venue, you can easily begin asking for a little money. Wait until you've shown the promoter something before getting on your high horse. Free is never actually free--it's a sample of what you can do and an investment in attracting future fans.

Booking A Tour

You followed my advice and you now have a great following in a lot of cities within driving distance and, weirdly enough, fans in other cities are writing to you on social networks, asking you to play their city. This is great news, but now you've got to take this to another level. You're going to go out for weeks at a time and take over new lands. Obviously, this endeavor will require much more planning.

In general, you're going to want to start small: An East Coast, West Coast or Midwest tour. Usually, you'll do whichever of these regions you feel is convenient and responding well your music. Later on, you can do a full North American tour and grow from there. Let's tackle one region first and then apply the same set of rules as you grow.

Go It Alone - You can head out on your own. If you have a good buzz this can be a good decision, but odds are, you're going to want to take another act with you who has a similar-sized fanbase in order to increase the draw in cities where you're both barely known. While you don't have to take someone with you, it often helps the tour go more smoothly. This will also mean you won't have to handle the booking duties on your own. Just remember that promoters might get scared away by tour packages with too many unknown bands--so keep it to you and one other band when you're starting out.

Jumping On With An Established Act - It pains me to even write about this subject. Every musician thinks touring with bigger bands is their ticket to success and they should be the one who gets this opportunity. Many musicians waste the entirety of their days writing bigger acts asking if they will take them on tour. This is usually a waste of time.
I know, I know--you think you're great and if they would only listen to you.. Stop! They aren't going to. In most cases, this is how you get on tour with an established act:

Connections - Acts who were submitted for support by another booking agent. Yep, cronyism at its finest. Once you have a booking agent, they get emails from other booking agents saying that one of their acts is looking for an opener. The qualifications to get this opportunity are detailed by this booking agent. Sometimes, they're a sales mark or how many people you can draw on a headlining tour each night. Other times they will want an act that will commit to contributing to the marketing budget of the tour.

Friends - Musicians who are friends with the established act. In general, the headlining act on a tour almost always ends up taking someone they're friends with--oftentimes for no other reason than they want to hang out and watch them every night. That's how it is. Accept it and learn to work within this system.

Buy-Ons - A headlining act sometimes puts a price on how much money they would want towards marketing their tour in exchange for a total unknown act to get to be on the tour. This "bribe" is called a buy-on. Usually, the buy-on act is the first of four or five acts in the night and play to half packed rooms and rarely get the value for the amount of money they put into this. If somehow you have crazy amounts of money to burn, this is a way to skip the line. But realize that it's quite rare to buy on a tour and see results.

If you're going to do a buy-on, make sure you negotiate a reasonable deal with terms that make sure you don't get the short end of a stick, especially considering what money you're going to be investing.

Making It Happen
How on Earth do you book a tour? The first thing you need to do is start finding the right venues to play. A great way to do this is use Facebook's geo-target function and start asking your fans from that area which venue to play at. If you have friends in acts from other venues, you can trade contacts. It helps as you meet promoters to keep their contacts handy in your contact database.

Once you know some promoters, think of how to sell the idea of you playing at their venue. If every act on your tour is relatively the same style of music with a decent buzz, it gets pretty easy. If you're going to promote the tour with ads, posters, appearances or whatever else, this can really help your chances of getting booked. If you have any major press going on this would be helpful to tell the promoter as well. The key is to sell promoters on why they should want to take a night out of their busy schedule to let someone they haven't heard of into their venue.

Growth - A lot of building a fanbase is about making investments in every city. Putting a little more promotion into each time you return can be helpful in increasing turnout. Making sure you're diligent about getting fans to sign up for your email list ensures that you'll be able to tell them the next time you're in town. Making sure fans know how to easily download your music for free will make it so they have the potential to become bigger fans, tell friends and bring more people each time you return.

Play Where Your Fans Live
Analytic technology offers the ability to find where you should be playing shows and where you shouldn't. Earlier in this chapter, I mentioned you shouldn't play in places where no one is going to show up. One way to see if anyone is going to show up is to turn to your analytics. Embedded in many services you use each day is the ability to see how many fans you have in each city. Here is what you can look at in order to determine if you should play in a certain city or not.

- **Facebook Insights** - Facebook will list how many of your Facebook fans exist in each city, state and country. This is great for gauging where you have enthusiasm for your music and where you should try to play.

- **YouTube** - You can use YouTube's analytic area to see where fans are watching your videos and where your subscribers live.
- **SoundScan** - If you have a record that is selling well, you can pay for the ability to see your SoundScan, which will also break down which cities your record is selling in.
- **NextBigSound Premier** - This software can pool all data from all of the above and put it all on a map for you. While it costs money, it's an amazing tool for marketing and booking tours.

Routing A Tour

It's easy to screw up the routing of your tours. It's great to think you can play that gig 14 hours away from the last one, but that isn't always the best idea. When routing a tour, you're rarely going to get to play cities in the perfect route you would like. Before taking a show on a tour, always think about the following first:

- **Gas** - Make sure the show pays more than the gas money it takes to get there. If it doesn't, be sure you have some money saved.
- **Grueling** - Make sure it's possible to get to the show and play well. If you're going to drive all night to get to a show with every member sitting upright in a cramped van seat, you may not play too well when you get there. Every musician has different needs in order to perform well. Make sure each show is within these bounds. Multiple excruciating drives in a row can bring a tour to a stop with sickness and exhaustion (which may lead to fighting among band members).
- **Possible** - Make sure it's physically possible to get to the next show. I've seen far too many musicians' book shows and not realize the distance on the map is greater than they think. Use Google Maps and make sure you can actually make the drive-in time for the next show. Montana is a *long* state, that's all I'm saying.

Knowing Markets

One of the keys to successful touring is to know your markets. There are no easy rules to touring and where you should play. Many musicians think they need to spread out and play every 200 miles across the country, but this neglects population density. For example, Maxwell's in Hoboken, NJ (and just recently closed after 30+ years) is about 5 miles from The

Mercury Lounge in Manhattan. Both are great gigs for an upcoming act and the overlap of fans that will go to both venues is small. Maxwells caters to the northern New Jersey crowd. Twenty-five miles away on Long Island is The Vibe Lounge. While that seems small, most of the attendees at these shows won't be at either of the other two venues. Depending on population density, different markets may need to be hit all very close to each other to get to different fans all packed in a close proximity.

There are also markets that are totally dead. Sixty miles to the East of the Vibe Lounge is The Hamptons, where no punk band is going to have any success playing. But if you're an electro-house DJ, you may do well there. Forty miles west of Hoboken is Sussex County, NJ--good luck getting anyone out to a show there unless you're the local cover band.

Research - The answer to all of these problems is to make sure you watch where the musicians you target play. Talk to your fans about where they go to shows. Don't make the mistake of skipping markets that seem close together or look like you should play them on a map. There are pockets where you need to play three shows to reach everyone and other areas that you should almost never play. Some acts can sell 20 million records and never need to play the top of Idaho.

How To Book A Tour With Guarantees?
The funny thing with guarantees is that they aren't actually "guarantees." Instead, they are promises, which are easily broken. You may deal with some shady promoters when you're out on DIY tours. However, if you have an established draw in a handful of cities (with demonstrable proof), a guarantee is something you can usually bank on.

Do Your Research - If you're going to try and negotiate with a promoter, make sure you know everything you can about the city and venue you're playing. What type of musicians play there and how often? What's the average turnout, capacity and ticket price? The more you know, the more likely you are to get a better rate.

Get Real - Musicians love to price themselves out of a club. It somehow makes them feel better about their music if they ask the club for an insane amount of money. Missing out on gigs because your guarantee is too high is exactly the opposite of being professional--it's completely amateur. It's also no way to build a fanbase. Your market value is what it is, which means that while you shouldn't take less than you're worth, you certainly shouldn't let your ego get in the way of planning a great tour.

Get Creative - Touring doesn't mean you have to play the same old tired dives all your friends play. Sometimes the Statesboro, GA Boys Club might have some extra cash lying around to bring a cool act to their gymnasium for some music-starved kids. Not only will you make money this way, but you're playing to hungry music fans that don't have 10 great venues in their backyard. Even small colleges often have entertainment budgets and can shell out actual cash for you to play. Just because it isn't the venue every other similar act plays in town doesn't mean that the show can't be cool and a great investment into fans that always support you.

Work Hard & Compromise - Remember that venues (no matter how slummy or crude) are businesses and they have a bottom line. They can't give you money they don't have, so do your best in negotiations and compromise when necessary. Sometimes they may not be able to give you a $300 guarantee but can offer you a door deal. If you're confident in your ability to bring in more than the promoter thinks you can, both of you are in for a pleasant surprise. No matter what, whatever you do is going to require lots of hard work and follow-ups. Your first few tours you might not have a guarantee on every show--but don't let that slow you down. Take the opportunity to show a venue what you can do and then perhaps you'll have more negotiation power next time around.

Playing Colleges
For many musicians, the college crowd is their ideal demographic. They consume so much music and even better, they usually pay really well whether anyone shows up or not. Here are some suggestions for how to get college gigs.

- **Fans -** The best way to get these gigs is to have fans solicit their college planning committees to have you play. If you have a strong following in a college town, make geo-targeted messages asking your fans for help.
- **Play In Town -** You're much more likely to get these gigs if you play at the desired venues that students prefer.
- **NACA -** The National Association for Campus Activities helps colleges plan events. You can get on their list by paying a couple hundred dollars. While this is steep, if you have a good buzz and have been doing some touring, one gig can make this money back.

317

If you have a booking agent, they're probably a member. You can also register as agents and split the costs between a few musician friends.

More Dates Doesn't Make It A Better Tour
When you're a young musician, it's an easy mistake to measure your worth by how many tour dates you can rack up and how long you can stay out on the road. Nothing could be further from the truth. It doesn't matter if you're playing Asia for a month straight or traveling coast to coast in the US for the entire year. If no one shows up to watch you, it doesn't mean anything. Playing live shows is inspiring and invigorating, but that novelty quickly wears off when the money runs out and the crowds stop showing up.

A fruitless tour can leave you frustrated, broke and at each other's throats. Don't think that adding a few more dates simply for the sake of making yourself feel better will improve things. Despite all of the excitement, tour life can be grueling. It's better to start out conservative and small and see how you do, instead of burning yourself while trying to do too much. While it might stroke your ego to tell your friends back home that you're going out on the road for 90 days, that doesn't mean it's the best thing for building your fanbase.

Relentless - There's a myth that you should be out on tour every day you're not recording. Not the case. Be *very* afraid of touring too much. If you're touring constantly and hitting new places, you continue to build a fanbase. But revisiting the same places too often will tire out your fans, lower your draw and make the region dead for you. Hit new places, give your best places some attention and build other areas appropriately. Don't overstay your welcome anywhere. Leave them wanting more!

Taking It To Another Country
Eventually if you are doing well touring the States, it may become time to plan a tour abroad. This is not something we suggest doing yourself. There are hundreds of pitfalls and money traps you can fall into that can make this a disaster if you don't work with someone who knows the terrain. If you feel you are gaining a substantial following in another country, it is often best to contact booking agents or a foreign label who would potentially release your music there and get them to handle bringing you over. Find these booking agents by talking to other musicians who have traveled abroad. There's many more risks for disaster if you don't have someone who knows the ropes taking you overseas. Especially if your crew has

someone with a criminal record where you need to secure tons of permits to get them across the border.

If you haven't built a fanbase that is excited in your home country, odds are it will not be easy to get anyone to take you on and bring you on tour elsewhere. However, if you are doing well and have made your way across this country, it may be time to start talking to your connections and figure out who you can talk to about getting you across a pond.

Tasks To Take Care Of Before The Show

Guest List vs. Getting Paid
One of the big debates at shows is the size of your guest list. It's unrealistic to think that a promoter is going to put all of your groupies, siblings and friends on the list, all because they're "down with the band." If you have a big guest list, the promoter is going to want to pay you less (even if you promise they will drink a lot). You also face the dilemma of having to balance friends with the many people who are important to put on the list, such as writers, label types, DJs, etc. Snubbing these people for a spot can breed resentment from powerful tastemakers and those who work hard on your music for little benefits other than this free show. It is worth taking the pay cut to get them in.

Your Rider
Bands dream of the day they can put all the ridiculous requests they have seen on The Smoking Gun on their rider. While you think it may be funny to put a drawer full of M&Ms with all of the brown ones taken out in a rider, this all cuts into the money you're making. A rider's true purpose is to ask for the needs that you don't have time to get before a show. Towels, a case of water, beer and a meal are practical. A rider is meant to make it so you don't have to leave your pampered backstage life while doing interviews and dealing with other inconveniences. It's not meant to be a contest to see how far a promoter will bend over backwards for you. When you make the promoter work hard for a ridiculous rider, they're going to pay you less or be less eager to have you back to play. Consider your rider carefully and think about what's important to you. If giving everyone a good laugh on The Smoking Gun when the world sees your rider is more important, have a go at getting those midget strippers in cages in your dressing room. Otherwise, get serious.

319

Your Input List

Bands constantly throw hissy fits when the venue's sound system can't accommodate them. One way to alleviate this in order to make sure the venue isn't going to charge you for rentals for sound equipment is to get them an input list (a breakdown of your setup and sound needs) when you book the show. Even if your setup is simple, having an input list is required by many venues and is expected if you get on a professional tour. To see what a standard input list looks like, head to this link. (bit.ly/inputlist)

Your Stage Plot

A stage plot is another important part of being a professional act. When shows are crammed together with far too many acts, a stage plot helps the soundman get a quick and easy mix and set up for your performance, not to mention ensure your monitors and sound needs are easily accommodated. These plots not only show where each member sets up on stage, their name and their instrument, but also what they like in their monitors. This can be a valuable asset and help keep your asshole singer from declaring war on the soundguy mid-set when he freaks out that the congas are in his monitors. To see what a standard stage plot looks like, head to this link. (bit.ly/stageplot)

Online Booking Tools

ReverbNation's GigFinder

If you want to submit directly to venues or search one of the largest, most complete directories of venues to find shows, you have it right here. GigFinder (reverbnation.com) uses your ReverbNation Press Kit to submit you for gigs at the venues of your choosing. You can search by area or even where musicians similar to you have played which makes this process very easy.

Sonicbids

Sonicbids (sonicbids.com) is one of the oldest networks for venues to find acts to play. Musicians simply make an EPK and submit to venues or festivals (like CMJ and SXSW). One point of contention many have with Sonicbids is they do charge to submit to many opportunities, which ignites a comment storm on our blog every time the Sonicbids name is mentioned.

You're able to submit to all sorts of opportunities on the service, including broadcast, licensing and tours.

MyAfton
A gig booking service that helps musicians connect with venues looking to book acts who can draw. The site works closely with those in its network to insure a mutually beneficial booking that has a good draw for both the musician and the venue. (myafton.com)

Concerts In Your Home Is Exactly What It Sounds Like
If you have the type of act that's "house-broken" (meaning you can play quietly), there is a whole network waiting for you. Concerts In Your Home (concertsinyourhome.com) is a service where musicians who want to play house shows can get in touch with hosts who would like to book them. The site is geared more towards the acoustic/folk circuit but is continuing to expand to many other genres. The bands I grew up playing in performed "basement shows" across the country in every "punk house" that would have us. With the help of the Internet, this movement has the potential to be stronger than ever. As someone who has hosted a handful of shows in my own living room, I can attest to how much fun this can be.

Eventful Helps You Plan Tours
To a lot of you, mentioning Eventful (eventful.com) is nothing eventful. They now boast 10 million users and 75,000 performers who use their awesome service. If, for some reason, you don't know about Eventful and how you can use it, here's a quick primer:

- Place a widget on your website using their Demand It! feature. It will tell you which cities your fans are in and where you should route your tour.
- Their widget allows your rabid fans to email it to other friends who like your music, so they can request you too, helping spread the word about you.
- If their users (any of the 10 millions of them) subscribe to your news, they're notified any time you're passing through their town--a great way to boost concert attendance.

Indie On The Move Takes DIY On The Road
Indie On The Move (indieonthemove.com) is a new comprehensive website that provides musicians with an up-to-date database of venues in the US, complete with ratings and reviews of clubs. The site also features a

personalized email system that allows you to contact music venues, booking agents and other acts directly using their large, frequently updated database. A quick dig around the site will find a decent list of tour tips. Especially considering that the service is free, there's no reason not to take advantage of it.

Book Your Own F*cking Life
Are you a punk band? Then this service is for you. This resource has been around since I was a teenager, in print form, but now it lives online. This is a resource that tells you about promoters who put on punk shows all across the country. It's older than the Internet and it's amazing if you're the right band. (byofl.org)

Additional Tools
TicketLeap - Helps musicians sell tickets and provides promotional tools. (ticketleap.com)

Chapter 18: Promoting Shows & Increasing Turnout

Play Events, Not Randomly Put Together Shows

If you're tired of playing shows where no one shows up, join the club. One of the main reasons no one shows up to the majority of shows is that there is nothing eventful about them. Many lazy show promoters will throw anywhere from three to seven acts on a bill whose styles of music mix so badly it makes the fans not want to watch the other acts. It's hard to get people to spend money on a show like that. The first way to increase attendance at your shows is to play with other musicians who your fans would appreciate. This isn't always easy, but it needs to happen unless you want to be playing open mics and half-packed rooms forever.

Diversity - Obviously, the opposite can work too--you'll see festivals where Jay-Z, Skrillex and The National all share the bill. This works because the event has some of the biggest names in music, all sharing a stage and they all have enthusiastic, diehard fans. But when you are playing with other acts that don't have much of a following, your audiences just get annoyed.

Bring It Together - If you can put together a night where all the musicians on the bill complement each other in some way, it's much easier to sell your show to potential fans. Something like "seven of the area's best hardcore bands," "an all-night dubstep assault" or "a celebration of the music of the '60s" captivates interest much more than seven random names on a flyer.

Something Special

If you have a bunch of like-minded people in one place, you can go even further and truly make your show an event. Are you an artsy band that plays in costumes designed by a fashion designer? Why not hold a fashion show in between the bands and bring in a group of people that wouldn't normally be interested in going out to your gigs? Do you play some old-timey '30s or '40s weirdo music? Maybe have the local steam-punk guy bring down his creations to display at the show. Is your fanbase a bunch of snobby yuppies? Maybe you can convince local organic food vendors to set up tents at your show so foodie-yuppies turn out. If you are a DJ who

323

plays some rock-friendly jams, maybe you should have a band do a set. If you write very smart songs, maybe have a local author tell some stories while you play instrumentally.

Fans want to attend special and unique events. Think about what makes you excited as a fan about going out to events. This is always what you should strive to make your shows.

Real World Promotion

Once you have your event planned, you need to promote it. Unfortunately for some, this means you might need to stop instant messaging your cyber-love for a few minutes and actually leave the house to promote a show effectively.

Flyering

One of the oldest ways to promote a show is to do the old flyering routine. No matter what future world you live in, every town still has a corner, coffee house, record store, high school, music store or even a venue that will allow you to hand out flyers. You can also hand them out at local shows when bands play and you think their fans would like you. A key to successful flyering is including a few details:

- **Credits** - Don't just list the acts playing--tell people in short form why they should be interested in attending the event. For example, "Gorilla Biscuits (NYC Hardcore, Revelation Records)" will immediately tell fans of this genre why they should care about going to that show.
- **Imagery** - Every genre or event has imagery that works. If you're doing a metal show, you don't want pictures of candy all over your flyers.
- **Color** - Colors give away genre well. A black metal show will almost always have a flyer in certain fonts and a mostly black flyer cries out to the eyes of fans of that genre. Neon colors are an instant nod to dance music fans. Figure out the colors and fonts and make sure they coincide with the crowd you want to have at your event. It's the difference between catching someone's eye that brings a group of friends to your show and playing to an empty room again.

324

- **Unavoidable** - The best advice I've ever gotten about flyering is to be unavoidable. Until your show happens, your promotions should be anywhere your fans might be. Drive to the record store on the other side of town to put up some flyers if you have to or the local bong shop so all the stoners know what you are doing.

Tour Posters

Tour posters are one of the best promotions you can invest in. They allow you to get free advertising space in places where potential fans will be. If you're going to be out on the road with the same acts for a while, it's usually a good idea to go somewhere and get tour posters made up. These are hundreds of posters mass produced with a blank spot where you can enter the date and venue information for each show on a tour. Printing posters with your latest album cover and then writing in the date, time, venue and acts you're playing with is a superb way to raise awareness of your music. You can find these posters inside or outside every venue touring acts play.

You then need to mail these posters along with some stickers (and a nice note) to your promoters. You can even mail these to street team members who are savvy enough to post them in the places potential fans hang out. You can also send CD samplers to the local record store if you want to put your all into the show and hope they may hand them out to customers who like music similar to yours.

Services like BandPosters (getbandposters.com) will print and mail posters to each of your gigs for $15, if you don't want to bother with printing, packing and personalizing them.

Appearances

Are you really cool in the eyes of some fans? You can sign autographs at a record store in town. Many musicians will do a meet and greet where you can meet up with fans and talk to them before the show to get them excited. Lots of musicians will also do this after the show and advertise that it's happening as an extra incentive to get fans to attend. This will involve posing for pictures, signing autographs or a quick hangout with some fans. Some musicians will do a special hangout with fans on the street team or fanclub to give back for their support and hard work.

In-Stores

Another way to get hype for your show is to do an in-store, meet-and-greet or performance at the local record store. A DJ set (record stores love when you play what's in stock) or acoustic performance is a great way to get added promotion for your show at a big venue you are playing later. This will also put you in good graces with the store and get your posters hung up and your record recommended. These record stores are often friends with local DJs and bloggers, who will announce this event and get you free publicity. Remember, many record stores are dying (literally, record stores are dying) to get people in the door, so it may be easier than you think to set this up.

Giveaways

Getting local blogs or radio stations to give away tickets is great way to get the word out. I have even seen local coffee houses and record stores do drawings for tickets to a popular show. No matter what, this is an easy way to sway an outlet that's on the fence about giving you press, since this helps them maintain their following too.

Interviews

Publicity

Doing interviews for local radio, blogs or newspapers are great ways to get the word out about your show. These interviews will usually mention your show and your music, helping get more fans out to the show. Promoters can often help arrange these interviews.

Concert Listings

Many radio stations and newspapers do concert listings. If you're playing a venue that doesn't send updates to the press, you can try submitting them yourself. Sites like SongKick and BandsInTown will do this for you automatically when you update your gig dates.

Friendliness

I have known many acts that get to town hours before load-in and hang out in the town center, skate park or mall. Be friendly and try to convince people to come out to the show.

Some musicians also get great success by tweeting to fans that they're hanging out at the mall or a town center before the show. They will then use the power of the crowd to tell others to come see the show that evening. They will play songs for passersby to raise their show attendance.

Musician Friends

Are your best friends playing the same venue the week before you? Hit them up and ask that they announce your show on stage to help turnout. This is crucial.

Mail Download Wristbands

All clubs that serve booze need to use wristbands to mark who is of age to drink. Why not order some download code wristbands (both CD Baby and TicketPrinting.com sell them) and give them to the club before you come to town, in order to promote your music before you even get there?

Backstage Is For Losers

While it is smart to meet the other musicians you're playing with and bond with them, you also need to get out from backstage after your set and talk to the fans that enjoyed your performance. Give them a chance to make a personal connection with you and give them an extra something to remember you by. This will help grow your relationship and get more fans out to your next show. There's almost nothing more important than this aside from playing a great show as this is the thing you can do to build fans bonds to you more than anything else.

Co-Ops

If you have a lot riding on a show or if you're starting to gain a following in a certain town, you can see if a local record store will do a co-op in the local paper. These co-ops are ads where your record is featured in an ad with the record store's name on it as well, mentioning that it's available there. This is often traded for special placement in the store.

Ads

Yes, ads in papers can help raise awareness of your show. While not the cheapest way of promoting your show, the right placement can help to raise awareness for your show in a big way. With that said, make sure the ads are worthwhile. You don't want to put an ad for your music in the wrong publications. For the money you're spending, make sure your ads are effective. Always consult your promoter and see where they've seen effective results from advertising.

Name Your Own Price Shows

Lately, I've been hearing more musicians using "name your own price" as admission to their shows. While this can get potential fans in the door, I've heard mixed results in how well it works out. One of the oldest tricks in the book is to pass the hat around after each act plays, which is a similar pricing model. Depending on the community you're in, this can be more profitable than charging a set fee.

Promoting Outside Shows

An obvious place to promote your music is outside your own shows and outside other similar acts' shows. Perhaps you played first when 15 people were watching and now there are 1,500 people at the venue. It could be a big stadium show for some corporate sellout band you hate, but their fans may love you when you show them the cool, fresh sounds you have. No matter what, there are some easy techniques you can use if you want to make new friends and fans.

- **Similar Shows**- There is no better way to get potential fans out to your next show than to target fans that are out at shows of similar acts. You already know they like going out to shows that are similar to yours. Hand out burned CDs, flyers, stickers or whatever else you can spare.
- **Headphones** - Playing your music for a new friend can lead to sales and new fan relationships. Ask fans wearing T-shirts of similar acts to hang out and play them your new music off your iPod. You can easily make a new fan that will be at your next show and hopefully many more to come if they like what they hear.
- **Target The Young** - The younger the fan, the more easily impressed they are. Trying to impress a 30-year-old isn't so easy. To a 15-year-old, everything sounds great. If you're the first artist to take the time to interact with them directly, you could build a lifelong fan. I've seen many musicians build followings by giving kids music for free.

Go Where Your Potential Fans Hang Out

While anyone can go to shows of other musicians and hand out flyers and CDs, that can get old after you do it for a few weekends. There are plenty of other places you can go where you can find potential fans. Think about where your fans would congregate aside from music clubs. Here are a few ideas:

- **Barbershops** - In his early days, Jay-Z would pull up outside the local barbershops blasting his music and then sell CDs from the back of his trunk. You can leave CD samplers and flyers at the local barbershop or do just as Jay-Z did.

- **Strip Club** - Everyone from Motley Crue to 2LiveCrew intentionally marketed their music to be played at strip clubs. Labels would service every strip club around trying to get them to play their song in the club, hang posters, etc. If this is your targeted fanbase, reach out to them.
- **Protests** - I attended Occupy Wall Street a lot when it first started up. It didn't take more than a month before I saw musicians handing out flyers all over or just playing there live. If your fans like to hang out protesting things, you should hang out protesting things too. *Just please, no more drum circles.* I can't take anymore of them.
- **Book Readings** - At a Chuck Palahniuk reading for one of his more violent horror books, I got a free CD from a band who had written that their lyrics were way more violent than Chuck's latest book. A bold claim indeed, but very creative.

Finding Places To Promote Your Show

- **Record Stores** - The Coalition of Independent Music Stores (cimsmusic.com) has a list of nearly every indie record store in every city across the country. You can use this list to call them and see if they're willing to work with you on stocking your record or putting up flyers.
- **The Promoter** - A lot times your promoter will know the writers to contact for press. Asking them this question can help get you some serious breaks on press if they have friends in the right places.
- **Radio Stations** - There is a list of every radio station and what they play at radio-locator.com. Finding the right DJ to send your music is a different story, but if you Google a bit you can find information on every station, including where to send music or a phone number. College radio stations are usually the easiest to contact.
- **Coffee Houses** - Use Yelp.com or Google Places to scope out spots that will potentially hang your flyers.
- **Fans**- Ask your fans or street team (more about that later) to put flyers, stickers or whatever you've got in the right places. If you have fans in a certain town, ask them where to go and oftentimes they're happy to help
- **Take A Walk** - It's good to walk around town and see where flyers are hung, talk to the locals and make friends.

- **Printing** - I've had great luck printing posters, flyers and postcards from both JakPrints (jakprints.com) and VistaPrints (vistaprints.com).

Online Show Promotion

Promoting your shows online is by far the most effective way to get your message to a lot of people on a tight budget. Below are a few ideas on how to do some obvious promotions a little more effectively:

- **Facebook Geo-Targeting** - Facebook updates from your page are great promotional tools, but don't annoy your fans and make sure to use geo-targeting. This is what that little location marker under your status update is for. This tool enables you to target fans around a particular area where you're playing and not annoy fans from other areas. This makes it far less likely you'll annoy your fans and get hidden from their feed.
- **Facebook Events** - Creating a Facebook event is a great way to let your friends and fans know about a show. Putting in details and making it lots of fun is smart (more about this in the Facebook chapter). Just be sure only to invite friends who live in the area of the show.
- **Twitter** - Twitter is great, but there are rules for Facebook status updates and Tweets. Tweet about the show no more than a few times. Tweet four to six weeks out to announce a show, then the week before as a reminder about it, then finally the day of the show to build excitement. Any more becomes annoying and will get you unfollowed.
- **Message Boards** - Message boards that are local or for your genre of music are a great place to get the word out to potential fans. Get to know your online scene.
- **Cover Photo** - You can add tour dates to your Facebook cover photo; that way if someone comes to your page they can see the upcoming dates immediately.
- **Email** - Email your mailing list. Employ geo-targeting since a lot of your fans are not going to want to hear about it. There are few ways as effective at getting fans out to shows as emailing people who live in the area you're playing and reminding them of a show.

Remember to get the zip code of every fan who signs up for your mailing list.

- **Listings** - List it on your page! BandsInTown, ReverbNation and SongKick all make great ways to do this for your Facebook page and website.
- **Blog** - If you have a separate blog other than your website, make sure the info is there.
- **Craigslist** - Craigslist has event calendars and listings. Many local papers will take from these and include them in their own listings. Be sure to put your show there.

Banner Ads, Facebook Ads & Google Ads

If you're setting out on a long tour, buying some Google Ads (more on this in the chapter on advertising) can be a small but worthwhile investment. These ads can target locations and fans of certain genres of music. Some local blogs will charge you pennies on the dollar to put up an ad for your upcoming show. Some can even be accessed easily by using Google AdSense.

Using Video To Promote Your Shows

If you're a video genius and can whip up smart, interesting videos fast, this is another great way to promote your upcoming show. Everyone loves a good YouTube video. Making a quick YouTube video is an eye-catching way to get fans' attention and get them to spread the word.

Annotate - If you have a YouTube video that is getting steady views, you can add an annotation to it with the show's details or a link to the show info. Remember to remove this annotation after the show has passed.

Live Video - You can post live videos from previous shows to get fans excited for your next gig. If you're on tour, it can also be a great idea to do tour updates or post videos from the road to help highlight remaining shows. Showing off your personality never gets old to the fans that love you.

The Four Places You Should Enter All Your Concert Dates

Entering concert dates is one of the most annoying parts of playing live. It's both time-consuming and annoying to keep up with. Thankfully, it gets easier and easier each year to do this menial task each year. Entering dates into the services we have outlined below increases the chance of getting both fans and potential fans to your shows. Some of them can put

331

them in the places where your fans go to hear and discover your music, where as others alert your fans that have liked you on Facebook that you will be in their town. Entering your dates into these services also increases your chance of being added to local concert calendars in local papers and radio stations. Making sure your dates are always up to date in these four services will increase the likelihood of getting fans out to shows and we will explain why.

- **SongKick** – With SongKick (songkick.com) fans can enter the acts they want to see into a well-designed service and be altered whenever they are playing near them. If that weren't enough the service offers a way to easily keep your dates up to date on your SoundCloud and Bandcamp pages. If fans navigate to your music on HypeMachine and YouTube and you are playing near them, the dates will display under your video. If that weren't enough if you employ the use of widgets you can display your dates on your WordPress, Tumblr and Facebook page. They also employ Spotify app, which will alert fans when the acts they listen to on Spotify are playing near them.
- **BandsInTown** – BandsInTown (bandsintown.com) service alerts those fans that have liked your Facebook page when you're playing nearby, by flashing an alert on that little globe on Facebook—making the alert hard to ignore. They also have a great looking Facebook concert dates App that lets you show fans when you are playing. Their Spotify app will not only tell fans who've listened to you on Spotify, but it will also alert fans who listen to similar acts you, when you are coming by and create a playlist of acts that they may enjoy, which you will be included in.
- **Facebook Event Page** – Making an event page helps Facebook show friends where other friends are going and spread the word about your music.
- **Your Email List** – Use a geotargeted mailing every time you are playing to draw out local fans. More on how exactly to do this in our email chapter.

Staying Organized

With any luck, you'll doing this for decades to come and hopefully you won't have to keep doing these duties yourself forever. Keeping track of all the record stores you visit, your DJ contacts, the places you post flyers and whatever else you do to promote shows in each town is helpful so you can do the same thing the next time you come through town. You can also trade this information for favors and contacts with other musicians.

You're So Much Better Live Than On Record? Why Does No One Know This?

If there is anything most musicians regularly hear from their adoring fans, its they're *soooo* much better live than they are on their records. While some of this hyperbole comes from the energy of live, loud music and enjoying it with others, there are many musicians who are truly great live and should let the world know it. Many musicians who are great live don't exploit it or show this off to their fans as much as they should. Here are some ideas to help you show off your live skills:

- **Free Live Download** - The easy and obvious way to show off your live prowess is to get a live recording (even as simple as two mics in the crowd) and put it up for free for the world to hear, in the form of a free download.
- **Blog It** - Acts who employ a lot of improv and perform new sets every night should record every show and post them to their blog regularly. This can show fans that they get a new experience every time they come see you.
- **YouTube** - Live videos are a great asset if you do more than shoegaze on stage. The more you record yourself live, the better chance you have of capturing something special and having it spread across the Internet.
- **Include Live Tracks On Your Records** - Bonus live tracks on your album downloads are a great way to show the world what they're missing. This way, everyone who falls in love with your recorded songs can see you're also worth seeing live.
- **Invest** - Do you constantly put on a fresh, new show with an amazing performance? Maybe you should put some money into a live recording rig to show it off. Taking the time to edit the best parts and put them out there for the world to see can help build your reputation. Get creative.

As the saying goes, "If you build it, they will come." If you have a great live show, make sure the world knows it. Far too many musicians fail to exploit their live show. Don't be one of them.

Allow Taping At Your Shows To Keep Fans Happy

If you're the type of act who prides yourself on your live show, always allow fans to tape your live show. Surprisingly, this practice is all too rare. You can even encourage taping by roping off a section in the middle of the

333

venue for fans that want to record you. Encouraging fans to tape your shows spreads your music and is an obvious move for anyone who wants to spread the word about their amazing live shows.

Give Superfans With Tattoos Free Admission

Once upon a time in the '90s, the band Rocket From The Crypt used to employ the policy that any fan that got a tattoo of their logo would get free admission to their shows. Not only did this encourage a lifelong loyalty to the band, but it showed that the group was extremely important and helped to build their buzz over time. If a fan is loyal enough to go this far, they definitely deserve a free show.

Chapter 19: Your Relationship With Your Fans & How To Mobilize Them

One of the best parts about being a musician is that you get to do something fun for a living. Even better, your fans will want to help you because they love your music. When starting off, you may have to do tons of work for your music and you may not have a lot of money to do it with. Thankfully, if you start to accumulate a fanbase, you can get them to do some of the work for you--and amazingly enough they'll be happy to do it. Almost too good to be true!

If you want to mobilize your fans, here are a few concepts that will help you do so in the best way possible.

Your Fans Should Feel Like They Owe You, Not Like You Owe Them
If you're constantly asking fans to request you on a radio station, vote for you in a contest or other calls to action, remember there's only so much a fan can take before they feel like you owe them more than they owe you. You need to always be rewarding your fans for their support with incentives they find worthwhile. If you're using crowdfunding for everything you do and if you aren't giving good enough rewards, your fans will eventually grow tired of always giving you money and will find a more worthy musician to give their limited funds to.

Constantly asking fans for favors can strain your relationship. Fans want to voluntarily tell their friends about musicians who "treat them well." Countless studies have shown that fans will always support the musicians they feel a bond with. And it's very hard to feel a bond with an artist who is selfish or not giving enough to them.

When mobilizing your fanbase, be sure to choose your battles. Maybe you don't need to enter seven contests at once and beg fans to vote in a different one every day. If you decide to do this anyway, make sure you give great rewards to the fans that help you. Take your relationship with your fans seriously and make sure you're giving them plenty of rewards for anything they do.

Desperation - While fans love to help their favorite musicians when they're in need, it can be very unattractive if the musician is too desperate. If your van flips in Wyoming and you need to have a merch sale or crowdfunding campaign to get it fixed, fans will understand you're in a desperate place and need help. If anything, this motivates fans to help you who may not have supported you before. When Man Overboard flipped their trailer on tour years ago, we needed money in a short timeframe. We put up a limited-edition T-shirt that fans could buy to show their support so we could get a new van. So many fans that had never bought merch from the group before paid for this T-shirt in order to support a group in need.

However, this can go too far. If every part of your music career is a tragedy and you need help all the time, you start to seem a little pathetic and it seems like you can't take care of yourself. If your fans can't find your new tour dates because they are buried under 40 tweets about voting for you to play the county fair, that doesn't give them much reason to keep following you or supporting you. If you're so desperate for your big break that you bury your content, updates and connections with your fans in a sea of begging for help, that doesn't give a fan much reason to keep a relationship with you.

Random Acts Of Wow
In Tony Hsieh's book, *Delivering Happiness*, he talks extensively about surprising customers of his company Zappos with surprise gifts or even just expedited shipping. This endeared customers to his company and made them thankful they bought from him. The same can go for your fanbase. If a fan is doing a lot to spread the word about your music or is particularly excited about your music, imagine how much more excited they are going to be if you surprise them with a small gift you may find to be almost meaningless. You may have some leftover postcards, guitar picks or a test pressing of your record that is near worthless to you. To superfans, this can mean the world and make them talk about you even more than they already do. Never underestimate how far a small random act of "wow' can go in making a fan want to tell the whole world about you.

Selling Your Fans Experiences
For years musicians have sold fans experiences like private concerts and meet & greets. As musicians continue to use the Internet to find new ways to monetize experiences with fans, we keep seeing more and more creative ways this can occur. Instead of selling merchandise to fans, musicians are selling experiences that give lasting memories and

connections to fans. These experiences are more than just a way to make money, they give fans something special that they tell friends about for years to come.

Some of the experiences you can sell fans include:

- **Covers** - A cover song a fan chooses for you to do.
- **Skype Chats** - Give personal time to fans.
- **Hangouts** - Go play pool, cook dinner or do something fun with a fan.
- **Lessons** - Many musicians sell private music lessons to fans.
- **Collaborate** - Record, produce or co-write a song with a fan.
- **Special** - You can get ordained a priest and marry two of your fans.
- **Backstage Access** - Sell fans guest list spots and time with your backstage.
- **Unique Art** - You can create a special piece of art unique to an individual fan.
- **Special Calls** - Allow fans to purchase a birthday, anniversary or even a prank call for a friend.
- **Personalized Mixtape** - You can make a fan a personalized mix based on some music they may have never heard before that you enjoy.

When Your Funds Are Low, Employ Your Fans For Cheap Volunteer Labor
If you haven't burned out your fans and they do feel the urge to help you, there are a lot of ways to take advantage of it. While it may feel a little like slave labor to have your fans help you out for little reimbursement, remember they're doing this because it's rewarding for them--they get to be around someone they find to be talented and who makes music that impacts them.

Mobilize - When you have fans, it's a great feeling that runs like a two-way street. You appreciate their adoration and support while they appreciate how your music makes them feel. With that said, there are often invisible lines that musicians draw when it comes to mobilizing their fans and getting them to help out. To some, it's fine to ask your fans to call and request your music on a local radio station or click on an online survey, but for some reason, it's not OK to actually be in the same room with them to work on promoting your music.

337

This invisible line is silly to say the least and doesn't need to be observed. In politics, candidates employ volunteer labor all the time from their followers who want to see them succeed. If you have fans, convince them to do the same for you.

Don't Be Shy - You might think that no one outside of your friends and family would ever want to spend time helping promote your music, but you're wrong. Fans are always looking to bond with others who have similar interests and the prospect that there are others who share their same passion (your music) will excite them. If you can show fans that this is a place where they can have fun and make friends, you may be shocked at how quickly you can mobilize a large group. Never underestimate what bored fans will do if you give them something to talk about.

If You Build It, They Will Come - There are countless tasks you can employ your fans to help with; all you need to do is ask them. If you have enough of a fanbase that you can draw around a hundred or so fans locally, odds are that once every few months you can get 10 fans to come help you for a day or two.

Make it clear they get to spend time with you and offer enticements, like hearing new demos, sitting in during band practice or treating them to a meal. Definitely explain how much this will help you. It's important to tell them what could potentially happen if they help out. People like to see clear results and to feel like they're working towards something. Be detailed so they know what the work will entail, though be sure to describe the day as being fun.

If you make it fun and are good to those who work hard on your music, they'll want to come back and do it again. Obviously you need to get work done but having a few beers on hand (not for the minors, of course) and having someone DJ will most likely keep fans wanting to come back and do this again.

What Your Fans Can Do
- **Recommendations** - As I've said many times before, one of the best ways to get exposure is when people tell their friends about your music. One of the first favors you can ask your fans to do is tell everyone they know about your music. Have they posted a Facebook status linking to your music? Have they tweeted about

you? Can they promote you on Last.FM and Jango? Do they have a blog where they can post your videos? If they belong to any Internet message boards, these are amazingly effective places to promote if done right. Have everyone bring their laptops (just make sure you have Wi-Fi) and put them to work posting about you on message boards and striking up conversations with potential fans across the Internet.

- **Merch** - One of the oldest tricks in the book is to get a bunch of people together to work on silk screening. Posters, T-shirts, patches, and bags can all be silk screened and made into merch that everyone sees as an advertisement.
- **Packing Envelopes** - If you have CDs, there are a million places to send them--whether it's radio stations, lawyers, A&R, friends in the business, magazines, websites, etc. If you want to do a full court press on the press for your music, you'll never have enough money or hours in the day to send out promos. Have your fans help stuff these envelopes.
- **Hit The Airwaves** - If you notice a radio station is playing your music, you should have everyone you know request it so it keeps getting played. Even if it's in a far-off town, having your fans call in to these stations and get you played more can help spread the word. Many radio stations also take requests via the Internet, so get those smart phones and laptops going.
- **Ideas**- Talk to your fans. What sites do they like? Are you on them? Do they have ideas for how you can promote your music? Do they know someone who can help you? You'd be surprised at how much those who have never picked up an instrument know about where you can promote your music. If you listen, you can learn a lot. Sometimes inviting fans over to talk about this can open new worlds for your music.
- **Your To-Do List** - Take a look at what you need to get done and see if anyone has any special talents that could be useful. Do you need a new YouTube layout? Maybe someone knows HTML and graphics. The possibilities are endless. If you listen and manage well, these parties can help get you ahead.
- **Motivate** – Groups like The Maine keep a leaderboard on their website that shows the fans who work hardest for them and reward them with hangouts and other motivations.

What's A Street Team?

One of the advantages musicians get on large labels is the mobilization of a great, well-organized street team. These street teams are made up of fans across the country and the label mails posters, flyers, stickers and other promotional items to them. The street teamers help promote and are paid back with rare merch, guest list passes and access to the musicians they love. The most common use of a street team is to put up posters that announce your latest recording or concert.

Here are some ideas of what your street team can do in each city:

- **Posters, Postcards, Wristbands, Flyers & Stickers** - The most common task for street teamers is to put up posters for your album or an upcoming gig. They hit the busy parts of town and places your potential fans would hang out. Have them take pictures and include them when they report back to you. It can help to tell them places where you'd like to see posters, if you know any.
- **Soliciting Record Stores** - Have them go to the local record store and make sure your music is on prominent display. If your music isn't in stock, have the street teamer request it.
- **Handing Out Flyers** - Have them go to shows of similar musicians or at the venue you're playing and hand out flyers.
- **Request** - Have them request local radio stations. If they have a school paper, maybe they can get a feature on you.
- **Internet** - If there are local Internet message boards or groups they're a part of, be sure to have them post on them about your music. Have them update their social networks and make sure there is a Facebook invite for your event, etc.
- **Banners** - Have them post banner ads and hang out on message boards with your banner ad as their signature.
- **Collections** - If you have an email-for-a-track tool, have fans post those wherever they can.
- **Comment** - Comment on blogs--a meaningful comment that links your website or a free music page.

Managing Your Street Team
The first thing you need to do is get some volunteers by calling out to your social networks. Remember even if you have 100 fans, if two of them want to help out in two different cities, this can be a big help in getting you established in these cities. Once you have them, keep them organized and efficiently promoting your music:

- **Locations** - You don't need more than one street team member in each city (unless it's one of the big cities like New York City, Los Angeles or Chicago), but it can help to have members in different surrounding cities. For example, NYC has New Jersey, upstate New York and the Long Island suburbs. All of those suburban areas are very different and it's rare they have overlap. The same goes for many larger cities. Have as many fans as you can spread out in the different areas you're playing.
- **Organize** - Assemble the street team members in a list and get their contacts into a spreadsheet. Enter all of their data and look at a map. If you have too many street teamers in one area, narrow them down by judging their enthusiasm. You'll want to keep everyone's information in case someone messes up or doesn't do his or her job.
- **Slackchat** – It is common in grassroots campaigns to keep a slackchat with everyone on the team so questions can easily be answered and the community can help each other and stay coordinated (slack.com)
- **Narrow** - Once you have some volunteers, you can narrow the candidates down. Make sure the fans know you have very little money. Send them a list of what they're expected to do. The day before you're going to mail them their materials, ask them if they're sure they have time to get the duties you're requesting completed. If you have multiple volunteers, let them know someone else is willing to do it if they aren't up for the job. This will narrow the chances of having someone flake out on you.
- **Mail** - Send the fans clear instructions on what they should do and what's expected of them. Make sure there is as little to mess up as possible. Write tour dates on posters yourself. If there is anywhere you know you want flyers, tell them explicitly.
- **Report** - Make sure fans know they're supposed to take pictures of everything they do. Even if they're boring pictures, make sure they know they need to email you a report filled with pictures of hung posters, them at a record store, whatever they can.

Motivate - You can motivate fans to do this by giving them rewards for their good work. You can say the three street teamers who do the best job will get a special prize. You can give all the fans that do a great job a free piece of merch at your show and guest list passes. What's great is you get both promotion and a deeper bond with everyone who participates. Most fans that do this end up being your fans for as long as you're around.

Giving special prizes to the street teamers who do the best work can promote competition but can also lead to disappointment if a losing fan feels they worked hard and also deserved a reward. While competition can help the team perform better, disappointing your fans with losing after they went out of their way for you is a bad place to be. Setting milestones they can hit for certain prizes, like hanging 12 posters or getting hits on your website from a link they posted, can set the rewards a fan will get in stone and makes sure they know what to expect.

Build - Most of your fans will know the cool places in their area. Be sure to get the names, locations and contacts for these places and add them to your database. You can even ask them to collect promoter, record store and radio info for you as part of their job.

Fanclubs: Giving Superfans A Special Place All Their Own
Many music fans go their whole life without ever joining a fanclub. In fact, you can be the biggest music nerd ever and never even join one. Despite that fact, a fanclub is a place where you can grow and nurture the fans that think about you all night and day. Joining a fanclub is a way for a fan to say they're so into you that they want to take your relationship to a higher level and will pay for more access and privilege. If you have a rabid fanbase, these fanclubs are a great way to grow relationships and make money from them.

Perks - The main element of a fanclub is that members get privileges other fans don't receive. Musicians will have fans either do promotional duties (being a member of the street team) or pay to get it done. Some musicians make it so that everyone who buys the top-tier package in their pre-order is a member; others will offer a special package you can only buy if you join the fanclub. Granted these tactics only work on the young, bored and super-enthused fans. But if that's your fanbase, here are some perks you can offer:

- **Exclusive Merch** - Many musicians make merch you can only get if you join the fanclub.
- **Exclusive Chats** - Only fanclub members get the password to secret monthly webchats with you.
- **Pre-Sales** - Offer super-fans the chance to buy tickets before anyone else, so they make it to all of your shows.

- **Meet & Greet** - Special fan hangout time before the show that only fanclub members get to go to.
- **Letters** - Giving fans a real response to letters they send.
- **Private Events** - Fans get access to limited events the public isn't able to attend.

A fan club is a great way to build relationships and get a little extra money from the fans that love you most. These moments are often some of the most enjoyable ones too, since the love from these fans is inspiring. If you hit the point where you have tons of fans wanting more from you, develop a fan club and enjoy the benefits.

Chapter 20: Effectively Promoting Your Tour

Obviously touring is an amazing way to promote your music. But it's not just about the shows. There are a lot of other chances you get while on tour that will help you grow your fanbase and promote your music.

Book More Than Just A Show In Each Town
Being on the road is often a rough experience: You're often hungry, dehydrated and tired. With that said, each new town is an opportunity to build a following for your music. Aside from the show you're playing, there are plenty of other events you can book that can help promote your music. The big successful acts do all of this every day on tour and it's what takes them over the top. Even when you're an unknown, trying to make these promotions happen can make a big difference. Here are some ideas for what you should do in each new city.

- **Radio** - Try to do a radio interview or stop by and meet a local DJ.
- **Local Press** - Try to schedule interviews with any writers in town.
- **In-Stores** - See if a record store will host a DJ set, acoustic performance or signing. If not, stop by and meet the owners to see if they'll stock your record in the future.
- **Meet & Greet** - Have a meet-up with fans to bond with them.
- **Public Places** - If nothing else is going on, go to places where your potential fans would hang out. Talk to people, meet them and increase your show turnout.
- **DJ An After Party** - Can you DJ? See if there's a cool bar that will throw an after-party. In NYC, it's common practice to play a show and then DJ a bar afterwards. This gets your name on two flyers with two venues promoting you and an added chance of exposure.
- **House Show/Party** - Many musicians will do a house show for die-hard fans. This can cater to fans that didn't make it to the first show or those who want to party after the first show. They also make for great footage and serious fun.

Use Your Talents On Tour To Make Money & Friends
Are you sweating it out on Warped Tour as you read this? Do you cruise across the America, meeting four different acts every night from show to show? I notice time and time again on the road, certain accommodations

are hard to come by. Over the years, I have met musicians with real skills and talents that would offer fans and the other musicians their services, gaining them money, friends and appreciation.

If you're good at haircuts, guitar setups, drum repair, tattoos, van repair, etc., many of the people you meet on the road would love your help. I've seen musicians who are good at haircuts bring their tools on the road and cut hair for tips. This is a great way to make a bit of extra money. This helps make friends and pay the bills on the road, not to mention winning you a good reputation. Anyone who's been on the road for 30 days and then gets some cheap help is very appreciative of it. If you have a skill that is helpful to the other acts in your situation, let everyone know. Life on the road is rough and if you can make it easier, everyone involved will be grateful.

Get Work Done On Tour
If you've ever been on tour, you know van rides from show to show have the potential to be a lot of wasted time. They don't have to be. With a wireless tether on your phone, you can get tons of the online work done in the van every single day. The $20 per month it costs to connect your laptop to your data plan can pay off quickly.

- **Virtual Office** - Musicians turn their vans into virtual offices all the time. Stuff envelopes for promo discs, mail posters and maintain social networks all from the van.
- **Rehearse** - Van time is also a great time to rehearse. Practice your vocal harmonies along with a battery-powered keyboard or laptop keyboard. Need to rehearse some acoustic covers for a future YouTube video? It can be done while driving through Montana (in warmer months).

Hire Employees, Not Roadies
Industry standard knowledge is that when you go on tour, you hire a tour manager, some stage techs (guitar, drums, etc.), a sound person, a merch person, a lighting person... the jobs go on and on. While your early tours probably won't have a crew this large, remember when you do start to hire people that there's a smarter way to do this than just hiring the standard roles. You can never have enough hands-on deck working to promote your music. In addition, most tour managers, techs and merch people are aspiring managers or label people. Why don't you get them started on

345

getting some experience? Most of your crew is bored in the van all day anyway and this will give them productive work to do.

You can have them do online marketing (much more about that later), graphic work, accounting, customer service, fan outreach and all sorts of other duties every day if they're competent. It benefits everybody--the roadies like this because it gives them experience in a field they want to go into. Some of them may want a few extra bucks for this work but getting countless hours of work done and promoting your music every day can is worth it.

Renting A Van
Many musicians don't have a van to tour in. Never worry, there are a few services that will rent you a van just for touring:

- **Bandago** - Bandago (bandago.com) has locations strategically placed around the country where you can rent various tour vans for your tour.
- **GreenVans** - Located on both the east and west coast, GreenVans (rentgreenvans.com) rent vans specifically for touring acts.
- **Bandvan** – A company that rents a size of vehicle between a van and a bus (thebandwagon.net)

Sleep Situations

Staying At Someone's House
While you might wonder how etiquette and staying at someone's house help spread the word about your music, allow me to lend you this wisdom. When you're a great act and good house guests, your hosts will tell everyone about how much you rule for years to come. If you're mediocre or rude, they're either going to say nothing or perhaps even curse you to high heaven. You may even lose them as a fan if you're the usual slobs that so many musicians are. So for the sake of your music gaining more evangelists and for just being a good person, learn to be a good houseguest.

Rise Above

On tour you might walk into someone's home that isn't exactly clean. This isn't an open invitation to be as much of a slob as the owner is. Instead, it's a situation where you should leave the house as clean or cleaner than how you found it. Just because you see a beer bottle on the living room table when you walk in doesn't mean you should add to the collection. It means that whoever lives there will eventually have to clean it up but doesn't want to have to clean up your mess on top of it. This theory can even be applied to when you're staying somewhere nice. If you want to be invited back to stay in other homes and not see nasty comments about your filthy habits all over the Internet, leave wherever you go a little neater than how you found it.

Walking The Walk
Odds are that you have no money so you can't pay your hosts for having you over. This doesn't mean you can't contribute a little labor. Below are a few simple things you can do to repay your hosts for their kindness:

- **Do The Dishes** - If there are dishes in the sink at any time, *just do them*. This will take 5-10 minutes of your life, but this small step of kindness can bring much good grace. Whether it's your mess or not, it shows you appreciate someone going out of their way for you when you go out of your way for them.
- **Cook** - If someone offers you food, offer to cook it. If there is anyone in the band with cooking skills, this is a great way to allow your host to relax a bit.

The Standards
As much it shouldn't be necessary to point this stuff out, years of having musicians stay at my house and studio have taught me to repeat these:

- **Bathroom** - If you see a dirty toilet and you think there's any chance it was caused by your filthy band of traveling slobs, clean it up! As gross as it is, I've seen major relationship wars over a musician that left a bathroom in shambles.
- **Make The Bed** - Make your bed. If you're kind enough to be given a bed to sleep in, at least make it when you're done.
- **Garbage** - Make sure you ask where a garbage bag is in advance if you're going to be drinking. Start putting your trash in there as soon as you get going and in the morning, ask where you can dispose of the mess you created. Your mommy won't be there to

clean it up while you're driving to the next town, so take some responsibility for your mess.

- **Shower** - If you're allowed to shower, ask where to put dirty towels. The floor isn't the correct answer. Also try and leave enough hot water for everyone, including your guest. No hour-long showers!
- **Respect** - If you're told to be quiet because someone needs to sleep, treat this as the most important rule in the house. I can't count how many times I've heard a fan complain of this behavior. Your reputation isn't worth laughing out loud at fart jokes in the wee hours of the morning while your kind host tries to rest for work the next day, when all you have to do is ride in a van all day.
- **Coffee** - If you make coffee, throw out the grinds.
- **Sponge** - If you make food, grab a sponge and wipe down wherever you made a mess.

If you follow the simple rule that you should leave the place you stayed in neater than you found it, you'll always have a place to stay, wherever you go. Just as word travels fast when you're total assholes, word also travels fast when you go above and beyond. It only takes a few minutes of your time to make someone a bigger fan of you and just a few inconsiderate moves to make someone hate you.

Couchsurfing May Get You A Free Place To Stay
Are you a young act putting your nose to the ground (aka the dirty floor you're staying on)? Couchsurfing (couchsurfing.org) can help you. The site is a very noble nonprofit that runs on the kindness of others. The idea is that you should offer your home to fellow couchsurfers and they will offer theirs to you. This is a great way for you to get a free place to crash after a long gig. When you're home, you can make friends with other musicians and get to know other people by having them stay with you. The site goes to great lengths to make sure its users are safe and held to a standard of kindness and participation in a "do unto others" sort of philosophy. Best of all, it's an international site!

Other Ways To Find Places To Crash On The Road
Don't forget to socialize with the other musicians (we may have told you this before). Those friendships and bonds you've built with local acts will come in handy when you stay with them on tour. Not only do they give you a place to stay, but this leads to stronger, lasting relationships that end up helping both acts. If there are no locals on the show, asking the crowd for

help can often get you a place to stay from a generous audience member. Saving the hotel fee each night is worth it.

Other Resources For Finding Places To Stay On The Road

- **TourSleeper** – This service connects musicians with fans who will give them a place to stay on the road. (toursleeper.com)
- **AirBnB** - A site where you can rent apartments or homes instead of hotels, this often makes for comfortable quarters and goes for very cheap--without the worries of sneaking the band into a hotel or worrying about thieves who target hotels. (airbnb.com)
- **Priceline** - You can find great deals on most of the hotel bidding sites. (priceline.com)
- **Hotel Tonight** – Good deals on hotels that are unbooked for the night. (hoteltonight.com)
- **Hotwire** - Same idea. (hotwire.com)

Chapter 21: Your Image & Graphic Design Promotions

Figuring out what imagery represents your music can be a serious creativity drain. Every act has their own identity and if your graphics don't fit your music, it usually results in lack of potential fans giving you a chance. If you don't design great merch, you miss the chance for the free promotion when your fan pays to be a walking advertisement for your music. It's important that you come up with designs that your fans are interested in. This takes time and experimentation. When you find imagery that resonates with fans, you will be greatly rewarded. There is a lot of work that goes into making sure this happens and your visuals help listeners become interested in your music.

Imagery
Think about a logo for your music. Many musicians mess this up from day one and don't invest enough thought into what their logo looks like. Simply putting your name on a T-shirt in ComicSans font is never going to sell--nor will it give fans a clue as to what you sound like.

It's important to start by establishing the level of quality you'll need to achieve in order to sell merch. All of the acts you choose to target earlier, most likely sell merch and you are going to need to make it of a quality that is on their level. Search out your favorite musicians' merch and see what you could be doing. Investigate the level of quality you're up against. Realize you're going to have to put that much effort into your designs to compete against all of the acts that share your potential fans.

Branding
I hate saying the word branding--perhaps it was growing up with a father who worked in advertising or one too many teenage readings of Naomi Klein's *No Logo*. Despite my reservations, however, music fans want to be a part of a movement and visual indicators showing what this movement looks like are very important. If you make your own unique look, it becomes synonymous with your music and your fans will use it to identify that they're part of what you do. If you do this poorly, odds are your music is never going to reach epic proportions.

350

If you think you don't understand branding, realize that it's something you see many musicians do--you just don't consciously think about it. Take Daft Punk for example--everything they do is robot-themed. Every time they have a visual that accompanies their music, it has the look and feel of the brand they've established. Branding even comes down to using the same logo on everything you do. The Misfits will always have some sort of horror imagery connected to them--usually on a black shirt with a skeleton. It can also be a moniker--Man Overboard had enormous success with their "Defend Pop Punk" mantra. A lot of their merch sales came from kids who believed in the slogan. By establishing a brand, fans know what to look for and you become all the more familiar. While it's not necessary for merch success, it can greatly help you establish an image for you and spread the word to new fans every single day.

The Graphic Design Workload
You're going to need countless graphic representations of your music. With every social network, music store or piece of merch you want to sell, you're going to have to create another image. Before long, this will become a full-time job. Below are some of the many places you'll need graphic design:

- **Merchandise**
- **Album Covers**
- **Logos**
- **Banner Ads**
- **Social Networks (Twitter cover and background, Facebook cover, YouTube channel, Tumblr banner)**
- **Your Website**
- **Tour Posters**
- **Print Ads**
- **Press Photo Tweaks**

Getting It Done
Now that you know what goes into good design, you may have come to the conclusion that there is no way to do this on your own, especially if you want a quality product. This isn't a problem, as most musicians hire out to freelance designers for this work. But how do you find the right designer? One of the best ways is to ask other musicians whose designs they like. If this seems out of the question, then it's time to use Google--there are countless merch designers out there. Nearly any graphic designer can do most of the graphic work you need for your music, but not every graphic designer will do the type of design you want. If you have a vision, hire a

graphic designer who you can communicate with. If you have no idea what you want, you'll need to find a designer who has a vision for you and hope for the best.

CrowdSPRING - CrowdSPRING (crowdspring.com) is a community of designers and writers ready to tackle all of your logo, merch or web design needs. Getting started is as simple as posting the specs of the job you want done and putting up a bounty price on the winner. According to their website, most entries get an average of more than 100 submissions, so you'll have a vast array of choices to get a great product from.

Use Threadless To Find Merch Designers - One of the more modern ways to find a merch designer is to search the T-shirt design community at Threadless (threadless.com). Simply go to their site and search until you find a design you like. Click the designer's name to get to their profile, which usually contains contact information. You can reach out to the designer and either offer to buy one of their designs or commission them to create a new design for you if you like their work.

99 Designs Gives You Countless Design Options

It can be hard to see the potential of how good your design can look. 99 Designs (99designs.com) allows you to run a design contest by posting a price and design requirements and let designers compete for your business. The service allows you to see a wide variety of options for where your design could go and can help get you a quality design on a budget.

Designing On Your Own

If you know you're over your head in the world of graphics and design, you may want to reconsider trying to wing it. However, if you have the talent, by all means, try designing your own merch. Some of my favorite musicians do a much better job designing their own artwork than if they hired someone to try to figure out their complex vision. Having the complete vision of sound and artwork together can be an amazing sight. If you're going to design your own merch, make sure you're aware of the sizing and graphical requirements from the company that will be producing your designs. If you're not an expert in Photoshop, Illustrator, Fireworks or GIMP (a free graphics program found at gimp.org), it's more than likely you have a friend who can at least help you get started. Most online merch production companies do a great job of offering templates and listing required guidelines, but if you have any doubt, it's best to call and speak to an expert who can double-check your work.

Pixelmator - Admittedly, I am graphically challenged. But from time to time, when I don't want to pay for a project or need to sketch a rough idea for a real designer, I have found Pixelmator ($14.99 in the Apple App Store) to be an amazing tool at the right price. Photoshop and GIMP are great for those with the time to learn these tools. With Pixelmator, it's much easier to jump right in and make your visual ideas happen.

Canva – Canva (canva.com) is an online graphic design service that makes simple design extremely easy. They have custom templates for everything from Facebook cover photos to album covers. This means you don't need to look up dimensions for various social media sites. For quick graphics Canva is the easiest tool I know of to make good looking graphics.

PicMonkey – This app has a free tier that is amazing for making graphics for every social network. (picmonkey.com)

Social Kit Pro – This service gives you templates and exact dimensions for make banners, avatars, ads and other graphics for all the most popular social networks. For $9.99 it integrates into Photoshop. (madebysource.com)

TinyPNG – Often times you will need to shrink photos and other graphics, but the quality degrades making them give you a bad representation. TinyPNG (tinypng.com) changes that by doing this in a high-quality way that maintains the integrity of your photos.

Your Logo
One of the most important considerations that will define the visual image of your music is your logo. This is the way your name will look for years to come. Think of many classic groups--usually when you think of their name, you picture it as their logo.

One of the keys to successful branding is making sure your logo does you a service. It should look how your music sounds. You'll use it for many years to come, hopefully becoming an instant cue in someone's mind for your music when they see it. This means you have to do more than just write your name and scroll through the fonts that came with your computer. While that is a great starting place, you're going to have to work harder than that if you want your logo to be memorable and bring to mind your music when someone sees it. This logo is going to be plastered on every flyer, poster, shirt and album cover you do for all of history. In fact, if you choose a bad font and go with it for a while, odds are it will stick around on the Internet for years to come--making it hard to shake. Choose wisely.

Identifiable - One of the greatest bits of advice I've gotten from the design world is that you should be able to recognize a logo from 20 feet away. Think of how many times you've recognized across the room that someone is wearing one of your favorite act's shirts. This means you should make sure your logo is a clear and recognizable image. Trust me, putting the effort into doing this right is well worth the reward.

You Need A Square Logo & A Rectangular Logo
You need one logo that works well horizontally and another one that works well vertically. You'll constantly be asked to send your logo to others who need to use it for designs and whether it's squeezing your name onto a tour poster so that it doesn't outshine the main act or getting it to work with your graphic designer's drawings, you'll need a logo that works in both orientations.

One quick trick to this is to just make sure your logo works as a square and a rectangular. If your logo is only a square, it's going to be hard to create banners. If it only works as a rectangle, it won't work in a small square ad for a website.

Other Logo Considerations
- **Vector -** In order to have your logo look good at small and large sizes, it needs to be a vector image. This will ensure that it works no matter what someone needs it for. If you don't make your logo a vector, it will get blurry and pixelated when it gets blown up.
- **Black & White Vs. Color** - Your logo needs to work in both black and white and color. Your logo will be used in many different formats and if your logo doesn't transfer well to black and white, it will not work for newspaper ads, flyers, etc. Make sure any logo works in this format before approving it.

Getting Your Album Art Right
To some people, album art seems less and less important these days as musicians are selling so few physical albums. However, album art is still a very important way to make your release stand out. When fans scan through stores digital libraries, they see your art and immediately make a

judgment about what you sound like. If you put in some smart consideration, you can make a great first impression that leads to potential fans checking out your music, instead of passing it by.

Does Album Art Still Matter?

Album art isn't dying as much as it is changing. While CDs and vinyl aren't the norm for every release today, album artwork still has a place in the world of music. Even as the way we all consume music evolves from CDs and vinyl to MP3s and streaming subscription sites, when music fans first see your song or album, they still see an image next to it. If this image is powerful and intriguing, it can help sway a fan to listen to your music over the millions of other options they have.

Even if you're releasing music with the sole intention of getting it blogged about, blogs love a strong image and are more likely to write about your music if you have a great image attached to it. Going with a poorly thought out image when you've put your heart and soul into a release can sabotage the success of what you're releasing. Whether you like it or not, a strong image is part of listeners' first impression of your music, so choose it wisely--it will either bring fans in or keep them away.

Vision - One of the keys to good artwork is making sure it works with your release. If you're a musician with a serious image, but then have a puppy on your record cover, you're going to give fans that could potentially love your music the impression that you might not be up their alley. Having a record cover that is both visually striking and represents your music will help brand you and communicate to potential fans what they're getting into if they give your music a listen.

Followers - Do you want to come across as a leader or a follower? Some musicians choose to market themselves as part of a genre by making sure they stick to some identifying marks (*read: clichés*) of the genre. For example, if you're an electro act, neon colors and sharp photoshopped images are a quick calling card. Meanwhile, a black metal group will have a hand drawn, nearly illegible logo that brings to mind evil imagery. If you want to be known as part of a genre, it's smart to take on some of these traits so your fans are able to tell you're a part of the movement. There is a happy medium between abiding by your genre's identity and creating images that are fresh and interesting. Be aware of what other similar musicians do and know what sets you apart.

Leaders - Some musicians will choose to stand out from the crowd and be leaders. This takes more work, but it's also what separates the leaders from the followers and the amateurs from the professionals. Being able to make a record cover that aligns with your themes without appearing to be derivative of the genre will help establish you as one of the leaders of your scene. While this can often be a subliminal result, it's an easy way to establish who you are in comparison to your peers.

Identity - It's been said that the best pieces of album artwork can be recognized from across a record store. While record stores are going the way of the Dodo, this still stands true in a digital world. A memorable record is recognizable from afar. It should be unique enough so fans won't think of other album art when they see it.

Bringing It Together
The best pieces of album artwork are visually striking yet still go well with the album's identity. When choosing album artwork, I find it helpful to think about which album covers have struck me in the past and what they did to bond image with the music. These thoughts can help translate to an artist what you need from them. Good artwork that melds with your music will leave you happier and help listeners bond with your release.

Getting Good Press Photos
It takes a seriously demented personality to find press photos to be one of the better parts of being a musician. Whether it's finding the right scenario, dressing everyone or choosing which photo to use, this process can be one of the most torturous parts of being a musician. Here are some ways to make it less painful.

Photographer - The first thing you're going to need to do is a find a photographer. You're going to want someone with more than an iPhone (though an iPhone can work in the right instance). Ask other musicians who they've had luck with or even get recommendations from fans. If you're a musician you've probably met someone who loves photography. Just make sure they're responsible and on board with your vision.

Scenario - It's usually a good idea to figure out a scenario for your photos in advance. If you're thinking about standing in front of your favorite local stage or on the railroad tracks, you need to think harder. The scenario should say something about you. It helps to put a lot of thought into how you want the world to see you. Even if this seems lame, it's still important.

Otherwise, potential fans will look at your photo and get the wrong idea about your music.

Look Like A Band - If you're in a band, look like you are in a band together. I know you're very diverse and each have your own special personality, but you need to find a commonality that brings you all together. If you all usually wear the same style jeans, this isn't the time to let your drummer wear his one nice suit. The same goes for your one band member who wants to wear khaki shorts. Nothing says boring like khaki shorts (unless that's your band's thing--I'm looking at you Vampire Weekend). You want to find a common bond in your look and meet in that middle ground.

Styling - Not every act needs a stylist, makeup artist and hair person. In fact, most don't. If you have a fashionably smart friend ask them to lend a hand. Most of these problems are easily solved with a fashionable eye pointing out the flaws in your look. If the idea of a fashion stylist coming near you makes you sick, I am right there with you. Do your thing. Just make sure you don't look like a slob.

Study On Sight - While taking the picture it helps to check and make sure everything is looking good on sight. If you're doing digital photos, it can help to look at them on a big screen (computer, iPad, etc.) to make sure you aren't missing a bad detail. A weird piece of graffiti that says "dick" above your guitarist's head may be accurate, but it may make the picture unusable when he throws a fit over it. Blow the pictures up and make sure they seem to be working.

Save It With A Filter - If the pictures come out terrible, all hope is not lost. Pixlr, Instagram and Prisma all have filters for photos that you can use for free. Even if you aren't a photographer, scroll through the filters until the problem you have with a photo either disappears or it looks cooler. These filters can usually gloss over flaws and get you something usable until you can get better promo shots.

Get Multiple Pictures In Multiple Resolutions - You should take your photos in as high a resolution as possible, in case you need it for something crazy like that cardboard cutout you're commissioning or perhaps your vinyl release. You also need to save every picture you like in more usable sizes so you can easily email them to press people. Remember, you're going to need huge pictures for desktop backgrounds, one sheet splash pages, Twitter backgrounds, Facebook covers, etc. These pictures need to work both in high resolutions and when they're shrunk down.

Black & White - You need a photo that works in black and white as well as color. A lot of press still works in black and white and if your photo looks bad, you may lose a press opportunity.

Animated Gifs Are The New Press Shots
If you're in the business of getting your music on blogs, having a great image to go along with your music will help grab a reader's attention and increase your likelihood of getting blogged about. One of the new trends in indieland is to make your promo shot an animated gif. If you're looking at this article with a bit of confusion, head over to Pitchforks' annual assembly of the year in photos, which is filled with tons of fancy animated gifs that are interesting, fresh and eye-catching. Obviously, it's impossible to print an animated gif in this book, but if you do some Googling, you'll surely get the point. These gifs are easy to accomplish by filming video during your photo shoot and then turning them into an animated gif in Photoshop. While this technology has been around for a long time, it's still steadily gaining traction now. Hop on the bandwagon!

Using QR Codes To Promote Your Music
Few technological innovations have been more hyped--with fewer results-- than QR codes. If you're not familiar, a QR code is a scannable bar code that your phone reads and takes you to a web address. It sounds really cool, right? You may even be salivating at the idea of the potential for this cool technology to market your music.

Well, I hate to burst your bubble, but data shows that no one actually scans these codes. It takes a lot of effort: You need to open a QR code reader on your smartphone and then scan it and then look at a website. These are too many steps for most people to bother with and you end up losing potential fans in the hassle. In general, it's rare that these cool little pieces of technology do you any good. If you have a simple website URL, interested users would rather type that in instead.

With that said, there is hope--you could be the musician who makes everyone start using QR Codes. Or maybe your fans are nerds and you want to try this out anyway. Here are a few ideas on how you can successfully use these codes to promote your music:

- **Merch Booth** - Make one that you hang up at your merch booth where you link your website or free music page.
- **Posters** - You can put a code on promotional posters and flyers so fans can preview tracks from the acts playing a show. You can direct fans to the Facebook event page or another page on your website with all the show information. Or better yet, direct them to a place to buy tickets.
- **CD** - Put a QR code on your CD or vinyl that unlocks a secret link to download your music digitally or even links to bonus material.
- **Postcard** - Put a QR code on a postcard and give it to fans to redeem for music.
- **On Stage** - Make a QR code and put it on stage (drummer's bass drum?). Have it link to a website where you'll host a download of the show you're playing now. You can also make it link to a download of your latest record.
- **Album Cover** - Odd Future had Jimmy Fallon hold a QR code up in lieu of an album when they made their national television debut on his show. It linked to their website, which had tons of free music and helped to make this huge exposure be a huge boost in their fanbase.

These sites will create a free QR code for you:
- **Kaywa** (qrcode.kaywa.com)
- **QR Hacker** (qrhacker.com)

Chapter 22: Making And Selling Great Merchandise

The Importance Of Merch

As the world accepts the reality of lower record sales--and more online streaming--one of the most important aspects of a musician's career is how to sell merch and more of it. Whether it's for financial reasons or for the fact that every piece of merch is a walking advertisement, merch is vital to building your fanbase.

You might remember the first time you went to the pizza parlor or local indie record store and saw some cool punk rocker wearing a bitchin' Minor Threat shirt (which naturally, was your favorite band at the time). He was older and was way cooler than you and was obviously a bad ass you could look up to. The next time you came back in the store, the same guy might have been wearing a Dead Kennedys shirt, so of course you went out and bought a Dead Kennedys CD and found your new favorite band (at least until Jello's vocals drove you too crazy to keep listening). Seeing someone who looks cool wearing a piece of merch is one of the strongest music discovery tools there is.

Recommendations - Remarkably, this is still very much how some music fans find their new music. If you're around any music scene long enough, you see it happen. You see a musician's name that is omnipresent on so many T-shirts, buttons, stickers, etc., that you eventually check them out to see what the hype is about. Perhaps the person you have a huge crush on walks by with a Crass patch--you then listen to them and buy their record in hopes of one day bonding with that person over your love of their music.

One of the basic ideas of advertising is to beat the public over the head until they're so unconscious they agree to finally buy whatever it is you're selling. The more merch you put out into the world, the more walking advertisements you have out there, making people want to investigate what it is you are about. Instead of looking at your merch as a dollar amount, see it for what it is--building the foundation of a promotional campaign. Sell as much merch as possible--you'll not only fund your music, you'll have legions of walking advertisements for it.

The best part of merch is that fans pay you to spread the word about your music! If you do merch well, fans will still continue to buy it by the boatload years after you're dead and/or retired. The world will continue to see your T-shirts and new potential fans will discover your music when they see someone they think is cool wearing your shirt.

So how do you make this happen?

Making Great Merch

Styles
Once you have a merch design, you need to decide what to put it on. Your fans will be receptive to many different types of merch; you just need to give it to them in the format they want. While hardcore kids love hoodies, try selling them to an artsy indie rocker in their 30s and you'll fail. A straight edge group shouldn't be selling bongs, but Sublime can sell them decades after their singer passed away. Every genre has different pieces of merch that work and every musician will have different types of merch that sell well. The key is to watch trends and tap into what you think your fans may be interested in buying. Doing this well is the difference between a basement full of unsold merch and merch you can't keep on the shelves.

The below list is the start of potential pieces of merchandise you can manufacture. But keep in mind, this is only limited by your own imagination.

- **T-shirts**
- **Hoodies**
- **Long Sleeve Shirts**
- **Crew Neck Shirts**
- **Phone Cases**
- **Tote Bags**
- **Lighters**
- **Bongs**
- **Ashtrays**
- **Frisbees**
- **Beer Cozies**
- **Scarves**
- **Varsity Jackets**
- **Skateboards**

- **Windbreakers**
- **Mesh Shorts**
- **Booty Shorts**
- **Thongs**
- **Belts**
- **Socks**
- **Shoes**
- **Pins**
- **Stickers**
- **Stencils**
- **Posters**
- **Temporary Tattoos**
- **"Live Strong" Style Bracelets**
- **Metal Water Bottles**

Viral Merch

Most of the time, viral incidents are thought of as YouTube videos of cats doing cute things, but your merch can be viral, too. By tapping into a feeling or a movement going on with your fans, you can all of a sudden see an explosion of merch sales. One-hit wonders Frankie Goes To Hollywood somehow made it cool for countless fans to walk around with shirts that said "Frankie Say Relax" (their hit single was named "Relax"). Some graphics nerds would argue that the shirts stood out by having a simple and LOUD graphic design that set them apart in an 80s world of busy hand-drawn graphics.

As I mentioned earlier, former MusforMGMT act Man Overboard made shirts with the mantra "Defend Pop Punk." The shirts tapped into the angst many pop punk fans had after watching their genre be demeaned--so that even fans who were lukewarm about Man Overboard bought the shirt en masse, simply because they agreed with the message. Their shirt became a membership card in a movement and as a result, the band continues to sell tens of thousands of them.

You'll see it other places too--the singer of a band wears a certain type of sunglasses and then hands out these same glasses with the band's logo printed on them at shows for free. This little investment then gets them hundreds of fans wearing these same glasses to shows, turning the glasses into a part of the band's underground movement.

Merch like this works when your fans want to be a part of something you're a part of. Give your fans a way to show they're a part of your movement by wearing the merch you sell. It will help you build a much stronger fanbase.

A simple song lyric that has profound meaning can also bring out the viral spread of merch. During a trip that Todd and I took to New York's famous Rockaway Beach, we were blinded by shirts with lines from LMFAO songs. Your viral merch will often be your witty lyrical quip that your fans feel passionately about--a good clue is usually the line that's always sung the loudest at your concerts.

Making Money & Using Merch As Advertisement At The Same Time
The funny paradox with merch is that musicians are still expected to make money off an avenue that most companies use as advertising. Most corporations try to give away free t-shirts, buttons and stickers, in an effort to get people to spread the word about their company. Yet today in music, we're all told these items are some of the last ways you can make money as a musician. So what's a musician to do?

While this is true and merch is one of the only ways left to make money in this business, you have options. You can use it both as a promotional tool and as a moneymaker.

- **Freebies** - Give away some free merch like stickers and buttons. These items are so cheap to make that charging for them is silly. You can also price them cheaply (like $.25 or $1.00 if it's online) and then give them away for free if someone offers the quarter. This ensures they really want it and increases the likelihood of them displaying it. Just don't think of this as giving away something that could be monetized. Think of it as fans posting free ads for your music. Remember, if you make another fan off this free promotion, it can lead to more income.
- **Clear Message** - This should be obvious, but make sure your merch shows your logo! All too often I see merch where the design is amazing, but I can't even tell if it's for a band. Make sure you have a legible logo in all of your designs. Yet again, if the world can easily see your name, you now have a free advertisement, not just a merch sale or money in your wallet.
- **Affordable** - Have an inexpensive T-shirt design. Musicians constantly disregard this idea, thinking that just because a product sells for cheap they won't make as much money. If every act at a

venue is selling T-shirts for $9 and you have a $6 shirt, it will help sales. If you sell a few more shirts at $6 than you would have at $9, you still made more money than the band selling the expensive shirt--and now have a few more walking advertisements out in the world. Also remember that there are many fans who are cheap or who don't have enough money for your full-priced shit. The $6 shirt makes it so that they can have your merch and promote you to more potential fans.

Don't Let Your Laziness Ruin Your Merch Profits - Get Your Merch Done Early

Go to nearly any merchandise site that does shirts/stickers for musicians and you'll almost always see the option for a "rush service" (naturally at a much higher price). Why is this? Because while every musician needs merch, many of them put off actually getting their merch ready before tours or shows. Getting good quality merch and selling it at a decent price is already a difficult task but adding on extra fees for overnight delivery and "rush fees" from a graphics company is certainly not going to help. Passing along a steeper price to your fans is not going to help your relationships and will almost always result in fewer sales. Check your stock and assess your needs early so you're not scrambling around right before your show or cutting a huge hole in your profits by paying unnecessary fees. Remember, merch is still one of the best ways you have to turn a profit. Don't let your slack behavior ruin a potential cash cow.

Always Be Available

You should always be available. How does this pertain to merch? Make sure you're stocked on every size of every type of merch you have. If you don't have the size someone is looking for and can't get them what they want, odds are they're not going to come back and try to get it again. Capitalize on your fans' enthusiasm while they have it. Whether it's at a show or in your online store, you need to be overstocked and also have the formats, styles and anything else you can think of that your fans want. Often you get one chance--you don't get to try to lure your fans into buying again. Selling your merch is always on your fans' terms.

Are there exceptions? Yes. There is a place for limited edition products. If you have die-hard fans and want to drive sales, limited edition merch is a fantastic way to do this. However, make sure your limited-edition items actually make sense to be sold as limited--they should be special and hard to produce in a great quantity. If your limited-edition item actually has mass appeal, it should be a constant fixture in your merch store--or else you're leaving money on the table.

Buying Merch In Bulk
Whether you're going to fulfill your own merch orders from online sales or sell it at shows, you're obviously going to want some merch of your own for friends, family and yourself. There are thousands of businesses that will print merch in bulk for you, but which do you choose?

- **Fulfillment Partner** - If you're going to have a company sell your merch in their webstore, it is smart to also buy it from them. They will often apply your online sales as credit for merch you can sell at shows.
- **Local** - The difference in price between getting merch shipped from a distant printer and picking it up from a local printer can be huge. T-shirts are heavy and sending 50+ merch items can rack up shipping charges fast. Look into price differences, including shipping from far away printers compared to a local one you can pick up from.
- **New Dimensions** - I've had great experiences dealing with the national merch printing company New Dimensions. They offer great quality, quick turnaround and convenient customer service. (newdimensions1.com)
- **Recommendations** - Ask local musicians where they get their merch printed. It will often take a little investigating to find a great provider who does good work for cheap.
- **On Your Own** - Remember, you can always make your merch yourself and give it a personal touch, which helps keep down rates. Just be warned--silk-screening can get boring and tedious very fast.

Selling Merch At Shows

Your merch booth is one of the most important places you can grow your fanbase. Most people who come near this area are potential fans. It's a huge opportunity to get potential fans interested and to get those who are already interested hooked on your music and your identity (and shelling out money for their addiction).

What Goes Into A Great Merch Booth?

While everyone should have different merch and tailor it to the type of fans they have, there are some things that are universal. Just putting out a piece of paper with your name and some prices won't get you any new fans. Instead, here's where to start:

- **Logo** - Let fans know this is your merch booth by displaying a banner with your logo somewhere prominent. If you have tons of T-shirts you can sometimes skip this step by hanging them from the wall or your pre-made racks (more below), as long as they obviously display your band name or logo. Fans can be drunk, stupid or high (or even all three). The more obvious you make yourself, the more likely it is that fans can find you.
- **Fan Addiction Tool** - You need a way to collect your fans' email addresses, so you can get them your music after the show. The simplest, cheapest form of this is a mailing list page in a notebook--there's more on this in a little bit.
- **Conversation Piece** - A great trick is to put an eye-catching and unexpected item at your merch table. A great example I recently saw was a merch guy who had a Furby doll sitting on his table. Tons of potential fans came up while they were bored or during an act they hadn't come to see, talked to the merch guy and sure enough got hooked in. Other options could also be a weird piece of merch you sell or, if you're a political band, a petition or literature for your favorite charity.
- **Flyers, Postcards, Wristbands, Stamps** - Have another local show coming up? You'd better have flyers! You should also always have a flyer or a postcard that says how to get free music from you when fans get home.
- **Nearly Free Stuff** - Stickers, pins, patches or whatever else you can make for under a dollar are great to either give away as a bonus when someone buys regular-priced merch or to sell at such a low price that even fans who are mildly interested strike up conversation.
- **Low Priced Merch** - Having a $5 T-shirt you silk screened yourself or made with a really simple design is an amazing way to get fans in the door and become your walking advertisement. It can also mean the difference between someone buying merch from you or the band in the booth next to you.

- **Regular Priced Merch** - There are the medium-priced items that you're going to try to sell. These are usually going to be your normal T-shirts, CDs and vinyl.
- **Big Ticket Merch** - This isn't good for acts that don't have dedicated fans yet, but once you do, you want to have a more expensive piece of merch with a high profit margin. This could be a skateboard, cuff links or whatever works for you. There is no reason to not capitalize on the high fans get from a live performance and sell them a special item that makes you a lot of money.
- **Change** - If you don't have proper change you'll most likely lose sales and fans.
- **Credit Card Machine** - If you don't have the ability to take credit cards, you'll lose sales. Fans who buy with credit cards often buy more than they would with cash. Don't miss out on this!
- **Light And Power** - If you haven't noticed, clubs are dark and no one is able to see you if you don't bring enough light (and power) to illuminate your merch booth. Without lighting, you may not get noticed at all. You'll also look like a clown when the other booths next to you look bright and intriguing.
- **Location** - You need a good location for your table. Next to the headliner is optimal, since you pick up scraps. Places where you're easily seen are also the best.
- **Video As Eye-Catcher** - If you have a visually striking video, keep it on loop at your merch booth with an iPad or similar tablet. Hook up some headphones and let fans gravitate to this eye-catching display. You'll sell more merch with it and give fans another chance to hear your music. However, if your merch booth is in the main part of the venue other acts play in, make sure you turn it off during their set as a courtesy.
- **Headphones** - If you're playing shows with more than five acts or at multi-stage events, it is helpful to give fans a way to hear your music. Having a nice pair of clean, over-the-ear headphones (so they can hear over the noise) can convince potential fans to check you out and buy more merch.

Fan Addiction Tool
Your goal is to turn everyone at your show into a fan of your music, but you can't do that unless you get them to hear you. You want to be able to keep in touch with everyone who likes your music. The best way to do that is via email. Every time you play a show, you have the opportunity to get the

people there addicted to your music, even if they weren't blown away with your live set or didn't get there early enough to see you blow the roof off the place.

How - Get every one of the concertgoers to actually hear you by signing up for your mailing list. At your show, instead of putting out a generic mailing list, you want to have sign that says, "SIGN THE MAILING LIST, GET FREE UNRELEASED MUSIC!" Throughout the night, try to get everyone who comes to the merch booth to sign that. If they're a dedicated fan, mention that they can get an unreleased song just by signing up. If they're a new fan, tell them they'll get some free music; it's hard for people to ignore something free. You can even offer this new potential fan a sticker or a button if they sign it, for extra incentive. Do whatever it takes to get them to put down their information.

When you're playing your set, say something like, "Hey everyone, this was really awesome and I'm glad we did this together. I am not going to forget this, so let's make sure you don't either. If you sign that list in the back, we'll send you some of our music for free." Emphasizing that you shared an experience with the fans really helps. Fans like feeling special and so do you, otherwise you wouldn't be up on that stage hogging all the attention. Mention the email list to everyone you talk to after the show.

The Tool - You can do this with a spiral notebook, tablet or a computer. Basically, find any way for your audience to give you their info. You don't want anything but their email; the more they have to write, the more likely they're going to lie or give fake information (this will happen no matter what).

Here are a few ideas on how to capture fans' email addresses:

- **Spiral Notebook** - Have them sign a spiral notebook. Write on the top of it that it's for your mailing list and attach a pen to it with a string (if you don't attach it, the pen will be gone within the first five minutes). Make sure you write the zip code of where the email addresses were captured on top of the page for later use.
- **Pre-Printed Sheets** - You can print out some nice sheets for fans to handwrite their email address on. Put your logo on the top and include a message. Remember, in these first two methods, you're going to have to enter the addresses into the computer. Some

people will have bad handwriting and you might lose a couple of emails.

- **Excel Spreadsheet** - If you have a netbook or tablet, you can get fancy and have your fans enter their email into a spreadsheet. Later you can export this file into your email program and access all of their email addresses easily. Remember to tag the zip code where you got them! This will help get more fans to your show the next time you're in town. Another helpful tip is for any mailing list option that uses a computer, wrap your computer in one layer of Saran Wrap to prevent spills and filthy fans from ruining it. This includes the screen. Also lock it up with a cheap computer lock!

- **Offline Signup** - Most of the major email list providers have an offline mailing list sign-up program. This will do the same thing as an Excel spreadsheet, except you don't have to export it.

- **Do It Online** - If there is a good Internet connection at the show, you can have fans can enter their address into a widget directly on your website.

The Incentive - How much free music you give away to fans is up to you. Obviously, giving away your full LP gives fans a huge incentive to give you their email, but also gives them less incentive to buy it from you. If this isn't your first record, my best advice is to give away a song or two from each of your releases. The more incentive you give fans, the less likely they are to give fake email addresses.

Making an exclusive track to give away for your email list is very important. This way, your big fans who already have all your other music will still have incentive to sign up for your mailing list. This doesn't need to be your best track. A cover, acoustic version or remix is fine. As long as there is something special for already existing fans, you're good to go.

You can also do this with a CD. Giving a fan a burned CD (or a real one, if you're generous) when they sign the mailing list is a workable and cheap incentive (burning a CD costs less than a quarter for each one). Especially, if the fan asks for it.

The Delivery - In order to get fans your music, you now need a way to send it to them! Most mailing list programs give you the ability to email these newly added fans right away with a message. If you captured the emails in handwritten form or from a spreadsheet, you need to add them and add them FAST. You have a much better chance of fans listening to your music if they're still high on your live performance. The faster you can get it to them the better.

In this message, include a link to download your record. Some cool ways to do this are:

- **Soundcloud** - If you already give away your music via Soundcloud, link the stream and allow all of the songs to be downloadable.
- **Splash Page** - You can make a page on your website that has a stream of your music and a link to download the free music. You can even add some items they can buy below the music download, so they know where to go if they want to take their relationship to the next level.

How I Do It
When I have used this method in the past, this is how I've done it:

- **TopSpin** - Using MailChimp, I create an Email For Download Widget. This widget allows me to automatically send fans an email with the link and it confirms that they signed up for the mailing list, essentially killing two birds with one stone.
- **iPad** - If there is Wi-Fi or 3G, I put an iPad (first generation ones can be bought online for cheap--and are useful for plenty of other music-related chores) on the merch table. Set it to display the online Email For Media Widget.
- **Delivered** - This method automatically sends them an email with the download link. They get the email within a minute of signing up and can download the music when they get home from your show--right when they're dying for more of your music. At that point, you'll seem like the best person in the world to them. They'll download your music, fall in love and you two will live happily ever after (at least until you enter your prog-rock phase).
- **Stream** – In this email you can also include links to stream your music on Spotify, Tidal and Apple Music, in case the fan only likes to listen on these services.

NYOP Merch
More and more musicians make their music available at shows on a Name Your Own Price basis. Do this by writing, "Price: Name Your Own" on your records at the merch booth. If a fan wants something free, you can email

them a copy. If they offer a quarter, hand them a burnt CD. If they offer a reasonable price, hand them a wrapped CD, vinyl or whatever else you have. If you believe in the good in people, you can give them whatever merch they want for this price--but you'd have much more faith in humanity than I do.

Stamp It!
I'm a big fan of customized stamps. Right when doors open and your merch person is bored, they can be stamping things! What do you stamp? Stamp where to get free music from you or your next local show on the back of all your stickers. If you have flyers for an upcoming show, stamp the back of those with the address of your free music site. If you have shirts, take little sheets of paper or flyers and write the size on them and stamp those.

If you're hosting a show or selling merch to fans, stamp the audience members with a custom made stamp that has your logo and website or free music page written on it. This stamp can mark admission or be a mark you tag your fans with. You can even sell the stampers to fans. I still have one I bought at a Nirvana show in high school.

Postcards
If you just put out a record, in my opinion, you should immediately make a postcard for it. I encourage all the bands I work with to make a postcard with their social network addresses, web address, good reviews for their record and most of all a big ad for your free music page. Make one side of it a good-looking piece of art your fans want to hang on their wall and the other where you put the important information. Hand these out to everyone you possibly can and make sure there is a sign that says "FREE" next the stack on your merch table. Once you've done that, congratulations--you've just sent tons of potential fans home with an ad for you and a reminder to check out your music.

You may also want to include quick phrases to tell fans why they should care. Did you get an amazing review from a well-known website? An endorsement from a famous musician? All of this can entice the fan into checking you out. But don't get too distracted. While all of this is important, giving fans a link to free music is the most important piece of information you'll put on the card.

Pre-made Racks

Do you play a lot of shows and have a lot of merch? It's easy to make a collapsible rack to display all of your shirts. Get creative and make a display that permanently has samples of all of your merch. This way you can always hang it up in a presentable way and not have to deal with constant setups.

Get A Charismatic Merch Person
More than any great designed merch, the number one way to sell more merch and get fans interested is to have a charismatic merch person. Time and time again, I go to shows and the act that is winning at sales is the act with the merch person who will chat people up, be friendly and connect with potential fans. Not only does having a personable merch person help your sales, it also builds fan bonding. Obviously, it doesn't hurt if they're good-looking.

Mobile Merch Booth
While it's not for everyone, one of the best ways to get new fans is to hang out in the crowd after you play. When people talk to you, make sure you make a connection. It doesn't hurt to walk around the bar/club after your show with your mailing list and some merch. If you happen to capture the interest of a new fan, make sure a to make a deeper connection with them. Ask them their name. Ask if they want to sign your mailing list. Give them a free CD or even a free T-shirt. Never let a new fan walk away empty-handed. Whether they have money or not, you're investing in them and their potential return in the future. Be nice and make real connections and it'll be easy to sell more merch and make more fans.

Use Your Merch Booth To Promote Future Shows
Your merch station is also a good place to advertise future shows. After someone has just seen you play an amazing show, let them know when they can have this great experience again. When selling merch, always try to find a way to include a show schedule. A small piece of paper can be slipped inside a disc sleeve or, if it's sealed, taped onto a CD case. If you're going to roll your shirts, slip a small show schedule under the rubber band so everyone who buys a shirt also knows when/where you'll be appearing next. Take advantage of the energy you've created after an electrifying live show and plant the seed for fans to come back and see you all over again.

Organize Your Merch

Sometimes selling merch is the difference in whether you have enough gas to make it to the next show. Take some time to organize your merch before going on tour and you'll maximize your efficiency to make more money. While your merch booth doesn't have to look like it was organized by The Gap, having your merch in order and easily accessible can mean the difference in a few extra sales.

After you've played a rocking show and have a huge line of folks ready to purchase your wares, you don't want potential customers getting impatient and leaving before they get the chance to buy stuff from you. Fold shirts (right down the middle), roll them up tightly from the bottom and wrap them (twice) with a thick rubber band. From here, pull the tag out so you can easily assess the shirt's size and move on (you can also use white duct tape and a sharpie to write the size so it's easily readable). Not only are these rolled shirts easier to handle, it also saves space in your merch bin.

Sell Exclusive Merch At Shows To Draw More People
If you're starting to build a decent following, have a piece of great merch that's exclusive to that show or tour. You can always sell it later online but selling it only at shows first can help get fans that are on the fence out to see your show. Tour EPs, exclusive shirts and special posters all work wonderfully.

Variable Merch Prices Can Reward You In Sales
When you're direct support or the local opener, it can be depressing to run the merch booth and see everyone flock to the headliner's merch booth. However, you can compete with their demand and net some extra sales by undercutting the competition and selling all your merch $1 or $2 cheaper than the headliner does.

Before doing this, make sure the headlining act has no "price matching" clause in their tour rider--this will mean you'll have to sell merch for the same price as the headliner. While this is great for your profit margins, it can make you look bad to fans and hurt your sales when you haven't earned the right to sell your merch for the inflated prices that some national acts do (this also means you can demand this when you are a headliner so the opening bands don't undercut your merch sales).

Draw Fans To Your Merch Booth

At festivals, it is tough to get fans' attention. Even if fans want to find you, you may not stand out when there are over a hundred tents to compete with. Here are some ideas to stand out and strike up a conversation:

- **Free Water** - Cases of water or paper cups fans can fill up at a cooler are cheap ways to help dehydrated fans while making them aware of your existence. GWAR takes this even further by having their own branded water at outdoor shows.
- **Programs** - If there are programs for the event you're playing, grab some and hand them out.
- **Free** - Free stickers, flyers, cookies or anything you can give away is always a huge draw.
- **Advice** - Free dating advice, horoscopes or anything else fun and wacky can get people over to your merch booth.

IndieHitMaker Will Help Get Your VenueScans Into SoundScan
One of the barriers that holds DIY musicians back from their label-having peers is the inability to do VenueScans. VenueScans enable musicians on labels to report to SoundScan the CDs they sell and have their sales count towards numbers on the Billboard charts. Major labels have long used this to hold their leverage over acts going it on their own. Lucky for you, this is no longer the case! IndieHitMaker (indiehitmaker.com) will take care of this for you if you join their service (*note: AtVenu also allows you to do the same*). They offer a few different pricing plans, none of which take a percentage. Remember you have to register your UPC with SoundScan two weeks before release in order for sales to count. They're enabling David to beat Goliath, not to mention show the world the success you're achieving out on the road.

Find Patterns In Your Merch Sales
When you start to sell a lot of merch, pay attention to the patterns in what you sell so you know what to order for tour. There's only so much room in the van and every time you have to reorder merch and have it shipped to the venue or a friend's place, there's that much more room for error. If you keep track of what you're selling and what you have left over, you'll start to get better at knowing what styles and sizes you need the most. You'll also start to learn tricks, like ordering more hoodies and fewer tank tops when it gets cold. Everyone will find different patterns but studying these on a long drive is a lot more interesting than hearing about the one time your drummer actually had sex for the 8,098,494th time.

374

Your Online Merch Store

A crucial part of your merch plan is how to sell your merch online. Selling merch over the Internet opens a world of promotional doors. If someone in Malaysia reads about you on a blog and falls in love with you, they can now order your merch and start rocking your sweet tank top halfway across the globe.

It also opens up a world of income. If you become popular and your fans know where to get your merch, there is PLENTY of money to be made off of this. Far too many musicians don't take advantage of the Internet-flattened world and the ability it opens up to sell merch directly to fans. They're missing out on forming bonds, getting new fans and funding their music.

Limited Run
Limited Run (limitedrun.com) is a merch platform that allows you to pay a flat monthly fee based on how many items you offer for sale. The price ranges from $10-$40 a month, with no percentage taken on your sales. You can bundle digital items and also sell physical items; you can also include a blog, SoundCloud player and many individual pages. They also offer the following features:

- **Custom Domains**
- **Discount Codes**
- **Analytics**
- **Digital Format Choices** - The ability for fans to choose which digital format they get their download in.
- **Email Customers** – LimitedRun has a fantastic email service that comes free with their service.
- **Ticket Sales** - The ability to sell tickets to your own events, including will call abilities.
- **Numerous Shipping Options**
- **Bundles** – You can bundle music with digital and physical releases.
- **Deep Analytics**

BigCartel Is An Easy-To-Use Webstore You Can Sell Merch Through
BigCartel (bigcartel.com) is one of the best online sites to manage all of your merch selling needs. With a tiered pricing plan that involves monthly

payments (free, $9.99 - $29.99), they make it easy to make your store work with as few problems as possible. They let you customize the store visually and set it up under your own domain.

In their system, you receive a payment to your PayPal account (it has to be a PayPal account) and you then ship the fan the merch they order. It's up to you to figure out merch prices, shipping prices and to coordinate customer service with the fan. If a fan has a problem with your fulfillment they can easily get the money refunded from PayPal--this means you have to ship it to them FAST and keep on top of your orders. You'll get email notices when you sell an item, but if you're the type of person who rarely checks their email, using BigCartel isn't going to be for you.

BigCartel has a sister company called Pulley (pulleyapp.com) that allows you to also deliver digital downloads to your fans. This means if you want to sell digital releases like your music or album notes, you can easily sell them or bundle them with your t-shirts. You can also do awesome tricks like bundle a sampler of your music every time someone buys some merch.

Manic Merch
Manic Merch (manicmerch.com), is the first affordable print-on-demand service for creators, enabling the tools to build a fanbase and monetize your creative endeavor off merchandise. In 10 minutes creators are able to upload designs and sell merch on every popular merch item, while Manic handles sales, shipping, customer services issues so the creators can create and not be bothered, while still profiting the way they would if they did it themselves

Manic has key features for creators including:

- **Set Up A Store In Minutes For No Money Down**—Upload your merch designs and tell us how to pay you and we'll take care of the rest. It takes a few minutes to begin selling high-quality merch to your fans with no customer service emails or packing up packages and heading to the post office. There's no financial risk or headaches for you to start selling merch.
- **Fans Buy More Merch When They Get To Choose How To Express Themselves**—Upload your merch designs in minutes

and sell more merch by allowing fans to choose colors and what they want each design printed on.

- **Set Your Own Prices**—You choose how much fans pay for each piece of merchandise so you can make what you want from each sale. Lower prices if you want to sell more and raise them if you want to make more from each sale.
- **Talk To Your Customers To Grow Your Fanbase**—You get the email addresses of everyone who buys from your store so you can let them know when you release new music, play shows near them or put up new merch.
- **Track Sales And Get Paid On Time**—You get paid every month, including detailed metrics on what was sold that you can analyze to sell more merch at live shows.

Bandcamp
While Bandcamp (bandcamp.com) is primarily thought of as a music store, you can also use it to sell merch. They take a 10% cut of your merch sales and no up-front costs. Their checkout is based on PayPal: You get the funds from your sales immediately and then fulfill the orders yourself. They offer a clean way to add merch items to your index page and get the fans that come to your page to buy merch. As an added bonus, you can bundle digital downloads with your merch so that all of your fans who buy merch also have your music.

Their merch service has all of the great features of Bandcamp's service, described in this book's Distribution chapter. They have a great interface for self-fulfilling orders as well as the ability to notify fans you have shipped their merch.

Shopify
When you are selling a lot of merch, Shopify (shopify.com) stores often the most options and flexibility to build a serious business in merchandise for your music. While they take on serious monthly fees their tools are superior to all else. You do need to find someone to fulfill your merchandising needs unless you DIY since Shopify is solely a storefront. The service is worth every dollar invested in its agility to run stores, market yourself, do SEO and do sales & discounts on individual items or sitewide.

WP eCommerce
WordPress has an easy plug-in that allows you to operate a checkout through your WordPress site. It offers a wide variety of checkout options,

including PayPal, and takes advantage of WordPress's CMS and SEO options, so that potential buyers are able to find your merch in search engines. (wordpress.org/extend/plugins/wp-e-commerce)

Amazon
Amazon (amazon.com) is the biggest marketplace on the Internet. If you're already selling a good amount of merch, using Amazon to set up a store has the added bonus of making your merch searchable in one of the Internet's biggest marketplaces. The widely used Amazon Wish List feature allows fans to ask for your merch as presents or simply broadcast their favorite pieces. There's no doubt that adding your merch to Amazon gives you the potential to pick up a lot more sales.

However, while Amazon is great, this shouldn't be your main merch store. They have large fees and they pitch competitors' merchandise while trying to sell yours, taking away your potential sales. It's good to have your merch on Amazon, but don't make it your main hub.

eBay
Music nerds and those looking for a deal often cite eBay as their favorite shopping place (ebay.com). This means if you have rare merchandise or some merch you can't get rid of, eBay is the perfect place to get it out the door. It's easy to set up a store, can you can keep the same items stocked and fulfill orders as they come.

Selling Your Merch On Etsy: When It Works
Perhaps you're an unfashionable, un-crafty, rural dweller and still haven't yet heard of Etsy (etsy.com). It's a huge community of DIY fashion and crafty artists who make their own clothing, jewelry, accessories and other crafts and then sell their wares within a network of like-minded individuals. Pretty much every crafty person in the world considers it the go-to community for such things. What this means for you is that you make some crafty, DIY type merch, you can sell it to this community and be a part of their unique search functions and amazing selling platform.

This community isn't for everyone. But for those who appeal to the indie rock, hippie, craft-loving community, this is a great place to have your merch. You may discover a whole new community of people you would be into your products.

In order to sell on Etsy, there are a few guidelines. To be a part of this community, your merch needs to fall into one of three categories – handmade, vintage or supplies. For most musicians, this means you'll need to sell handmade items. If you don't know what to sell, just browse around the site for a while to get some inspiration--Etsy is an endless wealth of creativity.

It's important to sell something that both your fans would want and that belongs in this community. Also, note that items with a great amount of effort put into them will go far in this community, as opposed to those that are cheap and thrown together.

Once you know what you would like to sell, you can easily set up an Etsy store by following their great guide (etsy.com) and pay the modest 3.5% commission to them. Be sure to link it on your website and let your fans who love Etsy items know you're there.

Zazzle, CafePress and Spreadshirt Are Not For Your Merch
While these services are great, since they put you in a marketplace and will print one-off shirts for you, they charge far too much for this service and will leave you with unhappy fans. The other on-demand options described above are far better options.

Selling More Merch

In your online store, you want to sell all of the items you normally sell at shows, plus some extra items. If you want the store to be successful, you need to make this store *the place* your fans go to find your merch. If you have to sell merch elsewhere, like on Hot Topic's website or your label's webstore, link to it from your main merch store. Your merch store needs to be your hub, where your fans can see every single item you offer on the Internet, even if they can't buy it directly from you.

Pricing
Just as you match or undercut other acts' prices at shows, it helps to know how much similar musicians are selling their merch for online. If you price your merch too high, fans will call you a sell-out monster and wonder why you're so cruel to your fans. If you sell for much less, you will have trouble making profit from your merch and funding your music. Find a happy

medium that keeps up with the prices other musicians similar to you sell their merch for.

Upsell
I know all of this talk of giving things away for free or putting money in and getting nothing out of it may have left you feeling a little sick. Now it's time to talk about actually selling to your fans. One of the keys to funding your music is to make sure fans have the ability to give you as much money as they want to. Price your items at $0, $5, $10, $25, $40 and even higher-- this will allow you to get more from bigger fans. If fans fall in love with your music and can't get enough, the only solution is to give them as much as you can and allow them to spend as much as they want.

If a bunch of fans are buying $10 shirts from you, maybe it's time to get a more profitable $20 option. Along those lines, if fans will buy a $50 item from you, maybe it's time to put a $100 item in your merch store. Give fans the chance to spend as much as they want. It is becoming more and more common for even smaller national acts to have $200+ high fashion items to take advantage of fans enthusiasm towards them.

Choices
As you sell more and more merch, you need to start giving your fans more merch options. The more merch options you give them, the more they'll be able to buy numerous items from you. If you are selling a lot of a shirt, it may help to put it in a different color or style (hoodie or tank-top?) to enable fans to have another reason to purchase it. If you don't give your fans enough choices, you leave money on the table you could be earning.

Clarity
The better looking your merch pictures are, the more of it you'll sell. Put the clothing on an attractive person in a real picture (as opposed to a mock up) and it'll not only show the fit, it will help sell the merch in a big way. Posting your mockups and photoshops of what a shirt will look like is a sure way to give fans no confidence in the quality of your merch. Look at the stores of popular musicians. They will often have models wear the merch. This takes very little time and can be the tipping point between a fan walking away from a purchase or clicking "buy."

Details
You know how there are record nerds who care about how many ounces the vinyl is and what color it is? This goes for all types of merch. Are your

380

T-shirts made on Gildan or American Apparel? How many colors is the print? What's the exact color of the shirt? Just saying blue doesn't cut it-- there are tons of shades of blue and some fans won't like certain shades by certain manufacturers. Your fans are trying to buy merchandise online. They haven't touched it or seen it with their own eyes, so providing them with a lot of details helps make them confident enough to plunk down the money for your merch. It will also cut down on questions coming into your inbox, so you can focus on getting more important work done.

Suggestions

Ask your fans what merch you aren't making. Do they wish you would print your shirts on American Apparel instead of Fruit of the Loom? Are you not making a size a lot of your fans want? This can all be answered by asking fans to tell you what you're missing. Have a note on your merch store that asks for fans input and include your email. You can make your fans happy and sell more merch.

Honest Communication

One of the keys to being able to sell merch is keeping your customers' (no longer just fans) trust. This means being clear and honest. Did you put up a shirt that you don't have in your hands yet? Make sure they know you're taking pre-orders and when you expect to ship them. If you don't check your mail or are going on tour, let the fans know the order may not ship for 30 days. The Internet has made the world very flat and when customers are scorned and lied to, they complain LOUDLY all over every social network they are on. Their complaints can discourage other fans from ordering from you and can turn your relationships sour.

One of the other keys to keeping fans happy is to include info on how to contact you all over the place. This should be an email address where customers can email you. When fans reach out to you, provide a polite and level-headed response. A lot of people are weary from bad experiences on the Internet. Customers are often scared to buy from a new person or an unknown entity. Showing them you're easily approachable will do a lot to quiet this concern and increase your sales.

Problems Happen

For no apparent reason, a package won't show up. Or it will come totally destroyed. Unfortunately for you, it's your responsibility to fix it when this happens. If the customer doesn't get their merch, check the tracking information. If it didn't make it, try to make good on the sale and keep this relationship in good standing. When you help a fan out and show a true interest in treating them well, they'll spread the word about how great you were. That also works in reverse: If you treat them like a crook and an asshole for complaining about a mishap, they will not only never buy from you again, they'll tell others how awful you were to deal with. <u>Remember, you're in the relationship business. This fan just upgraded your relationship to one where they give you money. Treat that with the respect it deserves.</u>

Bundle A Sampler With Your Merch

People who buy your merch are obviously big fans, but this doesn't mean they have all of your music. One way to get fans to want more of your music is to bundle a sampler with your merch. Services like Big Cartel, Limited Run, Bandcamp and TopSpin all give you the ability to easily bundle digital downloads with any merch item you sell. This means you can put a sampler with a T-shirt and have a fan discover you have more great music and other releases. You can even put your friends' tracks on these samplers and they can do the same for you. Not only does this help you bond with fans, it can help you sell more merch, since fans will see that they're getting free music with their merch.

Probabilistic Promotion

An easy way to bump up sales is to let your fans know there's potential they'll get something for free. If you tell them that 1 out of every 10 orders gets a hand-drawn picture from your drummer or a cute Polaroid of your dreamy lead singer, you'll see your sales go up. You can also follow standard practice and throw a limited piece of merch into the lucky winner's order. Once you have some customers, this will help turn borderline customers into paying ones.

Sale!

One of the concepts musicians seem to forget is that they're indeed a business. One of the things that businesses routinely do is have a sale to make some extra cash. Fans are always looking for a deal, so offering up a sale every three months or so can help entice fans into running to your merch store to pick up some extra merch. Also, remember to do holiday sales around the Christmas season.

Contests

Run contests that demand your fans see your merch. At your live show you can hold up a shirt that a fan can win if they answer a question correctly. Online, you can do this through your social media. It gives you a way to show off your shirt that isn't overbearing and can help get more fans interested in what you are selling.

Talk To Your Fans
Ask your fans what they want. Ask on social networks. Ask them from the merch table. You can even have a suggestion box on your merch site. They're the customers and may have suggestions you're not thinking about. You can even ask your fans to submit designs, though my experience with this is that it leads to a world of pain, when you inevitably receive countless horrible designs from your fans.

Thank You
You should show appreciation to fans that spend a lot of money on you. Many merch sales platforms allow you to see who your top-buying fans are. Surprise them with thank you notes, give them special privileges (backstage passes, private online access) and they will continue to show their support and then some. Everyone likes to feel appreciated and it takes very little time to thank them for their support.

Merch Drops
A common technique used in hip hop is to do merch drops where all of your merch goes up on a certain day in limited quantities. This creates urgency in fans to get the merch as fast as possible and make the items more valuable when they are scarce and limited. Many musicians now make this so much a part of their marketing they are now seeing themselves as half fashion brand half musician and the appeal of these drops has become immense in many genres.

Analytics
Just like you did with after your live show, you can go in the back end of your merch platform and look at the analytics. You may find that all your shirts with blue on them sell more, but all the shirts with green on them sell terrible. You just got a quick hint that you should be printing blue shirts. Maybe you always sell out of medium shirts before you sell out of small. Now you know to order more mediums and fewer smalls. You'll find tons of patterns--for example if one of your shirts get clicked on the most but isn't getting purchased, this is usually a hint that the price is too high. There are countless conclusions you can draw by looking at your analytics.

Fulfilling Your Merch Orders

Self-Fulfillment

Self-fulfillment means you're going to have to store all of your merch somewhere. Whenever an order comes in you're going to need to fill it, pack it and then ship it. While this sounds like one of the inner rings of hell, it can all be made easy and can be the right way to do merch sales.

Building Relationships - One of the biggest reasons I *always* set up self-fulfillment for the acts I work with, is that as you can use it to build fan relationships. The person you pay to fulfill your merch can also do other duties if you don't have enough merch work to fill their time.

Employees sound expensive until you realize that fans are paying for them. You know that ridiculous shipping and handling fee you pay every time you order something online? This is what the handling part is: The cost of an employee taking the time to pack orders and get them out the door. Whether you work out a rate for every package you ship or a flat fee for work by the hour, you can easily have an employee working for you once you have a couple dozen orders coming in. You can also keep doing this yourself and put that money into supporting your music or consider it your day job and pay yourself like an employee.

If you do choose to go this way, know it's an ever-expanding business. You might start off by hiring your little brother who needs a few extra bucks for spending money every week. Eventually, you can buy your own T-shirt press and offer the same service to all the musicians you know. It's possible to grow a big business from your merch and has been done many times before.

Owning Your Fans - I can't say enough how important it is to own your relationship with your fans. Doing your own merch is the ultimate direct-to-fan experience. If you treat your fan well and they like you, you can contact them every time you have something to sell. If your fan liked you enough to buy something from you once, chances are they'll do it again. However, if you let your fans buy your merch from someone else or even your music through iTunes, Amazon, etc., then you lose this chance.

Making It Work - If you're going to fulfill your own merch, you have a lot of lessons to learn. First your customer service has to be in the highest order. Not only are these fans customers, they're people you have established an intimate relationship with through your music. They like you now, but you have many chances to ruin that. They were kind enough to support your music when they had an infinite number of other options to choose from. That's special and means you need to make keeping them happy your utmost priority.

Special - The first way I like to make sure the customer is always happy is by giving them more than they expected. Every order should come with a sticker, postcard, note, drawing or something else special. Even a Xeroxed thank you note is nice, but the more special and personalized you make it, the better.

Viral - Man Overboard's merch fulfillment team got bored and started giving everyone who ordered merch a nickname on their envelope. This inspired the fans to post about it on Tumblr, Twitter and Facebook. Soon other fans started to want to order from them to get the same treatment. Not only did this endear fans to Man Overboard, but it spread the word about Man Overboard's music and increased their sales. Fans wanted a nickname of their own and would order merch just to get one. You can't do these personal touches when you don't fulfill your own merch.

Personal - When you have all of your customers' addresses, you can take time to thank them from time to time. You can buy postcards and send fans letters you write from the van, showing you care about them. Tons of huge acts like The Beastie Boys and Chester French are famous for doing this. This is the type of thing a fan will tell all of their friends about and most likely share on every social network. This personal touch can be an inexpensive way to get fans to talk about you and build your relationships in a way very few promotions can.

Wow! - Fans constantly tell all their friends about the freebies and special treatment they get from their favorite musicians. Those stickers, postcards or an old release you can't seem to sell will all get posted about and spread by word of mouth if you throw them in with fans' orders. If you have a label, you can promote your other acts by dropping their stuff in orders too. You can drop your friends' stickers and samplers in orders and have them do the same for you. You can even drop in burnt CDs of your friends' music (with their permission). This will make you seem like the coolest musician ever and help spread the word about your friends. Too easy!

Support - I can't tell you how many musicians have told me how they lost merch sales when they stopped fulfilling their own merch. A lot of fans are looking for a connection with the musicians they love. They also want to feel like they're supporting the musician. It doesn't feel like that when you buy a shirt from some corporate site and you don't get anything special in the mail except a shirt with a printed label.

Shipping & Handling - It can take some homework to figure out how much it costs to ship everything you have to every country. Be sure to include in the charges money for your labels, packing materials and time, but make sure you're not overcharging. One quick way is to see how much similar musicians charge in their shipping or to look up the international rates.

Screen Print Your Own Shirts
Do you have some spare time? Perhaps your friends do and you're having a get-together to get some work done? Your fans want lower priced merch and one way to give it to them is by doing the screen-printing yourself. This not only saves you money, it enables you to still make a good profit when you sell your merch at a lower price. Silk screening is easy to learn--just watch some YouTube tutorials. Every art supply store has the supplies to silkscreen and it's a great skill that can give you some extra sales and advertising.

How?
If you're going to ship your own merch, there are some ways to make it easier:

- **ULine** - ULine (uline.com) has a huge catalog of shipping materials and they're great to deal with. Here you can get bags to ship shirts (which cuts down on shipping costs), packing tape, labels, foam, whatever. They have it.
- **Bags Unlimited** - Bags Unlimited (bagsunlimited.com) has been making the best materials to ship vinyl, CDs and other media forever. They have great prices and specific shipping materials for media.
- **Endicia** - Endicia makes software for your computer to print shipping labels, all for a monthly fee. You can pay shipping costs off your credit account and can print your own shipping labels so you don't have to wait in line in the post office. There are startup costs involved, but if you're shipping more than a dozen items a month this will save you a lot of time and is worth the money and headaches. (endicia.com)

Third Party Fulfillment

What if you don't want to deal with printing and mailing your merch out yourself? There are some services that can take that torture out of your life, while still letting you take the orders through services like TopSpin and maintain control of customer service and your fan relationships. Your local T-shirt printing place is always an option, but here are some big companies who can take care of it for you:

Alliance Entertainment
If you choose to print and fulfill your merch through AudioLife, TopSpin or ReverbNation's ReverbStore, they're using Alliance Entertainment (aent.com) to print your merch on-demand. Alliance has software that integrates with various platforms, so you can sell your merch but have them ship it out for you. Easy enough.

Other Services
If you want to sell your own merch but have it fulfilled by another service which handles the printing and orders, two reputable companies are Paid (paid.com) and Whiplash Merch (whiplashmerch.com). Keep in mind they handle accounts, not the one order you get from relatives every so often. This is for when you're moving hundreds of orders of merchandise every month.

All-In-One Platform, Printing and Fulfillment Services
There are countless services that will take care of all your merch needs. Some even have their own designers. A lot of these services will penalize you with fees if you don't order or sell a certain amount of merch from them a month, but if that's not a problem, they can be a great no-headache solution that sends you a check every month for what you sell. They will also print merch for your tours and will even count your online sales as payment towards the merch you order for tour.

The two services I've had great experiences with are MerchDirect and MerchNow. They're both reputable, have been around the block a few times and are great to deal with. You can just use them to print your merch and deliver it to you and then choose to sell it yourself at shows or your online store.

Licensing Your Merch

If you start to sell a lot of merch, you may begin to get the opportunity to license it to third parties--usually stores, distributors or your record label who want to sell your merch in their own store or to stores they service. They'll pay you for the right to use a design with your name on it, often asking for an exclusive design, and then sell it themselves. For example, if Hot Topic wants your shirt, they will often ask for an exclusive design that only they will sell. They will take care of everything and send you a sales report and check either monthly or quarterly.

Your rate for this license will depend on what you're able to negotiate. It's best to let your lawyer negotiate it, since they're used to the normal rates for this kind of deal, though a few dollars per item sold is the most common rate I've seen. You can pursue these deals by contacting distributors who stock similar acts' merch and showing them your social media metrics or upcoming tours and promotions. You want to make them feel like it's worthwhile to license your brand. Foreign distributors are a great option too if you're touring a foreign country--it can help make some extra cash and have merch easily available overseas.

Chapter 23: Distributing Your Music In The Digital World

Digital distribution is one of the most important ways you'll share your music with the world. Having your music on the most common music discovery platforms like YouTube, Bandcamp, Spotify, Apple Music and Amazon can bring your music to many ears that may not otherwise hear it. Making sure your entire discography is on all of these services ensures your music has the potential to be discovered and spread to as many listeners as possible.

Doing Digital Distribution Right

Be Present
Make sure your record is available on every service possible. Think about your fans' listening habits--even in the digital age, music buyers act like they do in record stores: They find an outlet they like to browse in (Spotify, iTunes, Bandcamp or whatever), then search for music in their preferred store. If your music isn't available in their preferred outlet, you just lost a sale and potentially a lifelong fan. Make sure that potential fan can discover and buy your music on any service they could possibly use.

One note--this also applies to format. Make your music available in other formats like CD and vinyl, so that if a potential fan is only interested in those formats, you're still not losing out on their support.

Always Be Available
It's basically universally accepted that if you don't let fans buy your music, they will steal it. Even major labels (usually the last people to embrace progressive ideas) have gotten the message and now release singles on iTunes, Spotify, Apple, YouTube, etc., the second they go to radio. The memo is spreading--always be available or lose the chance to make a sale and build a relationship with a fan.

If a fan has the ability to obtain your music through illegal means, you need to immediately also give them the ability to obtain your music through sanctioned means. This can be anything--selling it to them or exchanging it for an email, tweet or Facebook like. But if your music is already available somewhere else and your fan can't get it from you, you're going to lose out.

This also applies to where fans get their music. The more places your music is available, the easier it is to find you and the more quickly you'll be able to solve your obscurity problem. If your fans like to buy from Napster as opposed to iTunes, put your music on Napster. If your fans are discriminate listeners and prefer FLACs (an audiophile format for digital music), make sure they can purchase them. Having your music on iTunes isn't enough for many fans who prefer high quality digital downloads or consuming music through subscription services (Apple Music, Spotify, Napster). Make sure you're available in any way a potential fan may want to discover and consume your music.

Here's an example: Let's say I'm a Black Keys fan, but they decided to not put their latest record on Tidal, Spotify or Apple Music. Because I only listen to music on Spotify these days and don't have time to go to my iTunes every time I want to their music, I've barely listened to their newest record (even though I still listen to their old records all the time on Spotify). Because of this, I also haven't been enthusiastic about going to see them live the past few times I've had the chance.

Not being available the way a fan wants to ingest your music can cripple your relationships with fans--and can cripple your fans' enthusiasm.

Allow People Who To Pay To Do
Some musicians have deemed selling music to be a boring and futile exercise and only want to make their music available for free. Other musicians want to promote their music by giving it away for free. While I am an advocate for having as few barriers as possible between your fans and your music, if you truly want to spread your music as much as possible, you still need to give yourself the chance to make money from the fans who actually want to pay you. If your music is being recommended to a friend of a fan, that friend will search for your music after being introduced to it via a paid platform like iTunes. If you have decided that you'll only offer it for free (failing to have it on iTunes), you lost out on a potential sale and a potential fan.

Putting your music on paid platforms also makes it easier for many fans to get your music. If a fan wants your song on their iPod while they jog, they can't get that unless it's on iTunes or they already have it loaded on their iPod. If they only listen to Spotify at work and your music isn't there, you lose the chance for this fan to become a bigger advocate of your music.

Give Fans The Option To Download Music Their Way

MP3, FLAC, WAV, AAC, WHATEVER! There are tons of different file formats that fans can use to listen to their favorite songs and many music nerds are particular about their favorite format. For some, MP3s are too low a quality and they need to listen to an Apple Lossless file. For others, that isn't enough and FLACs are the way to go. For the super nerd, the source file (usually a WAV) is the only thing they'll listen to. You can sell more music if you give fans the files they want. As an added bonus, they will hear a better sounding version of your music! The following services allow you to give fans the files they want to hear:

- **TopSpin**
- **Bandcamp**
- **Limited Run**

Ringtones

For a little while, ringtones were big money for some musicians. However, this is no longer the case. Both iPhones and Androids now make it easy to make your own ringtones, so sales have plummeted. This doesn't mean you can't give away pre-made ringtones on your website in exchange for email addresses. Trying to sell them may net you some cash if you have a die-hard fanbase, but most likely you'll be better off offering them as enticements. Most fans aren't going to plunk down money for them.

Digital Distribution Materials

Here's what you'll need to get your music into digital music stores:

- **WAV File** - This is the most common format mastering houses will send your song in. Many digital distributors and online services will not allow you to post an MP3 or other format, so make sure you receive WAV files.
- **ISRC Codes** - These are codes that help identify your music for a wide variety of purposes. They also help you get paid for publishing royalties. You can get them from your mastering house, digital distribution aggregator or from ISRC's website (usisrc.org)
- **UPC Code** - A UPC code is the barcode on the back of nearly every product available for purchase in a store. You need one of

these to sell your record online as well as in a store. Most digital distributors will give you one for free.

- **Art** - Most album art needs to be 1,600 x 1,600 pixels to get used by digital distributors. The file usually needs to be a .gif, .jpeg or .png.

Digital Distribution Aggregators

Unless you live under a rock, you know that each day CD sales falter, while digital music gains in popularity. You need to be distributing your music online, but you need to choose a middleman to get your music to online sellers. These middlemen are often called aggregators since they push your services to other services for a fee. They offer many bells and whistles for distribution and each one offers different benefits--you may find there is an unexpected service more suited to your needs.

While in years past each distributors partnerships would differ on whether they would get you into different stores or not. Now all of the aggregators get you to the same stores with little exception and their differences are fee structures and the bells and whistles they provide. But all of them provide the baseline of a UPC code, distribution to all of the major stores plus around 150 other music outlets and analytics.

Amuse
Amuse is modeled on aggregating your music to stores for no upfront costs as they use the data from who sells to scout artists. By being on their platform they are able to see who is trending in streams and see talent in advance. Because of this they allow free uploading and 100% royalties to be kept by the artist. (amuse.io)

Fees:
- The have a free tier that allows you to release music every 4 weeks.
- For $5 a month you can get advanced features, release music more often

CD Baby
CDBaby (cdbaby.net) has been on the Internet since dinosaurs ran it by running in mouse wheels. They have a well-established following of fans

that turn to them to find independent musicians. They also offer digital aggregation services to their artists and sell CDs and MP3s through their own store--a one-stop hub. They can get your music to:

Fees:
- 9.95-$55 price structure and they take 9% of all royalties.

Bells and Whistles:
- Distribute your CD to record stores.
- CD manufacturing through their parent company, Discmakers.
- CD Baby acquired Show.co which gives you free access to many marketing tools that allow you to trade fans Likes, Follows and Emails for music which are very powerful and some of my favorite tools in the business.
- The ability to collect advanced publishing royalties.

DistroKid
DistroKid (distrokid.com) is an affordable aggregation service that allows you to pay a yearly fee to keep your music online, as well as upload as music as you would like each year. This is ideal for anyone who wants to put out a lot of music each year and have it on all the most popular services. They allow you to keep 100% of your royalties and have some of the better bells and whistles.

Fees:
$20 a year to upload unlimited music for a single artist. There are packages for multiple artists for $35.99 and $79.99 with more features designed for labels. They include an option to pay $50 to keep an album on services forever.

Bells and Whistles:

- The ability to clear cover songs.
- Their FileVault service allows you to put up files for safe keeping.
- Includes a great tool for getting follows on Spotify as well as having your upcoming release saved to fans library automatically on release day.
- They have Spotify pre save marketing tools
- They claim to get your music in stores faster than any other aggregator.

393

- They have the ability to automatically split revenue saving you time having to do accounting.
- The ability to add credits and lyrics to your songs.

OneRPM

OneRPM (onerpm.com) offers an a-la-carte way to choose which stores your music is carried in. For $1.99 per store you can fill in holes in your present distribution or use them to choose specifically which stores you would like your music in. Each store you add your music to is $1.99, with no annual fees. They also offer free placement in their store, as well as a Facebook App to sell your music directly.

Fees:
$1.99 per store with no annual fee. They take 15 percent of your sales.

Bells and Whistles:
- Their own store where you can give away your music for free and collect emails.
- Free USB and ISRC codes
- Facebook store for Facebook sales.

Tunecore

Tunecore (tuncecore.com) is one of the most popular digital aggregation services. They also offer many facilities to track your music, like spreadsheet-compatible files of your sales and trending reports. Their service allows you to select which stores your music aggregates to, with a clean interface that allows you to read sales reports and research your marketing and sales information.

Fees:
- $14.99 to fully aggregate a single
- $29.99 per album
- $49.98 for album maintenance and storage per year

Bells and Whistles:
- Inexpensive CD pressing.
- They offer publishing collection services.
- In depth analytics.
- The ability to add credits and lyrics to your songs.

Other Aggregators
There are countless other aggregators but I find most of them to be too specified or just offer worse service than those listed above. These services are easy to use so tons of con artists are in this game so I have only listed those I deem reputable or to serve a function that differentiates them in the market.

Digital Distribution Platforms
If you run a label or are going to be prolific in your self-releases, you may want to move up to a digital distributor. These services offer special promotions, marketing and ad buys, and licensing and distribution options that many of the digital music aggregators do not. They also deliver to countless stores and platforms many aggregators don't send to. While they do take a cut and hit you with fees for these services, the benefits can easily outweigh the costs. They usually partner with some physical distributors, so it's easy to keep those services in sync. Many small and large indies sign up with these distributors to try to increase their streams and sales. If you have substantial sales and success using the digital aggregators, you can apply to be a part of any of these services (as opposed to all of the above aggregators which are open to anyone).

ADA (Alternative Distribution Alliance)
Handling many of the largest indie labels in the game, they also take on DIY artist labels and are the distributor behind the DIY success of Macklemore and Ryan Lewis having a huge hit album "without a label". They also handle physical distribution and merchandising. (ada-music.com)

Believe
Distributor focused on artist deals for both physical and digital distribution. Including label services like sync licensing and brand deals. (believemusic.com)

The Orchard
In North America The Orchard services a vast amount of labels and has countless marketing services and staff along with physical distribution to service artists. (theorchard.com)

InGrooves

Part of Fontana Distribution, which adds easy physical integration for their clients. (ingrooves.com)

FUGA
One of the biggest distributors in the business that primarily deals with larger labels. (fuga.com)

Red Eye Distribution
Huge indie distributor servicing smaller labels on up to huge ones like The Beggars Group. They offer marketing services along with physical distribution. (redeyeworldwide.com)

Secretly Canadian
Secretly is also one of the bigger indie distribution services for digital and physical items in North America. (secretlydistribution.com)

STEM
Stem is a unique bird in this realm in that like the others they only take on projects they see growth potential in but they aim themselves at handling independent artists instead of labels providing digital distribution and marketing tools. They also have a program called SCALE which will allow you to get royalties upfront from them. (stem.is)

United Masters
A similar service to STEM in that you apply to be a part of their digital distribution. (unitedmasters.com)

AWAL
Kobalt Music's version of the above two services. (awal.com)

Symphonic Distribution
Offering label services, marketing and playlist promotion Symphonic is a digital only distributor available to artists by application. (symphonicdistribution.com)

Digital Music Services & How To Promote Your Music Through Them

There are a number of services you can use to get your music to fans. But once your music is there, how do you use them to build a fanbase? Understanding the role each store plays in this ecosystem can help your strategy and make sure that your release gets as much exposure as possible. All of these services are aggregated to by using the previously mentioned digital music aggregators or distribution services. After you have chosen one of those services, your music will then get delivered to all or most of these stores and you can use these services to both earn money and get more fans.

iTunes

If fans are going to buy your music, they will most likely buy it on iTunes (itunes.com), but as of 2018 those sales are plummeting since everyone is moving to Apple Music, YouTube Premium or Spotify. Apple has by far the biggest cut of the digital music market, offering an easy interface to make sales quick and painless for the buyer. Whether your strategy is to give your music away or to sell it, it's important that your music is in their store, since this can still generate revenue through those who prefer to own your music instead of stream it.. Unless you go through a high-end digital distributor, iTunes will give you a standard price based on how much material you have on your record.

Making More Money On iTunes - One of the downsides of iTunes is that it takes a gigantic cut of your music sales (35% to be exact). This is pretty nauseating, especially when you're referring your fans there and doing all the work to make the sale happen. One way you can get some of this money back is by signing up with Rakuten LinkShare (linkshare.com) to get an affiliate commission for sending your fans to buy music from iTunes. LinkShare makes you money whenever someone buys something on iTunes via your recommendation. After you sign up with LinkShare, you simply paste a URL when you link to iTunes, and you receive a small commission if people buy music from your link.

Mastered for iTunes - Apple has announced a new section in the iTunes store entitled *Mastered for iTunes*. If you're thinking this is just another scam by the majors to get you to buy classic albums you already own, you're partially right. I am sure many of these records now have a fresh new coat of mastering on them and some of the releases in this section are actually current and new releases. In fact, throughout their white paper (bit.ly/masteredforitunes) on the subject, Apple makes no reference to any practices that would ensure your master for iTunes is different compared to what you would normally do to master a great-sounding record in the digital world. This seems like a way to revitalize the iTunes Plus platform that tacks on an extra 30 cents to each song for a higher quality download.

That being said, if you pride yourself on your recordings, you can use this service to allow fans to download higher-resolution files to enjoy. This is great, considering it offers musicians a good way to have mass archives from more high-fidelity recordings.

Go Straight To iTunes with iTunes Connect - If you have no interest in other digital services and aggregators, you can cut to the chase. Apple is happy to pay you directly and give you reports, as long as you fill out their application. If you want to upload eBooks or audiobooks you can also use this service to get paid directly through them. (itunesconnect.apple.com)

Apple Music
Apple Music (applemusic.com), is slowly rendering iTunes obsolete but we aren't quite there yet. While the streaming platform is the second biggest (up to Spotify) the ability to market your music effectively is still lacking.

Promoting Your Music On Apple Music - You can use major aggregator to get your music to Apple Music. Once it's there, Apple takes care of the rest. The big difference between Apple and the rest is they pride themselves on their curated playlists. Having your music on the service allows you to be added to these playlists and have fans share them with their friends.

You can also make playlists and link them all across the Internet. This is as easy making a playlist and then clicking the chain link button or Tweeting and Facebook sharing it from the page you're on. You can make a playlist of your discography, your local scene or even your friend's music and link the page on your website or on your social networks. Like Spotify, you can also link to any album by clicking the above-mentioned buttons. Use Apple to promote your record on your site and give fans a free way to listen to your music on the service.

The one trick to marketing your music on Apple Music is since they own Shazam encouraging your fans to play your music and Shazam it whenever they hear it, helps drive up your potential for playlist placement at Apple Music.

PreAdds - You can link your fans to your upcoming release and have them add it to their library in advance of your release by using Apple's link generator (linkmaker.itunes.apple.com/en-us).

Apple Music For Artists – Apple has access to analytics as well as embeddable widgets and links to show your fans Simply link your profile at their site (artists.apple.com).

Amazon

The other giant in the field of digital music sales is Amazon (amazon.com). Amazon not only will sell your physical products, but they also are the second largest seller of digital music. Having your music in the Amazon store needs to be an essential part of your digital distribution plan. Unfortunately, Amazon takes about the same cut as iTunes, so offering sales to them is a bummer. Still, selling music through Amazon has its upsides, since fans can also see the physical version of your catalog alongside the digital and an estimated 70% of physical media is sold through Amazon. Like iTunes, there are a few tricks you can use to become a bit more successful.

When you aggregate your music to Amazon, you can determine the price points for your record. From most to least expensive, your options are: Frontline, Midline, Catalog and Special. You can use this price determination to your advantage if you want to send your fans to Amazon to get a special price or aren't concerned about profiting from your record.

Prime Streaming – By uploading your music with any of the major aggregators you become part of Amazon's Prime music streaming service. When you upload your music to Amazon Music through an aggregator you are also granting them streaming rights. This allows your music to be played for Prime users on their Alexa devices which can help greatly with generating streams since many new releases are not available on the Prime format. As so many homes have Alexa this service is employed.

Affiliates - Like iTunes, you can make extra money from the referrals you give Amazon. Their affiliate program (affiliate-program.amazon.com) is one of the easiest to use and one of the most powerful. Not only can you make money linking your own records, you can also link to any product they carry and get money if your fans purchase these goods. This means you can add some personality to your page and recommend books, music, fishing poles or whatever will connect you to your audience by showing your personality, all the while making a profit.

Amazon For Artists – Amazon offers an app to correct information, view analytics and control your persona there. They offer little other marketing options for music aside from that.

Google Play
Google Play is Google's stab at a music service. This new service enables the millions of Android and Google products (Home, Chromecasts, etc.) users out there to purchase and stream your music. Their Artist Hub allows you to control how you're seen on the service but they take up such a small part of the market that few people pay much attention to this service as it offers very few marketing opportunities.

Spotify
Spotify (spotify.com) is a subscription-based music platform that, at the press of a button, allows you to listen to nearly any song out there. While there have been subscription-based apps before Spotify, none have had as many features, been as user-friendly or offer as many great opportunities to market your music. Boasting a detailed interface, huge catalog and the ability to download songs to mobile devices for offline listening, Spotify has set itself apart by also being a huge app platform. The most powerful part of the service is the easily shared user playlists, where users are able to trade off playlists with others. Spotify also offers easy sharing on social networks like Twitter and Facebook, which make it fun for users to spread what they're enjoying. You can see what your friends are listening to as they listen to it, making music more social than ever before and enabling friends to get automatic recommendations of what to listen to. If your music is getting played on Spotify, you're getting a stamp of approval from the listener that all of their friends can see.

How To Promote Your Music On Spotify - It's important you link to all your various social networks, especially to services like Spotify, from your website and any online profile or artist page you create. As potential fans discover your music, you're paid each time they listen and check you out (even if it's less than a penny, these listens add up). This also sends your new fans to a place where they can add your music to their favorites list and get locked into a lasting relationship if they like your music.

The most important part of promoting your music here is signing up for Spotify For Artists (artists.spotify.com). Once you are verified and your artist page is claimed it's important you get the right bio, photos and social media accounts linked, including your website. You can also type messages that mention your new single, tour or video. You can also use this message to tell fans you have new music coming soon. Spotify also allows you to feature a release so fans see this first.

Playlists On Spotify - Unlike many other music services Spotify's user playlists are searchable by any user. This means if you make helpful playlists they will be searched and listened to by other users. Here's some ideas.

- **Local Scene** – Get More Fans reader Douglas Kelley's band, Alberto Alaska made a playlist of their local scene in Rochester, NY which has helped both them and their friends gain a bigger fanbase locally.
- **Producers** - Noise Creators makes playlists of each producer on our service's discography so that musicians can listen to these producers work and decide if they want to work with them.
- **Nerd Lore** – A friend of mine made a playlist of every song he can find that uses a guitar pedal he loves.
- **Genres** – Make a playlist of your favorite in a specific genre you are in and label it so it comes up in searches. If your playlist gets popular you could see countless new fans finding your music.

You can pitch these playlists to blogs or link them on social networks. There's tons of potential in how you can market these playlists.

The Spotify Follow
One of the most important things you can get a fan to do today is follow you on Spotify. Since Spotify will notify and add your music to playlists the likelihood of this fan seeing what you are up to goes up be a factor bigger than almost any other opportunity I have ever seen in music. What makes it more consequential is Spotify claims to add you to 4 times the Discovery playlists than the amount of followers you have, so racking up followers dramatically increases your chances of converting new fans. Both Distrokid and CD Baby offer free services that enable you to have fans follow you on Spotify as well as save your future release to their library when its released. CD Baby's Show.co service is also available for $99 a month for those who don't use their service or the less expensive but more simple Feature.fm.

Pre-Saves

401

One of the cool features of Spotify is the ability to offer fans a button to save your next release to their library before its release date. Using buttons provided by Show.co, ToneDen or DistroKid you can make these buttons so that your fans are reminded to listen to your music in the future when they see it in their library.

Monthly Listeners
Spotify's Monthly Listeners is a metric featured on top of each artist page. For many people who are judging whether to give your music an opportunity or not this is a quick glance at whether you are big enough for that opportunity. This is another reason focusing on promoting on Spotify instead of Apple Music is often to your advantage.

How To Sell Merch On Spotify
Confirming your profile with Spotify allows you to connect a MerchBar (merchbar.com) account and make offers on your Spotify page.

Show.co Will Trade Your Content For Follows On Spotify
Show.co offers a way for musicians to gate audio, Soundcloud plays and YouTube views in exchange for a follow on Spotify.

Spotify QR Codes
Every song or album on Spotify has a scannable code to listen. These can be helpful to put on posters, CDs, postcards and other merch in order to encourage streams.

Ads - Spotify is ad-supported when you don't pay for the service. Once you pay for a subscription, the ads disappear. Many of the ads on the service are for other musicians, or feature musicians supporting products. This can be a strong promotional tool for your music. You can buy either 15 or 30 second ads where you do a voiceover to promote your new release or tour. Add placements can be narrowed by geography (country, US state or US Nielsen designated TV market), age, gender, platform (desktop, mobile Android, mobile iOS) and music genre. This can be highly effective in targeting and converting new fans.

Analytics - One of Spotify's strongest suits is their public and private analytics. I often argue if you want to judge an artist's fanbase you should look at the monthly listeners statistic Spotify has on every artist page. This is far more accurate than social media followers since you can look at how their fanbase is interacting with an artist presently and gauge their true enthusiasm. Spotify allows you to go deeper and see more about demographics if you sign up for their Spotify For Artist's service where you can see deep demographics of your listeners like location, age, sex and other helpful metrics.

Tidal
In 2015 Jay-Z along with a bunch of other mega stars bought a streaming music service named Tidal. While the launch was a huge misfire, the service does have users and allowing your fans to find you there, is in your best interest. Tidal will soon allow musicians to bypass aggregators and directly to the service. Until then use any of the popular aggregators to get your music there. The service is sadly quite under-developed so individually marketing to it is not only a bad use of time, but also very difficult. Hopefully that changes as time goes on.

Pandora
Pandora moved out of solely online radio and into streaming by purchasing Rdio in 2017. While the service is barely used, it is important to add your music there as Pandora tries to shift it's huge radio base to their streaming service. While their lister base is small Pandora actually has some great marketing tools for musicians on their platform that are effective.

- Pandora AMP allows you to record FREE short audio messages for fans to hear about your music and what you are currently promoting including tours.
- You can choose specific cities for messages to promote shows or other events specific to a region.
- Pandora Stories allow you to talk about your music and create playlists around it. These are great for album commentary tracks and other fan bonding including describing playlists of your favorite music.

Shazam
One of the most overlooked ways listeners discover music is through Shazam (shazam.com). Picture this–you start to get a local following of about 20 people at your shows. Because of your new found popularity, the cute girl at the local pizza shop is cranking out your songs and the local booking agent walks in and hears this song and wants to figure out who it is. Since the cute cashier girl is consumed by the delivery boy making the moves on her, the booking agent calls up the Shazam app in their phone to look you up, find your music, fall in love with it and wind up putting you as

the opening band on the next huge show they book. Or they can look you up in Shazam and you don't come up and you lose this great opportunity. Making sure your music is on Shazam can be the gateway to opportunities made or opportunities lost when someone looks up your music when they become curious about it. Especially considering Shazam's CEO says their app drives millions of streams a day.

So how do you make sure your music is there? A great first step is to play one of your songs from each release you have and make sure your songs come up on the service.

Simfy
Simfy (simfy.de) is a music subscription service available in Austria, Germany, Switzerland and Belgium. It's similar to Spotify, Tidal and Apple Music and is only important since its popular in the countries it serves. If you plan on touring in these regions, it's worth making sure your music is on these services. Nearly every aggregator and distributor services them.

Deezer
Deezer (deezer.com) is a French web-based music streaming service. It's similar to the other streaming subscription services, except that it also boasts a wide range of radio stations. However, it only services France and a few other European regions, but is extremely popular in these countries and gains more traction every day. If you are planning on touring these regions, be sure to get your music on the service.

We7
We7 (we7.com) is a free, ad-supported music-streaming site for music listeners in the UK. While the site is mostly based on stream, users have the option to purchase music from the service. They boast 2.5 million users, so this site is a strong tool if you're looking to promote in the UK.

Changes
These services come and go fast and this list could be out of date by the time you're reading this. In fact, every few months you can add or subtract another service from this list (we can pour out a 40 for the Zune, Turntable.FM and MOG that all died within a year of this book first being published). Because this landscape changes all the time, it's a good idea to see if you can add your music to any of the new stores available whenever you check in with your aggregator or distributor.

LinkFire Allows You To Link Your Music To The Services A Fan Uses

The biggest problem with digital music today is the person who has a YouTube Premium account probably doesn't have an Apple Music, Spotify or Tidal account. LinkFire (linkfire.com) allows you to link every service including your website and direct to fan sites so you can effectively link interested in fans where they can hear your new song or album. The icing on the cake is they can give you analytics on what fans are clicking so you can further figure out how to hone your promotions.

Services That Allow You To Do PreSaves, PreAdds And Follows

If you are looking to market your music to fans to rack up follows and presaves these services all offer tools to do so, they all change and are evolving so it is best to look through them and find which one suits your needs.

- **Show.co**
- **Feature.FM**
- **Presave.io**
- **ToneDen.io**
- **Found.ee**
- **Uncvrd.co**

Getting Your Music On Playlists

As streaming music takes over as the predominant way people listen to music playlists begin to be more and more important for both getting in front of potential fans ears as well as being a way to make income from your music. Because of this, the world is beginning to be obsessed with how to get on playlists. Thankfully, there's a lot of things you can do to get on them. This advice applies to Apple Music, Spotify, Google Play and Tidal unless we specify otherwise.

The Best Exploit Right Now

Right now getting on Spotify playlists are the best exploit around to gaining huge fans for minimal investment. You just need to know the rules you need to play by. Luckily Spotify tells you exactly what they want you to do. They even made a video series on exactly what you need to do to be considered for their playlists (artists.spotify.com/videos/the-game-plan). The key is to follow their best practices and they will promote you.

This is super important as playlists like Release Radar and Discover Weekly are in the top 5 ways most music fans hear new music and their other influencer playlists are just as big opportunities. Spotify publicly tells you they will serve your new songs to four times the amount of fans you have following you. This is why employing follow campaigns and releasing singles regularly increase your chances of gaining more fans than nearly any practice available right now.

It is important the best chance you have to gain a huge fanbase is to submit your music to Spotify YOURSELF using your Spotify For Artists by submitting your music to be released 4 weeks in advance and then writing a great pitch that tells Spotify why you are unique (see our chapter on your bio) and hoping for the best. Also remember to do all of Spotify's best practices including making your own playlists and filling out your own profile.

Making Your Own Playlists Gets You On Internal Playlists
Using the tools each streaming service gives you to make your own playlists helps up your chances for getting on their own internal playlists. The streaming services look for "good citizens" who use these features to add to their own internal playlists, so making your own playlists helps get you on the highly sought after internal playlists.

Your Own Playlists – The first thing you can do is make your own playlists from your artist profile. A common one to make is a playlist for fans who are just hearing about you in the order you would like fans to listen to your songs. These are often called "<Band Name> Discography" or "Welcome To <Band Name>" and for artists with big catalogs this can often be a greatest hits, whereas for younger artists it can organize the songs in a curated way, especially if some of your songs are collaborations or remixes on other artists profile. Most importantly, this playlist is great to share whenever you add a song to it since it will auto play more of your music once the listener hears the new song.

Commentary Tracks – You can set these up with your distributor and make a separate release or playlist where you record your commentary on your release about how songs came about. Be sure to encourage fans to follow you on your streaming services at the end of your commentary

Artwork & Description – Be sure to add artwork for all of your playlists, whether its custom or just your album covers. There is also a description field for each playlist that should be filled in with the information a fan would like to know. Doing all of this helps raise the odds your playlist will be featured in searches or in their recommendation algorithms.

What You're Listening To – A great playlist to make is what you're listening to as a group. This allows fans to bond, can help promote friends music and build community. The relationships this builds with fans when you show them their new favorite song can help build a lasting relationship and is one of the best tools ever made for making a long term memory with a fan by simply showing your personality. When you share this on your social media, be sure to @tag the groups you have added to your playlist in hopes of making friends and getting Retweeted for further promotion.

Festival Playlist – If you are playing a big bill make a playlist with everyone you're playing with's music included on it. Paste this on the Facebook invite comments as well as on your social media tagging your fellow performers. They will most likely help spread the word and be grateful for your kindness that took only a few minutes.

Getting On Influencers Playlists
Influencers are often the same people you pitched on blogs. If you see a popular playlist of your genre, you can always check who makes it by looking at the by ___ next to the name. Most often the influential playlists will be made by the streaming service themselves, but some are made by DJs and other influencers who you may meet in a Facebook Group. If that is the case do your best detective work for their email or blog address and submit to them in their preferred method. Keep in mind searching the name of various playlists on Google or Twitter you can often find the people who curate them since they link to brag about their influence.

Beware Of Playlist Promotion Services
In music there's always a place where the grifters go to take money from musicians aspiring dreams. This is where the majority of these people are working these days. Beware of any solicitations you get about playlist promotion. Unless you have a recommendation with someone you would trust with your first born's life, I suggest not hiring any of these people. With that said, if a trusted friend gives you a ringing endorsement, the payoff from those who do this well can make a huge difference in building your fanbase.

Playlist Push

407

Playlist Push (playlistpush.com) offers a paid service that will service your music to influencer's playlists in exchange for a fee. Two week campaigns start at $185 and you will receive direct responses from influencers who listen to your songs. In the campaigns I have been involved with that have tried this service the results have been mixed, ranging from worthless to a great value.

Tracking Playlists
There's a few startups that offer deep analytics for playlists so you can figure out where plays are coming from and analyze which playlists you should be following or trying to get on.

- **PlaylistSupply** – This service tells you what songs are playlists on Spotify along with graphs and other analytics so you can target playlist performance. (playlistsupply.com)
- **ChartMetric** – A similar service with advanced metrics for Playlist tracking on both Spotify and Apple Music. They offer a free tier that is useful and a $140 tier for more thorough searching (chartmetric.io)
- **Spotimatch** – A service that will show you similar playlists you can apply to. (spotimatch.com)

Once you find playlists to be on it can be hard to track people down. Looking them up on social media is often bet but tools like Tin Eye (tineye.com) can do reverse google image searches and show you everywhere else their picture appears so you can find them and contact them.

As this is an area that changes CONSTANTLY I encourage you to visit my YouTube channel as I regularly cover this subject and upload videos with the latest information.

Other Digital Music Services To Upload To Directly

Aside from the above services and social networks, there are plenty of outlets where you can post your music, getting it more exposure.

Bandcamp

Bandcamp (bandcamp.com) is one of the most powerful tools for getting your music out to the masses. The amount of different functions it offers is astounding. It also gives you the ability to give a solid first impression to fans and is a great way to let your fans easily listen to your music.

Bandcamp has two modes--a regular one, which is free, and a Pro version, which costs $10 a month and allows you to batch upload, host private streaming, access Google Analytics and sales maps as well as turn on and off streaming as you wish. In both modes, they take 15% of your digital sales and 10% of your physical merch sales. If you do more than $5,000 of merch through them per year, they will drop the digital rate to 10%. They do all of their transactions through PayPal and you will need an account with PayPal in order to get paid by Bandcamp. PayPal's fees are not included in Bandcamp's fees, so you have to factor that in as well, but they pay immediately, which can help a lot for getting fast money in dire times.

While the service is easy to use, there are tons of tips and tricks to make it an even better tool. It can be an amazingly dynamic way to bond with fans and give them extra special treats. Every song you ever release should be on Bandcamp.

Features - One of Bandcamp's coolest features is its immediacy. If you have a creative whim and record a song for a special occasion, the second you have a master it can be uploaded and sold or given away. With iTunes, Amazon, Spotify, etc. you always need to wait days to have your music go live. Because Bandcamp offers immediate turnaround, you can even upload a live show within an hour after leaving the stage.

Searchable - Bandcamp offers an extensive search function. You're able to tag your music for different search terms like genre or other words that describe your sound. You also include an overall genre selection and your location. So if fans are searching for new dance music from LA, you're easy to find. Many people use this to find collaborators, groups to trade shows with and tons of other opportunities.

Discover - Bandcamp has an awesome browsing tool that turns their service into a virtual Mom & Pop record store. You're able to browse by genre and a wide variety of qualifications, get recommendations, view charts or see new releases that have been uploaded to Bandcamp. This makes Bandcamp a great tool for letting music lovers stumble upon your release. And the best part is that as you drive sales on Bandcamp, you'll be rewarded for it by going up in the charts.

Your Profile & Index - Bandcamp allows you to add basic bio information. You have roughly about three Tweets (or 400 characters) to tell the world why they should care about you. You don't need to use this space to link your social networks, since there's another section for that or for your location, website and genre. Also remember your recording credits and information about each release can go right under its track listing, so save your breath on those details too. Instead, take this time to write a message to fans that may have just discovered you. Make this bio about who you are, not just your latest release.

Visually, you're able to show off in a few ways. First, you have the ability to add a press photo to your profile. Use one that you won't mind being featured on blog posts, Tumblr or anywhere else someone may want to share it. You can also choose a background image which will show up on all of your Bandcamp pages, no matter which of your releases a user clicks on.

One of the most important parts of your profile is your header image. In order to make sure your Bandcamp lives up to its full potential, be sure to take advantage of using image maps in your header image. An image map is more than just a picture, since it can allow you link to all of your other social networks and your website, from a good looking image on every page of your Bandcamp. If your Bandcamp page gets a lot of traffic, this link is a very helpful way to engage your fans and get them to follow your other social networks. If you do make a custom header, you can also make a separate header for Bandcamp's Facebook app and for when fans come to the site via their mobile devices.

Lastly, you can add concert listings to your Bandcamp page by updating your SongKick (songkick.com) profile. There isn't a way to manually enter dates on Bandcamp, which is helpful, since it means Bandcamp isn't just another site you need to keep updating. If you keep your SongKick tour dates up to date, your Bandcamp will always be up to date too.

Releases - Once your profile is set up, it's time to add your release. Adding music to Bandcamp works the same way many other sites do: Upload your music and provide the relevant information. As you add each track, you can add lots of other cool details, like an image for each song, credits or a description. You can also add the lyrics, which actually helps your Google search results--if a fan only remembers the lyrics to your song, they can type them in and be taken straight to the Bandcamp page where they can listen to the song and learn more about you. If you have UPC and ISRC codes, you can enter them and make sure your music sales are reported to Nielsen SoundScan, placing you on the Billboard charts.

Format - Bandcamp allows for music fans to download music in a wide variety of formats. Everything from MP3, AAC Lossless, FLACs, even Ogg Vorbis (the rare and weird format Spotify uses) are compatible. You will need to give them very high quality files (aka 16 bit WAVs at 44.1khz or CD quality) if you would like to use this service. If you only have MP3s of your music, they will not allow you to upload them unless you cheat and change them to WAV files in iTunes.

Pricing - You can set an individual price for each song or use Bandcamp's very cool option to make each price a minimum fans need to pay. This allows fans that really want to support you to pay as much as they want for your music. This effectively turns your Bandcamp into a tip-jar and means when it comes to fans showing how much they appreciate you, the sky's the limit. Lucky for you, Bandcamp is a community of music fans who enjoy supporting musicians. If you watch their front page, they have an interesting waterfall view of "What Is Selling Now." Many of the purchases are above the minimum price that musicians asked for--meaning that giving fans the option of paying more can be great for your wallet. This "Name Your Own Price" model (much like Radiohead's *In Rainbows* release) is a great way to get extra funding for your release and show fans you're someone who values a fair-and-square relationship. Fans appreciate this-- so much so that 40% of the time, fans pay more than the asking price for name-your-price albums.

You can also make that minimum price $0, but if you do this remember that Bandcamp only allows you only 200 free downloads per month (though if you sell $500 of merch, they will give you 1,000 free downloads). If you want to use Bandcamp as a place fans can come to get free music, you can purchase 1,000 downloads for $20 from Bandcamp. You need to buy them in advance though, so be sure to monitor your Bandcamp if you think you'll be giving away a lot of free music.

Because these prices are minimums, you can keep them affordable. It's also important to remember that since Bandcamp takes 10-15% of your profits, compared to iTunes or Amazon taking double that, you can take $1 off the price of each record or a few cents off of each song and still walk away with not only a higher profit as well as your fan's email address (win-win!). This enables you to seem cool, sell to your fans and keep building your relationship with fans that buy from you.

Capturing Fans - If you're giving away your music for free, make your fans give their email address in exchange for a free download. As we've talked about at length, this enables you to build your relationships with fans by keeping in touch with them. If you choose this option, it will ask fans for their email address and zip code, so you can geo-target them later.

Whether or not you chose this option, whenever a fan buys your music you also get their email address. This is a part of what makes Bandcamp an extra strong tool for staying in touch with fans and one of the many reasons you should drive fans to buy from Bandcamp instead of iTunes. You get to stay in touch with fans that like your music enough to buy it, whereas iTunes won't even let them know when your new record comes out. To get these email addresses, simply head over to the "tools" section of Bandcamp and export the .csv file of these addresses. You can then import this file into your email provider.

Follow - Bandcamp has a "follow" button that allows fans who are signed up to their service to be alerted whenever you release new music on the service. This means driving fans to download your music through the service--whether they give you their email or not--gives you a higher chance of your fans being alerted each time you release new music, unlike on iTunes.

Albums - Once you've added a few songs, you can add an album to Bandcamp, which will then open up a world of new options for your profile. As you add songs, it will make them available for streaming (unless you set your release to private--a setting to use if your record isn't being released until a later date). If you upgrade to Bandcamp's Pro account, you can also enter album credits and information on the release, as well as album art.

Bonus Material - One of Bandcamp's coolest features is the ability to bundle bonus material with your releases. You can add material in any of the following formats to be bundled with your digital download: png, jpg, gif, pdf, doc, docx, txt, ppt, pptx, mp4, m4v, m4r, mov, wmv, avi, mpg, mpeg, swf, flv, torrent, cue, afm, amxd, otf, sib, ptb, mid, midi, gp5, fxp, fxb, vst, mod, it, xm, mtm, nsf and ttf. You can bundle your vinyl sleeve layout, pictures, videos, stories of your songs, MIDI files and many other things. Your imagination is the only limit.

Bandcamp allows "Hidden Tracks," or songs that are only available if you purchase the whole album. Offering a Bandcamp-exclusive hidden track is a great way to get fans to buy from your direct-to-fan offering. You can also add bonus content like alternate versions, remixes or even a more dynamic mastering of your record for audiophiles. The possibilities are limitless.

Bundling - All music purchased from Bandcamp comes as a digital download, but you can also bundle physical items with those downloads that you'll then ship to your fans. This means you can add your CD, cassette, vinyl and even deluxe packages with T-shirts and other unique merchandise. This is a great way to upsell your diehard fans to a more expensive package that they'll appreciate. Each of these bundles needs to have detailed information: pictures, a price point and shipping and handling. It's also important you include how long it will take you to ship these items. You can set up pre-orders if you need to get sales going before your record hits the street and you start building the hype.

You can even limit quantities on this merch, so if you want to give away handwritten lyrics to the first 200 people who buy your release, you can add on $5 to the bundle and include them. Fans love getting something special and just because you don't have a CD or vinyl doesn't mean you can't create something cool to sell them.

Recommendation - Bandcamp is a community and one of the highlights is the recommendation section. When someone buys your music, they are presented with another album on Bandcamp you recommend to your fans. This means you can recommend your friend's album and they can do the same for you. You can recommend up to three other releases. It's a great idea to trade these with other musicians whose fanbase you think you appreciate you. It also helps to generate real, honest reviews that tell others why one of your fans would want to buy the record you're recommending. Remember, when your friends get a larger fanbase, so do you.

Download Codes - Bandcamp allows download codes. These codes allow you to give free downloads to your fans by giving them a password code that will be redeemed for a free download. This can be great if you want to bundle downloads with your LPs or send them to fans that do something special for you. Just remember these count against the free download credits Bandcamp already gives you, so make sure you have credits filled for every download code you give away.

Discount Codes - Discount codes can be a great way to offer a sale or reward to your fans and Bandcamp has an easy system to make them available. These codes can be anywhere from 5 to 95 percent off your regular prices and are a great way to drum up sales in times of need or just as a thank you to your fans. For example, you can put the code on flyers you give to fans at shows, in your email list to thank fans for signing up or tweet them out.

Facebook App - If you want to make Bandcamp an integral part of your fanbase-building strategy, use their great Facebook app. You can install it as a music player and music sales portal--meaning fans can stream your record and see what you're selling right there on their Facebook page. It's easy to set up and works very well.

Free Music Page - You can turn an album page into your free music page. Simply assemble all the material you would like to give free to your fans into an album and enable the email capture function. You can also bundle this album with your merch, so fans get all of this free music whenever they buy merch from your Bandcamp store.

Subscription - Bandcamp will allow fans to subscribe to all of your music for a yearly price you can set. This will enable subscribers to get any content you put on Bandcamp. As this service is implemented price points start around $20 and go up to $50.

Exclusive Streams – You can give an exclusive embed code to a blog so they can be the only one to post your new track. This can be used to effectively do premiers of your new song on blogs.

Videos - You can now post videos on your Bandcamp pages to promote your products or give fans a taste of your personality.

Best Practices

- **Credits** - Add recording credits and musician credits. This will help your album show up in search engine results. This way, if someone is a big fan of your producer or the guest vocalist on your track, they'll find you.
- **Add Visuals** - Obviously, you need album art. But if you're selling physical items, having a good-looking picture of your products (especially vinyl and merch) can go a long way. It also makes them much more visually appealing for potential fans browsing in the Discover tool.
- **PayPal** - Enable micro-payments through PayPal. Bandcamp's blog says that enabling this feature can save you "33 cents for a $1 payment, 45 cents for a $5 payment." Taking the five minutes to set this up means more profits whenever fans buy from you.
- **Special** - Offer fans special benefits through Bandcamp.
- **Buttons** - Bandcamp has buttons and badges available on their site that you can add to your website.
- **Custom Domain** - If you have a website, you can add a custom domain to your webpage and make it a seamless part of your web presence.

NoiseTrade
NoiseTrade (noisetrade.com) is a music store that allows you to give away your music for free or by allowing a fan to name their own price. As an added benefit, you can collect emails and addresses from every fan that downloads your music.

Bandsoup
Bandsoup (bandsoup.com) is a music discovery site where musicians can upload their own music and allow fans to discover unknown gems.

PlayMPE
PlayMPE (plaympe.com) is a service that will send your music to thousands of radio, TV and other music business folks for their catalog so they can draw upon it if they get requests.

Radio Reddit
The nerds on Reddit determine a lot of what spreads across the Internet. They also have a way for you to upload your music and get it heard by the citizens of Redditland on Radio Reddit (radioreddit.com). Simply submit your music and let this active community spread it for you.

Reddit Listen To This
Instead of Radio Reddit, there is also a sub-Reddit (a message board with a specific interest) to upload music that they think others may like. It's not pop-friendly and if you spam the board with your whole record, you'll quickly get down-voted. But, if you're a positive member of the community, you just may pick up some new fans (reddit.com/r/listentothis).

WFMU's Free Music Archive
NYC area radio station WFMU, along with affiliates KEXP, dublab, KBOO, ISSUE Project Room, All Tomorrow's Parties, PrimaveraSound and CASH Music, have launched the Free Music Archive (freemusicarchive.org). The idea of the site is this: You assign a Creative Commons License (more on this in the copyright chapter) to your music, with the theory that free downloads will increase sales by introducing listeners to music they wouldn't otherwise discover. The music will then be played by these curators without excessive royalties and made available to creatives to use in their projects. This is big news for those of you who work with samples in your music, podcasters and radio DJs. To explain the idea behind the site further and demonstrate their Creative Commons License, I offer you my awesome copy and paste skills:

"Radio has always offered the public free access to new music. The Free Music Archive is a continuation of that purpose, designed for the age of the Internet... Every MP3 you discover on The Free Music Archive is pre-cleared for certain types of uses that would otherwise be prohibited by outdated copyright law. Are you a podcaster looking for pod-safe audio? A radio or video producer searching for an instrumental bed music that won't put your audience to sleep? A remix artist looking for pre-cleared samples? Or are you simply looking for some new sounds to add to your next playlist? Inspired by Creative Commons and the open source software movement, the FMA provides a legal and technological framework for curators, artists and listeners to harness the potential of music sharing. Every artist page will have a bio and links to the artists' home page for users to learn more about the music they discover via the Free Music Archive. We also seek to compensate artists directly. Artist, album and song profiles will contain links to buy the full album from the artist and/or label's preferred vendor(s). Users can also "tip" an artist if they like what they hear, sending a donation directly to the artists' PayPal account. Artist profiles include tour dates, encouraging users to step away from the glowing computer screen and see some real live music."

416

Use Niche Genre Online Stores To Your Advantage

Many musicians exist outside the mainstream pop music bubble. If you are one of them, one of the smartest things you can do is to find a niche store in your genre and team up with them for promotions--be it exclusive merchandise, promotions, autographed merch, etc. Niche stores can help promote you in your genre and get your music to likely fans. Here are some of the more popular niche stores:

- **Smartpunk/District Lines** - District Lines (districtlines.com) is a site where bands can sell CDs, merch, vinyl, DVDs, etc. This is a great site if you're a pop-punk, hardcore, emo, screamo or modern metal band. If you have no idea what I just said, then move on. If those genres hit home, then this may be a great store for you. They sell many records from unsigned bands and feature them right on the front page.
- **Insound** - Insound (insound.com) is the place for Indie Rock. If your fans are hipster indie rock types, you should have your music here. Insound carries MP3s, CDs, vinyl and merch. If you think your band may appeal to these kids who fall into the hipster/indie snob category, your music should be here. The site has been around forever and treats its customers and labels very well.
- **Beatport** - Beatport (beatport.com) is the underground hub of dance/electronic music. If you're making music in these genres, you need to upload your music here--there are droves of kids in neon and baggy pants with pacifiers waiting to hear your 7-minute dance opus. If you're an act that does a remix or two, these should be on here as well. Unlike the other stores, Beatport only does digital downloads of songs, albums or mixes and nothing else.
- **Interpunk** - Interpunk (interpunk.com) is the place on the Internet for punk--like REAL punk, not kids in neon with 45 degree angled haircuts (though you can also find crossover musicians carried at Insound and Smartpunk). They carry CDs, vinyl, all sorts of merch and even books--but no digital downloads.
- **Bleep** - Bleep (bleep.com) is Warp Records' store and specializes in glitch/electronica/IDM music. This store is useless to you unless you're an experimental electronic artist, but if you feel your music falls into this category, this could be an important outlet. The service carries digital downloads, CDs and vinyl.
- **Beatstars** - A marketplace for beats and/or productions that don't have a completed composition yet. Usually they need a vocalist

and this is where vocalists looking for great production can go to find tracks and pay for them. (beatstars.com)

There are many other genre specialty stores out there. Talk to musicians who are similar to you and investigate and build bonds with these stores. It can be an easy way to get extra promotion for your music in front of fans that obsess over your particular genre.

Other Formats To Distribute Your Music On

Dropcards Allow You To Sell Digital Downloads At Shows

While many fans want to buy CDs at your live shows, others are done with the environmental footprint, not to mention the hassle of ripping a CD open and the clutter it creates. One way to give your fans the option of a small footprint and an easy way to get your music is to use digital download cards. Dropcards (dropcards.com) have been around for a while, but they become more relevant with every music fan that gets converted to digital downloads.

When you're out on tour, you need a way to get gas in the van *today*, not when you get paid from iTunes in a month. Download cards are cheap ways to get cash into the money box fast. Fans want to pay for your music on impulse while they're still high from the rush of your live show. Dropcards makes this process seamless, by selling fans a good-looking card that links fans to a simple download process to get your music. These cards have your own artwork, which fans can then hang up on their wall, giving your music free advertising for all of eternity. Get them today, so you can sell music to people like me who don't want another CD taking up space in their apartment.

CardIncluded Makes Download Cards You Can Print Yourself

Download cards are often derided by not being enough to entice fans at shows for the amount of money and effort they take to make. CardIncluded (cardincluded.com) fixes that problem by offering a cheap solution with minimal effort required to get easily deliver downloads to fans. With a low rate of only $0.01 per 20MB of downloaded data, the service allows you to design a card, upload audio and then print it out in a clean format for fans to download. They allow for instant access to download cards for those who need to get their songs out fast.

CD Baby Wristband Downloads

CD Baby (cdbaby.com) allows you to make wristbands (like the ones clubs use to identify attendees who are over 21 years old) where you can print download codes for your music. This is a fantastic marketing tool that can be used so fans remember to download your music or to give it away to everyone who attends a show. You can also get them from TicketPrinting.com.

USB Sticks

Many musicians get excited about selling USB sticks of their music to fans. While this seems like a new idea, very few musicians actually sell these sticks unless they are a special release. Some musicians get custom sticks that are designed around a theme. For example, the group Get Busy Committee did machine gun shaped USBs that could be bought during their pre-order. Other acts will put their entire discography on a USB in order to offer an extensive look at what they have done. If you choose to go down this road, just make sure you do something special with them or the pile of unsold USB sticks will be just as high as the pile of unsold CDs in your closet. No one wants to buy a plain old USB stick with your name on it.

Cassettes Are Back?

Many groups are getting nostalgic and doing cassette releases for fans that enjoy collecting a special novelty release. If your fans are record collector nerds, hipsters or those who can't buy enough merch, cassettes may be an option to explore. Since many listeners don't have a cassette player, cassettes are only useful to sell more merch to your fans, but don't expect it to be something that sells unless you have a rabid fanbase. If you are going sell cassettes to fans, be sure to remember that they are probably buying it for novelty's sake and you will need to include a digital download in order to get any substantial sales. You can easily get cassettes duplicated in a small run from services like Rainbo (rainborecords.com), Milwaukee Cassette Works (utechrecords.com) or by doing old-fashioned cassette duplication yourself.

Subscription Services

Subscription services have been a much-hyped idea of how to connect with fans. The idea is that fans will pay a subscription fee up-front to get a regular dose of music from you over the course of time. This can be a monthly or bi-monthly release sent to fans in physical form. They can be in digital form but keeping digital music behind a wall usually leads to illegal file sharing, making this all counter-productive and alienating fans who don't have the money to shell out for a subscription up front.

The downside to subscription services is that they can lock your music behind a wall, only accessed by fans that have the money and devotion to get your music. While subscriptions are a great way to deliver music to die-hard fans, they're not the best way to attract new fans. Because fans are paying for the music before they even hear it, this means you have to have an established fanbase that trusts you before this is possible. However, if you do have that fanbase and feel you can consistently get some music to them, this can be a great way to build up some fan-funding in advance.

Below are a few ways you can deliver subscriptions to fans:

- **SongAmpr** – SongAmpr (songampr.com) allows you to do one song at a time subscriptions to fans. They also encourage you to sell a one of a kid piece of merch with each song release. The service also handles the manufacturing and fulfillment for your merch.
- **TopSpin** - TopSpin (topspinmedia.com) has ways to give members of a fan club exclusive access to whatever you would like. This can include delivery of subscriptions to only those with fan club access.
- **Website Check Out** - If you're selling physical media for subscriptions, you can sell a subscription to them through any eCommerce checkout option (PayPal, Google, WP eCommerce) and then just fulfill the orders to your fans yourself.

iPhone & Android Apps

I am a generally optimistic person who gets excited by new technology, especially technology that can help musicians connect with fans in new and interesting ways. Sadly, the app phenomenon was one that has let me down. Heralded by many as the future of the album, that promise has yet to come true. Instead, I've seen countless musicians put their money into making apps to get attention or widen their fanbase, only to have it create a small ripple in the press and then die.

While apps are cool and all, their audience is limited. Only those using either iOS or Android phones will be able to access them--excluding everyone with a Blackberry, Windows phone or non-smart phone. On top of that, you'll have to convince your fans to download an app and then open it whenever you do something cool there. They're not constantly reminded that your music exists and won't think of your app when they open iTunes or turn on their iPod, unless they allow your annoying push notifications to come through. Instead, it lives anonymously in the sea of apps that swim in the deep screen of your fans' phones.

The other problem with apps is that they're expensive to develop and no one wants to pay for them. In fact, the three coolest apps from musicians that I've seen (listed below) are all quite different and available free of charge. They were all made by popular acts that were doing a cool project to give a bonus to their fans. Unless you have something special to offer and a fanbase that is hungry for more content from you, it is very unlikely your app is going to gain any traction. The few apps that have worked are all available in the iOS app store.

- **NIN:Access** - Nine Inch Nails was one of the first bands to make an iPhone app that actually had interesting features. And their app is still just as cool many years later. It lets fans that live near each other interact with one another, creating a community experience like never before. It also allows traveling fans to find like-minded friends through their favorite music no matter where they go. It boasts a newsfeed, music, videos, images and the ability to access the band's forum.
- **Apparatjik** - This app is an album for this group and delivers a choose-your-own-adventure storyline, an intellectual maze of games, visuals, videos and writing that's truly incredible. At the end, you can listen to the album as much as you like. The app serves as a visually stimulating ride to get to the grand prize--a new record.
- **Radio Soulwax** - Soulwax, aka 2 Many DJs, have put together tons of lengthy DJ sets that are accompanied by visuals. If you're a fan of the group's eclectic style, you can now listen and watch it from your iPad.
- **Mew's Sensory Spaces** – Before Radiohead made their app along the same lines, Mew released an App of augmented reality that allows you to navigate through your surrounding with an App

that enhance the sights and sounds you see. The group used this app to unlock new sounds as a bonus to diehard fans.

For whatever reason, you may want to make an app anyway. Maybe your fans are app-loving nerds or maybe you have a bright idea that could change the game. If so, here are some services that can help make it happen.

Tools

Max Rips Audio From A CD To Make Wavs, MP3s, FLACs, Etc.
Do you get requests for FLACs of your music? Need to make an AAC for a licensing opportunity? Need to make WAVs from your master CD to upload to your digital aggregation service? Max can do this for you. Max is free, open-source software that can convert audio to nearly any format you can imagine. Get a free copy of it and stop paying your engineer to do what can easily be done by your computer. (sbooth.org/Max)

MP3Cut Is A Website To Edit MP3s & Make Ringtones
If you're looking to make edits to a song or turn it into a ringtone or a DJ mix, you can use browser-based editor MP3Cut (mp3cut.net) to do the job. Simply upload your MP3, make the desired cuts and it will let you download a new file of your edits!

Chapter 24: Selling & Distributing Your Physical Releases

Music sales are shifting towards digital mediums, and by the end of 2015 we may see that CD sales are finally at their end. But today, if you want to take over the world you still have to press CDs and maybe even LPs too. With record stores going out of business daily, the leverage major labels had over DIY musicians is becoming smaller and smaller. Digital music stores allow DIY musicians the same availability as major label acts. With that said, if you have a release you're trying to make a big splash with, your plan will need to include physical distribution as well as digital.

The Role Of CDs Today

Many people write off CDs as a thing of the past, but anyone who is actually selling music today knows they still play a role in the grand scheme of things. What that role is will depend greatly on which genre of music you play and how you choose to promote your music. But as of 2020 we are seeing the sunset of CDs being smart to make for most artists. Unless you are selling music in rural areas or have a large fanbase CDs are probably not going to be selling very well as the market for them is continually shrinking and unless you have a massive following the number you will need to move them are probably not going to happen. The following are some scenarios where CDs are still relevant, many of which will stay relevant:

- **Live Shows** - Fans still like walking away with something physical. Many musicians will sell a CD at a show for $10, since this is how much the average digital download costs. Many fans prefer to grab the physical product and enjoy the liner notes, rather than having an intangible digital download. Once they own this CD, they know they also have access to this music on any computer they want.
- **Audiophiles** - While very few audiophiles would ever choose a CD over vinyl, there are still a lot of people who refuse to go the MP3/iPod route for its lack of fidelity. They still like to pop a CD in their car stereo or hi-fi system.

- **Luddites** - Some music fans are technophobes and haven't adapted to the times.
- **Collectors** - Some people just really enjoy having something physical and tangible to own. They want a physical CD, not a nonexistent download.
- **Slaves To The Car Stereo** - I still have a lot of friends who haven't plunked down the money to make their cars iPod-ready. They still buy CDs.
- **Adults** - It's remarkable to see the sales of musicians like Susan Boyle versus a group like Arcade Fire. Ms. Boyle's fanbase is largely composed of adults who still favor the CD format (as opposed to the hip youngsters buying those kooky arcade arsonists). If your audience is older or less hip, it pays to take CDs seriously.

CD Bells & Whistles

One way to get fans to buy CDs (even those who wouldn't normally buy them) is to offer added content. If this exclusive is something your fans can't get anywhere else, it will help drive your sales of CDs. Here are some ideas of what you can add to CDs to get fans to buy them:

- **Live videos**
- **Remix stems**
- **Video games**
- **Acoustic Bonus Tracks**
- **In-Studio** - Behind-the-scenes or making-of footage.

CD Packaging Considerations

Your CD packaging can help you sell more CDs. Many musicians will go for the cheap eco-sleeves, which are great if you plan on keeping the price cheap but are frowned on by many distributors who don't like to carry them since many record stores won't make room for them on their shelves. In addition, fans aren't as excited to buy a CD with the lack of effort that an eco-sleeve shows. On the other hand, digi-packs are a great-looking way to entice fans into buying CDs, but can get expensive with their very deluxe packaging. Standard CDs in jewel cases may not excite buyers in any way but will still demand value from a buyer. Just be sure to opt for a more fancy tray than the ugly brown that comes standard with many CDs.

Stickers Say A Lot

424

One thing that can help sell CDs both in stores and on the merch table is a big sticker on the CD with press quotes and a RIYL (recommended if you like) description. Many labels that still make CDs spend the money to print stickers after continually seeing the benefits they bring. If your release has valuable marketing information like guest appearances or famous members, these stickers can easily pay for themselves.

Getting Your Metadata To Show Up In iTunes
Normally, when you insert your favorite CD into iTunes, the program is smart enough to know who the musician is and the info pops right up in your window, because it's all listed by a service called GraceNote. Obviously, you want your CD to do this when a fan puts it into iTunes. Thankfully, this is very simple. When you get your CD back from the manufacturer, insert it into your computer. Wait for it to show up in iTunes and then click "Get Info" and start entering everything. Once you're done, go under the "Advanced" tab and click "Submit CD Track Names." Now every time someone puts your CD in iTunes, they will have the correct info.

How To Get Rid Of All Of Those CDs
There are few things more depressing than a pile of CDs sitting in your closet that you just can't seem to get rid of. Letting these CDs rot is a lost opportunity to make new fans and a waste of music you poured your heart. Here are some ideas on how to get rid of them:

- **Online Store** - Set up an online merch store to enable fans from far away to order the CDs. Make sure it's linked on your social networks and webpage.
- **Pre-Order** - Make sure to do pre-order bundles for your newest record that include CDs.
- **NYOP** - Let fans name their own price for CDs at shows.
- **Art** - Remember to make great art. A good-looking release can help seal the deal for a fan that can't decide whether to purchase your CD.
- **Lower The Price** - By the time your old release is out of date, you're probably embarrassed of this less mature material. After all, you have new songs that are much better now. Despite your shame, your fans may enjoy it anyway. You can use your old releases as a cheap promotional item. Sell it to fans for cheap or give them away with other merch as a surprise to your fans.
- **Distribution** - Explore distribution options. Many distributors will take on an unknown record if it's being heavily promoted. They will

take on a small quantity of your CDs at first and if you're selling them regularly they will buy more. Figure out which distributors you should go through by asking the buyers at your favorite independent record stores.

- **Online Stores** - Find niche mail order and online stores that work within your genre of music and ask them to carry your CD.
- **Consign** - Consign them at local shops in towns you regularly play in.
- **Amazon Advantage** - Another great way to get rid of your CDs is by carrying them on Amazon (amazon.com). Since Amazon recommends other CDs a user may like, this can be a great way to expose your music to potential fans. Registering with Amazon Advantage (advantage.amazon.com) is easy. They take on two of your CDs at first and will move on to larger quantities if your record begins to sell.

On Demand CD Printing
The price of CD manufacturing has drastically gone down in the last decade. This means you can earn a higher profit margin off your fans that do still buy them. In order to achieve reasonable CD prices, you need to order at least 1,000 of them to sell them. Sadly, you may know from the stacks of your last album in your closet that you probably will not be selling 1,000 CDs anytime soon. Nothing makes you feel like a waste of life more than a closet full of unsold CDs staring at you every time you go to put on your skinny jeans. Like the day your dad retired his 8-track and you threw out your Walkman for an iPod, the days of staring at the pile of unsold CDs are over.

These services allow you to press your CDs on demand. What does that mean? It means each time someone orders your CD, they will print them one at a time or 10 at a time, depending on your orders. You can also order CDs wholesale and sell them yourself, get them to stores or sell them at shows. They offer non-exclusive terms for sales and allow a musician to get a professional looking product for a very cheap price. Each of the services have their own special services that can work for different types of musicians.

CreateSpace - Amazon's very own on-demand printing service, CreateSpace, allows you to make your own e-commerce store or sell from Amazon and have them print the CDs and fulfill your orders. This service also supplies the Amazon on-demand service you see in some digital aggregation services. You can upload your artwork and tracks directly to the site and they give a volume discount for orders of more than 50 CDs.

CD Manufacturers
Below is a list of some popular CD manufacturers for bulk duplication that Musformation has had good experiences with:

- **Discmakers** - Owners of CD Baby, the largest CD manufacturer. (discmakers.com)
- **Furnace** - Serving many of the big and small indies for years, very reputable. (furnacemfg.com)
- **Nationwide Disc** - Great service with cheap options for cardboard sleeves, while still offering goods prices when you do small runs. (nationwidedisc.com)
- **Rainbo Records** - Veterans who have been doing this forever. A great and reputable service. (rainborecords.com)

Buy A CD Duplicator
With the lifespan of the CD coming to an end, a CD duplicator may seem like an odd investment. But depending on your needs, that may not be the case. High quality machines that make professional-quality labels and CDs have dropped dramatically in price. If you plan to do a lot of free or name-your-own-price CD sales, this can help make sure you have a quality product that costs very little to make. You don't even need to take the time to package the CDs. However, if you have the time, this can increase your profit margin dramatically.

Vinyl In Today's World

Vinyl sales have been steadily climbing for the first time in some twenty-odd years and as of 2019 outsells CDs. If you make music that appeals to twenty-somethings, hipsters, teenagers or audiophiles and you're not making a vinyl version of your record, you're missing out big-time. Despite the old folks who insist kids don't get it--teenagers, twenty and thirty-somethings buy more vinyl than anyone else. And no matter how much they annoy us, record-collecting nerds will never disappear. Vinyl is a great way to sell to them since they often want the rarest most obscure format you have to offer. Nerds or not, record collectors are influential and often are people who influence others. A vinyl release is an important way to reach these influential people.

While vinyl's resurgence is an important way to reach new fans, you need to understand how to do it right or you'll flush tons of time any money down the toilet.

What Goes Into A Vinyl Record?

The first time you press a vinyl record, the sheer number of options can be intimidating. There are many little details when you press vinyl, which, if overlooked, can cause huge problems for your release or leave you with a product you're unhappy with. Below are the decisions you'll need to make when pressing a record:

- **Size** - 7", 10" and 12" are the common parameters. Your vinyl pressing plant may allow you to get crazy with custom sizes and shapes, but most vinyl is one of these sizes, with 10" the least common. Depending on your genre, singles will vary in size. For example, it's common for dance and hip hop singles to be on a 12", whereas a punk single will usually be on a 7."
- **Speed** - 33 or 45 RPM. The slower of the two options allows you to put more material on each side of the record.
- **Weight** - As a record's weight increases, the quality of its sound also increases. If you're putting out a 12" full length, the standard is 140-160 grams. If you want hi-fi nerds to buy your record, you may want to choose a 160-180 gram weight. This consideration is important if you're marketing your record to fans looking for an amazing audio experience, not just a novelty. Specifically, reissues and audiophile-marketed records are almost always made on 180-gram vinyl. For 7"s, your choices are 40 or 70 grams.
- **Hole** - 7" records have the choice of having a large or small hole in the center. Some would argue that the small hole gives higher fidelity, while the large hole adds a more traditional feel to the 7" experience.
- **Etching** - If you look in between where the grooves end and the label begins on a vinyl record, there are often words etched into the vinyl. This is a nice way to be witty and have some fun on your record.
- **Color** - Keep in mind you're selling to total nerds, many of whom are collectors. You can make different color pressings of your vinyl in limited quantities and offer these up as limited incentives. Some

will even try to own a record in every color, just to get more nerd points with their fellow dorks. This means more sales for you, so rejoice in the silliness.

- **Center Label** - You'll need to choose a paper grade and decide if you want to print the center label in color or black and white. If you're opting to get special with your release, you may want a blank white label and stamp it yourself or hand write the labels. The pressing plant will give you the option to leave the center blank if you want to get creative.
- **Inner sleeve** - This is the envelope inside the cover that holds the record. You can print your liner notes on this or get a clear or white coat for it--whatever you chose. If you're going to be doing a "white label" printing you can also skip this part.
- **Insert** - You can also print your liner notes on a separate sheet of paper that you insert into the record cover. You can choose any paper grade the plant offers, with plenty of printing options for color, black and white or even pantone.
- **Jacket** - This is your record cover. You can get gatefolds (where it opens up and folds out--ideal if your release takes up two pieces of vinyl) or simple black and white or color printing.
- **Shrink-wrap** - If you're going to be selling your record in stores this is necessary.
- **Sticker** - If you're doing a white label release sometimes you'll want to put a sticker on the jacket. The plant can save you time and affix these for you. If you're shrink wrapping your release, you may want a sticker on the outside of the shrink wrap. The plant can take care of this as well.

Vinyl Bells & Whistles
There are many other esoteric options you can do to make your vinyl more interesting or appealing to buyers and collectors. These features give your buyers added incentive to buy a record they might otherwise illegally download or take a pass on:

- **Picture Discs** - One of the cooler tricks in the world of vinyl is that under the grooves of the record, you can have a picture printed. This can eliminate the need for a sleeve, though instead you'll need to purchase a plastic bag in order to keep the disc from getting damaged. These records demand a higher retail price and can help you make an extra buck.

- **Flexis** – Pirates Press makes flexible, light vinyl records that you can bundle inside magazines, tour programs or as bonus tracks inside regular vinyl records.
- **Exclusive Tracks** - Many vinyl releases will include exclusive tracks in on their vinyl to generate sales from true fans and collectors.
- **Bonus Discs** - Some records come with 7"s or even 12"s of bonus material. These can be vinyl exclusive tracks or just material there was no room for.
- **Digital Downloads** - It's becoming more and more customary to include an exclusive digital download with your vinyl release. Pressing plants like Pirates Press offer this service in addition to their vinyl pressing facilities.
- **Hand Numbering** - A lot of vinyl is sold in limited-editions and one-time pressings. Hand numbering can increase value for collectors and make the release a more rare prize nerds can show off.
- **Promo Materials** - Postcards and stickers can be inserted at the plant or by your own hand, to give bonuses to your buyers.
- **CDs** - It's becoming all the more common to throw a disc inside the vinyl release.

Vinyl Mastering Process Considerations

Making good-sounding vinyl is a lot of work. The first step in the process is to get your record professionally mastered. Once this is done, your mastering engineer needs to send the person cutting your vinyl a special vinyl split master. This is a master that designates where you split the sides (as well as the times when your songs split in order to put bands in the vinyl that show where each song starts). Nine times out of ten, your mastering engineer will not be the one who also cuts your vinyl. Your mastering engineer will make a master that translates well on CD and digital and you'll then pass it on to an engineer who will cut a vinyl lacquer, tweaking it to work best on this format. This will often be an engineer who works at a vinyl mastering company or at your vinyl manufacturer. This person is very important to your project and if you value your fidelity, you'll make sure you get a lacquer master (this is what your vinyl is duplicated from). If you went to a reputable mastering house, they can advise you on someone who will do a great job cutting vinyl for your release.

Once this lacquer is cut, it's a good idea to get a dub plate, which is a one-off pressing of the vinyl to ensure it sounds right to you. Sometimes the vinyl can distort or lose bass or treble in the pressing process. If you care about your fidelity, make sure to get this done. Listening to this or to the test pressing from your manufacturer will let you check the sound and let you catch mistakes before a mass pressing. A lot can go wrong in the process and once the records are pressed there's no turning back or returning them if something went wrong.

Vinyl Split - When sending in your record to be mastered for vinyl, keep in mind it will need to have a 2-minute gap between sides. You'll also need to make sure there are no crossfades between the side splits in your master. Your mastering house will need to send the engineer who cuts your lacquer a vinyl split master. In order to figure out this split, it helps to know much material will fit on a side of vinyl. Below are the recommended specifications for vinyl sides:

7" - 33RPM - 8.0 to 8.5 Minutes
7" - 45RPM - 6.0 to 6.5 Minutes
10" - 33RPM - 14.0 to 15.5 Minutes
10" - 45RPM - 10.5 to 11.5 Minutes
12" - 33RPM - 18.0 to 20.0 Minutes
12" - 45RPM - 14.0 to 15.5 Minutes

While many vinyl plants press records that exceed these times (to a degree), they warn that your audio fidelity will suffer.

Band Cuts - You will need to provide the pressing plant with a list of where each song starts in order to get the bands cut properly for your vinyl so that fans can find where each song starts.

Vinyl Lacquer Mastering Services That We Trust:

- **Salt Mastering** (saltmastering.com)
- **Chicago Mastering** (chicagomasteringservice.com)
- **SAE** (saemastering.com)

When White Labels Work
If you're not familiar with the term "white label," it's a term for a limited release, usually of copyright-infringing material meant to make the rounds with DJs and tastemakers. These releases often have only a white label on the vinyl and come in a blank white jacket that may have a sticker on it. They almost never have a UPC code or give obvious contact info for the musician. Musicians will buy stamps and stamp the white label themselves

with the release info. This helps prevent lawsuits for the distribution and makes it so there's no tangible record of its sale. While the Internet's anonymity has killed most of these types of releases, you'll still find them making the rounds in some genres.

Vinyl Manufacturers
Below is a list of some popular vinyl manufacturers that we've had good experiences with:

- **A To Z Media** – Great prices and service, we work with them a lot. (atozmedia.com)
- **Furnace** - (furnacemfg.com)
- **Pirates Press** - (piratespress.com)
- **Rainbo Records** (rainborecords.com)

Distributing Your Releases In The Real World

Use The UPC Code Your Digital Distributor Gives You For Your CD/LP
This is a simple little trick that saves a few bucks and makes your life easier, yet it gets lost on many musicians going the DIY route. When you upload your music to a digital distributor, you always get a UPC code. Use that same code on your CD/LP and you don't have to pay for a new code. Simply go to a barcode generator on the Internet (we use barcoding.com/upc), copy and paste in the UPC code your digital distributor gave you, save the PNG file it gives you and drop it into your album layout!

CDBaby Will Distribute Your Release And Sell It Online
CDBaby has long been one of the biggest online music marketplaces. You can shop for digital, CD or vinyl releases all from their service. If you wish to be a part of their service, they will stock, ship and fulfill all of your orders so you don't need to worry about a thing. They even offer distribution to record stores, if those stores want to carry your music. CDBaby will also get your release stocked through Amazon, Alliance and Super D One Stop (which services many record stores and pushes them to carry your music). CDBaby is an easy way to open up lots of sales channels for your physical releases. They charge $49 to start and then take a small fee on top of each release.

No Distribution? Make Your Release Available To Retailers With A Bulk Discount

Physical distribution can be a pain to deal with and gets a little less necessary with each record store closing. Getting paid by many distributors can be a hellish experience, especially if your record doesn't sell and your distributor decides to return product to you and bill you for expenses. But if you have a hot release and no distribution, you may have an opportunity lost. One way to get it to distributors and retail stores is through direct sales. Create a page on your website that allows retailers and distributors to order directly through you, taking away much of the pain and burden of distribution. You can set standard price points such as five CDs for $35 and five vinyl LPs for $90. This allows any distributor or retail outlet that wants to carry your record to do so, without the headaches of hoping they pay or return the product.

This won't work unless you're creating a huge demand for your music by building a substantial buzz for your release. However, if there is a lot of anticipation for your upcoming release, this can get your music distributed without all the hassles normally associated with dealing with middleman distribution companies.

How To Get Your Physical Items Carried By A Distributor

Getting carried by a physical distributor can open opportunities for exposure to new fans by putting you on the racks of record stores across the country. However, this is no easy feat. You must demonstrate that there's a demand for your music. In fact, if you have less than tens of thousands of followers on your social networks, this is going to be a waste of your time. Distributors carry a contingency that they're able to return any products that don't sell after a certain amount of time (somewhere between 90-180 days usually). This means all your work getting distributors to carry your release will be for naught if all of them end up returned to you. Unless you're doing serious promotion that's working to bring you a nationwide fanbase, it will all be useless.

If you are going to submit for physical distribution, make sure you include the following:

- **One Sheet** - A one sheet is a fast look at a release. In this one sheet you want to sell the distributor and retailers on carrying your release. Describe promotion, notable production credits, tour schedules, a short bio and social media metrics that will impress potential buyers. If you have previous releases that sold well, be sure to include SoundScan or other impressive figures.

- **Product** - Anything you want them to carry will need to be sent to the distributor. Having impressive packaging that looks good on record racks will help it get carried.
- **Promotional Items** - Posters, stickers or anything else you would be able to send to retailers should go in the pack. Let the distributor know of any retail promotions you're willing to do.
- **Co-Op Budget** - If you're willing to pay for ads in conjunction with record stores or for special in-store placements, let the distributor know.

Physical Distributors
Below is a list of physical distributors we've enjoyed working with. Please be sure to make sure they work with your genre of music before contacting with them, since many of them are specific in the type of music they work with:

- **The Orchard** - In addition to being a digital distributor, they also work in the physical world and are open to DIY artists and labels on a case-by-case basis. (theorchard.com)
- **RED Distribution** - They deal with a wide variety of genres but are open to labels with past performances that show substantial sales for an indie. (redmusic.com)
- **Redeye Distribution** - Indie rock-focused but deal with a wide span of artists and are open to working with DIY artists who are putting promotion behind their music. (redeyeusa.com)

Retail Marketing And How To Do It
While it's obvious that mass distribution was a huge advantages that large labels had over smaller ones, there were many hidden techniques major labels would employ to gain even more of an advantage. By building relationships with retailers, labels could get special promotion and treatment in stores that would raise awareness and drive sales. This promotion disappears more and more each day and labels refocus on other ways to promote their artists. However, you can learn a lot from this promotional technique and it can still help you promote your own music. Music fans still go to record stores to get recommendations from local shopkeepers. Being on this shopkeeper's radar can help get you recommendations when a young and impressionable listener is looking for new music to buy.

434

The Past - If you were a record label in the recent past, retail promotion was probably a crucial part of building a musician's fanbase. Depending on the size of the label, there would be employees whose only job would be to call retail shops--particularly mom & pop shops and small chains--all day long and ask them a few questions. These questions would usually be:

- Do you have <insert release name> in stock?
- How is it selling?
- You're down to ___ amount of records.... Have you reordered yet?
- <insert band name> is coming to town in two weeks. Would you be willing to hang posters and order more copies to make sure you have enough to supply the demand after their awesome live show that will make everyone want to buy a copy?
- Have you considered putting <insert release name> on display? It's doing very well for <insert record store name> and I know you deal with a similar audience.
- Did you know that they recently got a 10 out of 10 from <insert reputable blog's name>?

As someone who ran an indie record store and received these calls and was employed by an indie label to make these calls, I always had a unique insight into the absolute hell they would bring to a record buyer's life each day. The condescending nature of these calls would often make you hate the labels pushing releases you didn't like. If you did like what the act the label was calling about, you might consider helping them. Maybe the call would push you to favor an act you were previously lukewarm about. These calls would be especially helpful if a record store didn't have a record in stock from an act that your label had on tour. Every label's worst nightmare is to have someone come in to a store looking to buy one of their musicians' records and not have it be available.

In addition to the calls listed above, the retail promoters would do the following:

- Buy shared ads (aka co-ops), which advertise your record and the store where you can buy it.
- Buy featured placement at the end of racks and displays in stores that advertise the release.
- Get records into listening stations at stores, whether they're paid for or chosen by the staff of the store.

435

Obviously, these techniques gave major label musicians a big advantage over smaller acts. Depending on how good of a relationship you had with each store buyer, you could be granted huge promotional advantages and recommendations at stores across the world. Thankfully, this technique matters less and less each day as more and more record stores go out of business.

Now - Despite the decreasing importance of record stores, employing these techniques at crucial stores can still help you build a fanbase. Here is what you can do to get better results for your release:

- **CIMS** - Go to the Coalition Of Independent Music Stores website (cimsmusic.com) and call every store that sells your genre of music (no use wasting the call on a dance music store if you're a metal band) to see if they will stock it (you'll need to be distributed by a company they buy from; there is no shopkeeper who is going to buy directly from you). I would only advise doing this if you're getting exposure in the immediate vicinity of the record store. This exposure could be radio airplay, relevant tour dates or major press coverage. Remember that if you're not promoting your music in the area and the store still takes on your CD, they can return it if no one buys it, which your distributor will charge you for.
- **Tour** - If you're coming to town on tour and your CD distributor is one the local record store buys from, call and see if they will hang a poster advertising your CD or show or if they will order copies of your record.
- **One Sheet** - Email them a one-sheet so they will potentially order your CD.
- **Displays** - If you have the money or are a local band, convince the store to feature your release you in an end rack or a display feature. Cite other stores' success with displaying your release and write up a one-sheet explaining why this will help them.
- **Niche** - Find niche online stores that will sell your music. Nearly every genre has a specialty store, simply go online and start searching them out to see if you can get featured in one of these stores.
- **Co-Sign** - If you're targeting your retail plan on a local level some indie stores will still take your CD on co-sign if you show them that you're an active act, promoting your record in the store's customer area.

How Free CD Samplers Can Build Your Fanbase

When I was still playing in bands, I would get the word out about my band with compilation and sampler CDs. Pressing a small run of a three-song sampler would benefit us immensely. Before the days of Myspace, CD samplers and compilations were one of the best ways to discover new music. While I am one of those who wish the CD would die as quickly as possible, there is still a way you can take advantage of small runs of CD samplers and by using hustle and smarts. Use them to help your music get heard. While many musicians consider these samplers a thing of the past, there is a way to use them to get your music to potential fans.

Here's how to do it:

1. Pick a few songs from your catalog and press them to a CD. If you have friends, you may even be able to split the cost and each put three songs on the CD.
2. Do a limited run of a couple hundred CDs. Manufacture them through any of the normal means or buy yourself a CD duplicator.
3. Go to any of the local mom & pop music stores and talk to the clerks. Ask them if they can give this sampler out for free to anyone who buys a release in your genre. In other words, if you're a pop-punk band and Green Day has a new CD coming out, see if the clerk will hand it to everyone who buys the Green Day CD.
4. See if you can hang a poster or put up your sticker that advertises the promotion. This will help the record store move more copies by increasing value of the Green Day CD and helps get your music out to fans that'd be likely to dig your music too. Most local music stores are into this. These stores are more likely to support ideas like this every day as their business dwindles.

If you have a show coming up in town, you can print this on the CD artwork or put it on a mailing list sticker. You can also convince the record store to take copies of your EP/LP CD, since you are generating more of a demand for it. This is a great way to pick up some extra fans in a town and get heard by those who have the potential to like your music.

Dealing With Leaks

Leak Your Record Yourself (And Profit From It)

The Internet and file sharing have made trying to keep fans from hearing your music until you're ready obsolete. Nonetheless, many dinosaurs of the music business still try to fight it. When your record leaks before the intended release date, it can ruin many of the marketing and promotion plans you have set and can start to greatly damage the hype and sales of your release. But it doesn't have to be that way if you adapt to the times.

When it happened to a group I managed, I made sure we made the most of the situation and helped us immensely.

The Times - If you have any sort of fanbase, fans are going to be looking forward to your new release. This means if you decide to distribute it in any way before your release date, it's probably going to leak. Years ago, the group Thrice had a record leak 90 days in advance of their scheduled release time. What made matters worse was that the leak was not a properly mastered recording and contained an annoying voice-over on top of the music. It can be heartbreaking to work so hard on the sonics of a record, only to have a terrible-sounding 128kbps MP3 version with a voiceover be the first impression many fans get of your masterpiece. The old wisdom was that fans would buy your release after the leak because they want a good sounding copy of the record, but if you've watched any of the countless studies on this subject, you know better than to believe that. If your release leaks--no matter what the quality--it's very likely this is the version countless fans will hear and listen to when they want to hear your music.

The Ability To Pay

If your record leaks, you need to immediately have a high quality, paid option available. This gives your fans that want your release and want to support your music the chance to do both. Nothing tears at a fan's conscience more than knowing someone else has a record they want that's only available via illegal download. Even though this fan may have been looking forward to buying your record, they can't resist the option of an illegal download and are then less likely to pay for your release later. Often times this is what converts someone into an illegal downloader, instead of a paying customer.

Most digital aggregators can have your music on most music stores like iTunes within 24 hours. Every direct-to-fan service allows you to put your music up instantly. You can put your music up on sites like Bandcamp or

TopSpin, making it available for purchase instantly. The faster you make this available, the more of a chance you have to financially gain from the leak.

You can also put up one of those PayPal donate buttons on your site, but this will not be as effective as selling fans your music directly. Giving your fans the option to buy your music the second they can is crucial or else you risk your fans being already bored and on to the next thing by the time your record is finally available for purchase.

Working With It - Every release by a musician with a fanbase has the potential to leak. The second a stream or distributed listening copies are out in the world; you need to have a plan in case it leaks.

- **Direct-To-Fan** - The second your record leaks, you should make sure you put it up on your direct-to-fan method. This can allow you to capitalize on fans' interest, profit from them and gain their email addresses. By putting an exclusive bonus track not in the leak on this site, you can also drive even more sales.
- **Torrent** - If your leak is low quality, put up a high quality one as fast as you can, so that the poor quality torrent is not the version that is spread. Be sure to label it as high quality in the torrent title.
- **Aggregate** - Most services that are serviced by digital music aggregators can get your music up in 24 hours. Make this happen as fast as possible, so your fans that want to pay for your music are able to.

How Man Overboard Turned Their Record Leak Into A Good Thing
On Musformation, I constantly write about labels' refusal to figure out a way to take a leak and turn it into a good thing. As circumstance would have it, I had the chance to put my money where my big mouth is in the summer of 2010, when a group I was managing, Man Overboard, had their record leak 28 days before the intended release date. The strategy we employed made this become another event that won us both new fans and the loyalty of the fans we already had.

Background - To familiarize you with where the group came from and where they were in their career at the time of this incident, allow me to reintroduce them. Man Overboard is a pop-punk band out of New Jersey that have a decent following and a very devoted fanbase. Despite the fact that they are no household name, they have a passionate following across the country that had been eagerly looking forward to the release of their debut LP, *Real Talk*. In addition to managing the band, I also produced, engineered and mixed the record and consider it one of the strongest achievements in my long discography. It's safe to say I had a lot invested in this release. We knew the potential for it to leak was huge, since this is a scene of kids who sit on the Internet all day, sending files to one another. We had a lot of fans on Twitter and Tumblr looking for it from the day we announced we were finished recording the record. We decided to keep it very secure, not even allowing some of the band members to have a final copy of the record.

How The Leak Happened - Part of the plan for keeping the record on tight lock-down was sending it to only seven key writers from websites and publications that had great reputations and who would never allow it to leak. Or so we thought. Unfortunately, one writer who happened to be the most overzealous to receive it of them all gave it out to some friends. We started to see songs on the record get shared on Tumblr and numerous tweets about it (which thankfully, were very favorable). I dropped everything (canceling the date I had scheduled that evening), hopped on my 3G-enabled laptop in Union Square and sat on instant messenger begging a 16 year old girl from Canada to not leak any more of the record after she posted a song on her Tumblr. At this point, we realized the record would inevitably leak early. Not my idea of a fun Friday night and not the type of thing they tell you a manager does when you go to music business school. Eventually, Jeff who runs Run For Cover Records found the culprit of the leak by searching through Last.FM scrobbles, Facebook friends and Twitter followers--after finding the origin of the leaked copy and looking at the watermark, the leaker then admitted it.

I approached the band and their awesome label (Run For Cover Records) with the idea of releasing the record early. Both were immediately on board (it's great to work with smart and open people) and Jeff at Run For Cover approached his digital distributor about getting it on iTunes ASAP (which took about 48 hours). A few days later we saw enough Tumblr and Twitter posts that we knew it was time to put the record up. We got it up within 30 minutes of the full record hitting two of the biggest leak sites on the net.

Strategy - When we first started to see individual songs leak out, there was a lot of discussion about whether we should get out ahead of the leak. While this seemed like it might help sales, we also worried if we were perhaps just being paranoid and opted to wait. The band had a strong presence on Bandcamp and had long employed the philosophy that we should direct fans to buy records on Bandcamp rather than through other retailers. We especially liked that Bandcamp meant we could get fans' emails, stay in touch and also steer fans toward the large amount of free music we offered there (not to mention get a much bigger profit share than iTunes sales). Since Bandcamp allows you to hide releases, we decided to upload the record so that we could simply unhide it once the record leaked, to ensure we could get it up as fast as possible. We were happy that iTunes was a little slow to put up the record, since it meant fans came to the Bandcamp and we got their emails. Even better, they could easily find more of our free music and get hooked on the band.

Exclusive - Before we recorded the album, we had recorded a track we decided would be exclusive to Bandcamp in order to drive sales there instead of iTunes. This ended up working in our favor, since this track was not on the leaked version and gave our fans another reason to buy the Bandcamp version rather than the leaked version of the record. We also added physical packages to the pre-order, so fans could buy the CD or LP and get an immediate download to tide them over. Run For Cover used Bandcamp download codes to send to all of the fans that pre-ordered the record.

We crafted a news blast for our website, other blogs and websites and our mailing list that explained why we did this. It's an awful feeling to be a fan that wants to support a group by buying their music, but instead you have to stare down an illegal link to a record you really want. You would love to give the group the money, but because they won't be proactive and offer it for sale, you download the record and forget to buy it when it comes out two months later, when you're less enthusiastic about the record or just too broke.

We linked everyone to our website, where we had the Musformation widget that allows you to trade emails or tweets for a track, so that fans could get a taste of the record before buying it. By linking everyone to the website, they could also see what else we had going on as well as follow all of our social networks. It was very important to us that if this record was going to leak we could at least use it to build more fans by having them spread the word through tweets and getting them into our mailing list.

Response - The response couldn't have been better. Many fans praised us for being "adults" about the situation and countless fans were so thankful they got a record they had been waiting for a month early. Others said they would buy the record just to support group behaving in this fashion. Response on message boards and blog comments was amazing, with dozens of compliments on how cool it was for us to release the record to our fans early, instead of inflicting upon them the usual torture of having to wait.

We earned loyalty from our fans and turned them into evangelists by doing right by them, which coincidentally also did right by us. In the end, it was a win-win situation that most labels turn into a lose-lose situation. We could not have been more thankful to have a smart label and team that helped us benefit from an incident that's usually thought of as a catastrophe.

Rewards - We were also rewarded in sales: The record sold better than we expected! Of the six reviews the record got in its first two weeks, all of them raving, many awarded us perfect scores as well as record of the year accolades. We had numerous sites interview us specifically to talk about how well we handled the leak. The band got tons of write-ups on sites that had never written about them before (TechDirt gave us a particularly great write-up) but were now interested after seeing the huge reaction to this situation.

It should serve as a lesson that even when you're faced with a situation that can be potentially damning, you can turn it into one that grows your fanbase.

Physical Often Creates A Digital Leak

One of the other phenomenons of the digital age is that once you release your music physically it will often leak digitally. Trying to keep a release purely physical will no longer work. Fans know how to rip your release and upload it to torrent sites. One of the most troubling parts of leaks is that many record stores receive the physical copies from distributors days before your release date. Some record store clerks do the dishonest thing of leaking these releases early, in order to get a higher ratio (a form of clout in the torrent community) on torrent sites. This means most high profile releases will normally leak a few days before their release.

Tools To Help Prevent Leaks

Haulix Is A Secure Streaming System To Prevent Leaks
Haulix (Haulix.com) allows you to save press contacts and serve them watermarked streams of your music in order to keep them secure. The service is used by many of the big names in the indie world.

PlayMPE Is A Secure Watermarked Way To Distribute Advances & Prevent Leaks
PlayMPE (plaympe.com) is a great format to send out advanced records for press before a release date. It uses all the major formats and offers direct import into iTunes. Employing a secure watermark system and high security, they're able to assuage fears of your release being compromised by the all too common leaks of today's industry.

DIY Watermarking
If you're a small act on a DIY budget, you may have a little money to try to keep your record from leaking but don't have the money to get tons of copies watermarked. Not to worry, there is a simple way anyone with a DAW can watermark a record. Simply take the last song on your record into any DAW and consolidate it while adding an extra second. Add another second for each copy you make. If your original song is 2:40 you'll make the first watermarked copy 2:41 and the next 2:42. If you're making 20 review copies, this will result in your last track having 20 seconds of extra space at the end, which, truth be told, most reviewers will not even notice. Once this is done, make a document and notate how many extra seconds are on each version of the record and who you're sending them to.

If your record does leak, you can simply pull that song into your DAW and figure out which copy leaked by looking at who that version was sent to. Congratulations, you now have the culprit of your leak.

Chapter 25: Your Email List, Communicating With Fans and Growing Your Fanbase

When Myspace rose to prominence, physical mailing lists as well as email mailing lists became obsolete in many circles. It was easy and cheap to communicate with your fans using Myspace, and the website's engagement level was unparalleled. Unfortunately, this left a whole generation of musicians with non-existent mailing lists and without a clue on how to build them, despite that email still proves to be the single best way to communicate with fans and engage with them in a way that develops relationships and turns into sales.

When I tell musicians that their mailing list is one of the most important tools they have to build a fanbase, most look at me like I stepped out of a time machine from 1995. I don't care what style of music you play, where you're from, how cool your audience is or how old or young they are; amassing your mailing list will build you a fanbase that will stick around for years to come. Let me repeat myself: NO MATTER WHAT YOUR MUSIC OR FANBASE IS LIKE, GROWING YOUR MAILING LIST IS ONE OF THE MOST IMPORTANT TOOLS YOU HAVE TO MAKE SURE YOU GROW YOUR FANBASE AND KEEP IT!

Why Email Is Important

Gaining an email address from a fan is the beginning of a lasting relationship. Many fans will keep the same email address for far longer than the lifespan of any social network they use. Having an email relationship with a fan is a privilege. If you don't abuse it, you're rewarded with emails interactions with fans that have a much better chance of engaging your audience than most social networks. In fact, some fans are three times more likely to do what an email asks them than a social network update.

Myspace Death Lesson--Make Sure You Get More Than An Email For Your Mailing List

444

Remember when you were a user on Friendster and watched in disbelief as Myspace turned it into the first Internet ghost town and then Myspace did the same thing? It can happen again and if you watch the numbers, people are already leaving Facebook every time it betrays their customers trust. There are two pieces of information you should always capture from your fans when they sign up for your mailing list, whether at a show or on the Internet.

- **Email** - After all this talk about how important it is to get email addresses from fans, it is obvious this is the first thing you should try to get. Getting an email address leads to obtaining much more valuable information. Many mailing list providers are able to harvest social network information from the web and tell you a lot about your fans. You can also use a social network's friend-finding tools to search for fans with their email address.
- **ZIP code** - Almost every tool to capture fans has a facility to gain a ZIP code. By having a fan's ZIP code, you can then alert them every time you're doing something in their area. This will help you geo-target fans, which will help ensure you don't annoy fans with show listings when you're playing at a location across the country from them.

Asking A Lot
Asking a fan to fill out too much information can discourage them from signing up on your mailing list form. The more information you ask for, the less likely a person is to sign up. Making anything more than an email address and a ZIP code optional is a good idea but allow the option to provide more information.

Phone Number - Remember when Barack Obama texted nearly 20 percent of America at once to tell everyone he was going to be going steady with his new hair-plug-wearing main squeeze, Joe Biden? Well if you don't, now you know: He texted millions of followers at once and we all felt special after getting a message from our future president. Well, most of us did. Right now, you may be wondering, "What in the hell has this got to do with my life?" This technology is finally becoming huge which is why you see people constantly talking about this on TV and since 1999 I have seen more huge musicians doing text marketing since fans hang on to phone numbers longer than they do email. It's continuing to become cheaper to get software that will simultaneously text all of your fans when you do something eventful. There is even software that will allow you to choose certain area codes to text. You will be prepared for the new age and have another way to contact fans if you start collecting their phone numbers.

Social Network Handles - If you have a mailing list form, write "We Want to Follow You" and ask fans for their Twitter, Instagram or Facebook URLs so you can follow your fans. Hopefully, they will follow you back. Social networks increase your chances to interact with your fans. You can even write a fan to thank them for coming to the show--a great start to a relationship.

Email Is More Effective
For years there's been a lot of hype about how great Facebook and Twitter are for raising awareness of your music. While these are tools you should use to their fullest extent, you should not neglect email for several reasons.

- **Users Are More likely To Give An Email Address -** Musformation makes a tool that allows you to capture fans' email addresses, or trade tweets or Facebook likes. When we analyzed the results from this widget we found that, when presented with the option of tweeting for a track or giving their email address, users will choose to share their email address by a 2-to-1 ratio.
- **Social Networks Aren't As Effective -** When sending out messages on Facebook or Myspace, fewer than 5 percent of followers will respond and turn those messages into sales. In comparison, more than 16 percent of fans respond to email messages and, in the best-case scenario, buy something.
- **Email Is Long-Lasting -** Email addresses can last a decade or more, while there has yet to be a social network that has remained popular for even a half a decade.

Email Services

Once you realize you need to have a mailing list, you need to find someone to host it. There are a wide variety of choices, each with their own special features.

FanBridge

446

One of the best musician-aimed mailing list providers is FanBridge (fanbridge.com). The company has invested in becoming an amazing mailing list provider. They boast a strong feature set that makes it easy for musicians to keep in touch with their fans. Their powerful features include:

- Pricing is free up to 20,000 messages per month and then starts at $9.99 above that.
- In-depth analytics to see if your fans are opening and clicking through your email messages.
- Geo-targeting and scheduled email sending.
- Tons of widgets that can collect your fans' information and are embeddable on social networks and on your website.
- Text message campaigns to inform your fans of what you're up to.
- The ability to segment your fan mailing list and email them based on engagement and what type of contacts they are.

Collecting Fans - FanBridge's website has some phenomenal widgets that you can embed on your website or social networks. These widgets are able to collect tons of fan data. Their unique fields collect:

- Email address
- First and last name
- Address
- Gender
- Age
- Cellphone number

FanBridge offers two ways to collect fans. The first is a fan signup app for Mac or PC that allows fans to sign up for your mailing list from a netbook or a laptop at your shows. This can be a great tool to use to trade fans stickers, posters or other cheap promotional items for their information. The second way is an iPhone app that performs the same function.

Incentives - FanBridge also allows you to create incentives such as uploading free songs and allowing access to only the fans who have signed up for your mailing list. You can also use this to help guarantee the fans on your mailing list hear your new song. You can also track the success of this emailing through FanBridge's analytics.

Fan Landing Page - FanBridge also makes a webpage that allows your fans to sign up for your mailing list and aggregates your information in a nice clean layout. These fan landing pages are there so that you have a webpage that easily adds fans to your mailing list. They also have a neat function that allows fans to ask you questions. Directing fans with questions to this page can also encourage them to sign up for your mailing list.

Topspin

While Topspin (topspinmedia.com) has been discussed in previous chapters, one of the places the website really shines is by letting you seamlessly manage the fans you capture from widgets and purchases in your Topspin-powered web store. Their fan-relationship management tools give you a powerful way to funnel fans directly into your mailing list and gather information that will help you market to them.

Topspin's mailing list feature offers the following features:

- The ability to gain the age, sex and influencer score of your fans if Topspin has already harvested that information from other musicians' mailing lists the fan may have signed up for.
- Geo-target, schedule and execute advanced email targeting.
- Topspin widgets to trade email addresses for a wide variety of media. With their HTML5-ready widget you can trade videos, full albums, single tracks, PDFs and tons of other media.
- An advanced tagging system so you can tag fans and put them into various categories.
- The ability to target fans that buy a lot of your merch or to target fans you acquired in a certain way.
- The ability to discern customers from non-customers, so you can separate the die-hard fans from the casual fans.
- In-depth analytics about how your email campaigns are doing, directly linked to the sales in your Topspin web store.
- Fan club management and selective access for fans in the email system.

Topspin's service is priced between $9.99 per month and goes up to $99.99 per month for musicians who have a large mailing list and need more advanced tools.

Bandzoogle

While primarily known as a direct-to-fan website builder, Bandzoogle (bandzoogle.com) also has a great mailing list tool. Their prices go from

$9.99 to $19.99 per month, depending on how many fans are on your list. Features include:

- In-depth analytics
- Custom layouts
- Scheduled sending of emails
- Easy import and export of email addresses

Limited Run
Offering a basic email service that comes free with their service for email lists of any size, it makes them one of the best options for those who want to avoid huge monthly fees while still getting great features. They take 5% of merch store fees so the mailing list feature is essentially free. (limitedrun.com)

- **Value** – You can have as many subscribers as you want and email them as often as you want while not paying any additional fees.
- **Targeting** – You can target fans who bought a certain product or live in a certain zip code.
- **Templates** – There's a handful of templates to choose from.

MailChimp
MailChimp (mailchimp.com) prides itself on having a simple interface that still offers a strong tool for email marketing. When a musician is starting out and doesn't want to pay for an email service, MailChimp is one of the best options in the business but scales up to being some of the most powerful tools there are for musicians but gets dramatically more expensive once you cross 2,000 fans. The website features the following:

- The ability to trade email addresses for tracks through a website form.
- The ability to geo-target and track campaigns.
- In-depth analytics.
- Custom email capture forms.
- Free service for as many as 2,000 subscribers and 3,000 emails per month, and a $15-per-month service for 500 to 1,000 subscribers and more than 3,000 emails.

SendPulse

A new addition to the email game also offers plenty of interesting new ways to communicate with fans like SMS and website notifications. (sendpulse.com)

- Free up to 2,500 email addresses and offers extremely affordable rates.
- Other features offer Website notifications, Viber contacts and tons of other niche marketing features.

phpList

phpList (phplist.com) is an open-source email campaign manager. It takes a lot of web knowledge to figure out how to navigate this fantastic tool, so only consider it if you know how to read and write some code. Some of its features include:

- The ability to manage lists well past 100,000 recipients.
- Hosted option.
- The ability to track how often an email was opened and clicked-through.
- Multiple templates that allow HTML editing.
- No re-occurring fees.
- The ability to convert your blog or news feed RSS into email.

YMLP

YMLP (ymlp.com) offers a set of tools that are great for those not looking to go too far down the rabbit hole of email marketing for an affordable rate. Priced from free to $5 a month they are a great choice for those with a sizeable email list that don't want to pay excessively for it.

Constant Contact

A favorite tool of music publicists, Constant Contact (constantcontact.com), is a mailing list manager that offers great message customization tools. They offer a free option for small lists and then start pricing at $15 per month for other services. Their implementation of social media campaigns and message personalization make it a favorite for those who need to manage email relationships with countless contacts.

TinyLetter

TinyLetter (tinyletter.com) is a service from MailChimp that allows fans to opt into your email list for you to send personal, blog like entries to subscribers. Many musicians bemoan their personal thoughts being able to be commented on and shared on Twitter, Facebook or blogs, so this allows a more personal way to only reach those who care to regularly hear from you. This service can be ideal for musicians who want to start a mailing list and not pay fees, as it gives you a free service with a landing page that's easy to acquire fans through. You can also export subscribers and add them to whatever mailing list provider you use for other contact with fans.

Gmail

If you have a small fanbase or want to only mail those who regularly give you press, Gmail (gmail.com) groups can be a great option to use and keep track of who you should send certain emails to. It can be intimidating to pay a lot of money each month when you're only sending emails to a few people or only want to email members of the press. If you are sending email messages to more than a few dozen people, you should be sure to upgrade to one of the previously mentioned providers in order to avoid violating spam laws. Always comply with fan requests to be removed from your mailing list. There is also the add-on Gmass that allows you to use Gmail for mass mailing and analytics for $6-12 a month. (gmass.co)

Get More Email Addresses

Places You Can Acquire More Email Addresses:

- **Tumblr** - In your sidebar, paste an email collection widget.
- **Bandcamp** - Put up a free track that your fans need to give their email to download.
- **Your Website** - Put an email collection widget up.
- **Your Merch Store** - Every time someone buys your merch, you have a chance to get their email address if you set it up correctly.
- **SoundCloud** - Use their Email Unlock app to get emails.
- **WishPond** – Wishpond allows you to make a form to get to content on your website (early video premier, new track) and get a fan to fill out their email address and zip code in order to see the content. (wishpond.com)
- **Blogs** - If you get a blog to post your email for a track widget, you can collect emails every time someone finds this blog post.

Using A Netbook Or Tablet To Get More Email Addresses

451

The second I say the words "mailing list," many of you groan with the pain that accompanies copying names from a notebook into a computer. At a show, a bunch of the addresses will get copied incorrectly and the process is a boring pain in the ass that no one wants to do.

A simple solution to all this pain is to use netbooks and tablets. Not only are most of these devices available for about $100 to $600, they can help raise your productivity and in general make your life a lot easier. If you have no idea what I am talking about, allow me to explain.

Huh? - If you're not familiar, a netbook is a small computer that's easily portable and meant for running small applications like email, web browsing and word processing. You can run Windows, Linux or even hack it to run OS X (for info on this, Google the term "Hackintosh"). For our purposes, you'll be using it for your mailing list, despite the fact that you can use this computer to get plenty of work done on the road. The most common tablet is the iPad but many other brands make tablets using the Android platform. First generation iPads sell for less every day and many other tablets go for insanely low prices.

Offline - No matter what hardware you use, what you should care about is getting email addresses. There are a few ways to do this. If you have no Internet connection, you can use Microsoft Excel to collect email addresses by setting up a spreadsheet into which fans enter their info. If you're a real whiz kid, you can even customize your spreadsheet with illustrations to make it look cool. FanBridge has an offline email signup form which can do this job really well if you use them as an email provider. You can also have fans type their information into a text document, but make sure to monitor what they type.

Online - If you can get a steady Internet connection you can also collect email addresses. GoogleDocs (docs.google.com) has a spreadsheet document you can write into and export into your mailing list provider later. Like a Microsoft Excel spreadsheet, you'll want to export this document as a .csv file.

Tips - Despite making this look simple, there are some little tricks that can make it even easier to collect email in the real world:

- **Cover It Up** - The second concertgoers see a computer they're going to want to use it to check to see if their Internet girlfriend Lafawnda wrote back to their Match.com profile. One of the best tips I can give you when doing this is to take a piece of printer paper and cover the top inch or two of your hardware's screen with a sign that says "MAILING LIST (DOESN'T GO ON THE INTERNET)." Make it so this covers the top menu bar. You should write on this paper above each field what someone should enter like email, ZIP code, etc. Always enter a sample of an email address so fans know what to do here. It's amazing how computer-challenged some people can be.

- **Put A Lock On It** - A few hundred dollars is a lot of money for a touring act, and it can be tragic if your little computer gets stolen. Thankfully, there are tons of cheap laptop and tablet locks out there. There are also mountable iPad stands that can keep tablets from walking away. Simply lock the hardware to your merch table and put your mind at ease.
- **Put Saran Wrap On It** - Spills are deadly to a laptop, and you'll probably perform in clubs full of sweaty, drunk people with drinks in hand. An easy and quick security measure to take is to give a netbook two layers of Saran Wrap across the screen and keyboard. There are also tons of covers that are sold for netbooks to prevent spills from ruining your computer.
- **Incentive** - Remember, the easiest way to get people to sign up for your mailing list is to give them an incentive: a sticker, free sampler, download of an exclusive song or whatever you can think of to get fans to take the time to type in their information.

The Traditional Mailing List Notebook
Most musicians don't get fancy with computers to get email addresses. Instead they have a spiral notebook and a pen attached by a shoelace. Copying these emails into a computer is one of the worst parts of being a musician, but it really does help to expand your fanbase. One of the little tricks that can make this practice even more powerful is to write down the ZIP code of the venue where you acquired the email address at the top of each page, in case fans don't write it down.

Geo-targeting - Use your mailing list provider's geo-targeting feature and you can alert all the fans that were at this show to come to your next one. You know that these fans were willing to come out to a show in this ZIP code, so why not alert them the next time you're there? Make sure you enter this ZIP code for all of these fans when it goes into your mail list software. Also, don't be scared to ask for a Twitter or Facebook handle.

Mailing List Landing Page

The home page of your website should always have a mailing list signup form, but if you really want to concentrate on acquiring email addresses you can also make a page that's sole purpose is to acquire email addresses. Your free-music page may do the best job at this, but if you're going to send out tweets or news updates that encourage an email sign-up, it can be a little confusing to send fans to your home page. Instead, make a blank page or a page with a very clean layout and embed an email sign-up widget on it in a place that fans can clearly see. FanBridge includes fan-landing specifically for this purpose. Send links and remind fans of the benefits of being on your mailing list.

How To Get More Fans To Sign Up For Your Mailing List:

- **Email-Before-Download Widgets** - FanBridge, ReverbNation, Topspin, SoundCloud and all offer ways to trade free songs for an email address.
- **Web Stores** - Web stores like NoiseTrade, Manic Merch, Topspin and Bandcamp will capture your customers' email addresses for you.
- **Your Website** - Make an mailing list sign-up form available on your website. FanBridge, Topspin and ReverbNation all have fantastic widgets that allow you to do this.
- **Facebook** - ReverbNation Facebook app allows email signups. Be sure to grab these addresses and export them to your mailing list provider. This is not necessary if you use ReverbNation's app and mailing list manager together.
- **Mailing List** - Offer giveaways only to mailing list members, such as guest list passes, etc. Announce them on Facebook and Twitter so your fans hear about them and sign up for your mailing list.
- **Credit Cards** - Take credit card payments at shows through services like PayPal, which will capture your fans' email addresses.
- **Netbook Or Tablet** - Get a netbook or tablet at shows and navigate to a mailing list signup form and give away freebies like a sticker, button or patch to anyone who signs up for your mailing list at every show you play.
- **Crowdfunding** - Most crowdfunding services allow you to collect fan emails. This is great because these are fans that believed in you enough to give money to your band.

- **Tickets** - Sell tickets directly to fans through services like Topspin and gain the email addresses of fans that come to see you play.
- **Show Listings** - Put an email entry widget next to your concert dates on your website that says, "Get Email Alerts For When We're Coming To Your Town."
- **Online Radio** - Both Earbits and Jango will allow you to gain fan's email addresses.
- **Full Address** - Offer your fans rewards, such as postcards, for giving you their full address.

Getting Email Addresses From PayPal - While it may not exactly be legal (*it's legal if no one is looking, right?*) and I would never tell you to do anything illegal, but... PayPal has a function where you can export a .csv of all of your transactions. Included in that is the email address of everyone who has bought from you. This means if you're selling merch through Big Cartel or other PayPal checkout systems, you can gain all of the email addresses of your fans by simply exporting this .csv file and extracting all of their email addresses (you can do this for free in Google Docs). These are your paying customers, so it can be very helpful to have these addresses. Just remember, I am not telling you to do this.

Thoughts On Musicians Trading Mailing Lists - I am always for expanding mailing lists and hearing about new musicians, but not only can giving away your mailing list without getting permission from your fans make them mad, its illegal. Although this is the case, if my inbox is any indication, musicians and their team members do it every day. Here are some pointers if you're going to trade mailing lists with another musician:

- **Up Front** - Don't cloak it. It may even be a good idea to get a written endorsement from whomever you got the emails addresses from. Say that it was given because they thought the recipients of the email would enjoy their music.
- **Opt Out** - The ability to opt out of these emails is very important. Make it extremely visible, so you don't get flagged for spam and end up on a block list from an email provider.

How To Entice Fans To Sign Up For Your Mailing List
Just asking a fan to enter their email gives them little reason to do so. Here are some other incentives you can give them:

Make A Mailing List Exclusive Track - If there is one way to get more mailing addresses; it's to make a song that is only available if you sign up for the mailing list. This doesn't have to be your best song or even a C-side track. Granted, the better the song, the better the results you'll see. However, it wouldn't make much sense to use your best song for this purpose. A demo or acoustic version will do the job, but not as well as a song that fans are so impressed with that they want to tell the whole world about it.

FanBridge, Topspin and ReverbNation all have widgets that will automatically deliver this track to the fan once they sign up for the mailing list. Sending the track will be effortless once you put the widget on your website.

Give Away Something Unique To Get More Email Addresses - One of the easiest ways to build your mailing list is to give away something of value to your fans. Run a contest where fans that sign up to your mailing list can win prizes like test pressings, your drummer's underwear, one-of-a-kind merch, etc. This can be a powerful tool that will get fans that would not normally sign up for a mailing list to do so.

Tracks Are Not The Only Thing To Trade Email Addresses And Tweets For - While track downloads are an enticing benefit, they're not the only prize you can offer in order to build your fanbase. Whether it's poetry, zines, lyric books, enhanced artwork, video content etc.--anything you can come up with can be traded for an email address, pending your mailing list provider allows it. Free content is a huge part of promoting your music in the digital age. Trades are a great way to keep building your fanbase, get in the news cycle and give your fans something unique and special to enjoy.

Collect Email Addresses With Live Tracks While Promoting Your Live Show - Another way you can use the track-trading technique, while showing off your awesome live set, is to give away a live record. This kills two birds with one stone by getting people to check out your live show and grabbing their email address, making all of your future promotions a little easier.

Make More Twitter And Facebook Friends With Your Mailing List
From time to time musicians write in to Musformation and ask for help with their problems; Greensboro North Carolina's finest, We Are Masked, wrote

in to find out if there was a way to import the fans in their FanBridge mailing list into their Twitter friends. I suggested importing a .csv file of their contacts into a Gmail account, then add all of their Gmail contacts to Twitter. This technique works on Facebook and plenty of other social networks too. They took this one step further and created a new Gmail just for Twitter and imported the contacts from there, so that all of their contacts were from their FanBridge list. Good thinking! This technique will work on most mailing list management systems and most email systems, although Gmail is the easiest.

When Fans Unsubscribe From Your Email Blasts Ask Them If They Want To Follow You Somewhere Else
Many mailing list clients allow you to ask fans if they would prefer to follow you on a social network when a fan unsubscribes from your emails. This simple little trick can help you keep in touch with a fan for years to come.

Making Your Email Campaigns Work Better

Using Geo-targeting To Increase Show Turnout And Keep Your Fans Happy
Raising awareness for your shows is one of the best ways to get a big turnout. But when you have a national fanbase, annoying your fans about a show in Kalamazoo when they live in Brooklyn can get you a fan that chooses to unsubscribe from your mailing list. The solution to this problem is Geo-targeting.

Nearly every mailing list provider has a ZIP-code-based way of targeting fans whose address is within a certain number of miles of your next show. In order to geo-target accurately, it's a good idea to change the mile radius depending on the area you're working with. Perfecting this can take time. While a 100-mile radius may work well in Arkansas, targeting within 100 miles of New Jersey will annoy many people who live in this heavily populated state that borders on two major cities, New York City and Philadelphia, because it doesn't have much of a fan overlap for show attendance. Look at Google Maps and take some mile measurements, so that you don't overdo it and annoy fans that would never attend a show in the area you're going to perform in.

Even if you sent an email with all of your tour dates to your mailing list, you can also send a follow-up email that geo-targets fans in each city. Change the email subject line to reflect the specific show details. Consider including the venue, so fans get the hint you're coming to town and are more likely to open the email.

Tagging And Sorting Your Emails

Most mailing list providers have a fantastic ability to sort fans by a wide variety of criteria. This can very useful for trying to build relationships with your fans. Below are some ways you can tag and sort your email addresses to help you build relationships with your fans.

- **Recently Added** - You can sort your emails by when they were added. This means you can find all of your recently added fans and send them a thank you note for signing up. Got a free-music page on your website? Send this to your newest fans too, so they know where to find more of your music. If they all signed up after you released your newest video, link them to some places where they can buy that song.
- **Geo-targeting** - As I mentioned above, you can use this function to alert fans in certain areas whenever you're coming to town.
- **Purchasers Of An Item** - Topspin has a great tool where you can email everyone who bought a certain item. This is a great way to target fans that have been willing to spend money on big-ticket items and update them when you have a new piece of merch. You can also send them a discount code to thank them and make them feel special.
- **Tagging** - If you tag email addresses with the zip code of where you got them from, it can open a lot of doors. Many people travel far to come to festivals, so geo-targeting may not be efficient. If you tag the emails you got at a festival you can email them when you play their town again.
- **Users** - If you're getting emails from Bandcamp, SoundCloud or NoiseTrade, you can tag them as you import them. Then email these fans whenever you do something new on the site you've associated them with, because you know they like to get music there.

Writing A Good Subject For Your Email

Look at your inbox. Every time you see a new email, you're faced with the choice of reading it, ignoring it or deleting it. Often the sender of the email is the deciding factor as to whether or not you'll open it, but the email's subject line is the second-most important factor. Writing a subject line that lures fans in can be the difference between your fan reading your message or ignoring it. Below are some tips on writing subject lines that get your emails opened:

- **WTF** - Ask a question that's a bit shocking. For example, if your latest video got a lot of views you can write "Why Did Our New Video Get 47,903 Views?"
- **Friendly Question** - Asking questions like "Can You Help Us?", "Did You Catch This?" or "Will We See You Friday?" can get fans to open emails.
- **ALL CAPS** - CAN BE A LITTLE OVERWHELMING! Maybe, Try Just Capitalizing Each Word? Unless it's the most important email you have ever written, please turn off the caps-lock. Writing "BIG NEWS: New Album Out Now" is fine, but please refrain from all caps for the whole subject line.
- **Big News** - New albums, free singles and new videos are big news and worth putting in the subject line. Things like "New Album Out Today," or "Northeast Tour Dates Announced," can entice fans that are waiting for these big events.
- **Crazy** - If something crazy happened, start the email with that: "Our Van Flipped Over [What You Can Do To Help]." Remember though that long subject lines disappear in most email browsers. Often, only the first five to seven words of a subject will be read.

What's In A Good Email Blast To Fans?

How do you write a good email to fans? Use these small tricks to write a better email, ultimately getting a better result through your email campaigns.

- **Write To One Fan** - Instead of speaking in typical press-release fashion, imagine you're speaking to one fan when you write. Tell them what you think they would be interested in.
- **Show Some Personality** - Remember when I talked about your news updates and showing your personality? It goes for emails too. Show you're human and write something positive. You never want to sound like a computer or a corporate letter. Write to your fans in a language that shows that you speak like them. Feel free to use slang and show your sense of humor. Fans have grown

459

used to seeing their favorite musicians' personalities on sites likes Twitter and can get weirded out if they don't see this personality in email blasts.

- **White Space** - The worst thing you can do in an email blast is not have enough space between paragraphs. It's better to have too many paragraph breaks instead of too few and too much empty space rather than too little. A huge block of text is extremely intimidating and will discourage a fan from reading your message.
- **Get To The Point** - The fewer words you can use while still hitting all of your points, the better the email. Reread your emails a few times, to make sure there are no superfluous sentences or words.
- **Keep It Brief** - If your van died and you're pleading with your fans to donate money, it's tempting to tell them the 12-paragraph story to appeal to their sensitive side. Before you write that sob story, keep in mind that most fans are sneaking in a read of your email at work and don't have the time to read a long rant. Instead, explain the whole story in a blog entry and include a link to that in your email. If you're thinking about spending more than five sentences on a topic, think again. Summarize the story, or give them a taste of the tale, and then link to a place on the Internet (Tumblr, a blog, an article about it, Facebook note, etc.) where they can read it in full.
- **Link Often** - Draw attention to your social networks. If you drive email followers to your Twitter, SoundCloud or Facebook, it increases the chances that they'll become your followers. If you just started using a new social network like Instagram, make sure to inform your fans to follow you there too.
- **Tour Dates At The End** - Tour dates can be a long list and most of your fans aren't going to think of you as the modern day Grateful Dead and follow you across the country. Mention your upcoming tour and the dates in the subject and/or the first paragraph but list the actual dates at the end of the email.
- **Write What's Most Important First** - If you put out a new album, made a new video, have new tour dates or are selling new T-shirts, make sure you talk about your biggest priority first. Most fans aren't going to read all the way through your emails and if you have a lot to tell them, make sure what is most important appears at the top.
- **Social Network Links At The Very Bottom** - Always end your emails with links to other ways your fans can follow you. If they got that far, they're willing to hear more from you. You want fans to

follow you in as many places as possible, so you can still stay in touch if they change their email.

- **Never Write "Click Here"** - The words "Click Here" trigger spam filters. Write what you're linking to instead of "Click Here"
- **Pictures** - Putting pictures of merch with clickable links to buy can really boost sales. If you have a new video, take a compelling screen shot of it and make sure the image links to the video.
- **Recommend** - Give a recommendation in emails, whether it's to a friend or to something you think your fans would be into, like a great book or movie. It shows personality and gives fans an added incentive to open your emails when they know they're going to get a recommendation from you, as well as insight into your personality.

Don't Abuse The Privilege Of Email
By now you should know the importance of capturing email addresses of fans, maintaining your mailing list and using it for promotion. Just remember, don't abuse the privilege. The first email you send to fan is going to be a bit of a shock to them; they probably forgot they even gave you their email after all those Jagerbombs they drank to get up the nerve to dance at your show. Sending out five emails a weeks to talk about the same show at Trash Bar is going to get fans to click the unsubscribe button faster than you can say "no one comes to our shows anymore."

Keep your emails limited in frequency and make them relevant to fans. Be respectful and brief. While there may be some real super fans out there, most don't want to hear you clamoring on and on about yourself. There's no magical number of emails to send out each month, but a good general rule is the fewer the better. Remember that some fans are very private and protective of their accounts, so don't violate a fan's time by getting too happy with the send button.

But Really, How Often Should I Email Fans? - While there is no general rule, many popular musicians use email only a few times a year when they have something really important to say. My personal feeling is there is no reason you should send out more than nine email blasts a year to your full mailing list but send as many as you need to announce local events to specific fans. You can use geo-targeting and email fans whenever you're playing their area. If you play locally more than a dozen times a year, I would go easy on the geo-targeting and only email your local fans for the big shows.

When? - Just like when you're pitching bloggers, avoid sending emails on Friday through Monday. If you're emailing about your new release, you may want to avoid Friday since this is when new releases come out each week. Looks like Tuesday, Wednesday and Thursday are your days! Remember, nearly every email service will let you schedule an email. Just because you want it to send on Wednesday, doesn't mean you have to write it then.

Always Send A Test Email

These email blasts are special and you aren't doing them all that often. Every mailing list provider gives you the ability to send a test email before you blast out to thousands of people. Do this. It will help you avoid having to email your whole list an embarrassing correction. It helps to always have a second set of eyes and make sure you don't see anything wrong when the email goes through. You may catch a dumb error or realize that your old band name is the one that shows up in the inbox. Send a friend or bandmate a test, before you embarrass yourself in front of all your fans and friends.

Test Your Emails For Spam

When you're sending emails out for a large-scale campaign, you're going to want to check your emails for spam filters before you send them. Any number of problems that could set you back months can occur without you even knowing it. Recently, Todd was sending out emails for his band Sensual Harassment and noticed that some of the emails weren't arriving. After checking deep in the spam box he eventually found them. Turns out, the words "Sensual Harassment" aren't so email friendly. Changing the "From" setting in Gmail to read "SH" immediately fixed the problem. The same thing goes for spam-filter triggering subject lines. Make sure to test a few times, so all your hard work and marketing are not in vain. Sure it's annoying to take the time, but it's much less annoying than wasting your time emailing tons of fans who never get your emails.

What To Include In Email Signatures

Do you have a signature for emails? You should. In fact, without a signature you're missing the chance to get everyone you interact with to see where else they could be interacting with you. If you have a signature, you can optimize that space. If you're often asked for your phone number, website or address, include them in your signature. This also helps guarantee everyone who needs this information will have it, so that someone who was supposed to be on your guest list and is now mistakenly absent can get in touch with you easily. Including your two or three most important social networks can help get you more followers and make it easier for strangers to learn about what you do.

Avoid Hotmail, Yahoo And AOL As An Email Account

If you're a musician, you most likely use email all day, every day. Many of us have secondary email addresses, either to avoid spam or as a backup. If these are Hotmail, Yahoo or AOL accounts, don't use them to email your fans with. Microsoft will shut off your Hotmail account if it's inactive for nine months, meaning someone else can use that address again. With AOL, you're paying for inferior service that can become obsolete at any moment. Both platforms also have outdated restrictions on the size of files they allow you to send and receive, which make it difficult to send songs back and forth. Avoid them.

Updating Fans Via Text Message

There's a lot of buzz these days around the power of texting fans and getting them out to shows. While we all get the annoying text messages from our friends in bands trying to get us to come see them at whatever hellhole they're playing at on a Tuesday, the power of keeping fans informed by going right to their phone can't be underestimated. This is becoming especially important as fans read texts daily, and their phone numbers won't change after college. You will now see acts telling their fans to text a number to opt in to get texts from them since the potential to update on future events is extremely powerful. Here are a few prominent text message services:

- **Superphone** – A text messaging service used my many musicians to contact fans. (superphone.io)
- **Broadtexter** – Broadtexter/Tatango (broadtexter.com) will allow you to embed widgets around the web and collect fans' phone numbers. You can use these numbers to start a Mobile Club and set up alerts so fans are notified when you're in their area. Best of all, it's free!
- **SendHub** - SendHub (sendhub.com) offers an iOS App to text fans who have given you their number. It's free for the first 50 users and then pricing goes from $10 to $150 per month.

Your Email Analytics

Analytics are everywhere and yes, even your mailing list has analytics. Email analytics are important because they give you clues about whether things are going right or wrong. They can also give indicators of what you should be doing to reach out to fans and lend clues when you are making big mistakes.

Open Rate

Your email open rate should be at or above 22 percent. Any less means you're messing something up. The easiest way to improve your open rate is to email less. Email too frequently and you'll become the little boy who cried wolf; fans will simply stop opening your emails or unsubscribe if you annoy them constantly. Another fix is to make sure your subject line isn't boring and is giving fans a reason to open it. Maybe your email address isn't clearly stating who you are. You did email yourself and do a test email, right? Whatever the problem is, looking at your analytics will let you know whether or not your fixes are working.

Give Them Something Special

Give fans a reason to read your emails all the way through. Maybe your die-hard fans care about your life. Link them to a blog post about something that happened to your band or to your new favorite YouTube video. Maybe you link a special YouTube cover or demo you did in your bedroom. You can even get crazy and give a discount code at the bottom of the email as a reward to them for being so loyal. Maybe give recommendations for music and movies that you don't post anywhere but in your emails. If your fans feel like your emails to them are more than a sales pitch, they're more likely to open them. Word will spread and fans will take your emails more seriously.

Click-Throughs

Your email analytics will tell you not just the percentage of fans that open the email, but the percentage that click on the email's links. This number can give you a quick clue about whether you're getting your fans excited enough to actually do what you're asking of them. Watch this percentage from email to email; hopefully, it will keep improving. Otherwise, you're annoying your fans or doing a poor job at exciting them enough to do what you ask.

Unsubscribe

The clearest indicator that you're messing up is if a large number of your fans are unsubscribing. Every time you send an email, it's inevitable that some fans will unsubscribe. If more than a few percent are doing so, you're doing something wrong. You're most likely emailing them too much. If you have above a 5 percent or larger unsubscribe rate, you need to reevaluate what you're doing with your mailing list.

Check Your Other Analytics
Your emails should be trying to drive traffic somewhere. Maybe you're trying to get plays or sell some merch. No matter what, check your other analytics and make sure you're achieving your intended goal. Many analytics systems will tell you where your traffic came from. Bandcamp and Google Analytics will give you details about the email it came from, and you can determine how effective your campaign was at getting fans to click-through. Look at this data and try to keep improving it.

Chapter 26: Assembling And Spreading Information With Your Website And Blog

Why You Still Need A Website In The Age Of Social Networks

When Myspace was the top site for music discovery, many musicians wondered why they would ever need to have their own website. Myspace was easy to update and could give fans most of the information they were looking for in an easily organized space. Once the service became popular, many musicians stopped building websites altogether, brushing the pain and expense of building one out of their mind. Unfortunately, this wasn't a smart strategy.

A website has always been one of the most powerful ways to promote your music and build your relationship with fans. A good website will serve many different purposes.

First Impressions, Best Impressions - You always want to give a curious new listener a great first impression before they become a fan. A good website will tell them everything they want to know about you, in an easy-to-navigate format. For new fans, your website is the equivalent of window shopping; if a fan peeks in and the website is neat and organized, they will stay a little longer and see if they like the wares that you're hawking. If, however, your website is disorganized and difficult to navigate, it may send fans running. As you design your website, make sure you're giving someone looking to learn about your music the best experience they can possibly have. This starts, and continues, the relationship you have with each fan.

Deeper - A great website not only makes a great first impression, it is also a place where fans can find more information about your band. Sharing your lyrics, discography, and behind-the-scenes pictures will make fans come back and discover more about you. Make your website a place to connect with other fans and access rare music. A good website nurtures the super-fans and will keep feeding them more content. The more informative your website is, the more frequently fans will visit it.

466

A Place To Capture Fans - You want your website to be a place that captures fans, so enable it to do so. An email sign-up form is the most basic function for this, but you should also have tons of free music you're trading for emails and tweets. It should also be a place where fans can clearly see where your other social networks are, so you can send them there as well.

A Place To Raise Awareness - Your website should also be a news feed. It should also be a place where anyone can find information about you. Writers who need pictures of your band should be able to get them from your website. If a radio DJ needs clean versions of your tracks or a remixer needs stems, they should be able to easily find them. If someone wants your tour dates or to see where you are in the album cycle, your website should give them this information.

A Traffic Directory - Your website should point to where fans can get more of you. Whether this means linking to your other social networks, streaming channels or web store, your website should clearly show visitors where they can find what they're looking for. This traffic directory should be neat and clear, to ensure you don't confuse fans.

Call To Action - Every well designed website has a singular call to action. You should clearly ask your fans to perform a specific action. This could be watching your new video, streaming your new song, buying a T-shirt or trading an email for a download. Focus on the most important action you want a visitor to take and make it easy for them to take it.

SEO - Many musicians have a hard time getting to the top of Google, Bing and Yahoo! web searches. Doing some work on search engine optimization (commonly known as SEO), can be one of the best ways to get your site to the top of these searches. By mastering SEO, your site will become the first search result for your music and the first impression given to fan that search the Internet for your band.

Addiction - A good website will help you develop fan's addiction to your music. By capturing fans, giving away tastes of your band and then selling your music and merch, your website is the place where you can customize experiences that will increase fan interest.

A Place To Make Money - Your website should give fans many options of how to support you, whether through donations, merch sales or ticket sales. The website should pay for itself by encouraging and leading fans to support you.

Social - It should be easy for fans to tell other potential fans about what you do. Social sharing buttons are crucial to get your message spread. There is nothing more powerful than a fan recommendation to all of their friends. Reminding them and giving them the tools to easily share your music will increase the odds that they do.

But Why Direct Your Fans To A Website Over Facebook Or Bandcamp?

A good website will offer fans more options to learn about and ingest your presence than any social media platform. If a fan reads your news update on your website, they are also visiting a place to get free music, tour dates and merch all on the same website. If they read your news in a Tumblr feed, you lose the chance to show the fan everything else you have to offer. While Facebook is one of the best ways to spread your information, the inception of Timeline has made it more difficult for fans to see all great things you have to offer.

Capture

While there are many ways to capture fans online, a custom website give you the most options. Your ability to customize and embed options for fans to ingest content makes it the ultimate place to do so. Whether it's embedding widgets or offering tracks in exchange for an email address or a Facebook like, make your website a memorable experience for your fans.

Website Building Platforms

The first step in making a website is choosing a platform to build it on. These services make it easy for a layman website builder to create an online presence that exceeds their knowledge of coding. These services all have many different features and depending on how much time, money and effort you want to put in, they can be great for your needs. All of the services allow you to use your own domain name.

Below I've narrowed down which platforms musicians should use and spell out which require more effort and some understanding of HTML to use. While there are a countless number of platforms out there, these are the ones I think are great for building a musician's website. I've listed them in order of how difficult it is to set up a website on each service, going from least amount of effort to the hardest platform to master. Easy-to-use platforms often offer limited feature sets and possibilities but can build a site in minutes.

Squarespace
A fantastic service for those who don't want to type a single line of HTML code. Squarespace (squarespace.com) allows you to make really good looking sites that can be customized to present all the information you would like in a neat and modern way. They allow you to sell merch directly, put up a concert calendar and a drag & drop audio player. They have become my go-to service as they are stable with plenty of features that give fans a great experience.

In my opinion the choices you have for making a website is to either use Squarespace or WordPress. If you aren't a genius at making websites and want to do something on a small budget, Squarespace is the best option. While it won't give you all the options a WordPress site does, when you start out and don't need to cater to the needs of thousands of fans, Squarespace gives a set of tools that are both agile and easy to use and optimal for when you need to direct traffic to fans. Once you have greater marketing needs, move up to a WordPress site.

Tumblr
Tumblr (Tumblr.com) is a micro blogging platform as well as its own social network. It is easy to set up a Tumblr blog that will also act as your website. Although it is usually not the best looking option, you can simply pick a visual theme for your Tumblr, make a menu bar that links to a few pages and you're all set up. Tumblr will allow you to embed widgets, but its layout can be very limited. It can be difficult to keep news and updates separate from your website content. Because Tumblr is a social network, making it your main online presence does open a great social element, but many of the limitations of the platform make it a less desirable option. While Tumblr is free, many of its better themes will cost you around $50.

The upside of having Tumblr as your website is how easy it is to spread your posts. Fans can reblog you, and you can easily push the posts out automatically to Facebook and Twitter, making it easy to spread your content and have a website and news feed rolled into one. Tumblr is discussed extensively later in the book.

Bandzoogle

Bandzoogle (Bandzoogle.com) specializes in building great websites for musicians who don't want to learn a single line of code. Bandzoogle allows you to make a web store where you can sell merch, receive payments through PayPal and use a fantastic direct-to-fan platform. While there are many sites that will help you make money, Bandzoogle takes no percentage of your profits. The service offers a free trial and three levels of pricing plans, at $9.99, $14.95 and $19.95 per month, depending on your storage and feature needs.

The service has a host of features including the following:

- The ability to have a blog, forum, photo gallery and music player.
- Built-in email collection, including the ability to trade tracks for email signups.
- The ability to send email and text-message blasts.
- An amazingly customizable graphic interface that doesn't require knowing a line of code to make look great.
- ArtistData integration so you can update Facebook, Twitter and Myspace at once.
- Web stores to sell music and merch through and the ability get instant payments through PayPal. They also have a Topspin partnership to sell merch through.
- Deep analytics to analyze your marketing techniques.
- The ability to create limited-access fansites only members of your fan club can view.
- Easily blog and podcast away with their service.
- ReverbNation partnership means you can easily make the two services blend together.

CASH Music

CASH Music (cashmusic.org) is a non-profit site that makes free, open-source tools for musicians. Most notably, they have an easy to use way to set up a great looking music website. They offer self-hosted websites, or you can host it on their site. These sites have a diverse set of tools catered specifically to musicians including email collection, tweet-for-a-track tools, and audio and video players.

Shopify
If the main reason for your website is to sell merch, have a contact page and occasionally announce big news a Shopify merch store can kill all these birds with one stone. For most artists I work with I simply build their website with Shopify as it looks great, is easy to make and allows me to easily accomplish all of the goals of a website. (shopify.com)

Using WordPress For A More Complex Website

WordPress (wordpress.com) is the most versatile website and blogging platform around, with open-source layouts and the most extensive and up-to-date plug-in library in the business. If you're looking to build a diverse website that can handle your needs for years to come, WordPress is the way to go. While WordPress does require some CSS and HTML knowledge to use, it's easy to teach yourself the basic coding required. You can also hire any of the countless web developers and designers who work on this platform.

WordPress's feature set is almost limitless; whatever you've seen done on the web, you can usually do it in WordPress. I recommend it for musicians because it's easy to update once the site is designed and WordPress's easy to install plug-ins make it easy to keep your website up-to-date when new social tools come and go. Their layout is unlike other tools because it's easy for laymen to make small tweaks to their websites once the broad strokes have been developed. While the platform is free, you'll need to spend money to use your own domain. Most WordPress websites that experience any real traffic will need to buy their own hosting.

Some other WordPress features include:

- Extensive plug-in library, including many music-orientated plug-ins for easy integration.
- Social tools that help you always stay up-to-date and only require simple one-minute plug-in updates from time to time.
- By far the most customizable web experience; the graphic possibilities are endless.

- Versatile platform analytics and easy Google Analytics integration.
- HTML5 ready.
- Countless customizable themes.
- The choice to build a free site hosted by WordPress on their own network or to self-host.
- Sites built on their self-hosted version can be transferred to your own hosting once you feel comfortable with the platform.
- The ability to make private pages Google doesn't track and password-protected content to give fan club members or potential team members exclusive access.
- Extensive photo gallery, slideshow and lightbox possibilities.

Themes That Work Great For Music
WordPress has countless themes to help you start out your website's layout on the right foot. Here are some great themes for music websites:

- **Standard** - Every year WordPress updates its own standard theme. These can be fine for music websites, but everyone uses them, so it's a bit bland and generic. It comes with WordPress and is free.
- **Thesis** - A great and easy-to-use starting point for making a music blog. It comes with a price of $87. (diythemes.com/thesis)
- **Arrass** - Musformation's developers built my studio website (cannonfoundsoundation.com) and personal website (jessecannon.com) from this theme. It's free, with a suggested donation. Many web developers don't like working with this theme, because of its complex style. (arrastheme.com)
- **Backstage** - Another great theme many musicians' sites are built on. It has a price tag of $70. (woothemes.com/2009/12/backstage)
- **Unsigned** - Another fantastic starting place. Goes for $70. (wpkube.com/go/unsigned)
- **Foxhound** - Foxhound has a bunch of great themes for musicians including the awesome, DarkNGritty. Most carry a $70 price tag. (foxhoundbandthemes.com)
- **Custom** - Musformation's developers regularly build custom themes for websites. Contact us (musformation@gmail.com) if you have extensive needs.

Essential WordPress Plug-ins
WordPress has more great plug-ins than can be listed here, so I provided a list of some essential ones. To install them, simply go to the plug-in

installer inside WordPress, type in the name of the plug-in and install it in two easy clicks. All of the plug-ins listed below are free:

- **Jetpack** - WordPress's set of a wide variety of great tools for your blog.
- **Publicize** - Allows easy sharing on many social networks like Facebook, Twitter and Tumblr.
- **W3 Total Cache** - Makes your site load faster and run faster.
- **Smart 404** - Helps keep fans on your site after they get a bad or dead URL.
- **Akismet** - If you're using WordPress's commenting system, this is essential to avoid the misery of spam comments.
- **Facebook, Twitter, Share Buttons** - Exactly what is said.
- **Google Analytics for WordPress** - One-click integration of Google Analytics into your site.
- **Google XML Sitemaps** - This can help create one of those cool sitemaps for your site when it comes up on Google and help fans get the information they want more easily. Also will help with SEO.
- **Network Publisher** - Automatically publishes your content to many social networks.
- **SEO Smart Links** - If this helps more potential fans find you from Google.
- **WordPress Video Plug-in** - Makes posting videos from a wide variety of sources easier.
- **Yet Another Related Posts plug-in** - An easy way to keep fans on your site for longer. At the end of your post it will suggest them similar pages from your site.
- **SongKick** - List tour dates easily.
- **WordTour** - Event management plug-in for multi-faceted live show details.
- **Contact Form 7** - Makes creating contact forms for your site easy and without a lot of coding. Some knowledge of HTML is helpful, but not necessary.
- **Contact Form to DB Extension** - A fantastic companion to Contact Form 7 that saves all of the form submissions in a database and is easily accessible from the WordPress dashboard. You don't have to worry about missing an email because all the submissions are saved here.
- **NextGEN Gallery** - A great looking photo gallery for WordPress.
- **GigPress** - Lists your tour dates.

- **Instapress** - Will put your Instagram feed on your website in a great looking way.

WordPress Music - WordPress recently launched a music site (wordpress.com/music) which shows you the many themes, plug-ins and other tools that make it easy to make a website for yourself.

Other Services
WordPress is not the only website platform out there. Below are some other services musicians can use to build your website:

- **Drupal** - Some designers love Drupal (drupal.com). I don't recommend using this platform unless you know the platform well and are an experienced developer. It's not nearly as developed as WordPress and isn't as easy to use. However, once you master it, it allows you to accomplish much of what WordPress does.
- **MovableType** - I feel similarly about MovableType (movabletype.org) as I do about Drupal. Musformation did the first version of our site on it and later switched to WordPress. Why? Because Todd and I are nerds, but we aren't nerds who want to toy with code all day. It's too complex to do simple tasks and the plug-ins are either too expensive or updated too slowly. It just doesn't make sense for musicians to try to keep up with this technology. Your website should be easy so you can focus on other things. However, if you love code or are a total tech nerd, this may be for you.
- **About.me** - Another fantastic, good-looking and simple website builder. There are better options for musicians, but About.me can be a great option for you if you want a personal web presence in the music business. (about.me)
- **Wix** - Sure, it's easy-to-use and costs next-to-nothing. But it looks crappy and cheap and like everyone else's website who had no money or knowledge to work with. I recommend skipping this service.

The Elements Of A Good Website

Now you know why you need a website. So what elements go into making a good website?

News Feed

The single most important function of your website is being the place where fans go to get updates about you. Your news feed will also feed your social networks and the press written about you. Post whatever big news you have on your news feed. Making your news feed a clear and noticeable part of your website is crucial if you want fans and writers to gather information about what you're doing.

Posts - A post is what an individual news item is called in the back end of your website. These posts will appear in your blog timeline and also link to their own separate pages with their own URLs. These are different than "pages," because pages don't exist in a timeline.

The Difference Between Your News Feed And Your Blog - Earlier, I talked a lot about the need to separate where fans and writers get news about your music, such as updates on releases and concerts, from where you talk about your personality and what you're interested in. It's important you create one feed that is just for news on your website and keep it separate from your blog. *Note: You don't have to blog, but you should.*

Design And Impression

A good website will be at the top of all Google searches for your music. *Note: It takes time for your website to get to the top of Google searches, so don't cry if it isn't at the top on day one.* This means your website is the first impression many potential fans will get of your music. You'll need to find appropriate graphic design that gives a visual impression that works well with your music. Having a black and white, mysterious website when you make party-rock anthems is probably a bad idea. Think about the first impression you want to make and other sites that have made good impressions on you, and then work from there.

Header

The header is usually the top of your website. It will appear on every page of your website. This is where that fancy logo or band picture will go. It should at least have your name in it.

Sidebar

The sidebar is also present on every page of your website. Just because it's named the sidebar doesn't mean it has to be on the side either. It will usually have a handful of widgets that appear on every page you click. These widgets should usually include:

- Music Player
- Email Capture
- Tour Dates
- Facebook/Twitter Feeds

Theme
A theme is web-design speak for the utility that provides your website with a consistent look and way of arranging your website's content. Most website platforms allow you to choose a theme and saves you the trouble of having to start from scratch. Choosing the right theme to start with is important for getting the flow of your website down.

Call To Action
As mentioned earlier, a call to action should be a big element of your website. This is what you're hoping fans will do when they get to your site. Common calls to action are asking fans to sign up for your mailing list, watch a new video or download a new record, whether that's for free or not. You want there to be a singular, clear call to action that grabs the attention of visitors to your website.

What's In A Good Call To Action? - Writing a good call to action can boost your website's effectiveness. Here are some helpful hints.

- **Make The Benefits Clear** - If the fan gets a free download or membership in the fan club for giving their email, that should be labeled clearly.
- **One Call** - You shouldn't have numerous messages on your website asking fans to do countless different actions. If getting more likes on Facebook is your main goal, suggest only that. Instead of having numerous requests like "Subscribe to our YouTube channel, mailing list and Twitter feed." Don't confuse your fans and focus on what is most important.
- **Make It Important** - Use language that sounds appealing and make it clear that they will be missing out on something. .
- **Eye-Catching** - Since your call to action is the most important part of your site, make sure it's located where fans can clearly see it. Set it apart in an eye-catching design that begs for attention.

Social Navigation

Directing fans to go where you want them to go is one of the most important aspects of a good website. Lead your fans to social networks, so that fans can stay in touch. If you do some Googling, most services your music is on has one of those cool social buttons that you can put in a sidebar on your blog or website.

You don't need to link every social network you exist on. Link to social networks you actively use and want to promote. Concentrate on pointing your fans to the networks you actually update, have a presence on and can use to build relationships with them.

Below are the common social buttons you'll find on a website:

- **Facebook**
- **Twitter**
- **Tumblr**
- **YouTube**
- **SoundCloud**
- **iTunes**
- **Spotify**
- **Tidal**
- **Apple Music**
- **Last.fm**
- **Bandcamp**
- **Email**
- **RSS**

Automatic Follow Buttons

Many of the social networks have buttons that will enable you to add followers with one click. These provide a frictionless way for fans to easily stay in touch with you and can help build your following. Use the service AddThis (addthis.com) to get buttons for each social media site you want to use.

Social Sharing

You want fans to be able to easily share all of the content on your website, whether it's news, blog posts, lyrics or merch. Every page should have social sharing elements, which means buttons for fans to easily share your content. Thankfully, most platforms have this feature built in, or the buttons can be easily integrated through plug-ins. All the services described above also have buttons to do this. Your sharing buttons should allow your content to be shared on the following sites:

- **Facebook**
- **Twitter**
- **Reddit**
- **Email**
- **Pinterest**

These sharing options should be displayed prominently on every page, making it easy for fans to share. Putting these buttons on every page on your website makes them easier to share with potential fans.

Navigation
Nearly every website has a navigation bar, which is the menu that allows you to navigate to different parts of the website. This navigation bar will appear on every page on your website, so your fans can navigate to what they're looking for from any part of your website. If you have separate pages for videos, free music, photos and merch, a fan needs to be able to find them. You also want to keep your home page clean and clear. Putting all of the content on your website there would be silly. This bar will help direct traffic and give fans the options to find what they want.

What's In A Navigation Bar?
You'll often find the following categories in a Navigation Bar:

- **Home**
- **Merch/Web Store**
- **Contact**
- **News**
- **Tour Dates**
- **Video**
- **Photos**
- **Music**
- **Forum/Message Board**
- **Bio**
- **Other Goodies** - This can be content for fans like lyrics, song meanings or whatever else you want to post on your website.

Pages

478

Pages are URLs within your website that don't get listed in your news feed or blog timeline. They are the pages you'll put all of your content on. These pages are especially useful for sharing your free music, contact information, tour dates, etc.

Splash Pages

Splash pages are pages that pop up before the home page. Often it's a huge graphic promoting your main objective, in order to make sure everyone sees this big news before they get to your website. This could be your pre-orders, tour dates, new video or an album announcement. These can be great if you don't want your existing fans to miss your big news, just be sure to have a clearly labeled button to get away from the splash page and on to your main website (a common mistake is to hide this button).

HTML5 Compatible

HTML5 compatible means your website and all its elements - including theme, widgets, music and video player - are written with HTML5, or HTML4, code instead of antiquated technologies like Flash. If your website has Flash elements, it will not work on iOS devices, including the iPhone and iPad, and wasn't made with the future in mind. Avoid Flash or you will miss out on website traffic from the countless people who use iOS devices to access the Internet.

If HTML5 is an option for widgets, music and video players, make sure you select this option. Some music and video services will automatically detect the device and browser that you're using and switch to Flash or HTML5 behind the scenes. For example, if you're using an iPad, the service will detect that and automatically play the media in a HTML5 player.

ReverbNation, SoundCloud and Topspin all have HTML5 compatible music players and widgets. Topspin, Vimeo and YouTube are also fully compatible for videos. It's also important to make sure your web store checkout system doesn't run on Flash. Although most of the popular e-commerce platforms don't have this problem, you do need to make sure your customers can checkout on iOS devices.

Browser Compatibility

Once your website is developed, you need to make sure it works on major modern web browsers. This is often quite painful because different browsers render the same code on a website differently. Test browser compatibility make sure your layout is consistent across different browsers and ensure everything on your website is functioning properly before you finalize it.

In addition to checking different browsers, different versions of browsers make behave differently. You should test your website on the most recent version of each browser and the previous two versions. BrowserStack will allow you to test your site in various versions of desktop and mobile browsers.

The worst browser for developers to work with is Internet Explorer. Some developers and web services will only support Internet Explorer 9 and some will support Internet Explorer 8 and 9. Getting your website to display well with older versions of Internet Explorer can be quite a task and your web developer may charge additional for this. Major sites such as Facebook no longer support Internet Explorer 7 and below. Google Apps recently dropped support for Internet Explorer 8 and below.

If you're working with a web developer, get a clear understanding of which browsers and mobile devices will be supported by your website. Here is a list of major modern browsers you should check your website on:

- **Firefox** - Mac and PC
- **Chrome** - Mac and PC
- **Safari** - Mac
- **Internet Explorer** - PC
- **iOS Safari** - iPhone, iPad and iPod Touch
- **Android**

Browserstack – Browserstack (browserstack.com) is a service that allows you to view your website on any browser, phone, computer, OS configuration you can think of. The service is free for most browser configurations and prices escalate if you want to do more extensive testing.

Widgets
Widgets are, well, widgets. They perform a small utility on your website, usually by being embedded somewhere on the sidebar or in your blog posts. The most common widgets are streaming music players, Facebook like boxes and email capture tools. These usually come from third-party services who allow you to put their content on your website. The most common widgets include the following.

Streaming Players - Streaming players allow you to easily play music on your website. There is a wide variety of streaming players available, each with their own features that you can customize for the web experience you would like to give your fans.

- **SoundCloud** - The popular SoundCloud Player allows you to assemble sets for its music. You can get SoundCloud likes, comments and follows, all from their player. Coupled with a great-sounding player and interface, this is a great way to get potential fans to hear your music and connect with you on SoundCloud. It's free to use.
- **ReverbNation** - The service has great widgets that sink up with music you have on their site. ReverbNation's widgets feature pleasing visuals and customizable features. This service is free but customizing your widget costs $2.99.
- **Topspin** - Topspin offers a customizable player with sharing options, the ability to have audio and video side by side in a playlist and links to the website of your choice. This service comes with their $9.99 per month and more expensive packages.
- **Streampad** - Streampad offers a music player in a bar at the bottom of your site. It's a free unobtrusive streaming widget. (streampad.com)

Email Capture Tools - You can either have fans sign up for your mailing list or give them an incentive by offering them a download for their email address. Many of the popular email collection tools offer a variety of ways to do this.

- **FanBridge** - FanBridge offers many customizable email capture tools that can trade tracks for email. These are available for free if you've signed up for a subscription with FanBridge.
- **Topspin** - Topspin has tools to capture emails in exchange for tracks or any other type of media for that matter. These widgets can be extensively customized. This service comes with their $9.99 per month and up package.
- **MailChimp** - MailChimp has many useful and versatile ways to implement email capture on your website.
- **Other Services** - Most other email providers have email signup tools so fans are added to your mailing list.

Tour Dates - Showing fans your tour dates is an important part of raising awareness and increasing turnout. There are a wide variety of widgets that can help you do that.

- **SongKick** - SongKick has a widget and a WordPress plug-in that will show your tour dates here and any of your other SongKick-enabled sites.
- **BandsInTown** - BandsInTown (bandsintown.com/widgets) makes a widget that will aggregate your tour dates and send the dates to other web services they aggregate to.

Social - Use widgets to broadcast your social network presence on other sites too. This lets you promote your social networks, give fans new content and push fans to follow you.

- **Facebook** - Facebook has a like box that's easily accessed from your Facebook page. You can customize this box to have it show the pictures of other fans or your latest updates.
- **Twitter** - Twitter has a very customizable widget that will display a stream your latest tweets.
- **Flickr** - Flickr (flickr.com) has a widget that will show off the pictures you've uploaded to your Flickr stream. This widget can be great if you have good visuals or want to show the press where to get your high-resolution photos.

Video - Embeddable videos are basically widgets. Anywhere you can post a video, you can also paste a widget. This means you can go to a video service and embed YouTube, Vimeo, Ustream, etc., where you would put any widget. You can also embed playlists if you want to get creative.

Other Cool Widgets - There are a few other widgets you can use that can add some flavor and interaction to your website.

- **Formspring** - Formspring allows fans to ask you anything anonymously and posts the answers for the public to see. (formspring.me)
- **IgnitionDeck** - IgnitionDeck (ignitiondeck.com) is a crowdfunding widget for WordPress that lets you raise funds from your website.

Don't Overload On Widgets

These widgets sound so cool, that you may be tempted to put them all on your website. Before you get too widget-happy, keep in mind you want your website to be informative but clean. You should only have one widget for each purpose. Choose one music player, one email capture tool, one tour date list and one social network to aggregate to for your website.

Content You Need To Have On Your Website
All of this info should be on your website and easy to find:

- **News** - A feed of what you've been up to, so fans and writers can stay up to date. This also shows potential team members that you've been staying busy.
- **Biographical Information** - Tell your story and why fans should care. This doesn't have to be some lame music industry bio. Just give fans and writers content to bite into so they can have something to ingest and tell others about. Make sure to list band members' names and the instruments they play.
- **Concert Dates** - Inform fans when and where you're playing.
- **High Quality Photos** - If press wants a high-resolution, or high-res, photo of you, they should find them here. If fans want a great photo of your band for their desktop background, you have them covered. Have your high-res photos separate from your web photos. Clearly state they're high-res and if they can be used for print. Images for the web and images for print have a different number of dots per inch, or DPI. Web standard is 72 DPI whereas print standard is 300 DPI.
- **Contact** - A list of the contacts on your team. If you have separate management, PR, label, booking, legal, etc., list all of them on this page. You won't have to waste time forwarding emails all day if you offer these contacts.
- **Streaming Music** - A way for people to stream your music and decide if they like it. This may be their first impression of your music, so it should sound good. No brainer.
- **Social Network Links -** Show fans where they can go to get more of you on their favorite websites.
- **Free Music** - You need to have a page that clearly advertises where fans can get your music for free. The more you're able to regularly update this page and trade email addresses, likes and tweets for this content, the better.
- **Live Music** - If you pride yourself on your live music, it's helpful to have a page that showcases it. Upload audio and video of full sets.

483

Post video of a lot of shows; its ok to use various recording qualities. Allow fans to see why they should come see you. The more great content you add to this page, the more reason fans have to come to your shows.

- **Video** - Without video you're missing out on all your website visitors who want a visual element. They're often too tired, brain dead or disinterested to actually read what you have written. A video can give a new fan a lot of information about you fast. Make it easily available.
- **Industry Information** - Clean versions of songs for radio, remix stems, FAQ, press kit link, press quotes, high-res press photos and graphics can all help make life easy for those who want to promote you.
- **Capture Tool** - You need to have the ability for fans to stay in touch. Preferably, you'll have ways to trade email addresses, tweets and Facebook likes for a track or membership in a fanclub. You should also have a separate page for your mailing list sign-up that you can link from social networks. This page should offer a clean and focused way for fans sign up for your mailing list.
- **Super Fan Info** - Give your big fans information, so they have a reason to keep coming back. Lyrics, song meanings, tablature, discography, vinyl pressing info, rare photos, rare songs, live bootlegs, art or whatever else you can think of.
- **Community** - Giving users the ability to comment on blog posts or chat in a forum can help build the community around your music that turns fans into promoters.

More Tips For Making A Great Website
- **Advertising** - You don't want other people's ads competing with your message. While it is tempting to try to make some money off the traffic you get, odds are you won't be making enough to justify the distraction and clutter these ads bring.
- **Open In New Window Or Tab** - Be sure to make all of the links to external sites, like your social networks or reviews, open in a new window or tab, so fans stay on your website and keep browsing.
- **Endorsements** - If you have endorsements, find a place out of the way to list them. While this won't be most fans' concern, having them can help attract other endorsements and give fans pertinent information. Just keep them below the fold or on a separate page.

Bells And Whistles

There are many other little details you can add to trick out your website. These are a few small ideas that can make a big difference:

Add A Favicon - One of those little details that make you look a bit more professional is a favicon. These are those cool little images that show up on your website tabs and bookmarks. They're a tiny logo that identifies a website. You can easily make them for free from any image you have with this online tool. (tools.dynamicdrive.com/favicon)

Animated GIFs - You can use animated GIFs to call attention to a place on your website. For example you can make an animated GIF of all of your merch and link it to your merch store. A lot of musicians are now using them as eye-catching press photos. They can easily be made in Photoshop or for free online with Gifninja. Just make sure to keep these to a minimum or your site will never open for those with slow Internet speeds. (gifninja.com)

Fan Promotion Tools
Make a page on your website where your fans can get tools to promote your music.

- **Banner Ads** - Make banner ads for your music that fans can put on their Tumblr, blog, message board signatures or website. Make them in the three most common sizes 468x60 pixels, 234x60 pixels, and 125x125 pixels. These can also double as ads you use for promoting your music.
- **Twitter And Facebook Covers** - Make cover photos that you fans can use on their Facebook and Twitter to show their devotion for your music. Encourage fans to use them on their own page and help to spread the word about your music.
- **Screen Savers** - These can easily be created by melding a few of your graphics together in PowerPoint.
- **Desktop Backgrounds** - For fans to have on their computer so everyone will see your graphic. All you need to do is make a high-res graphic that's 1280x800 pixels. With some size adjustments, they can also be used for Twitter and Tumblr backgrounds.
- **Avatars** - These are used for message boards, blog comments, AIM and other chat programs. An image sized a minimum of 75x75

pixels is usually best. Make sure it's square and clear when shrunk down to this size.

- **Ringtones** - Have fans promote your music by playing it whenever their phone rings. Make 30 second clips of your music that can be used for ringtones on both Android and iOS.

Make An Amazon Store For Your Music

The Amazon aStore widget is an amazing tool that can be pasted right to your website. But why would you want this? Through this widget, you can sell any of your merchandise that's available on Amazon on your website and earn an extra commission of four-to-15 percent, depending on how well your store does. This is on top of what you already make from sales! You can also recommend all of the equipment you play, books, records, movies you like, etc. If your fans buy it after clicking on the link from your site, you get the commission.

Don't Forget RSS

One of the ways writers and web-savvy, taste-making nerds keep up with you is to follow you through RSS. Since the advent of Facebook and Twitter, RSS has been neglected, but it's still used by a lot of important people to keep up with their favorite musicians' news. Make sure you have a place to allow fans to subscribe to your news feed with RSS.

Encourage Your Fan Community By Starting a Message Board

Message boards are where the rabid nerds of the Internet still congregate to discuss micro-interests. Despite the advent of social networks, die-hard fans still flock to these doldrums to discuss what they love and hate. Boards like phpBB (phpbb.com) are free, although not very easy to install, and can do wonders for getting fans to spread the word about you as well as bond with your music. Most modern musicians with a diehard fanbase make sure to have a message board ready for fans that want to bond with each other. This also enables you to control your fanbase and easily feed them news.

Donate Button

If you give away a lot of music you can use a donate button to encourage fans to repay you for the pleasure they get from your music. PayPal buttons are often found on musicians' free-music page, dropping the hint that fans have a way to help fund you to make music.

Disqus Offers An Advanced Commenting System

While nearly every website platform offers a blog commenting system, Disqus (disqus.com) offers the best commenting tools possible. With multiple login options, they invite members of the community to comment by logging in through Twitter, Facebook, Google or Disqus's system.

Advanced Website Tips For Musicians

There are many advanced tricks you can use to help you make the most of your website.

Maximize Your Promotions By Always Raising Awareness On Every Page

Musformation has designed a lot of websites for musicians. We've seen a huge difference when we make sure every page has the following:

- **Streaming Music/Video Player** - I like to use the Topspin Streaming Player so I can load whatever video or song a musician is promoting into the player. A streaming player on every page lets any fan who finds your website easily find a way to hear what your music sounds like.
- **Fan Capture Tool** - Email address for media or an email address signup needs to be on every page, to keep in touch with as many fans as possible.
- **Concert Dates** - Raise awareness about your upcoming shows.
- **Merch** - An animated GIF of your merch can take up very little real estate and be an eye-catching way to tell fans what merch you have for sale. Make sure the picture links to your merch page.
- **Social Network Links** - Show fans where else they can find you.

Make this information available on every page of your website. This awareness can make huge leaps in your fan relationships, as well as increasing sales and spreading the word about your band. Every page without this information is a lost opportunity to educate fans about what you have to offer.

Always Link Back To Your Website

Since your website is the ultimate fan-capture tool, source of information and traffic directory, it's crucial to get fans here. The smartest strategy is to always post any news you have, song streams, videos, etc., on your website and then link back to it on your social networks. With the exception of when you do an exclusive with a blog, creating content fans want on

your website can help solidify relationships. Never link to the YouTube page of your video if it's on your website and always link to your website for any news, tour dates or other content.
It can be argued that when posting a blog of big news it can be spread more if you do it on Facebook or a thread on Twitter, the viral reach of big news is far easier to share. I have noticed that the best way to optimize this is to link to more details of the blog that super fans may enjoy at the bottom or other media so you get the best of easy shareability and visits to your website.

Create Special Content Only Available On Your Website
In order to get fans back to your website, you need to create content that only exists there. Giving fans content they can't get anywhere else is the best reason they'll have to visit your website. Here are some ideas for that content:

- **Exclusive Tracks** - Free music, streams that are only on your website player, email and tweet for tracks etc.
- **Exclusive Videos** - Video updates or premiere a video on your website.
- **Video Chats** - Host a chat with an embedded video on your website.
- **Lyrics**
- **Discography**
- **Record Pressing Information (rare vinyl, quantities, colors, etc.)**
- **Tablature** - For those guitar players who want to know how to play your songs.
- **Pictures**
- **Personal blogs**
- **Message boards**
- **FAQ**

Small Website Tweaks That Make A Big Difference
There are tons of small tweaks you can make to your website that make a huge difference:

- **Never Use AutoPlay** - AutoPlay is the function that makes a song or video play once your site loads. Enabling this option is a bad idea and causes many people to leave websites. Most people browse at work or in the library where they can't make a lot of noise. If they want to hear your music, they will hit play. Give fans a choice or get ignored.

- **Site Load Time** - We've all clicked away from a site that takes too long to load. Large images, too many widgets and animated GIFs all bog down your website's load time. Google has a great tool that will test your site and tell you how to fix what's wrong. (developers.google.com/speed)
- **Quality Of Design Builds Trust** - Many fans may be skeptical of buying from you since many of them have been burned by other musicians poor customer service. Lucky for you, studies show that the better designed your website is, the more fans will trust you.
- **Whitespace** - Your website doesn't have to have a white background to have whitespace. The term refers to keeping from cramming information too close together. Some whitespace gives your site room to breathe.
- **Most Users Don't Scroll** - A whopping 75 percent of users will never scroll down your site. Make sure the content you want them to see is in view when the website initially loads.
- **Click Here** - Avoid writing "click here," and instead describe what's on the other side of the link. If you're linking your new song simply type, "Check out <u>our new song</u>!"
- **Tour Dates** - Make sure your tour dates link to where to buy tickets and/or Facebook event pages.

Your Website Shouldn't Be Your Art Project
Unless you make some seriously artsy music, you should keep your website clean and useful. This means having very little friction and being as simple to use as possible. While hiding links inside your Jackson-Pollock-style splatter masterpiece might be amusing to you, if you want your music fanbase to build, keep it as functional as possible.

Yes, some famous musicians get artsy and make crazy Flash video games where you need to pick the singers nose with your mouse to get a free song. While this is great for musicians who already have the attention of blogs and give a good laugh to their established fanbase, this is probably not the avenue you want to go down. Let people get to know you first, and then let them see that you recreated the maze from the movie *Labyrinth* and that they need to get through it before they can download your David Bowie cover.

Researching What Platform And Theme To Use

If you're on another musician's website and really enjoy it, you can usually find out the details behind it. Simply look through your browser until you find a function called "View Source." This will show you what platform the website was built on and the theme that was used to build it, if there is one. Simply scroll through the code and look for clues. Most coding rookies can still easily find the name of the platform, theme and the widgets used to build the site.

If you ask me, I think everyone should start off on Tumblr and when you need more advanced features move to a WordPress site.

Hiring A Web Developer
If you want to have a nice website with tons of features and not spend hundreds of hours learning how to code a website, you'll need to hire a web developer. Developers are also known as website designers, but a developer handles more than just the graphical look of your site, they also handle the functionality. These developers can create a website that suits your needs and leaves you with an open-ended structure that you can update and tweak yourself.

Benefits - There are many reasons to hire a web developer. While many of the easy-to-use DIY website designs for musicians offer a great product for the price, sometimes you want more advanced options for your website. If you're interested in hosting various features for your fans and offering interesting marketing promotions, you're most likely going to need to hire a developer who can accomplish these feats for you.

Once you build your site, you'll have a layout that you can build on for years to come. If you build on a platform like WordPress, as technology changes you can easily keep your website technologically relevant by installing plug-ins, doing updates on your own and occasionally having a designer doing a graphic refresh.

Finding - Web Developers are everywhere. In fact, you probably know someone who does this for a living. With that said, it takes some smarts to make sure you get a great website. All too often, developers charge too much for their services and give a lackluster product that's more geared to them impressing prospective clients than giving your fans a positive experience. Skip Craigslist searches and instead get someone to do your website who is either reputable or has designed a website you like the look

490

of. Most website designers have their info listed at the bottoms of websites they designed, making it easy to contact them.

Objective - Your number one priority is for your website to be a good experience for your visitors, which means it should be easy for fans to navigate to what they need. When hiring a web developer it's important they get this, otherwise you're going to spend a lot of money on a website no one likes to visit.

Wireframe - In order to make sure you're happy with your website's layout you need to make a wireframe. A wireframe is a rough outline of where you would like each feature to be placed. This is one of the most important needs to communicate to a web developer. Since your website graphics will usually be based on an album, logo and press photos you already have, this functionality can make or break your website.

Update It Yourself - Any designer should build you a site that you're able to update yourself. This includes news posts, concert dates, music and videos, as well as a wide variety of other content. Not only is it costly to have a web developer do constant updates for you, but they take too long to do the updates, holding up your progress.

You should be able to edit every bit of text on your site, photo galleries, music players, widgets, video etc. The layout that a web developer creates for you should be so easy to use that an adolescent could update it for you. Platforms like WordPress make it incredibly easy for nearly anyone to update once a developer has put everything in its right place.

Considerations - Here are a few more points to consider before hiring a web developer:

- **How To** - Your web developer should give you a quick tutorial on how to upload pictures, text, news, music and videos. If most of this is based around widgets and blog posts, it's extremely easy to keep up with.
- **Syndicate** - Have your designer build you a header or background that you can also use on sites like YouTube, Bandcamp or Twitter to save you design costs.
- **Budget** - Most websites start at $500 and go up to the tens of thousands of dollars depending on your needs. Be realistic about

what you need. Remember, if you start small, you can keep adding to it as you go.

- **Timeline** - If you need a website built in four weeks, it may be best to tell the web developer six weeks. They're notorious for never finishing anything on time.

Choosing A Domain Name

In order to have a website, you need a domain name. A domain is the URL address you type into a browser to get you to a web address. For example: http://YOURDOMAINHERE.com. In order to get a domain, your desired name needs to be available and you need to go to a site that does domain name registration. Many of the services that do this change prices and have sales often; $5 to $10 per-year is the going rate. It's hard to determine the best website to register a domain name through, since they have similar features and prices. Below are some of the popular domain name registration sites:

- **1&1** - We use them to register domain names for Musformation. (1and1.com)
- **Namecheap** - With a lot of cool features, they also live up to their name and offer very cheap domain name registration. (namecheap.com)
- **Hover** – Hover does a great job of registering domains with a clean interface. (hover.com)
- **GoDaddy** – While the service is very popular, many of our community members have had terrible experiences with their service. (godaddy.com)

You Don't Need A Website To Put Your Domain Name To Use
If you aren't ready to put up a website quite yet, you can still buy your domain name to hold it so no one else can have it. In the meantime, you can use it to start getting traffic to any of your social networks. This is especially a good idea if you're having trouble with SEO. Use domain forwarding to point your URL to one of your social networks, or any website. Simply go to your domain registration site, log in and forward your domain name to whatever social network you would like to point to, whether it's your Twitter, Facebook, SoundCloud or ReverbNation profile.

What Domain Name Should I Buy?

The obvious first choice is to buy the name you go by. "Yourbandname.com", for example. If that's taken, try adding "music" to the end of it because it will help your SEO. If both of those are taken, you may want to consider a name change since someone obviously has a hold on this name in the music world. Registering to .net can work, but the way to close the deal on getting good SEO on your domain is to simply add the word music and/or the name of your genre of music after your name. When most people can't find a musician on Google they will then type "music" next to the musician's name. If you can't get "yourbandnamemusic.com" try "yourbandnameband.com" or something else memorable. If you play an uncommon instrument like the harp you could try tagging that onto your name or find something else distinguishable people may think of you for. This will improve your SEO and allow you to have a much better chance of connecting with fans when they Google your name.

Own Your Misdirected Domain Names

Do you go by a name that's constantly misspelled? Does your name have an alias such as its initials or a nickname that fans call you? If so, it's very important to own the domain on these names too.

People constantly think the name of my site is either Museformation or Musinformation. If you go to museformation.com or musinformation.com they all redirect to Musformation.com, so that you find our site. I bought these names after realizing users were constantly making those errors. It cost me $14 and 15 minutes to set this up. It gave our blog tons of traffic, and, if someone goes to Google and types in museformation or musinformation, they now find our site. Approximately two percent of our traffic comes from misdirected searches each month.

Years ago, the band Brand New made shirts that said Brand Nizzle as influenced by Snoop Dog's slang in the early 21st century. These shirts were so popular, people would often wonder, "who is Brand Nizzle?" If they had gone to Google they would only come up with some links for a shirt and an Urban Dictionary name (*Note: Another good way to own your aliases is to add them as a definition on Urban Dictionary*). Another potential fan lost.

Every time someone types in your name wrong and doesn't find your music, you miss out on a new fan. It's cheap and easy to make sure this doesn't happen. Make sure you have your bases covered.

Other Domains To Buy
While the name you go by, and its misspellings, are the most important domains you can get, it can help to buy some other domains too. Here are some ideas:

- **Album Name** - If you have a strong album title that fans may look up, buy that domain and point it to your website or your direct-to-fan site.
- **Song** - Same goes for songs. Especially if you're promoting a single with a catchy title. If it's a hit, someone else might buy the domain and do something shady with it. This happens more times than it should.
- **Free Music** - If you give away a lot of free music it is helpful to own "www.freeYOURBANDNAMEmusic.com." Make this domain forward to your free-music page and see great results. This is also easy to write on postcards, wristbands, stickers and posters so fans remember it.
- **Torrent** - Concerned about fans torrenting your music (even though you shouldn't be)? Well you can try to divert them from torrenting by buying "www.YOURBANDNAMEtorrents.com" and pointing it to the page of your choice. A smart move would be your free-music page, since that's what the listener is looking for.

Hosting Your Website

After you have a domain and a platform, you need hosting. This is the place on the Internet where you store the files for web browsers to read. You pay a company to safely store your information, avoid crashing due to too much traffic and provide security. For most musicians, this will cost between $5 and $20 per month. While this price can be steep for some, it enables you to have a versatile promotion tool for your music and to build your fanbase.

If Your Music Goes Viral, Don't Miss Opportunities! Use Media Temple

494

Over the last decade of dealing with web hosts, the incompetence of some companies never ceases to me. I have seen too many musicians complaining about their hosting going down the second they get a rush of attention. Despite it being 2017 we still see musicians websites crash when they get a lot of attention and miss out on huge opportunity to gain new fans. It seems any time a musician who isn't on a major label goes viral, their server crashes. This is unacceptable. It means that one of your biggest opportunities to convert new fans is lost, all due to the incompetence of a company you pay every month.

With that said, allow me to recommend the host that will make it so that if your music starts to blow up, you won't lose the chance to make countless fans. Media Temple (mediatemple.net) is a hosting site that actually has a cheap plan geared toward keeping your server up and running even if you get more traffic than usual. Not to mention they have the best customer service I have ever witnessed. It makes me furious when a band I've helped out loses exposure to an incompetent host. Don't be that band. Use a host that for $20-per-month will really help you.

They also do domain registration and charge as little as $4 a domain. Give them a look.

Other Hosts
- **Amazon** - If you're doing a big project, Amazon hosts many of the larger websites on the Internet. (aws.amazon.com)
- **Bluehost** - If you're not worried about crashing and want to cheaply host a simple website, Bluehost (bluehost.com) has hosting options for as little as $5-per-month.

Chapter 27: Using SEO And Web Analytics To Get Your Music Discovered And Name Your Group

If your name doesn't come up as the first listing on Google's results, you're at a huge disadvantage. Many potential fans will type in your name after they see it on a T-shirt, hear your name mentioned or read about you and want to find out more. Sadly, more than 75 percent of searchers on Google don't scroll past the first three search results. This means being at the top is super important, if you want lazy fans to discover you after all the hard work you put in trying to get them to hear your music.

While you may feel like you have everything covered because you have a Facebook and a Twitter page, keep in mind those platforms' in-site searches are often horrible and glitchy. We've all done a Facebook search for a musician we liked and been frustrated when they don't come up because of improper punctuation or some other stupid reason. If you rely solely on your social network presence, you may miss out when a promoter searches Google for your name and nothing comes up.

Using SEO To Help Your Music Get Discovered

Unfortunately, getting to the top of these search results isn't the easiest thing in the world. It requires a bunch of smart moves and adherence to rules set by these search engine companies. Whether you're having trouble with your SEO or want to improve it so no one can unseat you, there are tons of tricks you can use.

SEO Mistakes
Make sure to avoid these SEO mistakes:

- **Images** - If your website is just a bunch of images and no actual HTML text, you won't come up on searches.

- **Flash** - Building your site on Flash will not only make fans not able to see your content on iOS devices, it will diminish your SEO and make it harder to find.
- **Spamming Comments** - While spamming blog comments used to help with SEO, search engines have wised up to it. You shouldn't be afraid to link your website in the comments of blog posts, but if you go around spamming every blog possible, you'll not only annoy the blogger to death, you'll diminish your chances of getting good SEO.
- **Don't Pay For Scams** - There are tons of services that claim to help you with SEO. Google is on to these scams. Avoid them and spend your money elsewhere.

Improving Your SEO
If you're not the first search result when someone Googles you, there is some work you can do to improve this situation.

Never Type your Name
One way to start helping your SEO improve is to never type in your website's URL. Instead Google it every time you need to go there and then click on the link. Make sure you're not signed into Google and do this whenever you're at your friend's house, on a different device or on a different Wi-Fi network. Get your friends and family to do it and you'll start to have fewer SEO problems.

Domain
Nothing helps more than having the .com address of the search term you want to come up high in the search results of. This is why having the .com for your name and any other search term you want to come up is so important. Buy every term you want to come up when people Google you.

Use Wikipedia
One of the best ways to get to the top of Google is to have a Wikipedia entry. Not only will the Wikipedia page be a top search result on Google, but you can also make sure your website is linked from this page and it will help your website climb in search results tool.

Title
You see that catchphrase at the top of nearly every website you visit? Besides your domain, this is the most important asset you have in search. Put a description of your music in this place. Genre affiliations are great.

The titles of each page you make are also HUGE for SEO. For example, the name of every Musformation article is right after the domain name in the URL. This really helps SEO.

Keywords
There are certain words that are going to be associated with your music. If you play intelligent dance music, it's a good idea to have that written somewhere on your site, probably your bio. If you're known for a song, a band member's name or are famous for something else, be sure that also comes up. Many fans will search these keywords alongside your name on Google and either be directed somewhere else, possibly a news article or even a bad review.

Get Linked
The more websites who write about you and link your website, the better your SEO. It gives you authority, the measurement for how important you seem to search engines. The more authority you have, the higher you will rank on search engine results. This means that getting reviews and linking your website from your other social networks can really help your cause.

Meta Tags
Many platforms allow you to enter what are called Meta tags. These are keywords you enter to help your search results. While they will not guarantee you a high place in the search results of these words, they can give you a bit of a boost as long as you type in relevant information. If you're an R&B act and type in Rihanna as a Meta tag, despite not having any real relevance to her, it isn't going to do you any good. Type in words you think people would search next to your name and it will help you out.

Lots Of Content
Having a website filled with many pages of merch, discography, lyrics, blog posts and news gives your site an authority ranking on search engines. If you're posting relevant and helpful information on your website, your SEO will go up.

SEO Tools
Most platforms have a plug-in to help improve your SEO. Read the manuals for these and use them as directed to help every page in your website get the best SEO possible.

Install Google Analytics

Google won't say why this helps, but it does. You should do it anyway.

Webmaster Tools
While I refer to Google throughout this book as being the search engine to care about, that's only because it's the most popular search engine. Bing and Yahoo! are also used by millions of people every day and checking your SEO on them is important. Thankfully, all of the practices listed above work great for your SEO on them as well. All of them also have webmaster tools that can greatly help your SEO. Each of them will ask you to add and verify information about your site, which you can then use to enhance your SEO. Below are where to find webmaster tools for each of the big three search engines.

- Google (google.com/webmasters/tools)
- Bing (bing.com/toolbox/webmaster)
- Yahoo! (same as above)

These tools can also contact you if your website is hacked, infected with malware or having trouble with search engine crawls.

Testing SEO With Analytics
If you were smart and installed Google Analytics, you can look up and see what search terms get you traffic. The service will produce a list of search terms that people have used to find your website. Make a target list of search terms you want people to use to find you and make sure all of them are coming up. If you see search terms coming up that you're shocked people are searching, find a way to utilize these search terms.

The Name You Go By And SEO

A lot of thought should go into naming a band or even the name you go by as a solo artist, DJ, producer or whatever. If you're forming a band with the intent of building a huge fanbase, you need to think about what hurdles certain names may put in your way.

What's In A Name?
Some people will tell you that your band name needs to fit into your genre, whereas others will tell you to buck the trends in order to stand out. How you choose to go about this marks much of who you are as a band. Do you

want to be seen as a maverick? Or as a member of a genre? This decision is not the most important one, seeing as in 2001 there were a million rock bands named The <insert plural noun here>. Similarly, in today's heavy metal scene there are a million bands whose name follows the formula of "Verb The Noun" (genre naming credit goes to Steve Evetts). Your name will not be the main determinant of your success, but it is one of the first impressions every listener will get of your music.

I remember the first time I heard the name ...And You Will Know Us By The Trail Of Dead. I immediately checked out the band based on its name alone. It brought to mind such an extreme image, I needed to know what this band sounded like. Sure enough, I ended up becoming a fan. Although that band name is violent enough that it summoned the imagery of a death metal band in my mind, I was wrong. It turned out to be an indie rock band. Still, the name demanded attention, much like The Airborne Toxic Event, whose intriguing name doesn't tell you what they sound like. Then you hear their mellow rocking ways and learn they're named after a part of a Don DeLillo book.

There is a way to make sure your band isn't generic but still fits your genre. Pop-punkers Can You Keep A Secret have a band name that, while not being a genre cliché, instantly gives you a hint what genre of music they play. Having a cliché name doesn't mean you're never going to rise to the top of your genre either. My Chemical Romance is as cliché a name as you can get, and they still have ruled rock for years.

Figuring out how to name your band is a very personal experience and should come from your own personality, while embodying an image you want to give everyone who first hears of you. After you find a band name that you like, it's time to test it and make sure the name will enable you to spread your music easily.

Testing A Name
You want to make sure that the name you choose gives potential fans the image you want to invoke. One way to do this is to ask friends what they picture when they hear your desired band name. Ask them what they think a band with the name you're thinking about using will sound like. If this matches the type of image you want to invoke, you have a winner and can keep testing it. Until this matches up, you should keep trying to find a great name. With any luck, you'll be known for this name for decades to come, so it better be a good one.

Googleability

If a potential fan can't easily type your band's name into Google and get what they're looking for, you're going to have a miserable time promoting your music. Jesse Keeler of the group MSTRKRFT points to Google as the reason his band chose to omit the vowels from their name; MGMT anyone? If you choose a name where someone else has a strong SEO presence, you're dead in the water. I dare you to name your band Huffington and attempt to get on Google search page 20 up against Huffington Post.

Why do I place so much emphasis on this? If I am out with a friend and they tell me about a band that is sure to change my life, the first thing I do when I go home is Google them. If that fails to work, I might Google the band's name and put "music," "Facebook" or "Bandcamp" in the search query. If that yields nothing, I'm most likely over it. Many potential fans that hear about your music may never even get to that step. The band missed an opportunity to get me as a fan, have me fall in love with their music, buy their merch and tell all my friends about them.

Why This Is So Important

I've worked with a lot of bands. There is a huge difference in how easy it is for a hardworking act to build a fanbase, depending on which bands' names come up at the top of Google searches and which bands' don't. If you don't have a favorable ranking in Google searches, you're going to have lots of trouble promoting your music. When searching Google Alerts and Twitter for your name, it will take FOREVER as you scour through others talking about something else aside from your music. If you name your group something unique, these searches will always lead to opportunities for your music. Working against a common name or phrase can take away countless hours you could otherwise be using to build your fanbase and will make you work harder than a band who has their name pop to the top of a Google search.

Spelling

While it's great you decided to name your band Kaffeine, verbal communication of your band name is going to be difficult. Alternate spellings may get you the imagery you want for your music, but they also hold you back from being easily discovered when a fan doesn't realize you decide to get creative with the spelling of a word.

Symbols

One a big trend in the indie world right now is to use hieroglyphics and symbols, as if everyone was a modern-day Prince. While this may get you attention on the blogs, you'll likely be regretting this five years from now when no one knew what to call your band aside from "option T on the keyboard; you know, †." Cool gimmick, bro.

Symbols And Voice Search

The biggest trend in search is voice search, meaning when you tell Siri, Alexa or Cortana to play an artist or to lookup information on them on Google. This method of search will be growing ever year especially with Alexa, Homepod and Google Home sales going through the roof. If your band name has a symbol or isn't easily pronounced on search you will miss opportunities for fans to discover your music when they search this way.

Another Band Has The Name I Love

Surprisingly, this may not be the end of the world! There are three places to check to see if you have a problem. Let's say you've already Googled the band name and found a potential problem. Type the name into the following sites: AllMusic (allmusic.com), Facebook and the iTunes Store.

If you found a band on iTunes or AllMusic that put out a record in the past 10 years, give up and move on. If their last record came out more than 10 years ago, see how active they were. If the band put out one record 15 years ago on a small label, you may have to deal with some trouble down the line, but odds are, you're in good shape. If the band has been inactive and not using the name for 10 years, you're most likely fine.

If you see another band using the name on Facebook but not iTunes, you could also be fine. Copyright law states whoever can prove they made interstate commerce with the name first is the owner, as long as they are actively using it. This means whoever sold goods over state lines first owns that name, i.e. you need to sell a CD or a T-shirt to someone in another state. Call up that cute dude with the stupid haircut from Wyoming you talk to in the chat room and beg him to buy a T-shirt from you. Convince your crazy aunt who is in some cult in Arizona to buy it. Don't be a fool and run straight to the copyright office, because whoever can prove they made interstate commerce first will usually win in a court of law, and most lawyers will never let it get that far in the first place. While it is smart to copyright your name, you need to sell something related to your band across state lines before you can do so.

You're probably thinking your Googleability is destroyed by this other small band that's on Facebook. Well, if your aspirations are higher than how popular that band is now, you might as well duke it out. Get a Facebook, Twitter and domain name ASAP. And if any of them are unavailable, add your state abbreviation or something else descriptive to the end of the name. Once you have made that interstate commerce, get any lawyer to send out a cease and desist letter to all the other bands using it. Most of the time this will make the other bands wet their beds and run. No one wants to fight a legal battle unless they've already made a ton of fans using that name. Remember, if you can't get the best Facebook and Twitter URLs, you may be at a disadvantage in promoting your music for a long time, as people always assume your handle is your name instead of another you pick like @coolestbandofsexyd00dzever.

Bands change their names all the time once they get signed to major labels to avoid having to deal with a long court battle over a name. Almost no one goes to court over this. At most, two lawyers argue a little and it's done.
.

Once you have the name you love, make sure you can claim it everywhere you go. Here are some places you should make sure your name is available:

- **Web Domain**
- **Facebook**
- **Twitter**
- **Tumblr**
- **Instagram**
- **iTunes Store**
- **Spotify**
- **Namechk** - This service will allow you to check on dozens of sites at once to see if your desired username is available. (namechk.com)

What If It's Your Name?
Unfortunately, the same rules apply to your name as a band name. You have no extra rights to a name, even if it's your birth name. For example, if your name is Billy Joel, you can't market yourself as a musician using the name Billy Joel. He has registered that name and retains the rights to it in

this field to use it for music trade. If someone else has made interstate commerce and registered that brand already, you're out of luck. I hope you have a great middle name. All hope is not lost, however, you just need to do better. Just think about David Bowie. His birth-name was actually David Jones, but the Monkees already had a very popular David Jones in their band.

If You Are Doubting Your Band Name, Now Is The Time To Change It
Musicians often rush into naming their project. As time passes they eventually either have a better idea for a name or circumstances change and they need to change their name. Whether you have found a better name or you're worried about another person that is using your name, the time to change it is now. The time is not tomorrow when you get more popular and have to alert thousands of fans of this name change, losing many of them in the process. Before you get more fans, change your name to something better.

If you have a huge following like Prince and you change your name, the whole world will know and probably still refer to you by your old name instead of the stupid symbol you choose for your shark-jumping career. The problem becomes when you're mildly well-known and are then forced into a name change or want something better. It's best to get a good name as fast as possible and start building off of it.

Why?
There are millions of reasons bands change their name. I once worked with an amazing indie-prog band named Twilight City Fracture. At the time of the recording they were going by the name, Royal Crime Syndicate, which gave the impression of a bunch of gangster-thug dudes, not some skinny indie rock nerds playing hook-filled spacey guitar songs. Before they released new songs that they hoped the whole world to hear, they decided to change their name and make their lives easier. Fun fact: They actually were named Twilight City Fracture originally, before Royal Crime Syndicate. The new name fit their genre of music better and helped them make better impressions, opening doors instead of closing them.

We've all had the experience of not wanting to listen to a band because of their name and then being shocked when we listen and grow to love the band. In other cases, bands have such a great name that we immediately want to hear what they sound like. Here are some common scenarios why it may be a good idea to change your name:

- **Plenty Of Options** - Despite it being common wisdom, make sure you realize there are plenty of names available. If you're worried that another band has your name, it may be better to find a better name now. Odds are there is a better name out there.
- **Bad Luck** - Circumstances can sometimes ruin your life. Popular Indie-Rock band Burning Airlines couldn't get anyone to put their name on a billboard or flyer after 9/11, despite the fact they had been around long before that sad day. Bad luck! A supergroup could form tomorrow with nearly the same band name as yours and you'll forever live with the world thinking of that band when they hear your name. Potential fans might even think you're a cheap rip-off.
- **Improvement** - You may have a better name in mind. It's going to bother you until you switch to it. If your name isn't making the right impression on people, it's time for it to go. It's hard enough to get ahead without your own name working against you.

Do It Now!

While I think it's a good idea to get your ball rolling by choosing a name, if you haven't found the perfect one, it's also a good idea to keep thinking of a better name. Switching your name after you have played fewer than ten shows isn't a crime against humanity, it's coming into your own as a musician.

Odds are your fanbase is only going to keep growing. When your band is formed is when the least amount of people will ever know about your music. This means that when you're attempting to inform the world you changed your name, it will be easier to make the transition closer to your band's inception. The biggest problem comes when you've generated a mild buzz and then decide to change your name. It isn't as easy to get out the news of the name change to everyone who has been introduced to you and is interested in your music. With each day that passes you're going to have to change more social networks and contact more writers to get this message out. Start today and thank me tomorrow. And start claiming all of your URLs and social networks, so no one takes that great name you found.

Once You Choose A Name

After you have a name you like that has passed all of the tests, make sure to register it on every website, service and social network as soon as possible, so no one else takes it. After this make sure to contact your lawyer or a legal service like LegalZoom (legalzoom.com) and get a trademark on the name in order to avoid the pain of legal fees in the future. While this can cost about $600, it can save you a lot of money and headaches in the future.

Website Analytics Put To Use

The analytics for your website are an amazing help not only for understanding your fanbase, but also seeing if your promotions are working. Google Analytics is one of the most powerful tools in the business, and it's totally free. All you need is a platform that supports it and a Google account. You can then figure out information ranging from when you should release a new song to which of your promotions are working and which are not.

Using Google Analytics
Connecting Google Analytics to your website allows you to see a wide variety of metrics about your visitors. Most platforms make this process as easy as copying and pasting a line of code. After a couple of days of having it installed you can see a wide variety of information about your visitors.

Breaking It Down
When you open Google Analytics you're presented with a wide variety of data. While this can look a bit overwhelming, there are many easy deductions you can make. The following is some valuable information you can gain from your analytics data:

- **Unique Visitors** - This is how many individual people come to your website per month. If you're working hard and pushing traffic to your website, this should be increasing every single month. If it's going down, it may be time for some new promotion, like releasing new music, a video or eventful content.
- **Page Views** - This can show you if fans are clicking on other pages on your site. Ideally, this number is exponentially higher than your unique visitors, since you want your fans to be looking at more than one page on your site on a regular basis.

- **Bounce Rate** - This is how many people leave after only looking at one page on your site. You want to try to keep this to 50 percent at the highest.
- **% New Visits** - This number is how many people have come to your site who have never visited it before. This is a good way to see whether your website is mainly attracting fans who get a first impression of your music or a dedicated fanbase. It can tell you which types of content you can nurture and if your promotions are working. If you aren't getting enough new visits, perhaps you should try to get fans to use a tweet for media widget so they recommend your page to their friends. You could also put more effort into your SEO. If you want more fans to come to your website on a regular basis, develop more content that fans are interested in.
- **Demographics** - This will show you what countries, cities and languages are coming to your website. If you see a lot of visits from a country or city in which you don't currently play, perhaps schedule a show there. It also may be a big clue you aren't ready to play in another city if you have a huge number of visits from one city and zero in others. I have worked with bands with millions of website visitors, but no visitors have come from Montana and Wyoming.
- **Devices** - If you don't see iOS and Android ranked in the top five operating systems visiting your site, you may have serious problems with your mobile site you need to test out. iOS is often ranked third on most sites and Android fourth. If this isn't the case, take a look at your site on these devices.
- **Ad Campaigns** - You can measure the success of your Google Ad campaigns in these analytics under its own separate area. These can show you if these campaigns are worth the money.

Traffic

You can get valuable information about your site traffic. This information can help to make sure you're promoting your music properly.

Search

You can see how much search engine traffic is coming to your site. Most search engine traffic is potential fans checking you out. You can quickly see how much traffic these searches are giving you. Every site will get a different amount of search traffic. What's much more important is to look at the search terms that get people to your website. You want to make sure your name, album name and any other relevant terms are getting people there.

Sources

If you see your news get posted on a handful of blogs that link back to you, it's easy to see which one generates you the most traffic. This is helpful to know which blogs to give exclusives to. While one blog may have a higher traffic, that higher traffic is useless if that blog's readers never click on the links that take them to your site. This is a great way to get solid data on which blogs help you the most.

You can also see which of your social networks get you the most traffic. You may have more Facebook likes than Twitter followers, but if every tweet gets you more traffic to your website, you have more engaged fans there and should place focus more of your attention to them.

You can also discover people and blogs who like you. You may find out an influential Twitter user is your fan after being linked by them and seeing it in your analytics. It would be helpful to follow, thank them and nurture this relationship. You may have gotten some press and not seen it in your Google Alerts, yet it's getting you a ton of traffic. Without checking your analytics, this could all be missed.

Popular Pages

Your analytics will show you which are the most popular pages on your website. Your main page will usually be the top hit. If you have a free-music page with tons of free music that isn't near the top, then maybe you're not calling enough attention to it? If you have a really popular video page, this is a hint to make more videos.

Conversions

You can hook up your e-commerce, usually your online merch provider, to Google Analytics and see if you're selling merch to your visitors. There are many ways to tweak your site to get the number of people you sell, known as conversions, higher. If you host your merch on your website and you see that a T-shirt is getting a lot of clicks but isn't a good seller, maybe your page isn't selling the shirt well enough. You may need a new picture or description to sell that shirt better. Is a random page getting a lot of traffic? Look at your search terms and see if it's getting traffic from search engines. Maybe you should make more pages like that one.

Live Intelligence

Google Analytics has a great feature to see what traffic is happening live. This way you know where to nurture your website fans. Set up email alerts so that Google will alert you if you have a traffic spike. This is helpful so you can jump on your social networks and try to pour gas on the fire if there's suddenly a spike in fans talking about you.

So Much More

The more traffic you get, the more you can extract from your analytics. This is some of the most powerful data you can have about your music. While it may seem boring at first, it can become fun and will help you build your fanbase.

Chapter 28: How To Make The Most Of Social Networks

The whole world is obsessed with social networks, be they the big networks like Facebook, Twitter and Tumblr or exciting up-and-comers like TikTok. In addition to being an easy way to waste the best years of your life, social networks do an amazing job of spreading the word about your music.

With that said, all this social networking gets confusing and time-consuming after a while. It's easy to look at other musicians who have great success with it and wonder why you're not having the same results. Odds are you may be imitating the habits of groups who have an established fanbase when you are still starting out.

While conventional wisdom is to blindside potential fans with links and pleas to listen your music, there is a better way to create fan relationships than spamming. By becoming an active member of social network communities, you can build bonds, friendships and, most importantly, fans that will tell everyone about you. <u>All you need to do is talk to them, instead of at them. Converse with them, instead of telling them what to do. Talk to them in the real language you speak, so they see you are authentic, not a PR bot.</u>

A single interaction with a potential fan saying something as benign as you saw a mistake in the last episode of Empire, instead of just telling them you have a new song is a million times more effective. Rabid music fans investigate who they are interacting with regularly on social networks, and if they are looking for new music and think you are similar to them, they will check it out by their own free will and will be much more likely to enjoy your music.

Remember every social network update, email blast, press placement and piece of content you create is a way to remind your fans and potential fans that you exist and they should remember to give your music attention because of a bond you share. Giving these reminders on a regular basis allows you to stay on the mind of everyone who is interested in you. They'll remember to stay in touch and tell their friends how great you are. Just make sure that you don't post frequently enough to annoy your followers,

Throughout this book I've talked about capturing fans and getting them to stay in touch with you. Once they do, it's very important you don't abuse the privilege of them listening to you to talk about your daily activities. There are many nuances to keeping this relationship a mutually beneficial one, but that is the key term: mutually beneficial. Your fans benefit from this relationship by hearing about updates of interest to them. You'll benefit from them sticking around and continuing to support you.

Doing Social Networks Right

What's The Goal Of Your Presence On Social Networks?
Some musicians are overwhelmed by the vast landscape of the Internet and by social networks especially. They don't see the potential for promoting their music. No matter who you are, there are some goals everyone should have for their social network strategy.

- **Don't Annoy** - You want fans to keep paying attention to what you do. If you have the privilege of accumulating followers, you do not want to annoy them. Watch what others do. Look for what's annoying and excessive and avoid it like the plague.
- **Gains** - You want to gain new fans. This happens by getting linked and shared. You need to create and post interesting updates so that your fans will spread the word. Social networks enable your band's news to be spread like crazy if you do something remarkable.
- **Share** - Getting your music shared is most important. If it's important for you to have an outlet for your photography skills, how cute your cat is or your reviews of your lunch, there may be a better place to share that than the place fans are coming to hear about your music.

Whenever you're in doubt about what to post, remember those things. Just because one of your favorite musicians posts an update every time they enter Chateau Marmont, doesn't mean it's cool for you to post to all of your social networks every time you walk into the place where you party with the former cast of some trashy reality TV show in your hometown.

Context is very important in what you share on social networks. Kanye West gets away with tweeting about looking at porn in the studio all day because his fans have come to know him as an eccentric. When no one knows who you are and you tweet about the same, you seem like some creep watching porn in your mom's basement while you make bad music that everyone is now too creeped out to hear. In time, you could gain fans that are so obsessed with you that they may care about your every move. Until you have built that fanbase, you must pay attention to making sure your social network content is as informative and interesting as possible. Five posts a day about how smart your cat is will not be interesting to those who barely know you.

How You Should Think Of Your Website, Facebook, Twitter, Blog, Etc.
Does anyone actually read Twitter or Facebook news streams? These questions may be debated until the end of time, but there are some practices you can employ to make huge leaps in gaining fans on every social network.

If you take a dozen music fans and ask them how they keep up to date with the musician they love, you'll probably get a dozen different answers. Realize if you don't to keep updating your profile on a given social network, you're eliminating a possible outlet where some fans may like to hear from you. Just because your friends on Facebook can hide you, doesn't mean they all will.

Saying that no one reads email blasts, Facebook, blogs, RSS, Twitter, etc. is ridiculous. While you and your friends may not, there are still people who keep up to date and prefer information on the musicians they're interested in different formats. Never assume that everyone who likes your music likes to hear news about it in the same way as you and your friends.

Different fans aggregate information in different ways. If you choose to not participate in any of the major social networks, you miss out on countless potential fans that would follow you and spread your music if you enabled them to. Deleting your profile or ceasing updates on a given social network cuts off fans that prefer that medium. If you find individual updating to be a pain, try copying and pasting or employ aggregate services that post to more than one social network at a time. Realize though, that is best to customize your updates on each social network. Otherwise, face the wrath of losing fans that want to like you, but are thwarted by your failure to give them information in the format they prefer.

Do Not Use Your Social Networks As A Place To Impress The Music Business
Some musicians will never understand that littering their pages with electronic press kits, press photos and bios meant for music business insiders won't make a good impression on fans. This says you're looking to impress the music business, instead of talking to your fans about what they care about. Fans don't care who you opened for, and they aren't going to browse through your electronic press kit. Dominating your website with these items says you're concerned with being scooped up for stardom, rather than working to build a fanbase. Make your social networks a useful place for making new fans, not a place to brag about having opened for Puddle of Mud's reunion tour and other not-so-glowing achievements.

Instead of posting whole reviews, tell the stories that inspire your songs. Instead of posting all of the acts you have opened for, tell visitors about experiences you had at these shows. Focus on making new fans instead of talking to potential team members about your achievements. This will make attracting new team members much easier, when they see how mature and interesting you are. Always think about what a fan would want to hear, not about a booking agent who might be following your social networks.

The Flaws In Every Social Network And How You Fix Them
While social networks are very powerful, each one has flaws to consider. It's a huge mistake to get fooled into thinking that only one of them can handle all your promotion needs. The number of friends, followers, likes, etc. you have can be deceptive. Despite your perceived online presence, you may not be as well-known as you think in the real world. Just because you have followers doesn't mean that these "fans" haven't blocked you out using the many ways to do so on social networks.

- **Facebook** - While you may look at your page and see a huge number of fans, the real shame is that a lot of them have hit the hide button on your updates in their news feed, just like you did to your cousin who writes what she eats for every meal. Even worse, if they aren't on at the time you make a post, your update is buried easily and never seen by your fans AND Facebook hides it from 85% of your fans who liked you, just to get you to pay for ads.

- **Twitter** - With lists and muting apps to exclude annoying tweeters, your followers may not be hearing what you say. To make matters worse, many people are complaining about a trend where many users don't actually read what others say and only send out "selfish tweets" about their own actions.
- **Instagram** – People scroll to fast through the content each day and most of it gets missed.
- **Tumblr** - While Tumblr is thought of as Twitter with more characters, there is much more to it than that. While Twitter has many ways for you to ignore undesirables, Tumblr's problem is that it's the over-sharing capital of the Internet. It's easy for your updates to get lost in all the clutter. On all of these sites, your news is buried if your fan doesn't read your update within hours of sending it.
- **RSS**- While RSS is a great tool, nobody uses it. It takes a particular info maniac nerd to enjoy the ease that RSS readers bring to their life. Even if you make it available, odds are, not a lot of people are going to take advantage it. However, many of those who do subscribe via RSS will be your most important followers, since they're usually press and tastemakers.
- **Email** - By this point, everyone in the world knows how to sign up to a mailing list with a junk account or send unwanted email updates to their junk folder. Even if it passes by those guards, they can still choose to not open your email. Just because you have a ton of email addresses doesn't mean anyone is reading your emails.
- **YouTube** - Getting a YouTube subscription is a great thing. But if your fans don't check on YouTube's page the day you post your video, you may be lost in the endless barrage of other channels they have subscribed to.

Fixing These Problems - The way you fix these problems is to try to keep your presence on every social network as optimized to their use as possible. You want to share the type of content Facebook likes on Facebook and the type of content Instagram likes on Instagram. You also want to make sure you are sharing on every one of these networks so you don't miss fans that may be ignoring you.

How To Not Get Ignored On Your Social Networks

With all these flaws, social networks might seem like a big waste of time. But there are a few practices you can employ on every social network that will help you be more successful:

- **Don't Annoy** - Updating all of your social networks every time two of your band members go see a movie together may inspire one or two bored fans to interact with you; do it too often, and the rest of your audience will slowly begin to abandon you. Talk to your friends and gain insight about what annoys them on social networks. Once you know, avoid these habits. If you investigate what makes your friends stop paying attention to updates, you'll be way ahead of the crowd.
- **Make Aware** - All of your social networks should be interlinked. When you blast out emails they should all be linked for those who would rather follow you in another way. For example, I hate non-business or personal messages in my email inbox, but I love to get updates from everyone via RSS. But other people are totally different. If you show fans there is another way to follow you, they may choose a format that is better for them. The superior format is based on the individual fan. Always link your other social networks so that fans can follow you the way they prefer and hopefully on more than one network.
- **Watch Your Stats** – All of the social networks have great analytic tools to show if you're losing fans. Analytic tools like Next Big Sound and ChartMetric and can also show if you're losing or gaining fans. If you remain ignorant of this you could end up in fan bankruptcy.
- **Don't Ignore RSS Or Email** - Most data shows that email and RSS are very effective when compared to social networks. Push your emails with rewards and make sure links to your RSS feed are abundant. While neither are as cool or as exciting as the latest social network, they both are extremely important in keeping fans up to date.
- **Reward People For Paying Attention** - Putting giveaways inside emails, Tweets and Facebook updates will keep your moderately enthusiastic fans paying a little more attention. Whether it's free merch, tickets or interesting content, if you make it exclusive to certain formats you can keep fans paying attention.
- **Be Everywhere** - Just because your updates on a certain social network aren't effective for you at first, doesn't mean that nurturing them won't eventually give you huge returns. Make sure to care for

all of them and remember it takes time to build a fanbase. Just because a few posts won't turn you into Billie Eilish overnight, doesn't mean your social network isn't working.

- **Summarize** - If you can keep your news consolidated, do so. Got an upcoming show and a small review to post? Maybe you can do it in a two sentence Facebook post instead of two posts in the day. Keep your followers news feed free of clutter, and they will reward you with a long lasting follow.
- **When In Doubt Do Less** - Think you're updating too much or being annoying? You probably are. Most fans don't need an update from you more than five times a week on your social networks. You also don't need to feel obligated to even do it that much. Remember it's much more rare to lose a fan from saying too little, rather than too much.
- **Inside Jokes** - Inside jokes between your friends get old fast. They're fun here and there, but extended tweets of them can get exhausting.
- **Sales And Promotions** - If a service is having a sale or special deal, make sure you call attention to it. If your record is on sale this week through Amazon or another outlet, tell fans.
- **Bigger Isn't Better** - Just because you see a celebrity doing something on a social network doesn't mean it will work for you. Remember, celebrities have a much bigger, more rabid fanbase than you. Their fans will put up with a lot more from them than they will from you.

What To Do To Increase Your Social Network Followers
While there are tons of things you can do to scare fans away, there are just as many things you can do to attract them, no matter what service you're using.

- **Nurture** - If someone reaches out to you on a social network, it means they want to be your friend. If they follow you, follow them back. If they start up a chat, be friendly.
- **Converse** - It's totally great to ask questions to your followers and it can help you meet people. It's great to keep conversations going when someone starts one up. Take advantage of this friendliness to form bonds with your fans that will last for a long time.
- **Be Human** - Don't let your management run your social networks. Even Justin Bieber and Lady Gaga type their own tweets a lot of the time. The tweets are in their voice and sound genuine to fans.

Fans don't enjoy talking to a dull corporate drone; they want to see the real person who has charisma and personality that originally drew them in.

- **Talk The Way You Talk** - The slang you use is part of you. While it's good to be professional, you're also a musician and if you sound like a corporate, neutered version of yourself in order to avoid offending anyone, fans will see this and be turned off.
- **Show Personality** - Are you funny? Why not let it show? As you gain fans, they like to see your human side and what makes you tick. With that said, if you're an avid sports fan or cat lover, no one needs to know how you feel when your favorite athlete scores or your cat yawns.
- **Lead Discussions** - Has it been bugging you whether Five Guys or Shake Shack makes a better burger? Are you having an internal band debate about whether Ben Sherman or Fred Perry is more stylish? Why not ask your fans what they think and share the best answers? Twitter, Instagram and Tumblr are great for these types of discussions and fans love to be a part.
- **Conversations, Not Just Affirmations** - Writing "Hell yeah" and "Thanks" in response to fans is the minimum you should do. If you want to make bonds you need to converse, have fun and lead interesting discussions. I'm not saying you need to discuss the literary works of Proust here, but write back a response that is interesting instead of the normal "awwwwww yeah."
- **Start A Discussion Not A Spam** - Don't say "Buy My Album." Have a conversation. Ask your fans questions like, "Have you heard our new album?" or "What's your favorite song on our new record?" This will get fans talking and have your message spread without being spammy.
- **Help People Who Help You** - Social networks are a great way to give recognition to those who help you. Give thanks to cool promoters, fans who help out, a musician who lends you something or a cool blog. Giving a link from your social networks to those who deserve is a great thank you for the help they gave you.
- **Cross Promotion** - Make sure to work in links to your other social networks. Keep diverse content on your social networks. This will allow fans to stay in touch if they're growing tired of the one social network.

The Science Behind How To Act On Your Social Networks

As we have impressed throughout this book, the music business is all about forming honest relationships with people you have commonality with. While that is lovely that I've seen that work, what about actual facts? In 2013 MTV commissioned a study on musicians' interaction with fans. The study found:

- 53% of music fans say the more an artist shares online about themselves, the closer they feel to them.
- 91% say it's OK if an artist has some flaws – it makes them human and likeable.
- When they buy, it's because they want to support an artist that they respect and connect with.

What I extract from that is you should be a humble version of yourself. No one is going to buy your music because you barrage them with links to it on iTunes or SoundCloud. They will buy it if they feel a connection to yourself that is honest and feels real. Do not spam fans, make connections with them.

How Often Should You Post About Your Upcoming Concert?
Trying to promote your shows without annoying your followers is a balancing act. While there is no easy answer to deciding when to post about your upcoming concert, I can give you some definite times:

- **When You Find Out** - Early notice helps fans to mark their calendars.
- **One Month Out** - Post on all of your social networks a month before the show. It will not be the time when fans are looking to lock up plans, but the post can help generate fan interest.
- **Two Weeks Out** - Some fans are more whimsical than others. This can lock them in.
- **Two Days Before** - Fans may have had other plans fall through or forgotten about your show.
- **Day Of** - Find a way to casually talk about the show the day of. Give one last reminder for fans looking for something to do that evening.

Make these announcements different on your social networks. You may just want to send event invites and one or two reminders on Facebook. On Twitter and Tumblr you can make regular announcements. Posting the flyer once on Instagram and taking a picture of the venue on the day of the show is smart promoting.

Social Network Strategy - Be Available But Don't Call Attention
One of the biggest pains in the music business today is that the sheer amount of websites that can promote your music on. These sites can help spread the word about your music, but sometimes it's best not to draw attention to them. Many musicians put too many social network links on their website and in their email signature. The problem is that many of these sites don't deserve to have your fans directed toward them, because they don't allow you to keep in touch with the fans that go there. A visitor to one of these websites, is essentially useless. You won't be able to stay in touch with them. Point fans to your preferred social networks and let them find you on other networks if they happen to be surfing the web.

Do you have a ReverbNation or some other low-traffic social network page? Great! If someone is browsing around one of those sites they can now find you. The problem is getting them to stay in touch and buy music from your preferred web store. There is no foolproof way to do this. This is why you need to be present on many of the smaller social networks, but never link them. Instead link to sites like Facebook, Bandcamp, SoundCloud or your own website, where you can put mailing list widgets up as well as widgets to buy and listen to your music from your favorite stores.

If a site doesn't allow you to stay in touch with your fans, you shouldn't promote them. Simply use them for what they're good for: Make a profile and take advantage of any traffic they may have. Realize there is no reason to direct your fans to them. The only sites you should promote are those that allow you to keep in touch with your fans and potential fans.

The Effectiveness Of Social Networks At Selling Music
Your presence on social networks can turn into sales. At Musformation, we frequently measure the effectiveness of links sent out on the various social networks. While nothing can beat email, which can give as high as 28 percent returns, the other social networks can still give you solid performances. We have determined that Twitter links can generate sales from around three percent of your followers, but for acts on Twitter, that number can get much larger when the band has a huge following. This number gets closer to five percent when you post a link on Facebook. These numbers may seem small, but they can translate to a large amount

of sales when you gain a lot of fans on your social networks. Remember most musicians have way more social network followers than email addresses.

To Link To Your Press Or Not To?

It's often debated if musicians should link their good press, interviews and articles in their social network feeds. The argument against posting this content is your followers are already your fans and don't need to hear how amazing you are all the time. This is a reasonable point, but fans enjoy interviews, and press helps to build your bonds with fans. A well-written review can expose your fans to valued opinions about the music they love. This makes interviews worthwhile content to bring to fans' attention.

It can be tacky and frivolous to always post your good reviews, especially if they're pouring in. Your fans will see it as clutter and eventually get annoyed. The dilemma is many online outlets create content hoping the musicians they cover will link their material. These media outlets can turn on a musician, giving up on the musician if they don't link to the review or article. Other outlets will also be attracted to write about your music if they know you'll link their article, because they're also searching for web traffic. If you're starting to have very engaged fans, they'll also appreciate a well-written review.

My philosophy has always been that you should overshare on one of your social networks--I prefer Tumblr--and keep it all business on the rest. Every now and then, drop a hint to your fans that they can find more of your content there.

Know Your Followers

Look at who is liking, following and favoriting you. It can open up opportunities. I've worked with musicians who discovered that their favorite musicians, A&R people and celebrities follow them and are fans of their music, all from looking at their followers list. Contacting these esteemed followers can lead to opportunity and relationships with those you would like to know. Read through your followers list from time to time and get to know its occupants. Check out their profiles and see if they're someone you should nurture a relationship with.

Interact With Your Followers

If someone is interested enough in you to follow you, be sure to interact with them. Follow back everyone who follows you and take every chance you can get to make a personal interaction with your followers. Each of these interactions is an investment in turning the follower into a bigger fan. If you don't believe these personal interactions work, take an example from Thomas Nassiff, who edited this book, about building his relationship with Man Overboard.

He posted on the band's Myspace wall after hearing a song he enjoyed from the group. They gave him a friendly reply and a few other pleasant interactions, so he purchased their EP and went on to become a fan of the group. The same interaction occurs between musicians and fans every day. If you are unwilling to take the time to interact with one fan every day, you are going to be at a disadvantage to the countless musicians who are willing to take part in this smart daily practice.

What's Crowdsourcing? And How Can It Help Your Music?
Crowdsourcing is when you ask your fans for help with a task. This means logging into your social networks and asking your fans for their opinion or knowledge on a subject you're thinking about. If you're wondering where the best place to play in a certain city is or which bands to play with, you can crowdsource an answer by asking your fans. If you want to make sure your fans enjoy your set, you can ask them what songs to play. Social networks have opened a dialogue that allows you to make wise and informed decisions to choices you can't always find the answer to by searching Google.

You don't always need to do exactly what the crowd says but use fans opinions to make the best decisions possible. Asking your fans a question can make them feel like they're a part of your music, as well as giving you an answer you may not have already thought of. Your fans love to be involved in these decisions and are grateful that you respect their opinions. Some questions that are easy to crowdsource are below:

- Which merch designs should you press?
- Which songs should you play on your next tour?
- What your next single should be?
- Which venue you should play in a town?
- What bands you should go on tour with?
- What towns have you been missing on tour?
- Who should remix your song?

You can also crowd source to get work done. Imogen Heap crowdsourced the writing of her bio to promote one of her records. Some musicians run contests to design their latest tour merch by crowdsourcing submitted designs and then enlisting the crowd to choose the winning artist. It has become popular in dance music to crowdsource the vocal performance on a track and allow fans to vote on submissions. The possibilities are endless.

Outsource - Musicians are always asking me to write their bio or news blasts for them. Many musicians are musicians because they did not enjoy similar writing assignments in school. I tell them to outsource this task. Why not ask your Twitter followers if they want to do it? Fans love being involved with the musicians they follow. You may even get multiple bios with different interesting points, which you can compile into one amazing piece. This is much better than asking a busy third party to write your bio.

Should You Trigger All Of Your Accounts To Post At Once?
Posting to all of your social networks one by one with the same message is a huge pain. There are many ways to link one of your social networks to post from another like Instagram posting to Twitter and Facebook. While this seems like a great and easy answer, be aware this will take the personality out of your posts. Fans are looking to see your voice, not an automated robot making posts for you. They want to think you're there watching if they ask you something. It's worth the extra time to post across more than one social network at a time with copy, paste and a little customization, instead of using automated tools that take the personality out of your updates.

Personal - One of the keys to making your social networks effective is that updates need to be written in your own voice. Fans want to feel like these updates are from you, not your manager or your label. Even the most famous musicians understand this and make sure to give their fans a taste of their own personality. Fans are much more likely to keep following you if they think there's a chance they'll get to interact with you and forge a bond. If fans think your manager is the only person seeing their cries for attention, they will become disengaged and lose interest.

Making Concert Updates Easier
Updating your concert listings is really annoying. Thankfully, technology has made the task easier. Here are some ideas for how to setup your social networks, so you have to update as little as possible.

SongKick & BandsInTown - We're big fans of SongKick (songkick.com), BandsInTown (bandsintown.com) and how much easier they make updating your concert dates. If you update these services once and have your social networks set up right, it will be the only update you need to make. If you use BandsInTown or Songkick's Facebook app, it will automatically update after you post dates in Tourbox. If you have a website or Tumblr that allows Songkick's widget or plug-in, your dates will get updated there. They also aggregates dates to Bandcamp, SoundCloud and your YouTube videos, Spotify Apps, etc. getting your dates in many places at once.

Always Link To A Playlist Instead Of A Single Video
Anytime you link to a YouTube video be sure to make a playlist first and link to that. This gives you an opportunity to cue up another one of your songs to introduce a listener to since many people will stick around after the first song finishes. Instead of letting YouTube suggest them a Justin Bieber video, suggest your own with a playlist.

Meme Marketing Is The Unseen Hand Shaping Our Thoughts
One of the most interesting changes in how many of the biggest artists are marketing themselves today is by having "meme accounts" create content around them. Both Post Malone and Mac DeMarco have full time employees making memes about them to keep them in the conversation and Atlantic Records has a whole department that spends the majority of their times developing this content for their artists. They will often disseminate these memes to popular accounts that aggregate the best content, helping to spread their image to a wider audience. While it is not a strategy for everyone and at times it can turn your image into a laughing stock instead of viral hit, devoting resources to develop memes around your music can often have it spread more effectively than many other marketing methods.

If you are interested in an agency who does this try Songfluencer (songfluencer.com)

Tools To Make Social Networks Easier

HootSuite: A Real Time Dashboard To Post To Your Social Networks

HootSuite (hootsuite.com) allows you to post to a wide variety of social networks via a dashboard inside their own app. In its suite you can post to many networks including Facebook, Twitter, WordPress, FourSquare and LinkedIn. It also has the ability to schedule posts and view deep analytic data. It has a few tools for collaboration as well, which can be very useful for musicians. They acquired one of our favorite services Seesmic Ping and for $9 a month they allow you to manage your social networks better than any toolset out there.

Buffer App Can Help Schedule Your Social Network Posts

Buffer (bufferapp.com) is a free App (or a little over $100 a year if you want advanced settings) that will allow you to schedule posts on Facebook or Twitter It can be simply installed as a Chrome extension and allow you to get work done when it is convenient. It is also available for iOS and Android.

If This Then That Will Forward Your Social Media Posts

While forward your social media posts to other social networks can take some of the personal touch out of them, occasionally it's appropriate and saves time. IFTT (ifttt.com) will allow you to make a hashtag that will forward posts to whichever social networks you designate, saving you time copying and pasting the same message over and over.

Piqora Is A Visual Marketing Tool

If you are big on marketing using visuals for Pinterest, Tumblr and Instagram, Piqora (piqora.com) has great tools for you to help make the most of them. Their tools allow you to make landing pages, track link analytics and a host of other tools to make sure you are making the best of your visual marketing.

ToneDen

Toneden (toneden.io) has a variety of tools that allow you to do both gating and landing pages that can link fans to services, get you more followers, or sell more tickets. They provide a great interface and clean analytics. If you plan on taking social media marketing seriously they make one of the best tools for musicians to do more thorough marketing. Best of all it has a free tier.

Headliner Will Make Animations For Social Media

Headliner is a service that allows you to do a bunch of cool animations you have probably seen on social media. Most notably the app will allow you to create videos for your Instagram, Twitter or Facebook feed that either put transcriptions of what's being said on the screen or waveforms over a graphic to catch the eyes of those scrolling through social media. Use this to highlight interview quotes or make a sample for people to hear new music on social media. It has both free and pair tiers, but I have found the free tier suits most of my needs. (headliner.app/)

Using Link-Shortening Services
One cool trick for your social networks is to use link-shortening services. These services will allow you to make custom URLs like bit.ly/musformation that point to whatever web address you choose. This is an especially great way to give your fans an easy-to-remember URL instead of a complex one. Make sure you use this if your free-music page has a complicated web address.

As an added bonus, these services have great analytics built into them. Let's say you're promoting a free download from a YouTube video. If you make a unique, short link to this video, you can view analytics and see how many people are clicking it. If you're getting lots of clicks, you may want to add these links to all of your videos or make more videos.

Here are a few services that do link-shortening and analytics:
- **Bit.ly** - Popular and free link shortening site with deep analytics.
- **Ow.ly** - HootSuite's link service that integrates right into their awesome social media service and analytics.
- **SmartURL** – A link shortening service that offers pre-saves and a handful of other tools. (smarturl.it)

Chapter 29: Connecting With Fans Through Photos And Videos On Instagram, TikTok & Snap Chat

One of the most entertaining services to come to the Internet is the picture sharing, social network Instagram (instagram.com). It provides many cool filters and photography tools and allows friends to easily follow you and comment on your photos. Often described as the last happy place on the Internet, it's also a place where avid music fans congregate. According to a Nielsen study it's users spend 42% more money than the general population and listen to 30% more music.

The service allows you to import all of your friends from Facebook, Twitter and your contact list. Your fans also have the ability to follow you if they see a picture you posted to Facebook, Twitter or Tumblr. So what good is it to have your fans follow you on a social network where you only post pictures? You'd be surprised.

Here are a few ways you can promote your music on Instagram:

- **Photo Sharing** - You can get your content shared with friends of friends by taking interesting pictures. In Instagram's news section you can see what your friends have been liking and commenting on. If you're taking pictures fans like, others will discover you from the social aspect of the site.
- **Business** – A business account allows lots of extra features but most notably the ability to put links in your stories where fans can swipe up to promote links (make sure to prompt them by asking them to "swipe up"). This only extends to Spotify links until you meet some metrics on followers though.
- **Promote** - Post pictures of your latest album or press you have gotten so your fans know to go check it out. While you may want to do this sparingly, this is a great way to make sure fans don't miss when you have something new and exciting out.
- **Geo-Tagging** - Instagram has geo-tagging built in. Tag yourself at soundcheck at the venue you're playing to remind your fans you have a show that night. You can also take cool pictures around the

venue or even make a great looking flyer for your show with Instagram.

- **Behind The Scenes** - You can show behind-the-scenes glimpses through photos and bond with fans in the comments section. Show your fans how you live when you aren't on stage.
- **Discovery** – One of Instagram's strongest features is recommending to others the photos their friends like. This means when you post high quality photos that rack up likes, friends of your fans who like them see your photo and name and you begin to break down the listening barrier to get your music heard.
- **Hashtag** - Make use of their hashtag system by using tags like #recording, #recording studio, #giglife, #guitarporn or #bandshirts. Many users will search these hashtags to look at photos of what they're interested in. I'm addicted to the #recordingstudio tag, where musicians show off pictures of themselves in the studio. Tag appropriately, and you can get your music discovered by others who share similar interests.
- **Profile** - Be sure to fill out your profile and web address. If users find you through the social aspects of Instagram, they can learn about you and where to get your music for free.
- **ReGram** - You can capture photos from other users by taking a screenshot. Be sure to credit them by writing "ReGram" and crediting the author by tagging their @symbol. This is helpful if a fan took a great picture of you that you like. You can also use apps like regram.me to automate the process.
- **Spread** - Instagram is a great way to get pictures onto your other social networks. Remember, great-looking images get shared fast on social networks like Facebook, Twitter and Tumblr. Use Instagram to make your pictures look better and they will raise awareness about your music.
- **Filter** – Making sure your photos are optimized by seeing if a filter helps improve them is crucial to getting more like.
- **Follow, Comment And Heart** - Just like Tumblr, you should follow your fans and then heart and comment on their photos. Interact with them and build better bonds.
- **Album Credits** – Do a carousel post with the credits for each song on your album and be sure to tag everyone who worked with you on it. This enables easy sharing, and will help get you in the Discovery tab.

- **Tag** – If you post a show announcement, a new song or some cool merch, encourage your fans to @tag friends that would want to know about your announcement.
- **Trailers** – Since Instagram allows you to post short videos, you should take advantage of this and post the 10-14 seconds that are the most interesting from every video you post on YouTube.
- **Personalize** – Instagram allows you to send private messages to your followers. This means for your supportive fans who buy a lot of merch, comment a lot or join your fan club, you can regularly send them pictures of what you are doing that other fans don't get. This can encourage them to keep spreading the word about your music.
- **Webstagram** - Don't want to do all of this from your phone? You can comment, heart, etc. all from your computer with Instagram's own website.
- **Scheduling** –Schedugram (app.schedugr.am), Planoly (planoly.com) and LaterGram (latergram.me) allow you to schedule Instagram posts.
- **Links** – Use LinkTree (linktr.ee) to make a link that allows multiple destinations (Spotify, YouTube, Apple Music to stream your latest single) when you link something in your bio.

Stories Let You Bond With Fans Who Want To Hear From You All The Time
One of the best parts of Instagram adding stories to their service is it allows oversharing to become less obtrusive. By keeping stories on their own clickable path it allows those who follow you and want to gain a deeper look at your life to do so. This allows you to keep important news and more exciting content in your main posts, while using stories to feed those who are hungry for your every move. Consider the balance between the two when you post as well as utilizing Instagrams multi-picture upload feature to keep your feed nimble while still keeping fans excited.

Here's how to do stories well:

- **Show Your Personality -** Filters, captions and other fun can allow your personality to come out. That's what your audience is here for so don't be shy.
- **You, Yourself -** Fans who care enough to watch your stories also want to see you. While many artists treat their Instagram feed as a

place where they are photographing the world around them, if there's one place to show yourself it's here.

- **Regular Posts** – Like much of the advice in this book, if you want to get the rewards of stories like your fans spreading the word about them, you need to do them on a consistent and sustained schedule.
- **A Look Deeper** – While you would never put the dullest moments of recording or setting up a show in your main feed, this is exactly what is great about stories. Your computer skipping on your newest song or being unable to get all the equipment in the van is exactly what people want to see here.
- **Polls** – Instagram allows you to poll your fans in your stories which can be great for set choices or figuring out which merch to sell.

Analytics

Since Instagram has many fans enthusiasm and is effective for communicating with your fans, their analytics are some of the most valuable you can see. In order to see your Insights, you need to upgrade to a business account in the setting and once you do you can gain valuable information on gender, age, as well as which posts perform best in order to hone in on what spreads with your audience.

Contests

Fans connecting with you on Instagram can raise awareness about your music. Encourage them by telling your fans whoever takes the best Instagram photograph of your show, and tags you in it, can get a free piece of merch after the show. Having them tag you will show all of their friends what they were missing by not coming to see you.

Scheduling Posts

Since Instagram is very closed off with letting other apps post for you it can be a pain in the neck to schedule posts. Planoly (planoly.com) allows you to plan in advance your Instagram posts and post them to Instagram.

Follow

If you want fans to follow you on Instagram, all you need to do is tell them to go to instagram.com/yourusername. This means you can make buttons and badges (instagram.com/accounts/badges) for your website and link them to your profile.

Turn.Audio

Turn.Audio is a fantastic free Instagram video maker that will take an mp3 of your song and it's album cover and make it into a Instagram optimized video for you to share with your fans. I regularly make these instead of single screen videos for songs since they are more visually striking. Take advantage of this great free tool.

Your Own Filter
One of the new parts of an album roll out today is to create a striking Instagram Filter that ties into the imagery of your record. Instagram allows anyone that can develop AR to put up their own filter and all you need to do is share it from your account and your fans can use it on their own.

Getting Your Lyrics To Match Your Song
If fans are posting your song it can be insanely annoying that they don't show the lyrics like all your favorite artists. To do this you need to add them on MusixMatch (musixmatch.com)

Stickers
If you want your fans to be able to use a sticker you have created you need to get a Giphy Branded Account (Giphy.com) which allows you to add them to Instagram.

Strategy
While there is no one size fits all strategy for any social media platform here's some ideas that I think work for most people.
- Look to post at least once a day to remind your followers to think about your music.
- Let's remember what's in the caption is often more important than the picture. Instead of making a blog update, an Instagram post can often say much more and be more effective in getting it to your answer and spread around the web. This is where emotional bonds are made.
- Remember Instagram is often mistaken as a place to show visually stunning images, but I find the posts that do the most for musicians are those where they use the comments to write about things that connect musicians to their fans emotionally.
- Let stories be less eventful things, but also remember you can make a post one day and put something similar in your story the next day to remind people of big events.

- While you shouldn't be posting in the feed more than once a day unless it is a really eventful day, feel free to overshare in stories since they are easily skipped.
- Making your own memes or sharing ones that will help resonate between you and your followers is an amazing way to bond and should be something you do regularly.

Let Snapchat Show Your Fans Your Life

Snapchat (snapchat.com) is a social network based on finding friends and message their usernames with pictures they can only see for 1 - 10 seconds. This can be great for sending your fans special and fun pictures that make them feel special. They can also tune into "stories" in your profile, which can document what you have been doing the past few days. If your fans are 13-25 years old and predominately female, Snapchat is *the* way to keep you in their thoughts. While Instagram is slowly, but surely taking their users away, the service still has millions of users actively looking to be entertained. This can be ideal on tour or while filming a video.

The worst part of Snapchat is that nothing is permanent. You aren't creating content that lasts and can be ingested by new fans. This can also be liberating for finding your voice. Anything you do will never be seen again a day later and you can see how fans react to you as you find your voice. To make matters worse, Instagram aping all of their features is sending their traffic to a quick death.

Here are a few other Snap Chat ideas:

- Send coupons for merch or the location of special events to Snap Chat followers.
- Send fans on a scavenger hunt for tickets you hide in a part of town and let whoever gets there first get a special prize.
- Show fans the fun, silly and interesting things you do.
- Show what your day is like through stories.
- Take a key from DJ Khaled and give advice and funny scenarios to entertain followers.

Strategy

Snapchat at this point is mostly used to take the filters and send them over to Instagram. But if you want to entertain the fans that are here think about repurposing your best Instagram content and syndicating it here.

Let TikTok Show Everyone Your Moves

If your fans are teenagers, you should be making content on TikTok. Much like Vine, the service is where people are going to make fun videos, but the difference is that you can use copyrighted content on this service as they have agreements with most PROs so you are able to use your music as content. While the clips are only 15-60 seconds you can do clips in succession in order to prolong your song being played out.

How To Do TikTok Right

- The venn diagram of what makes a good TikTok is to be visually performative while saying something that is also entertaining.
- Many musicians when they want to be informative about their latest song's subject or something in their life will do it in a ridiculous or overly performed way.
- You can run contests here, have your fans making content around your music as well as make your own.
- Create challenges where you can have your fans to do performative things that tie into your music videos and get your fans to reenact what you have done or do a stunt you are capable of.
- As well will discussed on Instagram you can use hashtag marketing.
- Localized content is great, TikTok users get a kick out of seeing people do things in places that are recognizable.
- Don't use your own music in every post. This is a great platform for boosting others!
- Remember mangling your songs for danceability can go great here. Many TikTok hits are making a song weird or dancey that doesn't fit that context. Lykke Li "Sex Money Feelings Die" was even re-released in a slowed down version after it became a TikTok hit.
- Use duets to collaborate with your friends in music to expose each other to one another's audiences.
- Use response videos when a musician you enjoy does something and you have a fun reply.

- Tik Tok videos can be shared on other platforms so feel free to spread them out, especially when they have received a good reaction.

TikTok For Artists – TikTok has a specific app for musicians to monitor their content on the app.

Chapter 30: Using Facebook To Raise Awareness

Unless you're living under a rock, you may have heard that Facebook is the largest social network on the Internet. When a social network has your grandmother updating her status on a daily basis, you need to do whatever it takes to make it work for you. Despite of Facebook's shortcomings, there are many ways to make it be a powerful tool in your social network presence.

Getting Started

Setting Up A Profile
It's no secret that Facebook isn't friendly to their users. The site's navigation facilities are different than most. In order to make a page for your music, you need to first make a personal profile, which you can hide from the world if you want no part of Facebook in your personal life. You then need to make a page for your music. On the right hand side you'll see a choice that says "Pages." (*Note: Facebook has changed this 4 times in the last 18 months, so please check our website for the latest information on making a page)* You now want to choose the "Artist," "Band" or "Public Figure" button and type in your group's name. There is no difference between a band and musician page, so choose what you feel best represents you.

Personal Profiles
While you may be tempted to make your personal profile your music profile, this isn't smart. You'll be capped at only 5,000 friends and unable to add music to your page. Facebook erases these profiles for spam regularly. Skip this idea.

Use your personal profile to grow fan relationships by accepting your fans' friend requests. Put all of your fans in a group, and you can keep the annoyances to a minimum and maintain whatever privacy you would like. It can make a fan's day to wish them a happy birthday on Facebook. These personal interactions only take a second but can be a moment that makes a fan happy for years.

534

Your Profile Picture

If no one knows who you are, use a picture or logo associated with your music. Don't use the picture of your drummer barfing all over a nightstand in Ohio. When potential fans are hanging out on Facebook, they will see friends becoming fans of your music in their news feed and have becoming your fan suggested to them. The more recognizable your photo is in that stream, the more likely they will recognize you and like you.

We hope you're a fan of your own music, so make yourself the first fan by clicking the like button next to your name up top. This will get added into your news feed and your friends will see that you now have a page for your music. Hopefully, they will add you. If you have your doubts, you may want to give them a nudge by sharing this like with them.

Your Cover Banner

Your cover photo is the large photo that goes on top of your Timeline page. Ideally, this is a high-resolution picture that looks good as a panoramic.

Cover Banner Tricks - Cover banners can have text. You can put your website address, tour dates and tons of other information in your cover photo. This gives all fans a clear view of whatever you're trying to promote at the time.

Call To Action

Facebook allows you to put a button of your cover banner that can direct fans to do what you would like them to do. Here are some examples:

- **Sign Up** – You can point fans to your free music page or somewhere where they can get an email for a track.
- **Watch Video** – Link to your latest video or an introduction video.
- **Shop Now** – Send fans to your merch page.

About

In this area, you have a chance to tell the world who you are. You can use either your one-paragraph bio or your two-sentence bio. If you use your two-sentence bio, you should also leave room to link your other social networks.

Extras

This space also has room for you to put lots of relevant info for fans, writers and potential team members. Many people know they can get relevant information here, so be sure to keep this area up-to-date. The following is some info you can fill in:

- **Biography** - Keep it short and speak to your fans, not the music business. This is for fans, so try to write something they would be interested in.
- **Website**
- **Genre**
- **Members** - Make sure you list names and instruments. Nicknames are fun too.
- **Record Label**
- **Description** - For some reason this is different than your biography. Have fun with it.
- **Hometown**
- **Current Location**
- **Artists We Also like**
- **General Manager** - Put your managers email address here. If you're self-managed include that info and a contact email.
- **Press Contact**
- **Booking Contact**

Username
Facebook allows you to set your Facebook URL. Choose a simple and easy to remember name, so that your URL will read facebook.com/YOURBANDNAME. This is very important because you want fans to remember it. Try to make it as close to your band name as possible and if it doesn't work out, add music to the end of your name.

If your desired URL is taken, there is an easy workaround. Go and buy a domain from your favorite provider such as www.<yourbandname>facebook.com and have it redirect to your Facebook page URL. You obviously want anyone who Googles your music to find a presentable page and this technique is a cheap way to make that happen.

Setting Admins For Other Band Members
If you're in a band or you have a manager, you'll probably want to allow those people access to edit your Facebook page. First, make sure anyone you want to be an admin likes your page. Once they're a fan, you can add them as an admin. They can now edit everything you can on the page.

Application List
536

The photo app can't be moved from the first position, but it isn't the end of the world. Photos are some of the most powerful tools you have and it pays to always keep them easy to find. You can order any of the other apps you have installed, as well as re-title them and change their default picture. It's smart to move your music player and tour dates to the left position and to choose wisely when picking which other tabs are visible to fans. You can also get a direct link to any Facebook tab by clicking this edit mode. This helps if you want to link fans directly to your music player or tour dates.

If you want to link your website, merch store or free-music page, you can do it with custom apps like Decor or My Tab. Simply search Facebook apps and use their easy to use interfaces.

Doing Facebook Right

Remember Facebook Is A Flawed Fan Communication Method
Perhaps you have seen a link on your Facebook timeline where your poor musician friend links to an article about how Facebook doesn't allow updates from pages to reach all of the people who have liked them. Unlike the links your Uncle posts from Fox News, this is actually true. Sadly, Facebook wants you to pay to "promote" your posts each time you post them. If you choose not to promote them, an average of 15% of those people who have liked your page will see each update. To make matters worse, the rumor is they plan to keep shrinking that number.

You may be thinking "Why on Earth would I try to get people to like my page then, if it's going to be so inefficient?" Well, because all of the social networks are inefficient; tweeters don't read every tweet, no one opens all of their "junk mail", etc. But this one feels particularly awful since Facebook does it intentionally and is trying to get you to pay a huge fee to interact with the fanbase you built. Regardless whether Facebook makes you pay to talk to your fans or not, even reaching that 15% can do big things to spread the word about your music. It's worth it to try to get likes for your page, but remember, email is always the best fan communication tool.

Unless your audience skews much older, I suggest putting minimal effort into Facebook since it does little to grow a fanbase. While you should answer fans comments and messages and post your news here since it may be where they see them – leaning into Facebook for marketing is not good use of your time.

Making A Timeline
While not the most exciting or interesting thing to do with your time, an actual timeline with event milestones can give fans and writers a sense of history and about your music. If fans don't bother looking through your Timeline history, it can be a waste of time setting it up. If you do want to go through with this, here are some ideas of what you can add:

- Formation
- Past Tours
- Member Changes
- Album and Single releases
- When you signed to your label

Making a picture that goes with each event can be enjoyable for fans. You can add text to the pictures and make them fun for fans to share. This can help your news feed as you add new milestones. If you add past milestones to your history, be sure not to share all of them in the news feed.

Making It Fun - If you're an act that has a knack for taking embarrassing pictures of one another, you can make your Timeline a load of fun. Make milestones that show your horrible haircut at an early rehearsal. Maybe your guitarist passed out naked on tour--be sure to blur the bad stuff out. All of these are fun milestones. You can have a sense of humor if that's your thing. Let your fans enjoy your laughs and make the most of this tool.

Fan Of The Month - Some musicians use these milestones to celebrate a fan every month (or even every week, but that makes it less special, right?). They make a graphic with a picture of the fan and it shows up as a searchable milestone that fans will share amongst their friends.

What To Post About
You should keep your Facebook a little less personal and definitely less prolific than your Twitter or Tumblr feeds. As many social media nerds have written, Facebook users have grown weary of too much clutter. This means posting less frequently is crucial to keeping you from getting hidden and to making sure fans stay updated on your news. Facebook should be

fun, but most of your updates should be infrequent and with the intention of keeping fans informed.

- **News** - Facebook is the social network where you should almost always filter out the self-indulgent posts. Only post your news and exceptional updates, such as releasing a new song or tour dates. You can even audition posts on Twitter and Tumblr. If they do really well, post them on Facebook. Keep posts about clutter and the view from your van on your other social networks.
- **Behind The Scenes** - Pictures and quick stories are great ways to get fans excited. As long as these updates are occasional and not the majority of what you post on Facebook, you'll stay in your fans' news feed and avoid the dreaded Hide button.
- **Crowdsource** - Ask fans to reply in comments about input on set lists, where to play and which musicians you should check out. Fans love this and will feel like they're a part of what you do.
- **Pictures** - Individually post any exciting pictures you have into your pictures section and remember to trickle out different pictures of a recent event over days at a time.
- **Questions** - Asking for a quick opinion from your fans or even a simple "yes or no" answer to a question can do wonders for getting fans commenting and interacting with you.

Captioned Pictures - One of the most powerful ways to get fans to share your pictures is to make them text pictures. Pictures with quotes are one of the most shared type of Facebook posts and it's easy to use this to your advantage and turn your content into a meme.

First, find a great picture of you from a live show or a press shot. Next, find a great quote. This can be a popular lyric, a line from an interview or text from your bio. Go into your favorite photo editing software and write your quote on the picture in a cool font that matches the mood of your quote. Be sure to use the quote as the picture's caption too.

Finally, put your name and web address at the bottom of the photo. Make it part of the image but out of the way. Post the picture in your news feed and ask your fans to share it. Watch your message spread and new fans be introduced to your music.

Flyers - Flyers are not dead. If you can make a great flyer that fans love and post an image of it on Facebook, it will only spread farther. Encourage fans to hit the Share button if they like the flyer.

Ask Questions With A Poll - Facebook gives you the ability to ask questions of fans and allows them to hit a button to choose their answer. Simply click the "+" button where you select the type of update you're going to post. You can use this to poll fans on a fan-picked setlist, choose your album title or simply make conversation. Questions are show up in fan's timeline, making it easy for fans to share the poll. This can help you gain insight, have fun, bond with fans and get the word spread about your music.

Steal From The Thieves - One of the very best things you can do is like media outlets like Vice, Huffington Post, Vox, etc. and watch how they use Facebook. These outlets throw piles of money at learning the most effective ways to use Facebook posts.

Digest Posts
When you post an update, it should be about more than a single subject. Say you're promoting a new song, T-shirt and a show on Friday. You've already posted about all three of them this week but want one last post to drive it home. Simply post something like this:

"Did you guys hear our new song yet? Awesome! We'll be playing it and selling our new T-shirt at our show Friday at The Elks Lodge In Freakerstown"

You can link where to get the song and shirt in the post's comments but keep the update concise. You could even link to a blog post that has information on all three, so fans can find everything they need in one place.

Scheduled Updates
Many people don't have the time or patience to sit in front of a computer and make sure their news gets posted numerous times a day. Thankfully, Facebook now allows you to schedule posts so you can get all of your social media updating done at once, when you have the time (HootSuite and TweetDeck have long allowed this feature). Simply click the clock under your post and it will appear when you want it to.

Facebook Pages App

540

Facebook has a neat app you can download to your iOS or Android device that allows you to see who is talking about you and interact with fans. It provides thorough analytics and makes it easy to look after your presence on Facebook. (facebook.com/about/mentions)

Geo-Target Your Show Posts To Not Clog Up The News Feed
It can get pretty annoying for your West Coast fans to be bombarded with updates about your shows in Brooklyn three times a day. Facebook has a way for you to target your updates so that only fans in select geographical areas will be able to see them. Simply click the little globe sitting under your Facebook update. This will dramatically cut down on how often you're hidden from fans' news feed or unliked by them.

How Often Do I Post?
Here are some general guidelines for how often you should post:

- **Daily** - You should post once a day. If you don't have a lot going on, you can make that once a day only five days a week.
- **Twice A Day** - It's totally acceptable to post twice a day, as long as you keep the posts more than five hours apart.
- **Seven Times A Week** - In general musicians have the most success if they post around seven times a week. This means either once a day, every day, or more than once some days, while abstaining from posting on other days. You can go over seven posts a week when you have big news, but in general seven is a good goal.
- **Nights And Weekends** - Posting between 8 p.m. and 8 a.m. can be very successful for some musicians with night-owl fans. Experiment with posting at various times of the day and night and watch the reach of each post to figure out when is effective for you.

Don't Get Lost
The average Facebook post has a lifespan of about three hours. Even worse, it's estimated that only 10 to 15 percent of your fans will see each post, and only one percent will like it. Facebook has enough posts that yours could either be pushed down the timeline immediately or their weird algorithm will hide it from the news feed before the overwhelming majority of your fans will ever get the chance to see it. This can mean posting big news twice, at different times of the day, is helpful. Contrary to our prior limited posting rule, big news every month or two is an exception. All fans

don't check Facebook at the same time, so there is a lot of potential to get lost.

So how do you make sure your fans don't feel spammed? One way is by posting the same news in different ways. First, post a link to your website. Second, link to a blog who picked up the news. The third time, perhaps the next day, post a reminder with a new message. The fourth time maybe make another post to your website. Remember, Facebook allows 10-20% more fans to see posts with no link or text, so just communicating with your fans can keep you on their mind and also shows how hopeful it is to not always be promoting your music and create genuine bonds.

Most users don't check Facebook at the same time every day, so making sure big news gets posted at various times can really help make sure your message reaches fans. However, if it's just a simple update to show you're alive or a fun musing about life for die-hard fans, there is no need to drive the point home numerous times.

What Not To Post About
Getting hidden or unliked is the death of your relationship with a fan. Here are some rules to help you avoid that death:

- **Constantly Asking For Favors** - Fans will get really tired if only ask for favors and never give anything in return. They like you for what you give, not for being a beggar. If all you're ever doing is asking them to come to shows, vote for you or to check something out, your relationship will be very one-sided.
- **Anticipation Posts** - Giving fans a warning that an event is happening tomorrow is great. Writing a countdown for 10 days till you premiere your new video is only for musicians with thousands of mega fans. If you're not one, you're just asking to be hidden from your fans' news feed.
- **Posts About Boredom** - Facebook is the last place where you want to talk about the little things. Use it for your most exceptional updates and you won't lose the attention of those who have liked you.

Using Facebook Event Invites
Event invites are one of the most powerful ways to alert fans and potential fans about what you're doing. There are many tricks to doing event invites successfully. This is important because if you annoy your fans, they can

block themselves from ever getting your event invites in the future. Every show or event you play should have an event invite that you share in your timeline.

A few tips to making your event invites successful:

- **Be Informative** - Include as much information about the event as possible, including contact numbers and emails. The more information there is, the more likely you'll have good attendance.
- **Map** - Make sure you include a map. Many fans assume there will be a map. If they get in the car and all of a sudden they can't find the show, you lose out on paying fans.
- **A Great Flyer** - Flyers are not dead. Making a great flyer will get your event shared all the more. You can alternate between posting the event and the flyer picture on your wall.
- **One Event** - It's important you make one event and then assign hosts for each band and the promoter of the event. Potential attendees will see that it's going to be big event that lots of people are invited or going to.
- **Geo-target** - You can choose to only invite friends who live near where the event is happening. You can even choose to only share the event with them. This will make sure you don't get your event invites blocked from fans not in the area.
- **Videos** - Post YouTube videos of every band you're playing with in the comments section and write something nice about each of them. Not only does it show what a nice person you are, it can excite undecided fans about the show. It also puts you in the good graces of the other musicians you're playing with, before you've even played together.

Other Events - You can also make events for album and single releases. It's important not to do this often since your fans will likely block you, especially if lots of fans are posting comments inside the event's wall.

Don't Betray Your Relationships - If you don't strictly target your invites, they will most likely be largely ignored as more friends begin to block you. If you betray your relationship with fans by constantly inviting friends who live nowhere near your event or making up fake events, you're sure to get blocked and lose the chance to interact with a fan. If your events have lots of comments or if you're constantly updating the reminders, you can drive your fans insane.

543

Events Subscribe – Facebook has added a tab on your page where fans can subscribe to hear anytime you have an event near them. Periodically encourage your fans to click this feature so they are alerted when you play close by.

Facebook Groups Are The New Message Boards

If you have ever been to Musformation's message board, you know we use a Facebook group to power it. The Facebook groups we use have a way of keeping their members engaged and constantly reminded of their content. Former MusforMGMT group Man Overboard's bulletin board got to be too much of a mess to administer. I made the Defend Pop Punk group on Facebook, and it proved to be a success that gives 30,000 members a place to bond over the music they love. It also gave the band a place to post news that reached tons of fans that may have never subscribed to our other social networks.

The message board can be a great marketing tool that brings in new listeners. It allows fans to meet like-minded individuals and keeps them in a place discussing your music. Best of all, Facebook posts these updates in users' news feed to remind members what's going on in the group. These groups are also how you find community, doing a search for your genre of music is often where influencers, DJs, writers and others who make moves in your genre congregate and find out about new artists.

How To Get More Facebook Likes

A few ideas to get more likes to your Facebook Page:

- **Invite** - From your personal page you can invite all of your friends to like your page. This is a great place to start since they are your friends, right? Simply click the Build Your Audience tab and every few months you can invite your Facebook friends to like your page.
- **Trade Likes With Other Facebook Pages** - Your Facebook page will display five of the pages you have liked. This means you can help your musician friends out by Liking their page. Trade this like with a friend's band and enjoy the free advertising as their fans see this recommendation.
- **Support Other Musicians, Have Them Support You** - Posting an update when your musician friends do something important builds a community and can help encourage them to do the same for you.

Fans take the recommendation of their favorite musicians very seriously; so make sure to help each other.

- **Encourage** - When a fan takes the time to make a nice comment, the least you can do is click the like button on their comment, if not take the time to write back. The more you give to fans, the more they will give back to you, usually by telling their friends about your band.
- **Link** - Make sure your Facebook address is on your other social networks, in the about section on all of your YouTube videos, etc.
- **Like Box** - Facebook has a great tool where you can post a Like Box widget onto your website. This widget allows any fan signed into Facebook to like you with one click.
- **Make Sharable Content** - Upload pictures and videos that fans will want to share.. Make sure that when you post this content that the photos and their captions are clear and able to be seen in a feed.

Use Your Other Contacts To Get Likes On Your Facebook Page - Under the tab that says, "Build Your Audience," there's an option to invite friends by email. You can use this function to invite friends directly from your Skype, Apple Mail, ICQ, Microsoft Outlook and iCloud contacts. You can also hack this system to export your mailing list from your provider into Microsoft Outlook or your Apple Mail address book, which is totally free with any Mac, and then add them to this address book. This will invite everyone on your mailing list to like your Facebook page.

How To Make Your Facebook Message Grow
- **Acknowledge** – When fans say nice things about you in the comments click like on their posts.
- **@Tag** – Encourage fans to tag friends who would want to know about your show or new song to @tag their friends in the comments.
- **Share** – Click share on the main announcement from your music page. Share on your personal timelines, in Facebook groups or any other pages you manage.

What To Not Do
- **Spam Other Musicians' Walls** - While this may seem like a great idea, Timeline has minimized the comments on the wall so they're much less visible. There are many more effective promotions you could be doing in the time it takes to spam another musician's wall.

545

- **Post Too Much** - While your posts may disappear from the Timeline, that doesn't mean you always need to be there. Getting hidden and unliked is a lost opportunity you can't regain.
- **Pay For Likes** - There are lots of sites that will get you fake followers. This does nothing for you. If you think it's impressing potential members of your team, you're wrong. Nearly everyone can tell the difference between fake fans and engaged fans.

Put Your Latest Set List In Your Player To Make Gigs Better
If you want fans to participate at shows and increase attendance, you simply need to make the experience more enjoyable for them. Fans enjoy shows more when they know all your songs. Stream the songs you're going to play in your live set from your Facebook player and on your website too. Then make an easy post like this:

"Hey Everyone, Most of the songs we'll be playing at our show on the 23rd are now on our Facebook player. Learn them, sing along and let's have a good time."

You can also do this on your event page. Fans will get to know your material better, become engaged and enjoy your shows more.

Do Not Send Important Messages Over Facebook
A little known fact about Facebook is it has a secret spam filter that destroys thousands of business opportunities every day. To see what I mean, click the Messages button. Now look at that button on the left that appears that say "Other." That contains all the messages Facebook thinks are spam. Facebook will classify most messages not from your friends as spam. What's worse is they don't let the sender know they're doing this.

Too many connections are lost to this box every single day. When you want to send someone a message or an introduction, do it over email. Look at the person's profile or their music page and see if an email is listed. If not try their website. Avoid the trap that is Facebook spam unless you really have no other choice.

Also remember that every page you have on Facebook has an inbox, as does your personal profile. Be sure to keep up with both inboxes, because many important messages will come to both of these boxes even though they really shouldn't.

546

Facebook Apps For Your Page

Once upon a time Facebook would be a place you would go to listen to a band's music for the first time. Thankfully, those days are gone and you now get paid when someone does that on a streaming site. With that said there are some apps you can still use to curate your Facebook page to make it a better experience for your fans.

Videos
The way we now show fans the music you have is to upload the videos you put on YouTube to Facebook and they live under a videos tab. Facebook promotes videos uploaded to their platform more than YouTube links so it's especially helpful to upload them here until you have a sizable fanbase and need to employ a more complex strategy.

Show Listings On Facebook
It's very important to list your tour dates on Facebook, and these apps offer a way to showcase them. Have a separate link for tour date listings and keep them in sync with their respective services.

- **SongKick** - SongKick has a great app that allows you to list show dates with a banner image and the website's usual feature set. (songkick.com)
- **BandsInTown** - If you use BandsInTown for your concert date listing, it will stay in sync with the BandsInTown Facebook app. (bandsintown.com)

Facebook Creator
Facebook has their own app that can help you do marketing and video content including live videos for your pages. This app has streamlined features to help you market yourself better that cater to creatives like musicians.

Use Facebook Insights To Optimize Your Promotions

One of the coolest features of Facebook is that it allows you to see if you're actually doing a good job promoting your music. These insights give you valuable information about your fanbase and can teach you how to improve promotions.

Likes
Under the likes tab, you can see the number of likes and unlikes you're receiving. Use this to determine if your promotions are working or if you're just annoying your fans. If your likes are going up, you know you're doing a good job. If they aren't, perhaps your promotion strategies need to be refined.

Keep in mind that unlikes are going to happen. Getting an unlike for every 20 likes is common and not something you need to be losing sleep over.

You can also see where your likes are coming from. If you have a Like Box on your website and you receive a lot of traffic there, the website should be one of your top-ranking sources. It can also show you if fans are recommending you to other people.

Age/Gender/Location Check
You can see your fans' age, gender and location. Use this to determine who you should be targeting with your Facebook ads. Know if you should be making all-ages shows a big part of your tours. Knowing the gender distribution of your fans will tell you which gender to gear more merch toward. Checking fan locations makes it easy for you to see where you should be touring. Make sure your tours hit the top cities and countries on this list. You can break these demographics down by both who has liked your page and who is constantly posting about you.

Posts
Facebook makes it easy to see a ranking of your most effective posts. These analytics will show you what type of language works best with fans. You can also see what days of the week and times of day get the best reaction from your fans. Every post says how many people viewed it along the bottom. Use this information to figure out when the best times to post will be.

Strategy
Facebook at one time was an amazing opportunity to grow a fanbase but now it is best served as a necessary supplement to your promotions.
- The greatest exploit right now on Facebook is groups are where many artists communities are now built. There are so many groups

where artists find their early fanbases and teams and your time spent on Facebook is best spent interacting in the ones you belong in.

- I would only post major announcements and your best performing social media posts from other platforms onto Facebook.
- While it is totally exploitive it is often worth the ROI to put some advertising money onto big announcements you want to make sure all of your fans see. Doing this every 1-3 months can be helpful to make sure your fans see what you're doing, especially after your fanbase exceeds 10k or more.
- Remember unless you are regularly getting over 50,000 plays on your videos to also upload every video to Facebook. The platform gives preference and increases the reach of your posts when you post them there instead of a YouTube link. While this drives down your YouTube views, this is a necessary evil to employ until your YouTube views matter when you are going out for larger tours.

Chapter 31: Building Relationships With Twitter

Once thought of as an over-hyped trend, Twitter has proven itself to be a potentially life-changing technology and valuable communication tool for musicians. It has broken down many of the walls between fans and the musicians they love and given fans a direct source for band information and communication. For musicians without a fanbase, it's created a direct line to build relationships with fans.

Here are some reasons why you should be on Twitter already:

- Your fans and potential fans are there waiting for you.
- It's a fast and easy way to tell your fans what you're up to.
- It's one of the best tools for building relationships with your fans.
- It's a fantastic way to bond with fans, other musicians and potential team members.

Twitter Is like A Party
When thinking about how to behave on Twitter, think of it like a party. Who do you want to be around at the party? Naturally, you want to be around the interesting people who are social, having fun and actually participating in the party. The people who don't use Twitter a lot are the people who are already passed out on the couch. Why even bother with them? They're going to be no fun at all. Instead, focus on interacting with the people who are participating in the party, people with whom you have things in common. Interact with all of the fun and interesting people and let the annoying, boring people do their own thing.

Just like at any party, there are people acting like idiots and doing all sorts of dumb things on Twitter, but you don't have to hang out with them. Once in a while the annoying people will fall into your line of sight or even get in your face, but all you need to do is ignore and avoid them and keep having a good time. Find people who you have something to talk about with and you form a beneficial relationship.

Getting Started

Now that I've got your attention, sign up for Twitter (twitter.com). Here is what you need to get started:

- **Name** - Choose a name that tells the world who you are. Fans are going to search for you on here so make sure it's a name they will search for.
- **Profile** - Fill out your profile using a 160-character description. That short two-sentence bio you worked on before will come in handy right now.
- **Picture** - Put up a picture. A lot of musicians use their current album cover or logo. Press pictures are often tough to decipher if you're a band, so skip those unless you're a solo artist.
- **Cover Photo** - Upload a cover photo. Your Facebook cover photo may work if none of the text in it clashes with the text Twitter puts over your banner.
- **Website** - Be sure to list your website so people can hear your music.
- **Private** - Don't make your account private or else fans won't be able to retweet you and will have a difficult time following you.

Design Your Own Twitter Background
You can choose your own background image for your Twitter profile. Use a large, high-resolution picture that looks great in a full-screen view. Press photos, logos and album covers all work really well, just make sure they're large and high-resolution. You can also put all of your social network information and a bio on the sides of the background. This trick can drastically improve your chances of getting Twitter followers to check out your other pages. Twitter users with larger monitors can see this and will learn where else to follow you.

An easy site to make a design like this with is Free Twitter Designer. Its easy-to-use interface can get you a great Twitter background with legible URLs in minutes. (freetwitterdesigner.com)

Here is what you can link in your sidebar:

- **Free Music Page** - Give bored Twitter users an easy way to hear and get your music.
- **Your Website** - Where you ultimately want fans to go.
- **Facebook**

- **SoundCloud**
- **Merch Store**

Pin An Informative Tweet

When potential fans arrive on your page, the first tweet they see is will help them decide whether they follow you or not. Twitter allows you to pin a tweet so that it is the first tweet people see when they arrive on your page. This is a great time to advertise your newest release, campaign or a funny tweet that shows off your personality.

Use An Animated GIF To Grab Attention

You can use an animated GIF as your profile avatar and grab attention in the Twitter timeline. This can help you stand out in the timeline and afford you some attention you may not otherwise get. Find a cool image to cycle through and you'll stand out from the pack when you show up in potential fans timeline.

Get Some Friends

Next, you need some friends. When you join up, Twitter will suggest you become friends with a bunch of people like Fred Durst. Most likely, you don't want to be friends with Fred Durst--not that he's a bad guy or anything. In order to become friends with a user click "Follow" on their profile. Here is a list of everyone I suggest you start following:

- **@musformation** - See every time we update a post. We also retweet deals and big news from other sites.
- **@sensualh** - Todd's band. He keeps it tight and minimal. He always shows the utmost taste in posting just the right amount of news and insight.
- **@jessecannon** - I have two twitter feeds: a personal one (@jessecannon) where I post about my life and politics and the @foundsoundation one, where I only post about music. You can do the same thing if you don't want to bore fans with tweets they may not be interested in. I know most of my followers only want to hear my thoughts on music, not my thoughts on Chris Christie.
- **@hypebot** - Daily music business news.
- **@musically** - More great music business news.
- **@buzzsonic** - The best music business links on Twitter.
- **@pitchfork** - Whether you love them or hate them, they're constantly tweeting which musicians are doing the latest and most

interesting marketing techniques or cutting edge videos. Great for inspiration, no matter what.

- **@wfmu** - Tweets out some of the best musical oddities in the business.

You can also import contacts from your email address book into Twitter at any time or find all of your fans by clicking "Find People" and then "Find on Other Networks". After you've added fans, make sure your Twitter account is linked on your website and all of your other social networks.

Next, start to find your own friends on Twitter. Look up musicians you've played with, your friends' bands, friends in the industry, musicians you respect, superfans, etc. This should get you started. As fans see your profile, they will add you.

You can also see if anyone has already posted about you by searching Twitter for your name (twitter.com/search). If anyone is writing about you, be sure to follow them, thank them and interact with them.

Doing Twitter Right

What Do You Post About?
As you spend time on Twitter, you'll start to notice the tone everyone uses to interact. Spend time reading and picking up on what you should be doing. As you get it together remember these things:

- **Personality** - Show your personality; talk about what makes you unique, show something awesome you found on the Internet. Show your followers what you're interested in. If you're a big science fiction geek, it can be great to post links to telescopes and whatever else you nerds tend to like.
- **Extraordinary** - When you see something you think is great, show your fans. Found a new YouTube video of cats crawling on couches? Great! Read an article that really blew your mind? It will probably blow your fans' minds too.
- **Music** - Tell your followers what you're listening to. This is one of the quickest ways to bond with fans, because you all love music and fans are curious to know which bands the musicians they love are listening to.

- **News Feed** - Don't forget that you want this to be a place where fans can go to find out your news. While Twitter is great for showing personality and building relationships, your goal at the end of the day is to make sure fans stay updated on your news.
- **Show Announcements** - Announce your events. You can even have fun and announce when you're in town by making jokes or observations about the town. Tweet incrementally, announcing each show, but don't overdo it. Tweet about each show no more than four times.
- **Observe** - Look at what other musicians are tweeting. Twitter is always evolving, as are the ways people use it. Find and follow musicians you like and learn the smart things they do on Twitter.
- **Interact** - Write @replies to fans and thank them, converse with them and be yourself. Twitter is great for growing your bonds with fans. Make sure you aren't sending @replies out to your whole feed by starting the tweet with the Twitter handle (@theirname) you're replying to.
- **Crowdsource** - Twitter is a great place to crowdsource and ask questions. Get opinions from fans and make them feel like they're a part of your process.
- **Threads** – If you want to rant or share something personal that's long, try doing a thread by replying to your previous post. Twitter has made these easily sharable or you can use a service like Storify (storify.com) to collect it easily.
- **Special Treatment** - Give your followers special benefits. You can create discount codes for merch or run contests that only followers qualify for.
- **Find Collaborators** - Deadmau5 gave a musician his big break after searching for a collaborator on Twitter. You can use Twitter to find others to work with.
- **Ask** - If you ask fans to retweet your important message, many will oblige you and help.
- **Help** - Need a place to stay on the road or to know which bar is open all night? Twitter can help.
- **Guide** - Your fans will look to you for advice and support. Your lyrics may resonate with them and they'll search you out for comfort. Groups like Passion Pit, who often sing about issues such as mental illness, reach out to fans going through similar problems and advise them on getting help.

- **Educate** - If you are knowledgeable about music history within your genre, show fans where the roots of the music they loves comes from.
- **Phenomenomize** - Do you have a crazy prop, mascot or picture fans can take pictures with? Encourage them to tweet pictures of this so fans' friends hear about your music.
- **#FollowFriday** - Aka #FF is a way to tell your followers who you think they should follow each week. This hashtag is a popular way to give thanks and spread the message about people you like every Friday. Simply tweet some @names for your followers to check out and #FF each Friday.
- **#MusicMonday** - Music Monday is a great way to spread the word about the music you love and bond with fans every week. Simply use the hashtag on your post and tweet a link to some music.
- **#ThrowbackThursday** - This tag is a great way to remind your fans of something that happened in the past. Want to promote an old album or video or just make your followers laugh with a picture of you from you were younger? This is how to make it relevant.

Retweet Your Bad Press And Have Fans Come To Your Defense
Twitter is where your gang lives. Your gang stands by you and will help defend you. While it seems weird to call attention to someone who cries for attention by saying bad things about you, you can shame these trolls by having your fans come to your defense. This also makes your fans feel like a part of what you do. Whenever someone makes a ridiculous or stupid comment on the musicians I work with, I tweet it out so that the musician's fans can set them straight. This reinforces the musician's bonds with fans and also shows you have the confidence and humility to take others' criticism.

Getting Your Tweets To Spread A Bit More
While none of these things will make huge differences for your tweets spreading in the span of a single tweet—over time using some smart techniques can get you way more Re-tweets and have your content spread.
- **Afternoon** – Most Re-Tweeting happens in the afternoon, towards the end of the day and after school is out.
- **Pictures** – Use Twitter's picture system as well as a link and your content will catch more eyes.
- **Link** – When you add links to tweets, work them into your text instead of putting them at the end.

- **Tag Others** - @tagging others that involved with your tweet reminds them to re-tweet it.

What To Not Post About?
There are some updates that you don't need to post on Twitter:

- **Oversharing** - Some tweeters will tell you every time they eat breakfast. While this may be all you're thinking about, it also gets old fast and can cause you to quickly lose followers. Tell your followers something extraordinary and interesting, not how mundane, average or boring your life is. Twitter isn't meant to be a place where you express how you feel at regulated intervals. Even Justin Bieber's fans don't need that type of update and they're some of the most rabid fans on Twitter. Twitter is a place to build relationships by talking about something interesting, and it's not interesting that your pet rabbit just moved six inches.
- **Fights** - A lot of beginners on Twitter think it's a great idea to start fights to get attention. Trust me, this doesn't work. If you do feel passionate about trash-talking someone else, do it for legitimate reasons, but know that it's probably not going to make you more popular on Twitter in the long run.
- **Over-Indulged Interests** - If you tweet every time a sports team scores or a politician says something dumb (these both happen at about the same frequency), you'll lose followers. Odds are most of your fans are not watching that game or that speech and weren't following you to hear your commentary on it anyway. A tweet on these subjects here and there shows some personality. Fifteen tweets in a row about how much a coach sucks will get you a swift unfollow.
- **Inside Jokes** - An inside joke here and there is great, but if the only thing you ever tweet about is a joke that 95 percent of your audience doesn't get, 95 percent of your audience is going to be annoyed and want to unfollow you.

Do Not Spam
Twitter takes spam very seriously and next to every tweet there's a button to report spam. If you get reported more than once, that's the end of all your hard work. Instead of carpet-bombing tweets at potential fans asking them to listen to your music with a spammy message, cater each message to the user to introduce them to your music. Better yet, don't even ask a follower to check you out until you've had a meaningful interaction with

them and there's a seamless way to work it in. This isn't a self-promotion forum. This is a place where you need to participate in the community to get ahead.

The Party

Let's take Twitter back to this party analogy. You don't want to be the person at the party who talks too much, says dumb things all the time and annoys everyone. This is a great party, don't ruin it for everyone. If you're the person who is cool, fun and interesting, others at the party will talk to you, retweet you and tell others how cool you are. If you're lame and annoy everyone, the party will move to another room to get away from you.

As well, you don't need to do anything you find to be lame. If you don't want to use every little social media trick in this book, you don't have to. Lorde famously told her label's social media people that if she used #hashtags she would alienate her audience. She instead tweets her real emotions and is barely self-promotional. And plenty of other smaller artists make bonds with new fans by just tweeting what they are passionate about. Remember, people at the party like you if you act like yourself and find a commonality with one another. Don't pretend to be something you are not, look around Twitter and find the language and technology you feel comfortable with using.

People often leave a party because they find the crowd lame, usually because they didn't give the party a chance. One of the biggest reasons people leave Twitter is they follow idiots or people they don't have commonality with. Do your best to find people who don't just write about their cat and their lunch. There's plenty of people here interested in what you are. It can be an amazingly fulfilling medium, you may have to put some effort in and walk around the party to find those who you bond with. It never ceases to amaze me how much people can get out of Twitter if they search out likeminded people and join a vibrant and supportive community.

You Can Have a Personal Twitter Too

Twitter can be really fun. Sometimes you may want to say things that will cost you followers. Don't worry, there is a solution. You can also set up a personal Twitter, that isn't the one you use to promote your music. Plenty of musicians have a Twitter they use to tweet about their personal life and all sorts of over-indulgent nonsense that only their friends, family and die-hard fans care about. You can even occasionally retweet your personal account from your music account and vice versa to get both more followers.

Interacting

While it's important that fans don't unfollow you, it's also important that you build relationships and connect with fans. How? Here are some tips:

- **@reply** - Use the @twitteruser terminology and click reply to friends' tweets. Discuss things, talk about last night's show, share similar experiences. This will keep the message out of the news feed of users who don't follow the user you're talking to. If your followers also follow the person you're @replying to, then they'll see it and possibly join the conversation.
- **Favorites** - Twitter gives users the ability to favorite any tweet. This is a great way to show your fans you appreciate when they write about you. Whenever you see a fan write about you, favorite it, so they're encouraged to keep talking about you without having to share it with the world. You can also favorite good tweets you read from fans that follow your targets so they can see that you exist and appreciate what they say. Favoriting tweets you like, agree with or find funny is a great way to endear yourself to a Twitter user and begin a relationship with them.
- **Community** - Support and help the other musicians you're friends with or enjoy. Retweet their tweets when you want to help them. Your audience appreciates seeing your community as long as you do it in moderation. Converse with other musicians and have fun. Your mutual fans will appreciate it.
- **Crowdsource** - Use Twitter as a place to learn. Ask questions publicly and retweet the best replies so everyone can see the answer!
- **Include** - If you don't know which song should get cut from your set list on your next tour, why not ask your fans? This helps fans feel included and a part of something, as well as giving you an answer that will make sure they're happier at your next show.
- **Direct Message** - Remember, if you have something to say that isn't for the public's eye, be sure to say it on Twitter the correct way. Use the 'direct message' function for anything the public shouldn't see. I once leaked private information regarding an unannounced band recording to the Internet when I @replied to a band member and gave away their secret (Google "Anthony Weiner" if you want to see how this can really go wrong). Don't let

this happen to you. Keep anything private in direct messages only or off of Twitter entirely.

Using Twitter To Seem Like The Most Caring Touring Musician On Earth

You know what's a great feeling? Seeing your fans tweet about how great you were after you play a show. Even better is seeing a fan tweeting how much they're looking forward to seeing you at your tour date in their town. While this feels great for you, you can make the fan feel even better with a little effort that you can do right from your tour van.

Whenever you see a fan tweet about a show you played, simply go into your Twitter client and make a new "Private List." Add each fan to a list for the city they're from. The next time you're rolling through town, take the time to tweet or direct message the fans a few days before the show. Not only will they be amazed that you acknowledged them, your show turnout and their passion for your band will increase. Seconds of boring work in the van every day can yield high returns.

Courtesy

When you meet someone or play a show with a musician you liked, reach out on Twitter and say something nice about this person to your followers. For example, if you played with a great band, tweet "We played with an awesome band of soft rockers called @greatsoftrockband. Check them out!" When you meet someone, get their Twitter handle and do the same, especially the fans who do favors for you. It's the modern way of texting someone to say you had a good time. They will usually retweet and return the favor, helping both of you get more exposure.

Enable Community

Giving a way for fans to meet other fans and bond with them is using Twitter on a professional level. If you can introduce one fan to another or lead discussions on subjects, you'll be rewarded with many more fans. Use #hashtags to assemble tweets and lead discussions amongst fans. If you ask a question to your fans, retweet the best answers. Twitter is a place where you can bring fans together on fun subjects like Team Edward or Team Jacob, or any other crucial questions that plague pop culture. Musicians are finding better ways to build a community through Twitter every day.

How Often Should You Tweet?

Tweet when you have something interesting to say. Some say you should tweet every 24 hours. Twitter even has a nudge feature where the website will text you if you haven't Tweeted in 24 hours. If you only tweet when you have something spectacular to say, you'll probably never bore or annoy your followers. At minimum, Tweet news or remind fans you're alive at least once a week. Tweet more than a dozen tweets per day, however and it starts to become a bit too much.

When Should You Tweet?
Every musician will have different times when their message is best received. Their fans may be night owls, after-school readers or the type who read Twitter at work all day. The service Tweriod (twheriod.com) will tell you when your fans are online, so you can plan your tweets accordingly. You can also experiment. Some musicians have great luck starting conversations with their nerdy friends who are home on Friday nights. Others will have the best luck on Monday mornings when their corporate drone fans are bored and procrastinating at work. Experiment and take note of when your tweets get the best reaction.

Once you figure out the best time to Tweet, you can use services like HootSuite and TweetDeck to schedule when your tweets go out then.

Follow And Lead
You should try to follow everyone who follows you. Be aware that this isn't Facebook or Myspace where everyone you follow automatically follows you in return. If you follow your followers, you end up on their followers lists, which their friends look at instead of paying attention in class. This can get you more followers and visitors.

It also enables you to see what your fans are talking about, so you can build relationships with them. When they tweet something and you reply it can create a friendship. You can build on these relationships with simple interactions like discussing favorite movies, food or opinions on current events. If you have a good sense of humor, make fans laugh their way into discovering your music.

If some fans are too annoying to follow, use the Mute function on most Twitter apps to ignore them, but not be bothered by their frivolous tweets.

Twitter Tools For Building A Following

HashTags - How To Use Them Properly

Hashtags are the most misused tools on social media. Contrary to popular belief, they're not used to express extra intent, #idiots. They're not meant to say what you're actually thinking, #youfools. They're actually a smart way to sort all of the tweets on Twitter, so everyone following a subject can do so easily. For example, at the SXSW festival, attendees looking for a happening party or the leak of a super-secret event can search #SXSW to find this information out quickly. If you're playing a surprise show at 4 a.m. and you have a mounted Twitter army, you could get a greater turnout by flooding this channel with news of the event. This is a crucial skill at music festivals or industry events.

Hashtags can also help you get on the front page of Twitter via their Trends chart. When there is a spike in a topic or #hashtag, it will show up on the chart as Trending. Twitter is kind enough to provide a short explanation of what each hashtag means at the top of all searches that begin to trend. While it's not easy, some musicians try to gain extra exposure by getting their fans to tweet hashtags of their song name. If this works, you can see great exposure (it takes thousands upon thousands of users tweeting this hashtag in a given hour to get you anywhere near the front page of Twitter).

Participate - Look at which hashtags are trending and try your hand at writing a popular tweet in this hashtag. For example, if you see that #kanyekimbabynames is trending and you think you have something funny to say, post the tweet. If you get retweeted by a lot of users, you could see a huge spike in followers.

Twitter Analytics

In 2015 Twitter came out with free, in-depth analytics for all users. These analytics allow you to take a look at your growth and make helpful analysis of how Twitter can work better for you. (analytics.twitter.com) There's also FollowerWonk which can give you deeper understanding of your audience (moz.com/followerwonk)

Twitter Search

Twitter Search (twitter.com/search) allows you to see who's tweeting about you. Searching for your name or other words associated with your music will let you see what fans, writers and even trolls are saying about you. You should follow everyone who tweets about you and interact with them.

Thanking a fan for saying something nice about you can make their day. Talk to them about what you're both interested in. Keeping up on Twitter Search and interacting with those who tweet about can ensure you're able to pounce on big opportunities you might never have known about otherwise.

Using The Advanced Search Function On Twitter To Get People To Your Next Gig

If you're looking to make friends with new musicians or promote your gig in another city, Twitter search can help. Simply go to the advanced section of Twitter Search and enter a ZIP code from the city you'd like to target. You can also set how many miles out you want to target from your show's address. Search for a musician whose fans you want to target or even your own name, if you want to see if you have any fans or potential fans in this ZIP code. Remember searching a 25- mile-radius on a New York City address would be useless, since most concertgoers won't travel more than five miles to a show, but in Arkansas, traveling 50 miles might be acceptable.

Once you locate some fans, follow them and find a casual way to tweet at them and give them show information. You can try to be subtle, tweeting something like "Hey, we'll be playing in your town next Wednesday. Any recommendations for a good BBQ joint?" If the fan follows you back, they will see your show announcement in your feed. If they don't follow you back, maybe they'll tweet about needing something to do. Be coy and don't make let your tweets read like spam.

Targeting Fans

You need to target potential new fans across social networks. Twitter is a great place to find new fans by targeting musicians similar to you. Take the list of targeted musicians you made earlier and Twitter Search for fans of your targets who are interacting with them. Don't scour another musician's follower list, a beginner mistake many tweeters make. Find Twitter users who are very active and who follow your target.

The Twitter party analogy is applicable here too. You want to target the most popular and active users who follow the other musicians you targeted. Use Twitter Search to see which of their fans are actively using Twitter. Look at the tweeting habits of these users tweeting about musicians. Do they have a lot of tweets and followers? If so, follow them, interact with them and maybe they will give your music a spin. Many users follow anyone who follows them, so you easily have a good chance to gain a potential fan that is very active on Twitter.

Too Much, Too Fast

In order to prevent spam from destroying Twitter the way it did Myspace, Twitter has some rules about how many interactions you can have in a given time. You cannot follow more than 1,000 users in a day and if you follow too many users too fast, they will disable your account for a few days. This is a good thing. You shouldn't be following too many users at once. Your fan base should be a pyramid you're slowly building by pushing big rocks into place every day to form a huge and amazing structure; not a bunch of rubble you throw into a pile and don't care about.

Use Twitter Lists to Find Fans and Industry Folk

Are you looking to find musicians who are similar to you and have super fans? Want to connect with music business people on Twitter? If so, Twitter lists can help you. Every user has the option to make a list for anything they want. See if musicians you've targeted have made some lists. You can also find and follow any public lists they're on. These lists usually contain superfans or other people musicians know in the music business. Lists can help you easily identify other potential fans and industry professionals to follow..

Automatically Direct Message On Follow

You can use tools like SocialOomph (socialoomph.com) to automatically send a direct message to everyone who follows you. While some Twitter users think this strategy is tacky and awful, I've seen it get great results in convincing casual followers to listen to your music and become fans. Even if they don't immediately listen to your track, they may see your message and want to get to know you better.

The downside to automatically direct messaging is that it is very impersonal and doesn't set your relationship with a fan off on the best foot. Be sure to also link to a page with a free music stream and download, it will give potential fans a great first impression.

Use Twibbon To Identify Your Movement/Clique/Followers

Have you ever seen those weird pieces of Blingee writing across some people's Twitter avatars? These are called Twibbons, and you can use them to promote your music. Simply go to Twibbon and make a design that will identify you to your fans. Consider using your logo. Ask your fans to use this Twibbon to identify as part of your movement. Their friends on Twitter will have their curiosity piqued and ask about your music. (twibbon.com)

Twitterfeed
If you find tweeting every time you make a blog post annoying, you can use Twitterfeed to automatically tweet whenever you post on your blog. If you add the RSS of your blog and authorize your Twitter account for the service to use, it will take care of the rest. (twitterfeed.com)

Spreading The Word On Twitter

Tweeting For A Track
As mentioned numerous times in this book, tweeting for a track is an important way to spread your music to new potential fans. Followers telling their followers they like something is the most valuable social-media currency. It's essential that you make tweeting for a track part of your online strategy.

There are a bunch of great services that allow you to trade tweets for a track:

- **CASH Music** - CASH Music makes a fantastic code to install on your website to allow users to trade a tweet for a track. Although the code is free, if you're HTML illiterate or don't have a website, you may not have an easy time making this happen. (cashmusic.org)
- **Pay With A Tweet** - A free service that will allow you to trade a tweet for a track. (paywithatweet.com)
- **Tweet For A Track** – Fanbridge recently took over this service and it can be used for an inexpensive effective Twitter campaign. (tweetforatrack.com)

A More Personal Way Of Trading A Tweet For A Track
You don't need some high tech web service to trade a tweet for a track. If you want to keep your relationships more personal with fans you can just tell them to follow you and tag you in a tweet about your new song. You can then send a direct message with a private link to listen to your song to

everyone who does this. While it may take more time, you're trying to build relationships and this method gives a nice personal touch.

Other Twitter Tools To Utilize
Here are a few other Twitter tools that may make your life on the service easier.

- **Electoral** – Search other user's Twitter lists and find potential connections and fans. (electoralhq.com)
- **SocialBro** – While the name makes me want to barf, this tool has many helpful features including helping you find what time to tweet each day to reach the most followers. (socialbro.com)
- **MyTopTweet** – This feature shows you your top tweets so you can find what tweets get your message across best. (mytoptweet.com)

Strategy
I think there are a few general rules for Twitter that work well.
- Trying to find something to post 5-7 days a week is optimal to remind your fans to listen to your music, without explicitly asking them to do so.
- If you aren't sending out a tweet that is specifically promoting something, try to put into words your authentic emotions and tweet things others can relate to that will start a conversation.
- The best part of Twitter is you can use Retweets to share insight that rings true to you and put a comment with your own thoughts on it. Often times Retweeting someone else's insight or a meme is the best way to build the community you want to build on Twitter.

Chapter 32: Other Social Networks To Promote Your Music On

Don't limit your social network potential to Facebook, Twitter and Myspace. There are many other smaller social networks that may receive less traffic than Facebook, but also have less clutter and better ways to directly interact with potential fans. There are tons of fans waiting to find their favorite musician on other social networks, so don't miss out on reaching them.

Using Tumblr To Spread Your Message

If you aren't a teenager, habitual sharer, hipster or GIF addict, you may have a hard time understanding the appeal of Tumblr (tumblr.com). Even if you don't "get" it, understand this: Tumblr presents a huge opportunity to market your music. This is especially true if you market toward teenagers because many of them use Tumblr more than they use Facebook. Even if Tumblr doesn't boast the numbers of Facebook or Twitter, they have a community of users who are passionate about what they like, with tools to spread what they love and influence their friends. Ignoring this social network means ignoring one of the ten most visited sites in America and a website that has some of the easiest tools for building a fanbase around.

Just like Twitter

Many say Tumblr is just like Twitter, but with a less constraining character limit. This description only begins to scratch the surface of Tumblr. The service's true potential is how easy it makes to present and share visuals, audio, news, ideas and links with one another. It's often said that Twitter is like a friend recommending something, but Tumblr is like a friend showing you something. It's much easier to share and make personal bonds without the constraint of 280 characters and with the ability to easily embed pictures, audio and video.

Spread And Socialize

566

The best way to get Tumblr working for you is to be social. Post audio and video of what you do, make posts about what you enjoy, what you're listening to, etc. Tumblr for musicians tends to be less about tour dates and show announcements, and more a way to talk about what you're seeing, doing and interested about. While Facebook and Twitter are ways to blast out news, Tumblr works best when you use it to talk about what you're into. You can still use it to announce news, but make sure you're using it to be personable for the best results.

The reblog function is one of Tumblr's strongest tools. When you follow your fans, you can see what they're writing. When you see a post you like, reblog it. This builds a bond with your fans by showing you have things in common. You can also reblog when fans post your songs or mention you. This is a nice way to show that others recommend you.

Heart (essentially Tumblr's like button), every time you're mentioned in a post, and reblog the posts that are cool or interesting to your fans (like the way you would favorite a tweet that is nice to you and Re-Tweet one that is interesting to your followers on Twitter). This helps acknowledge fans and make them aware you care because your fans don't see what you heart but do see what you reblog. Fans are excited by this behavior, it helps to build their enthusiasm. They will often mention you again, helping spread awareness about your music.

Making Friends On Tumblr
What you ultimately want to do on Tumblr is build relationships with your fans while spreading your music. There a handful of fun, effortless ways you can do this..

Follow Everyone Who Follows You - Like we tell you with every social network, the key to Tumblr is to follow anyone who follows you. Once you announce you're on Tumblr on your various social networks, you'll start to pick up a few followers. Put up buttons for Tumblr on your website and do everything you can to raise awareness that you're on Tumblr. You should be taking the time to look at your fans content, heart their posts and interact with them. This will help to build relationships with your fans and get them to tell their friends about you.

If your music starts to spread, you'll also have fans' Tumblr posts about you show up in your Google Alerts. Follow all of these fans and they'll see that your Tumblr exists. Many popular music blogs also have Tumblr versions of their site. This strategy in invaluable when it comes to ensuring the press is getting your updates. If you post cool content, blogs who follow you will often reblog it to their followers. This can lead to massive exposure and a huge increase in fans if you're reblogged by the right people.

Search
The next thing you should do to make Tumblr friends fast is to search Tumblr and see who has already written about you there. When you find them, be sure to follow them. This will most likely result in a return follow. You can also heart and reblog when your fans write about you. Once you have made one of these searches, save the search in the right hand bar of your dashboard.

By hearting posts your fans make about you and reblogging those worth sharing with your fans, you can bond with your fans and encourage them to keep promoting you. This is the single best way to keep your fanbase growing via Tumblr. The more you encourage your fans by acknowledging them, the more they will spread the word about you to their friends, giving you new fans.

Ask Me Anything
Tumblr also has an "Ask Me Anything" function, which allows fans to ask you questions that get answered publicly in your feed. It puts a button in your profile, and when fans can click it, they can ask you whatever they want. This is another way to bond with your fans and publicly answer frequently asked questions. Be sure that when you answer these questions, your services don't automatically post them on your Twitter or Facebook feeds. It can quickly get annoying to have these Tumblr links clogging your other social networks. Also remember, if you are going to answer more than a few questions at a time, you can schedule posts to trickle out later on, so that you don't annoy your followers.

Function
Tumblr is also easy to update. You can do so through WordPress, via Jetpack, HootSuite, Tumblr's iOS & Android Apps or from their site. You can even schedule posts to go up later. If you need to have a blog with an RSS feed, Tumblr is just that. If you link to your Tumblr from all your social networks, you can send interested writers there to get updates from you. This is a little more useful than Twitter because you're able to write long news updates. Make sure writers and fans can easily find the Tumblr link and inform them this is where your news will be coming from.

Interchangeable
Do you already update a blog? Do you not want to update another site? Can you not stand the idea of tweeting out another website you updated? No worries! Tumblr is a great site to use as your main website. Tumblr has a built in way to update Twitter or Facebook every time you post content. You can just update Tumblr and not have to worry about the other two. This makes your updates less personal, but if you're pressed for time, it can be done.

Customize
You can install all sorts of widgets on your Tumblr and even put up links of where to get your music. You can create custom backgrounds or select from a wide variety of themes and header options to make your Tumblr fit the theme of your other sites. With a little bit of HTML knowledge, you can easily customize your blog with music players, widgets, comment management systems, etc. One tricks is to add HTML5 widgets to your Tumblr sidebar. You can put widgets to trade email addresses for a track, or music players in this sidebar. Musformation has lots of success with trading email addresses for a track, and fanclub incentives in the sidebar.

Themes
Tumblr has many cool themes that will not only help you get a great layout, but also easily add widgets and other content to help market your music. Sadly, many of the themes that make it a great tool for music marketing cost money. Themes like Tumblrcamp (tumblrcamp.com), which allow you to make your Bandcamp and Tumblr play nice cost $50. But if you have the money, you can easily browse themes inside Tumblr's dashboard and pick out one that will work well for your needs. It can be helpful to get your web designer or web developer to tweak a theme. Making your reblog, share and follow buttons prominent in your theme can help make your content go as far as it can.

Diary
Tumblr works great as more than a place to do your news blasts. Many musicians use it as a personal blog and post pictures, writing and fun content they find on the Internet. I have a personal Tumblr where I write about anything I wouldn't normally write about on Musformation, like political views or every keyboard cat video I can find. If it creates a bond with your fans, then you're successful on Tumblr. It's very easy to create separate Tumblrs from one account and you can make different Tumblrs

so your fans can get what they want from you. Many musicians have a personal Tumblr and a separate one that is for their music marketing, so don't be afraid to go both ways. You can lend fans of your music the hint that you have a personal Tumblr with an occasional mention or reblog.

Pages

Tumblr allows you to make pages that aren't published to your followers' news feed. These can be great for FAQs, an about me or even a page that has a bunch of free music widgets that you link in your Tumblr sidebar. Pages are especially helpful if you use Tumblr as your main website.

Social

Users search through Tumblr for content, namely specific genres of music. They have features that will enhances recommendations and a hashtag-like tag system that helps users easily search for their interests. Tagging your posts about skateboarding, cooking, art or whatever with that tag can get you discovered through readers' shared interest in that hobby. If you have a great interest or talent in something other than music, this can be a great way to introduce potential fans to your music. I know one musician whose great skills with the video game StarCraft gained him tons of fans, just from his regular Tumblr posts about the game. Fans of his StarCraft Tumblr then discovered and became fans of his music.

Other Features

Tumblr also has some other great features:

- **Keep Up -** Tumblr allows fans to message you. Many fans will also message you publicly by tagging you. If you start a Tumblr, understand it can be poisonous to your relationships with fans if you don't keep up with it regularly. Once you commit to using Tumblr, keep up with it, or risk missing countless opportunities.
- **Community -** If you do start to clog up your Tumblr timeline with 'Ask' questions, you can add a comment section to your Tumblr using the social commenting service Disqus (disqus.com). This will allow fans to comment on your Tumblr posts and converse with one another as well as with you. Make open threads or question threads. You can even start conversations with fans. You'll see a lot of the big rockstars doing this. If your community on Tumblr grows, this is a great way to keep it under control.

- **Pinned Posts** - If you have big news, like a new song, tour dates or cool merch, Tumblr now allows you to use pinned posts to make sure your followers don't miss the news. These ads will remain in your followers' faces for the day, reminding them they should take note of what you have done. These posts cost $5 and will allow you to have your ad stay at the top of your followers' feed for 24 hours. Even if you only have 100 followers, this is a powerful marketing tool to make sure your fans hear about your latest news.
- **Highlighted Posts** - If you're feeling cheap, like $2 cheap, you can do a highlighted post, which will draw extra attention in your followers' feed. Just be sure to not abuse the feature or you'll be phased-out from your followers.
- **Google Analytics** - If you use Tumblr as your website or your blog and are curious about its performance, you can install Google Analytics on your site to view metrics and learn how to promote better marketing with your Tumblr.

Strategy
Unless your fans are under 21 or your music revolves around a lot of visual art I would not put a lot of effort into Tumblr. While it is helpful to syndicate your important posts here, there's no need to put marketing time here unless you find you have a strong community here to bond with.

SoundCloud As A Social Network

SoundCloud (soundcloud.com) may not seem like a social network upon first glance, but it's social features make this service more than just the best streaming player in the business. SoundCloud made streaming music on the Internet a pleasant experience, not to mention one that's easier to use with every new feature they add. It's also a presence you should take seriously and use to its fullest extent.

SoundCloud exists in its own web community, an iOS & Android app and on countless websites and services throughout the Internet via embedding tools. You'll see SoundCloud used as the streaming player of choice on many musicians' websites and also how many blogs share music. It can also be seen in streams hosted on many of your social networks.

SoundCloud is free for the basic user. If you need more stylish widgets or more than two hours of music, prices vary from $63 to $135 per year depending how much storage you need. Most users don't need more than the basic service, but if you do, the extended feature set is well worth the price, especially if you have a lot of music to upload.

Profile

When you make your SoundCloud profile, the first thing to do is add a picture, your name and a short description about yourself. Keep this to one paragraph or less and make it something fans would want to read. Try using your one-paragraph bio. In this profile, you're able to list your Facebook, Twitter, Last.fm, Tumblr and YouTube profiles. You can also list your website or your free-music page. You can enter a nickname for this site like "Buy My Music" or "Free Stuff" and link to the website you have for your fans to do those things. If you link your SongKick profile and keep it updated, your concert dates will show up on your SoundCloud page.

You can connect your Facebook, Twitter and Tumblr profiles to SoundCloud, so you can easily share your songs on those networks and find your friends on these services. You can also enter whether you're a musician, producer, manager or DJ in order to join different communities and enable different feature sets on SoundCloud.

Quality

SoundCloud is best known as the high-quality streaming player that took online music listening out of the ghettos of Myspace and Facebook's internal streaming widgets. It famously brought the world full-bandwidth audio with a wide variety of options and abilities. You are able to upload high-quality files that can be streamed from SoundCloud's site or embedded all over the Internet. SoundCloud's embedded player is commonly used to host streams of tracks on blogs, enabling you to get your music to be a part of many different blog communities.

Feed

SoundCloud also serves as a feed that allows music fans to keep up with your audio updates. Music fans have the ability to follow musicians on SoundCloud and whenever you add new tracks it will appear in their dashboard when they login. This means fans are alerted whenever you add new music, DJ sets, playlists or an audio update where you tell fans what you've been up to. If you're a record label, this can be a great way to keep fans up to date as each release happens. If you're a remixer or a prolific songwriter, this is an easy way for fans to stay up to date with your frequent new material.

Making sure your fans know you constantly update SoundCloud. Add demos and every part of your discography to ensure fans know this is a place to stay in touch with you. This can increase fan bonding. It's also a great way to get your music spread because bloggers learn to expect updates from you and know their ability to share your music is one click away.

Information

There is an information section under every SoundCloud track. Be sure to fill this in and let your fans know the vital information about the track. Include the following information:

- **Call To Action** - Offer one call to action, whether to buy the track or download it for free. Anything more is overwhelming.
- **Purchase** - Tell fans where they can buy the song. If they can get it for free, give that address.
- **Free-Music Page** - Tell fans where they can get more free music from you.
- **Suggest** - If you have more songs from this record or remixes of this song, point fans to them.
- **Link** - Suggest the viewer follow you on the social network you're having the best luck with. Your website can also be a good idea.
- **Credit** - Be sure to credit the producer, engineer, musicians, and anyone else whose credit would be appreciated here. This is one of the only ways those who work hard on your music get credit.
- **Lyrics** - Add lyrics so they will show up in search engines and help fans sing along at shows. Many times fans only know the lyrics to a song and not the title, so including lyrics is often an immense help in getting your music discovered.
- **Equipment** - Many SoundCloud communities are based around music nerds. If you're using equipment that's of interest to other musician nerds, feel free to tell them. SoundCloud has whole communities built around creating music with specific pieces of gear. If this context helps fellow music dorks appreciate your song, let the community know.

Comments

SoundCloud enables comments on your tracks, and followers can even comment on specific parts of the song they want to talk about. This is an amazing tool for feedback, fan interaction and community building. These comments can also give you some great advice from your community on what you could be doing better and add a social element where you can bond over your music.

You are also able to tag anyone who comments to you, just like on Twitter. This is a great way to build bonds and friendships, as well as give thanks to fans. Make sure you engage those who are interested enough in your music to comment on it.

Other Services
Music creation apps like Ableton, Cubase, Pro Tools and Studio One all allow you to export your mixes directly to SoundCloud. Once your music is in SoundCloud, you can easily add it to the following services, without having to upload it again:

- **Tumblr**
- **Jango**
- **Hype Machine**
- **CD Baby**
- **Limited Run**
- **FanBridge**
- **Flavors.me**
- **Flipboard**

Raising Awareness With SoundCloud
When someone sees your SoundCloud song streaming, they have the option to share it on Facebook, Twitter, Tumblr or via email. They can also favorite it on SoundCloud or embed it on their own blog. You also have the option to let fans download the song you posted. If a fan shares the song on Facebook, Twitter or Tumblr, it plays in a nice clean interface right in the website's window without fans having to click through to SoundCloud's website or leave the page they're on. SoundCloud is an ideal way for fans to spread your music to potential fans. It's also an ideal way for you to share your own music.

Trades - SoundCloud has a service to trade email addresses for a track (unlock.fm) or tweets for a track. This is a great way to get a fan's contact information using a clean interface from SoundCloud. Both apps are found in the App Gallery on SoundCloud's website and are easy to setup.

Exclusives – You can give exclusive embeds to blogs, by disabling the ability to share an embed code. This can help you get blog coverage by offering exclusives.

Curate - You can post other users music in curated sets that will be seen in your feed and by your followers. You can trade a place in a curated set with other SoundCloud users so you can expose your music to each other's fanbases. This is a great way to use SoundCloud to grow a fanbase while getting an endorsement from another act that has a fanbase. Just reach out to like-minded musicians and ask to trade places in these curated sets.

More Tricks - SoundCloud provides an endless world of possibilities to promote your music. Here are a few more:

- **Submission** - When submitting to blogs, link the song on SoundCloud, so the writer has an easy way to put it onto their blog.
- **Tags** - Make sure to thoroughly tag your music with any term someone may search for. These tags help your music get discovered by bloggers and fans alike and are one of the most powerful parts of SoundCloud.
- **Image** - Make sure to upload a unique image for each of your songs. Give a visual that will identify your song.
- **Downloadable** - SoundCloud also allows users to download your music. If you're trying to give away as much free music as possible, this is a great way to do it.
- **Buy** – You also have the choice instead of giving your file a download button to give it a buy button to link to the store of your choice.
- **Custom Download Sites** - You can link your music to other sites for free downloads. This can be your direct-to-fan site or a free music page.
- **Comment** - Leave positive comments on other people's tracks and then reach out to them privately. It's a great way to make friends and one of the easiest ways to find musicians you'll share fans with.
- **Follow** - Follow everyone who follows you and make sure to follow the musicians you target, friends and the blog you want to be on.

There is very little spam on SoundCloud so following someone means you'll be subjected to much less annoying nonsense. Listen to the tracks of those who follow you and participate in this community. The potential here is huge.

- **Remixes** - If you like your music to be remixed, you can host the stems on SoundCloud--make sure they're downloadable--and then host a remix contest there. You can assemble all of the entries on a playlist and have fans vote on it via comments.
- **Pulse** – Soundcloud has an app that allows users of their service to easily do what they need to keep up on comments and their profile.
- **Analytics** – Pro accounts can see what cities their music is listened to it, to be sure to tour there.

Private Comments

If your song is still a work in progress, you can select to have your song be private and only heard by those you invite to the file. Those you invite can comment on the song and give feedback on what they're hearing. Many producers do this when getting feedback on a mix, so that listeners can comment on specific parts of the song's timeline. This can also be useful as a centralized place to get feedback on a track without worrying on exposing it to the world.

Use SoundCloud To Send Mixes, Demos, Songs To Potential Team Members

As a musician in the modern world, you need to send your tracks to other people, whether to get mixes approved, try to get signed or collaborate. Using sites like WeTransfer and YouSendIt comes with annoying wait times and file size restrictions. When you're trying to get someone in the industry to listen to your track, these wait times can decide whether your track is listened to or forgotten about.

SoundCloud eliminates the wait time on these files and has a few other awesome features:

- **Quality** - You can upload high-quality files, rather than low-quality PureVolume or Myspace streams.
- **Download** - Downloading is optional, which can help prevent leaks.

- **Private** - You can make files private! Making them only available to a few recipients rather than risk your file's secrecy if a URL is leaked.

Strategy
Soundcloud is a great place to put your music especially if you make Hip Hop or EDM. Many fans and tastemakers watch their feeds and communities for tracks that come up so it's crucial for building an early fanbase. If you are in these genres commenting, messaging and building community can be crucial.

Spreading Your Music With Pinterest

While many are puzzled with the success of Pinterest (pinterest.com), there is no doubt that its users are obsessed with the service. It's based around users finding a visually stimulating image and pinning it to their board. Because Pinterest is light on the reading, it makes it an easily enjoyable experience for users. By creating Pinboards, users are able to create posts based on a wide variety of themes. These themes can attract other users to look at your Pinboard, give take the time to learn your interests and share your posts with others.

One of the more interesting things about Pinterest is it's predominantly used by women and parents, unlike many other social networks. Pinterest can be a great marketing opportunity for musicians who make music for an older crowd or with a strong female following.

Getting Started
Link Pinterest to your band's Facebook page and Twitter. Since Facebook is based around your personal profile, link the Twitter account you use for your music to gain some early Pinterest followers. You can then connect your Facebook account and start pinning. Pick a subject you're passionate about and create a board for that theme. For example, let's say you really like expensive suits. You can make a Pinboard about suits and then subtly drop in the song you wrote about your favorite suit into this board.

Tips
Below are some ideas for making Pinterest work for marketing your music:

- **Pinboards** - Make Pinboards your fans would enjoy. If it's of interest to you, it can also show fans your personality and build a better bond with them.
- **Interviews** - If you give great interviews, you can make a pinboard of all of them. Direct your fans there so they can get to know you better and become a bigger fan.
- **Photos** - Make a pinboard for whenever you get a great live photo or press photo.
- **Re-Pinning** - Encourage re-pinning by reminding your fans they should share what you do.
- **Like** - Just like every other social network, it's important to follow anyone who is your fan. Comment on, like and re-pin their content. Most importantly, bond by discussing your posts on Pinterest. Every Pin has the ability to leave comments.
- **Link** - You can also link cool things your fans do on Pinterest on your other social networks. If you see an amazing Pinboard you can always tweet it out and make that fan's day.
- **Images** - Anytime you see a great image involving your music or a fashionable fan wearing your merch, pin it!
- **Merch** - Make a pinboard of potential merch designs. Invite fans to like the designs they want or comment on what they would do differently.
- **Think Out Loud** - Assemble Pinboards of equipment you want to buy, ideas for your next video, outfits you want to wear on stage, etc. The possibilities are endless.

Tools
Pinterest has made itself very open to outside tools. Some of the more helpful tools are listed below:

- **Buttons** - Pinterest has a wide variety of buttons available to get others to pin content from your website or follow you on Pinterest. (pinterest.com/about/goodies)
- **Bookmarks** - You can also get bookmarklets for easy pinning on the same page. They have an iOS and Android App available if you want to work on the go.
- **ShareAsImage** - ShareAsImage is a helpful app that can take any quote and turn it into a good-looking image for sharing on Pinterest. This can be great for pinning song lyrics. (shareasimage.com)

Strategy
Unless your fanbase is adult females spending time marketing here will probably not do you much good, but if they are taking the time to curate and bond here and find a community can do worlds of good for your marketing. Sharing Pintrest boards with like-minded fans can excite them greatly.

The Hype Machine Can Proliferate Your Fanbase

You may be asking yourself what the big deal is about The Hype Machine. Let me put it simply, the website have more than a million registered users who are among music's biggest tastemakers, DJs and cool kids who tell other kids what's cool in the music scene. The Chainsmokers famously made their way to pop stardom by scowering the site daily to look for the best collaborators to make tracks with. Pretty sweet, huh? The Hype Machine has a chart that these cool kids are watching all the time in order to discover the next great act, which they will tell all their friends about. If you chart here, you could have the chance for a huge number of potential fans to hear your music. The catch is The Hype Machine aggregates from thousands of blogs. You must be featured on one of the blogs in their network to get put on the site, and then users of the Hype Machine need to "heart" your music in order for it to get on the charts. The chart also resets every couple of days, so you must act quickly. (hypem.com)

If you want to go for it, the first thing you need to do is set up a search for yourself so that you know when you make it onto The Hype Machine. In order to do this, go to The Hype Machine. Look at the top navigation bar and type in your name to the Search Blogs field. The website will show if you've been written about on any of the blogs in The Hype Machine's network. Even if no one has covered you yet, subscribe to an RSS feed that will let you know when someone does write about you and you end up on Hype Machine. *Note: Click the RSS button in your browser and subscribe to this search.* If you make it onto The Hype Machine, it will now show up in your RSS Reader.

Seizing The Opportunity
If you do get written about on The Hype Machine, capitalize on this opportunity. Click the link in your RSS Reader, and it will take you to a page showing you where your song was blogged about. If this happens,

you, your bandmates, friends and family should all immediately be hearting your music on The Hype Machine and participating in the website's community, otherwise the hearting will be seen as spam. Click hearts on songs you like and be a part of the community. Hopefully you have an army of friends who can heart your song and help drive it up the chart. The other way you can promote music is to have your friends tweet a link to this page and rank high on their Twitter chart. Just be sure to not sign up tons of fake accounts to make this happen, because The Hype Machine watches for any fraud that might be driving musicians up their charts. Instead, encourage your fans to be members of The Hype Machine community. Make sure you post on all of your social networks and get fans ramping you up the charts.

Reddit - The Ultimate Viral Community

Do you often wonder how the world finds out about all the cool things going on across the Internet? The answer is Reddit (reddit.com). If something is funny, cool, exceptional, weird, interesting or noteworthy, Reddit is the place it gets spread first. Before something is considered viral, Reddit has already seen it, shared it, rolled its eyes at it and called it old news. If you want your music to be heard by those who seed content around the Internet, Reddit is the place to go.

On Reddit, users post content and community members either vote that content to move up or down on the website's feed. Users can also comment on and spread content from the site. Users can choose what they're interested in and follow sub-Reddits, which act as vote able message boards for whatever specific interests you have, such political humor, dubstep, cat videos or old-school punk. While Reddit isn't known for being a music community, it has hundreds of sub-Reddits that deal with music. These sub-communities can be fertile ground for sharing your content.

Promoting Your Music On Reddit
If you want to promote your music on Reddit, you need to find the sub-Reddits you belong in. After you sign up for Reddit, you're automatically subscribed to the music section. Go there and then click on the sub-Reddit directory, it will take you to a huge list of sub-Reddits. Subscribe to any you

might be interested in or you think might be good to promote your music in. Next, start to participate in the community: Vote on things, comment and share links that are interesting. Don't just engage in self-promotion, post content others will enjoy.

Once you have a feel for the community, add your own music. It helps to have some karma, the feature Reddit uses to show how much you participate in the community, so that your links are taken seriously. If you post your own music, adding some context usually helps. Be sure to tell it to the community if there is a good story behind your song. At times there will be threads to share your music, and there are whole sub-Reddits devoted to sharing music. Participate and be a real member of the community who contributes regularly so your links will get taken seriously. If you abide by the idea that you should post 10 helpful posts to the community for every one that is even the least bit self-promotional, you will have much more success getting your music heard. Stick with it, I have been a member of some Reddit communities for years and I will go a month without self-promoting. When I do drop a self-promotional mention the community respects it.

Other Tips To Promote Your Music On Reddit
- **Listen To This** - The sub-Reddit r/ListenToThis is specifically for posting music that the community should hear.
- **Radio Reddit** - Upload your music to Reddit's music discovery channel. It acts as a radio station for the community. (radioreddit.com)
- **Ads** - Reddit has an advertising option that can get you in front of the website's community. It's covered more extensively in the chapter on advertising.
- **Don't Fake** - Making a ton of fake accounts and upping your content will do you no good. It's one thing if a few of your friends up-vote your content, but anything more will be caught. This is a community of smart, bored people, don't underestimate their BS detectors.
- **The Right Sub-Reddit** - One of the most important parts of promoting on Reddit's huge community is to make sure you post in the right community. Do your research and make sure you post in the right community for each post, otherwise it will see little reaction.

- **AMA** - If you start to get some popularity you can hold an AMA session where you take questions. Reddit promotes these events and can they can mean some good exposure for your music.

Using Reddit
Best of all, not only is Reddit a great place to spread your music, it's a place where you can find tons of great content to show your fans and just have fun. Here are some sub-Reddits I enjoy:
- r/WeAreTheMusicMakers
- r/MusicBloggers
- r/PopPunkers
- r/ElectroHouse
- r/TheCure
- r/ListenToThis
- r/RadioReddit
- r/Drums

Strategy
Find communities where like-minded people are on Reddit can be one of the most consequential things you can do with your time. Reddit is where tastemakers and the most avid music fans are exchanging ideas, thoughts and the best new music, so maintaining a presence here and being help in your community can have huge results.

Some Social Networks To Not Forget About

Make Gifs on Giphy
Giphy (giphy.com)is a social network of Gifs where people looking for a fun image to friends can scour their service to make texting or social network interactions more fun. Giphy also allows you to make a profile and upload your own. If you are smart like Chris Farren (giphy.com/chrisfarren) you can make your own page of you doing various common text reactions with accompanying images, spread the word to your fans and let them promote you by spreading your image around while creating a deeper bond with your personality.

Make A Goodreads Book Club For Your Music
Is your audience a bunch of literate, book reading, NPR-listening dorks? Well, lucky you! If this is your audience, odds are you're one of those types

582

too. Bond with your fans, showing each other what huge bookworm dorks you are by creating a Goodreads book club. This can encourage camaraderie and build a fun and interesting community around your music. It will also lead to much better conversations at shows. (goodreads.com)

Genius
Genius is a site that allows fan to annotate lyrics, but this doesn't mean artists can't get in on the fun. Artists commonly correct or tell stories around their songs in this context and it's a great way for fans to get a glimpse into what lyrics are about or what inspired them. (genius.com)

Other Social Networks That May Be Of Interest To You
- **Clubhouse** – Clubhouse is an app for your phone where you can listen in on on conversations or host them and allow others to listen in. It's a public space for hanging out and having conversations. (In the app store)
- **OurStage** - OurStage is a battle-of-the-bands-type social network that gets winners exposure and the opportunity to be heard by industry professionals. (ourstage.com)
- **PureVolume** - At one time, PureVolume promised to be the next MP3.com, but now it's a dwindling music site with mild social-networking possibilities. While it still proves to be a decent place for emo, punk, hardcore and metal bands to get exposure, it dies a little bit more every day. (purevolume.com)
- **LinkedIn** - If you fancy yourself someone who wants to meet people in the music business and gain networking accolades, this is the place to do it. LinkedIn doesn't offer much in the way of music discovery, but you can find industry professionals fairly easily. It will also help you make introductions and stay in touch with the people you meet in the music world. (linkedin.com)
- **Medium** – The blogging platform from the people that brought you Twitter is a great elegant way to write and have your writing discovered if you want to write long form pieces about your music or any subject for that matter. (medium.com)
- **Discord** – Discord Chats are chatrooms you can make for your fans to chat with them or for your scene or microgenre and invite members of message boards to do live chatting. (discordapp.com)

Other Places To Maintain A Presence With Your Music

583

A key to getting your music around the Internet is to have information readily available. Sites like Wikipedia and AllMusic are aggregated by services like iTunes, Spotify, Tidal, Napster and Apple Music, to provide their users with information on your music. This can also help improve your SEO and raise awareness about your releases, relevant info and how fans can stay in touch with you. Try to get your information on all of these resources and let them help your music spread.

Wikipedia

Having a Wikipedia (wikipedia.org) entry is a great way to easily provide your backstory and relevant facts to the world. Not only does it make you feel important, it also ensures that when potential fans or writers look you up, you'll be easy to find and at the top of search engine results. Sadly, there is a catch: you need to be important. Wikipedia wants you to be able to link news articles and show that you're a relevant part of the Zeitgeist, in order to be featured on their service. In fact, you should make sure you explain why readers would know who you are as fast as possible in your entry and include links that illustrate your relevance.

Once you feel you have reached the point of notoriety where you should be written about, you can then look up Wikipedia's writing guidelines. The other option is to read some other musicians' Wikipedia pages, copy and paste their information and replace it with your information in Wikipedia's format. They're quite picky in their Ivory Tower of information; so give this some serious effort. It helps to have been a part of the Wikipedia community and familiar with its writing style. If this is your first entry and you haven't added small tweaks to other entries, it's very likely your entry will be rejected. Below are some tips to help make sure your entry gets approved.

- **Source** - Cite sources! You need to be able to point to interviews or articles for biographical information. Awards and significant events with dates and links really help your entry get past the inspectors.
- **Discography Details** - Fill out discography and members section with ACCURATE AND DETAILED information.
- **Link** - Use the external links section to link your various social networks and website.

- **Third Person** - Don't write from the perspective of a group member. Wikipedia wants this page to be written as if an outside fan or journalist wrote it.

AllMusic Lists Record Credits

With the rise of digital music over physical albums with artwork, no one seems to see album credits anymore. As this becomes the norm, AllMusic (allmusic.com) becomes an invaluable resource. AllMusic is a place where you can read reviews and discographies of various musicians. Perhaps the coolest feature they offer is compiling album credits in a searchable directory.

All this makes it valuable for figuring out who you would like to work with. Let's say you wanted to see every record a certain producer worked on or that a certain musician played on. Simply type in the person's name in the search box, click credits and you'll see a chronological discography of their work. If you hear an amazing guitar solo, you can easily look up who played it. If you like the way a record sounds, it's easy to find out who worked on it. If the album art of a record blows you away, you can find the artist here too. While their listings are renowned for having inaccurate information, AllMusic does offer submissions to correct incorrect information. This service is becoming more and more valuable with each year that passes. As album credits become more scarce, AllMusic should be supported for providing such useful information.

To get your music listed on AllMusic send your CD, DVD, Vinyl or whatever to:

All Media Guide
1168 Oak Valley Drive
Ann Arbor, MI 48108
The listing will be up 4-6 weeks later.

Song Meanings

Song Meanings (songmeanings.com) is a site where fans discuss, you guessed it – song meanings! You can upload lyrics and talk about your songs here for fans to discover.

Other Resources That Can Help

Here are some other sites to add your information to, in order to help improve your SEO and spread your music.

- **Urban Dictionary** - If your name or song names are slang fans may not know, add them to Urban Dictionary. If you're the inventor of a slang expression you can also add it and credit yourself as the inventor. (urbandictionary.com)
- **MusicBrainz** - MusicBrainz is a database of metadata for your music. They provide a service that will aggregate metadata for a wide variety of music services. If you want your song titles, credits and other information to show up properly, be sure to add it to MusicBrainz. (musicbrainz.org)
- **Gracenote** - Gracenote is the service that makes a CDs metadata appear when you insert it into iTunes. They provide this data to many different services. Adding your music and information to their database will help make sure it's correct across the web. (gracenote.com)

Lyric And Tablature Websites: Promotion Or Poison
There are tons of websites on the Internet that compile the lyrics and tablature of popular records. It can be great promotion to have this information on the Internet, allowing fans to find your lyrics and sing along at shows. Tablature websites let fans fall in love with your songs while they try to learn how to play them.

While this is great, it's not getting fans to your website. So if you have your lyrics and tabs available, why not get the traffic to your own website? Put this information on your website instead of to sites that have nothing but lyrics and ads for other musicians. In fact, you can use lyrics to draw traffic to your YouTube videos by posting them there. Bandcamp also gives you the ability to add lyrics and tablature to your songs, to help drive Google traffic there.

Lyric Sites - If you do want your lyrics on these site here are a few you can get them on.

- **A-Z Lyrics Universe** (azlyrics.com)
- **LyricsFreak** (lyricsfreak.com)
- **Song Lyrics** (songlyrics.com)

Tablature Sites - Here are some sites where you can upload your tablature.

- **Ultimate Guitar** (ultimate-guitar.com)
- **All Tabs** (alltabs.com)

Music Industry Listings

If you want access to submit to countless music industry figures, there are many services, which will provide you with contacts for them. Remember though, cold emailing potential team members is a poor use of your time. Do this at your own risk.

Here are a few services that can provide you with tons of access to music industry professional's contact information, with a price.

- **Music Business Registry** - The Music Business Registry has a humongous listing of music business contacts that are separated into all sorts of fields, including A&R; Licensing and Publishing. (musicregistry.com)
- **MusicSocket** - MusicSocket has a list of over 2,000 record label and manager contacts as well as many other contacts. (musicsocket.com)

Submit To Award Shows

The music business loves an award show. If you look around your community long enough you'll see them happening. Many medium-to-small-sized cities seem to have them. Submitting to these award shows can raise awareness of your music, increase concert draw and boost sales immensely if you happen to get in the door. Look around your local area and be prepared to submit about a year in advance for any opportunities. Here are some fairly well-known award shows that you can submit to:

- **The Grammys** - We all laugh at how clueless they are, but boy do they help sell records and establish musicians. In order to submit, you need to submit your media company, aka your record label/LLC, to them first. You can do that at their submission website (mediaregistration.grammy.com) and then follow this year's guidelines for submitting your music.
- **Independent Music Awards** - These awards honor the best in independent musicians, although not necessarily indie rock musicians. The submission process is a paid one, through Sonicbids. (independentmusicawards.com)

Chapter 33: Planning And Promoting Your Music Video

Making a great music video is the best advertisement for your song. I often tell musicians that once their record is completed the most important thought they can devote their attention to is developing the images the will go well with their music to help it emotionally resonate more. When a great video is paired with a great song, it makes us all get excited. We want to tell everyone we know about it, giving free promotion to this great video, giving a huge endorsement to all our trusted friends. This is exactly the type of promotion every musician dreams of.

In order to make a great video, you need some serious planning and consideration. Whether you do it yourself or hire a director, making a video is a lot of effort even in the planning stages. Making it happen on a shoestring budget is even more of a challenge. The good news is that we live in a day and age where if you make a great video, even for a couple hundred bucks, it can get shared with millions of potential fans and give you the exposure that musicians could only have dreamed of a decade ago.

Planning Your Video

Budget
Before going any further, you need to figure out your budget. This will determine if you need to shoot the video yourself, recruit a charitable friend or hire it out and make a huge production of it. The great thing about living in the digital age is that videos with budgets less than $500 regularly get airplay on major video networks.

OK Go's famous backyard dancing video could be made for nothing, if you have an iPhone and a free afternoon. And it was played millions of times online and all over national TV. We're in an era where a cheap, well-done video will often leave a bigger impression than one someone spent $10,000 on. If you are creative and come up with a great concept that can be accomplished on the cheap, the sky's the limit.

589

Keep in mind that if you're going to hire someone to film and direct your video, you may also have to pay for a wide variety of other production costs. Make sure your budget takes into account every expense you might possibly have to pay for. Budgeting a video is more than just the fee the director will need. While some directors will choose to take on the responsibility of keeping the video within this budget, that needs to be agreed upon beforehand. Also remember, almost every video will go over budget by 25 percent. In general, you're going to need at least $750 to get a director on board who has a mild amount of experience and at least quadruple that for a director who regularly makes great music videos. With that said, there are plenty of younger directors who can do great work for $250 to $500.

Remember, unlike many other parts of working in music, videos are usually paid for upfront because so much of the budget is spent on the production. Be sure to have your budget in hand before you start filming.

Treatment
The first thing you need to do to make a video happen is to come up with a treatment. A treatment is the idea and approach to the video. If your video matches a song well, then you have a combination that your fans are going to enjoy. Getting a good vision for the treatment and figuring out cool details that will add to your video are crucial to making a music video fans want to watch again and again.

When coming up with a treatment, you want to brainstorm as many ideas as possible that can help visually convey the idea behind your video. The funny thing about music videos is that most of them have no dialogue, so you have to convey all of your meaning visually or match it to the song lyrics. This means coming up with many clever ways to convey your message. It's a good idea to assemble a list of videos you enjoy that are in the style of the video you want to make. Identify what you like about them and work from there.

When making a great video that will go viral, it's important to ask, "what would make anyone want to watch this video more than once?" Most successful videos demand to be watched numerous times to take in all of their greatness. Without this ingredient, it won't be shared by your fans or have any lasting power after a viewer sees it one time. Think about what's made you watch a video over and over and try to incorporate those attributes into your own video.

Even more important than wanting your fans to keep watching, it's crucial for them to think your video is so remarkable they want to tell all of their friends. It's important to ask yourself what's so remarkable about it that your fans would tell their friends about it. If you don't have a solid answer, it's time to go back to the drawing board.

It's often said there's three types of videos that help a band:

- **Emotion** – A video that enhances the emotion of the song that's already there.
- **Entertains** – A video that entertains the audience with a display of something that captivates their attention
- **Shifts Perception** – A video that changes the audiences perception of who the artists is.

When I think of the videos that I have shared or watched numerous times I think of these:

- **Psy "Gangnam Style"** - There are so many details to take in, so many shots in this video that are just absolutely ridiculous, it begs to be watched numerous times.
- **OK Go "Here It Goes Again"** - The moves on the treadmills are insane. There is so much going on that you want to take it all in and tell your friends to watch it.
- **Aphex Twin "Windowlicker"** - My favorite video of all-time. This one is so ridiculous and visually stunning, you almost don't want to watch it again because it's so disturbing. You can't help but watch it again though, because you want to make sure you don't miss a single detail.
- **Red Fang "Prehistoric Dog"** - These guys are so ridiculous, and they always make the coolest videos. It's hard to believe they made a video so funny for so cheap. They're the ultimate example of a band that consistently makes great videos that match their image, for very little money. Whitey McConnaughy deserves high marks for always coming to bat for these guys.
- **Sensual Harassment "Disco Heart"** - Todd's band made a fantastic video that shines as an example of something you want to watch over and over. It fits the song and the band's image perfectly.

- **Eric Wareheim's Work** - Any Eric Wareheim video begs to be watched again. He always finds the way to match a song with imagery you want to watch over and over. In fact, sometimes it's so gross you never want to see it again, but you have to torture your friends by making them watch it. I will never forget where I was the first time I saw Flying Lotus' "Parisian Goldfish" video.

I would never begin to make a video until I have a list of a dozen videos that are similar to the one I'm trying to make. Watch them repeatedly and dissect the elements that make them work. Make a list of these elements and make sure you get your video to reach the same marks.

Utilize Your Resources
One of the best ways to make a great video is to figure out what resources you have to make one. For example, if a band member's father is a firefighter, maybe they will let you use the fire station for a scene. Perhaps your drummer's girlfriend is a fire-breather who you can use for a scene? The talents and resources of friends are the easiest way to make your video awesome and easy to make. Your resources often influence what you choose as a treatment or add an element to that treatment.

Videos With A Mission
A video is often an introduction that tells your audience who you are while helping to define your image. One of the best examples I have ever seen of this ideology was Sum 41's video for the breakout hit "Fat Lip." At the time, it was not cool for most punk bands to embrace any elements of hip hop, despite the fact that many of them had listed hip hop as a guilty pleasure. Sum 41's first video showed familiar faces of punk fans, skaters and BMXers all hanging with the band and doing the ridiculous things punk kids do. The video started with them beatboxing and rapping in an obnoxious punk way. It aligned them with the punk scene and showed kids that looked just like the fans they wanted to get, embracing this new sound and loving it. It immediately made a risky transition for this genre totally acceptable to a more mainstream audience.

If you're worried about how your diverse sound or image will affect your crossover appeal, a video can help you define how you want to be viewed. Giving the audience hints of your image can help align you with whoever you want. Lana Del Rey may have been another forgettable female artist, lumped in with every other mainstream singer vying for big media attention. But her first video for "Video Games" was chock full of hackneyed hipster imagery and teenage clichés. She established herself as part of indie culture instead of mainstream culture with her imagery. The video allowed her to be accepted by a hipster audience as well as a mainstream one.

Knowing how you want to be seen and thought of by the world is a great clue into many of the decisions you will make for your video. Lead the world in what they should be thinking of your music by putting in visual imagery that reinforces what you want your audience to think about you.

Some Songs Should Just Be A Lyric Video
If you have a song with lyrics that are really striking it can often be helpful to call attention to them. Sometimes the most powerful video for a song is to let the words speak for themselves. In fact, if your lyrics really are striking I would plan on making lyric videos even be the feature. You can also appear and perform in lyric videos. One of my favorite examples of this is Snail Mail's video for "Pristine".

Hiring A Director
If you don't know what you want for a treatment or want help making it better, it's smart to hire an outside video director. Many musicians contact a few potential directors who will all listen to your song and write a treatment for it. If your budget works for them and their treatment works for you, you can make a video together. It's common for musicians to read two or more treatments from the same director and then choose which one to go with.

If you don't know any directors, it's easy to find some.

- **Local** - Check out the videos of some local musicians. Even if you don't like their music, they may have a great director who lives close to you.
- **YouTube** - The credits for a video usually come at the end or in the description box below the video. If you enjoy a video, write the director's name down.
- **College** - Local film schools are crawling with aspiring music video directors. Post a bulletin or talk to a teacher and have them inform their students that you're looking.
- **Craigslist** - Craigslist is riddled with aspiring directors who will work on a shoestring budget. (craigslist.org)

- **Radar Music Videos** - A cool network where musicians can post their needs for a video and directors will give treatments in hopes of getting the job. (radarmusicvideos.com)
- **Promo News** - This website is a steady stream of cool music videos and director information, which is great for scouting talent. (promonews.tv)

Your budget will be a determining factor in who you get to work with. When you only have $500, contacting the director of your favorite Skrillex video is going to be a big waste of time. When approaching a director, you need to make it clear whether you already have a treatment or not. Some directors are better at accomplishing other people's visions, while others only want to do videos where they write the treatment. It's also important you and the director can get to the same location to shoot the video.

When deciding on a director, make sure to look at their reel. This will be a collection of videos they have done before. Just because a director did a video you love, doesn't mean they can deliver great results all the time. You want to look for the director making quality videos at least a handful of times before you trust them with your hard earned money. While the videos don't all need to be ideas you love, seeing that they're high quality and well-done should be enough to pass the test. If you want to do some quick homework, see if they're on Vimeo because most directors post a reel or a playlist there. This homework will ensure you don't waste countless hours, money and momentum on someone who doesn't live up to your expectations.

Not Just Directors
Directors are not the only people who make videos. Motion graphic artists, animators, choreographers, photographers and other talented people can all make great videos for you. Maybe your friends are amazing interpretive dancers? Go film them. Music video ideas can come from a variety of places.

Other Duties
In addition to your director, you may need a handful of other talents on deck to help with your video:

- **Choreographer** - If your video involves complex dancing, someone will need to handle the choreography. Without a good choreographer, your dance moves may come off as amateur, lacking coordination and style.

- **Casting** - Do you need actors, dancers or extras for your video? Thankfully, you can usually find these talents in your fanbase. Send out messages on your social networks and recruit fans that will be excited to be a part of your music. If that doesn't work, Craigslist is filled with talent.
- **Fashion Stylist** - If your image is important and looking stylish is a part of what's going to make your video work, you may need a fashion stylist. Fashion stylists give you an objective perspective on your look. They make sure your suit isn't five sizes too large, that your shirt is tucked properly and a wide variety of other details that make your look something fans are in awe of. You can find stylists on Craigslist, through your director or, if you're on a limited budget, by asking your fashionable friends to pitch in and give you some help. If you have a local fashion school, you may be able to get free help from a student.
- **Hair/Make-up** - If you need to look especially glamorous in your video, a hair and makeup person can make sure your skin and hair are in place. There are tons of people who do this for a living. If you have a hairdresser friend, they can often take care of the hair part. You can also find this talent through your director or on Craigslist. The local beauty school can often get you free help from those looking to build a portfolio.
- **Video Editor** - Sometimes your director will hire out a separate editor for the video. This will usually be administered by your director. If you filmed your own video but are unhappy with the edit you're getting, you can find good editors by contacting other directors you would work with, because they often are editors themselves or would have a good recommendation.
- **Remote Recording** - If you're filming a live video, or one that requires dialogue to be recorded on set, you're going to need someone to handle this duty. Many recording studios offer remote recording facilities. My studio, Cannon Found Soundation in the NY/NJ area, provides these services (cannonfoundsoundation.com). Asking your record producer for a recommendation can often yield a good result.
- **Cameos** - Getting famous friends or fellow musicians to do a cameo can give your fans a treat, not to mention get more people to pay attention to your video and promote it.

Crowdsource It

You can crowdsource many elements of your video. Your fans will always be willing to help out and be a part of music they love. Here are some ideas for how to crowdsource your video:

- **Casting** - Get actors, extras or dancers from your fans. Any talent you could want can often be found in your fanbase.
- **Filming** - iPhones and other smart phones can shoot great video that can later be filtered for footage. Enlist your fans to film you. Allow free admission to shows for fans who bring high quality cameras to film you.
- **Performances** - You can have your fans film themselves doing something for your video.
- **Recommendations** - Ask your fans for recommendations for who to work with on your video, videos they like or what song you should do a video for.

Scheduling

Scheduling is an important part of making a video. If your video requires being outdoors, it's crucial you have a rain date. Many videos start production before the sun even comes up so they can get as much daylight filming as possible. You have to make sure everyone involved in the video can be there on the same day. This gets crazy if you have a large cast and crew all working for little money. Be sure to schedule your video far in advance to deal with any scheduling problems ahead of time. A director and treatment is often settled on 60 to 90 days before filming even begins.

The other painful part of scheduling on low budget projects is that it's rare video editing gets done on time. When you're trying to get a video into your promotion calendar so you keep momentum going, waiting for the editing to be done can be depressing, since it stalls your promotions in a major way. Be sure to allow for some extra time for the editor to go over deadline or emphasize the severity of your deadline to whomever is handling the editing duties.

Having a Plan B, and even Plan C, is crucial with videos that have very specific needs. Remember Murphy's Law: Everything that can go wrong, will go wrong. This seems to always be the case when filming a video.

Common Video Mistakes

When videos don't come out well, it's usually because of the same problems. Watch out for these common mistakes that inexperienced filmmakers make.

- **Coming Up Short** - Not filming enough good footage is the most common video mistake. Many times, inexperienced filmmakers will assume they have enough good shots, but they come up short and end up needing to use mediocre footage. You also must make sure you film enough B-roll, which are the cut-away shots you'll use to make sure you keep your viewer's attention. Think about single shots of images that will reinforce the feeling of the video and use these as cutaway shots. Film more than you would ever need and from multiple angles to be safe.
- **Lighting** - Bad lighting is one of the most common afflictions to a video. Filming footage and assuming it's lit properly is a tragic mistake that makes video painful to watch. Proper monitoring and checking your footage on site can help alleviate this problem.
- **Color Correction** - Color correction is to video what mastering is to audio. It adjusts the overall feel of the video's color contrast and a wide variety of other settings. When a video looks cheap or unprofessional it's often because of bad color correction. You can find a good color-corrector through recommendations from your director.
- **Unclear Narrative** - It can be tough to get what you're trying to say across without using dialogue. If your video has a meaning or a narrative that needs to be followed, you want to make clear. Make sure you screen your video for some viewers who don't know the narrative and see if they can pick it out, without any guidance from you.
- **Back That Thing Up** - Since most videos are made digitally, you need to treat them like any file and back them up. Make a second copy of everything as soon as it is done being shot. Try not keep the copies in the same place in case your equipment is damaged, lost or stolen.
- **Don't Be Shy** - Don't let there be weak performances in your video. It's best to go too far and outrageous in your performance and then edit it out, than to hold back and be shy. No one has a reason to watch and spread a video with boring performances.
- **Playback** - Make sure you're creating the video in conjunction with the recording of the final mix of the song. Your video editor will need to lock it up later and will not tolerate out of sync cues. Your

editor can easily fix other out of sync elements that make your video look bad or unprofessional, but it takes away precious time that can be devoted to improving your video.

DIY
The tools you need to make a great video on a low budget continue to become more readily and financially viable. We've seen great videos filmed on smartphones, Go-Pros and iPhone cameras countless times. Renting or buying a nice Canon camera with some lenses can be an amazing investment for your music, but not everyone has a few thousand dollars sitting around. iMovie comes with every Mac. Final Cut Pro is used to edit movies seen by millions of people and can be bought for $300. All of these tools are becoming cheaper every day, and you can easily access them. Start experimenting and learning to make great videos yourself if you have the time and ambition. While hiring a professional can save you time and money, if you have the ambition and vision to do something great, it's within your reach.

Final Product
Once your video is done you'll need it in a couple of formats. You'll want to output one version in the highest quality possible for any TV or high-definition Internet viewing. You'll also want a medium resolution and low resolution version. Some video players can't handle high-definition video, so these versions will come in handy to make sure you're able to upload your video to whatever service may want it. You may also need a DVD copy if you're going to be sending it to TV networks or video promotion companies.

Be Sure To Get The Content You Need
When filming a video you need to remember you need to get tons of other content to promote around each video. Matt Healy of the 1975 says this about this concept, *"I see the 1975 live show as like our daily marketing exercise: the show is content based, and acts as a sort-of frame for all of the visual marketing assets that we've produced to date. We use video as a light source as opposed to conventional lighting, and that enables us to build this huge canvas that we can drop the visual identify of the band into, that has evolved over the years, "*The following is some content to consider capturing while making your video.

- With the advent of vertical videos it is crucial that you get them so you have content for Spotify Canvas, Instagram & Facebook stories, TikTok or Snapchat

- If you do visual on stage you may want to tie parts of your video intro your projections. Specifically using B roll or other looks.
- Many groups give their single another life by doing a Vertical video of outtakes and B Roll or a simple performance in a vertical format since fans don't demand as high production value from it.
- Imagery from the video may also be used for future branding, merchandise or social network posts. Keep an eye out for visuals that can be recontextualized.

DIY Lyric and Visualizers Resources
If you are looking to do lyric videos or visualizer yourself there's a handful of resources that are free you can utilize.

- **Davinci Resolve** – Free video editing software that is great for editing videos in or making lyric videos. (blackmagicdesign.com)
- **Hitfilm** – Their express version is a VFX environment ideal for making visualizers. (fxhome.com)
- **Urmusic** – You can generate a visualizer based off the music you upload. (nassio.io)

Promoting Your Video

Once you have a finished video in hand, you'll want to get it to as many places that will promote it and allow it to be shared as possible. The following are some ideas on how to get your video to as many outlets as possible:

- **Press** - Any blogs or news sites that regularly write about you should be alerted. Negotiate an exclusive premiere with a blog to get extra push and exposure for your video. Try to make the premier a big deal by getting someone to push it.
- **Social** - Post the video to your social networks and ask fans to share them.
- **Website** - Make sure your video is on prominent display on your website and any social networks.
- **YouTube/Vimeo** - Make sure your video is on both of the top two online music video networks. The promotion of your video on these two networks is discussed in-depth in their own chapters.

- **iTunes Store** - You can make your video available for sale using TuneCore. (tunecore.com)

Hit The Video Blogs

YouTube has many channels that cover musicians, with more popping up every day. Search Google and YouTube's analytic sections to find the video blogs that are covering the musicians you targeted. Approach these bloggers with your video. Here are some cool channels that have come across Musformation's radar:

- **THECOOLTV** - THECOOLTV is on a bunch of cable stations and the Internet. Best of all, they take fan requests. (cooltv.com)
- **BlankTV** - Huge YouTube channel and website hosting tons of videos from punk, metal, emo/ and hardcore groups. (blanktv.com)
- **LP33.tv** - YouTube channel featuring tons of emerging musicians. (youtube.com/lp33tv)
- **BalconyTV** - Interviews and performances with tons of musicians. (balconytv.com)
- **Nervous Energies** - Punk bands stripped down to acoustic performances. (neverousenergies.com)
- **$99 Music Videos** - A YouTube channel that posts videos made for almost no money. (youtube.com/99dollarmusicvideos)
- **Antville** - An open blog posting cool videos and information about them. (videos.antville.org)

Video Promotion Companies

There are many companies who'll promote your video for a price. Most publicists will also work with your video and get it placements, but the video-specific companies often have access to many outlets normal promotion companies may not. These companies can often get you on outlets like on-demand video promotions for cable companies or mtvU. These services can really help you build your fanbase. Be warned, some of these companies are scams and will only upload your video to a few places and then run a bot driving up your YouTube views, comments and likes. While this can help your video's search results, it can look bad to fans and potential team members.

Sadly, getting your video played on major networks, on-demand services and video jukeboxes still depend on paying for promotion to get through gatekeepers. If you are doing extensive promotion and have built a good buzz for you music that you're able to demonstrate, a video promotion company may be able to help you get through these gates. However, they don't do a lot to help musicians who don't have a substantial following and buzz already. They're not a service that will break you on their own, they're help to enlist when you've come far and need an additional boost to get through the door of some guarded outlets. Make sure you're employing a well-rounded promotion campaign and have a good following on all of your social networks before sinking thousands of dollars into a video promotion company.

Here are some services Musformation has enjoyed working with:

- **HIP Video Promotion** - Highly recommended. The best video promo service we know of. (hipvideopromo.com)
- **Trendsetter Marketing** (trendsettermarketing.net)
- **Rive Video Promotion** (rivevideo.com)

Chapter 34: Youtube - The Biggest Music Social Network, Search Engine And Music Video Channel

It's hard to say what YouTube is when it has so much going for it. It's a social network where you can build relationships with fans and communicate with them in a meaningful way. It's the second most-used search engine on the Internet and the most used for music. It's also the largest music website on the Internet, where more than a two hundred million people stream music every day. In 2018 it was announced that more music is played on it than all other platforms combined. This means it's a pretty big deal and it always amazes me when musicians don't put their all into YouTube. It's a place where teenagers and adults spend all day browsing and looking for the next thing that will bring some joy to their life.

You can see it in the numbers. There's a lot of videos that have over a billion views. To put that in perspective, there are about 320 million people living in America. On a smaller scale, Tay Zonday's insanely viral "Chocolate Rain" is a video with zero marketing dollars, but 200 million plays. That means that without a dollar of promotion, your song could be heard hundreds of millions of times. That's pretty exciting!

Very few social networks can single-handedly make someone go from having a dozen fans to a million in a week's time. While results are not commonly that drastic, YouTube has the power to spread your music like few of the other tools in your arsenal, yet too many musicians don't take their presence there seriously enough.

Never before has the field been so level for smaller musicians with no budget but a great song and video. YouTube's searchable lexicon has made nearly any song ever recorded easily accessible. Fans know this and use YouTube to search for music every day, so your presence there is too important to ignore.

Your YouTube Channel

Your YouTube Channel can be like a TV station: a channel where you choose what's on. Add any original programming you come up with to your channel and if fans like it they can subscribe to it just as they would HBO, Showtime or MTV (though If you want to show other people's copyrighted material you need their permission). Your channel can be an interesting place to see what's going on or a place that clearly illustrates that you aren't very active.

Every day another person cancels their cable subscription because there is nothing that interests them on TV. They buy an Apple TV, Roku or use their computer to watch TV instead. Once they do, they subscribe to their favorite YouTube channels, replacing Fuse, The Voice and The Real Housewives with a channel they find more interesting. If they love your music, it could be your channel they subscribe to for constant programming.

It's Called A Channel For a Reason
Far too many musicians look at their YouTube as an afterthought, where you place your music videos instead of programming that you curate. You can put anything you find interesting on this channel. While your fans may not find it too interesting if you stray from your channel's stated intent, like when MTV started to show fewer music videos and more reality TV. This is your space to get creative and serve the millions of people who are bored and looking for the next great thing to watch.

As fans subscribe to your channel, they give you permission to program for them and keep them entertained. Take your YouTube channel seriously and make it a great place to visit.

Your Channel's Profile
You can customize your YouTube channel and give it a look and content that appeals to fans. Keep in mind YouTube looks at your page to make sure it is optimized when deciding whether to promote your videos or not so doing all the best practices they suggest is crucial to making YouTube work for you. Your channel can be optimized in a number of ways.

- **Background Image** - You can upload a cool background image. It's not a bad idea to use the same background as your Twitter account or Facebook cover photo. Keep in mind this image will be seen on 70" smart TVs so they should be high resolution.

- **Banner Header** - Use an image map that links your other social networks, website, merch store and free-music page. It takes a little tinkering, but this is a great way to make the people who find your videos explore the rest of your web presence.
- **Social** - In your About section, YouTube allows you to connect all the same pages with links in a neat format.
- **Avatar** - This is the picture that will go next to your name. A 1,600 x 1,600 pixel photo works best. It helps to use a logo that translates to the small thumbnail image used when you leave a comment on a video. Album covers also work great.
- **Trailer** – YouTube promotes the channels that obey their best practices so you get discovered by more new fans. To get this added promotion you need to create a trailer that introduces fans to your music.
- **About** - Use your one paragraph bio to let fans know who you are. Focus the bio on what videos you'll have on your channel.
- **Playlists** – Be sure to give your fans an easy way to see what you do. If you vlog there should be a playlist of blogs separate from your music videos or concert videos that entice your fans to come see you play live.
- **Layout** - YouTube allows you to choose a few different templates. If you want to specifically choose the videos to be featured on your landing page, choose that layout and categorize the videos you want viewers to see as feature videos.

The Feed

The feed appears on YouTube's front page and shows users the activity of every channel they've subscribed to. Unlike many other social networks, you're able to easily customize what goes into your feed, separating what content you keep to yourself and what your fans see. You don't want to pollute fans' feeds and have them unsubscribe from your channel, so it's important you give these settings a glance. This can also be a great way to give fans relevant content while you're between updates. Here are some ways you can use your feed:

- **Create** - The main thing your feed does is show fans when you upload a video or put one on a Facebook page.
- **Like** - You can show your fans whenever you like a video. If you're going to be a social butterfly and like tons of videos on YouTube, this can get a bit much for fans trying to sort through the feed. You can also use this function to call fans' attention to fan videos you

think others would enjoy. Only click like on these fan videos and ensure your feed stays relevant to your music.

- **Comment** - Fans will be alerted when you comment on a video. Again, if you're going to be a social butterfly this can be a bit much for fans to take. If you're only going to comment to your fans, this can show other fans that you're gracious and encourage them to make content involving your music.
- **Favorite** - Your favorites can bring fans' attention to videos about you that are not on your channel. Disable showing fans the videos you like and continue to be a social butterfly. Then use your favorites function to show subscribers videos you want to bring to their attention.
- **Subscribe** - If you're going to subscribe to a lot of channels this can get annoying for those who follow you, but it can also give fans a glimpse into what you enjoy.
- **Thumbnail** – Your thumbnail is one of the most important things you can make for each video to get a potential fan to click on your video. Every top YouTuber will tell you spending time to design the best thumbnail possible is crucial to YouTube success.

Tips For Getting More Channel Subscriptions
- **Add A Subscribe Card** - Adding a subscribe annotation to your videos will help you get more subscriptions, even when fans are viewing your video off the channel.
- **Keep A Schedule** - If fans know you regularly post content, they will keep checking back. Otherwise, they will forget you exist.
- **Personality** - If you assemble great playlists and let fans know about them on your other social networks, they will heed your call and subscribe to your channel.
- **Share More Than Your Own Videos** - Channels that point out other videos get more subscriptions.
- **Don't Split** - Only upload one version of your song to YouTube. Do not upload it to both the musician and the label's channel. Instead favorite the video from the account it is not posted from so it will show up in your subscriber's feed. Note that some distributors have options so that you can aggregate your music through them and have your video also show up on your own channel.
- **Custom URL** – Be sure to take advantage of YouTube allowing you to make a custom URL for your channel to ease your linking.

Videos Every Music Channel Should Have

Now you know you should be using YouTube, what types of video should you have on your channel?

Lyric Videos - The lyric video is one of the best tools for marketing today. It's funny how a simple video that shows the lyrics to a song can help fans forge a stronger bond with a song and become a bigger fan of your music. These videos can increase sing-alongs at shows and give fans content to watch that takes very little effort for you to make. Adding behind-the-scenes photos and other rare videos in the background can give your fans even more of a reason to watch lyric videos. If your lyrics are what fans will find appealing about your song, having a lyric video for the song is even more important.

These videos can be made using any video editing software that comes with a computer. If you're a true luddite, you can make a single-frame video and use YouTube's Video Cards system to make lyric videos. You can even get prehistoric and rip off Bob Dylan's "Subterranean Homesick Blues" or INXS's "Mediate" by filming yourself showing the lyrics on cards. If you're a great artist, you could make a lyrical drawing for each lyric. This format is open to many cool ways to hold fans' attention while they learn your lyrics.

Music Videos - Just like you used to see on MTV. Obviously, a great video can go viral and give your fans content to watch while they listen. When a music video is done well, it's the ultimate marketing tool. With every music video you make, you up your chances to have it go viral and have your fanbase exponentially increase. Many musicians have built careers by making great videos and spreading them.

Live Video - If you want people to come see you live, having an impressive taste of how good the experience will be can lead to more people coming out. The better the quality of your video, the more likely it is to be shared and thus ensure a good turnout.

While videos shot from a single camera can be honest, a video with a bunch of shots edited together can sell fans on coming to see you, especially if you get a good mix from the board. Remote recordings can work too. If you're a musician who prides yourself on your live show, put a lot of effort into making sure there are as many great live videos of your band as possible.

I've had the experience of trying to woo a potential team member, only to have them fear the band I was working with was bad live, because they had no videos of themselves performing on their YouTube channel. The experience made me realize YouTube is a place where many potential team members are auditioning musicians to work with. Live video needs to be a part of your YouTube presence.

Interview - Giving fans a way to watch and get to know your history and personality, and your little personality quirks, can go a long way when it comes to making your fans feel like you're someone they want to tell the world about. Filming an interview and answering some frequently answered questions is a great way for fans to get you to know.

Even if you don't see the interviewer or the questions flash on the screen, this is a great way for fans that don't want to read your bio have an enjoyable look into your personality and history. Cee Lo Green even made a video where he interviewed himself. The Dead Weather made a video where they answered all the interview questions they were tired of being asked.

Single Frames - If you can't make a music video, live video or lyric video for your song, you should at least have a single-frame video for every song you've released to the public. YouTube is the biggest music discovery medium out there. Not having your music on YouTube means you're missing out on the biggest opportunity for potential fans to discover your music. This is insane, considering it takes five minutes to put your song on YouTube.

Updates - Give fans a look behind the scenes and tell them what you have been doing. Not everyone wants to read a blog, so give them something good to watch.

More Ideas For Videos You Can Make For Your Channel
- **Trailer** – YouTube allows you to make a video that introduces you when potential fans navigate to your page. This is a great way to let fans know what they can find on your channel.
- **Personality** - Do you like to cook? Maybe you're really good at a video game? If this is part of your shtick, nothing is better at showing it off than YouTube. Against The Current garnered tons of fans attention by doing makeup tutorials.

- **Your Story** - If you have a great story behind your music or a special cast of characters (bandmates, roadies, collaborators), you should document it in order for fans to grow a greater appreciation for your music.
- **Welcome Video** - YouTube's new One Channel design allows you to make a welcome video where you can show new viewers who you are and direct them to some content to get to know you.
- **Tour Update** - Fans love seeing all the fun you're having on the road. Just make your tour update isn't filled with inside jokes and gives a good insight into your life and personality.
- **In The Studio** - Show fans how you create the music they love.
- **Updates** - Keep fans abreast of what's been going on with a video, instead of 20 paragraphs on how you have been writing in your parents' basement and eating at 7-Eleven. It is much more interesting to show them the oh-so-exciting lifestyle you're living than to tell them about it.
- **In-Studio Performance** - The kings of the in-studio performance are Pomplamoose. Look at their channel for some real inspiration. Making an interesting video of yourself creating a song in the studio never gets old to fans.
- **Dance Videos** - Are you a great dancer? Or maybe a horrible one? For some reason, YouTubers love nothing more than watching a choreographed dance performance to a song, especially if you have an abnormally-shaped butt. OK Go built a career on this.
- **Acoustic** - Recording an honest, stripped-down version of your song right into a camera can move your fans.
- **Sheet Music** - Post sheet music or tablature in your video and have it scroll with the song. This is great if you have many musicians for fans.
- **Lessons** - Teach fans how to play your song or even another musician's song.
- **Record Preview** - Make a funny or informative video preview for your next release.

YouTube Gold - The Cover Song
Nothing has propelled more unknowns into becoming well-knowns faster than a fantastic cover song posted on YouTube. Fans are constantly using YouTube to search for songs, and part of the website's beauty is that sometimes a fan covering the song comes up instead of the original

version. Many super fans seek out the cover versions of songs since they can't get enough of the song or are sick of the current version.

Cover songs get thousands, even millions of hits if done right. Many acts use cover songs as gateways for interested listeners to hear their original songs. Some musicians cover and cover and cover until there is an audience just for their covers. No matter what you do, covers are an easy way to get a larger audience.

Honest Vs. Polished - There is something about the honesty of a cover recorded on the camera microphone or your laptop that makes this video genre work. While doing a little mastering and polishing afterwards can really help sell a video (check out our service youtubemastering .com), using in-depth editing or pitch correction defeats the purpose of many of these cover videos. Fans want to see you have true, raw talent.

With that said, if you're able to do an incredible cover with some studio trickery, no one ever says "no" to a great song that's well-recorded. Just be sure you're doing the right thing for your approach and, most importantly, DO NOT LIP SYNC!

Put Every Song You Have Ever Made On YouTube
YouTube is the ultimate music discovery tool. It's where millions of music fans search for music. If someone hears your music, they're most likely going to search for it again on YouTube. If they can find it and fall in love with your band, you have another fan to build a relationship with. If they can't find your song on YouTube, you just lost a potential fan because they've already found another song to fall in love with.

Whenever you release music, make sure you have a YouTube video for every song you release. Not only does it allow fans to discover your music, it gives you another chance for someone influential to easily link your videos and send you lots of fans. It isn't easy to link songs from a Facebook page, but everyone knows how to link a YouTube. Watch celebrities on Twitter. If you don't think many careers are made by celebrities linking their favorite song and bringing the video thousands of plays, you're dead wrong.

Having a YouTube for all of your songs is a license for unlimited promotional potential. While some luck and hard work are usually necessary, this is the first step in opening unlimited possibility.

More Reasons You Need A YouTube For Every Song - As if that rant wasn't enough, here are a few more convincing points.

- **Blogs** - There are tons of YouTube blogs that only post YouTube videos instead of SoundCloud or other streaming audio services.
- **Playlists** - There are many fans that make playlists of their favorite songs every day. By having all of your music available on YouTube, you allow fans to include your music in the playlists they share with friends.
- **Social** - Fans comment on YouTube videos, then their friends and fans see those comments and check out the video. Remember, everyone has a feed on YouTube, so even fans that only upload videos of their cat have friends following them. Users' friends see their activity and interact with the same content.
- **Viral** - Few avenues increase the chance of your video spreading widely as much as YouTube does. Most likely, even your Grandmother knows how to share a video on YouTube and post it on her Facebook.
- **Google** - YouTube videos come up high on Google searches. This helps increase the chance that you'll get heard and discovered by potential fans.
- **Message Boards** - You can post YouTube videos on message boards, which may have disabled other music players.

Promoting Your Music On YouTube

YouTube Playlists

YouTube Playlists are not only a presentable way to sort videos with a common theme, they're also a great way to sort videos for your fans to consume. I believe you should never post only a single video. Instead, post playlists for your fans, and lead the playlist with the video you most want fans to watch. Playlists increase the chance viewers will watch your other videos once the first one is over. Playlists are powerful tools and there are countless ways to use them.

Here are some playlists you can make for your fans to enjoy:

- **Your Record** - Put your record in order. Present the album the way you intend fans to hear it.
- **By Type** - Do you make a bunch of acoustic covers or remixes? Sort these tracks into playlists by type.
- **Interviews** - You can assemble all of your video interviews in a playlist for fans who want to learn more about you. Writers searching for background information on your band will also appreciate this.
- **Updates** - Put all of your updates in one playlist for fans who are curious what you've been doing.
- **Fan Videos** - Do your fans make covers or dance videos to your tracks? Show them some appreciation, and encourage more fans to do the same, by assembling these fan videos into a playlist. You could even go one step further and make a remix video from your favorite videos.
- **Personality** - Are you a total geek for particle physics? Have you just discovered Can's music and want to tell the world? Maybe you pride yourself at being better than Tosh.0 at finding viral videos and want to arrange a monthly digest. Assemble your favorite videos that fit a theme and share it with your fans.
- **Live** - Some fans will post noteworthy videos of your shows. Assemble the best videos in a playlist and encourage more fans to upload similar videos.
- **Crew** - Make a playlist of your friend's music. They might do the same for you.
- **Favorite Songs** - Fans love learning about what you love. You can keep playlists of what you've been listening to or watching recently. This is great content for your blog or Tumblr.
- **Your Local Scene** - Assemble a playlist of the best local acts around you. Name them things like "Wyoming Dance Scene." When someone searches for that scene, your playlist will come up.
- **Long Content** - If your video exceeds YouTube's upload length, you can break your video up into parts and use a playlist to string them together. Similarly, if you made five studio updates in five separate videos, you can assemble them into a playlist.
- **Video Nerd Stuff** - If your videos use something like stop motion, cartoons or some other nerdy video technique, you can make a playlist of other videos that share the same qualities.

Spreading The Word With Playlists - Here are some ways you can put playlists to work promoting your music:

- **Embed** - Embed playlists on your blog and Tumblr. Share them with fans and they will spread across the Internet.
- **Social** - Tell your fans on your social networks if you assemble a cool playlist. Be sure to remind them you do this regularly and to subscribe to your channel to stay updated.
- **Search** - You'll get views if you name playlists with terms potential fans will search. If you make sweet songs about your love of The Legend Of Zelda, make a playlist that mentions it, so fans of the video game will find your music.

Using Intros And Outros To Grow Your Fanbase And Mailing List - YouTube allows you to make intros and outros for your playlists. Use these to give the address of your free-music page or a place where you can build fan relationships and acquire email addresses. Make a video that tells fans where they can go to get free music from you and make it either your intro or outro. If the song in one of your videos is available for free, be sure to include that information too.

Playlist A Single Video - You can make a playlist that's just an introduction and one song. Take the playlist embed code, embed it on your blog, and share it on your social networks. All of your fans will now see the music video with this intro.

Getting More Plays For Your Video
After you've put your video on YouTube, you want to get as many plays as possible. The first step is to make a great video with a great song. After you accomplish that, there are plenty of things you can do to spread your video on the Internet. Making sure your video gets a lot of plays is important, because the more plays your video gets, the higher it comes up in searches.

- **Four Minutes** - Plays of YouTube videos drop off dramatically if the video lasts longer than four minutes. Fans are used to short bursts and often fit watching videos during short lulls between other activities. You'll get more views if you keep it brief. If possible, break a long video into parts.
- **Press** - You spent weeks making your video, but you don't need to spend weeks trying to get it to spread. Make sure your video gets on every blog, channel and playlist you can once you release it.

- **Premiere It At A Show** - If you have a big show coming up, you can play your video before you take the stage. The new content will get fans talking.
- **Get Endorsements** - Contact all your musician friends and have them link to your video from their social networks. In return, do the same for them.
- **Embed** - Embed your video on your website, Tumblr, Facebook Music Player and in your news feed. Tweet it and take a screenshot of it to post on Instagram. Exposure is key to driving up views.
- **Premier** – Set your YouTube video as a premier so that if fans scroll through their subscriptions they will see it before its posted and hopefully remember to come back and watch it later.
- **Behind-The-Scenes** - Post a behind-the-scenes video two weeks after your music video is released. Embed it in a playlist with your video, and watch your old video be given new life. Make sure to link back to your main video in the information box and cards.
- **Let It Play At Your Merch Booth** - If you have a visually striking video, you can keep it on loop at your merch booth on an iPad or similar tablet. Hook up some headphones, and let fans gravitate to this eye-catching display. You'll probably sell more merch with it. This works especially well at big festival shows.
- **Metadata** - The more information you put in the information box, the more likely it is to come up in searches and be discovered by potential fans.
- **Watch Your Own Video** - You can run up plays on your video every time you go to a new location. Just be sure you're not signed into Google. You can hit play on your video every time you're in a new location and rack up a few more views.
- **Thumbnails** - Thumbnails are the frames you see when your video isn't playing. Since this is what most fans see before they play the video, it's important to choose a still frame from your video that will draw them in. Find a great shot from your video that will make fans want to watch, and you'll get more plays.
- **Category** - Be sure to put music as your category on YouTube. This will help to sort your music from other videos.
- **Caption** - If your video is of a speech or prepared remarks, add a caption file to your YouTube video so that it can be easily read.
- **Chat** – Host a chat for your fans in the comments of your video. This will push it up the YouTube search results and get more new fans eyes on your videos all the while bonding with fans.

Tube Buddy – One of the best free resources out there is a Chrome Extension called TubeBuddy that helps you find the right keywords for your videos and tons of other optimization tips. (tubebuddy.com)

Community
One of the best ways to promote yourself on YouTube is to participate in a community. Interacting with commenters on other musicians' videos is a great way for them to see your name and that you're a member of the community too. Many YouTube reputations are built by fans becoming familiar with a name in the comment section. Here are some other ideas on how to build community and get noticed on YouTube.

- **Respond** - Thank or interact with every fan that comments on your video. It's especially important you respond to them if they ask a question.
- **Comment** - Commenting on other musicians' videos is great for establishing the community you're a part of. It's also important to comment on your fans' videos, especially if they make ones that involve you.
- **Feed** - Be sure to show your friends' videos to your fans in your feed.

Getting Spammy
Although I don't condone this behavior, it does help some musicians. Many musicians will create a separate YouTube personality that they only comment and promote from. They will go to other musicians' YouTube videos and suggest a video of their band while pretending to be someone else. It can be effective, but there's plenty of more effective work you could be doing to build your fanbase.

What I have seen other musicians do, that's also much more successful, is become a positive member of a musician's community. Add a signature on all of your comments that links to what you would like to promote.

Getting Fans To Promote You On YouTube
It's easy to get fans to promote you on YouTube, if you inspire them.

- **Contest** - Hold a dance or cover contest and reward the fan that creates the best one. They will inevitably share the video they made for the contest on their social networks, thereby giving you free promotion.

- **Fan Of The Month** - Many musicians hold contests to find a fan of the month, where they honor a fan that helped promote them. Encourage fans to share or promote your videos on YouTube in order to win this honor.
- **Ask Them To Share** - The easiest way to get fans to spread the word about your video is to simply ask.

Horrible Promotion Idea: Putting Your Music On Someone Else's YouTube Video

Some not-so-bright minds think it's a good idea to rip the video from a popular song's music video and to put their own song on as the audio track, annotating it with their Facebook or iTunes link. Clever? Yes! Bad idea? For sure! Not only is this a defamation lawsuit waiting to happen, but also it pisses the listener off because they didn't find the music video for which they were searching. They could have liked your song, but now they're angry at the YouTube system failing them, and they're probably not in a good mindset to enjoy your music. Sure, you may reach a viewer who hears your song for the first time, but their confusion will probably cause them to avoid becoming your fan or buying your track. Promote your music in a smarter way instead of wasting time on this stupid trick.

Promoting With The Information Area

Below every video is a place to add information and context. It's important you add this information as soon as you upload your video. If your video gets a lot of traffic while you're sleeping, you could lose the chance to take advantage of a big opportunity. It's also important you don't overwhelm the viewer in your information section with requests to do something. Here are some ideas for what to put there:

- **Call To Action** - Offer one call to action, either to buy the song or download it for free. Anything more is a bit overwhelming.
- **Other Content** - Suggest another video you have viewers may enjoy.
- **Purchase** - Tell fans where they can buy the song. If they can get it for free online, link that web address.
- **Free-Music Page** - Tell fans where they can get more free music from you.
- **Suggest** - Suggest another great video for viewers to watch before asking them to buy music from you.

- **Link** - Suggest the viewer follow you on the social network you're having the best luck with. If that's YouTube, you can always link your YouTube channel, or you can save that for the cards. Linking your website is also a good idea.
- **Credit** - Be sure to credit the video's director and anyone else who would appreciate recognition. Including this information is one of the only ways those who work on your video get credit. You can also add credits at the end of the video itself.
- **Inform** - In the title of the video, inform fans what kind of video it is. If it's a lyric video, tell them. If you and a fan upload a video for the same song, mark yours "Official" if you don't want the fan to take down their video.
- **Lyrics** - Add lyrics so that they show up in searches. Many fans only know the lyrics to a song and not its title, so this can be an immense help in getting your video discovered.

If you want to see how well all of this linking is working, you can use a service like Bitly (bitly.com) for analytics and to see how often your links are clicked. You can use this information to decide what to put in your information box.

The Fold - The information box has what's called a fold, meaning that users can click "Show More" if they want to see all of the information you've included. Put all of the actions you would like fans to do above the fold. You can put as much information as you would like below the fold. You can include lyrics and extensive production credits here. This can improve your search engine results.

Banner Ads
If you're a YouTube partner (more info on this later in the chapter), you can add a banner ad to the bottom of your videos. This banner can show where to buy the song, promote your website, tour or whatever you would like. It's one of the perks of being in a partnership with YouTube. This is a great place to link your free-music page.

Using Cards To Promote Your Music
When a video is shared in Facebook's news feed, viewers can't see any of the information listed in its YouTube description unless they click the "Show More" tab on the video. Adding cards can help you solve this problem. Cards are also a great way to give viewers more information

about your video. Unfortunately, cards can also be very distracting to viewers and can get in the way of your video's awesomeness.

Regardless, cards are helpful when your video is embedded on blogs and social networks, because the information listed on your YouTube page won't be there. These cards can also give fans relevant information while they watch your video. Here are some ideas for using cards in your video:

- **Optional Cards** - Inform the viewer they can turn the cards off. Be sure to do this if you're going to use a lot of cards. Tell viewers they can click the box at the bottom of the video player to turn cards off.
- **Inform** - Annotate some of the information you put in the video's description box, perhaps the director or a place to download the song.
- **Buy-Download** - If you're giving this song away for free, or you want to sell it, let fans know. This kind of annotation is most effective at the end of the video in the fade out. You could also put this annotation at the beginning of the video, before it gets visually stimulating.
- **Short Run** - Cards don't need to run through the whole video. They can pop up for just a few seconds.
- **Guest Star** - Do you have someone cool or famous in your video? Use annotation to point them out.
- **Commentary** - You can use cards to make commentary about your video while it's playing. Try informing fans with fun facts, sort of like Pop Up Video on VH1. Use speech bubble cards for commentary.
- **Dialogue** - If you don't want dialogue spoken in your actual video, but you want to show what the actors in your video are saying, use the speech bubble cards.
- **Subscribe** - YouTube allows you to create a one-click subscribe button for your channel inside your video. You can even link other channels. Consider linking your label or director's channel. If your video is premiering on a blog or your label's channel, ask them to add a subscribe annotation for your channel.
- **Update** - Be sure to point to your newest video from your older videos if they still get traffic.
- **Upgrade** - If you make a music video for a song you already have a single-frame or lyric video for, be sure to link to it in your cards and the information section.

- **Merchandise** - YouTube has a merchandise annotation tool. Use it to point to your merch on any YouTube approved site.
- **Links** - You can't make clickable links to anything outside of YouTube's website unless you're a partner in good standing with YouTube. However, if you are a partner you can link to your own website which is the perfect opportunity to link to your free music page or a direct-to-fan purchase of the song or album in the video.
- **Questions** - Use cards to ask your fans questions and get them commenting. You can even ask which song you should make a video for next.
- **Spotlight** - Use the spotlight cards to make buttons in your videos, which go to other videos, parts of a running theme or subscribe to your channel.
- **Open In New Window** - It's a good idea to use the "Open in New Window" function for any links you make.
- **Like** - You can ask for likes or comments in your cards. If you ask for comments, ask a specific question fans should give an opinion on--not something vague and open-ended. It can also help to ask for the like at the end of the video after you have impressed the fan.
- **HD** - If your video is in HD and looks great, you can use cards to suggest turning on the HD settings.
- **Next** - At the end of your video suggest another video for fans to watch so they get even more hooked.
- **Live Shows** – YouTube is picky about who you can link in Cards, but your BandsInTown page is able to be linked if you want to promote upcoming shows.

InVideo Programming - InVideo allows you to recommend other videos on your channel to viewers. This means you can recommend old videos or your latest video from your old videos so that fans see more of your content.

Tagging Your Videos
While tags may seem boring to type, they're how potential fans find your video. These terms help you get a higher rank in the results when people do a YouTube search. It's important you tag your videos thoroughly using keywords (things fans would search for) relevant to potential fans searching YouTube.

Here are some ideas of what to tag:

- **Name**
- **Song**
- **Album Title**
- **Genre** - Don't overlook this detail, since it can help a lot in coming up high in searches.
- **Themes** - Is your song about a drive-by shooting? Make sure that it's tagged as that.
- **Guest Stars**
- **Guest Musicians**
- **Director**
- **Contents Of Video** - This is especially important if someone is going to describe it as "the video on the space pirate ship."
- **Mood** - If your song is a baby-making jam you may want to tag it just like that. Whatever the mood, tag it explicitly so it comes up in searches for that feeling.
- **Location** - Fans may recognize something in the video or look for a location they have been to and discover your video.

Don't forget, you need to use quotation marks around your multi-word tags for them to register as a single tag. This means you need to tag "Sweet Child O' Mine," not Sweet Child O' Mine as four separate tags.

Trade Recommendations With Other Musicians To Promote On YouTube
Every musician wants potential fans to see their videos. An easy way to do this is by writing to musicians who are your friends or have a similar fanbase to you and asking them to trade recommendations. Once you figure out some musicians you could do this trade with, there are three ways you can show your fans each other's music:

- **Channel Recommendation** – On your YouTube channel page you can show your fans some other channels that you enjoy. You can make a small list below your featured playlists with a custom title and recommend another channel for your fans to watch. Every YouTube channel page can make this by clicking the Other Channels button while customizing their page.
- **Playlist** – Make a playlist of your favorite music or all of your friend's music and feature it on your channel. You can see this in action on our YouTube channel (youtube.com/user/Musformation) where I have made a YouTube playlist called "Music I Love". This

playlist can get shared in your feed and linked on other social networks exposing all of your followers to your friend's music and the same when they do this for you. You can embed the playlist on your blog, Facebook, Tumblr, etc. and easily expose each other's music to your fanbases.

- **Feed** – You can choose what your fans see in their subscription feed by clicking on your Channel Settings. You can like friends' videos and share it, show when you create the playlists we described above, comment on a video or subscribe to a friend's channel. You can turn these settings on before you give your friends an endorsement, and they can do the same for you so that all of their subscribers see this public display of affection for you.

What Many Of YouTube's Biggest Musician's All Have In Common
While not every big YouTube act does the same things, in my years of writing about DIY musicians I see a few common traits with all of the musicians who do big numbers on YouTube.

- **Regular** – Most of them post a new video weekly if not bi-weekly.
- **Cards** – They make interesting and fun cards to their videos as well as cards that point to their subscription, downloads for the song and a website.
- **Description** – The video description links where to buy and/or download the song for free as well as lyrics for the song and credits.
- **Try Again** – Most accounts have low video counts at first and they keep getting better. Persistence is key. Many of YouTube's stars videos did terrible for a year or more. YouTube success doesn't happen overnight and takes commitment.
- **Social** – They socialize in the comment sections with their fans.

YouTube Analytics - A Powerful Look Into How You Can Promote Better

YouTube's statistic tools are available for everyone on every video on YouTube (as long as the channel doesn't turn them off), simply by clicking a little bar graph or integrating Google Analytics. They can give a powerful insight into whether your promotions are working and how you can do them better. Best of all, they're super clear and easy to use.

Press

Remember when I told you how important it was create a Google Alert for your name so you know who's writing about you? Google Alerts may not pick up on someone who is embedding videos of your music. You could have a huge writer, blogger or message board personality posting your videos and you wouldn't even know it. To find this, click the stats button and click "show more stats." Clicking this shows you a graph of where your views are coming from. You can click each of the graph parameters to get data. The most important one for our purposes will be the embedded player, which shows you all the sites that posted this video. Visit these sites, collect their contact information and add them to your press mailing list. Comment on the blog posts--thank them and you're setting up a great relationship for the future.

Touring

Click on the Demographics tab in the left column and learn about who and where people are viewing your video (if you don't have a lot of views, this may be unavailable). If you click on the countries in the graph you can even see which states are giving you the most views. Wherever you see a lot of plays coming from are places you should visit on tour. You can also see the gender of your fans so you know who to aim your merch toward.

Momentum

You can see when your YouTube views peak in traffic and when they start going downhill. This may be time to kick up the promotion for this video or to move on to release another one. This section can also be helpful in making sure your ad campaign is working well. Be sure to also check you old videos and see if they're getting any new, interesting trends that you can use to your advantage.

Making Money On YouTube

There are a few ways you can make money right on your YouTube channel, aside from linking to where to buy your music.

Make Money From Ads On Your YouTube Channel

If you have been on YouTube before, you may have noticed they have a lot of ads all over the place. You can get a portion of the money made on your channel by simply opting into YouTube's partner program. YouTube will give you a portion of the profits they make, as long as this service is turned on. If your video goes viral, this can mean seeing some serious money from it. It only takes a minute to sign up. Depending on who you ask you will get paid .325-.6 of a penny for every YouTube view so that minute can be worth your while. After all, even at the lowest estimates a million plays on YouTube will get you a few thousand dollars in royalties. (youtube.com/partners)

Hold Off On Ads - Some labels like to hold off ads on unknown act's videos for a little while. This way fans don't get discouraged when they have to sit through a five- or 30-second ad just to see if they like a song.

VeVo - VeVo is of course the big time for YouTube music videos. You can get an increased royalty rate and recommended to more users by being a part of the network. In order to get the video on VeVo you need to upload it through a digital distributor that has partnered with VeVo.

SongKick Will Display Your Tour Dates And Sell Your Concert Tickets On YouTube
If you're updating your tour dates on SongKick they will show up on your YouTube page to viewers based in the areas you're touring. Their service will also provide viewers with links to buy tickets if the buy link is available. In order to get this going, you need to do nothing more than add your dates to SongKick. Another great reason to always keep SongKick up to date!

Sell Product Placements
If you're getting tons of YouTube plays, you can team up with brands that may want to be a part of your demographic and get them to give you some money for putting their product in your video. YouTube mega-stars like OK Go did this with State Farm Insurance. It can also be more subtle where the product is worked into a video.

Endorsements
While it isn't exactly money, having a YouTube channel with tons of views that shows you use a company's product can entice them into a nice endorsement deal. Be sure to approach the companies you want endorsements with numbers from your YouTube channel.

YouTube SEO
Many musicians will try to game YouTube to get higher results in the search function, so more new potential fans will discover their video. However, this doesn't just come down to gaining a lot of views. While

YouTube will look at your tags, metadata and the information in your description box when deciding if you'll come up in a search, what's most important is engagement. Fans need to like and comment on your videos, otherwise your search results are doomed. You can encourage these interactions with cards or in the end credits of your video. By doing so you may be helping yourself to be discovered by tons of new fans.

Here are some other tips to make sure you're discovered in searches more often:

- **Tags** - Tags are much more powerful than your title or description. Make sure you take your tags seriously and do a thorough job tagging your video with every term someone may search for when looking for your video.
- **Regular** - Keeping your channel active with regular uploads makes YouTube rank your content higher in searches. If you have an active channel and are getting views regularly they will give you priority over those who don't.

Tools For YouTube

The following are a set of tools both within YouTube and from outside services.

Private/Public/Unlisted
If you aren't ready to show the world your video there are three options for privacy right inside YouTube. This is especially helpful if you want to upload your video, maybe show it to some friends and make sure everything works before going public. Here are your options and how to use them:

- **Public** - Anyone can see your video. It is listed in playlists, on your channel, Google and YouTube.
- **Private** - If your video is set to private, only you and up to 50 other users who you invite to view the video will be able to see it. The video will not appear on your channel, in search results or in playlists etc.
- **Unlisted** - Unlisted means that only those who know the link to the video can view it. This is great if you aren't too worried about

anyone seeing it and want to send around the link to a few people before the video goes live. Note that anyone who has the link can see it, so someone can leak this link and the whole world can find it.

Enhancements

YouTube has a few options to let you touch up your video after it's uploaded. If you didn't quite nail it when editing your video you can do the following with YouTube:

- **Auto-Fix** - YouTube will optimize lighting and color for you.
- **Fine Tune** - You can tweak lighting and color on your own.
- **Stabilize** - This will help to fix shaky camera motions.

Live Streaming

YouTube allows you to live stream and alerts your followers when you do. These can often be higher quality and better production than Instagram since you can use more than your phone.

Stories

YouTube has stories that you can use to update your fans just like Instagram, Facebook and Snapchat. You can aggregate the same content here but most users report very little engagement on these.

Improving Sound On YouTube

If you're recording YouTube videos in your bedroom or on a camera, the audio can sometimes be harsh. This sucks because you just gave a great performance, but the sound is either quiet or not as pleasant as you would like. The best option is to master your YouTube video. YouTube Mastering (youtubemastering.com) will perform this for you for $25-50 depending on your needs. They can clean up noise and make your YouTube video sound more full and louder. Basically, if there is a problem they can fix it. This is ideal for those hoping to go viral from a video they recorded themselves.

What about Music Videos? - Most music videos don't need special mastering for YouTube. If your music was mastered, it's usually fine. If you do notice that your video is having bad sound problems, you can send it into the service and they will do what they can to fix it.

Use Show.co To Capture Fans And Add Bonuses

Show.co has an amazing tool that can help you promote your video, get email address and give fans free tracks. The tool allows you to link fans to your YouTube page (or any page for that matter) and a widget of your choice will pop-up in a Lightbox. You can use their email-for-media widget and trade fans a download for their email for the video you're linking.

This Lightbox will only happen when fans click the link you give them not when they surf to the video on their own. This can work very well if you get blogs to use this link. It can greatly up your mailing list if your video becomes popular. You can also use this link in the information section on your YouTube to allow fans to grab this download even if they didn't come to the video from this link.

Content ID
Content ID is YouTube's anti-piracy function. With it you can tell YouTube what material is pirated or uploaded by fans. You can then choose whether to take it down or whether to enable the ability to make ad money from the plays on the fan's channel. I don't think it's a good idea to make money from the ads on a fan's channel but instead would ask them to take it down and put the video on your own channel. You want your fans to think of your channel as the place they can go to get all of your music, not a scattering of videos across fans channels.

Asking Fans To Take Down Your Video - If you achieve any level of success, you'll probably deal with fans uploading your video to their YouTube channel. Yes, this is illegal, but don't treat them like criminals. These are your fans and are big enough fans that they want the world to hear your music. Simply try to message them via comment or find them on another social network. Do whatever it takes to avoid taking down a video through YouTube's Content ID system and having that fan's YouTube channel deleted and instead just claim it and monetize it so you get the money from the streams.

MP32Tube Will Make A Single Frame YouTube Video Of Your Song
Making a single frame YouTube is a little too much video editing for some musicians who aren't good with technology. MP32Tube (mp32tube.com) is a service that will do this for you with just a few clicks. Simply upload the song and the picture and it will make you a single frame video straight to your account. If you want to get rid of their logo and have a more advanced set of options, you can pay $10.99 for their premium function.

Additionally, the service TunesToTube (tunestotube.com) will do the same for free.

Strategy

There are some general truths that work for every artist on YouTube.

- Pay attention as YouTube changes best practices in their creator guides and follow them. They promote the creators who follow their instructions and the rewards are worth the little bit of time you need to take to keep up with what they want.
- Take the time to annotate videos and keep your promotions up to date on every video that is getting plays. This can be a great way to have your old content do work for your new promotions.
- Make sure to take the time to develop other content outside your music your fans will find interesting. YouTube is the greatest opportunity musicians have today to connect with new listeners so take advantage of it in every way you can.

As this is an area that changes CONSTANTLY I encourage you to visit my YouTube channel as I regularly cover this subject and upload videos with the latest information.

Chapter 35: Other Video Services To Help Promote Your Music

While YouTube may be the best known video service, that doesn't mean there aren't other services that have niches and features that can help your music. These services all have a role in the social video world that can help you build bond with fans and get you discovered by influential listeners.

Using Vimeo To Promote Your Music Video

Many think of Vimeo (vimeo.com) as a competitor to YouTube--I don't. The numbers don't show Vimeo even coming close to competing with YouTube, but that doesn't mean Vimeo isn't very important. Instead, think of Vimeo as a community of viewers who are interested in great quality videos. Vimeo prides itself on having a great looking player and its users appreciate it. This is why it's the place where directors, animators and other high-tech geeks go to get inspired and show off what they have.

My advice to musicians is to not put every video you have on YouTube also up on Vimeo. Instead let Vimeo be the place where you show off the high-quality videos you have to a community that will appreciate them. Putting up your single-frame video or lyric videos on Vimeo diminishes the plays it would get on YouTube. Instead, put up the videos you put a lot of effort into and shot in high-quality video. Vimeo is a place where other users will appreciate it.

While writing this book I often clicked Vimeo on my Apple TV and watched their music channel. It's filled with tons of great-looking videos. Others do this too and with Vimeo's Tumblr-like news feed, video nerds are able to stay up to date with their favorite musicians and directors on the service. In fact, if your video director has a strong presence on Vimeo, it can sometimes be best to let the video be hosted on their channel.

Vimeo Music Store
Vimeo's music store isn't like most music stores. It's much more of a place where the creative users in their community can access music to license.

Not only is this a great way to make money, it's also a cool way to promote your music in an artistic community. Having your music in this store exposes you to a community of creative users of a vibrant video community. So how do you get your music there? That is a little more complicated.

The licensing company AudioSocket (audiosocket.com) has exclusive rights to curate the paid music on the service. In order to get your music here, as well many other places where AudioSocket pitches and aggregates, you need to be accepted by their service. If you offer up your music for free, it would be a great idea to get your music on WFMU's Free Music Archive (freemucharchive.org). If you license your music with a Creative Commons attribute on the FMA, you're able to get your music on to the Vimeo Music Store.

If you think your music is ideal for web videos soundtracks, follow one of these avenues to get your music in the store:

Vimeo Password Protection
One of the features Vimeo users love is the ability to password protect a video. This is great for when you want others on your team to be able to watch an unfinished product and not worry about the video leaking. Many directors prefer doing this stage of the video-editing process on Vimeo since it provides a much better-looking video stream. This can also be great to protect a video you want to pitch to bloggers for potential placements.

Protected Embed
If you want to give a blog an exclusive embed of your latest video, the options are scarce (Topspin's streaming player will also disable embedding). YouTube doesn't allow this function and neither do a lot of the cheaper video services. Vimeo offers the ability to disable the embed code option on a video so you're the only one who has it. This allows you to give an exclusive video stream to whichever blog you want to partner with.

Promoting
Promoting on Vimeo is similar to YouTube in that you have comments and the ability to subscribe to other channels. There is also a feed which shows activity. If you're going to be making lots of high quality, visually stimulating videos, this is a great place to nurture and build community.

Vimeo Tools
- **Montage** - Vimeo has some great widgets where you can embed a whole slew of good-looking videos in a clean format.
- **Download** - You can download Vimeo videos easily (if enabled) in all sorts of different sizes. This is great if you want to give fans that option.
- **HTML5** - Vimeo is HTML5 friendly so it will work great in iOS.
- **Tipjar** - If you're a Vimeo Pro or Premium member you can hook your PayPal account up and get tips from fans deposited directly to your account.

Live Streaming Services

Live streaming is a great way to bond with fans, right on the spot. The excitement of being able to chat with fans live can get them excited and feel a part of what you do. As the Internet gets faster, this mode of communication will get more and more appealing to fans.

What You Can Live Stream
Here are some ideas for live streams you can host for your fans:

- **Shows** - Set up a camera or a few and send fans a feed of the live show.
- **Recording** - Live stream your recording process to get fans psyched for your new record.
- **Q&A** - Fans love to get this access and ask you what they want to know.
- **DJ Sets** - Play fans some music and let them watch the action.
- **Private Concerts** - You can set up concerts in your practice room to play for fans. This is great for building hype for a tour and giving something to fans in areas you have never toured.

Twitch – The First Live Streaming Service To Really Break
For years, every service that tried to do live streaming would ascend and then descend as fast as they rose. That is no longer the case since Twitch came to town. While it's is commonly used as a live streaming site for gamers, but more and more musicians are using it to stream live shows and their recording process. The service allows revenue sharing and great features to take questions and interact while broadcasting. Many musicians bond with fans while announcing on social networks they are going to go

on to chat with them while they play video games or do other interactions. (twitch.com)

One of the emerging marketing schemes on Twitch is to find popular players who listen to your genre of music and guest on their streams. Twitch also offers a royalty free music library (music.twitch.tv/) which you can add your music to in order to get exposure. In addition to gamers streaming your music while they play there are emerging DJ channels which take music submissions. There also some musicians who do regular streams performing covers and other improvised performances. The artist Hana recently interacted with her fans while recording her whole new record on Twitch. The format is still young and have plenty of room to do creative things with. This can be an amazing exploit to get exposure before it gets crowded.

Services That Will Allow you To Live Stream
There are a handful of services that will allow you to host live streams to your fans each with their own feature sets:

- **YouTube** - Hangouts are group video chats that you can host with fans. Google has now enabled them for everyone to easily use.
- **Facebook/Instagram Live** – Going live on Facebook/Instagram allows you to capitalize on where eyes are when they are bored. It's becoming more and more common for part of an album launch to include Facebook Live broadcasts of shows, practices or Q&As.
- **Periscope** – Twitter's live streaming service allows you to stream live video from your phone. The videos also remain for 24 hours if fans miss what you did. (periscope.tv)

Chapter 36: Advertising Your Music

Doing something eventful that's worth talking about is the best advertising, but sometimes you just want to pay some money to get yourself in front of some eyes, in order to get discovered by more potential fans. Advertising used to be an essential part of building a fanbase in the old music business. With the flattening of the music world there are musicians who barely spend any of their budget on advertising and still manage to gain lots of fans. With that said, if you're seeing some success from your grassroots promotions and then have the budget to spend to go further, advertising can open new worlds to you.

Many musicians make the mistake of thinking advertising dollars thrown at a problem will equal sales. This is not true in the Information Age. Advertising is merely a reinforcement in a well-rounded strategy. I would argue that if all of your social network and distribution avenues are not in place, advertising is going to be pretty useless. Ads work when there is a lot of content for a fan to ingest. They are a best way of starting a relationship with a fan by building familiarity instead of making a direct sale. If you want to see sales go up from ad campaigns, you'll usually be disappointed. If you want to see more people be more aware of you and hear your music, you can have a lot of success.

If you're anything like me, you rarely see an ad for a musician and click on it. Instead, you see a name on a news site, an article somewhere or their name playing a show with a musician you like. All of these things lead you to break down and give a spin to a new song. Sometimes that leads to becoming a fan; sometimes the music is not for you.

That is most likely how your ad campaign will go too. Advertising is the way to start some hype, but as discussed in this book again and again, you're not going to sell music to those who don't yet consider themselves fans of your music.

The other crucial thing to consider with advertising is that nothing will kill a bad product faster than good advertising. If you are not putting the majority of your budget into making great music, you may as well burn that money instead of advertising. Advertising should never be more than 10-15% of your overall budget and even that may be far too much.

Internet Advertising

Advertising on the Internet is a gift to everyone with a limited budget. Before the Internet, it was extremely hard to build a national brand without millions or billions of dollars. Now with a good product, smart social media and some smart advertising you can build a national following for far less money than ever before.

There are many services that allow you to place online ads and each of them have their advantages. One disclaimer: My advice is aimed toward those of you who are not ad executives, but rather have a limited budget of somewhere between $100-$10,000. This advice is aimed to be cursory and focused to those who want to make a little money go far. If you have more than $10,000 to spend, do more research and read a book that is devoted specifically to online advertising. Maybe even some blogs. My advice on how to make a lot of money go far in that situation would be far different. This is serious money and it is easy to blow it in a stupid way.

Google Ads
Google ads or Google AdSense is the most popular advertising channel on the Internet. It's in your Gmail window, at the top and the right in your Google searches and in ads all over your favorite websites. They're the most popular form of ads on the Internet. They also are highly effective and can get you in front of potential fans that are interested in whatever you want to target. This means if you're in a KISS cover band you can pay to show up every time someone Googles "KISS cover band" or even "KISS." While it's expensive to target a search term that specific, it can be highly effective.

The great thing about Google Ads is you have a lot of control over them. In fact, you can keep experimenting and refining them until you find one that gives you better results. There are tons of parameters to tweak in every ad.

- **Daily Budget** - Google Ads will allow you to set a limit on how much you spend on advertising every day.
- **Words To Target** - You can target specific searches or interests. If you want to be one of the top results for a search, you can type in

that search. If you want your banner ads to show up on a certain type of site or interest, target that.

- **Location** - Only target where you're trying to build your fanbase. Don't waste money on targeting potential fans in New Zealand if you're not touring New Zealand and have no music out there.
- **Age/Sex** - Target your most common fan profile. If your music is about equal between sexes, you can target both, but no one's music is universal in age. Look at your analytics on other sites and identify the common age of your fans.
- **Interests** - You can target the interests of the potential fans who see your ads.
- **CPC**- This is cost-per-click. You can tell Google how much you're willing to pay for a click, which will let them decide on the type of placements they give you with their users.

Types Of Ads - Google offers a few different types of ads. Each one has advantages and specific strategies to make them work.

- **Text** - Text ads appear in places like Gmail and on websites with text ads enabled and the right hand of your Gmail or search feature. They have no picture; instead, they pitch you on what they're selling in a sentence or two. While these are not too common for music campaigns if you're creative they can work.
- **Display** - These ads are displayed on websites or over YouTube videos. While they are effective, it's usually smart to make something more visually appealing for music marketing.
- **Image** - Banner and square ads are the most common displays ads. These are commonly used to promote musicians' campaigns. You can use text and a nice graphical representation to catch a fan's eye.
- **Search** - These ads focus on keywords your potential fans might search for. When they do, your results will come up in the results at the top or on the right. If you want to come up in the search for a certain website or another group, this is the way to do it.
- **Mobile** - These ads come up within apps on mobile devices. They aren't the most common type of ad for your music, but if you have something clever up your sleeve you can give it a try.

Google ads are one of the easiest ways to get a great bang for your buck in advertising your music. If you do some thorough research and serious targeting you can run an effective campaign that starts a relationship with more fans.

Advertising On YouTube

Advertising on YouTube is a great way to get your video more plays. Many consider your YouTube video to be advertising for your music. Music videos were the ultimate advertising in the MTV age, but even then was a lot of money poured into promoting and marketing these videos. One way to do this this promotion in the present day is by employing a YouTube ad campaign (youtube.com/advertise). These campaigns will allow you to show up in promotions across YouTube, such as being the featured video (Video Discovery Ads), being played before a video a viewer chooses (In-Stream Ads) or coming up at the top of YouTube searches.

Getting Started - The first thing you'll need to do is tell YouTube how much you're willing to spend each day for a budget. Then you need to decide which video to promote. Once this decision is made, there are four types of promotions to choose from:

- **Search** - You'll show up in the YouTube search feature as a result at the top.
- **In-Slate** - These are the advertisements where YouTube tells you to watch a video uninterrupted after you choose an ad to watch.
- **In-Display** - This allows you to become the featured video next to the YouTube someone is watching.
- **In-Stream** - Your video will be played before another video on YouTube.

You'll then tell Google how much you're willing to pay for each click. This will greatly determine the quality of YouTube videos your ads are placed on.

Focus - Like all Google ads, you can then greatly narrow your demographics. You can focus on age, location, interests and "viewing content in." Look at your analytics and use them to save your money by keeping it to users who would be interested in your music. Be smart and target searches for similar acts and your genre.

YouTube Advertising Considerations - There is an art and understanding to this that could fill a whole book and there are many on this subject. Know that this is just an overview--if you're going to take Google and YouTube ads seriously, buy a great eBook on the subject.

Here are some other considerations:

- **Target** – The easiest way to run YouTube ads is to find bigger bands who's fans would like you and buy ads that target their fans. While these ads cost more it can be highly effective if you narrow on regions you play regularly and age groups that are within your audience.
- **Sales** - Like most ads, don't expect these to lead directly to sales. These ads are just the start of a relationship.
- **Plays** - While these ads may generate plays, they're worthless if they don't begin a fan. relationship. Make sure you're interacting with your video's comments and that your video is set up with proper information to capitalize on this promotion.
- **Quality** - If your video doesn't blow the potential fan's socks off, it is all for naught. If you're going to put promotional money in, make sure you worked hard on both the music and video.
- **Buying Plays** - For no more than a penny per click, $10 can buy you about 1,000 plays if all you want is to inflate plays. Sadly, most of these clicks will be useless and not very well targeted.

Reddit

As discussed before, Reddit (reddit.com) may be the biggest community of tastemakers and over-sharers on the Internet. What gets popular on Reddit, gets popular on the rest of the Internet. This means advertising in this community can do a lot to get your message to those who will spread it. Reddit offers many advertising options where you can place your content--be it articles, videos or pictures--right into their community. You can target just the Reddit communities and interests you feel would be relevant to your music in order to maximize promotions.

Reddit ads are unique, in that they can be voted up or down and you get real-time comments on the content you placed. If this content does well, you can effectively get free advertising and an introduction to a supportive community. You can see analytics and set a daily budget for your ads, along with a growing list of other features. If you're trying to go viral--with your latest video of pandas and cuddling kittens--advertising here can give you a boost in the community that makes or breaks your viral aspirations.

Twitter Advertising

Twitter has stepped into the advertising game with the following cool and coy advertising options:

- **Promoted Account** - This will make your account show up in users' "who to follow" suggestions list. It will appear only to users who follow users similar to you (at least in Twitter's eyes). Twitter says you can expect 3-5 new followers a day for just $1. This is great for musicians looking to be suggested to potential fans and especially musicians with an established fanbase who have never promoted their Twitter account.
- **Promoted Tweets** - You can choose one of your Tweets to appear in potential fans' Twitter timeline. This is a way to tell new fans about your new single or an introduce yourself. For $1 a day you can expect 3-5 clicks.
- **Geo-Target** - If you're only interested in promoting in a certain location, you can geo-target your promotions.

For as low as $30 per month this could make a difference in introducing new fans to your music.

Tumblr Advertising

As mentioned earlier, Tumblr allows you to use pinned posts to make sure your followers don't miss the news. These posts cost $5 and will allow your ad to stay at the top of followers' feed for 24 hours. Even if you have only 100 followers, this is a powerful marketing tool to make sure your fans hear about your latest news. If you're feeling cheap, you can also do highlighted posts ($2), which will draw extra attention in your followers' feeds. Just be sure to not abuse the feature or you'll be phased out from your followers.

Spotify Advertising

Many muscians get very excited about Spotify and with good reason. There's no better way to advertise your music than to get people to listen to it, especially right where fans are listening to music. With that said a thing to keep in mind is you can head to any managers forum on the Internet will tell you unless you spend around $10,000 or more the results aren't enough to move the needle on Spotify advertising and that's if you have an amazing song fans are responding to.

Advertising On Facebook

Facebook advertising has always been annoying. You do all the legwork to get fans to like your page and they then charge you to reach all of them. With that said there's never been a more cost effective way reach your fans and make them aware of what you're doing as well as potential fans. Facebook has ways to retarget people who've visited your website/store, target fans of musicians similar to you as well as targeting them by locations you'll be touring in.

Facebook/Instagram Advertising In A Nutshell

Facebook ads allow you to populate the newsfeed, the small ads you see throughout Facebook on sidebars or below pages as you scroll. They also allow you to make your ads syndicate to Instagram.

Elements - There are a number of options for Facebook ads:

- **Posts vs. Page** - You can choose to promote either a specific update or your page. If you want potential fans to hear that your new single is out, you can promote the post announcing it. If you only care about getting more likes and having potential fans hear your music, you can promote your page.
- **Stories vs. Ads** - You can choose to have features that show friends of friends have liked your page (a powerful recommendation) in the news feed or ads that appear on the right-hand side of Facebook.
- **Targeting** - You can target a wide variety of interests on Facebook, including the fans of certain pages. You can also geo-target and target fans in a wide variety of demographics.
- **Optimization** - If you create multiple ads, Facebook will look at which ads perform best and show those to fans.
- **Mailing List Targeting** – You can import your mailing list and have Facebook target those who have already shared their email address with you.
- **Retargeting** – By placing a pixel on your website Facebook can allow you to retarget those who have gone to your website before but may have not purchased your items.
- **Budget** - You can choose to budget how much you would like to spend each day and the maximum you're willing to pay for a like.

Facebook Ad Considerations- Facebook ads work for some promotions, but you should also know their strengths and weaknesses:

- **Slippery Slope** – Remember, because Facebook will not show your updates to everyone who likes your page (most estimates say 15% of those who've liked you will see your updates), meaning that promoting Likes on your page instead of an outgoing like or an event, you are just paying for an inefficient method to communicate with fans. Paying to get likes, means you need to keep paying to talk to these fans.
- **Narrow Your Targets** - It's important to target your demographic as much as possible. Limiting ages, location, language and even sex can help your ads be more successful.
- **Promote Something That Builds** - Sending those who click on an ad to a page where they have to click like to hear you is needless friction and gives potential fans a bad first impression in the relationship. Send potential fans somewhere that builds a great fan relationship like your free-music page.
- **Optimize** - Facebook has tons of analytics as well as Think Insights. Use them to see how you can make your ads work better.
- **Canvas** – Facebook has a feature called Canvas which will help you design ads to be as eye catching and clickable as possible.
- **Instagram Only** – You can choose to only advertise on Instagram if you think your audience will be best served there.

Ad Syndication Services
If you want to advertise across various music blogs there are a few services that will allow you to advertise using certain keywords to make sure your ads go on a wide variety of blogs and are seen by your potential fans. This can be helpful if you don't know all the outlets you could potentially advertise to find your audience.

- **Wavo (wavo.me)**
- **Feature.FM**

Advertise On Music Websites Directly
While the above services offer a way to get on many top music sites, most of these sites offer takeover ads where you're the only ad for a certain amount of time and as well as other special perks.

You can place an ad on most every music blog. In fact, if you're a big fan of a blog your potential fans are also into get ad rates from them. Smaller blogs can have great rates and a readership that is the type of hip potential fans you want familiarity with. You can even search some similar musicians on HypeMachine and Google, see where they're written about. Inquire around and spend wisely. Below are some suggestions:

- **Pitchfork** - This is expensive ad space and their coverage is all over the place. They cover everything from metal to gangster rap. Look for smaller blogs with a similar focus.
- **Rolling Stone** - Insanely expensive and while it's filled with your idols, you can find a blog or website that has lower rates and a more focused audience. They cover every style of music and get a lot of their hits from political articles. Find an outlet with a more narrowed interest set until you have some real money.
- **Google Ads Can Buy You Cheap Access** - While a lot of these big sites sell their own ads, at times they don't have ad space to fill. Most often they fill it by displaying Google Ads. You can get your ad on their site if you target right.

Effective Online Advertising Tips

Recommendations
If you got an album of the year recognition or someone famous said something good about you, showcasing this is the best way to get potential fans to click your ad. Placing a Google ad on the search for sites that gave you a good review and quoting that review is a great strategy. The same can be done for other musicians who have given you a press quote. If the singer of the band, Nintendo Boyfriend called you the best punk band since the Sex Pistols, you can buy an ad on the search terms "Nintendo Boyfriend" and "Sex Pistols" and get a highly effective campaign.

Curiosity
If you create curiosity in a fan, you'll have a much stronger likelihood of getting a click. Writing an ad that makes you wonder what's behind the link is an effective strategy. If you're advertising on a site like MOJO that specializes in classic rock and your ad says, "What if Jim Morrison was a 7-foot-tall transgendered badass?" you're probably going to get some clicks. Of course, you need to find that singer for your group to back up the ad. Don't lie, instead find qualities in your music that will create curiosity.

Start In One Area

If you aren't going to be doing a national tour any time soon, it may be best to start your advertising around where you're going to be playing live and make your dollars turn to building a local following first. This can make sure they're well spent establishing a following in a place that can help you before you take over other areas.

If you think your local scene is going to be hard-pressed to accept you, there are other options. If you're an indie or dance group it may be smart to focus on Brooklyn and Los Angeles since there is a higher concentration of fans than anywhere else. A punk band may want to focus on big-city suburbs. If you're the next Miranda Lambert, you may want to avoid all of the areas I just mentioned. You can eventually promote everywhere, but first focus your limited budget on somewhere that will make a big difference.

Persistence
Advertising takes time to work. It takes numerous times seeing a name before a potential fan breaks down and gives you a try. Commit to it and give it time to work. Don't spend a ton of money to advertise for just two weeks. Instead, stretch your budget for a while and let potential fans see an ad a second time. Be something that potential fans feel they should check out since you're always popping up on their radar.

Advertise When You Have Content To Bite Into
Major label acts are always advertising months before their record is even out. This is because they want to be able to brag about hitting the top of the charts. This is probably not going to happen for you and you don't have the budget to do this. Instead, focus your ad money when you have content to sell. It's unlikely a new fan is going to be so impressed with you that they will come back when you have something to sell them. Get them to listen with your ad and then sell them something while they're excited.

Retargeting
Retargeting is the term used for when you go and look at a product on a website and then you get served an ad for it on another website. This is accomplished by installing a pixel on your site which will then tell sites like Google, Instagram or Facebook you purchase ads with to target people who were interested in your product. This method of advertising often raises sales as it continues to tempt those who were interested in your product. Setting up retargeting campaigns and pixels is easy for anyone with light experience and are one of the keys to a successful promotional

campaign. Companies like Ad Roll (adroll.com) will set up these campaigns and make them more effective.

Group Discount Sites
One of the biggest Internet phenomenon's in recent years is the rise of coupon sites. These sites offer group discounts to a limited number of users. The idea is that by offering a great deal, many people will purchase the deal and give the brand extra business and familiarity. These sites used for concert promotion every day, offering discounted tickets or drink deals at a venue.

You can try doing a group deal to entice people to come to a show or get extra promotion by being on these services massive mailing lists. The financial investment can get you lasting fans and bigger turnout than you expected. You be the judge if it's worth it.

Here are some sites that allow you to do group deals:

- **Groupon** - The biggest group discount site, Groupon (groupon.com) works with their partners to create an enticing deal that makes the site and the client (you) money while increasing your business.
- **LivingSocial** - The other big name in this game. It's very similar to Groupon with a few small differences. (livingsocial.com)
- **Facebook Offers** - Facebook Offers are coupons you can offer over Facebook to those who have liked your page. Let's say you don't care about making a ton of money and just want to fill out your show. You can offer a discount on admission or a coupon for merch all for free on Facebook.
- **Google Offers** - Google's foray into game. The offers blend into their advertising system, which can add to some extra exposure. (google.com/offers)

Advertising In Print Publications

While this isn't recommended for limited budgets, you may have your eyes set on print ads. In general, these are not as effective or inexpensive as online advertising. While they can make you seem like a big player in a genre and like you have big bucks, they can drain that budget with an ineffective message. There are some instances where print ads can be highly effective:

Local Papers
If you're promoting an upcoming show, local music and culture papers offer options that are affordable enough to make them worthwhile. There is also the option for co-ops with the local venue or record stores. It's best to discuss these options with your concert promoter who can tell you how to go about making it happen. Many record distributors will also help you place these ads and give you affordable group buys for them.

Zines And Micro-Genre Magazines
Zines are often focused on a specific genre and are a great way to establish your name familiarity with that genre. While print is dying, the smaller zines and magazines still standing have the added advantage of a narrow demographic, which may be the one you're looking to reach. The rags that are still standing and command a lot of respect with an audience that appreciates them. They're often where the tastemakers and super-fans of a genre go to find out about the next big thing. Getting in front of those people's eyes can be a big help in building your fanbase. I would advise you to not buy an ad in these magazines unless you can afford a half-page or full-page. Any of the other ads are usually loaded toward the back and are too small to make an impression.

Major Magazines
These are not worth it in my eyes. They cover too wide a base of interests to give you any effective name familiarity and you'll be spending your limited funds to advertise to far too many people. While your dream may be to be in Rolling Stone Magazine because they put John Mayer in there, it may be best to look elsewhere until you have John Mayer's advertising budget.

Chapter 37: Internet Radio Gets Your Music Heard By Potential Fans

Radio was once one of the most important parts of making or breaking a musician. We live in an era where musicians can sell hundreds of thousands of copies without ever getting much radio airplay. Radio is one of the many parts of a broad promotion scheme, while Internet radio has become one of the most powerful ways to market your music and get in front of listeners who are likely to become fans.

If you think radio is a thing of the past, think again. While it may be going downhill in influence, the top albums still have a strong correlation to what's picked up by major radio stations. Tens of millions tune into Pandora and use Spotify's radio functions every single day. These stations employ targeting algorithms that learn a listener's taste and recommend music based on their specific tastes. This enables fans to easily find new music they love and maintaining a presence on these stations means it could be your music fans fall in love with. Radio raises awareness of your music and introduces you to new fans that have the potential to love your music.

Even terrestrial radio still has a big role. There's a direct correlation to the indie bands who sell big and those who premiere their records on NPR. Top 40 and adult radio still determine who sells big and who doesn't. Tons of radio DJs can still take you from obscurity to a growing fanbase with a few spins. Radio in any form is an important part of getting new fans, who then spread the word about your music. While this world seems intimidating, it's a lot easier than you might think if you follow a few simple rules.

Promoting Your Music On Internet Radio Services

In case you haven't noticed, Internet radio has taken off in recent years. Pandora now boasts tens of millions of users and the other Internet radio outlets adding up to a huge audience that gets bigger every day. Pew Research has found that more people now listen to music on Internet radio than terrestrial radio. Your presence within Internet radio is extremely important to maximizing your promotions and getting your music to the right people.

It's no secret that Internet radio is one of the best ways to find new music you may like. Through the powerful recommendation engines Internet radio outlets offer, you're able to efficiently target potential fans--something that was nearly impossible just a few years ago.

Upload Your Music To Pandora
Pandora is by far the biggest Internet radio site in the business. Sixty million people and counting go to it to hear music and get recommendations for other artists they may like. When someone types in a musician similar to you in Pandora you could be one of the songs played for the user. Unlike Jango and Last.fm, which have similar services, Pandora is free to get your music featured. Since Pandora upholds a high standard for which artists they work with, Pandora users trust the quality of the recommendations more than most other services. Their discerning tastes and lack of a pay-to-play function keeps their quality high and users happy. All of this is why this is one of the most important sites to get your music played.

Most digital distributors now upload your music directly to Pandora, but if you have not, here is what you'll need to be a part of Pandora:

- Provide us with your basic contact information
- Give us details about your submission including your name, release information and links to your tracks
- Ensure that you have legal rights to your work and it is available on iTunes (US only), Amazon.com/MP3, CD Baby or Bandcamp
- Verify your account
- The legal rights to your music.
- MP3 files for two of the songs from your CD.
- A free Pandora account, based on a valid email address, which can be associated with your music.

After you have this in order, head over to Pandora's Submission Page (submitmusic.pandora.com) and submit your music. Don't wait!

Aggregators - Some aggregators will submit your music to Pandora's system, but you still need to go through the above process. The larger digital distributors will add your music to Pandora's system automatically.

Marketing On Pandora

Pandora has a feature called AMP (amp.pandora.com) where artists can log in, see analytics and optimize their pages. They can correct artists information and feature tracks that will be played on your station. This can help to rack up streams for your new single when you are selected to be played on an artist station.

AMP also has a platform where you can buy commercials that encourage fans to listen to your artist station to divert fans of similar artists to check out your latest release. You can record a message and have potential fans get hip to what you are doing. You can even geotarget messages to promote a tour.

How To Get Your Music On Jango And Make It As Effective As Possible

Jango (jango.com) is a channel-based Internet radio service that boasts an audience of more than six million listeners every month. It operates off a simple system that allows you to select a channel. Say for example you select the group Justice. They will play acts similar to Justice (a concept very similar to Pandora).

They offer musicians a pay-to-play method for getting your music on the site via their Airplay campaign (airplay.jango.com). For a $30 fee you'll be introduced into the site's playlist and guaranteed 1,000 plays. The listener is then presented with the chance to either delete the artist from regular play or promote them. If you receive 50 promotions you are graduated into regular airplay.

This is a very cheap way to start marketing your music to listeners who will likely become fans. While some may find this to be a form of payola, it can be argued that it evens the playing field and allows small acts the same chances as larger acts.

Let's take a look at how to get started using Jango and what exactly you'll need:

- A high quality MP3 of the single you have picked out
- $30 (at least) on a credit card, which you're ready to use to promote your music.

- The URLs of your iTunes, Amazon and direct-to-fan sites (you don't need these but you should have them).
- A dozen or more of the musicians you targeted earlier in the book, whose fans you'll have Jango target with your music (it can be no less than five).
- A bio so that potential fans can read about you.

Once you have all of that, make a login and enter your credit card. You'll now need to choose a payment plan. Buy as much credit as you would like but start with no less than $30 for 1,000 plays. You need at least that many plays to make the promotion worth your time. If you're going to spend $1,000 or more on getting a ton of plays, please make sure you don't set it and forget it---leave time to come back and tweak the targeting.

Next, you'll need to upload your song. It has to be an MP3 and under 10MB, which means that if the song is long you'll have to lower its bitrate until it fits. If you already have your music in a downloadable format on SoundCloud you can link your songs and the work is already done for you!

Once this is done you'll be asked to enter your websites and places to buy your music. This is an important part of making Jango not only a great tool to get new fans, but also to make you money. Make sure to put up links to iTunes, Amazon and a direct-to-fan method (Bandcamp, Limited Run, etc.). You can also link your website and social networks.

Jango is going to ask you what genre you belong to and subsequently will choose a bunch of musicians that you probably sound nothing like. Next to these musicians you'll see a trash can--click this for any artist you think doesn't belong on your list. Next, add the list of the musicians you would like to target. You can enter between 5-30 artists at this time, but if you have a clear idea and not much money for this campaign, you may want to only enter the one whose fans you most want to target.

If you get 50 likes you'll be added into their regular rotation on their various stations. If your goal is to get added to regular rotation off as few plays as possible, it may be a good idea to choose the artists you target wisely and stay with a few similar artists. If you hope to get heard by a lot of people in a short amount of time, enter in some obscure references.

After you have received a hundred or so plays you can start to see some results of what your play stats are. By clicking the reports feature you'll start to see who is liking your music broken down by age, gender and location. One of the coolest stats is the fan overlap chart, which will show you what the listeners who like your music also like. You can use this chart to improve your targeting by looking at the artists you may have missed that show up on this list. If there are artists on here that you missed, start adding them to your targeting.

You can also implement premium targeting but be warned this costs half of the plays you bought. If you fancy yourself a marketing whiz, you can choose age and gender for people who you would like to target. While that on its own isn't too thrilling, the geo-targeting should be. This means that you can do neat tricks like only targeting a certain area for plays. This works great for a few reasons:

- **Local** - This is helpful if you're trying to build a local fan base and then move to the rest of the world later. This feature will allow Jango to play your songs multiple times to anyone who doesn't skip or give it the thumbs down that way you don't lose repeated plays to those who don't like you. It gives you time to grow on the listener and make the song feel familiar. With sustained promotion this can make a big impression on your local area.
- **Tastemakers** - If you're an indie rock band, whose sole concern is getting written up by blogs, you could strictly target NYC where many influential blogs are based. You could also add Chicago, LA and London and you'd have 98 percent of the big blogs targeted in your genre. If you're a country songwriter looking to make a splash in Nashville, you can choose to keep your plays focused there.
- **Tour** - Target only the countries you'll be playing if you're planning on a European tour and want to focus on getting fans out to the shows.

Email - Jango allows fans to opt-in and reveal their email address to their favorite musicians when they become your fan. Anyone who becomes your fan allows you to contact them via email in Jango's internal structure. You can even get some fan email address and then export their emails into a .csv file. Look at what country and city they're from and message them when you're coming to town. If you're smart, you'll click on the Fan screen. Message all of the users who haven't given you their email and send every one of your fans a letter thanking them and linking them to some way to trade whatever free goodies you have for their email. You can also post bulletins that all of your fans will see when you put up new songs or have other eventful promotions.

Other Cool Tricks Inside Jango

Jango has also become more and more of a social network. It now has many features that make their service a great place to direct fans to in order to preview your music. Here are some cool tricks you can do with Jango that you may have missed:

- **Video Embeds** - You can now add videos to your profile and set them to show up when a fan navigates to your Jango profile.
- **Concert Dates** - You can also add concert dates to your profile.
- **Overlays** - You can capture fans' emails and promote your latest songs, album and tours with custom overlays that drop down while fans listen to your channel.
- **Referrals** - If you refer other musicians to Jango and they sign up for an Airplay account, Jango will give you free play credits.

Using Last.fm To Promote Your Music

Last.fm is still one of the biggest Internet radio services on the Internet. They're also able to report and show what listeners have been listening with the power of their scrobbling service - the publishing of music-listening habits in order to track when and how often certain songs are played. In addition to providing a great recommendation engine for listeners, they also have social features, which allow users to see what similar listeners are into and make friends. All of this makes them a popular site for the kids of today, and if you're looking to market to them you need to make sure you're making the most of your Last.fm profiles.

Setting Up Your Profile - To promote your music on Last.fm you need to log into their music manager (musicmanager.last.fm). If you have already been scrobbled a lot you'll need to go through the claim process for your music. This involves proving that you're actually who controls the rights to your name. Once your name is claimed you can then upload your music. Once your music is uploaded, you have three options for how your music will be handled by Last.fm: a 30-second preview, a full stream or allow it to be downloaded.

RSS - Once your music is uploaded, take your blog's RSS feed and import it into the service so that your fans will always see the latest news you have when they come to the site.

Making Friends - As you gain listeners and fans, you can try to gain their email addresses and get them on your other social networks. If you see fans leaving you shouts in the shout-out section of your page, you can leave them shouts back and advertise whatever you're currently promoting. This can mean sending them links to free music you have etc.

When you setup your account, make sure to friend everyone who listens to your music. This bonding is a great way to see what fans of your music listen to through their listening stream. You can also see which of your albums they have been tuning into. Send them some free music from your other releases and start a lasting relationship that will expose them more of your music they may like.

Target - Another way to promote your music is to find similar musicians and follow their fans and see if they follow you back. You can send shout outs and start a relationship recommending them music, including your own.

Earbits
Earbits (earbits.com) is a streaming radio station that suggests music for a fan to listen to based on their tastes. It focuses on independent and do-it-yourself musicians, so the service is geared toward fans who are searching to find the next big name in music. Earbits is a great place for your music to be discovered.

Like Last.fm, Jango and Grooveshark, EarBits also offers a way to buy plays to reach potential fans. The cost is about 1 cent per play. Unlike the other services, you need to be approved by EarBits get your music played on the website (earbits.com/submissions). Earbits keeps its music's level of quality a bit higher than other services. This strategy keeps the website's users happy, so if your music is accepted to the website, listeners will be predisposed to believe it is of higher quality than an unaccepted band's music.

Social Currency - Earbits offers what they like to call a "social currency" where fans can stream free music by liking musicians on Facebook or giving their email address. This means having your music on this service can not only expose you to new fans, it can begin relationships with them as well.

Slacker Radio

Slacker Radio (slacker.com) is one of the most popular Internet radio stations. It has pre-programmed stations and user programmed stations that offer suggestions about what music a listener will like. Users can create and share customized stations that are available on the Internet, smartphones and on TVs through the streaming entertainment device Roku. Many popular musicians, including Metric and Karmin, curate their own stations on Slacker Radio as a promotional vehicle.

Promoting Your Music On Slacker Radio - Many of the larger digital distributors will aggregate to Slacker Radio. Most digital music aggregator's aggregate to the service. Once your music is on Slacker Radio, you can search for stations on the service in its main window. If you find a popular station you can often find its DJs on Twitter or other social networks. Try to build a relationship with the stations' DJs. Once the relationship is established, show them your music and hopefully they will be spinning you soon. You can also create your own channel on Slacker Radio where you play your favorite tracks.

Songza

Songza (songza.com) is a popular Internet radio app that allows anyone to create a station that users can listen to. You can also get station recommendations via a Netflix-like engine that determines what stations you may like based on other users' with tastes similar to yours. Whereas Pandora relies on complex algorithms and analysis of music to deliver suggestions, Songza only pays attention to the songs fans like and their similarities. Most music aggregators allow you to get on to this quickly growing service.

AmazingRadio

AmazingRadio (amazingtunes.com) allows you to upload your music and find new fans by getting played for fans of a similar artist. They link to your music to be purchased by fans where you get 100% of profits.

Radical.fm

Radical.fm enables musicians to make their own Internet radio stations for fans. You can invite fans to your station with the website's artist dashboard and then play your music. Like our dearly departed friend Turntable.fm, there is a chat box and you DJ by making playlists. Radical.fm is still developing a following at the time of this book's publishing.

Blip.fm Is A Social Radio Station

While Blip.fm may not have as much traffic as Pandora, Jango and Last.fm, it's more than a *blip* on the radar. This popular service can be a great way to make connections with fans, especially if your music is based around DJ communities.

Promoting To Traditional Internet Radio Services

You can find other Internet radio stations to promote your music on by clicking the radio tab in iTunes. This will present a list of many stations, which are sorted by genre. Research to find which stations you want to play your music. You can also search iTunes' podcast area to find podcasts that may play your music. Look at the Wikipedia entry on Internet radio to see an extensive list on the subject (en.wikipedia.org/wiki/List_of_Internet_stations).

Here are some more of the larger Internet radio stations that play music in a traditional radio format:

- **BBC Radio Introducing** – A station that's broken hundreds of huge acts in the UK has a submission form where you can send your music to be listened to. (bbc.co.uk/introducing)
- **Absolute Radio** - U.K.-based Internet radio with tons of popular Internet radio programs. (absoluteradio.co.uk)
- **Idobi** - Internet radio with many popular bands in specific genres. Idobi can be great for promoting your music on a national level if you're able to link up with the right DJ. (idobi.com)
- **Live365** - Tons of curated music channels that you can submit your music to. (live365.com)
- **AOL Radio** - AOL still curates many radio stations. (music.aol.com)
- **Yahoo! Music** - Yahoo! provides a similar service to AOL. (music.yahoo.com)
- **More** - There is a Wikipedia entry that keeps a current list of Internet radio stations. (wikipedia.org/wiki/List_of_Internet_stations)

Promoting Your Music With Podcasts

Podcasts are listened to by millions of people every day and can be used for music promotion. These radio-like broadcasts are curated by a DJ to expose their fans to new music. Being played on the right podcast can help your music reach your target audience. Search the following websites to find podcasts that may play your music.

- **iTunes** - iTunes has a devoted music podcast section. Unfortunately, searching through it means a lot of scrolling through podcast titles. You can try typing in your genre name, or an interest name, and see what comes up. Once you find a podcast you want your music on, find the website listed on the podcast's page. There is usually a way to submit your music through the podcast's website.
- **Podcast Alley** - Podcast Alley (podcastalley.com) is much easier to search through than iTunes. The website's search function will give you an extensive list of podcasts who are affiliated with your search term. If you want to find podcasts that play punk, simply type "punk" in the search bar and start scrolling through the results. Each podcast has an information page with a link to its website. Submit your music through the website of each podcast.

Community - Most podcasts are based around a website with comments, a message board or some sort of community. If you want to be covered by the podcast, devote some time to participating in its website's community.

Free Music Archive
One way to submit to tons of Internet radio, terrestrial radio and various other music outlets is through WFMU's Free Music Archive. Putting your free tracks here will allow more than 100 outlets access to play your music. (freemusicarchive.org)

Getting Paid
Remember, many of the Internet radio outlets that play your music will pay you for the plays you receive through a performance rights organization, like SoundExchange (soundexchange.com). If you're going to put the effort into promoting through these outlets, make sure you're registered with a performance rights organization to get your dues.

Chapter 38: Promoting Your Music On Terrestrial And Satellite Radio

Big radio is a corrupt institution where gatekeepers keep musicians who make meaningful music out of the limelight and put generic puppets in the forefront. Fortunately, the power of mainstream radio is slipping away with every Internet radio subscription and iPod purchase. Regardless, you may want to try to play the game of terrestrial and satellite radio in order to give your music a well-rounded promotion.

Getting On Mainstream Audio

Mainstream radio is almost a necessary evil because of how much it can help you. Unfortunately, you're going to have to hire a radio promotions service to have a chance at getting on mainstream radio. You'll need to hire a promotion company geared toward your genre of music.

Be warned, all the cash you spend on these services could be for naught if you don't already have significant buzz and other promotions. Mainstream radio may play dumb music, but they people running it are not too stupid to see past someone thinking they can pay to get played. Even though you may have paid your way to be heard by these stations you may get shelved right from the get-go if your song isn't up to par with the station's level of quality.

The Backdoors

There are backdoors into mainstream radio. Befriending a DJ is one way, but don't count on this method. Many stations have shows where they play local artists. Mobilize your fans to put in calls for requests after receiving airplay and you could regularly be played on this station. If you're a regular on one station, use your popularity to leverage play on other stations.

If you're building up a local buzz, many local DJs will begin to play your music if they think it's something special. Mobilize your mailing list and social networks to get fans to put in requests, so the radio station keeps playing your music. Calling the radio station and figuring out how to schedule interviews, special sets and giveaways can help keep you in the station's regular rotation.

Depending on the city you live in, this will be a unique struggle. Some big cities, like Los Angeles, have rock stations that nurture the local scene, whereas New York City has a hip-hop scene that loves to feature up-and-coming talent. Research your local scene and find out how to get through this gate.

Getting On College, Independent Or Local Radio
Small radio is a big deal for many genres of music. Getting played on college-targeting stations could be where the buzz lies for your music. There are also independent stations like WFMU (PO Box 5101 Hoboken, NJ 07030) and KCRW (KCRW Music Library, 1900 Pico Blvd., Santa Monica, CA 90405) that can launch you into heavy airplay on other stations because they're trend setters for the rest of the country. You can also try huge taste-making websites like KCRW, WXPN, KCMP, KEXP, and WBGO. The BBC has a new music uploader that can launch you into the playlist of some of the most influential DJs on Earth (https://www.bbc.co.uk/introducing). All of these stations regularly start the landslide of radio play for a wide variety of less-known musicians.

As someone who worked at one of the largest taste-making radio stations, WFMU, for nearly a decade, I frequently saw the inner workings of how nobodies became somebodies after a few plays from an influential DJ. You need to find the exact DJs who have tastes for your music, but if you can, the rewards are well worth the work.

Promoting to college radio is a venture many indies take on themselves. There are also many college-radio promotion companies you can hire to undertake these tedious tasks for you, but it's an easy process to do yourself if you have the time and money.

How To Do It Yourself - To promote your music to a college radio station you need to send a CD or an LP to the station. If you have crazy merch like a flash drive attached to a bong, send that also. You'll attach two thing with the CD or LP:

1. Include information about the release. This makes it easier for the station's music supervisor to figure out what to do with your record. If you don't include this info you may be put into a pile of CDs that are never heard, because the station's employees don't want to waste extra time figuring out whether a musician is playable. These labels need to have the following information clearly displayed on them:

654

- Artist name.
- Album name.
- Recommended songs, aka singles.
- Label and release date.
- Recommended If You Like, also known as RIYL. List two to four bands whose music your fans also enjoy.
- A list of any songs with profanities along with a second mark of where the profanities occur. If there are countless profanities, state that clearly. Some savvy labels send an additional censored CD.
- Two-sentence bio about the music.
- Contact name, email address and phone number. If the DJ wants to have you on their show, don't make it a hassle for them. They are busy people.
- Web addresses of your two best social networks, or websites, for finding more of your information and music.
- Don't get crazy with the font, make this purely a utility.
- Sending an electronic press kit or a package full of materials is wasted time. Music supervisors make snap judgments and don't have time to read all of your interviews or to care about your cool new hairdo. Unless you have a press kit that is really eventful or written in blood, skip it.

2. A simple bio, preferably one with good reviews and exciting updates about your band.

Finding Stations To Send Your Music

- **Google** - Search Google for radio playlists that feature bands similar to yours.
- **Radio Locator** - This is a list of every radio station and what music they play. You can go to the station's website and submit your music to the program director or music supervisor, but it would be smarter to research specific DJs. (radio-locator.com)
- **Social Networks** - Head to your social networks and mailing list and ask your fans to send you the contact information of any college radio DJ who may play you.
- **Tour** - When you're coming to a college town on tour, call up a local station and offer CDs, guest-list spots, posters, T-shirts, etc. for giveaways from the station in exchange for mentions of the show on the air.

- **Lists** - Use Google to look at the many lists of college radios stations on the Internet. Visit stations' websites and see if there is a DJ with a playlist that you think should include your music. You can also contact station directors and see if there is a DJ that would play your music. If so, send them a CD.
- **DMDS** – DMDS (dmds.com) is a company that will electronically submit your music for radio airplay at countless stations across the country. This will net you a very small result unless you have a good buzz going in your genre.

Making It Happen
Once you have a list of stations to send your materials to, you need to actually deliver the goods. Here are some ways to get that done:

Shipping - Standing in line at the post office is awful and postage can get expensive. Think about using the tools available from companies like Endicia (endicia.com) and Uline (uline.com) to make shipping easier.

Clear Information Is Everything - Your music can easily be lost in the hustle and bustle of a radio station's operations if it's not directed to the correct person. Make sure it's VERY clear who should get your music. In addition, make sure you write clear information on what tracks are relevant to them. If you have a specific song or an event you're promoting, type up a short note and tape it to the disc to bring attention to it. Although you're aiming to be professional, try to keep everything simple. A CD and a short bio in the form of a one-sheet should do the trick.

Make It Easy - Remember that you're trying to make station employees' lives easier and set yourself apart from the deluge of discs sent to them weekly. Take the time to remove the plastic wrap from your CD, that's one step less the DJ has to take to listen to your music.

Follow Up - Because of the frantically busy nature of college radio stations, it's important to follow up with your contact to make sure they got your music and information. Don't just throw a CD out there and hope it ends up in the right hands. If you get a Google Alert that you've appeared on a playlist, make sure you thank the DJ and station manager for playing your tunes. They'll be much more likely to spin your music in the future.

- **Printer** - Get a printer and some large mailing list labels to print out the labels described above. You can also go to your local print shop and pay for this service. In some cases this may be just as cheap as printing the labels yourself considering the cost of paper, ink and programs to make the labels.

- **Budget** - If you only have the money to send to either a music supervisor or a specific DJ, I suggest mailing to the DJ . Try to also mail the music supervisor a copy if you have the money to do so, because they can be finicky about DJs playing music not in the library of the station.
- **Supervisor** - If you don't know which DJ may play your music, address it to the music supervisor.

Requests - Tons of college radio stations, and even some mainstream stations, still take requests. If your music's been added to a station, you can mobilize your fans or call yourself and request your music be played. The reward is great if it comes through.

Guest List - If a DJ is playing you, make sure to reach out to offer them a guest list spot at your show to meet up. DJs always talk about the shows they went to, and this practice can build a relationship with someone who is often knowledgeable about the music business and is cool. Add DJs who will come to your shows to your contacts database and always reach out when you're in town. Most famous musicians practice this strategy. It can help you climb radio playlist charts and get fans. Handing DJs a T-shirt, CD and some stickers can go a long way.

Getting Paid - While radio is a great promotional tool, let's remember that radio plays also get you paid by your publisher--more on that in the publishing chapter. If you're going to make radio promotion a serious part of your marketing, be sure to have everything squared away with your publisher in advance.

Satellite Radio
In case you haven't gotten the word, Sirius and XM is now one entity, which means satellite radio is really only one company. Thankfully, this makes submitting to the company easy. Satellite radio is a huge entity and has millions of national listeners. Getting your music through this gatekeeper can make-or-break your radio promotion strategy.

To put your best foot forward, practice the guidelines described in the terrestrial radio chapter. It can help immensely to send a copy of your CD to a music director, as well as individual copies to the DJs who you think may play your music.

To submit your music to SiriusXM, send it here:

Attn: Music Programming Department
SIRIUS
1221 Avenue of the Americas
New York, NY 10020

Remember that satellite radio payments are handled just like your Internet radio plays are, by a performance rights organization such as SoundExchange.

Radio Promotion Companies
Today many marketing plans neglect radio promotion, but this can be a back door into reaching many potential fans. If you make the type of music college aged kids will enjoy, taking the time to seriously concentrate on servicing radio with promotional CDs and call about making appearances can help make great leaps in your promotion. Below are a few companies who do radio promotion that we've had good experiences with:

- **The Syndicate** - Radio marketing and other services. (thesyn.com)
- **Powderfinger Promotions** - Works with many do-it-yourself bands on promotions. (powderfingerpromo.com)
- **Landshark Promotion** - Works with musicians of all sizes on radio promotions. (landsharkpromotion.com)
- **Tinderbox Promotion** (tinderboxmusic.com)
- **Team Clermont** (teamclermont.com)

Chapter 39: Licensing Your Music

As record sales decline, more songs are popping up in ads and TV shows. Musicians are looking for ways to get their music licensed now more than ever. Licensing becomes an increasingly important way to obtain exposure and revenue. Although we have discussed that you shouldn't waste your time sending cold emails to music business figures, licensing is the exception. The folks at these services are looking for your music. They screen music searching for a hidden gem to show to those with less time to sort through all the new music out there.

We've all looked up a great song from a commercial. Licensing can help raise awareness about your music, gaining you new fans and funding. These opportunities have the ability to align you with massive cultural experiences. If your music is in the right movie, you are forever recognized of as being part of that cool scene and experience.

How To Increase The Chances Of Getting Your Music Sync Licensed

What do you do to increase your chances of getting your music licensed? Aside from writing and recording better songs, there are a few key practices to employ.

Have It Ready To Go At Anytime
The advertising, TV, film and licensing industries can work at breakneck speeds. It is not uncommon for one license to fall through and need to be replaced within the hour. This is not a "what if" scenario but an occurrence that happens every day. Musicians can lose a potentially huge license because they could not deliver a track in an hour's notice.

The smartest thing you can do is to have your mixes in a folder that are ready to send. If you don't already have a high-quality version online, make sure you know how to upload one on short notice. Myspace and MP3s don't count as high-quality files!

Instrumentals
Having instrumentals of your music is crucial! Most of the time, someone who wants to license your music is going to want an instrumental version

included. Even when they're using the version with the vocal track, they may want to loop a part without a vocal. Make sure you get instrumentals when you mix down the regular version of your song, so you can have it ready at a moment's notice. It can take your mix engineer weeks to make you an instrumental, even in a dire situation. Don't leave the studio without instrumental mixes.

Have Your Contact Information Written Everywhere
Creatives, the people in charge of licensing songs for agencies, often get in over their heads. A client will ask them for a "down-tempo indie rock dirge," and the creative will have no idea what their client is talking about. Hypothetically, they will call a friend who is into indie rock and happens to have a crush on your drummer. She mentions your band along with three other groups. The girl looking to give you tons of money in this potential license deal wants to call you to license your awesome "down tempo indie rock dirge," but she can't find your phone number. She needs to have a tentative placement in about two hours, so she moves on to the next band and gets a hold of them. You lose! The moral of the story is to make sure you have an email inbox that someone is always checking and/or a contact phone number on all of your websites.

Get Your Music Mastered
I shouldn't even have to tell you this! Because most placements are going to be for TV or film, creatives want music that sounds clean and fresh, not tracks they're going to have to apologize for in a boardroom and say "we'll get it mastered or remixed." Your song needs to be ready to go.

Avoid Samples
If you have samples in your music, the odds of getting licensed drop immensely. The creatives don't want to deal with clearance and administration. If you're pursuing getting a song with a sample licensed, make a version without it to use for licensing.

Be Present
When you read interviews with creatives, they all have a different method to choose which songs to license. Some scour SoundCloud, Hype Machine and YouTube, some ask friends, and some download mixtapes and DJ sets. The point is, no one method is going to get you more licenses. Make your music available in as many places as possible so that it is easily discovered.

Don't Bicker

Although driving a hard bargain can get you many benefits in this business, licensing is not always the place to do the bickering. Licensing is a buyers' market, meaning that if you aren't into a buyer's terms, odds are they're going to walk away from the deal and go find someone who is. There are millions of musicians who want a licensing spot, and it's often a gift if a creative wants to use your tracks. While exclusivity may be a concept to discuss, the monetary amount and terms most licensing agreements present you are not up for negotiation.

Your compensation and terms are often budgeted in advance with little room to move, until you have a big following and can negotiate around this brand that wants to be associated with your popularity. Creatives are simply looking to place music somewhere that they believe it will fit well. Unless they want you because you bring a "cool factor" to their lameness, odds are their terms are not moving. Phoenix, M83 and CHVRCHES are all wanting to get their music in a placement, so take this easy money for what it is. If you get too particular about an issue, the license buyer knows they can find someone else to work with. Be wise about how far you push these licensing negotiations, because the numbers are not usually in your favor.

Show Presence

You want to be active on your social networks. Many licensing professionals want you promote the production your music becomes a part of. For example, if a TV show about vampires is looking for a song to use, they want to license from a band that has a rabid audience of social network followers that are likely to love a show about vampires that will tune in to hear this song. If you have an active social network following, you will give creatives incentive to use your song.

Going For It On Your Own

Often, when I am sitting in the studio with a band, group members will say "this would be the perfect song for a _____ ad." If that's the case, why don't you tell a licensing company that? All you need to do is do some searching on Google. Find a brand your song caters to and look up who is running their current advertising campaign. Most advertising agencies have a personnel list on their website. Find the Music Supervisor and Creative Director and email them. Just be sure to really sell them on your idea. They're enthusiastic people who deal with ideas all day long, and they are usually HUGE music and art fans who love to talk to other creative people.

They also hear pitches all day, so make yours better than the competition's.

Keep It Simple
If you're only submitting music, Music Supervisors and Creative Directors usually don't need a full press kit. They don't care if you have an arm growing out of your head or a double chin, they just care if your music fits their needs. Keep in mind who you're submitting to and try to appeal to them in a simple way that doesn't go overboard on the sell.

Impressions Matter
Nearly every creative I know is wise enough to look at a band's social networks if they their song. They want to give a quick background check to make sure who they're about to be associated with isn't a liability. This means if you just retweeted someone calling the President a "Kenyan socialist," intelligent people may not want to deal with your ignorance. This also goes for your gratuitous drug use, sex life, etc. If you're trying to get a song on a children's video, taking Instagram photos of you hitting the bong may keep that from happening. It may also get you a sweet commercial for a Vaporizer. Be aware that these brands are going to have your name tied to theirs, and they're going to want someone who is in line with their image.

Exclusive vs. Non-Exclusive Licensing
One of the biggest differences in the type of licenses that you will encounter is whether they are exclusive or non-exclusive. This distinction in a contract is whether only this company will be able to use your song (exclusive), as opposed to another licensing company being able to shop your song or another service being able to license it (non-exclusive). In the case of exclusive licenses, agreements will differ, but for an exclusive license you should always get a higher percentage and upfront fee for the license. For non-exclusive licenses you are able to have multiple services shop your song or use your song. This also means you are usually less of a priority and therefore merit less of a percentage and fee.

Which Is Better? – They both have their benefits for non-exclusive licenses, it can be great to have tons of services shopping your music and be in tons of libraries since many ears will hear your songs as they browse these libraries. However, trusted licensing companies often make exclusive agreements with deep connections to creatives who buy licenses, who are able to place licenses for your songs more commonly and bring in higher dollar licenses.

Services That Will Help You With Sync And Games Licensing

A common way of getting your music licensed is to go through intermediaries. These are organizations that work closely with creatives, companies and whomever else needs music to license. Below is a list of licensing companies that Musformation knows to be reputable.

Pump Audio
Pump Audio (pumpaudio.com) is a division of Getty Images, one the biggest names in image licensing. One of the benefits of listing with Pump Audio is that you get pushed to Getty Image's large clientele. The down side is their rates aren't very musician friendly. They feature the following:

- No submission fee.
- More than 100,000 placements.
- Musicians get 35 percent of earnings.
- Non-exclusive, so you can use other sites/services to license your music.

Rumblefish
Rumblefish (rumblefish.com) does just about everything a licensing company can do, but is most famous for getting your music inside retail store playlists through its unique sonic branding. They do strong placements for soundtracks in stores and other branded experiences for consumers. The feature the following:

- No submission fee.
- Non-exclusive.
- You receive 50 percent of net licensing fees.
- One-year-term.

They run Friendly Music, which licenses music for YouTube videos so that YouTube and low-budget video directors can get high-quality music. They also partnered with Shutterstock to license music to video creators.

YouLicence
A marketplace for licensing that connects musicians directly with people looking to license music. YouLicense takes a fee off the transaction, and

you do the rest of the negotiations. All of their deals are non-exclusive. (youlicense.com)

Music Xray
Music Xray (musicxray.com) is a website where you can submit your music to a wide variety of opportunities. They facilitate licenses and marketing opportunities for brands including MTV and NBC.

Ricall
Ricall (ricall.com) boasts much of indie rock's royalty; as well as old-school chart hits from the '50s and modern-day pop hits. Ricall is much harder to get involved with, but it is reputable and has huge numbers for revenue and songs licensed.

Beatpick
Beatpick (beatpick.com) takes your music to all forms of media. You can easily submit your music to their website. Beatpick's terms vary according to different agreements with each act.

Audiodraft
This is a marketplace where you can get hired to create original music for companies. (audiodraft.com)

Broadjam
Submit your songs for more than 100 music-licensing opportunities per day. (broadjam.com)

Prescriptive Music
A background music curator. Prescriptive (prescriptivemusic.com) uses music to set vibes for restaurants, hotels and other high-end establishments.

iStock Photo
Although this is a popular site for stock photos, you can get licensing opportunities when company clients look for audio to accompany the website's images. iStock Photo also draws heavily from Pump Audio's catalog. (istockphoto.com/audio.php)

Sonicbids

Sonicbids (sonicbids.com) has tons of licensing opportunities for musicians. For those on a cramped budget, please be aware there are fees associated with maintaining a profile on the website.

TAXI
TAXI (TAXI.com) is a member service, with fees, that can help songwriters get licensing opportunities.

Jamendo Pro
Jamendo (pro.jamendo.com) is a popular website for free music downloads. Its professional package offers artists a way to upload their music for licensing opportunities. Based in Luxembourg, this is a great way to open up European licensing opportunities for your music.

LicenseQuote
If you have a big catalog of music that you're regularly pursuing licensing opportunities for, you may want to look at LicenseQuote as a solution to go directly to your buyers, rather than sending them to massive catalogs where they may find other choices. LicenseQuote gives you your own licensing storefront in order to facilitate licensing sales direct from your own website. (licensequote.com)

Magnatune
Magnatune is a licensing company for independent artists. The company claims to have a high standard for whom it selects to present to their clients. Magnatune deals in a wide variety of music and offers its clients previews by browsing through their subscription-based music catalog. (magnatune.com)

Audiosocket
Audiosocket (audiosocket.com) states stock music is crap. The company offers real songs from real artists. Audiosocket deals with a handful of artists trying to find them great licensing opportunities. The company also is a curator of the Vimeo Music Store which, aside from the Free Music Archive (freemusicarchive.org), is the only way to get your music on to the service.

Music Dealers
Music Dealers offer a huge catalog of music and a non-exclusive agreement which enables you to get inside its extensive catalog and

increase your chances for placements. The company offers both sync and gaming license opportunities. (musicdealers.com)

Naxos Licensing
Licensing company exclusively for classical music. (naxoslicensing.com)

Sentric Music
Sentric Music looks for sync and gaming placements for independent artists. They're a U.K.-based company that handles opportunities for both sync and games. (sentricmusic.com)

Soundlounge
U.K.-based licensing company that's been bringing placements for 30 years. (soundlounge.co.uk)

More Services
The following are music licensing services that accept unsolicited music, that we haven't had the chance to extensively review:
- **1000 Tracks** (1000tracks.com)
- **300 Monks** (300monks.com)
- **A&G Sync** (agsyncmusic.com)
- **Affix Music** (affixmusic.com)
- **Agoraphone** (agoraphone.com)
- **Aperture Music** (aperturemusiclibrary.com)
- **Audiomachine** (audiomachine.com)
- **AudioMicro** (audiomicro.com)
- **Beatclock** (beatclockmusic.com)
- **Black Toast Music** (blacktoastmusic.com)
- **BossHouse Music** (bosshousemusic.com)
- **Brand X Music** (brandxmusic.net)
- **Bright Mind Music** (brightmindmusic.com)
- **Crucial Music** (crucialmusic.com)
- **d2 Music** (d2music.com)
- **Jingle Punks Music** (jinglepunks.com)
- **Magnatune** (magnatune.com)
- **Mainstream Source** (mainstreamsource.com)
- **MusicSupervisor** (musicsupervisor.us)
- **Nightingale Music Productions** (nightingalemusic.com)
- **Princess Blue** (princessbluepublishing.com)

- **RipTide Music** (riptidemusic.com)
- **Transition Music** (transitionmusic.com)

MusikPitch Is A Songwriters Marketplace For Songwriting On Demand

For those of you who pride yourself on your ability to write a song for any occasion, MusikPitch (musikpitch.com) may have just opened up a wonderful world for you. Buyers post what they need from a song on the website, whether they want a tune for a commercial, film, TV or video game. MusikPitch provide songwriters with feedback and the winner gets paid in the end. This website is a great opportunity for songwriters to get noticed and make some extra cash!

On Bigger Licensing Deals

One of the most sought-after deals is to be represented by a big licensing company like Bank Robber Music or Ocean Park Music Group. Most of these deals are made by having the right team on your side and being associated one of the label, management or legal teams these licensing companies work with. Instead of soliciting to a big licensing company with your music, work hard on attracting a great team to your music. It will be much easier to get in their door.

There are many smaller licensing firms who will make small, non-exclusive deals with you and submit you for placements with music supervisors. Many of these contracts are easy to negotiate and very standard. These smaller licensing companies can often be the start to a relationship that will take you to a larger music licensing deal and more placements. Don't be close-minded to smaller licensing deals. They can be the first step to bigger things.

Getting Your Music In Film

Many musicians dream of the day their music is in a film. Not only is it amazing to see your music set to film, but also how cool would it be if you got to impact the mood for a whole movie? Don't forget that some big movie company will pay you to create music, you'll be on an official movie soundtrack and you'll get tons of promotion for your contribution. Here are some ways to make this happen.

- **Interviews** - One of the easiest ways to set yourself up to make music for films is to talk about it in interviews. Directors are always looking for musical collaborators and clearly stating your interest to the media can make it happen.
- **Social** - The film industry is always having a party. Even in smaller cities, movie premieres happen monthly. Film festivals are fertile breeding grounds for meeting people who can help you. Immerse yourself in the film scene and meet those who run it. This is how a shocking number of musicians end up becoming film composers. Tell directors you would love to work with them on their movie.
- **Licensing Companies** - There are companies who do a lot of film licensing, but you usually need some fans or experience to get near them. You may find a licensing company to build great relationship with if you search Google after you have some experience.
- **Website** - Make a section of your website where you upload music that would potentially go in films. Start making music with textures for film today. The possibilities are endless and you can bring your music to a new medium and audience.

Use A Gratis License To Get Your Music In Indie And Non-Profit Films
The brilliant marketer and electronic artist Moby created a gratis license so that non-profit and indie filmmakers can use his music for free. This is a fantastic idea and is a great way to allow your music to be heard by more people. Many people will sit through five minutes of movie credits to identify a song they loved in a movie so they can buy that song. Having your music featured in indie and non-profit films shows other filmmakers the potential your music has to set the mood of a film. It also gives back to a deserving community that is far too underfunded.

Obviously, just slapping a gratis license to your music isn't going to get you very far in becoming featured in hundreds of films. If you want your music to be used for non-profit purposes, make sure you disclose that in your liner notes and website. Leave flyers at film schools and post to message boards in the film community if you're serious about getting your music in these kinds of films. The more you promote, the more likely you'll get placement and free promotion.

Licensing Your Music To Other Regions

One of the easiest ways to get free money is to license your record to a label in another country or region. Not only is it lucrative to get another label pushing your music in another country, but it can also lead to successful tour opportunities and an income stream that can last you for years to come. You can also book better tours in the countries you're licensed to. With all that said, getting this going is more tricky than you might think.

Finding A Label To License Your Music In Foreign Regions
The first thing you need to do to spread your music in another region is to find a label to license your music. Look at other musicians in your genre and see which labels are releasing their records in other regions. This information will often be found on websites or Facebook pages and may take an afternoon of investigating to find. There are four to six regions musicians can look for licensing in:

- North America: US and Canada
- South America: Mexico or Brazil primarily
- Europe
- Japan
- Australia/New Zealand
- Other: Some genres will have exclusive licenses to specific countries in Europe, South America and/or Asia.

Once you have found labels to target in the various regions, the best thing to do is email them a sell sheet. Point out good reviews and other bands you've toured with that can show the caliber of your music. This raises the chances the label will bring you over on a tour to promote the record they license.

Terms - Every genre has different terms that are customary for foreign licenses. Get yourself a lawyer who knows your genre well and have them look at the license. Standard contracts include:

- An advance payment.
- A fee per unit.
- Some sort of touring promotion.

Chapter 40: Copyrights, Covers & Sampling - Using Them To Help Promote Your Music

I know I promised there would be no boring law talk in this book, and I intend to keep this promise. As strange as it sounds, copyright can do a lot to help you get more fans. The copyright you assign to your music can help you protect what you have made and help you earn money from it. Copyright can also free your music so other creative people can use it as a part of their compositions.

Too many musicians spend their time thinking about copyrighting their music to make sure no one steals it, instead of about how to promote their music so that more people can hear it. The likelihood of your music being stolen and you being unable to reap any financial benefits past the exposure of blogs and YouTube videos is next to none. Songwriting theft is a less than one-in-ten-million occurrence. Sampling is different than songwriting theft and is usually either pre-cleared or settled it gets to court. In most sampling cases, whether you actually sent your copyright forms to the government or not is an afterthought compared to if the artist admits they stole from you, which they usually will. Remember, someone sampling you can get you exposure. Dido was just another English major label act who hadn't caught on in America until Eminem sampled her for his hit song "Stan." The exposure launched her American career. The way you administer your copyright allows you to deny those chances or open them.

Worry more about getting your music out to the world than making sure you keep potential fans from stealing it. Take care of the copyright in a fast and efficient manner and get back to work on promoting your music. Don't sweat over the details of your copyright for months on end, always thinking about the small possibility that someone may steal your music.

Legal Disclaimer: Let me remind you again, we're not lawyers. We make no claims, promises or guarantees about the accuracy, completeness or quality of the information contained in this book or our website. The advice in this chapter is presented as opinion and not legal advice.

Creative Commons And Traditional Copyright

When musicians think of traditional copyright, they think of sending their music with a form to the government. This does happen, but what many musicians don't think about is many of the ways copyright holds back their music from being promoted or integrated into other artists' work. However, you still need to pursue a copyright through the government before you can spread your music through Creative Commons.

Obtaining A Copyright
In order to obtain a copyright for your music, you need to have an actual recording of the song and fill out an application at the Electronic Copyright Office (copyright.gov). The recording needs to be a WAV, MP3 or AIFF file. You can use a demo, but it's recommended you copyright the final version of the song. It costs $35 to file for the copyright, which can be paid online. This fee can cover a whole album if you register all of the songs together.

Poor Man's Copyright
The myth goes, you can mail a postmarked letter to yourself or send an email to a friend in order to copyright your music. Others say your music is copyrighted once you release it and put a copyright symbol on it. This information isn't reliable. Courts have both upheld and not upheld the copyright of materials done this way (remember laws are up to each individual judge's discretion). If having your music protected under a copyright is important to you, take the time to fill out the official forms and copyright it. If you doubt you'll be one of the very few musicians who ever goes to court for copyright, release your music and carry on. Remember, as long as you can prove a song was written on a date before the other person wrote theirs and that they heard your song, the law is on your side. Releasing a song to online stores helps prove that point easily. With that said, if you get a real, legit copyright you can save thousands of dollars in legal fees if there is a problem down the line.

Creative Commons
Creative Commons is a way of saying to fellow creators and musicians that you're OK with them using your music under a set of conditions. These conditions can be set by you, depending on what you find fair. If you want to encourage your music to be given away, shared by fans or used in other creative works, you can signal it is legal to do so with a Creative Commons license. If you want to allow non-profit films to use your music or allow sampling or remixing of your music, you can specify that with a Creative Commons license. Services like the Free Music Archive

(freemusicarchive.org), which host Creative Commons licensed music, allows you to be a part of a community of creative people who can help promote your music in a wide variety of ways. If you often sample and remix, sharing your music with these services is a way to give back to the medium you use to create music. If you value being sampled, remixed and used in other artistic endeavors, this is a way to allow your music to be easily used and spread.

Below I have copied the Creative Commons website (creativecommons.org), which is legal because they allow it under their license. I have put their description in quotes and italics. My comments appear outside of the quotes and italics.

- **CC BY** - *"This license lets others distribute, remix, tweak and build upon your work, even commercially, as long as they credit you for the original creation. This is the most accommodating of licenses offered. Recommended for maximum dissemination and use of licensed materials.* "This license essentially says anyone can take your music and integrate it into their own if they give you sufficient credit. This allows your music to be integrated into film, remixes or sampled in other songs. This is a great way to get free press and give back to a community you participate in if you also engage in sampling or remixing.
- **CC BY-SA** - *"This license lets others remix, tweak and build upon your work even for commercial purposes, as long as they credit you and license their new creations under the identical terms. This license is often compared to "copyleft" free and open source software licenses. All new works based on yours will carry the same license, so any derivatives will also allow commercial use. This is the license used by Wikipedia and is recommended for materials that would benefit from incorporating content from Wikipedia and similarly licensed projects."* This means that if someone is going to use your work, they also have to attach the same Creative Commons license to it. They're not able to take your work and then apply a more restrictive copyright. They have to allow any song they sample your music in to be spread just as you did.
- **CC BY-NC** - *"This license lets others remix, tweak and build upon your work non-commercially and although their new works must also acknowledge you and be non-commercial, they don't have to license their derivative works on the same terms."* This license

allows others to sample, excerpt and remix your music but they can't profit from this content. They don't have to use the same Creative Commons attribute as you to do.

- **CC BY-ND** - *"This license allows for redistribution, commercial and non-commercial, as long as it is passed along unchanged and in whole, with credit to you."* This allows your music to be used for free by those profiting from it or no. It doesn't allow others to sample, remix or excerpt it.

- **CC BY-NC-SA** -*"This license lets others remix, tweak and build upon your work non-commercially, as long as they credit you and license their new creations under the identical terms."* In order for someone to use your material, they need to use the same license as you without collecting a profit from it. This is the license we used for this book.

- **CC BY-NC-ND** - *"This license is the most restrictive of the six main licenses, only allowing others to download your works and share them with others as long as they credit you, but they can't change them in any way or use them commercially.* "This license allows others to spread and share your works, but they can't change your content in any way. If you want to maintain your rights and restrict sampling use, but you want to allow your music to spread by being given away for free, this is probably for you.

Creative Commons has made it easy for you to decipher its legal lingo. All of the laws are in laymen's terms on the Creative Commons Chooser (creativecommons.org/choose). This service will allow you to click through some questions to get the license you want.

Not Enforcing Your Copyright Music Can Help Your Music Spread
Psy's "Gangnam Style" is the most-watched video in the history of YouTube. Almost every musician would love to have this distinction. One of the hidden secrets to this success was the lack of copyright enforcement on the song. This allowed countless parodies, performances, dance videos and other videos that promoted the original song as users uploaded their own versions of the video. The lack of copyright also enabled fans to spread the video in any way they chose, even if it was as silly as a baby dancing to the song. As those creating videos uploaded their creations to social media, their friends who hadn't yet experienced "Gangnam Style" would need to go see the original video to get the joke.

Lack of copyright enforcement made the music video phenomenon easy to spread. Copyrights can be limiting. When you, your label or publisher, are taking down fans' versions of your music, you keep fans from promoting your music. However, a lack of a copyright is not necessary to enable this kind of spreading. If you control your own music, you can simply choose to not pull down these videos or use a loose Creative Commons license to allow them while still maintaining a copyright.

How To Secure The Rights To Cover A Song

Cover songs are a great way to get press and tons of views on YouTube. However, clearing your covers and getting the rights to play them is important. After all, you don't want to face a lawsuit or to be shamed for ripping off other musicians. Here is how you do it:

Clearing The Sales And Downloads Of A Cover Song
A mechanical license will pay the mechanical royalties to the songwriter you're covering. Mechanical royalties are for when you actually sell a copy of someone else's song and make money off of it. You'll need to purchase the right to cover a song in advance. You pay in advance for these streams and downloads. Contrary to popular belief, you need to pay this fee even if you're giving away a cover song for free. The downloads you're paying for in this license cover paid or unpaid downloads. Be warned, if you don't pay these fees you are subject to huge fines in addition to the royalties you owe. It's no joke.

Clearing The Right To Cover A Song On YouTube
Right now, this process is undergoing a huge change. YouTube bought the company RightsFlow and is trying to make it so the company will administer YouTube covers. YouTube is presently trying to get publishers to opt-in to their system, in order to make clearing a cover on YouTube easier. Until then, musicians can only hope to get paid by their publishers and YouTube's Content ID system. Unfortunately, you're at the risk of having your cover song taken down from YouTube at any time. While deletion of your account is rare on YouTube, the work you put into this cover could be for naught if it's suddenly deleted. Here are some ways to help make sure that doesn't happen:

- **Publisher** - Contact the publisher of the song and get a license. This is time consuming and going to cost you thousands of dollars.
- **Three Strikes** - YouTube gives three strikes before they delete an account. If you get two strikes, you may want to reconsider doing covers without permission.
- **License** - Remember, the owner of the content gets to choose whether they delete your cover using YouTube's Content ID system. Linking to the original song, acquiring a license through any of the services below if you sell the cover and linking to buy the original song may help you not get deleted.

Cover Song Clearance
The following services will help you clear the recording of cover songs to post on digital distributors or YouTube.

- **Loudr** – A helpful service that clears your songs for $15 a song (loudr.com)
- **Affordable Song Licensing** – A service that clears your songs for $10 a song as well as offering other services. (affordablesonglicensing.com)

Playing Covers Live
The venue you're playing takes care of this. Venue owners pay publishers money in order to have live music and this includes the cost of your cover. Have fun with that "Free Bird" request, because you can't tell the audience you can't afford to cover it.

Clearing A Sample
If you sample someone's audio, you're going to need to get in touch with their publisher directly. This can be a long process requiring lawyers and contracts up front. It's best if you have a lawyer who is experienced with this kind of work. If you don't have a serious budget, sampling an established band is probably not going to happen.

Chapter 41: Publishing Your Music And Making Money From It

Publishing your music is the way you get compensated for others playing, using and distributing it. Once you release a song to the world there are a wide variety of royalties it can earn if it's making the rounds. It's your publisher's job to find the royalties you're entitled to. Their job also includes giving you opportunities to gain more royalties.

Choosing the right publisher can create opportunities for gaining revenue and spreading your music. This includes radio and TV performance, covers, public performance, jukebox plays, karaoke and DJ spins at a club. Getting someone on your team to take care of publishing can be a huge stepping-stone in promoting your music.

There are a few different avenues you can go down with publishing. Each of them works for different musicians in different ways, but one thing is for certain: You're going to need to sign up with these services to get the money you deserve.

Publishing Services

The Big Three PROs
There are three main publishing companies that are open to a large base of applicants and that most musicians use: ASCAP, BMI and SESAC. These companies are called Performing Rights Organizations, or PROs, because they're advocates who collect money for your music being performed. All three of them have a wide variety of services for musicians and provide similar royalty collection and opportunities, but they also differ in some major ways. You'll need to choose one of these PROs to deal with unless you sign a publishing deal.

ASCAP
ASCAP (ascap.com) is one of the most popular PROs in the world. It represents the biggest and smallest artists out there.

- **Application** - $35 fee for membership.
- **Contract** - Contracts are on a year-to-year basis and can be terminated at the end of that year.
- **Insurance** - ASCAP has a vast insurance program. Their partners offer discounts on medical, dental, studio and touring insurance.
- **Credit Union Access** - If you're looking for financial advantages, ASCAP is partnered with a musician-friendly credit union.
- **Pay Schedule** - ASCAP sends checks three times a year.

BMI

BMI (bmi.com) is the other big hitter in the publishing game. Most of the top musicians in the world use ASCAP or BMI.

- **Application** - You are automatically accepted with no fee, but you need to pay $250 to join.
- **Contract** - If you're a writer, the contract is two years long. For a publisher, it's five years.
- **FedEx** - Get a 25 percent discount from FedEx, which can come in handy once you start shipping a lot.
- **Insurance** - Access to a musician-friendly health insurance plan.
- **Loans** - Access to a musician-friendly loan program.
- **Pay Schedule** - BMI pays royalties quarterly.

SESAC

SESAC (sesac.com) claims that by being selective of who gets to join their organization, they're able to offer you a more personal relationship. They have some of the top musicians in the world, and many indie artists also use SESAC because of the organization's favorable profit splits that give what is thought of as a more fair share to smaller acts.

- **Application** - You must apply and interview to become a member, but there is no fee for membership.
- **Contract** - A standard three-year contract is used.
- **Insurance** - Musician friendly insurance through MusicPro Insurance.
- **Pay Schedule** - SESAC pays quarterly.

Other Royalty Collection Services
After you choose whether to use ASCAP, BMI or SESAC, you can also register with the Harry Fox Agency and SoundExchange in order to get royalties you're entitled to that the PROs don't collect.

678

The Harry Fox Agency

Harry Fox (harryfox.com) is not a competitor to ASCAP, BMI and SESAC. Instead, the agency collects mechanical royalties. This means it will seek out and collect the royalties when sales of your music occur. The Harry Fox Agency only works with publishing companies. Songwriters can't affiliate with the agency unless it's through a publishing company. To affiliate with the HFA, your publishing company must have had at least one song commercially released by a third party within the last twelve months. This is particularly important for songwriters who wrote a song that's being performed by another act, covered by someone or being used on someone else's record. The HFA will get you your money for any copies of this song that have been sold.

Even if you're putting out your own music, the HFA can help get you paid if someone else is selling the songs you wrote. Remember, anyone can cover your song without your permission as long as they don't change the lyrical intent. This agency can help ensure you get your share if someone does take the initiative to cover your music and sell it.

SoundExchange

Satellite radio and Internet streams offer a whole new frontier for collecting royalties. SoundExchange (soundexchange.com) is here to help you get paid for it. Once you register for free with SoundExchange, you're entitled to royalties paid quarterly from streams on the Internet like Pandora Radio, Sirius XM Radio or cable music channels. If you haven't registered with them, they have a huge list of musicians who they have collected money for already and haven't claimed it. It's free money waiting for you after you fill out a form, so you might as well get started.

Royalty Collection Services

While you'll need to choose whether to publish with BMI, ASCAP or SESAC, you can then choose to hire a service which will more efficiently collect royalties for you. These services are a new part of the publishing game, but they are collecting tons of money for musicians that may have never received it otherwise.

TuneCore - In addition to being an aggregator to music stores, TuneCore (tunecore.com/songwriters) has gotten into the publishing game. They offer an advanced system that allows them to collect royalties that weren't able to easily be collected before.

- **Application** - After paying a $75 fee, you fill out an application and are automatically accepted into the service.
- **Cut** - TuneCore takes 10 percent of your royalties in exchange for chasing them down.
- **Benefit** - TuneCore claims to be able to recover 25 percent of songwriters' royalties that are lost in frivolous, out of date methods.
- **Royalties** - TuneCore is able to collect publishing, mechanical print and sync royalties for you.
- **Pay Schedule** - TuneCore pays out quarterly.
- **Maintain Complete Ownership** - TuneCore allows you to maintain control of your copyrights.
- **Get Separate, Additional Royalties You Are Owed As A Songwriter**
- **Register Your Songs Globally** - More than 100 collection agencies and digital stores worldwide.
- **Get Royalty Payments** - Detailed accounting reports are available on your TuneCore dashboard.
- **Administer Licensing Requests**
- **Unlimited Song Uploads**

Songtrust - Songtrust (songtrust.com) is a next-generation songwriting collection services. They handle the collection of your royalties and offer a streamlined service that takes away many of the pains of most collection services. Started by the Downtown Music Group, it is housed with the forward-thinking label and its other services.

- **Application** - Songtrust offers two plans: Solo artists for $50 per year and bands for $100 per year.
- **Contract** - Contract is on a year-to-year basis.
- **Cut** - You keep 100 percent of your royalties.
- **All Around** - Collects your royalties from ASCAP, BMI, SESAC, the Harry Fox Agency and a wide variety of other sources.
- **Sync** - Allows you to get sync opportunities through Downtowns dms.FM licensing service.
- **Internet** - Songtrust collects the same royalties as satellite radio and Internet radio that you would normally go through SoundExchange for.
- **Mechanical** - Songtrust will collect mechanical royalties from The Harry Fox Agency for you.

- **Pay Schedule** - Songtrust pays quarterly.

CD Baby Pro
CD Baby Pro (members.cdbaby.com) gives musician the ability to collect both international and US royalties they were previously denied, while still retaining 100% of the rights to their music.
- **Collection** - Like Song Trust and TuneCore they allow you to optimize the royalties collected through the PROs you are already with.
- **Price** – Their rates to upload to their service and use their songwriting collection service is $99 per album and $39 per single.

Doing Publishing Right

Songwriter or Publisher?
When you register with a PRO, you need to register as either a publisher or songwriter. You're setting up your own publishing company if you register as a publisher. You'll often see each member of a band has their own publishing name inside a record cover. For example, your drummer may be Homeless Without A Girlfriend Music (SESAC) and your singer may be Annoying Illiterate Guy Music (BMI). Both members have their own publishing company. You can use this distinction to have your publisher split up the money, or your whole band could be under one publisher and split the money amongst yourselves. There are a handful of other reasons to become one or the other, but it's best to talk to the rep at your PRO or your manager about how you would like to do it.

Getting a Publishing Deal
One of the most sought-after opportunities in the music business is to sign with a publishing company that will pay you a huge advance on your songwriting. This is a sign the publisher will be working hard to get your music placements and other opportunities that make both you and the publisher money. This can range from placement in films to hooking you up with other musicians to write songs for. The publisher will handle the work of going to the PROs and getting the money from the organizations. After your advance is recouped, a profit split will be agreed on for the publisher's work. Many dream to be published on EMI, Warner Chappell or House Of Hassle, but this isn't so easy. In order to attract one of these deals, cold emails will not cut it. Instead, focus on the following:

- **Team** - Most publishers are attracted to you from connections within your teams. Make sure you have a solid team.
- **Body** - Publishers want to see that you have written more than a dozen great songs, and that you show the promise of writing dozens more.
- **Momentum** - Publishers want to see that the hard work is happening to create opportunities. This excites publishers.

There are smaller publishers who will offer you a few hundred or thousand dollars upfront for your songs. Many musicians will be skeptical of these publishers, but a little bit of research can show you if they're a scam or not. Friends of mine have had great success with smaller publishers, while others have gotten that upfront money and never saw another dollar again. Often, the upfront money is more than they would have seen anyway. Do your research and talk to the publisher's other clients to see if it's worth the hassle.

Directory - If you do want to reach out to publishers with submissions, the MusicRegistry (musicregistry.com) has a directory available for purchase.

Tips For Getting The Most Of Your PRO

- **Set Lists** - You can collect royalty payments for your performances you're playing in venues. Make sure you upload your set lists and enter your concert dates to be compensated for your dues of playing live.
- **Radio Promotion** - If you're providing your record to radio stations or paying someone to promote it, make sure you're signed up with the appropriate PROs. You can make a lot of the money you paid to promote your music back in publishing earnings if you're successfully getting airplay. Remember, satellite radio airplay is handled separately than terrestrial. You'll need to be registered with SoundExchange if you're promoting heavily on satellite or Internet radio.
- **Register Your Old Music** - Just because you forgot to register your first record doesn't mean you can't do it now. If your current record takes off, your other material will follow, and you can earn money from it.
- **Register Everything** - You never know when a demo is going to get spun by some DJ.

Resources

- **SongSplits** – SongSplits make easy forms for you to figure out the royalty splits across multiple songwriters for your publishing deals and save you tons of time on the phone with managers and lawyers. (songsplits.com)
- **MusicMark** – A registration format that helps make the music registration process more uniform across the various PROs. (musicmark.com)
- **TuneRegistry** – A service that consolidates and streamlines song publishing, metadata, splits and other information (tuneregistry.com)

Chapter 42: Last Thoughts, Things To Remember And Resources

You have taken an important step by educating yourself on how to build your fanbase. The next step is continuing to learn and working hard on your music. It takes creative and hard work every single day to build a huge fanbase. You now know what you should be doing every day to make your dream come true. The next step is continuing to learn and working hard on your music. Good luck!

Here are a couple points that I would like to hammer home one more time. We all get in ruts, and it becomes unclear what we should be doing during them. I like to think of these as a few thoughts you can revisit over and over again from this book, as you need more inspiration for building your fanbase.

Things To Remember

Promoting Your Music
- Your biggest problem is no one knows who you are. Constantly think of how you can get more potential fans to hear you by making it as easy for them to do so as possible.
- Be eventful, do things that are worth talking about. Think about what makes you tell your friends about a musician and do similar things.
- Think of your fans experience. You should always be thinking of what makes you love a musician. Do the same things for your fans.
- You need to have a steady stream of content that keeps you in the news. If you slow down or have multi-month lapses in activity, your momentum will slow down. Fans will forget about you and move on to someone else who keeps them more captivated.
- Getting fans to recommend your music to their friends is the most powerful and most affordable way to gain new fans.
- No single promotion is going to build you a fanbase. You need to employ countless different methods of promotion by accumulating tons of small pieces of the puzzle until they form a whole picture.

- Promote yourself using grassroots methods instead of hoping the record label fairy magically leaves you a contract because you got lucky. Instead of counting on luck for your success, employ one on one connections with fans to grow your fanbase.
- You need to be willing to go out of your way to make one fan at a time when you first start building a fanbase. Eventually, you will have many fans, and they will do more and more of this work for you.
- Your goal should be to be so great you can't be ignored, not just good enough. Think about what will draw attention to your band.
- Instead of spending time researching and figuring out which labels you can send your songs to, research the fans of similar musicians and send them your songs. They will talk about you enough that it will get labels' attention.
- The first week you release a record isn't the most important week when you are an up-and-coming act. You are never going to make a big splash the first week. Concentrate on sustaining your promotions and aim to have your biggest week nine months after your release.
- Do a small promotion every two weeks and a big promotion every month. Continue these promotions with minimal lulls in your momentum.
- Make a press calendar so you have promotions planned out and will always able to know what you should be promoting.
- Making smaller releases more frequently keeps you on fan's minds and your name in the news cycle so you continue to build your fanbase.
- Whenever you think of a way to promote your music, think about whether you would tell another friend about this promotion because it is so exciting. Think of eventful promotions that fans who barely know you would still tell their friends about.
- Podcasts, remixes, covers, videos, tour updates, mixtapes, pre-orders, fan experiences, events and other news keep you in the news cycle and on fans minds. Always be thinking of way to continue promoting to your fans.
- Advertising isn't as effective as most other ways of promoting your music, but if you are employing every other promotion possible, it can be smart to let advertising help you get in front of some more ears.
- Concentrate on promoting your music in one area first and continue to spread as it begins to work there.

Free Music

- Free music is a gateway to getting fans. You cannot make money or gain fans unless people can easily hear your music first.
- Just because you give a song away for free does not mean you can't also charge for it. Some fans will still buy songs from their preferred outlet, such as iTunes, even if you give it away for free on your website.
- Just because your song is free doesn't mean it always has to be. You can repackage your music and sell it as you gain fans.
- Many musicians find the songs they give away for free are the songs that sell best.
- Free music is a gateway for fans to buy merch, concert tickets and other experiences that have a much higher profit margin than selling a single song's download. Be sure to have items they can pay for so you can fund your music in the future.
- No one buys music today because they have to, they buy it because they want to. It is easy to acquire nearly any record for free. Fans buy so they can have music in the form they want it and to support the musicians they love.
- Having a free-music page where fans know they can go to get a dose of your music builds fan relationships. It also serves as a great place for new fans to get a regular dose of your music and become an addict.

Building Relationships With Fans

- Fans buy from the musicians they feel they have the closest connections with.
- Make sure to have a direct-to-fan method setup so you can build relationships with fans and gain their contact information.
- Offer special benefits, lower prices and content to your fans who buy direct from you.
- Always talk to your fans the way you would if you were speaking to them at a show. Never send out press releases or talk like a corporate drone. Be yourself and utilize the vocabulary you and your fans speak.
- Although it is ok to occasionally ask your fans for help with funding and promoting your music, if all you ever do is ask your fans for favors instead of rewarding them, they will get tired of your begging and find a musician who rewards them more often.

- Always be available to your fans. Make sure your music is in every outlet possible and you are always stocked with what merch fans are craving.
- Build relationships with your fans. Don't expect them to start buying from you after hearing just one song. Bond with them until they become addicted to your music and are willing to pay bigger prices to get what you have been giving to them for free.
- Building a fanbase builds you a stable career, not music business connections.
- Trade fans music downloads for email addresses and tweets as much as possible. Giving a download in exchange for nothing is a lost opportunity to stay in touch and build a relationship with a fan.
- Surprise your fans with unexpected acts of kindness, and they will tell their friends about you.

Managing Your Music

- Manage yourself before you get a manager so you can learn what goes into the job.
- Not allocating your time properly costs you opportunities. The more efficient you are with getting the work done to promote your music, the more time you have to get it in front of more ears.
- Do what is important, not what is easy. It can be fun to sit on Twitter talking to fans and put off making a new website or video. Make sure you prioritize the work that needs to be done according to what will help build your fanbase the most.
- For every five opportunities someone promises you, only one will come through. Make sure to create so many opportunities for yourself that you are never desperate to have one happen.
- DIY means Decide It Yourself, not Do It All Yourself. You are in charge of making decisions and should build an organization behind your music that suits your own needs and ethics. You should build a team behind you that fills in your blanks and needs as you grow.
- Make sure you get objective perspectives to give your intuitions a second check.
- Make sure to keep every contact, record store, blog, place to hang a flier, manager etc. all organized in a clean contact database. You will be using this information for years to come. Trying to find this information a second time is wasted time.
- Taking too long to accomplish small tasks will turn off potential team members. You need to keep up your momentum, otherwise

no one will want to work with you. Diligent work attracts potential team members, laziness does not.

- You are not an unsigned band if you don't have a recording contract. Instead, you are a DIY musician.
- Don't be afraid to say unique and original things. While following other groups may seem like an easy way to get fans, musicians who are remembered are those who do their own thing.
- Having bad photos and low-quality recordings tells potential team members you aren't resourceful. Take pride in everything you do, and make sure you always strive to do everything as well as possible. It will speak volumes to fans and potential team members that you should be taken seriously.
- As music fans we are all looking for someone who makes something exceptional and above the rest. If you want fans you need to strive for this goal, since it is what you yourself look for in the musicians you love.
- Even when something goes wrong, there is usually a way to turn it around and make it benefit you. Always look on the bright side and don't get bogged down when setbacks occur. Figure out how to make them into opportunities.

Targeting
- Target similar musicians so you can find writers, promoters and fans who are likely to enjoy your music. This will save you the trouble of trying to get people who may never enjoy your music to listen to it.
- Follow similar musicians and set up searches and alerts so you can find as many contacts as possible who have a high likelihood of enjoying your music.

Social Skills
- Be friendly and reach out to other musicians who are similar to you.
- Be a part of your scene. Participate on message boards, join social network conversations and attend shows to meet others similar to you.

Impressing Potential Team Members
- Managers, A&R, booking agents, etc., do not go to school to learn how to see talent in its raw form. You need to leave nothing to their

imagination and to be a finished product that needs little development.
- If you show potential team members demos, unmixed songs or unmastered material, their lack of imagination may not see your potential. Many of these people just want to hear a finished product and are unable to imagine how good your song could be with some more work. Show them a great song that is finished.
- Find something impressive and brag about it. If you have an unusually high amount of YouTube views, concert attendees or fans who get tattoos of your lyrics, be sure to let the world know.
- Potential team members are impressed by the musicians that fans are buzzing about. Concentrate more on getting fans to talk about your music than mailing your demo to record labels. They will be more likely to hear your music and be impressed by it when fans keep mentioning you.
- Understand what makes you special and find a way to tell people it in two sentences or less.

Funding Your Music
- Crowdfunding your next project is a great way to build anticipation and get more fans before your next campaign.
- Crowdfunding is about connecting with your fans just as much as it is about getting the funding for your music. Take this opportunity to offer your fans special rewards and experiences for contributing.
- Sponsorships and endorsement deals not only get you funding, but they also can help you increase your band's exposure. Take the time to search for plausible and interesting partnerships that are mutually beneficial to both you and the brand you team with.

Planning Your Recording
- How good a recording you get of your newest song determines your potential until you release another song.
- No matter how hard you work and how much money you put into your promotions, you will receive diminished returns if the world doesn't enjoy your music. Be sure you walk away with a recording of every song you are confident is the best you can do.
- It's not smart to record as many songs as possible in a recording session. Concentrate on recording as many quality tracks as you can.

- If you have to qualify you recording with context before someone hears it, you are going to have trouble promoting your music. You need to have music that takes no explanation to be appreciated.
- Do not walk into the studio with half-finished songs that you hope will come together. Rehearse and refine your songs until they are the best you can make them.
- Recording bonus tracks to use for fan bonuses can help build your fanbase.
- Mastering your music with a great mastering engineer helps your music sound "right" and makes you competitive against the records of similar musicians.

Getting Press

- Many writers will copy and paste your bio and other materials verbatim. Make sure you write what you would like people to say about you.
- Most people who write about you will be fans of your music. The blogosphere is filled with people writing about the music they are passionate about. Treat these writers like fans, not someone you are trying to sell a product to.
- Little blogs with small readerships matter because bigger blogs' authors use them to see who they should write about. Big blogs matter because they have a huge audience that pays attention to them, looking for who to listen to next.
- Exclusive content will help you get covered by a blog that may not always cover you.
- If you want to be covered by a blog or music site, participate in their community and get to know them.
- Cultivate stories around your music. You will get covered more often if you have an interesting and unique story around your music as opposed to just a "new song."
- Do not send corporate-style press releases to bloggers. Speak to them like they are your friends and fans.
- A blog is for personal opinions, stories and pictures of your cat. A news feed is just updates on your music. Make sure you keep them separate even if the content from your news feed makes it into your blog at times and vice versa.
- Musicians who say interesting things during interviews, get more interviews.
- Thank those who write about you and return to their site, comment on their posts and friend them on social networks.

- Going viral usually means you will have flash-in-the-pan fame and not a lasting presence.
- If you do go viral, be sure to capitalize on it by having more content for fans and a way to capture their email addresses so you can build a relationship.

Playing Live To Promote Your Music

- At empty shows talk to the other musicians and few fans that are there. An intimate show can often lead to a relationship that leads to bigger things in the future.
- Touring is not always the smartest first step, or even third step. Build a following locally and slowly expand to weekend trips before touring.
- Give incentives for fans to sign up for your mailing list.
- You should try to make sure no one leaves any show of yours without having a way to get free music from you.
- Give other musicians, promoters and sound guys T-shirts because fans will see them with them on, giving your music a free advertisement.
- Contact other musicians who are similar to you about trading shows.
- Once you are drawing in a big crowd at shows, put on your own shows and ticket them yourself with tools that will allow you to acquire your fans email addresses so you can contact them the next time you play.
- Use analytics software in your social networks and website to find where your fans live and be sure to play there.
- Play events with a theme your fans would enjoy instead of shows thrown together with a bunch of random acts. Employ non-musical acts and other interesting locals who can bring depth to this event.
- Plan other appearances while you are in town at record stores, malls, radio stations, colleges or anywhere your fans may hang out.
- Your flyers for each show should be unavoidable. Figure out where potential fans hang out and make sure your flyers are there.
- Employ a street team by giving incentives to them to help promote your music.
- Online promotion is very powerful and there is much more to it than just making a Facebook event.

- Stay with fans and musicians friends on tour instead of hotels. Go out of your way to thank them for their hospitality.

Your Merchandise And Visual Image
- The images associated with your music should be easily recognizable from 25 feet away.
- The most effective images fit in with the standards of your genre, while not being generic and showing a characteristic that matches your music.
- Merchandise not only helps to fund your music, but it also turns fans into walking recommendations for your music.
- Have a wide variety of merch at various price points so fans who are willing to spend a lot on you can and so those who aren't that committed you can still walk away with something.
- Try to have merch available in every way your fans desire it so you can capitalize on the huge potential of it to make profits and help promote your music.
- Being good to the fans who buy from you is crucial. If you go above and beyond the call of duty for them, they will tell everyone they know on their social networks. If you do them wrong, they will also do the same.

Distributing Your Music
- Even if you give a song away for free, it should be in every online store possible.
- CDs allow friends to give gifts to one another. CDs also allow those who prefer physical media to own something tangible.
- Vinyl is important to diehard music fans. Having vinyl can help expose your music to more people.
- iTunes, Spotify, Apple Music, Tidal, Bandcamp, etc. all have different features that can help your music get heard by fans. Utilize each of them as we described.
- There are plenty of other services to distribute your music to that aren't aggregated by digital distributors, TuneCore, ReverbNation, Distrokid or CD Baby. Don't miss them.
- Torrents are a powerful way to get your music to fans.

Using Email Effectively
- Email is the most effective way to get fans to do what you want and the best way to develop a lasting relationship.

- Email addresses often last longer than the life of most social networks.
- Emailing with a fan is a privilege, don't overuse it.
- Geo-target your emails so you don't annoy fans with messages about shows 1,000 miles away from where they live.

Your Website

- Your website should be a great first impression for a new fan to find whatever they want.
- It should be a place where someone can find any information they want about you.
- It should be a place where fans can hear more of your music and connect with other fans.
- It should be a place where fans can always easily find what you are up to right now.
- A fan should easily be able to find you other web presences like social networks.
- You should be able to capture fans email addresses so you can email them and easily show them what you have for sale.

Social Networks

- Talk to your fans, not at them. Start conversations instead of telling them to do things.
- Follow everyone who follows you and participate in the conversation they start in order to improve the relationship you have with them.
- Thank, commend and appreciate the fans who promote you.
- While it is tempting to focus on self-promotion, it subtly pays off here. Focus on developing relationships with fans and they will spread the word for you. Don't spam people asking them to check out your music.
- Think about your fans experience by following you on a social network. Is it fun and enjoyable to follow you or are you always saying the same self-indulgent things?
- Remember most of these social networks will die like Friendster and Myspace. Be sure to make your fans aware that you are on other social networks.
- Be yourself and talk the way you talk. Don't sound like a commercial for your music or your manager.

- Myspace is dead because no one checks it anymore. Devote your time to other social networks.
- Facebook is a great tool, but it isn't everything. Make your updates less plentiful than other social networks.
- Create sharable content, like pictures with lyrics and fun questions, to keep Facebook followers engaged.
- Twitter is like a party, and you want to be the person everyone wants to talk to. Ignore the people who are being stupid and find those you get along with and have fun.
- Tumblr is the oversharing capital on the Internet. If you want to overshare, do it here.
- Follow, reblog, retweet and heart your fans as much as possible and show them you appreciate them.
- YouTube and SoundCloud are the most popular ways listeners discover new music. Nurture your page, participate in groups and socialize there the way you would any other social network.
- There are many other social networks aside from Twitter and Facebook. Maintain a presence on all of them since they are a huge opportunity to make new fans.
- Reddit is the place content goes to go viral. If you want your content to spread, participate in this community.
- Connect with fans by doing video chats on video services like Google Hangouts.

Making A Great Video And Spreading It With YouTube
- Videos can help establish who you are to your fans. Think about what you would like your fans to think about you and make your video explaining that to them.
- Every song you have should be on YouTube because it is the most common way for a listener to discover new music. If your songs aren't on YouTube, they lack the potential to be easily discovered by hungry listeners.
- Every song doesn't need a full-blown music video. You can make single-frame videos or lyrics videos.
- Your YouTube channel should be just like a TV channel: A feed of video content you want your subscribers to see. It doesn't only need to be your music.
- Cards are a powerful tool that can promote your new album, an upcoming show or direct those watching your old video to your newest and vice versa.

- YouTube can be a profitable medium to fund your music, so be sure to join their partner program.
- If you want more people at your shows, be sure to make quality live videos to put on your channel.
- You can trade recommendations with other musicians on YouTube.
- YouTube metrics can help get you on better tours and through other gates. Concentrating on promoting your music on here can do big things for your music career.
- Make playlists of your music along with similar bands' music.

Internet Radio
- Internet radio is one of the most powerful ways to get in front of the ears of people who would potentially like your music. Get your music on there and let it do the work of making you new fans, with minimal effort on your part.
- Get your music on every Internet radio outlet you can, it is worth the time since the outlets can target listeners who are likely to be your fans.

Licensing Your Music
- Make all of your music easily available to be licensed.
- Have instrumentals on hand because most licensing offers require them.
- Even if the monetary compensation for a licensing contract is small, it may get you in front of many new ears.

Copyrighting And Publishing Your Music
- A traditional copyright can hold your music back from being spread. Explore a Creative Commons license that will help allow your music to spread.
- Register your music for publishing so you can obtain money you are due from your promotions.

How To Keep This Going

This book is self-published by just Todd and I, with no big promotion budget, corporate machine or experience in the book world, just the two of us working hard. If you enjoyed this book and want us to keep making this information available for free on our website, the biggest way you can help us out is to tell your friends about the book. Go to Facebook and share a link to it with your friends. Send a tweet or a mass email. Most importantly, we really need reviews on Amazon.com because that helps more people hear about our book. Look up our book and leave a kind review if you liked what you read. Thank you for the support you already gave us by buying this book; we really appreciate it. With your continued support, we can keep updating our website with more articles, just like the content in this book.

If you did get this book for free, please at least tell your friends about it or give us a review on Amazon.

We update this book every year and offer free updates to the e-book if you help us promote it. Simply write us and we will send you an updated copy! We also have a regularly updated mailing list where I tell you for free what I am discovering as I consult on projects. You can sign up at http://getmorefansbook.com/sign-up/

If you enjoyed this book and are interested in reading a book on how to avoid the pitfalls that happen when creating music as well as how to make music listeners find emotionally powerful, Jesse has written *Processing Creativity: The Tools, Practices And Habits Used To Make Music You're Happy With. It has received immense praise and is the best-selling book on songwriting of 2017. For more information go to* https://processingcreativitybook.com/

As stated much of this book changes CONSTANTLY I encourage you to visit my YouTube channel as I regularly cover this subject and upload videos with the latest information.

I also host a Facebook group that is only helpful tips for DIY musicians, no playlister con artists or bs. We have great discussions every single day about the latest ways to promote your music and it is very active. Facebook.com/groups/musformationdiy

Thank you for reading.

Bonus: How To Go From Zero Fans To 10,000

One of the criticisms of this book has been that it didn't explicitly spell out how to go from no fans to 10,000 so I wanted to make a section filled with the advice I give bands on this when I do consulting work. Below is what I see as the most current methods that are working to explode your fanbase as well as some of the under discussed ideas and methods I think everyone should be employing each day to build a fanbase.

Find Community - Before you start releasing music or put any more effort into it, start finding your community. Refer to the chapter on targeting and do everything you can to find the blogs and message boards where your fans hang out as well as the Twitter, Instagrams and Facebook pages where they are posting. Find any subreddits or Facebook groups that your potential fans are active in and be a member of that community. Be active in the comments and community so your name becomes familiar and you make friends in the community. This will allow you to meet the like-minded people who you will team up with and the fans who will boost you up. You should also observe what is working for other musicians in your community and figure out how to make that work for you. I would devote at least 30 minutes to this a day 300 days a year and make this a very high priority.

Realize We Live In A Singles World, Your Release Strategy Should Reflect It - Employ the release strategy of releasing a new single every 6-8 weeks for 12-18 months that we discussed in Chapter 14, while doing something eventful every two weeks and something smaller every week. This only takes 8 songs per year to fill up an entire calendar year. This way you are reminding people you exist regularly and create the impression you are an exciting phenomenon that should be paid attention to and can harness the power of algorithmic recommendations as often as possible. Use Distrokid's subscription service to get your music on Spotify, Apple Music, etc. so you don't incur costs for release many small releases. You should be knowing what you are posting 4-6 months in advance on a bi-weekly basis. Since it takes weeks or even months to get songs and videos ready this will ensure you have the runway time to prepare all the content around your song releases.

Go Hard On Spotify - Right now Spotify gives you the biggest opportunity of all of the streaming sites to explode your fanbase. Every time you release an audio track use a Show.co campaign to try to drive up your follows so with each song you release Spotify will put you on more

Discover Weekly playlists which has the potential to really up your fanbase. Regularly make playlists and link them on your social media that include your music and follow all of Spotify's current best practices so the likelihood of them promoting you increases.

Take The Time To Make A YouTube Strategy - YouTube holds the great opportunity for growth for your fanbase and taking the time to think of how you can make both music videos as well as other content that will keep people engaged with your YouTube. I would not only be releasing a single screen video, lyric video and music video for every song but also finding other content to post on a regular basis. I would make this one of the top priorities on your to do list and hold regular brainstorm sessions with your team on this, since the ROI on doing this is superior to almost any other way you can spend your time outside of recording great songs.

Have A Real World Strategy - Make a merch store with LimitedRun or ManicMerch so that fans can become advertisements for your music and to earn income. Make sure you have stickers and flyers anywhere potential fans hang out to increase the likelihood you will convert potential fans into listeners by appearing as someone they should know about. It's shocking how well IRL promotion works with posters at venues and around town in making you seem like someone people should be paying attention to since so only larger acts do it now and far less people are doing it now.

Find An Alternative Promotion Strategy - If you make music that will go over well with college students consider a college radio promotion program (not because college radio is listened to by lots of people, but because those who do work in these departments are often tastemakers). If you're making amazing videos consider a video promotion campaign. If you are good talkers or have a unique interest consider making a podcast or doing a series on your YouTube channel. If your music has a sense of humor or a strong image, be sure to devote resources to making memes around your music and even approaching influencers to spread these memes. Find something unique to do that amplifies your strengths and explore channels beyond the obvious thing every artist does.

Take The Time To Consider And Pitch Stories - The great power of social media is you don't need to wait for a journalist to tell your story. If you have a powerful story about a song, your art or life you can tell it on social media and if people connect with it, it will spread as long as you've built up some small platform to launch it from. One of the most important parts of getting people talking about your music is figuring out how to tell that story best and how to get it into the conversation. Find the most interesting thoughts you don't see other people talking about and develop them and get them out with your music via social media. When I talk to people who regret their music's marketing it often stems from them underestimating how many other people are fighting for their audience's attention. This is why taking the time to create strong stories, images and content plans around your music is crucial since the competition is so vast and strong.

Extend Yourself - The biggest thing I hear from people who fail to grow their fanbase at first and then have a breakthrough is they spend more time reaching out to new people and talking to them. Be as proactive as possible in expanding who you know or even talking to your most passionate fans to expand the people who keep you top of mind for opportunities. Push yourself to talk to someone new all the time and even when you fail continue to reach out and meet new people in your community.

Analyze and Introspect - While the only way music ever connects with an audience is when you are making music you yourself love and emotionally react to, it also helps to take in criticism. Make sure you pay attention if people say your music is lacking production or a player isn't carrying their weight. You can do all of this work, but if your music has fatal flaws the work is going to yield minimal results. Be honest with yourself and weigh criticism.

Develop Images That Reinforce Your Music's Emotion - With YouTube and Instagram being the way so many fans discover music today, having images that match your music, adding more emotional resonance to what you've created is one of the best ways to get your music to spread more. Devote time and attention to this pursuit.

Keep Up On Your Databases - Early on in this book we discussed keeping spreadsheets of contacts. Making sure those stay up to date and you keep in regular touch with them is one of the practices that can make monumental leaps for you. Especially considering many of the people you meet on the way up regularly ascend up to bigger things, staying in touch with everyone in the business you meet is a practice that give great rewards.

Social Media Strategy - I think the biggest mistakes artists I talk to make about social media is they don't remember that fans support the artists they feel the closest bonds with. Often times what is written in the caption is more important than a good looking picture on Instagram. A tweet where you share insight and truth can expose you to more fans than an announcement. Think about how you start conversations and show your unique self while also being informative about what you have going on. There is a balance between oversharing and not telling your fans about your music enough and just being a boring press release factory. I believe the artists that find a balance between these two poles get the most mileage out of social media. Here's a few other thoughts -

- There's nothing wrong with posting more than 1 Instagram story each day or a few Tweets. Keep Facebook posts to only 1-2 a week as bigger reminders or your bigger events.
- While I believe big announcements should also be on your website since you give fans the chance to stick around and see everything you have going on. If you don't have a website do this on Instagram since your chances of it spreading are greatest here through the Explore option and it's easy ability for others to share.
- "Going Live" on Facebook and Instagram right now is still a great exploit since the platform promote it and send out alerts to all of your followers. This is a great exploit right now.
- If being funny or visually performative is your thing TikTok and Triller are presently the best exploit in the game to get people to pay attention to what you're doing.
- If your music is popular with "gamers" consider hanging out in Twitch streams where the creator plays your genre of music. There's also many emerging DJ channels on the stream and it's worth investigating if any of them are in your genre since this is a great way to get exposure. This can also be a great place to find your community.
- In all of the chapters in this book on social media we have a section called "Strategy" that can give you further ideas on how to make the most of your time using social media.
- Remember Twitter and Facebook can schedule posts, so you can take time each week to schedule most of your posts in advance and you can write your Instagram posts in a notes app. Most people's weekdays are jam packed and if you worry about getting content out you can make it easier by taking the time to put it together when you have time.

Make Progress On The Other Things You Need To Do - Be proactive and go through this book and make sure you are utilizing every service we talked about in her that may be helpful for your music.

Essential Services
Show.co - I would use this whenever you share links with fans to build campaigns that also build your Spotify and YouTube followers.
Song.Link - A free service that you can use to share the link for your song on every streaming service.
TweetDeck - Schedule tweets and even follow up tweets for the anniversary of hallmarks in your career when you have spare time as well as monitor your mentions on Twitter.
Turn.Audio - Make good looking videos for songs on Instagram.
Distrokid - I would use Distrokid to aggregate all music since their fees are the lowest while giving you the best tools.

I will be updating this as anything relevant comes to mind. If you want to be on a mailing list to receive free updates go to
http://getmorefansbook.com/sign-up/

Index

What People Are Saying About Get More Fans

"This is the most up to date, reliable source of information I've seen in any form for up and coming bands" - **Ross Robinson (A&R I Am Recordings – Slipknot, The Cure and Glassjaw / Producer – At The Drive In, Korn and Deftones)**

"Comprehensive insight, observations and DIY strategies are offered, not force-fed, to provoke thought, instill common sense, and inspire ingenuity in those with the perseverance to permeate the rapidly changing ozone of the modern day music business." - **John Cafiero (Manager of the Misfits & the Ramones/Record Label CEO/Producer/Director/Writer & Editor – *Commando: the Autobiography of Johnny Ramone*/Musician – Osaka Popstar)**

"This is a must read for anyone marketing themselves in this new age of media. Jesse has one of the most diverse ranges of real life DIY music industry experience I've ever seen, it's perhaps his realization that the new music industry is not about finding a solution but about constant evolution that makes him so qualified to present this information to us." - **Benjamin Weinman (Guitarist, Songwriter, Manager for The Dillinger Escape Plan)**

"At a bit over 700 pages, it's hard to take in as a whole yet so far I cannot find anything I would describe as padding or filler. It's simply an amazingly complete guide to taking charge of your music career in hardcore DIY fashion… The general vibe I get is one of being very clear about the fact that they're speaking to musicians who want to take charge of their career in order to be able to make their own decisions. In the process they advocate building a solid, lasting foundation that takes advantage of the overwhelming array of online tools available for DIY artists… If you had to go with just one book on DIY music biz, this would be the one." - **Clyde Smith (**Hypebot.com**)**

"Astonishingly packed… $10 well spent indeedy" – **Adrian Fusiarski** (Buzzsonic.com)

"For anyone out there in a band or with an interest in the music industry, check this book out… As kids in bands growing up, we did A LOT of stupid stuff… This book will teach you how to 'play it cool' and make some smart/innovative decisions." - **Man Overboard**

"It may very well be the most essential text written in recent years for anyone in the music industry." - Thirty Roses

"If you play in an aspiring band, it is a must read!" - **Transit**

"Comprehensive, 700-page look and DIY guide to the real way the music industry works today" - Free Williamsburg

"A HUGE undertaking and completely worth people's time" - **Run For Cover Records**

"If you're serious about your career and are looking for a comprehensive guide that you'll want to refer to repeatedly and isn't likely to be outdated any time soon, then be sure to pick this up." - **Christine Infanger** (Think Like A Label)

"This book is a complete DIY guide for independent musicians. It's full of knowledge, wisdom, and resources. It's super long, and fun/easy to read. A must for the independent musician." - Dave Herring

"This comprehensive guide book of over 700 pages tears through everything you need to know to get yourself more exposure." – Unveil Music

"If you are looking for a vote of confidence from us here at Indie-Monster you've got one. This book is not only full of useful information, but the timing of its release is impeccable. Bands could use this information today

now more than ever. New technologies and DIY outlets are popping up on a daily basis. All are helping to level the playing field for musicians. This book aids in leveling it even more. We vote it a must read!" – Indie Monster